Evolution and Social Psychology

FRONTIERS OF SOCIAL PSYCHOLOGY

Series Editors:
Arie W. Kruglanski, *University of Maryland at College Park*
Joseph P. Forgas, *University of New South Wales*

Frontiers of Social Psychology is a new series of domain-specific handbooks. The purpose of each volume is to provide readers with a cutting-edge overview of the most recent theoretical, methodological, and practical developments in a substantive area of social psychology, in greater depth than is possible in general social psychology handbooks. The editors and contributors are all internationally renowned scholars, whose work is at the cutting-edge of research.

Scholarly, yet accessible, the volumes in the *Frontiers* series are essential resources for senior undergraduates, postgraduates, researchers, and practitioners, and are suitable as texts in advanced courses in specific subareas of social psychology.

Recently published

Close Relationships, Noller & Feeney
Negotiation Theory and Research, Thompson

Forthcoming titles

Affect in Social Thinking and Behavior, Forgas
Automatic Processes in Social Thinking and Behavior, Bargh
Culture, Chiu & Mallorie
Personality and Social Behavior, Rhodewalt
Political Psychology, Krosnick
Science of Social Influence, Pratkanis
Social Cognition, Strack & Förster
Social Communication, Fiedler
The Self, Sedikides & Spencer

For continually updated information about published and forthcoming titles in the *Frontiers of Social Psychology* series, please visit: **www.psypress.com/frontiers**

Evolution and Social Psychology

Edited by

Mark Schaller, Jeffry A. Simpson, and Douglas T. Kenrick

Psychology Press
Taylor & Francis Group
NEW YORK AND HOVE

Published in 2006
by Psychology Press
270 Madison Avenue
New York, NY 10016
www.psypress.com

Published in Great Britain
by Psychology Press
27 Church Road
Hove, East Sussex BN3 2FA
www.psypress.co.uk

Psychology Press is an imprint of the Taylor & Francis Group, an informa business

Typeset by Macmillan India Ltd, Bangalore, India
Printed and bound in the USA by Sheridan Books, Inc., Ann Arbor, MI, on acid-free paper
Cover design by Lisa Dynan

10 9 8 7 6 5 4 3 2 1

Library of Congress Cataloging-in-Publication Data

Evolution and social psychology / edited by Mark Schaller, Jeffry A. Simpson, Douglas T. Kenrick Arizona State University.
   p. cm. – (Frontiers of social psychology)
  Includes bibliographical references and index.
  ISBN-13: 978-1-84169-417-7 (hardback : alk. paper)
  ISBN-10: 1-84169-417-7 (hardback : alk. paper) 1. Social psychology. 2. Human evolution. 3. Social evolution. 4. Social perception. 5. Group identity. I. Schaller, Mark, 1962 – II. Simpson, Jeffry A. III. Kenrick, Douglas T. IV. Series.
  HM1033.E96 2006
  303.401–dc22

                              2006005428

ISBN13: 978-1-84169-417-7 (hbk)

ISBN10: 1-84169-417-7 (hbk)

Contents

About the Editors   vii

Contributors   ix

1   Evolution is the New Cognition   1

     Douglas T. Kenrick, Mark Schaller, and Jeffry A. Simpson

2   The Evolution of Accuracy and Bias in Social Judgment   15

     Martie G. Haselton and David C. Funder

3   Modular Minds, Multiple Motives   39

     Robert Kurzban and C. Athena Aktipis

4   When and Why Did the Human Self Evolve?   55

     Constantine Sedikides, John J. Skowronski, and R. I. M. Dunbar

5   The Ecological Approach to Person Perception: Evolutionary Roots and Contemporary Offshoots   81

     Leslie A. Zebrowitz and Joann Montepare

6   Social Functionalism and the Evolution of Emotions   115

     Dacher Keltner, Jonathan Haidt, and Michelle N. Shiota

7   An Evolutionary Perspective on Social Identity: Revisiting Groups   143

     Marilynn B. Brewer and Linnda R. Caporael

8   Evolutionary Bases of Prejudices   163

     Steven L. Neuberg and Catherine A. Cottrell

9   Accuracy and Bias in Romantic Relationships: An Evolutionary and Social Psychological Analysis   189

     Garth J. O. Fletcher, Jeffry A. Simpson, and Alice D. Boyes

10   Evolution, Relationships, and Health: The Social
      Shaping Hypothesis   211

      Shelley E. Taylor and Gian C. Gonzaga

11   The Altruism Puzzle: Psychological Adaptations for
      Prosocial Behavior   237

      Mark Van Vugt and Paul A. M. Van Lange

12   The Evolution of Aggression   263

      David M. Buss and Joshua D. Duntley

13   Evolutionary Social Influence   287

      *Jill M. Sundie, Robert B. Cialdini, Vladas Griskevicius, and
      Douglas T. Kenrick*

14   Groups as Adaptive Devices: Human Docility and Group
      Aggregation Mechanisms in Evolutionary Context   317

      Tatsuya Kameda and R. Scott Tindale

15   Evolution and Culture   343

      Ara Norenzayan, Mark Schaller, and Steven J. Heine

Author Index   367

Subject Index   383

About the Editors

Mark Schaller, Ph.D., is a professor of psychology at the University of British Columbia. He is the author of dozens of scholarly articles on a wide variety of topics, including group stereotypes and prejudices, person perception, kin-recognition, helping behavior, and the psychology of scientific inference. Within that context, he explores broader questions about the psychological foundations of culture, and the evolutionary foundations of human psychology.

Jeffry A. Simpson, Ph.D., is a professor of psychology at the University of Minnesota, Twin Cities Campus. His primary research interests center on adult attachment processes, models of human mating, idealization processes in relationships, the management of empathic accuracy in relationships, and social influence strategies. He is a fellow of the American Psychological Association and the American Psychological Society. From 1998 to 2001, he served as editor of the journal *Personal Relationships*, and currently serves as an associate editor for the *Journal of Personality and Social Psychology*. He has also served on grant panels at the NSF and the NIMH.

Douglas T. Kenrick, Ph.D., is a professor of psychology at Arizona State University. His research has attempted to integrate traditional social psychological theory and research with theoretical and empirical developments in evolutionary biology, and more recently, dynamical systems theory. Recent work focuses on how fundamental motives (such as self-preservation and mate-search) might affect selective attention, encoding, and memory for other people. He is a fellow of the American Psychological Association.

Contributors

C. Athena Aktipis
Department of Psychology
University of Pennsylvania
Philadelphia, Pennsylvania, USA

Alice D. Boyes
Department of Psychology
University of Canterbury
Christchurch, New Zealand

Marilynn B. Brewer
Department of Psychology
Ohio State University
Columbus, Ohio, USA

David M. Buss
Department of Psychology
The University of Texas at Austin
Austin, Texas, USA

Linnda R. Caporael
Department of Science and
   Technology Studies
Rensselaer Polytechnic Institute
Troy, New York, USA

Robert B. Cialdini
Department of Psychology
Arizona State University
Tempe, Arizona, USA

Catherine A. Cottrell
Department of Psychology
University of Florida
Gainesville, Florida, USA

Robin I. M. Dunbar
School of Biological Sciences
University of Liverpool
Liverpool, United Kingdom

Joshua D. Duntley
Department of Psychology
University of Texas
Austin, Texas, USA

Garth J. O. Fletcher
Department of Psychology
University of Canterbury
Christchurch, New Zealand

David C. Funder
Department of Psychology
University of California
Riverside, California, USA

Gian C. Gonzaga
Department of Psychology
UCLA
Los Angeles, California, USA

Vladas Griskevicius
Department of Psychology
Arizona State University
Tempe, Arizona, USA

Jonathan Haidt
Department of Psychology
University of Virginia
Charlottesville, Virginia, USA

Martie G. Haselton
Communication Studies &
   Department of Psychology
UCLA
Los Angeles, California, USA

Steven J. Heine
Department of Psychology
University of British Columbia
Vancouver, British Columbia, Canada

Tatsuya Kameda
Department of Behavioral Science
Hokkaido University
Sapporo, Japan

Dacher Keltner
Department of Psychology
University of California
Berkeley, California, USA

Douglas T. Kenrick
Department of Psychology
Arizona State University
Tempe, Arizona, USA

Robert Kurzban
Department of Psychology
University of Pennsylvania
Philadelphia, Pennsylvania, USA

Joann Montepare
School of Communication Sciences
    and Disorders
Emerson College
Boston, Massachusetts, USA

Steven L. Neuberg
Department of Psychology
Arizona State University
Tempe, Arizona, USA

Ara Norenzayan
Department of Psychology
University of British Columbia
Vancouver, British Columbia, Canada

Mark Schaller
Department of Psychology
University of British Columbia
Vancouver, British Columbia, Canada

Constantine Sedikides
Department of Psychology
University of Southampton
Southampton, United Kingdom

Michelle N. Shiota
Department of Psychology
University of California
Berkeley, California, USA

Jeffry A. Simpson
Department of Psychology
University of Minnesota
Minneapolis, Minnesota, USA

John J. Skowronski
Department of Psychology
Northern Illinois University
De Kalb, Illinois, USA

Jill M. Sundie
Department of Marketing &
    Entrepreneurship
C.T. Bauer College of Business
University of Houston
Houston, Texas, USA

Shelley E. Taylor
Department of Psychology
UCLA
Los Angeles, California, USA

R. Scott Tindale
Department of Psychology
Loyola University
Chicago, Illinois, USA

Paul A. M. Van Lange
Department of Social Psychology
Free University
Amsterdam, The Netherlands

Mark Van Vugt
Centre for the Study of Group
    Processes
Department of Psychology
University of Kent
Canterbury, UK

Leslie A. Zebrowitz
Department of Psychology
Brandeis University
Waltham, Massachusetts, USA

1

Evolution is the New Cognition

DOUGLAS T. KENRICK, MARK SCHALLER,
and JEFFRY A. SIMPSON

*I*f there had been a *Frontiers in Social Psychology* series 30 years ago, it would surely have included a volume on the exciting new developments at the interface of cognitive and social psychology. In the mid-1970s, a growing number of social psychologists were exploring the subtle effects of cognitive processes on social behavior. At that time, many social psychologists viewed these developments with skepticism and concern. To some, the study of cognition seemed an arid exercise outside the disciplinary boundaries of social psychology. To others, it seemed plain unnecessary to posit invisible mental processes in order to predict and explain behaviors.

That latter form of skepticism echoed the behaviorist critiques of cognitive psychology, which had dotted the psychological landscape for years (e.g., Skinner, 1950). Behaviorist warnings about the futility of the cognitive approach appeared in prominent places even into the mid-1970s. On the pages of *American Psychologist*, Ebel (1974) colorfully likened "attention, perception, memory, reasoning, will power, and the like" (p. 486) to dryads—fanciful nymphs that were once believed to animate the personalities of trees. Ebel dismissed these cognitive constructs as "ad hoc, imprecise, unverifiable" (p. 487), and concluded that these "dryads of the mind" are "useless...in our search for understanding of behavioral phenomena" (p. 491).

Today, these criticisms seem quaint. The ostensibly useless study of cognition has proven to be indispensable in the advancement of the psychological sciences in general and of social psychology in particular. The cognitive revolution in social psychology has been a huge success. By explicitly including this additional level of conceptual analysis in social psychological inquiry, our theories are more sophisticated, our empirical database is much richer, and we now have a much more coherent and integrative understanding of social behavior.

So what does all this have to do with a book on *Evolution and Social Psychology*? This: There are remarkable parallels between the status of cognitive social psychology 30 years ago and the status of evolutionary social psychology today. Indeed, there is an eerie similarity in the flavor of the critiques initially lodged against the cognitive perspective and those that are still commonly lodged against the evolutionary perspective today. And there is a striking resemblance in the scientific trajectories of these two perspectives as well—indicating, among other things, that those common criticisms are largely irrelevant to the scientific utility that these perspectives offer. Despite many reactionary critiques, the cognitive approach to social psychology revolutionized the field, and social psychologists who ignored these developments did so at their own intellectual peril. Today, the conceptual utility of the evolutionary perspective is just as unignorable. More and more social psychologists are drawing on an evolutionary perspective to inform their research—with salutary effects on our collective understanding of social cognition and behavior.

EVOLUTIONARY SOCIAL PSYCHOLOGY IS EVERYWHERE

Once upon a time, social cognition represented a relatively small and austere little niche in the study of social behavior. Today, it hardly makes sense to treat social cognition as a specialized domain of inquiry or to separate the study of social cognition from the study of social psychology more broadly. No longer is cognition relevant merely to, say, the study of person perception and impression formation; it is fundamental to our understanding of aggression, altruism, close relationships, intergroup prejudice, social influence, and every other form of interpersonal or group behavior discussed in any introductory social psychology textbook.

The same trajectory now characterizes the evolutionary perspective on social psychology. Although an evolutionary perspective had been lurking on the fringes of certain social psychological topics for several decades—during which time biological scientists of all kinds were embracing evolutionary analyses to elucidate the behavior of animal species (see Alcock, 2001)—the power of evolutionary models was not at first widely recognized by scientists who studied human beings. Early explorations in evolutionary social psychology focused on a few specific domains of behavior—especially altruism, aggression, and interpersonal attraction—for which the implications of evolutionary principles were most immediate and obvious (e.g., Buss, 1989; Daly & Wilson, 1988; Sadalla, Kenrick, & Vershure, 1987). Until quite recently, though, social psychologists working on most other topics found the evolutionary perspective easy to ignore. Well, things have changed. This book is a testament to how much has changed in a very short period of time: The logical tools of evolutionary psychology now inspire insights into myriad aspects of human social behavior.

As this book demonstrates, the evolutionary perspective has remarkably fecund implications for generating hypotheses about topics that cover the entire range of social psychology. There are, of course, chapters in this volume that revisit topics that have appealed to evolutionary theorists for years—aggression, prosocial behavior, and interpersonal relationships (see, for example, the chapters by Buss & Duntley; Fletcher, Simpson, & Boyes; Taylor & Gonzaga; and Van Vugt & Van Lange). Each of these chapters offers new insights on these traditional evolutionary psychological topics. Other chapters explore evolutionary insights into a whole range of basic intrapersonal processes, including emotional experiences and self-concept (e.g., the chapters by Keltner, Haidt & Shiota; Kurzban & Aktipis; and Sedikides, Skowronski, & Dunbar), as well as impression formation, stereotyping, and other classic topics in person perception (e.g., the chapters by Haselton & Funder; Neuberg & Cottrell; and Zebrowitz & Montepare). There are additional chapters that apply evolutionary theorizing to the study of interpersonal influence (Sundie, Cialdini, Griskevicius, & Kenrick), group processes (Brewer & Caporael; Kameda & Tindale), and human culture (Norenzayan, Schaller, & Heine). Just as no domain of social psychology has been untouched by the insights of cognitive science, these chapters demonstrate that the same is fast becoming true regarding the insights of evolutionary psychology.

UNVERIFIABLE, UNNECESSARY, AND UNDENIABLY USEFUL

Evolutionary thinking may be increasingly ubiquitous across social psychological topic areas, but that does not mean that its ascendance is accepted uncritically. Of the many different kinds of criticisms that have been—and sometimes still are—leveled against evolutionary explanations for social psychological phenomena, perhaps the two most common are exactly those that were lodged against cognitive explanations years ago—the hypothesized processes are unverifiable and unnecessary.

Whether applied to cognitive psychology or to evolutionary psychology, the charge of unverifiability is both logically valid and largely irrelevant to scientific progress. Cognitive constructs reside in an abstract conceptual space and cannot be observed directly; they must be inferred from more superficial forms of measurable data, such as verbal self-reports, reaction times, and blood-oxygen levels assessed by functional magnetic resonance imaging (fMRI). Despite these limitations, the study of social cognition has been hugely successful, mainly because hypotheses about the nature of relations between constructs are eminently testable (and subject to falsifiability). The same is true of evolutionary psychology (see Conway & Schaller, 2002). Evolutionary processes—operating on whole populations, rather than mere individuals, over vast stretches of prehistoric time—are also inaccessible to direct observation. Their operation must also be inferred from other forms of data. And as with the cognitive perspective, evolutionary speculations can yield eminently falsifiable hypotheses and have resulted in numerous useful empirical strategies for testing their unique implications (see Ketelaar & Ellis, 2000; Öhman & Mineka, 2003; Schmitt & Pilcher, 2004; Simpson & Campbell, 2005).

Critiques based on explanatory necessity are also valid in a very limited sense, but they are also irrelevant to scientific progress. The case of cognitive psychology is again illustrative. If our goal is merely to predict outcomes in the most parsimonious manner, it may be subjectively unnecessary to consider additional or deeper cognitive levels of analysis. But this is a very timid goal. Science progresses not from the mere prediction of empirical facts, but from the deeper explanation of those facts, from the discovery of new facts, and from the development of richer theoretical structures that coherently link facts together (see Lakatos, 1970; Thagard, 1992).

The cognitive perspective has proven indispensable to social psychological inquiry not because it offers satisfactory explanations for behavioral data, but because it offers a *deeper and richer understanding* of these findings and, most importantly, suggests vast new domains of scientific discovery.

The same is true of the evolutionary perspective. Social psychological data are almost always limited to observations in the here-and-now, and social psychologists in particular tend to be skeptical of explanations that go beyond the given data. But, as a science, the epistemic objective of social psychology is not to explain data in the most minimally satisfactory way. The objective is to explain social psychological phenomena as completely as possible and, in the process, to discover new phenomena. An evolutionary perspective thus serves as a powerful intellectual tool for prediction and discovery (see Buss, Haselton, Shackelford, Bleske, & Wakefield, 1998; Ketelaar & Ellis, 2000; Schaller, 2002), a fact that is highlighted by every chapter in this volume. If judged by its ability to stimulate new discoveries, an evolutionary approach to social psychology is much more than necessary; it is indispensable.

HERE'S WHY

That last point demands a bit of elaboration. Why is an evolutionary approach indispensable? Exactly what does an evolutionary perspective bring to the scientific discipline of social psychology? The chapters that follow articulate at least four partially overlapping answers to these questions. An evolutionary perspective offers (1) a unique set of powerful logical tools for deducing social psychological theories and hypotheses; (2) unique hypotheses about both general processes and specific contents of social cognition; (3) clues about the specific kinds of social situations that have especially important influences on human cognition and behavior; and (4) a unique, meta-theoretical framework within which many superficially different phenomena can be coherently integrated.

Tools for Theory-Building

Social psychologists are trained to cherish and celebrate theories. But good theories are hard to come by. Indeed, there is growing concern about the state of theory in contemporary social psychology, and there have been concerted attempts to rededicate the discipline to serious theory-building (see Kruglanski, 2001; Kruglanski & Higgins, 2004).

When it comes to theory-building, there is nothing so practical as a rigorous meta-theoretical framework. Cognitive science provided one such framework. Evolutionary theory provides another (Brewer, 2004). The literature in evolutionary biology is replete with theoretical concepts that have been remarkably generative. For example, the concept of sexual selection (Darwin, 1859) has helped biologists understand the function of certain features of animals that exact a clear cost to survival (such as a peacock's feathers or an elk's antlers). Similarly, the concept of differential parental investment (Trivers, 1972) has helped biologists understand why such costly features are more likely to be found in males rather than females. When applied to human psychology, these same ideas have had tremendous heuristic value in generating novel theories that have predicted a wide variety of sex differences in cognition and behavior (see, for example, Archer, 1996; Buss & Schmitt, 1993; Geary, 1998; Kenrick, Trost, & Sundie, 2004). Even more impressively, these same theories have generated dozens of novel hypotheses—and hosts of empirical discoveries—that specify the circumstances under which these effects are more or less likely to occur (e.g., Gangestad & Simpson, 2000; Li, Bailey, Kenrick, & Linsenmeier, 2002; Maner et al., 2005; Simpson & Gangestad, 1991). These concepts have contributed to the meta-theoretical framework within which new theories are being deduced—theories not only about sexual behavior, but also about many other forms of social behavior (for examples in this volume, see the chapters by Buss & Duntley, Fletcher et al., and Sundie et al.).

Similarly, the evolutionary concepts of inclusive fitness and kin selection have had enormous impact on biologists' understanding of animal behavior. These ideas have been imported into social psychology to derive novel theoretical perspectives, hypotheses, and discoveries, especially in the domains of helping behavior and aggression (e.g., Burnstein, Crandall, & Kitayama, 1994; Daly & Wilson, 1988; Laham, Gonsalkorale, & Von Hippel, 2005). Recent research has begun to apply these concepts to social cognition and person perception, with implications extending to interactions involving both strangers and kin (e.g., DeBruine, 2005; Park & Schaller, 2005). More generally, an evolutionary perspective brings into sharper focus the social importance of kin relations of all kinds—sibling relations, parent–child relations, etc. In this volume, for instance, Taylor and Gonzaga unravel several subtle implications of specific types of kin relations on social support, stress, and health. Sundie et al. identify a series of new and intriguing hypotheses about the ways in which kinship moderates social influence. The fact that many of these hypotheses still await empirical scrutiny attests to the heuristic value that evolutionary concepts offer in terms of novel theory-building and hypothesis generation. Several years ago, Daly, Salmon, and Wilson (1997) referred to the psychology of kinship as a "conceptual hole" in our field. It is only through the rigorous application of evolutionary principles that this huge conceptual gap is now beginning to be filled with the development of new theories, new hypotheses, and new empirical findings.

In addition to these and other core concepts, an evolutionary framework brings with it a toolbox full of logical tools that can be applied profitably to social psychological theorizing. The assumption of functional modularity that is so central to evolutionary psychology (see Barrett, 2005; Tooby & Cosmides, 1992) has begun to lead to new models and insights into the complexities of social cognition, as illustrated in the chapter by Kurzban and Aktipis. An evolutionary cost–benefit analysis (in which the costs and benefits of thoughts, feelings, and actions are defined not by their immediate consequences on the resources of individual organisms, but by their long-term consequences on reproductive fitness) has emerged as an invaluable tool in the development of novel theories about human cognition and behavior (see, for example, Gangestad & Simpson, 2000; Nesse, 2005). The chapter by Haselton and Funder is especially illustrative of the heuristic power of this kind of cost–benefit analysis. An evolutionary perspective, which demands that one consider dynamic relations between individual- and population-level processes, also provides a set of rigorous analytic tools—such as evolutionary game theory—for exploring those dynamic relations and their implications for social psychological outcomes (e.g., Axelrod, 1984, 1997). Several chapters in this volume, especially those by Van Vugt and Van Lange and by Kameda and Tindale, accentuate the productive application of these tools to topics such as prosocial behavior and group processes.

The multitude and diversity of useful evolutionary tools mirrors the multitude and diversity of the tools provided by cognition science. The adoption of a cognitive perspective in social psychology has never implied commitment to any one particular social cognitive theory or hypothesis, but rather to a broad set of meta-theoretical assumptions that sometimes lead to very different and competing derivations. The same is true of an evolutionary perspective (see Ketelaar & Ellis, 2000). Many of the chapters in this book demonstrate this point very nicely. Buss and Duntley, for example, postulate a particular "homicide module" and contrast their theory to other evolutionary views that view homicide as an incidental by-product of other mechanisms. Zebrowitz and Montepare discuss two very different evolutionary explanations purported to explain psychological responses to physically attractive people. And Brewer and Caporael distinguish between evolutionary processes that focus on the fitness consequences of intergroup conflict vs. those that focus on the consequences of within-group coordination. In doing so, they re-engage the controversial topic of group selection, a concept that is currently discounted by many evolutionary theorists, but has recently been reconsidered in various forms of multilevel selection (see Richerson & Boyd, 2005; Sidanius & Kurzban, 2003). As these and other viewpoints illustrate, an evolutionary approach to social psychology offers a fertile framework for the deduction of many new, conceptually distinct, and sometimes competing hypotheses.

Emphasis on Both Process and Content

Social psychology addresses not only questions about the processes through which thoughts, feelings, and actions are produced, but also questions about the specific contents of those thoughts, feelings, and actions. One side effect of the cognitive revolution was a de-emphasis on content. Indeed, it is often considered an appealing aspect of many cognitive models that they apply universally across different domains of social and nonsocial thought (Markus & Zajonc, 1985). In social life, however, content matters. As important as it is to understand the processes through which attitudes, impressions, and other knowledge structures are acquired, encoded, modified, activated, and associated, it is just as important to understand the actual contents of those knowledge structures—because different contents have different consequences. For example, two qualitatively different trait concepts (e.g., "ignorant", "hostile") may be methodologically interchangeable as stimuli in an experiment studying impression-formation processes, and may even be equivalent in their overall evaluative tenor; but when actually encoded into an actual personality impression or group stereotype, those two traits have very different implications for subsequent interpersonal behavior (see the chapter by Neuberg & Cottrell). In recent years, there has been a resurgence of interest in the actual contents of attitudes, impressions, stereotypes, and social norms. It has become clear that certain kinds of knowledge structures (e.g., fearful attitudes toward ethnic outgroups) are especially likely to be acquired, activated, and to comprise the collective beliefs of most human populations (e.g., Olsson, Ebert, Banaji, & Phelps, 2005; Schaller, Faulkner, Park, Neuberg, & Kenrick, 2004). It is important to understand why this is so and to explore the implications for social cognition and behavior. It is toward this goal that an evolutionary approach to theorizing is uniquely valuable.

One of the most fundamental tenets of an evolutionary approach is that thinking (and feeling) is for doing: The specific thoughts and feelings experienced in a given social context are likely to be those that, during evolutionary history, facilitated specific kinds of behaviors that typically enhanced (or at least did not diminish) reproductive fitness. What one feels or does in a social situation depends critically on what the goal is. Accordingly, the specific contents of affective states and cognitive knowledge structures really do matter—the same feelings and behaviors that will facilitate finding a mate will not facilitate taking care of a child or protecting oneself from a mugger. The common social psychological tendency to lump emotional states into broad categories of negative and positive affect misses the fact that there are evolutionarily-important differences between different kinds of negative and positive states, with very different implications for contemporary social behavior (see the chapter by Keltner, Haidt, & Shiota). The same logic applies to the contents of attitudes, impressions, stereotypes, and other social knowledge structures. Specific, fitness-relevant kinds of social information are particularly likely to draw our attention (Maner et al., 2003). Specific, fitness-relevant kinds of knowledge structures are also learned with special efficiency, and tend to be activated in specific, fitness-relevant kinds of social situations (see Öhman & Mineka, 2001; Schaller, Park, & Faulkner, 2003). An evolutionary approach—with its focus on reproductive and inclusive fitness—has been instrumental in discovering and fully explicating these and many other phenomena. The evolutionary tools that Keltner et al. applied to comprehend the specific nature of social emotions can be extended to develop novel hypotheses about the specific contents of self-concepts, social impressions, intergroup attitudes, and other important social knowledge structures (see the chapters by Haselton & Funder, Neuberg & Cottrell, Sedikides et al., and Zebrowitz & Montepare). And as the chapter by Norenzayan, Heine, and Schaller highlights, these tools can also be used to predict the contents and practices of specific human cultures.

Social Situations that Really Matter

Social psychology is a science that emphasizes social situations and the power of those situations to govern the thoughts, feelings, and actions of individuals. To folks who are naïve about the implications of evolution (and who mistakenly assume that evolution implies inflexibly "hardwired" behavior), the context-dependent malleability of social behavior is sometimes thought to be at odds with an evolutionary analysis. Nothing could be farther from the truth. An evolutionary approach to social psychology not only allows the potential for variability across situations; it provides us with tools to identify the types of situations that should matter most, leading to novel hypotheses about specific social situations that ought to trigger specific kinds of thoughts, feelings, and actions.

What kinds of social situations matter most? Evolutionary inquiries in social psychology focus on mental processes that have been "designed" to solve particular kinds of problems posed by certain social environments. Some problems are more directly relevant to reproductive fitness than others, including problems of self-protection, group affiliation, mate acquisition and retention, and care for one's kin (see Bugental, 2000). Situations bearing on these sorts of problems have particularly powerful and wide-ranging consequences on social perception, cognition, and behavior. For instance, some physical features of people may have historically signaled opportunities that might have enhanced reproductive fitness (e.g., morphological symmetries that convey the attractiveness or "viability" of a potential mate) or threats that might impair it (e.g., morphological oddities that connote the possible presence of parasitic infection). The perception of such features may trigger a cascade of psychological events—specific emotions, specific thoughts, and specific goal states—that facilitate behavioral responses that, on average, enhanced the likelihood of availing oneself of those opportunities or avoiding them during evolutionary history. The potential fitness benefits of any such psychological response, however, must be weighed against the potential costs associated with those responses. These costs and benefits are likely to vary from situation to situation. And so, evolved psychological responses to other people are further calibrated to the particular contextual cues that signal whether those responses are likely to lead to costs or benefits.

A wide variety of novel hypotheses and discoveries have emerged from applications of this logical template, as revealed in every chapter in this volume. For example, Fletcher et al. apply this sort of evolutionary cost–benefit analysis to make predictions about context-specific variation in bias and accuracy within close relationships. Sedikides et al. consider how an evolved predisposition toward self-enhancement might be functionally flexible across different kinds of social contexts. Buss and Duntley's evolutionary analysis of aggressive behavior leads to the specification of qualitatively different kinds of aggression, each of which is linked to a conceptually distinct influence on reproductive fitness, and each of which should be triggered by a distinct set of contextual cues. Similarly, Neuberg and Cottrell develop an evolutionary model of prejudice that not only predicts different forms of enmity toward different kinds of groups, but also predicts specific situations in which each specific prejudice is likely to be exacerbated or mitigated. In sum, these chapters showcase how and why an evolutionary approach to social psychology can help social psychologists improve what they do best: Discover the subtle influences of situations on social cognition and behavior.

Conceptual Integration

One of the classic complaints about social psychology is that it appears to consist of a list of interesting, but largely unrelated, empirical phenomena, each explained by a different ad-hoc mini-theory (e.g., Hogan & Emler, 1978). The cognitive revolution helped to change that perception. With the tools of cognitive science in hand, it became clear that a consistent set of underlying cognitive processes influenced assorted social psychological phenomena. An even more comprehensive conceptual integration can be achieved by combining cognitive science insights about how the mind works with evolutionary insights into what the mind has been designed to work on and why (see Kenrick, Becker, Butner, Li, & Maner, 2003). An evolutionary perspective can bring greater conceptual unity to diverse phenomena within a topic area. It can reveal many subtle points of conceptual contact between ostensibly dissimilar social psychological topics. And it can help build important conceptual bridges between social psychology and other disciplines within the social and biological sciences.

This first point—conceptual unity within a topic area—has been most amply demonstrated in applications of differential parental investment theory to the study of interpersonal attraction and romantic relationships. This single theoretical structure provides a means of conceptually connecting a wide range of physiological phenomena (e.g., predictable variability in the development of secondary sexual characteristics, and in hormone levels across the female ovulatory cycle), affective phenomena (e.g., predictable variability in sexual arousal, and in sexual jealousy), perceptual and cognitive phenomena (e.g., predictable variability in attention to specific kinds of morphological features, and in inferences drawn from those features), behavioral phenomena (e.g., predictable variability in strategies used to find romantic partners, and in exchange patterns in ongoing relationships), and societal-level phenomena (e.g., predictable variability in cultural norms promoting specific forms of marital arrangements, and preventing specific forms of sexual harassment). Similar kinds of conceptual unification are currently being discovered in other social psychological topic areas. In this volume, for instance, one can discern how specific aspects of an evolutionary approach can illuminate connections between very different kinds of phenomena within the literature on the self (see, for example, the chapters by Kurzban & Aktipis and by Sedikides et al.). Many other chapters also highlight integrative utility within specific topic areas.

Even more impressive is the way in which an evolutionary perspective can conceptually connect phenomena across seemingly disparate areas and domains. These lines of conceptual integration go well beyond the obvious observation that modern human beings and our social groups are ultimately the products of natural selection. Although this may be true, it does not tell us much. Far more informative is the fact that the evolutionary consequences of differential parental investment have predictable implications not only for sexual attraction and close relationships, but also (and less obviously) for aggression and other forms of interpersonal influence, including a range of phenomena in the realm of social cognition. Novel conceptual connections also emerge from the fact that an evolutionary cost–benefit analysis can be fruitfully applied to such varied topics as person perception, aggression, prosocial behavior, group dynamics, and intergroup prejudice, to name just a few. These and other cross-topic conceptual commonalities reveal a fundamental set of common processes underlying diverse social psychological phenomena that, at a superficial level, appear to be conceptually unrelated.

Finally, the evolutionary perspective provides the unique service of connecting social psychological phenomena with phenomena in other disciplines. Social psychologists—and the scholarly community more broadly—have benefited enormously from the fact that the cognitive revolution provided novel links to computer science, linguistics, and other cognitive sciences. Similar benefits will accrue from the fact that an evolutionary perspective provides a lattice of connections to theoretical biology, behavioral ecology, physical anthropology, and other life sciences. Research within these disciplines can inspire creative exercises in social psychological theorizing. Furthermore, the empirical findings documented within those literatures are likely to be essential to develop more complete and more detailed explanations of important social psychological phenomena. Years ago, some of Sigmund Freud's erroneous assertions about incest motivations and group psychology resulted from misinformation about evolutionary prehistory and its contemporary consequences. Freud can hardly be blamed, of course, given the limited knowledge of the biological sciences at that time. That excuse does not hold anymore, despite the fact that many psychologists remain fairly ignorant of basic biological facts and findings. Such ignorance—and the mistaken assumptions that accompany it—can lead to erroneous conclusions about the bases of social psychological phenomena (see Kenrick & Simpson, 1997). Just as it behooves us to be familiar with work in the other cognitive sciences, it also behooves us to keep abreast of recent developments in fields such as behavioral ecology, developmental biology, comparative neuroscience, and other evolutionary sciences. Indeed, if we are to develop a truly coherent science of social psychology, such an approach may not be a mere intellectual luxury; it may be a necessity.

THE UNIGNORABILITY OF EVOLUTIONARY SOCIAL PSYCHOLOGY

The cognitive revolution did not occur overnight; it just seems so today. But still, given the passion and prevalence of early objections, it is striking how quickly the cognitive perspective moved into the mainstream of social psychology. The pace of progress in evolutionary social psychology is proving to be just as swift. No longer does it lurk at the outer fringes of social psychological inquiry. Increasingly, evolutionarily informed inquiries are found in the front and center of our field.

The evolutionary approach is still young, of course, and it is still raw, rough, and adolescent in many respects. A host of complicated issues still need to be resolved, and many perplexing questions must still be addressed. There is much that we still do not know about exactly how evolutionary pressures that operated on ancestral populations might have been translated into the cognitive and behavioral tendencies we observe in people today. What are the complex genetic substrates that underlie these psychological processes? What are the specific neurological structures that affect social cognition and interpersonal relationships? What are the developmental processes through which evolved genotypes gave rise to these neurological structures? How is this all influenced by the developing individual's local environment, local culture, and local opportunities for and constraints on learning? Conversely, how does our evolved psychology affect the very cultures we construct? Answers to these and other pressing questions are yet to be discovered. The fact that we do not yet know these answers does not diminish the increasing importance of evolutionary social psychology. If anything, it makes this approach all the more scientifically stimulating. It is only by asking such big questions that big answers will emerge. When they do, those answers will depend upon discoveries in other disciplines (e.g., human genomics, developmental biology, cognitive neuroscience, and cultural psychology) that, like evolutionary social psychology, still represent an exciting scientific frontier. And, just as those other domains of inquiry are increasingly unignorable features of our scientific future, so too is evolutionary social psychology.

REFERENCES

Alcock, J. (2001). *The triumph of sociobiology*. New York: Oxford University Press.

Archer, J. (1996). Sex differences in social behavior: Are social role and evolutionary explanations compatible? *American Psychologist, 51*, 909–917.

Axelrod, R. (1984). *The evolution of cooperation*. New York: Basic Books.

Axelrod, R. (1997). *The complexity of cooperation*. Princeton, NJ: Princeton University Press.

Barrett, H. C. (2005). Enzymatic computation and cognitive modularity. *Mind and Language, 20*, 259–287.

Brewer, M. B. (2004). Taking the social origins of human nature seriously: Toward a more imperialist social psychology. *Personality and Social Psychology Review, 8*, 107–113.

Bugental, D. B. (2000). Acquisition of the algorithms of social life: A domain-based approach. *Psychological Bulletin, 126*, 187–219.

Burnstein, E., Crandall, C., & Kitayama, S. (1994). Some neo-Darwinian rules for altruism: Weighing cues for inclusive fitness as a function of the biological importance of the decision. *Journal of Personality & Social Psychology, 67*, 773–789.

Buss, D. M. (1989). Sex differences in human mate preferences: Evolutionary hypotheses tested in 37 cultures, *Behavioral and Brain Sciences, 12*, 1–49.

Buss, D. M., Haselton, M. G., Shackelford, T. K., Bleske A. L., & Wakefield, J. C. (1998). Adaptations, exaptations, and spandrels. *American Psychologist, 53*, 533–548.

Buss, D. M., & Schmitt, D. P. (1993). Sexual strategies theory: An evolutionary perspective on human mating. *Psychological Review, 100*, 204–232.

Conway, L. G. III, & Schaller, M. (2002). On the verifiability of evolutionary psychological theories: An analysis of the psychology of scientific persuasion. *Personality and Social Psychology Review, 6*, 152–166.

Daly, M., Salmon, C., & Wilson, M. (1997). Kinship: The conceptual hole in psychological studies of social cognition and close relationships. In J. A. Simpson & D.T. Kenrick (Eds.), *Evolutionary social psychology* (pp. 265–296). Mahwah, NJ: Lawrence Erlbaum Associates.

Daly, M., & Wilson, M. (1988). *Homicide*. Hawthorne, NY: Aldine de Gruyter.

Darwin, C. (1859). *On the origin of species*. London: Murray.

DeBruine L. M. (2005). Trustworthy but not lust-worthy: Context-specific effects of facial resemblance. *Proceedings of the Royal Society of London, B, 272*, 919–922.

Ebel, R. L. (1974). And still the dryads linger. *American Psychologist, 29*, 485–492.

Gangestad, S. W., & Simpson, J. A. (2000). The evolution of human mating: Trade-offs and strategic pluralism. *Behavioral & Brain Sciences, 23*, 573–587.

Geary, D. C. (1998). *Male, female: The evolution of human sex differences*. Washington DC: American Psychological Association.

Hogan, R. T., & Emler, N. P. (1978). The biases in contemporary social psychology. *Social Research, 45*, 478–534.

Kenrick, D. T., Becker, D. V., Butner, J., Li, N. P., & Maner, J. K. (2003). Evolutionary cognitive science: Adding what and why to how the mind works. In K. Sterelney & J. Fitness (Eds.), *From mating to mentality: Evaluating evolutionary psychology* (pp. 13–38). New York: Psychology Press.

Kenrick, D. T., & Simpson, J. A. (1997). Why social psychology and evolutionary psychology need one another. In J. A. Simpson & D. T. Kenrick (Eds.), *Evolutionary social psychology* (pp. 1–20). Mahwah, NJ: Lawrence Erlbaum Associates.

Kenrick, D. T., Trost, M. R., & Sundie, J. M. (2004). Sex-roles as adaptations: An evolutionary perspective on gender differences and similarities. In A. H. Eagly, A. Beall, & R. Sternberg (Eds.), *Psychology of gender.* New York: Guilford.

Ketelaar, T., & Ellis, B. J. (2000). Are evolutionary explanations unfalsifiable? Evolutionary psychology and the Lakatosian philosophy of science. *Psychological Inquiry, 11,* 1–21.

Kruglanski, A. W. (2001). That "vision thing": The state of theory in social and personality psychology at the edge of the new millennium. *Journal of Personality and Social Psychology, 80,* 871–875.

Kruglanski, A. W., & Higgins, E. T. (2004). Theory construction in social personality psychology: Personal experiences and lessons learned. *Personality and Social Psychology Review, 8,* 96–97.

Laham, S. M., Gonsalkorale, K., & von Hippel, W. (2005). Darwinian grandparenting: Preferential investment in more certain kin. *Personality & Social Psychology Bulletin, 31,* 63–72.

Lakatos, I. (1970). Falsification and the methodology of scientific research programs. In I. Lakatos & A. Musgrave (Eds.), *Criticism and the growth of knowledge* (pp. 91–196). Cambridge, UK: Cambridge University Press.

Li, N. P., Bailey, J. M., Kenrick, D. T., & Linsenmeier, J. A. (2002). The necessities and luxuries of mate preferences: Testing the trade-offs. *Journal of Personality and Social Psychology, 82,* 947–955.

Maner, J. K., Kenrick, D. T., Becker, D. V., Delton, A. W., Hofer, B., Wilbur, C. J., & Neuberg, S. L. (2003). Sexually selective cognition: Beauty captures the mind of the beholder. *Journal of Personality and Social Psychology, 6,* 1107–1120.

Maner, J. K., Kenrick, D. T., Becker, D. V., Robertson, T. E., Hofer, B., Neuberg, S. L., Delton, A. W., Butner, J., & Schaller, M. (2005). Functional projection: How fundamental social motives can bias interpersonal perception. *Journal of Personality & Social Psychology, 88,* 63–78.

Markus, H., & Zajonc, R. B. (1985). The cognitive perspective in social psychology. In G. Lindzey & E. Aronson (Eds.), *Handbook of social psychology* (Vol. 1, pp. 137–230). New York: Random House.

Nesse, R. M. (2005). Natural selection and the regulation of defenses: A signal detection analysis of the smoke detector principle. *Evolution and Human Behavior, 26,* 88–105.

Öhman, A., & Mineka, S. (2001). Fears, phobias, and preparedness: Toward an evolved module of fear and fear learning. *Psychological Review, 108,* 483–522.

Öhman, A., & Mineka, S. (2003). The malicious serpent: Snakes as a prototypical stimulus for an evolved module of fear. *Current Directions in Psychological Science, 12,* 5–9.

Olsson, A., Ebert, J. P., Banaji, M. R., & Phelps, E. A. (2005). The role of social groups in the persistence of learned fear. *Science, 309,* 785–787.

Park, J. H., & Schaller, M. (2005). Does attitude similarity serve as a heuristic cue for kinship? Evidence of an implicit cognitive association. *Evolution and Human Behavior, 26*, 158–170.

Richerson, P. J., & Boyd, R. (2005). *Not by genes alone: How culture transformed human evolution.* Chicago: University of Chicago Press.

Sadalla, E. K., Kenrick, D. T., & Vershure, B. (1987). Dominance and heterosexual attraction. *Journal of Personality and Social Psychology, 52*, 730–738.

Schaller, M. (2002). The evidentiary standard of special design is a little bit like heaven. *Behavioral and Brain Sciences, 25*, 526–527.

Schaller, M., Faulkner, J., Park, J. H., Neuberg, S. L., & Kenrick, D. T. (2004). Impressions of danger influence impressions of people: An evolutionary perspective on individual and collective cognition. *Journal of Cultural and Evolutionary Psychology, 2*, 231–247.

Schaller, M., Park, J. H., & Faulkner, J. (2003). Prehistoric dangers and contemporary prejudices. *European Review of Social Psychology, 14*, 105–137.

Schmitt, D. P., & Pilcher, J. J. (2004). Evaluating evidence of psychological adaptation: How do we know one when we see one? *Psychological Science, 15*, 643–649.

Sidanius, J., & Kurzban, R. (2003). Evolutionary approaches to political psychology. In D.O. Sears, L. Huddy, & R. Jervis (Eds.), *Oxford handbook of political psychology* (pp. 146–181). New York: Oxford University Press.

Simpson, J. A., & Campbell, L. (2005). Methods of evolutionary sciences. In D. M. Buss (Ed.), *The handbook of evolutionary psychology* (pp. 119–144). New York: Wiley.

Simpson, J. A., & Gangestad, S. W. (1991). Individual differences in sociosexuality: Evidence for convergent and discriminant validity. *Journal of Personality & Social Psychology, 67*, 870–883.

Skinner, B. F. (1950). Are theories of learning necessary? *Psychological Review, 57*, 193–216.

Thagard, P. (1992). *Conceptual revolutions.* Princeton, NJ: Princeton University Press.

Tooby, J., & Cosmides, L. (1992). The psychological foundations of culture. In J. H. Barkow, L. Cosmides, & J. Tooby (Eds.), *The adapted mind* (pp. 19–136). New York: Oxford University Press.

Trivers, R. L. (1972). Parental investment and sexual selection. In B. Campbell (Ed.), *Sexual selection and the descent of man 1871–1971* (pp. 136–179). Chicago: Aldine.

2

The Evolution of Accuracy and Bias in Social Judgment

MARTIE G. HASELTON and DAVID C. FUNDER

*H*umans are an intensely social species and therefore it is essential for our interpersonal judgments to be valid enough to help us to avoid enemies, form useful alliances and find suitable mates; flawed judgments can literally be fatal. An evolutionary perspective implies that humans ought to have developed sufficient skills at solving problems of interpersonal judgment, including gauging the personalities of others, to be useful for the basic tasks of survival and reproduction. Yet, the view to be derived from the large and influential bias-and-error literature of social psychology is decidedly different—the social mind seems riddled with fundamental design flaws. We will argue in this paper that flawed design is probably the least plausible explanation for the existence of so many errors. We present an evolutionarily based taxonomy of known bias effects that distinguishes between biases that are trivial or even artifactual and lead virtually nowhere, and those that have interesting implications and deserve further study. Finally, we present an evolutionary perspective that suggests that the ubiquity, automaticity, and success of interpersonal judgment, among other considerations, presents the possibility of a universal Personality Judgment Instinct.

ADAPTATIONS FOR SOCIAL LIFE

Archeological evidence and behavioral patterns observed in extant hunter–gatherer groups indicate that the human species has been intensely social for a long time (e.g., Chagnon, 1983; Tooby & Devore, 1987). Human offspring have a remarkably extended period of juvenile dependency, which both requires and provides the skills for surviving in a complex social world (Hrdy, 1999). Humans evolved language and universal emotional expressions that serve the social purpose of discerning and influencing the thoughts of others (e.g., Darwin, 1872; Ekman, 1973; Pinker, 1994), and humans will infer social

intentions on the basis of minimal cues, as Heider and Simmel (1944) demonstrated in their classic experiment involving chasing triangles and evading circles. Recent work has shown that children above age 4 and adults in disparate
cultures (Germans and Amazonian Indians) can categorize intentions—chasing,
fighting, following, playing, and courting (for adults)—from no more than the
motion patterns of computerized v-shaped arrowheads (Barrett, Todd, Miller,
& Blythe, 2005).

Most notably, humans have a deeply felt need for social inclusion.
Deprivation of social contact produces anxiety, loneliness, and depression
(Baumeister & Leary, 1995); indeed, as William James (1890) observed: "Solitary
confinement is by many regarded as a mode of torture too cruel and unnatural
for civilised countries to adopt." Participants in laboratory studies who are left
out of a face-to-face triadic ball toss respond with depressed mood and decreased
self-esteem (Williams & Sommer, 1997). These effects can even be produced by
a computerized version of the game in which participants use key presses to
"toss" the ball back and forth to human-like figures on a screen (Williams,
Cheung, & Choi, 2000), and persist when participants are told that the other
players have been scripted or are mere computer programs (Zadro & Williams,
2003, cited in Williams, Case, & Govan, 2003). Neuroscience evidence suggests
that being ostracized activates the same brain regions involved in the sensation
of physical pain (Eisenberger, Lieberman, & Williams, 2003). Rejection hurts,
literally.

This acute social sensitivity makes sense in the light of the many problems of
social adaptation that have long faced members of our species: the formation of
cooperative alliances for hunting and protection (e.g., Tooby & Cosmides, 1988;
Tooby & Devore, 1987), hierarchy negotiation (Kyl-Heku & Buss, 1996), mate
choice (Buss, 2003; Miller, 2000; Symons, 1979), choice of allies and friends
(Tooby & Cosmides, 1996), and social exchange (Cosmides, 1989), to name a few.
Given the importance of these problems, we should expect finely honed adaptations for forming social judgments and making social decisions that are, at the very
least, good enough to promote survival and reproduction. We would certainly *not*
expect thousands of years of social evolution to yield a psychological apparatus
fundamentally prone to social misperception, judgmental flaws, and maladaptive
interpersonal behavior. Yet, this is the picture one gets from a good deal of conventional research in social psychology.

IS THE SOCIAL MIND DEEPLY FLAWED?

A large part of social psychology—including some of its most famous and influential research programs—consists of a loosely connected set of nonintuitive and
curious effects, each of which demonstrates a context in which humans can be led
to make incorrect judgments according to one or more standards of logic, statistics, or even morality (Krueger & Funder, 2004). An especially famous error is the
putative tendency for people to infer that dispositions (enduring aspects of personality) have stronger effects on the behavior of others than do situations, coined

the *fundamental attribution error* (Ross, 1977; but see Funder, 1982). Humans also have been accused of false consensus, confirmation bias, overconfidence bias (as well as pessimistic bias), hindsight bias, and the sinister attribution error. And, experimenters have caught humans in the act of committing the planning fallacy, the external agency illusion, and the transparency illusion. These are just a few examples from a very long list (for reviews see Fiske & Taylor, 1991; Gilovich, Griffin, & Kahneman, 2002), a list that grows longer all the time. One recent example is the *dud-alternative effect* in which adding an implausible alternative (e.g., a "dud" in a horserace) increases the judged likelihood that a good alternative will win, when in fact the inclusion of more alternatives must reduce the probability of success for any given candidate (Windschitl & Chambers, 2004). An especially terrifying recent example is the *bias blind spot* (Pronin, Gilovich, & Ross, 2004), which is the bias to not know you are biased! The cumulative effect of this ever-growing list is a view of the human social mind as fraught with shortcomings, a view that is almost always detectable implicitly and often is expressed explicitly as well (Lopes, 1991).

The emphasis on bias and error is understandable to some degree. Bias effects tend to be counterintuitive (Funder, 2003; Lopes, 1991), funny—they make for good anecdotes and amusing classroom demonstrations (Crandall, 1984)—and to the degree they really do afflict cognition and associated life outcomes, they call out for study so that they can be fixed. However, the view of human judgment as dominated by error is both implausible and theoretically impoverished.

When a putative error of human judgment is discovered, there are three possible explanations. First, the error might not be an error at all. The experimental situation or instructions to subjects or the standards by which error has been defined might be misleading or incorrect, so that the putative error is better considered an experimental artifact. Second, the error might be one that, on balance, leads in realistic situations to adaptive decisions more often than not. The error might be produced by a usually adaptive heuristic, or be the result of a tendency to favor less costly errors over more costly ones (see below). For example, to the extent that behavior really is predictable from stable traits and attitudes, the fundamental attribution error (to the extent that it is itself not an artifact) will tend to produce correct decisions in realistic circumstances. Third, the error might reveal a flaw in psychological design such that the mind is fundamentally prone to get a broad class of decisions wrong. This explanation is the most frequently offered of the three but is, we submit, the least plausible one.

Furthermore, these loosely connected findings, despite their number, do not add up to a broad, coherent theory of human social thought and behavior. The reason is that demonstrations of error characteristically begin by assuming human judgment to be perfect, and attain their news value from the conclusion that it is not. But this conclusion does not provide even the beginnings of an explanation of how judgments are ever made correctly; the initial assumption of perfection bypasses any possibility of a broader account. Instead, the long lists of errors powerfully convey the usually implicit, sometimes explicit and surely misleading message that good judgment is rarely achieved.

WHERE DO BIASES COME FROM?

Setting aside the possibility of fundamentally flawed mental design, we suggest that each of the many documented biases and errors may be (1) *artifacts* of inappropriate research strategies, and surprisingly many of the most famous ones may belong in this category, (2) may stem from *heuristics*, usually effective judgmental strategies that are subject to systematic breakdown, or (3) be the result of *error management*, a special case of a heuristic in which less costly errors are favored over more expensive ones (see Table 2.1; after Haselton, Nettle, & Andrews, 2005). We consider each of these causes in turn.

Artifacts

Before beginning a serious analysis of the source of perceptual and judgmental bias, the first step is to set aside those that are little more than experimental artifacts. Researchers have found it easy to design artificial research settings in which individuals can be shown to err. But do such demonstrations reveal flaws in the design of the mind? Similarly, if the testing strategies researchers use to conduct research are more sensitive to error than to accuracy, people will appear error-prone. But are they really?

TABLE 2.1   Evolutionary Taxonomy of Evidence of Bias and Error in Social Psychological Research

Cause of Apparent Bias	Examples
Artifact: Apparent biases and errors are artifacts of research strategies. Biases result from the application of inappropriate norms (e.g., Cosmides & Tooby, 1996), the placement of humans in unnatural settings (e.g., Gigerenzer, 1997), or testing within the *error paradigm* (Krueger & Funder, 2004)	• Some instances of base-rate neglect (Hertwig & Gigerenzer, 1999) • Some instances of confirmation bias (Cosmides, 1989)
Heuristic: Bias results from the use of heuristics, which work well in most circumstances but are prone to systematic breakdown. Heuristics are compromise solutions to problems of judgment given time or processing capacity constraints (e.g., Tversky & Kahneman, 1974) or ecological/informational constraints (e.g., Gigerenzer, Czerlinski, & Martignon, 2002)	• Fundamental attribution error • One-reason decision strategies (Gigerenzer, Todd, and the ABC Research Group, 1999)
Error Management: Selection favors bias toward the less costly error (Haselton & Buss, 2000). Error management causes overall rates of error to increase, though net costs are minimized	• Auditory looming (Neuhoff, 2001) • Sexual overperception by men (Haselton, 2003) • Commitment skepticism in women (Haselton & Buss, 2000)

Problem Formats   Gigerenzer (1997) proposed that the human mind should be better at likelihood estimation when presented with information about discrete events as compared to numerical probabilities. Frequencies of events are what are observed in nature, he argued, whereas probabilities are invented, numerical abstractions that lack any direct connection to sensory input. Moreover, the computation of probabilities loses information about base rates (Cosmides & Tooby, 1996), so even if human sensory systems could take probabilities as input, frequencies may convey superior information.

In the famous Linda problem, subjects were asked to read a personality description: "Linda is 31 years old, single, outspoken, and very bright. She majored in philosophy. As a student, she was deeply concerned with issues of discrimination and social justice, and also participated in anti-nuclear demonstrations." They were then asked to determine which of two options was more probable: (1) Linda is a bank teller, or (2) Linda is a bank teller and active in the feminist movement. Although the conjunction cannot be more likely than either of its constituents, between 80 and 90% of subjects select (2) as the more probable option, committing the "conjunction fallacy" (Tversky & Kahneman, 1983). However, simply changing the format of the problem from probabilities to frequencies (e.g., how many out of 200 women are bank tellers and how many out of 200 are bank tellers and feminists) dramatically improves performance [Cosmides & Tooby, 1996; Fiedler, 1988; Hertwig & Gigerenzer, 1999; Tversky & Kahneman, 1983, but see Mellers, Hertwig, & Kahneman (2001); also see Hertwig & Gigerenzer (1999) for related issues about violation of conversational norms in the classic problems]. This insight has implications that go beyond identifying artifacts; Gigerenzer and his colleagues point out that in the relatively rare but important cases where exact probability judgments are important (e.g., in medical diagnosis), it is important to give decision-makers (e.g., doctors) relevant information in a form they can use (Hoffrage, Lindsey, Hertwig, & Gigerenzer, 2001).

Problem Content   Often researchers compare human performance to idealized rules of logic or specific statistical computations. Ironically, the very fact that it is feasible to present judgmental problems to humans using words, numbers, and abstract concepts may be precisely why it so easy to demonstrate that people make mistakes in solving such problems. Imagine, by contrast, a study that tried to demonstrate fundamental irrationality, or even imprecise reasoning, in a dog. Would this be possible? We would guess not, which does not mean that canines are smarter than humans, at least not in most cases. Rather, the presentation of difficult abstract problems presented in complex verbal and numeric formats is something that can only be inflicted on humans. You would not do it to a dog. From an evolutionary perspective, the important problems of judgment are probably not very abstract. They involve estimations of others' specific motives and intentions (such as distinguishing friend from foe), predicting whether a patch of land will contain prey animals or predators, and, perhaps, detecting cheaters in social exchange.

As statistics teachers can attest, people do not find falsification logic either intuitively sensible or easy to employ. It comes as little surprise, then, that people are not especially good at testing the abstract conditional rule, if *p* then *q*. Wason (1983) showed that subjects correctly recognized that confirmatory evidence (the presence of *p*) is relevant to testing the rule, but they typically failed to test for falsifications of the rule (the absence of *q*). In the same line of research, however, a variety of content effects augmented performance on the task (e.g., Johnson-Laird, Legrenzi, & Legrenzi, 1972; Wason & Shapiro, 1971). Cosmides (1989) argued that many of these content effects reflect the operation of a cheater-detection algorithm. When the conditional rule involves social exchange (if you take the benefit [*p*] then you pay the cost [*q*]), people look not only for benefits taken (*p*) but also costs not paid (not *q*), increasing performance dramatically from 25% correct (Wason, 1983) to 75% correct (Cosmides, 1989). Similar effects are elicited by hazard-detection content, in which people are also induced to detect violations of a precaution rule about hazards (e.g., if you touch a contaminant [*p*] then you wash your hands [*q*]; Pereyra, 2000). Cosmides hypothesized that performance increases dramatically in these problems because the content elicited mechanisms for cheater detection or reasoning about hazards, both of which necessarily use falsification "logic" given the nature of the adaptive problem they are designed to solve [Cosmides, 1989; Fiddick, Cosmides, & Tooby, 2000; Pereya, 2000; see Cosmides & Tooby (1992) for an extensive discussion, including a description of the many variants of the task devised to rule out confounds and alternative explanations]. The conclusion to be taken from this work is not that humans actually do reason according to abstract rules of logic; in fact, results from the same line of work demonstrate cases in which adaptive responses systematically violate normative rules (see, e.g., the work on switched social contracts, Cosmides, 1989). Instead, the key message is that adaptive performance cannot be evaluated unless researchers present subjects with problems for which their minds are designed.

The Error Paradigm   The most basic reason to be skeptical of many of the putative demonstrations of error is that that the error paradigm, upon which most of these demonstrations are based, makes it extremely easy to detect error and almost impossible to detect accurate judgment. In the typical study, the normative response, whether it is derived from formal logic, abstract principles, or math, is a point prediction. For example, people have been asked to estimate other persons' attitudes, frequencies of behavioral compliance, probabilities of events, or even exact degrees of association between two variables. Only if subjects exactly attain the experimenter-defined correct estimate of the correct number will they be treated as accurate; needless to say, this almost never happens. The average estimate by real subjects will not exactly match the point-prediction; if enough subjects are in the sample, this deviation will be statistically significant, and a new bias will be born (Krueger & Funder, 2004). The abundant evidence of error in the literature must be qualified by noting that the basic research strategy makes error easy to find.

Heuristics

As Herbert Simon famously observed, the best solutions to problems of judgment are often good enough—*satisficing*—rather than the best imaginable, because perfection may not be worth the extra cost (Simon, 1956). This observation inspired much of the most influential research on social judgment and decision-making. Kahneman, Tversky and many others (see Gilovich et al., 2002, for a recent review) proposed that information processing time and cognitive capacity are limited and thus people use heuristics that trade-off accuracy for speed and efficiency. Surprisingly, however, many researchers forgot Simon's important message that such trade-offs still ought to yield decisions that are reasonably good. Instead, study after study was designed to show how the use of heuristics caused people to be, quite simply, wrong. For example, Tversky and Kahneman documented a variety of effects suggesting that humans do not use probability information properly.

For example, the "Linda problem" which we have already mentioned, led people to estimate Linda to be more likely to be a feminist bank teller than to be merely a bank teller. In studies in which subjects judged the likelihood of series of coin flips, subjects tended to say that HTHTTH was more likely than the sequence HHHTTT or HHHHTH, when in fact the former contains too many alternations and too few runs (Tversky & Kahneman, 1974). People seem to expect chance to be a self-correcting process (for a series of Hs to be corrected by a T), but of course each new flip is independent of the last, and in large samples correction has not occurred but rather repeated Hs or Ts have merely been diluted (Tversky & Kahneman, 1974).

Tversky and Kahneman (1974, p. 1124) attributed these effects and a variety of others to the use of mental short-cuts: "people rely on a limited number of heuristic principles which reduce the complex tasks of assessing probabilities and predicting values to simpler judgmental operations." Indeed, when people are rushed in forming judgments, under cognitive load, or less motivated to be correct, their tendency to be biased (and presumably their use of heuristics) is more pronounced (see, e.g., Kahneman, 2003). Tversky and Kahneman (1974) offered the heuristic *representativeness* as an explanation for the conjunction fallacy and misconceptions of chance. When using the heuristic, people base their answers more on what is deemed representative of the category (feminist, random sequence) than on assessments of probabilities.

These investigators and others operating in the same paradigm have observed that they did not intend their findings to be taken as belittling the capacities of human judgment, and that heuristics such as representativeness might very well be part-and-parcel of good judgment under most circumstances. However, the consistent research strategy has been to show how these heuristics lead to errors, not how they ever, let alone typically, enhance accuracy or produce otherwise adaptive judgments. The widespread impression produced by this body of work, therefore, is of a massive number of studies demonstrating how heuristics produce errors, against few if any showing their adaptive possibilities. This impression has been encouraged by some of the rhetoric employed in research summaries (Funder, 1992; Lopes, 1991).

Only recently has this imbalance begun to be corrected. Gigerenzer and colleagues (e.g., Gigerenzer et al., 1999) developed a very different take on Simon's classic message. They observed that in addition to constraints imposed by time and cognitive capacity, the environment imposes quirky *informational* constraints (Gigerenzer, Czerlinski, & Martignon, 2002). People can only be expected to use information that is actually available to them in the current environment, or was so in the evolutionary environment in which decision-making strategies were forged. (As we discussed in the artifacts section, this perspective offers an alternative explanation for subjects' well-documented failure to use some forms of probability information correctly.) People are also expected to possess strategies that exploit features of the informational environment leading to efficient—*fast-and-frugal*—decisions that are, as Simon would expect, valid enough to be useful (Gigerenzer et al., 1999).

Gigerenzer and Goldstein (1996) showed that a family of simple decision-making rules that use only one datum can work as well or better than more complex algorithms (e.g., multiple regression) that use all possible information. An example is the recognition heuristic. When asked to make judgments about which of two alternatives will be higher on some criterion variable (such as who will succeed in a soccer game, or which city is larger) someone who uses the heuristic will choose the more familiar alternative. For example, when asked which city has a larger population, San Diego or San Antonio, German students tend to guess right: San Diego (Goldstein & Gigerenzer, 1999). American students tend to get this question wrong. This is the *less-is-more* effect—American students cannot use recognition since they have heard of both cities, so they rely on other cues that turn out to be invalid. The advantage reverses when German cities are compared; American students generally do better. Native residents know too much—both cities in their own country sound familiar to them—and therefore they cannot exploit the general principle that names of foreign cities are likely to seem more familiar if their population is larger.

The essential function of a heuristic is to guide someone who has little relevant information toward one or a few valid cues within a sea of possibilities. In this case, the cue is recognition. The heuristic would not be adaptive, and thus it would not persist as a feature of human cognition, if it did not produce useful decisions in most cases.

Error Management

The most common interpretation of biases involves trade-offs against constraining factors, such as time, cognitive resources, and the availability of information, as we have seen. But such an interpretation does not explain the particular *direction* of the bias exhibited. We suggest two possible solutions to this problem (also see Kenrick & Maner, 2005; Krebs & Denton, 1997). The first is that the bias may actually serve, in most cases, to nudge inferences based on limited information in the direction of a valid or useful conclusion. For example, to the extent that human behavior really is affected by personality dispositions, an inference based on limited information that is biased in the direction of the fundamental attribution error is more likely to be correct than an inference not influenced by this bias. This process is analogous to the case in visual perception, where errors such as the Ponzo illusion or the Müller–Lyer illusion reveal mechanisms that cause limited two-dimensional stimuli to be misjudged but allow correct judgment of size and distance in three-dimensional contexts (Funder, 1987).

A second explanation for directional bias draws on the fact that judgments are not merely abstract outcomes; they are bases for action and therefore affect survival and reproductive success. As Kurzban and Aktipis (this volume) explain, the mind is not designed for logic or truth, per se. In some domains, such as representing certain aspects of the visual world, reasonable accuracy is adaptive, whereas in others, what is adaptively useful might systematically misrepresent the truth.

Biases may, for example, be directed by trade-offs in error costs. Judgment mechanisms can make two general types of errors, false positives (false alarms) and false negatives (misses). For any given decision or judgment these two types of errors often differ in their costs. Sometimes a false alarm is highly costly. This is the case in scientific hypothesis testing, in which researchers have set the criterion for affirmation very high. In other cases a miss is more costly, as when people react to a threat too quickly but they are "better safe than sorry." Error Management Theory (Haselton & Buss, 2000, 2003; Haselton & Nettle, 2006) proposes that whenever the costs of errors in a given domain were consistently asymmetric over evolutionary history, judgment or decision-making adaptations should evolve to bias inferences toward the less costly error. Systems designed according to this engineering principle will tend to make more errors overall, but the errors will tend to be relatively cheap.

Haselton and Nettle (2006) argue that many apparent biases—from sensory perception to estimating the likelihood of events in the future—can be understood from this perspective. In perception, Neuhoff (2001) documented *auditory looming* in estimations of the time-to-impact of approaching sounds. When people try to estimate the time of approaching sounds, they tend to underestimate the time of arrival, whereas when sounds move away, their estimates are unbiased (Neuhoff, 2001). Underestimation may have been favored by selection. When an object (such as a falling rock) is traveling toward you, it is better to anticipate its arrival too early than too late.

Haselton and Buss (2000) documented two error management effects in courtship communication. Abbey (1982) found that during brief cross-sex interactions men tended to rate women's sexual interest more highly than the women themselves did. Haselton and Buss (2000) proposed that this effect may reflect an evolved sexual overperception bias in men. They hypothesized that the fitness costs of underestimating a woman's sexual interest and thereby missing a sexual opportunity were greater on average than the costs of overestimating her interest and spending effort on fruitless courtship. Given women's selectiveness in mate choice (Trivers, 1972) and men's relatively greater willingness to engage in sex (e.g., Schmitt & International Sexuality Description Project, 2003), the same asymmetry does not hold for women's estimations of men's sexual intent. Three studies using diverse methods confirmed Abbey's original finding and showed, as predicted, that women do not show the same bias in interpreting men's sexual intent (Haselton, 2003; Haselton & Buss, 2000). In a recent set of experiments, Maner et al. (2005) found converging results. Men who were placed in a romantic frame of mind were particularly likely to see sexual arousal in women's facial expressions, especially when the women in the photographs were attractive. These results suggest that cues to increased reproductive benefits, which should further shift cost asymmetries to favor the false-positive bias, tend to yield corresponding increases in sexual overperception by men.

Haselton and Buss (2000) also predicted that women would be biased in interpreting men's courtship communications. They hypothesized that the fitness costs of overestimating a man's interest in forming a long-term relationship were greater ancestrally than the costs of underestimating it: the former could result in reproductive abandonment, whereas the latter would result in modest reproductive delays. As predicted, women appear to be commitment-skeptical—relative to men, they tend to underestimate the degree of commitment conveyed by various dating actions (Haselton & Buss, 2000). Men show no such bias in interpreting women's commitment on the basis of the same cues (Haselton & Buss, 2000).

Many other biases may also be understood from the error management perspective. Defenses such as allergy, cough, and anxiety should be somewhat over-responsive to threats (Nesse, 2001). Indeed, doctors can dampen these defenses with drugs and cause few untoward effects on their patients (Nesse, 2001). People may have a natural tendency to avoid diseased or injured persons to a greater extent than strictly necessary to avoid becoming ill themselves (Kurzban & Leary, 2001). There is evidence that this bias overextends to disabled individuals or individuals expressing phenotypic extremes (e.g., the obese) who pose no true threat (Park, Faulkner, & Schaller, 2003; Park, Schaller, & Crandall, 2004). Two sets of studies also indicate that cues linked with harm increase defensive biases. First, ambient darkness, a cue suggesting increased risk of hostility by others, increases subjects' stereotypes connoting violence in outgroup males, whereas other negative stereotypes do not change (Schaller, Park & Faulkner, 2003; Schaller, Park & Mueller, 2003). Second, subjects who are induced to feel fear in the laboratory see more anger in neutral facial expressions of outgroup males as compared with subjects induced to feel romantic arousal or those in the neutral emotion condition (Maner et al., 2005).

"Positive illusions" (Taylor & Brown, 1988) may be understood as biases for promoting striving when the costs of expended efforts are lower than the costs of passivity, as trying and failing may not be very costly relative to failures to try at all (Nettle, 2004; also see Kurzban & Aktipis, this volume; Taylor & Brown, 1988). For example, feeling optimistic and therefore increasing one's striving for uncertain fitness goals, such as finding an attractive mate or achieving status in the eyes of peers, results in a greater chance of success than failures to try because of a sober perspective. Considered together, the error management effects we have reviewed suggest that people should be optimistic in some circumstances but paranoid in others (i.e., they should be *paranoid optimists*, Haselton & Nettle, 2006). Whichever strategy dominates in a given situation will depend on the relative costs of errors.

In sum, biased solutions may often be better than strategies that seek to maximize accuracy. Evolutionary models of specific adaptive problems of judgment and the relative costs of errors have helped guide researchers to undiscovered adaptive biases, as well as explaining some known to exist.

Clean House and Shift the Focus

Our brief review of the errors-and-biases literature has two implications. First, now may be a good time to *clean house*. The taxonomy in Table 2.1 provides principled standards for deciding which biases do and do not deserve extensive study. If a bias is likely to be an artifact of a research strategy, it is unlikely to have an impact on humans' daily thoughts and actions, and surely, then, we should not devote abundant effort to studying it.

Second, a shift in focus may be in order. If errors are produced by useful heuristics that sometimes break down, they are best thought of as by-products of otherwise adaptive systems. We wonder, then, shouldn't the focus be on the adaptations themselves? Errors resulting from the use of heuristics demonstrate how the system fails, which reveals only a limited amount about its design. In investigations of personality attribution, for example, the focus has typically been on repeated demonstrations of the fundamental attribution error. The question of how observers use behavior to make reasonable inferences about enduring dispositions (a formidable task, as we will see) is neglected, leaving us with little information about how this is actually done. Similarly, with respect to error management effects, one can investigate how and when these biases translate into adaptive social behaviors (or those that were adaptive in ancestral environments).

PERSONALITY JUDGMENT

After years of debate, most social scientists agree that personality exists—people have enduring personality traits that are useful in predicting their behavior (the only thing shocking now about this is how long it took to arrive at this conclusion; see, e.g., Kenrick & Funder, 1988.) Given personality variation along important social dimensions such as cooperativeness, competitiveness, and dependability, being able to discriminate between individuals who are high and low on these dimensions poses a crucial adaptive problem. In short, when deciding with whom to cooperate and whom to avoid or whom to select as a long-term mate, better personality judgment leads to better behavioral prediction, which leads to better social decisions.

The Realistic Accuracy Model

One description of how judgment of personality characteristics might be judged accurately is the Realistic Accuracy Model (Funder, 1995, 1999). Consider an individual who has managed to accurately judge the cooperativeness, competitiveness, or conscientiousness of another. How is this possible? According to the model, four things must happen. First, the target of judgment must do something *relevant* to the trait in question. An individual cannot just sit around thinking cooperative thoughts, he or she must actually do something characteristic of cooperativeness or his or her disposition will remain forever unknown. Second, this behavioral information must be *available* to the judge. A common example is physical presence. An individual might be cooperative with her family, but uncooperative at work, or vice versa, leading co-workers or family members (respectively) to underestimate her general capacity for cooperation. Third, relevant and available information must be successfully *detected* by the judge. He or she must not be so inattentive or distracted or unperceptive as to miss essential clues as to what is going on. Finally, successfully detected relevant and available information must still be correctly *utilized* by the judge, which includes being correctly remembered, compared to existing knowledge, and interpreted.

The most important implication of this model for present purposes is that it reveals how and why personality judgment is so difficult. Unless all four stages of the model are successfully traversed, accurate personality judgment is impossible, and partial imperfections at each stage combine multiplicatively (Funder, 1999). If the target does not do anything relevant, if the relevant behavior is in a context not shared with the judge (e.g., if the target deliberately conceals uncooperative behavior), if the judge misses important information, or if he or she misinterprets the information—any of these failures is sufficient to sink accuracy. Perhaps even worse, the Realistic Accuracy Model is a description of the core of the process of accurate judgment that oversimplifies the problems entailed. The model describes a one-cue one-judgment sequence, whereas in realistic contexts judges evaluate multiple traits simultaneously on the basis of multiple sources of behavioral information that vary in credibility and which derive much of their meaning from the ways in which they interact with the social context and with each other. Indeed, when one considers how difficult it is to correctly judge personality, it is possible to feel the same way some observers have felt when contemplating the formidable task of learning, comprehending and producing language: it must be impossible.

And yet, of course, people do sometimes judge personality accurately. Decades ago, Gordon Allport (1937, p. 353) observed that often we *are* able "to select gifts that our friends will like, to bring together a congenial group at dinner, to choose words that will have the desired effect upon an acquaintance, or to pick a satisfactory employee, tenant, or room-mate." Without getting into a debate about whether people are usually right or wrong, it is easy to observe that it would be difficult to survive in a social environment if our personality judgments were not correct at least sometimes. Moreover, extensive evidence from the Riverside Accuracy Project and other sources shows that personality judgments often show impressive construct validity when evaluated against the criteria of self–other agreement, consensus, and the ability to predict future behavior (Funder, 1999).

Evidence also suggests that people can make valid inferences from very subtle appearance cues. A range of personality traits can be judged with surprising accuracy from very brief observations (Ambady, Bernieri, & Richeson, 2000), including traits associated with personality disorders (Oltmanns, Friedman,

Fiedler & Turkheimer, 2004). Strangers can discriminate "cheaters" in experimental social exchange interactions from noncheaters based on facial photographs alone (Yamagishi, Tanida, Mashima, Shimoma, & Kanizawa, 2003). Women and men tend to judge men with masculine and symmetrical faces as sexier, more sexually experienced, more dominant, but less faithful and less likely to be good dads (Johnston, Hagel, Franklin, Fink, & Grammer, 2001; Penton-Voak & Perrett, 2001). Research has shown that more symmetrical men (who also tend to be more facially masculine) tend toward a short-term mating strategy (Gangestad & Simpson, 2000), and thus these judgments have validity.

A Personality Judgment Instinct?

The achievement of accuracy under such difficult circumstances creates a dilemma. People seem to go way beyond the information given, to know more about personality than they should know given each individual's limited social experience, and to be better at judging attributes of others than they would be expected to be given the complex and multifaceted problem such judgment presents. A similar dilemma was resolved in the domain of language by theory and research on the "language instinct." Researchers proposed that humans are able to learn language because the infant mind already contains many language rules and specific language-learning devices (e.g., Pinker, 1994, 2000). This proposal was of course controversial, so we are aware of venturing across thin ice when suggesting a personality judgment instinct. Yet, it is worth considering the possibility that, like language, the ability to judge personality emerges during development as a result of specialized learning mechanisms. These mechanisms help developing humans to sift through cues linked with personalities by entertaining privileged hypotheses about them. In its mature form, the personality judgment instinct leads people to quickly form and utilize valid personality judgments, and thus helps to explain how accurate judgment is possible even in the face of seemingly overwhelming obstacles.

By instinct, we mean that the ability to judge personality is undergirded by a set of evolved, relatively autonomous, and specialized computational devices (or "modules"). A module, as we use the term, is similar to an organ of the body—organs are often linked and their operations can certainly affect each other, but they take in different types of bodily input and their functions are specific. Like body organs, cognitive modules might interact in some ways (Barrett, 2005), but they are sensitive to only a limited range of input and they have specific functions. Fodor (1983) described many features of cognitive modules, including domain specificity, obligatory firing, rapid speed, inaccessibility to consciousness, characteristic ontogenetic course, dedicated neural structure, and a characteristic pattern of breakdown. As Fodor himself suggested, none of these features is necessary or defining [also see Barrett (2005) for an extended discussion], but observing these properties in the personality judgment system would render it unlikely that a central, general processor that is designed to achieve many different functions is responsible for personality judgment. Thus, we consider whether some of these features might exist.

Testing the Personality Judgment Instinct Theory

We have derived several hypotheses and predictions from the proposal that there is a personality judgment instinct [inspired in part by predictions by Pinker (2000) made about language]. Available evidence already supports some of these expectations, whereas others await future empirical testing.

Hypothesis 1. People should be naturally proficient in personality judgment.

We have already reviewed some evidence that people form quick and generally valid personality judgments. More can be mentioned. Judgments of college professors based on 30 s silent videos predicted the professors' evaluation scores at the end of the term (Ambady & Rosenthal, 1993). Meta-analyses demonstrate that inferences based on these thin slices of behavior are generally good (e.g., they produce moderate effect sizes in predicting criterion variables; Ambady & Rosenthal, 1992). People can even correctly judge the sexual orientation of others based on brief films of nonverbal behavior or still photographs (Ambady, Hallahan, & Conner, 1999). The literature contains many examples of this nature.

Like the parsing of one's native language or the visual recognition of objects, personality judgments should also feel effortless and natural, and we may not be able to "turn them off." Trait inferences are made without much effort, outside of awareness, and even under conditions of distraction (e.g., while simultaneously attempting to remember a long string of digits; Winter & Uleman, 1984; Winter, Uleman, & Cunniff, 1985). Indeed, it is difficult if not impossible to prevent yourself forming a first impression. If you met someone new today and shook her hand, could you prevent yourself from forming any judgments about her at all? Courtroom judges appear to understand that personality judgments are a part of human nature. They explicitly instruct juries to remain "unbiased" and to avoid jumping to conclusions about the character of the accused and the witnesses. Anyone who has served on a jury knows this is difficult if not impossible to do.

In short, people do appear to be naturally proficient. Personality judgments also seem to be characterized by three features of modules: rapid speed, inaccessibility to consciousness (at least to some degree), and obligatory firing. It is not a requirement, of course, that evolved adaptations operate in an "automatic" or nonconscious fashion. There is nothing in evolutionary theory that requires selection to design psychological adaptations that are unresponsive to contingencies involving conscious thought; and indeed, no one yet knows what the function of consciousness is (Cosmides & Tooby, 2000). Some personality judgments may be altered by deliberation and reflection and therefore the system may be cognitively penetrable. We do contend, however, that finding that some cognitive operations occur quickly and unavoidably—as appears to be the case for the parsing of language and perhaps for initial judgments of personality—suggests that they may be produced by a dedicated system.

Hypothesis 2. Personality judgment abilities should form a distinct part of the phenotype.

If there is a personality judgment instinct, it should form a distinct part of the human psychological phenotype, characterized by its own specialized input conditions and decision rules, a dedicated neural structure, and subject to catastrophic breakdown (it will exist intact or its components will appear to be missing entirely).

Important components of social judgment may be missing in some individuals. People with Asperger's syndrome, a mild form of autism, have difficulty reading others' emotional expressions and understanding some subtleties of social interaction (such as when someone has committed a *faux pas*), but their other cognitive capabilities may be normal (Baron-Cohen, Wheelwright, Stone, & Rutherford, 1999; Stone, Baron-Cohen, & Knight, 1998). Similarly, damage to a region within the limbic system that is implicated in social reasoning impairs reasoning on a cheater-detection cognitive task, but not on a closely matched and logically equivalent precaution task (Stone, Cosmides, Tooby, Kroll & Knight, 2002). These two tasks are equally difficult for subjects without brain damage (Stone et al., 2002). In our original draft of this chapter, we wrote that we knew of no cognitive dissociation studies specifically investigating trait inferences, but that we would expect similar dissociative patterns. In the several months that followed, Heberlein and Saxby (2005) published an fMRI study showing that personality judgments of point-light walker stimuli resulted in activation of different brain regions than did emotion judgments of the same stimuli (also see Heberlein, Adolphs, Tranel, & Damasio (2004) for converging evidence from patients with specific brain lesions).

Hypothesis 3. The ability to form personality judgments should emerge without explicit training and perhaps in spite of incompatible social inputs.

Children begin to spontaneously use global trait-like terms and some specific trait terms as early as age 3 (Eder, 1989). Beginning at age 4, children can use trait labels like "shy" vs. "not shy" and "nice" vs. "mean" to make nonobvious inferences about mental states (Heyman & Gelman, 1999). Children from age 5 understand that two individuals who have different traits— e.g., generous vs. selfish, honest vs. dishonest—will have different emotional reactions in response to the same event (Yuill & Pearson, 1998). There is some evidence that spontaneous personality judgments also emerge early (between 3- and 6-years-old) in Japan (Matsunaga, 2002).

In sum, this evidence suggests that the development of personality judgment begins spontaneously and early. Further work is needed, however, to examine whether trait inferences by children can be fully accounted for by explicit training by parents and peers. Proficiency in language use does not seem to require explicit education—people in lower class rural environments use language as complex as that of an Oxford professor. Likewise, we would expect effective personality judgment to emerge even in impoverished informational environments, and the existence of a personality judgment instinct would imply that children may develop normal abilities even if their primary social models are deficient (e.g., unaffected children of parents with autism or Asperger's syndrome).

Hypothesis 4. Personality judgment should be ubiquitous.

A personality judgment instinct should be a universal part of human nature. Its behavioral manifestations may be variable, but its underlying developmental and psychological design should show evidence of universality.

One aspect of universality is that children should pass through similar developmental sequences across cultures (also see Hypothesis 3). There are several clues about the developmental sequence in children from studies conducted in the United States. For example, children may first begin using general evaluative terms, then global traits, and then specific traits (e.g., Alvarez, Ruble, & Bolger, 2001; Eder, 1989). Children everywhere may use information about motives to infer traits (Heyman & Gelman, 1998) and take hints from the lexicon about what characteristics are enduring vs. transient. For example, traits picked out by nouns (*Rose is a "carrot-eater"*) result in greater attributions of stable and internal characteristics than do possible traits that are not (*Rose eats a lot of carrots*; Gelman & Heyman, 1999).

There is also evidence that personality judgments around the world converge on several personality dimensions. McCrae and Costa (1997) have amassed evidence that the *big five structure* replicates across cultures. Specific studies find that more or fewer dimensions may be needed to account for individual differences in a given culture, but four of the five factors—extraversion, agreeableness, conscientiousness, and neuroticism—appear universally robust (see Triandis & Suh, 2002, for a recent review).

Buss (1991) argued that the emergence of extraversion and agreeableness as the two major axes of individual differences reflects the universal importance for humans of discriminating others' tendencies to climb the social hierarchy and to be good partners in alliances. It seems likely that other dimensions that also had important fitness consequences will emerge consistently across cultures. Key candidates include sexual restrictedness, attractiveness (or *mate value*), health, and physical strength. We predict that people around the world will be especially proficient in forming these judgments (also see Gangestad, Simpson, DiGeronimo, & Biek, 1992).

The most robust universal, however, is that people everywhere should form personality judgments. We predict that nowhere in the world will people choose mates and friends randomly with respect to personality, and even when marriages are arranged for political or financial purposes, we suspect that personality will not be irrelevant. People across the globe will also infer enduring traits in others, these inferences will generally be valid, and they will use them in making important social decisions.

Evidence of universality should also be observed within cultures. Within cultures, neurologically intact individuals who do not show evidence of specific impairment of the personality judgment system should not differ much in their abilities to form valid personality judgments, whereas they may differ widely in other abilities and preferences. A lack of variation in performance in nonverbal judgment tasks in the West may reveal that most people perform at a generally high level, perhaps near ceiling given the difficulty of the task. An enduring problem in the study of accuracy in personality judgment is that consistent individual differences in judgmental ability have been surprisingly difficult to establish (Funder, 1999; Schneider, Hastorf, & Ellsworth, 1979). Perhaps this is because personality judgment is such an essential life skill that nearly everyone can do it well enough to get by.

A further speculation is that an evolved propensity for accurate personality judgment might be particularly likely to arise for traits that have particular importance for survival and reproduction. For example, it would certainly be adaptive to be able to judge deceitfulness in one's fellow humans. But unfortunately, it would be equally adaptive to be able to feign faithfulness, so the evolutionary outcome could be a sort of "arms race" with no clear winner. By the same token, perhaps females might have a special ability to judge dominance or status (and its survival advantages for her and her offspring) in male targets, whereas males are especially sensitive to indicators of parental nurturance. But counterbalancing such possibilities is the equally likely chance that sexual selection according to these indicators might lead to their mimicry, where nonprotective males would evolve misleading signs of dominance, and non-nurturing females also develop the capacity to seem other than they are. This analysis highlights the heavy task for the personality judgment instinct, which is to help people not only to detect essential attributes in others, but to see through attempts to mimic desirable traits and to mask undesirable ones.

CONCLUSIONS

Social-cognitive psychology's focus on judgmental imperfection has led research astray from focusing on the phenomenon of interpersonal judgment that truly is fundamentally important: the ability to judge personality with a useful degree of accuracy in the face of daunting obstacles. Evolution can be expected to produce a mind that produces judgments that are sufficiently accurate given cognitive and informational constraints, not perfect. Imperfection is therefore not only surprising, it is foreordained. Many putative demonstrations of judgmental error are also artifactual. The relatively rare and especially interesting demonstrations of error are those that (1) are not merely produced by unrealistically difficult or obscurely framed experimental tasks and (2) show misjudgments not evenly distributed around the midpoint of accuracy, but systematically biased in one direction or the other. Such findings remind us that the human cognitive system was evolved not for abstract accuracy but for survival and reproductive success. When false positives are more costly than false negatives, we should expect a bias in the direction of false negatives, and vice versa. But even judgments that are biased in this sense would still be expected to be reasonably good, as Simon pointed out long ago.

Nonartifactual findings of error and bias deserve a closer look, and a different sort of look than they have traditionally received. Rather than shaking our heads sadly at yet another demonstration of incompetence or having a "chuckle about our goofs" (Crandall, 1984, p. 1499), we should be led to ask what adaptive purpose is or was served by the cognitive system that produced these errors. Such an inquiry may lead to a deeper understanding of errors, the cognitive mechanisms that produce them, and human cognition in general.

Finally, our outline of the possible nature of a personality judgment instinct is obviously far from the final word on the matter. At present we wish to suggest that it might be heuristically useful to entertain this possibility, and to see if it helps to integrate otherwise scattered facts about personality judgment including its ease, ubiquity, universality, and general accuracy. Whether our hypotheses in the end are supported or not, evolutionarily based analyses of interpersonal judgment are yet rare, which means the field is wide open. Those readers of the social psychological literature who find the regular delivery from the "error of the month club" a little less thrilling than it used to be, might consider the possibilities that an evolutionarily informed approach could offer to reinvigorate a tiring field.

REFERENCES

Abbey, A. (1982). Sex differences in attributions for friendly behavior: Do males misperceive females' friendliness? *Journal of Personality and Social Psychology, 42*, 830–838.

Allport, G. W. (1937). *Personality: A psychological interpretation.* New York: Henry Holt.

Alvarez, J. M., Ruble, D. N., & Bolger, N. (2001). Trait understanding or evaluative reasoning? An analysis of children's behavioral predictions. *Child Development, 72*, 1409–1425.

Ambady, N. Bernieri, F. J., & Richeson, J. A. (2000). Toward a histology of social behavior: Judgmental accuracy from thin slices of the behavioral stream. *Advances in Experimental Social Psychology, 32*, 201–271.

Ambady, N., Hallahan, M., & Conner, B. (1999). Accuracy of judgments of sexual orientation from thin slices of behavior. *Journal of Personality & Social Psychology, 77*, 538–547.

Ambady, N., & Rosenthal, R. (1992). Thin slices of expressive behavior as predictors of interpersonal consequences: A meta-analysis. *Psychological Bulletin, 111*, 256–274.

Ambady, N., & Rosenthal, R. (1993). Half a minute: Predicting teacher evaluations from thin slices of nonverbal behavior and physical attractiveness. *Journal of Personality & Social Psychology, 64*, 431–441.

Baron-Cohen, S., Wheelwright, S., Stone, V. E., & Rutherford, M. D. (1999). A mathematician, a physicist and a computer scientist with Asperger Syndrome: Performance on folk psychology and folk physics tests. *Neurocase, 5*, 475–483.

Barrett, H. C. (2005). Enzymatic computation and cognitive modularity. *Mind and Language , 20*, 259–287.

Barrett, H. C., Todd, P. M., Miller, G. F., & Blythe, P. (2005). Accurate judgments of intention from motion alone: A cross-cultural study. *Evolution and Human Behavior, 26*, 313–331.

Baumeister, R. F., & Leary, M. R. (1995). The need to belong: Desire for interpersonal attachments as a fundamental human motivation. *Psychological bulletin, 117*(3), 497–529.

Buss, D. M. (1991). Evolutionary personality psychology. In M. R. Rosenzweig & L. W. Porter (Eds.), *Annual review of psychology* (Vol. 42, pp. 459–491). Palo Alto: Annual Reviews, Inc.

Buss, D. M. (2003). *The evolution of desire: Strategies of human mating* (revised ed.). New York: Basic Books.

Chagnon, N. (1983). *Yanomamö: The fierce people* (3rd ed.). New York: Reinhart & Winston.

Cosmides, L. (1989). The logic of social exchange: Has natural selection shaped how humans reason? *Cognition, 31*, 187–276.

Cosmides, L., & Tooby, J. (1992). Cognitive adaptations for social exchange. In J. H. Barkow, L. Cosmides, & J. Tooby (Eds.), *The adapted mind: Evolutionary psychology and the generation of culture* (pp. 163–228). New York: Oxford University Press.

Cosmides, L., & Tooby, J. (1996). Are humans good intuitive statisticians after all? Rethinking some conclusions from the literature on judgment under uncertainty. *Cognition, 58*, 1–73.

Cosmides, L., & Tooby, J. (2000). Evolutionary psychology and the emotions. In M. Lewis & J. M. Haviland-Jones (Eds.), *Handbook of emotions* (2nd ed., pp. 91–115.). New York: Guilford.

Crandall, C. S. (1984). The overcitation of examples of poor performance: Fad, fashion or fun? *American Psychologist, 39*, 1499–1500.

Darwin, C. (1872). *The expression of the emotions in man and animals*. New York: Philosophical Library.

Eder, R. A. (1989). The emergent personologist: The structure and content of 3 1/2, 5 1/2, and 7 1/2-year-olds' concepts of themselves and other persons. *Child Development, 60*(5), 1218–1228.

Eisenberger, N. I., Lieberman, M. D., & Williams, K. D. (2003). Does rejection hurt? an fMRI study of social exclusion. *Science, 302*, 290–292.

Ekman, P. (1973). Universal facial expressions in emotion. *Studia Psychologica, 15*, 140–147.

Fiddick, L., Cosmides, L., & Tooby, J. (2000). No interpretation without representation: The role of domain-specific representations and inferences in the wason selection task. *Cognition, 77*(1), 1–79.

Fiedler, K. (1988). The dependence of the conjunction fallacy on subtle linguistic factors. *Psychological Research, 50*, 123–129.

Fiske, S. T., & Taylor, S. E. (1991). *Social cognition* (2nd ed.). New York: McGraw-Hill.

Fodor, J. (1983). *The modularity of mind*. Cambridge: MIT Press.

Funder, D. C. (1982). On the accuracy of dispositional vs. situational attributions. *Social Cognition, 1*, 205–222.

Funder, D. C. (1987). Errors and mistakes: Evaluating the accuracy of social judgment. *Psychological Bulletin, 101*, 75–90.

Funder, D. C. (1992). Everything you know is wrong (Review of *The person and the situation*). *Contemporary Psychology, 37*, 319–320.

Funder, D. C. (1995). On the accuracy of personality judgment: A realistic approach. *Psychological Review, 102*, 652–670.

Funder, D. C. (1999). *Personality judgment: A realistic approach to person perception*. San Diego, CA: Academic Press.

Funder, D. C. (2003). Toward a social psychology of person judgments: Implications for person perception accuracy and self-knowledge. In J. P. Forgas & K. D. Williams (Eds.), *Social judgments: Implicit and explicit processes; social judgments: Implicit and explicit processes* (pp. 115–133). New York: Cambridge University Press.

Gangestad, S. W., & Simpson, J. A. (2000). The evolution of human mating: Trade-offs and strategic pluralism. *Behavioral and Brain Sciences, 23*, 675–687.

Gangestad, S. W., Simpson, J. A., DiGeronimo, K., & Biek, M. (1992). Differential accuracy in person perception across traits: Examination of a functional hypothesis. *Journal of Personality & Social Psychology, 62*, 688–698.

Gelman, S. A., & Heyman, G. D. (1999). Carrot-eaters and creature-believers: The effects of lexicalization on children's inferences about social categories. *Psychological Science, 10*(6), 489–493.

Gigerenzer, G. (1997). Ecological intelligence: an adaptation for frequencies. *Psychologische Beitrage, 39*, 107–129.

Gigerenzer, G., & Goldstein, D. G. (1996). Reasoning the fast and frugal way: Models of bounded rationality. *Psychological Review, 103*, 650–669.

Gigerenzer, G., Czerlinski, J., & Martignon, L. (2002). How good are fast and frugal heuristics? In T. Gilovich & D. Griffin (Eds.), *Heuristics and biases: The psychology of intuitive judgment; heuristics and biases: The psychology of intuitive judgment* (pp. 559–581). New York: Cambridge University Press.

Gigerenzer, G., Todd, P. M., & the ABC Research Group (1999). *Simple heuristics that make us smart.* New York: Oxford University Press.

Gilovich, T., Griffin, D., & Kahneman, D. (2002). *Heuristics and biases: The psychology of intuitive judgment.* New York: Cambridge.

Goldstein, D. G., & Gigerenzer, G. (1999). The recognition heuristic: How ignorance makes us smart. In G. Gigerenzer, P. M. Todd, & the ABC Group, *Simple heuristics that make us smart* (pp. 37–58). New York: Oxford University Press.

Haselton, M. G. (2003). The sexual overperception bias: Evidence of a systematic bias in men from a survey of naturally occurring events. *Journal of Research in Personality, 37*, 43–47.

Haselton, M. G., & Buss, D. M. (2000). Error management theory: A new perspective on biases in cross-sex mind reading. *Journal of Personality and Social Psychology, 78*, 81–91.

Haselton, M. G., & Buss, D. M. (2003). Biases in social judgment: Design flaws or design features? In J. Forgas, K. Williams, & B. von Hippel (Eds.), *Responding to the social world: implicit and explicit processes in social judgments and decisions.* New York: Cambridge.

Haselton, M. G., & Nettle, D. (2006). The paranoid optimist: An integrative model of cognitive biases. *Personality and Social Psychology Review, 10*, 47–66.

Haselton, M. G., Nettle, D., & Andrews, P.W. (2005). The evolution of cognitive bias. In D. M. Buss (Ed.), *The evolutionary psychology handbook* (pp. 724–746). Hoboken, NJ: Wiley.

Heberlein, A. S., Adolphs, R., Tranel, D., & Damasio, H. (2004). Cortical regions for judgments of emotions and personality traits from point-light walkers. *Journal of Cognitive Neuroscience, 16*, 1143–1158.

Heberlein, A. S. & Saxby, R. R. (2005). Dissociation between emotion and personality judgments: Convergent evidence from functional neuroimaging. *Neuroimage, 28*, 770–777.

Heider, F., & Simmel, M. (1944). An experimental study of apparent behavior. *American Journal of Psychology, 57*, 243–259.

Hertwig, R., & Gigerenzer, G. (1999). The 'conjunction fallacy' revisited: How intelligent inferences look like reasoning errors. *Journal of Behavioral Decision Making, 12*, 275–305.

Heyman, G. D., & Gelman, S. A. (1998). Young children use motive information to make trait inferences. *Developmental Psychology, 34*, 310–321.

Heyman, G. D., & Gelman, S. A. (1999). The use of trait labels in making psychological inferences. *Child Development, 70*, 604–619.

Hoffrage, U., Lindsey, S. Hertwig. R., & Gigerenzer, G. (2001). Statistics: What seems natural (response to Butterworth). *Science, 292*, 855.

Hrdy, S. (1999). *Mother nature: A history of mothers infants, and natural selection.* New York: Pantheon Books.

James, W. (1890). *The principles of psychology* (2nd ed.). Chicago: Encyclopedia Britannica (published in 1990).

Johnson-Laird, P. N., Legrenzi, P., & Legrenzi, M. S. (1972). Reasoning and a sense of reality. *British Journal of Psychology, 63*(3), 395–400.

Johnston, V. S., Hagel, R., Franklin, M., Fink, B., & Grammer, K. (2001). Male facial attractiveness: Evidence for hormone mediated adaptive design. *Evolution and Human Behavior, 21,* 251–267.

Kahneman, D. (2003). A perspective on judgment and choice: Mapping bounded rationality. *American Psychologist, 58,* 697–720.

Kenrick, D. T., & Funder, D. C. (1988). Profiting from controversy: Lessons from the person-situation debate. *American Psychologist, 43,* 23–34.

Kenrick, D. T., & Maner, J. (2004). One path to balance and order in social psychology: An evolutionary perspective. *Behavioral and Brain Sciences, 27*(3), 346–347.

Krebs, D. L., & Denton, K. (1997). Social illusions and self-deception: The evolution of biases in person perception. In J. A. Simpson & D. T. Kenrick (Eds.), *Evolutionary social psychology* (pp. 21–47). Hillsdale, NJ: Erlbaum.

Krueger, J. I., & Funder, D. C. (2004). Towards a balanced social psychology: Causes, consequences and cures for the problem-seeking approach to social behavior and cognition. *Behavioral and Brain Sciences, 27,* 313–376.

Kurzban, R., & Leary, M. R. (2001). Evolutionary origins of stigmatization: The functions of social exclusion. *Psychological Bulletin, 123,* 187–208.

Kyl-Heku, L. M., & Buss, D. M. (1996). Tactics as units of analysis in personality psychology: An illustration using tactics of hierarchy negotiation. *Personality & Individual Differences, 21,* 497–517.

Lopes, L. L. (1991). The rhetoric of irrationality. *Theory and Psychology, 1,* 65–82.

Maner, J. K., Kenrick, D. T., Becker, V., Robertson, T. E., Hofer, B., Neuberg, S. L. Delton, A. W., Butner, J., & Schaller, M. (2005). Functional projection: How fundamental social motives can bias interpersonal perception. *Journal of Personality and Social Psychology, 88,* 63–78.

Matsunaga, A. (2002). Preschool children's inferences about personality traits. *Japanese Journal of Developmental Psychology, 13,* 168–177.

McCrae, R. R., & Costa, P. T. J. (1997). Personality trait structure as a human universal. *American Psychologist, 52,* 509–516.

Mellers, B., Hertwig, R., & Kahneman, D. (2001). Do frequency representations eliminate conjunction effects? An exercise in adversarial collaboration. *Psychological Science, 12,* 269–275.

Miller, G. F. (2000). *The mating mind.* New York: Doubleday.

Nesse, R. M. (2001). The smoke detector principle: Natural selection and the regulation of defenses. *Annals of the New York Academy of Sciences, 935,* 75–85.

Nettle, D. (2004). Adaptive illusions: Optimism, control and human rationality. In D. Evans & P. Cruse (Eds.), *Emotion, evolution and rationality.* Oxford: Oxford University Press.

Neuhoff, J. G. (2001). An adaptive bias in the perception of looming auditory motion. *Ecological Psychology, 13,* 87–110.

Oltmanns, T. F., Friedman, J. N. W., Fiedler, E. R., & Turkheimer, E. (2004). Perceptions of people with personality disorders based on thin slices of behavior. *Journal of Research in Personality, 38,* 216–229.

Park, J. H., Faulkner, J., & Schaller, M. (2003). Evolved disease-avoidance processes and contemporary anti-social behavior: Prejudicial attitudes and avoidance of people with disabilities. *Journal of Nonverbal Behavior, 27*, 65–87.

Park, J. H., Schaller, M., & Crandall, C. S. (2004). Obesity as a heuristic cue connoting contagion: Perceived vulnerability to disease promotes anti-fat attitudes. Manuscript under review.

Penton-Voak, I. S., & Perrett, D. I. (2001). Male facial attractiveness: Perceived personality and shifting female preferences for male traits across the menstrual cycle. *Advances in the Study of Behavior, 30*, 219–259.

Pereyra, L. (2000, June). *Function variation of the hazard management algorithm.* Paper presented at the Human Behavior and Evolution Society Conference, Amherst, MA.

Pinker, S. (1994). *The language instinct.* New York: William Morrow & Co, Inc.

Pinker, S. (2000). Language as an adaptation to the cognitive niche. In M. Christiansen & S. Kirby (Eds.), *Language evolution: Report from the research frontier.* New York: Oxford.

Pronin, E., Gilovich, T., & Ross, L. (2004). Objectivity in the eye of the beholder: Divergent perceptions of bias in self versus others. *Psychological Review, 3*, 781–799.

Ross, L. (1977) The intuitive psychologist and his shortcomings. *Advances in Experimental Social Psychology, 10*, 174–214.

Schaller, M., Park, J. H., & Faulkner, J. (2003). Prehistoric dangers and contemporary prejudices. *European Review of Social Psychology, 14*, 105–137.

Schaller, M., Park, J. H., & Mueller, A. (2003). Fear of the dark: Interactive effects of beliefs about danger and ambient darkness on ethnic stereotypes. *Personality and Social Psychology Bulletin, 29*, 637–649.

Schmitt, D. P., & International Sexuality Description Project. (2003). Universal sex differences in the desire for sexual variety: Tests from 52 nations, 6 continents, and 13 islands. *Journal of Personality & Social Psychology, 85*, 85–104.

Schneider, D. J., Hastorf, A. H., & Ellsworth, P. E. (1979). *Person perception.* Reading, MA: Addison-Wesley.

Simon, H. A. (1956). Rational choice and the structure of the environment. *Psychological Review, 63*, 129–138.

Stone, V. E., Baron-Cohen, S., & Knight, R. T. (1998). Frontal lobe contributions to theory of mind. *Journal of Cognitive Neuroscience, 10*, 640–656.

Stone, V. E., Cosmides, L., Tooby, J., Kroll, N., & Knight, R. T. (2002). Selective impairment of reasoning about social exchange in a patient with bilateral limbic system damage. *Proceedings of the National Academy of Sciences, USA., 99*, 11531–11536.

Symons, D. (1979). *The evolution of human sexuality.* New York: Oxford University Press.

Taylor, S. E., & Brown, J. D. (1988). Illusion and well-being: A social psychological perspective on mental health. *Psychological Bulletin, 103*, 193–201.

Tooby, J., & Cosmides, L. (1988). *The evolution of war and its cognitive foundations.* Institute for Evolutionary Studies Technical Report #88–1.

Tooby, J., & Cosmides, L. (1996). Friendship and the Banker's Paradox: Other pathways to the evolution of adaptations for altruism. In W. G. Runciman, J. Maynard Smith, & R. I. M. Dunbar (Eds.), Evolution of social behaviour patterns in primates and man. *Proceedings of the British Academy, 88*, 119–143.

Tooby, J., & DeVore, I. (1987). The reconstruction of hominid behavioral evolution through strategic modeling. In W. Kinzey (Ed.), *Primate models of hominid behavior.* New York: SUNY Press.

Triandis, H. C., & Suh, E. M. (2002). Cultural influences on personality. *Annual Review of Psychology, 53*(1), 133–160.

Trivers, R. L. (1972). Parental investment and sexual selection. In B. Campbell (Ed.), *Sexual selection and the descent of man, 1871–1971* (pp. 136–179). Chicago, IL: Aldine Publishing Company.

Tversky, A., & Kahneman, D. (1974). Judgment under uncertainty: Heuristics and biases. *Science, 185,* 1121–1131.

Tversky, A., & Kahneman, D. (1983). Extensional versus intuitive reasoning: The conjunction fallacy in probability judgment. *Psychological Review, 90,* 293–315.

Wason, P. C. (1983). Realism and rationality in the selection task. In J. Evans (Ed.), *Thinking and reasoning: Psychological approaches.* London: Routledge & Kegan Paul.

Wason, P. C., & Shapiro, D. (1971). Natural and contrived experience in a reasoning problem. *Quarterly Journal of Experimental Psychology, 23,* 63–71.

Williams, K. D., Case, T. I., & Govan, C. L. (2003). Impact of ostracism on social judgments and decisions: Explicit and implicit responses. In J. Forgas, K. Williams, & W. von Hippel (Eds.), *Responding to the social world: Implicit and explicit processes in social judgments and decisions.* New York: Cambridge University Press.

Williams, K. D., Cheung, C. K. T., & Choi, W. (2000). Cyberostracism: Effects of being ignored over the internet. *Journal of Personality & Social Psychology, 79*(5), 748–762.

Williams, K. D., & Sommer, K. L. (1997). Social ostracism by one's coworkers: Does rejection lead to loafing or compensation? *Personality and Social Psychology Bulletin, 23,* 693–706.

Windschitl, P. D., & Chambers, J. R. (2004). The dud-alternative effect in likelihood judgment. *Journal of Experimental Psychology: Learning, Memory, & Cognition, 30*(1), 198–215.

Winter, L., & Uleman, J. S. (1984). When are social judgments made? Evidence for the spontaneousness of trait inferences. *Journal of Personality & Social Psychology, 47,* 237–252.

Winter, L., Uleman, J. S., & Cunniff, C. (1985). How automatic are social judgments? *Journal of Personality & Social Psychology, 49,* 904–917.

Yamagishi, T., Tanida, S., Mashima, R., Shimoma, E., & Kanazawa, S. (2003). You can judge a book by its cover: Evidence that cheaters may look different from cooperators. *Evolution & Human Behavior, 24*(4), 290–301.

Yuill, N., & Pearson, A. (1998). The development of bases for trait attribution: Children's understanding of traits as causal mechanisms based on desire. *Developmental Psychology, 34*(3), 574–586.

3

Modular Minds, Multiple Motives

ROBERT KURZBAN and C. ATHENA AKTIPIS

*A*s the scope of the contributions in this volume illustrates, the evolutionary approach has the potential to inform many of the content areas of interest to social psychologists, such as relationships (Fletcher, Simpson, & Boyes, this volume), cooperation (Van Vugt & Van Lange, this volume), and emotions (Keltner, Haidt, & Shiota, this volume). However, in addition to informing hypotheses about the *content* of human social cognition, the evolutionary approach also brings to the fore an important idea about the *structure* of cognition: that information-processing systems sculpted by natural selection are likely to show *functional specificity*. Because information-processing systems gain in power by restricting the domain of problem space on which they operate, natural selection favors functionally specific mechanisms over mechanisms with a broader domain of application (Tooby & Cosmides, 1992). This leads to a cognitive architecture that consists of a large number of specialized information-processing systems each with its own narrowly defined function as opposed to a small number of very general systems that are responsible for performing a wide range of functions (Rozin, 1976; Symons, 1979).

This idea might have particular relevance for the study of a central issue in social psychology, the "self." Historically, the "self" has often been construed as a relatively unitary entity, as evidenced by the use of broad terms such as "self-concept" (see Baumeister, 1987, for a historical account; Baumeister, 1999a; Markus & Wurf, 1987). However, substantial numbers of notables across time and disciplines have expressed dissatisfaction with the idea of a single unified self in one form or another, including René Descartes, William James, Sigmund Freud, Marvin Minsky, Daniel Dennett, Michael Gazzaniga, Richard Restak, and Joseph LeDoux. As Rorty (1996) puts it, "Neo-Freudians, cognitive psychologists and social theorists … agree in characterizing [the self] as constituted by relatively independent subsystems whose interaction is often only precariously integrated" (p. 83; see also Rosenberg, 1997). The evolutionary view that the mind consists of a large number of autonomous but interacting systems resonates deeply with this emerging convergence in perspectives.

MODULARITY

We begin by endorsing the computational theory of mind, the view that the mind can be understood as an information-processing device (e.g., Marr, 1982), and we further assume that its features were designed by natural selection to take in information and process it to derive functional inferences and generate adaptive behavior (Tooby & Cosmides, 1992). Again, because the operations that must be performed on information vary depending on the adaptive task to be solved, different cognitive mechanisms will perform different computations in order to perform their functions (Tooby & Cosmides, 1992).

We therefore take the mind to consist of a large number of *modules*, which take only a very narrow range of inputs, perform computations on these inputs, and generate particular kinds of outputs, typically other representations, which are then subject to additional processing. The terms "module" and "modular" have, of course, been the subject of a certain amount of debate (Barrett & Kurzban, in press; Coltheart, 1999; Fodor, 1983; Sperber, 1994). As opposed to entering into this debate, we will simply endorse a particular view: that the defining property of modular systems is functional specificity, and that they consequently show *informational encapsulation*, meaning that a given mechanism processes only a certain class of inputs (Fodor, 1983, 2000, 2001).

Informational encapsulation can be seen most easily in sensory systems. For example, photoreceptors are designed to take as inputs only electromagnetic radiation, and even then, only within a narrow range of frequencies; no other input (under normal conditions) will be subjected to processing. Similarly, other systems in the brain process only narrowly defined inputs in the form of particular kinds of representations. We endorse the "massive modularity" hypothesis, that modularity exists not just at the level of sensory or "peripheral" processes (Fodor, 1983), but at higher, more central processes as well (Barrett & Kurzban, in press; Carruthers, 2004; Sperber, 1994, 2002), including, of course, mechanisms designed to serve social functions (Gigerenzer, 1997). Illustrative examples of modular systems are discussed below.

Encapsulation and Enzymatic Computation

Barrett (2005) has proposed a useful metaphor for thinking about modularity: enzyme systems. Enzymes' binding sites, acting like a lock, allow only precisely formed substrates to attach and then be acted upon. Barrett has proposed that representational systems could plausibly function in a similar way. In this model, information gets "tagged" as it undergoes preliminary processing. These tags can be thought of as shapes that will then "fit" into a processing subsystem and allow the information to enter only certain cognitive-processing subsystems.

For example, the enzymatic computation model can account for the finding that individuals are better at reasoning about social contracts than logically identical problems (Cosmides, 1989; Cosmides & Tooby, 1992). The hypothesized cheater detection subsystem is designed to take inputs with information about social contracts, but not logically identical information without the appropriate tags. Social contract information would be able to enter the information-processing system specialized for "cheater detection" because it has "cost" and "benefit" tags in the appropriate configuration (Barrett, 2005).

We do not claim (nor does Barrett) that the enzymatic model describes the physical instantiation of information in the brain. Barrett's enzymatic computation model is an existence proof of a modular, informationally encapsulated system that can perform computations that are necessary for processing information about the physical and social world. In other words, it is a plausible model for a cognitive design that is modular yet flexible and powerful in information-processing terms. This model also does not run afoul of the problems critics have used to undermine the modularity thesis in the context of the computational theory of mind (Fodor, 2000), the details of which are beyond the scope of this chapter. The enzyme model also provides a convenient way to think about how mutually inconsistent representations can simultaneously exist in the same brain.

Modularity, Truth, and Consistency

Some cognitive systems' functions depend critically on generating accurate, veridical representations of the world. A system designed for navigation, for example, must preserve spatial relationships in some form in order to accomplish its function (Gibson, 1950). This implies that at least some subset of evolved cognitive mechanisms should be expected to be designed to generate something approaching a logician's version of "truth"—more or less accurate representations about facts and relationships that exist in the physical world.

However, natural selection should not be expected to cause mechanisms to come into existence that generate truth, per se. Instead, natural selection should be expected to fashion systems that generate adaptively useful information, inferences, and behavior. That is, cognitive mechanisms are sifted by the sieve of evolution not by virtue of their ability to generate true inferences, but by virtue of their ability to generate adaptively useful inferences (Barrett, 2005). It is an open question the extent to which these overlap in any given domain, and it is at least plausible that there is relatively little overlap in some domains. Indeed, as Ghiselin (1974) puts it, "We are anything but a mechanism set up to perceive the truth for its own sake" (p. 263).

Consider, for example, the application of signal detection theory to behavioral ecology. A gazelle with a cognitive mechanism that was designed to maximize the probability of being "accurate" about the presence or absence of a cheetah, fleeing only when its best guess indicated that a cheetah was present, would be at a severe selective disadvantage relative to a gazelle that made systematic errors, representing the presence of a cheetah with only minimal evidence to this effect (Hauser, 1996). Considerations of costs and benefits of errors clearly illustrate that maximizing accuracy is not necessarily a goal that an evolved mechanism should have. Haselton and Buss (2000) have recently taken an innovative approach that has expanded this reasoning in the domain of human mating (see also Haselton & Funder, Chapter 2, this volume).

Indeed, human cognition might be distinctive in its ability to maintain false propositions (for which we adopt the logician's notation, and refer to propositions as "P's"). Cosmides and Tooby (2000a) have argued that a signal feature of human cognition is its ability to represent things that are not true, and, have further added, that the modular architecture of humans provides a means of doing so that protects the broader cognitive system from harm that might be done by allowing untrue representations to circulate freely.

To take a simple example, consider representations of the form [agent – believes – P] often referred to as "metarepresentations" (Baron-Cohen, 1995; Sperber, 2000), because they consist of representations of other representations (in this case, a representation of a belief). While an individual might think that another agent has a particular representation P, this fact P need not be something that is true about the world. For example, if P is that "the sky is falling," this proposition should not generate a host of downstream inferences that would be tainted by this false premise. This can be accomplished by encapsulating the potentially offending representation P in the protective shell of the metarepresentational composition (Cosmides & Tooby, 2000a). This form of encapsulation allows untrue representations to be represented without undermining inference systems. So, if you believe that [Chicken Little—believes—"the sky is falling"], this belief does not cause you to take cover, though you might make the inference that Chicken Little will do so.

So, while P exists within a metarepresentation that insulates it from entering into inferences, not-P—here, that the sky is safely bound to the heavens—can be represented elsewhere in the cognitive system. The point is that different representations *about the very same thing* might be encapsulated in different cognitive systems, and, because of the insulation that modularity supplies, *there is no particular reason for these representations to be mutually consistent.* Beliefs therefore need not be held at the "expense" of one another (Gur & Sackeim, 1979; Surbey & McNally, 1997). A logical consequence of this view of modularity is the entailment that *representing a belief P does not limit representations inconsistent with P elsewhere in the brain.* Before continuing, it is worth pointing out that this consequence of modularity implies that there is no reason to believe *a priori* that reconciling or resolving "dissonant" representations is a problem in need of a solution, an idea that lies at the root of theories surrounding cognitive dissonance (Festinger, 1957), a point to which we return below.

Let us assume, as is likely, that certain cognitive systems might be designed to maintain a store of representations that are not the best possible estimate of what is true, and that these untrue representations can be stored in an isolated modular subsystem. Taken together, these two assumptions imply that representations that do not reflect the best estimate of truth in some global sense can nevertheless be treated as "true" within the context of a particular encapsulated subsystem for purposes of entering into inferences within this subsystem.

An easy way to see this is in the context of plans and goals (Tooby & Cosmides, 2000a). Imagine planning taking place within a given informationally encapsulated module. This module might represent a situation that is, currently, contrary to the actual state of the world, such as, the (hypothetical) idea that I have just entered the gates at Disneyland. This subsystem can make inferences based on this piece of information, such as the inference that I have the opportunity to go on various attractions, without any concern about this representation, "I'm at Disneyland," being treated as true by other systems. This modular system allows planning, counterfactual thinking, and so forth, while ensuring that other systems do not use the representation for inferences before doing so is warranted.

In summary, *certain cognitive systems might be designed to maintain a store of representations that are not the best possible estimate of what is true, but are nevertheless represented as true within that particular subsystem* (Cosmides & Tooby, 2000a). This idea follows straightforwardly from the idea that the optimal design for a cognitive system might not be one that accurately represents the world (Ghiselin, 1974). Some systems' functions might be best served by representing incorrect information.

Critically, another representation, more congruent with the actual state of the world, could be stored elsewhere, insulated from the system designed to use the incorrect or perhaps biased representation (e.g., Pinker, 1997). These more accurate representations might be accessed when the appropriate inferences require them. Elsewhere, we suggest that a substantial variety of representations about the self are of precisely this nature: that they are not necessarily the best estimates of what is objectively true about one's self and that other, more accurate representations about the self are stored in separate systems for other purposes (Kurzban & Aktipis, 2004).

Evidence of Modularity and Inconsistency in the Brain

Research from neurology, perception, and social psychology supports the idea that our cognitive systems are modular, allowing encapsulated information to enter into some computations and not others.

Psychological Disorders Mutually contradictory representations in the same brain can be most easily seen in extreme cases. Consider patients who have undergone a commissurotomy, the severing of the corpus collosum, the connection between the two hemispheres of the brain. In one classic experiment, the left hemisphere of such a patient is shown a chicken claw, and the right a wintry scene. An array of objects is shown (to both hemispheres), and the subject is asked to point, with each hand, to an object related to what they have seen, and verbally explain these choices. The left hand (controlled by the right hemisphere, shown the wintry scene) pointed to a snow shovel, and the right hand pointed to a chicken. The left hemisphere, not having access to the information from the right, but having control of the vocal apparatus, explained that the shovel was for cleaning up after the chickens (Gazzaniga & LeDoux, 1978). In this artificially modularized brain, two separate reasons for selecting the shovel are represented. One system, the one that generates speech (which Gazzaniga refers to as the "interpreter"), had access to only one of these (Gazzaniga, 1998). The subject does not report confusion about this contradiction—the two contradictory reasons are encapsulated from one another.

A variety of other unusual cases illustrate the same principle. Consider "phantom limbs," cases in which amputees report pain and other sensations from their absent arm or leg. Patients report that they know that the limb is absent, but there is clearly a representation of the limb somewhere in the brain. Ramachandran and Blakeslee (1998), discussing one patient, put it this way: "When John decides to move his phantom arm, the front part of his brain still sends out a command message, since this particular part of John's brain doesn't 'know' that his arm is missing—even though John 'the person' is unquestionably aware of the fact" (p. 45).

There are any number of other examples of patients with conditions that cause mutually incompatible representations within the same brain, from cases such as "blind sight," in which patients clearly have a representation of the visual world while denying any such knowledge, to even more extreme cases such as anosognosia, in which patients deny that they have what should be obvious illness or debility. For example, an anosognosic patient might have a limb that is completely paralyzed and yet deny that this is the case, even when presented with seemingly unambiguous evidence, such as their inability to perform simple tasks with the limb in question. As Restak (1994) puts it, "in the presence of anosognosia, beliefs can become modular and exist independently and even in contradiction to one another" (p. 50).

The clinical literature suggests that in some unusual cases, there might be multiple "selves" encapsulated from one another in the same brain. Dissociative Identity Disorder (formerly Multiple Personality Disorder) is one such case. Klein (2001) points out that "each identity typically is able to recollect events and experiences that took place only while it was in control" (p. 33). Each identity seems to tag episodic representations as happening to that "self," and these episodes cannot be recalled by other "selves." Indeed, the DSM–IV (American Psychiatric Association, *Diagnostic and Statistical Manual of Mental Disorders*, 1997) states that Dissociative Identity Disorder "reflects a failure to integrate various aspects of identity, memory and consciousness" (p. 484). Although there is still controversy surrounding the exact nature of the disorder, substantial work supports its existence (Bearhs, 1994; Cardena, 1997; Elzinga, Phaf, Ardon, & Dyck, 2003; Gee, Allen, & Powell, 2003; Gleaves, 1996; Gleaves, Hernandez, & Warner, 1999, 2003; Spanos, 1994).

Normal Subjects Evidence of modularity is by no means restricted to patients with pathologies. There are any number of examples illustrating how particular psychological mechanisms accept only particular types of input and, similarly, cases in which two mutually incompatible representations exist simultaneously within the same brain. Here we present two cases of each to illustrate the broader point.

First, interesting cases of the exquisite sensitivity of psychological mechanisms can be seen in the work of Gigerenzer and his colleagues (Gigerenzer, 1998; Gigerenzer & Hoffrage, 1995) in the context of even high level processes such as reasoning and decision-making. Gigerenzer and Hoffrage (1995) suggested that peoples' purported inability to perform Bayesian inferences might not be due to a lack of computational ability to do them, but rather to the format of the information in which problems were put to participants. By using precisely the same information (in terms of mathematics) but changing the format from probabilities (.2) to frequency formats (2 out of 10), they showed that participants were able to achieve substantial gains in performing Bayesian computations. This suggests that the mechanism that executes the computations exists, but is specific in the inputs it accepts, a conclusion consistent with the view that informational encapsulation is by no means restricted to "peripheral" systems, but extends into "higher" domains of cognition as well.

Striking examples of informational encapsulation can also be found in the developmental literature. Hermer and Spelke (1996) conducted a series of cleverly designed experiments with young children (roughly 2 years old) and were able to show that the mechanisms that these children used for navigating were exquisitely selective in the information used to perform a task—in particular, the researchers found that children who were disoriented used only information such as the geometry of the room that they were in, but neglected nongeometrical information such as markings on the containers in which toys were hidden, despite the fact that these markings could have been used to correctly complete the task. As Hermer and Spelke put it, "children's reorientation depends on a process that is both encapsulated and task-specific: a process that is guided by only a subset of the information that the child detects and remembers" (p. 226). This suggests to them support for the presence of a "geometric module" (Gallistel, 1990), which takes in only geometrical information for purposes of reorientation because of the value of this type of information for this function in ancestral environments.

Beyond cases of informational encapsulation are examples of mutually contradictory representations. For example, Ramachandran and Blakeslee (1998) discuss a method by which you can experience your nose as "stretched out about three feet in front of your face" (p. 59), while you presumably maintain the knowledge somewhere in the brain that your nose is of normal size. More generally, consider perceptual "illusions," such as the well-known Muller–Lyer illusion, a frequently used example to illustrate modularity (Fodor, 1983; Sperber, 2002). In this illusion, two lines of equal length appear unequal because of either inward or outward facing arrows. Once a viewer is told—or more likely, shown—that the two lines are equal, the illusion persists, and the lines continue to appear to be of unequal length. The perceptual system maintains a representation that the lines are unequal, even though another part of the brain has a representation (in some form, possibly propositional) that they are equal.

Another demonstration of mutually inconsistent representations is Gur and Sackeim's (1979) classic study in which participants heard their own and other peoples' voices played back to them and were asked if the voice they heard belonged to them. Simultaneously, their galvanic skin response (GSR) was measured. Peoples' GSR did indeed correlate with samples of their own voice, while participants' identification of their own voice did not always do so. The GSR indicates that there was a representation that the voice was the participant's own in some modular system (which has a causal effect on the physiology underlying this response), while the participants' own responses indicate a contradictory representation. In our terminology, the information that led to the GSR was encapsulated within a system that did not pass this information along to the system generating the participants' self-reports.

MODULAR MIND, MULTIPLE MOTIVES

The modularity of mind has any number of implications for theories in social psychology. Our focus here is on the set of motivations that have been associated with the "self." Modular systems with distinct functions must be dynamically activated and deactivated to cause the organism to perform appropriate actions at appropriate times (Cosmides & Tooby, 2000b). We take the different motivations that have been discussed within the context of the "self" to be examples of this dynamic process, which gives the appearance of multiple, sometimes contradictory, motivations. There is, of course, nothing paradoxical about this. Simply because a satiated organism does not forage does not mean that there is no "hunger" motivation, or that other motivations are "dominant" over hunger; it simply means that its current state or context brings other systems' motivations to the fore. Here we discuss motivations, including information-seeking goals, which are the result of the constellation of modular mechanisms (see also Sedikides and Gregg, 2003).

Accuracy

Accurate information about one's self can be useful for any number of purposes, so it would be unsurprising to find cognitive mechanisms designed to gather information that is correct and useful for either strategic purposes or generating true inferences. Learning about one's skills, abilities, and so forth, particularly relative to others (Festinger, 1954), can be useful for tasks such as making oneself a valuable social partner and understanding the social niches one can occupy (Tooby & Cosmides, 1996; Trope, 1986). Mechanisms designed to gather correct information do not, of course, always necessarily dominate, and other mechanisms can take precedence under a variety of circumstances. Indeed, experimental evidence suggests that the motivation for accurate information is frequently subordinated to other types of information-seeking motivations (Sedikides, 1993), though there might be substantial individual differences in this regard (Roney & Sorrentino, 1995).

Self-Enhancement

Substantial evidence suggests that, under certain conditions, people are motivated to find information that casts them in a positive light, even at the expense of accuracy (e.g., Greenwald, 1980). This might seem somewhat surprising from a functional perspective: Surely adaptive behavior would have been facilitated by maintaining accurate information. However, the maintenance of biased representations is not surprising if one postulates that there is an additional representational system that separately maintains a representation of what is "true," or at least maintains one's best estimate of the truth, so that these representations can be accessed and used for purposes in which truth is more important than the representations one makes to the social world. It is fine to discuss one's fictional prowess as a lion tamer, but using that information when deciding whether or not to enter the cage would be a mistake. As Pinker (1997) puts it, "...the truth is useful, so it should be registered somewhere in the mind, walled off from the parts that interact with other people..." (p. 421).

Pinker's view mirrors our own, that inaccurate information might be maintained in a separate pool of representations that are useful for various social processes, such as negotiation and persuasion (Kurzban & Aktipis, 2004). To the extent that what is true about an individual is negotiable, it makes sense to design a mechanism to find information that can be presented to the social world that indicates that one has positive qualities (Jones & Pittman, 1982). Because people make inferences about others based on their behavior, individuals can take an active role in shaping others' representations (e.g., Swann, 1985).

This view suggests that the motivation for self-enhancement should dominate therefore only under particular circumstances (Brown, 1990; Greenwald & Breckler, 1985). Where there is ambiguity, self-serving representations make the most sense: If the situation or content at stake is one in which there is inherent uncertainty about the true state of the world, one might expect self-enhancement motives to be active. To take just one example, what counts as important is debatable in many contexts, and it should therefore be unsurprising to find that people are motivated to view their particular abilities as especially, even uniquely, valuable (Campbell, 1986; Tesser & Campbell, 1983; Tooby & Cosmides, 1996). It is important to note, however, that there might be substantial cross-cultural variation in the strength of the self-enhancement motive (Heine, Lehman, Markus, & Kitayama, 1999).

Consistency

When peoples' behavior violates consistency, they will be seen as liars, hypocrites, mentally impaired, or worse (e.g., Swann, 1985). Further, if I am motivated to induce people to believe P, and if I occasionally act in ways that are inconsistent with my belief in P, then I undermine my influence (Sperber, 2000). Both of these facts point to the importance of projecting consistency to the social world.

Maintaining consistency might represent a serious computational problem if the modular view we advance here is correct. If different modular systems with different underlying representations are active in different contexts, then this could easily lead to inconsistent behaviors. Hence, the cognitive system should be designed to maintain representations of what others know or could know about one's past behavior and attempt to maintain consistency relative to others' beliefs and expectations. Consistent with this view, Tice (1992) claims that behavior that is "public" changes the self-concept more than "private" behavior (see also Baumeister, 1982; Baumeister & Cairns, 1992; Schlenker, Forsyth, Leary, & Miller, 1980; Schrauger & Schoeneman, 1979; Tice & Baumeister, 2001), a claim at odds with early views that inconsistency between action and belief per se motivates resolution of dissonance (Festinger, 1957; Festinger & Carlsmith, 1959), but consistent with later refinements to theories surrounding cognitive dissonance (Carlsmith, Collins, & Helmreich, 1966).

Maintaining consistency is particularly important in the context of morality. Inconsistent morality evokes a reputation for hypocrisy, undermining one's standing in a social community. However, maintaining a fully consistent moral stance can be problematic, as one's goals are not always well served by the reasoning that follows from moral principles one has publicly endorsed. As Haidt (2001) puts it: "From an evolutionary perspective, it would be strange if our moral judgment machinery was designed principally for accuracy, with no concern for the disastrous effects of periodically siding with our enemies and against our friends" (p. 821). Haidt (2001) further suggested that, "moral reasoning is produced and sent forth verbally to justify one's already-made moral judgment to others" (pp. 818–819) in order to influence others' beliefs and judgments. This view, which could be applied to domains beyond moral reasoning, obviously resonates deeply with our own.

IMPLICATIONS OF A MODULAR MIND

Existing views already countenance, at least implicitly, a certain degree of modularity. The idea of multiple selves can be traced at least as far back as Freud, with his tripartite system of id, ego, and superego. More recently, Sedikides and Brewer (2001) suggested a different tripartite system (individual, relational, and collective selves) with associated motivational systems (Sedikides, 1993).

We agree that these selves "coexist within the same individual" (Sedikides & Brewer, 2001, p. 2), but think that the modular view does not lead naturally to the idea that there is one "self" that is "primary" (Tice & Baumeister, 2001), that the selves might be "opponents" (Sedikides & Brewer, 2001, p. 2), or that it is going to be productive to ask questions such as, "what version of the self is the real and true one?" (Baumeister, 1999b, p. 67). Instead, the modular view implies that encapsulated information-processing systems that together comprise what some psychologists have referred to as the "self" are activated and deactivated dynamically in response to cues in the environment that indicate when the functions of each system are relevant (Sedikides & Gregg, 2003). In short, we deny that there is a "real" self in there somewhere (Minsky, 1986) but instead that there are modular systems with particular evolved functions (Swann et al., 1987; Turner, 1976).

This modular view should lead us to call into question theoretical perspectives that turn on the notion of consistency within the cognitive system. For example, although cognitive dissonance theory (Festinger, 1957), and its descendants, such as self-consistency theory (Aronson, 1968), have long and distinguished histories (Jones, 1985), the fundamental premise—that dissonant "cognitions" (representations) motivate resolving dissonance—frequently does not apply (Cooper & Fazio, 1984; Steele, Spencer, & Lynch, 1993). Establishing consistency among various representations should perhaps be considered a specific cognitive function relevant under particular conditions (Cooper & Fazio, 1984) rather than a broad psychological principle (see Harmon-Jones & Mills, 1999, for current views in this area).

The modular view similarly demystifies superficially puzzling phenomena such as self-deception, cases in which an individual mind simultaneously contains two mutually contradictory beliefs (Demos, 1960). Because these beliefs can be encapsulated within different cognitive systems, this phenomenon per se does not require special explanation (Gur & Sackeim, 1979). It is possible, as discussed above, that while some systems are designed to generate accurate representations, others are not. Two such systems, if collecting information about the same content, could easily generate mutually contradictory representations. For example, some systems might be designed to generate overly optimistic representations about the self (Taylor & Brown, 1988), whereas others might be designed to generate accurate representations about the self. The existence of two such systems, operating autonomously would give rise to phenomena associated with self-deception and positive illusions (Kurzban & Aktipis, 2004).

Despite the broad and explicit denials that there is a unitary self, discussion persists that implicitly endorses such a view, possibly because the intuition of the self as a unitary entity is a powerful one (Pinker, 2002; Restak, 1994). Sperber (2002), for example, says that "*I* have the information that the two lines in the Müller–Lyer illusion are equal…" (p. 51, emphasis original), using "I" in a way that parallels the way that Ramachandran and Blakeslee talk about John "the person." It might be time to discuss purging language from scientific discourse that points to a unitary self which might not reflect the actual state of cognitive affairs (Katzko, 2003). At minimum, researchers need to exercise exquisite care in their use of the word "self" (Leary, 2004). If there is no "I" (e.g., Minsky, 1986), then it might be better to discuss information simply in terms of which systems have access to it. In short, modularity entails deep skepticism about seemingly simple claims about agents having beliefs.

Our goal was not to introduce a revolutionary way of thinking about the "self," but merely to suggest that the modular view provides potentially valuable tools for thinking about the multiple systems that together comprise the "self." In addition, our hope is that this analysis will help to make researchers more aware of their implicit commitment to a unitary self embodied in terms such as "self-deception." We hope that considering evolved cognitive functions will shed light on some of the vexing problems surrounding the "self" and related issues.

REFERENCES

American Psychiatric Association. (1997). *Diagnostic and statistical manual of mental disorders* (4th ed.). Washington, DC: American Psychiatric Association.

Aronson, E. (1968). Dissonance theory: Progress and problems. In R. P. Abelson, E. Aronson, W. J. McGuire, T. M. Newcomb, M. J. Rosenberg & P. H. Tannenbaum (Eds.), *Theories of cognitive consistency: A sourcebook* (pp. 5–27). Chicago: Rand McNally.

Baron-Cohen, S. (1995). *Mindblindness: An essay on autism and theory of mind.* Cambridge, MA: MIT Press.

Barrett, H. C. (2005). Enzymatic computation and cognitive modularity. *Mind and Language, 20*, 259–287.

Barrett, H. C., & Kurzban, R. (in press). Modularity in cognition: Framing the debate. *Psychological Review*.

Baumeister, R. F. (1982). A self-presentational view of social phenomena. *Psychological Bulletin, 91*, 3–26.

Baumeister, R. F. (1987). How the self became a problem: A psychological review of historical research. *Journal of Personality and Social Psychology, 52*, 163–176.

Baumeister, R. F. (1999a). The nature and structure of the self: An overview. In R. F. Baumeister (Ed.), *The self in social psychology* (pp. 1–20). Philadelphia: Psychology Press.

Baumeister, R. F. (1999b). Self-knowledge. In R. F. Baumesiter (Ed.), *The self in social psychology* (pp. 21–23). Philadelphia: Psychology Press.

Baumeister, R. F., & Cairns, K. J. (1992). Repression and self-presentation: When audiences interfere with self-deceptive strategies. *Journal of Personality and Social Psychology, 62*, 851–862.

Bearhs, J. O. (1994). Dissociative identity disorder: Adaptive deception of self and others. *Bulletin of the American Academy of Psychiatry and the Law, 22*, 223–237.

Brown, J. D. (1990). Evaluating one's abilities: Shortcuts and stumbling blocks on the road to self-knowledge. *Journal of Experimental Social Psychology, 26*, 149–167.

Campbell, J. D. (1986). Similarity and uniqueness: The effects of attribute type, relevance, and individual differences in self-esteem and depression. *Journal of Personality and Social Psychology, 50*, 281–294.

Cardena, E. (1997). Dissociative disorders: Phantoms of the self. In S. M. Turner & M. Hersen (Eds.), *Adult psychopathology and diagnosis* (3rd ed., pp. 384–408). New York: Wiley.

Carlsmith, J. M., Collins, B. E., & Helmreich, R. L. (1966). The effect of pressure for compliance on attitude change produced by face-to-face role playing and anonymous essay writing. *Journal of Personality and Social Psychology, 4*, 1–13.

Carruthers, P. (2004). Practical reasoning in a modular mind. *Mind & Language, 19*, 259–278.

Coltheart, M. (1999). Modularity and cognition. *Trends in Cognitive Science, 3*, 115–120.

Cooper, J., & Fazio, R. H. (1984). A new look at dissonance theory. In L. Berkowitz (Ed.), *Advances in experimental social psychology* (Vol. 17, pp. 229–262). Hillsdale, NJ: Lawrence Erlbaum.

Cosmides, L. (1989). The logic of social exchange: Has natural selection shaped how humans reason? Studies with the Wason selection task. *Cognition, 31*, 187–276.

Cosmides, L., & Tooby, J. (1992). Cognitive adaptations for social exchange. In J. H. Barkow, L. Cosmides, & J. Tooby (Eds.), *The adapted mind* (pp. 163–228). New York: Oxford University Press.

Cosmides, L., & Tooby, J. (2000a). Consider the source: The evolution of adaptations for decoupling and metarepresenation. In D. Sperber (Ed.), *Metarepresentations: A multidisciplinary perspective*. New York: Oxford University Press.

Cosmides, L., & Tooby, J. (2000b). Evolutionary psychology and the emotions. In M. Lewis & J. M. Haviland-Jones (Eds.), *Handbook of emotions* (2nd ed., pp. 91–115). New York: Guilford.

Demos, R. (1960). Lying to oneself. *Journal of Philosophy, 57*, 588–595.

Elzinga, B. M., Phaf, R. H., Ardon, A. M., & Dyck, R. v. (2003). Directed forgetting between, but not within, dissociative personality states. *Journal of Abnormal Psychology, 112*, 237–243.

Festinger, L. (1954). A theory of social comparison processes. *Human Relations, 7,* 117–140.

Festinger, L. (1957). *A theory of cognitive dissonance.* Evanston, IL: Row Peterson & Co.

Festinger, L., & Carlsmith, J. M. (1959). Cognitive consequences of forced compliance. *Journal of Abnormal & Social Psychology, 38,* 203–210.

Fodor, J. (1983). *The modularity of mind.* Cambridge, MA: MIT Press.

Fodor, J. (2000). *The mind doesn't work that way: The scope and limits of computational psychology.* Cambridge MA: MIT Press.

Fodor, J. (2001). *Review of Evolution and the Human Mind.* [Online]. Available: http://www3.oup.co.uk/phisci/hdb/Volume_52/Issue_03/pdf/520623.pdf

Gallistel, C. R. (1990). *The organization of learning,* Cambridge, MA: MIT Press.

Gazzaniga, M. S. (1998). *The minds' past.* Berkeley, CA: University of California Press.

Gazzaniga, M. S., & LeDoux, J. E. (1978). *The integrated mind.* New York: Plenum Press.

Gee, T., Allen, K., & Powell, R. A. (2003). Questioning premorbid dissociative symptomatology in dissociative identity disorder: Comment on Gleaves, Hernandez and Warner (1999). *Professional Psychology: Research & Practice, 34,* 114–116.

Ghiselin, M. T. (1974). *The economy of nature and the evolution of sex.* Berkley: University of California Press.

Gibson, J. J. (1950). *The perception of the visual world.* Boston: Houghton Mifflin.

Gigerenzer, G. (1997). The modularity of social intelligence. In A. Whiten & R. W. Byrne (Eds.), *Machiavellian intelligence II* (pp. 264–288). Cambridge: Cambridge University Press.

Gigerenzer, G. (1998). Ecological intelligence: An adaptation for frequencies. In D. D. Cummins & C. Allen (Eds.), *The evolution of mind* (pp. 9–29). New York: Oxford University Press.

Gigerenzer, G., & Hoffrage, U. (1995). How to improve Bayesian reasoning without instruction: Frequency formats. *Psychological Review, 102,* 684–704.

Gleaves, D. H. (1996). The sociocognitive model of dissociative identity disorder: A reexamination of the evidence. *Psychological Bulletin, 120,* 42–59.

Gleaves, D. H., Hernandez, E., & Warner, M. S. (1999). Corroborating premorbid dissociative symptomatology in dissociative identity disorder. *Professional Psychology: Research & Practice, 30,* 341–345.

Gleaves, D. H., Hernandez, E., & Warner, M. S. (2003). The etiology of dissociative identity disorder: Reply to Gee, Allen, and Powell (2003). *Professional Psychology: Research & Practice, 34,* 116–118.

Greenwald, A. G. (1980). The totalitarian ego: Fabrication and revision of personal history. *American Psychologist, 35,* 603–618.

Greenwald, A. G., & Breckler, S. J. (1985). To whom is the self presented? In B. R. Schlenker (Ed.), *The self and social life* (pp. 126–145). New York: McGraw-Hill.

Gur, R. C., & Sackeim, H. A. (1979). Self-deception: A concept in search of a phenomenon. *Journal of Personality and Social Psychology, 37,* 147–169.

Haidt, J. (2001). The emotional dog and its rational tail. *Psychological Review, 108,* 814–834.

Harmon-Jones, E., & Mills, J. (1999). *Cognitive dissonance: Progress on a pivotal theory in social psychology.* Washington, DC: American Psychological Association.

Haselton M. G. & Buss, D. M. (2000). Error management theory: A new perspective on biases in cross-sex mind reading. *Journal of Personality and Social Psychology, 78,* 81–91.

Hauser, D. (1996). *The evolution of communication.* Cambridge, MA: MIT Press.

Heine, S. J., Lehman, D. R., Markus, H. R., & Kitayama, S. (1999). Is there a universal need for positive self-regard? *Psychological Review, 106,* 766–794.

Hermer, L. & Spelke, E. S. (1996). Modularity and development: The case of spatial reori-entation. *Cognition, 61,* 195–232.

Jones, E. E. (1985). Major developments in social psychology during the past five decades. In G. Lindzey & E. Aronson (Eds.), *The handbook of social psychology* (3rd ed., pp. 47–108). New York: Random House.

Jones, E. E., & Pittman, T. S. (1982). Towards a general theory of strategic self-presenta-tion. In J. Suls (Ed.), *Psychological perspectives on the self* (Vol. 1, pp. 231–262). Hillsdale, NJ: Erlbaum.

Katzko, M. W. (2003). Unity vs. multiplicity: A conceptual analysis of the term 'self' and its use in personality theories. *Journal of Personality, 71,* 83–144.

Klein, S. B. (2001). A self to remember: A cognitive neuropsychological perspective on how self creates memory and memory creates self. In C. Sedikides & M. B. Brewer (Eds.), *Individual self, relational self, collective self.* Philadelphia: Psychology Press.

Kurzban, R., & Aktipis, A. (2004). *Modularity and the social mind: Why social psycholo-gists should be less selfish.* Unpublished manuscript.

Leary, M. R. (2004). Editorial: What is the self? A plea for clarity. *Self and Identity, 3,* 1–3.

Markus, H., & Wurf, E. (1987). The dynamic self-concept. *Annual Review of Psychology, 38,* 299–337.

Marr, D. (1982). *Vision.* San Francisco: W. H. Freeman.

Minsky, M. (1986). *The society of mind.* New York: Simon and Schuster.

Pinker, S. (1997). *How the mind works.* New York: W.W. Norton & Company.

Pinker, S. (2002). *The blank slate: The modern denial of human nature.* New York: Viking.

Ramachandran, V. S., & Blakeslee, S. (1998). *Phantoms in the brain: Probing the mysteries of the human mind.* New York: HarperCollins.

Restak, R. M. (1994). *The modular brain: How new discoveries in neuroscience are answer-ing age-old questions about memory, free will, consciousness, and personal iden-tity.* New York: Charles Scribner's Sons.

Roney, C. J. R., & Sorrentino, R. M. (1995). Self-evaluation motives and uncertainty ori-entation: Asking the "who" question. *Personality and Social Psychology Bulletin, 21,* 1319–1329.

Rorty, A. O. (1996). User-friendly self-deception: A traveler's manual. In R. T. Ames & W. Dissanayake (Eds.), *Self and deception: A cross-cultural philosophical enquiry* (pp. 73–89). Albany: State University of New York Press.

Rosenberg, S. (1997). Multiplicity of selves. In R. D. Ashmore & L. Jussim (Eds.), *Self and identity: Fundamental issues* (pp. 23–45). New York: Oxford University Press.

Rozin, P. (1976). The evolution of intelligence and access to the cognitive unconscious. *Progress in Psychobiology and Physiological Psychology, 6,* 245–280.

Schlenker, B. R., Forsyth, D. R., Leary, M. R., & Miller, R. S. (1980). A self-presentation-al analysis of the effects of incentives on attitude change following counterattitudi-nal behavior. *Journal of Personality & Social Psychology, 39,* 553–577.

Sedikides, C. (1993). Assessment, enhancement, and verification determinants of the self-evaluation process. *Journal of Personality and Social Psychology, 65,* 317–338.

Sedikides, C., & Brewer, M. B. (2001). Individual self, relational self, and collective self: Partners, opponents, or strangers. In C. Sedikides & M. B. Brewer (Eds.), *Individual self, relational self, collective self* (pp. 1–4). Philadelphia: Psychology Press.

Sedikides, C., & Gregg, A. P. (2003). Portraits of the self. In M. A. Hogg & J. Cooper (Eds.), *Age handbook of social psychology* (pp. 110–138). London: Sage Publications.

Shrauger, J. S., & Schoeneman, T. J. (1979). Symbolic interactionist view of self concept: Through the looking glass darkly. *Psychological Bulletin, 86,* 549–573.

Spanos, N. P. (1994). Multiple identity enactments and multiple personality disorder: A sociocognitive perspective. *Psychological Bulletin, 116,* 143–165.

Sperber, D. (1994). The modularity of thought and the epidemiology of representations. In L. A. Hirschfeld & S. A. Gelman (Eds.), *Mapping the mind: Domain specificity in cognition and culture.* New York: Cambridge University Press.

Sperber, D. (2000). Metarepresentations in an Evolutionary Perspective. In D. Sperber (Ed.), *Metarepresentations: A multidisciplinary perspective.* New York: Oxford University Press.

Sperber, D. (2002). In defense of massive modularity. In E. Dupoux (Ed.), *Language, brain and cognitive development: Essays in honor of Jacques Mehler* (pp. 47–57). Cambridge, MA: MIT Press.

Steele, C. M., Spencer, S. J., & Lynch, M. (1993). Dissonance and affirmational resources: Resilience against self-image threats. *Journal of Personality and Social Psychology, 64,* 885–896.

Surbey, M. K., & McNally, J. J. (1997). Self-deception as a mediator of cooperation and defection in varying social contexts described in the iterated Prisoner's Dilemma. *Evolution and Human Behavior, 18,* 417–435.

Swann, W. B. (1985). The self as architect of social reality. In B. R. Schlenker (Ed.), *The self and social life* (pp. 100–125). New York: McGraw-Hill.

Swann, W. B., Jr., Griffin, J. J., Predmore, S., & Gaines, B. (1987). The cognitive-affective crossfire: When self-consistency confronts self-enhancement. *Journal of Personality and Social Psychology, 52,* 881–889.

Symons, D. (1979). *The evolution of human sexuality.* New York: Oxford University Press.

Taylor, S. E., & Brown, J. D. (1988). Illusion and well being: A social psychological perspective on mental health. *Psychological Bulletin, 103,* 193–210.

Tesser, A., & Campbell, J. (1983). Self-definition and self-evaluation maintenance. In J. Suls & A. Greenwald (Eds.), *Social psychological perspectives on the self* (Vol. 2, pp. 1–31). Hillsdale, NJ: Erlbaum.

Tice, D. M. (1992). Self-presentation and self-concept change: The looking-glass self is also a magnifying glass. *Journal of Personality and Social Psychology, 63,* 435–451.

Tice, D. M., & Baumeister, R. R. (2001). The primacy of the interpersonal self. In M. B. B. C. Sedikides (Ed.), *Individual self, relational self, collective self* (pp. 71–88). Philadelphia, PA: Psychology Press.

Tooby, J., & Cosmides, L. (1992). The psychological foundations of culture. In J. H. Barkow, L. Cosmides & J. Tooby (Eds.), *The adapted mind* (pp. 19–136). New York: Oxford University Press.

Tooby, J., & Cosmides, L. (1996). Friendship and the banker's paradox: Other pathways to the evolution of adaptations for altruism. *Proceedings of the Royal British Academy, 88,* 119–143.

Trope, Y. (1986). Self-enhancement and self-assessment in achievement behavior. In R. M. Sorrentino & E. T. Higgins (Eds.), *Handbook of motivation and cognition* (Vol. 2, pp. 350–378). New York: Guilford.

Turner, R. H. (1976). The real self: From institution to impulse. *American Journal of Sociology, 81,* 989–1016.

4

When and Why Did the Human Self Evolve?

CONSTANTINE SEDIKIDES, JOHN J. SKOWRONSKI, and R. I. M. DUNBAR

*T*he construct of self is central to psychology and allied disciplines. This construct has captivated and enchanted philosophers and scientists, religious and political figures, writers, and poets. The self has been hailed as the basis of motivation, emotion, and behavior, and has also been heralded as the key to a deeper understanding of human nature. At the same time, the self has been mystified as enigmatic and fleeting, and has also been vilified as a direct route to personal miseries and societal woes.

Given the increasing relevance of natural selection principles in psychology, it is not surprising that a construct as multifaceted and influential as the self has begun to attract the attention of those psychologists who are interested in the evolutionary origins of various human psychological attributes (e.g., Gilbert, Price, & Allan, 1995; Leary & Buttermore, 2003; Sedikides & Skowronski, 2003). These psychologists conceptualize the human self as a trait that evolved in response to the environmental pressures that drive natural selection.

However, whether this conceptualization is likely to bear fruit is the subject of some debate. This debate is driven by the realization that our knowledge base concerning the conditions that influence the early evolution of humans is still thin. Consequently, one must make a number of plausible suppositions in an attempt to use principles of natural selection to understand the evolutionary origins of the self. For some researchers, such speculation—no matter how informed—is futile, and even potentially misleading. This is particularly true for those selection pressures, such as social organization, that leave only faint physical traces. For example, Bahn (1990, p. 75) argues: "I hate to break the news, but social organisation *is* unexcavatable, when the best one can hope for is a hypothesis based on inference and analogy.... In fact it is quite possible that all the interpretations of Palaeolithic life yet put forward are hopelessly wrong, and in any case we shall never know which of them are correct."

However, other researchers believe that the generation of informed speculation facilitates, and may even be necessary to, the development of an understanding of how evolution has shaped human psychological characteristics. As noted by Quiatt and Reynolds (1993, p. 262): "Anthropologists who have managed perfectly to subdue their imagination make dull company. Only informed speculation can give us a sense of how our society evolved."

In this chapter we side, rather unapologetically, with the latter of the two debate camps. After all, evolutionary theorizing and hypothesis generation pertain to the design and functions of psychological attributes rather than ancestral conditions. We use our current understanding of the self and combine it with the work of paleoanthropologists, primatologists, archaeologists, and archeolinguists to offer informed speculations about the evolutionary origins of the self. These speculations will include consideration of facets of the self that may have been subjected to the pressures of natural selection, why those facets might have been selected, and when (in evolutionary time) these self-facets may have begun to evolve. We conclude the chapter with a description of some of the empirical implications of these ideas.

DEFINING AND CHARACTERIZING THE SELF

Before we address these evolutionary ideas, however, we would first like to define and characterize the construct, the self, that is the focus of this chapter. We are specifically concerned with the evolution of the *symbolic self*. This term refers to both the ability to consider the self as an object of one's own reflection and the ability to store the products of such reflections (which may be abstract and/or language-based) in memory. We do not claim that the abilities comprising this adaptation are uniquely human. Instead, we accept that, in evolution, an attribute rarely arises *de novo*. That is, evolution generally proceeds by reworking, amplifying, or diminishing existing characteristics. One consequence is that there is often a fundamental continuity between related species. This continuity implies that evidence of the precursors of a symbolic self, or even a rudimentary symbolic self, should be found in other species, especially those that are close to humans on the bush of evolution. Indeed, recent evidence now suggests that higher primates (e.g., chimpanzees, bonobos, orangutans, gorillas) do possess rudimentary forms of a symbolic self-representation (Mitchell, 2003). However, this evidence also indicates that the human self is substantially more complex than the self possessed by other higher primates (Sedikides & Skowronski, 1997; Skowronski & Sedikides, 1999).

A distillation of research that explores the psychology of the self suggests that the human self has three interrelated capacities (Sedikides & Skowronski, 2000). One capacity is *representational*: The self serves as the repository of mental structures that store and organize self-relevant information. These self-relevant representational structures can be concrete or abstract, negative or positive, and can depict the past (e.g., autobiographical memories), present (e.g., how our writing of this chapter is currently going), or future (e.g., aspirations and possible selves). The representations can also include meta-cognitions (e.g., ideas about how others perceive one's behavior), information referring to dyadic relationships, information about one's position within the group, and information about intragroup dynamics and intergroup relations. Furthermore, the representations might contain attributes that can be: (1) unique and distinct from attributes that characterize related others or ingroup members (*personal self*), (2) shared with a related other (*relational self*), or (3) shared with the ingroup (*collective self*) (Sedikides & Brewer, 2001).

The second capacity of the self is *executive* and involves the regulation of its relation with the social and physical environment. Three classes of motives play a crucial role in guiding this capacity (Sedikides & Skowronski, 2000; Sedikides, Skowronski, & Gaertner, 2004): *valuation* (i.e., protecting and enhancing the self), *learning* (i.e., pursing a relatively accurate image of the self, improving skills and abilities), and *homeostasis* (i.e., seeking and endorsing information that is consistent with the self). We will discuss these motives at length later in the chapter.

Finally, the third capacity of the self is its *reflexivity*, defined as the organism's ability to depict itself in its ongoing relation with other objects. Reflexivity is manifested in the interplay between the representational and executive capacities. For example, reflexivity allows the organism to alter long-term goals and render them congruent with anticipated environmental changes. Because of this reflexive capacity, the organism can respond flexibly and dynamically to environmental changes, such as alterations in social contingencies, by selectively activating or de-activating portions of stored self-knowledge. More generally, the interplay of the representational, executive, and reflexive capacities allows the organism to process information in a way that is detached from the immediate environment, travel mentally in time, imagine and contemplate the future, simulate the consequences of own actions, and take preparatory steps for what might come as well as reparative measures for what has come. The interplay of these three capacities accounts for much of what it means to be human. We will elaborate on features of this interplay in the second half of the chapter, where we consider the evolutionary significance of the motives that influence the executive self.

A TIMELINE OF HUMAN EVOLUTION

Having addressed definitional issues, we now turn to the consideration of a timeline for human evolution. The construction of such a timeline serves as a context that greatly facilitates one's ability to locate the emergence of the human self. However, the proposal of such a timeline is a tricky business. Successive paleoanthropological discoveries necessitate the continuous updating of timelines and speciation patterns. Indeed, evidence that has been reported since we previously reviewed the timeline of human evolution (Sedikides & Skowronski, 1997) prompts us now to update and refine that timeline. While change might appear to be gradual on geologic time scales, when considering smaller time slices, evolution often proceeds in a series of fits and starts in which change is disorderly and nonlinear (Caporael, 2004; Klein, 1999; Klein & Edgar, 2002; Lahr & Foley, 1998; Leary & Buttermore, 2003; Tattersall, 2000). One reason for this disorderly pattern is that the environmental conditions that drive natural selection often change in a disorderly and nonlinear manner. Indeed, human evolution occurred in such a context, with periods of relative stability intermingled with dramatic and global climatic fluctuation. These fluctuations altered climates (from glacial to more temperate and vice versa) and changed ecosystems (from forests to grasslands to deserts). Geological activity (e.g., volcanic eruptions) may have similarly served to alter local climatic conditions, and may have even had global climatic consequences.

As noted earlier, it is commonly believed that this climatic instability critically influences evolution. For example, Caporael (2004) argues:

> "There is not slow gradual progress of a single lineage evolving through time in a stable [environment]. Instead, the evidence indicates changing environments and habitats breaking up. Fragments of populations would become isolated. They might speciate from the parent population through gradual selection to a new or changing environment, stay unchanged by following their preferred habitats, or simply become extinct. On the ground, evolution is … the complex responses between climate, biogeography and populations that may fragment, expand and collapse." (p. 195).

In this regard, consider some of the climatic changes that occurred in the context of the evolution of our human ancestors and some of the changes in our human ancestors that are correlated with such changes. Approximately 7 million years ago (mya), the warm rainforests of Africa were populated by a remarkable diversity of apes. Between 6.5 and 6 mya (end of the Miocene era), an acute temperature drop occurred. Woodland and savannah began displacing rainforest. During this same time, almost all of the Miocene apes went extinct. One surviving lineage, however, is thought to be a common ancestor to contemporary apes and humans (Haile-Selassie, 2001). By 5 mya, with the temperature rising and with evolution proceeding, diversification in the ape lineages is again observable. One of these lineages was apparently especially well suited for life in seasonal habitat and for consumption of gritty food. This lineage is thought to have given rise to bipedal apes with relatively small-sized brains relative to body mass, the best known of which are the australopithecines. Indeed, evidence from the most famous australopithecus, Lucy (Australopithecus afarensis), reveals a brain only slightly larger than a chimpanzee's.

The australopithecines were specialized for both walking and tree climbing and, consequently, were well suited to life in diverse habitats (e.g., savannah, forest). They had ape-like bodies with cone-shaped trunks and narrow shoulders. They were characterized by substantial sexual dimorphism (i.e., males were bigger than females), suggesting male competition for females and less male parental investment. They also likely had the intelligence for crude tool-making (e.g., wooden implements). The australopithecines were also thought to be a relatively social species whose members spent at least some time in the company of other conspecifics.

It is currently believed that *Australopithecus afarensis* spawned at least six species, including *Paranthropus boisei*, *Homo rudolfensis*, and *Homo habilis*. The appearance of *Homo habilis*, approximately 2.5 mya, coincided with a general cooling of the environment, which resulted in another recession of the rainforest and re-emergence of the savannah. It has been argued that the lack of rainforest safety and the ecological demands of the grasslands precipitated the achievement of evolutionary milestones such as the development of simple stone tools (i.e., splintered rocks). There is also evidence that these *Homo habilis* hominids carried their tools from site to site, even when these sites were separated by several kilometers, and reused these tools. Moreover, these tools (Oldowan choppers and handaxes) appear to have had multiple purposes, which included cutting flesh from bones and smashing bones open for the marrow (Potts, 1984). The evidence for tool-reuse and tool-carrying suggests the presence of at least two critical mental capacities. First, *Homo habilis* species members must have been able to anticipate the future. Second, these hominids were capable of some form of meta-cognition, as they would need to cue themselves for remembering where tools were abandoned or hidden and for hiding them in predetermined places. Indeed, the proposal for emergent meta-cognitive abilities among *Homo habilis* is compatible with their slightly larger brain to body size ratio (when compared to the australopithecines) and a trend toward change in their diet, namely increased consumption of meat (Tobias, 1987).

Current reconstructions of hominid evolution suggest that between 1.8 and 1.7 mya, *Homo habilis* had given way to *Homo ergaster,* which spread out of Africa and by 1 mya had evolved into *Homo erectus*. It is now believed that the latter species was an evolutionary dead-end that later became extinct in Asia (Klein & Edgar, 2002), but we will discuss the two species in combination given the similarities in their anatomical characteristics, cognitive faculties, and lifestyle. *Homo ergaster/erectus* had a less ape-like appearance, with longer legs, a smaller pelvis, a moisture-conserving external nose, and a barrel-shaped chest. Indeed, the body of *Homo ergaster/erectus* had lost the specialization for climbing, was fully adapted for terrestrial life, and was particularly well adapted for life in hot and dry climates. In particular, exposure of more surface area (relative to body mass) for cooling the body and brain likely contributed to effective thermal regulation, whereas the small pelvis facilitated more efficient walking. Additionally, sexual dimorphism decreased, with females getting bigger, suggesting that competition for females decreased while male parental investment increased.

It is likely that meat was a regular component of the diet of *Homo ergaster/erectus* species members. This high-quality nutrition made possible a significant reduction in intestine volume, thus allowing a shift of energy from the gut to the brain. In accord with this reasoning, this species had a large brain (i.e., neocortex) relative to body size. Evidence for a corresponding increase (Jerison, 1973) in the cognitive ability of *Homo ergaster/erectus* is manifested in several ways. First, this species was able to maintain naturally occurring fires and, by 790 thousand years ago (kya), to start and control fires (Goren-Inbar et al., 2004). Second, the species was able to produce better stone tools. An example is the Acheulean bifaces, an almond-shaped wedge with a point and a butt at each end, which appeared to conform to the designer's mental template rather than to trial-and-error stone knapping. Third, the species displayed unprecedented dispersion patterns. Specifically, *Homo ergaster/erectus* immigrated to many regions of the habitable world (e.g., Middle East, China, Indonesia, and Southern Europe). Fourth, this species was likely capable of at least rudimentary speech. Although there is some dispute about this, it has been claimed that Broca's area appeared approximately 1.5 mya. However, some argue that the increase in the emergence of Broca's area may simply reflect an amplified need for breath control, which was an original function of Broca's area (although precise breathing control is also essential for both speech and singing).[1] At the very least, suggestive evidence of frequent communication (not necessarily using language) exists in the widespread use of fire and the standardization of stone tools.

It may be the case that deliberate nonverbal communication (e.g., pointing, gesturing, facial expression), referred to as *mimesis* by Donald (1991), might also have evolved during this time period. While it is possible that such nonverbal communication was the origin of spoken language, the emerging consensus is that language has vocal rather than gestural origins (Barrett, Dunbar, & Lycett, 2002). Nonetheless, even mimesis requires sophisticated mental capabilities. These include knowledge of: (1) what it is to be communicated (self-reflection), (2) what others know (theory of mind), (3) what others need to know (tactical self-presentation), (4) how one would feel following the communicative message (affective forecasting), and (5) how or whether one would be in a position to control purposefully the message (knowledge of self-regulatory ability) (Gallup, 1997; Hopkins, 2000; Leary & Buttermore, 2003). Regardless of whether it was verbal or nonverbal, improved dyadic and group communication (for, say, hunting or foraging) likely facilitated both dispersion and successful group living. In this regard, it is interesting to note that *Homo ergaster/erectus* lived in larger groups than *Homo habilis*, groups characterized by flexible hierarchies with shifting roles and alliances (Aiello & Dunbar, 1993; Foley & Lee, 1989).

In summary, the larger neocortex in *Homo ergaster/erectus* coincided with relatively sophisticated tool-making and other markers of enhanced performance, suggesting enhanced cognitive abilities (Jerison, 1973), as well as with increasing social complexity and skill (Byrne & Whitten, 1988), thus facilitating efficient food acquisition strategies. We argue that these evolutionary milestones provided the foundation for the mental capabilities that were later combined to produce the emergence of the human self.

Homo heidelbergensis was a descendant of *Homo ergaster* or *Homo erectus*, appearing in Africa around 600 kya. This species is associated with a somewhat refined tool production (i.e., the Late Acheulean hand axe) and increased communicative ability (at approximately 500 kya; Mithen, 2000). By 150–130 kya, a lineage of *Homo heidelbergensis* is thought to have given rise in Africa to *Homo sapiens*. At about 130 kya and during a glaciation period, it is thought that a limited population of *Homo sapiens* survived an evolutionary bottleneck (when death rates far exceed birth rates, with a concomitant drastic reduction in the number of individuals who contribute to the gene pool), leaving a relatively small set of approximately 10,000 breeding individuals. This remaining population expanded greatly at the beginning of the interglacial period and dispersed out of Africa to Europe, the Far East, and into the Americas around 70,000 years ago. The fossil record shows sophisticated tool production characterized by considerable variety of form and a high turnover (5–10 kya) of tool types from about 40 kya. This explosion in tool production is considered the signature of a larger neocortex. The fossil record also testifies to sophistication and variation in stone transport, diet, hearths, and built structures. Hunting and gathering techniques seem to have increased in complexity and efficiency, and so did group living and social networking. It is during this time, we would argue, that the modern human self had finally arrived in full.

WHEN DID THE HUMAN SELF ORIGINATE?

While there is general agreement that the human self was certainly in place by 5–10 kya (i.e., within what is effectively historical times), there is no agreement on the time when the human self initially began to emerge in a form that bears resemblance to the modern self. In fact, dating the emergence of the human self has recently generated some controversy.[2] In our earlier work (Sedikides & Skowronski, 1997, 2003), we speculatively placed the origins of the human self in *Homo erectus* (or *ergaster/erectus*, according to the current taxonomy). As noted earlier, this species possessed a large and complex neocortex (manifested, in part, in advanced tool-making and fire control), pursued cooperative hunting with remarkable efficiency, witnessed the emergence of more advanced communicative and, eventually, linguistic capabilities, and demonstrated sophisticated social organization characterized by group stability, flexible social hierarchy, use of home bases for nomadic hunting, and widespread dispersion. We argued that, given the presence of these indicators of sophisticated cognitive abilities, it was plausible to surmise that a rudimentary human symbolic self had begun to evolve during this time.

Leary and Buttermore (2003) have challenged some of the bases of our conclusion. They argue that it is not clear how large or complex the brain needs to be in order to sustain a self, that cooperative hunting is exhibited by both primate (e.g., chimpanzee) and non-primate (e.g., wolves, wasps) species, and that *Homo ergaster/erectus* did not leave behind artifacts (e.g., art, religion, culture) that a researcher would normally associate with the human self. In contrast, Leary and Buttermore placed the emergence of the human (i.e., symbolic or conceptual) self in the late Paleolithic epoch (50–60 kya), as indicated by both the widespread emergence of technological advances (e.g., tools, clothing, housing, boats) and the widespread presence of artifacts (e.g., body adornment, art, ritualistic burial) in the paleoanthropological record.

We believe that debating the issue of origination of the symbolic self is not just a matter of satisfying intellectual curiosity, although this is an important matter. In addition, this debate is relevant to broader questions of how deeply rooted or central the symbolic self is to the *Homo* species. Is the symbolic self an adaptation that appeared merely 50 kya, or, alternatively, has the symbolic self been inextricably linked with practically the appearance of the *Homo* species?

Prompted by Leary and Buttermore's (2003) thoughtful and constructive challenge, we would like to clarify our own position and to question their rationale for providing a date of 50–60 kya for the evolution of the human self. To begin with, our thesis was that only a rudimentary human symbolic self appeared in *Homo erectus* (Sedikides & Skowronski, 1997, 2003)—a thesis acknowledged by Leary and Buttermore. We surmise that this adaptation undertook substantial transformation before it matured into the modern (i.e., *Homo sapiens*) self. Nonetheless, we believe that the evidence supports the earlier date that we proposed for the emergence of the self, and we believe that we can effectively rebut Leary and Buttermore's arguments.

For example, Leary and Buttermore (2003) asked how large the brain needs to be in order to sustain a self. Although we do not have a quantifiable answer to this question, we can respond to this question by weaving together several sources of evidence. The first of these suggests that cognitive capabilities were quite substantial in *Homo ergaster/erectus*. For example, there is a strong relation between intellectual ability and the ratio of brain size to body mass across mammals (Kuhlenbeck, 1973; Macphail, 1982). Given that there is a trend toward increasing brain size relative to body mass as the *Homo* genus moved from the australopithecines to *Homo sapiens*, it is hard to avoid the inference that intellectual ability was also increasing during that time. This conclusion is especially hard to ignore when considered in combination with the paleoanthropological evidence suggesting that, as time progressed, hominids possessed increased ability to inhabit inhospitable environments, which would increase diversity in food procurement. In addition, the *Homo ergaster/erectus* neocortex enlarged relative to that of *Homo habilis* at a time when tool production, cooperative hunting, communication, and group living also took a great leap forward. These capabilities, in combination, are suggestive of the presence of symbolic information processing capabilities, which are the heart of the symbolic self. In reply to such evidence, Leary and Buttermore point out that cooperative hunting exists in species that do not possess a human-like self. Indeed, we would be surprised if it did not exist, as we fully endorse the principle of cross-species continuity in many traits. In counter-reply, we point out that our argument was that hunting in the *Homo ergaster/erectus* period was remarkably more complex and efficient than hunting in the *Homo habilis* period, thus suggesting improvement in underlying cognitive abilities.

An additional thrust of our argument concerned social organization and communication. Evidence suggests that group size began to rise substantially toward the end of the *Homo ergaster/erectus* period (i.e., approximately 1 mya; Aiello & Dunbar, 1993), increasing thereafter at a rapid rate. Living in relatively large groups contributes to the solution of many ecological or survival problems, but it also entails costs and challenges. For example, given the pressing feeding requirement of group members, the length of daily journeys undertaken by large groups can increase relative to those undertaken by smaller groups, thus incurring additional energy and time costs (Dunbar, 2003a); contests over access to and distribution of food can disrupt foraging (Dunbar, 2003a); and the expenditure of energy and time, along with food contests, can contribute to reduced fertility in females and lower birth rates (Bowman, Dilley, & Keverne, 1978). The challenges of group living are also social: Large groups require the investment of large amounts of time in social grooming in order to ensure their cohesion and functionality through times (Dunbar, 1991), which causes problems with adequate allocation of grooming time. Such time demands may necessitate role differentiation and increased structuring of groups (Dunbar, 1984; Kudo & Dunbar, 2001); the necessity for intragroup cooperation might also increase with group size, with the formation of dyadic alliances (Trivers, 1971) and the need to monitor other members' contributions to the alliances, manage free-riders, detect cheaters and oneself exploit opportunities to cheat (Byrne & Whitten, 1988; Cosmides, 1989; Dunbar, 1999), all of which consume cognitive resources. In addition, effectively managing group-related behavior can entail ongoing social rank calculations and the tracking of shifting alliances (Harcourt, 1988), intensification of intrasexual competition for mates (Parker, 1987), and increased intergroup competition for resources (Ghiglieri, 1989).

Consider the mental abilities that would help an organism to navigate the demands of a large, complex, and ever-shifting social context. Effective functioning in such an environment would be facilitated by knowing who might be a "good fit" to one's own abilities (Tooby & Cosmides, 1996). This ability to predict whether one can effectively interact with others seems to require a good deal of self-understanding. Indeed, the need for such information may have contributed to the formation of a *private self*. In addition, an individual would benefit if he or she were able to perspective-take and know how she or he was perceived by others through reflected appraisal processes. These skills are also important when an individual wishes to present him or herself to other group members in a desirable manner when attempting to form alliances or ingratiate oneself into relationships. Such needs may contribute to the capacity to "know" what people are like and what they might want—in essence, a theory of mind. Beyond this, however, the effective detection of cheating requires a rather advanced theory of mind (i.e., knowing what the potential cheater thinks that I know; Dunbar, 2003b). Such a theory of mind would enable a cheater to manipulate the impressions conveyed to others by deliberately engaging in behaviors that would be seen as differing substantially from prototypical "cheating" behaviors. Thus, the need to effectively navigate the social world may also have contributed to the development of a theory of mind that could be useful in manipulating one's own behavior via self-presentation—or to the development of what we now call the *public self*.

The social demands associated with group living can be thought of as selection pressures that drive evolution, and, in our view, it is important that such pressures coincided with the presence of augmented cognitive capacities in human evolution. Indeed, in support of this notion, the complexity of social organization is generally correlated with neocortex volume in anthropoid primates. Specifically, five indices of social complexity (i.e., group size, grooming clique size, utilization of social skills in male mating strategies, frequency of tactical deception, frequency of social play) correlate with relative neocortex volume (Dunbar, 2003a). Group size, in particular, correlates strongly with absolute neocortex volume (Dunbar, 2003a).

The implication, then, is that the computational demands of the complex social life of *Homo ergaster/erectus* may have been an important driving force in the evolution of human mental capabilities, selecting for a larger brain—and especially frontal lobe (Dunbar, 2003a). Why the frontal lobe? Self-reflective skills are related to the presence of a relatively large neocortex. Recent research suggests that this area of the brain has emerged as the locus of many processes (e.g., self-awareness, self-recognition, self-reflection) that are vital to a concept of the self (Feinberg, 2001; Kelley, Macrae, Wyland, Caglar, Inati, & Heatherton, 2002; Turk, Heatherton, Kelley, Funnell, Gazzaniga, & Macrae, 2002).

The evolution of the neocortex was also accompanied by the evolution of physiological structures necessary for language production (Aiello, 1996) and, hence, implicitly language understanding, since the use of language is itself indicative of a capacity for symbolic reasoning (a capability important to the human symbolic self). Indeed, a complex vocal apparatus and a brain capable of controlling it is one of the special provinces of hominids. In fact, it has even been argued that language drove physiological evolution, conferring advantages to those who were able to produce more complex language sounds (Bickerton, 1981). Regardless, the physiological evidence related to language production capabilities that has been amassed to this point again suggests an earlier rather than later date for the origins of the symbolic self.

As mentioned previously, brain casts have been interpreted as reflecting the emergence of Broca's area as early as 1.5 mya. The evidence that Broca's area was enlarged in the left hemisphere appears to indicate the beginning of precise vocal control (Corballis, 2003). Moreover, an expanded and lower larynx—which many claim is a physiological necessity for articulate speech—evolved in late *Homo erectus* (McHenry, 1992; Zeller, 1992).[3] Other scholars (e.g., Aitchison, 1996) note that as *Homo habilis* evolved into *Homo ergaster/erectus*, their skulls altered in ways that would allow individuals to increase the variety and intricacy of the sounds they could produce. Examination of skeletons that are increasingly "modern" show a gradual enlargement of orifices in bones that can accommodate the nerves required to control complex speech. This trend begins pre-*Homo sapiens*, which suggests that some rudimentary language capability might also be evolving prior to the emergence of modern humans.

Curiously, there appears to be an interesting paradox in the lower larynx position that apparently accompanies speech. Although it is important to the production of complex speech, the low larynx makes human beings more susceptible to choking than any other species on the planet. From this paradox, some have concluded that, because the benefits of communication seem to outweigh the costs of choking, it is logical to assume that this larynx position is a key adaptation in the origin of language. As Scovel (1998, p. 43) argued: "So the linguistic advantages outweigh the physiological disadvantages of a lower larynx, and if the emergence of language is as vital to our evolutionary history as most anthropologists believe, and if language is so indispensable to our species, it is no exaggeration to claim that the descent of the larynx has permitted the ascent of mankind!" Nevertheless, it is possible that such alterations reflected preadaptations—changes that occurred for other reasons (e.g., the establishment of a lower vocal range that can strengthen the potency of threatening signals), and only later in evolution were these changes found to be advantageous for speech production (Nishimura, Mikami, Suzuki, & Matsuzawa, 2003). However, such arguments apply primarily to the positioning of the larynx, and can not easily explain the evolutionary timing of the increase in the size of the speech-controlling Broca's area or the expansion in the size of the skull orifices that accommodate nerves related to speech production. Hence, the constellation of changes in hominid anatomy over time collectively implicate the relatively early evolution of complex vocal communication. This also implies the presence of symbolic thought, a cognitive component critical to the modern self.

Leary and Buttermore's (2003) date of the evolutionary origins of the self at 60–50 kya was largely based on the emergence of the cultural "big bang"—a period of time in which glimmerings of human "selfness" seem to be evident in art production and ritual burial practices (see also Mithen, 2000). However, if Leary and Buttermore's dating is correct, then no such evidence ought to exist prior to 50 kya. The record suggests otherwise. Evidence of culture, art, and burial has been generated from archaeological sites that are older, sometimes substantially older, than the Leary and Buttermore date.

At least three lines of evidence can be cited in this regard. The first of these concerns art objects. Recent finds from South Africa, including bone fragments and an engraved nodule of hematite, have now been dated to more than 77,000 years ago (d'Errico, Henshilwood, & Nilssen, 2001; Henshilwood et al., 2002). Additional finds suggest that inhabitants of sites in South Africa and Cyrenaica in the middle Paleolithic period (as early as 100 kya) made use of red ochre and specularite pigments and of seashells that were a by-product of expanded food procurement practices in the production of carved artwork or personal adornment (Clark, 1989, 1995). However, some researchers claim that rock art objects may have an even older history. That is, although the evidence is disputed, some forms of rock art may be substantially older than the dates of the South African finds. For example, Marshack (1997) claimed that the "Berekhat Ram figurine" (a real carved object and not a product of natural forces) can be dated to at least 250,000 years ago. Bednarik (1998) reviewed additional evidence for the early emergence of art, noting that rock art consisting of cup marks and a meandering line hammered into the rock of a sandstone cave was produced in India 200 or 300 kya and that, at about the same time, simple line markings were made on a variety of portable objects (bone, teeth, ivory, stone) in several locations. However, these particular examples remain subject to some dispute as to whether or not they are human-made.

A second line of evidence, related to the production of art, concerns personal adornment. Archaeologists have recently discovered that humans used paint for aesthetic purposes far earlier than previously thought. Specifically, over 300 fragments of pigment were found in a cave at Twin Rivers, near Lusaka, Zambia. This find included pigments and paint grinding equipment believed to date to 350–450 kya (Barham, 2002). The obvious significance of pigments is that they imply ornamentation, which is a sign of self-emergence.

A third line of evidence comes from burial practices. Although true burials (i.e., those associated with grave goods) are not found prior to ca. 25 kya, several Neanderthal cave sites dated to 90,000 years ago provide what is considered to be the first plausible evidence of deliberate disposal of the dead (Stringer, Grün,

Schwarcz, & Goldberg, 1989). In addition, Clark et al. (2003) reported that modern human crania from the Middle Awash in the Afar Rift, Ethiopia, dated to 160–154 kya provided indications of deliberate mortuary practices (such as defleshing and polishing), which would push the date of burial practices back even farther. Moreover, at the early archaic human site of Atapuerca in Spain, there is evidence of the intentional storing of bones (but not necessarily burial) from at least 32 individuals in a cave chamber by as early as 300 kya (although a more conservative date may be 150 kya; Arsuaga, Martinez, Gracia, Carretero, & Carbonell, 1993; Carbonell et al. 1995; Nieves & Mendoza, 1993). If burial practices reflect a sense of self, as has often been claimed, then we have additional evidence that puts an evolving sense of self substantially earlier than suggested by Leary and Buttermore (2003).

We also question Leary and Buttermore's (2003) dating on other grounds. Given that language signifies the presence of symbolic or conceptual abilities, if Leary and Buttermore's dating is correct, then no language ought to have evolved prior to approximately 50 kya. Although language probably arose in a series of stages rather than as a single phenotypic or genotypic event (Aiello & Dunbar, 1993), it is also believed that language, in a relatively advanced form, had already evolved by 0.5 mya (Dunbar, 2003a). In addition, if language had evolved after 50 kya, it would be difficult to account for its universality across the human species today, since modern humans last shared a common ancestor some time prior to 70 kya when the main dispersal across the Arabian landbridge occurred.

In summary, we have argued on both evidential and logical grounds that the symbolic or conceptual self emerged well before the Upper Paleolithic era. In our view, Leary and Buttermore's (2003) claim that the emergence of the symbolic self is indexed by the cultural "big bang" around 50 kya is untenable in the face of the paleoanthropological evidence. Indeed, the current view leans more toward the suggestion by McBrearty and Brooks (2000) and others that the Upper Paleolithic cultural revolution in fact began in Africa some time prior to 100 kya. The apparent explosion in Europe after 50 kya may thus have more to do with the fact that modern humans only arrived in Europe, complete with their Upper Paleolithic culture, some time after 50 kya. Regardless of the fine details of this or any other explanation (such as Tattersall's [1995] language push or Klein's [1999] genetic mutation that caused a reorganization of the brain) for the sudden outburst of cultural diversity in Europe after 50 kya, unless challenged by new evidence, we hold to our thesis that the human self was already substantively in place by the appearance of archaic humans round 500 kya, and hence that its first glimmerings may already have begun to emerge by the late stages of the *Homo ergaster/erectus* period.

FUNCTIONS OF THE HUMAN SELF: THE CASE OF SELF-EVALUATION MOTIVES

What are the functions of the self that might have contributed to its maintenance and propagation? We previously defined the self in terms of the interplay of the representational, executive, and reflexive capacities. In discussing the executive capacity, we referred to three classes of self-evaluation motives: valuation, learning, and homeostasis. We will now discuss the adaptive utility of these motives for the self-system as well as relational living (Fletcher, Simpson, & Boyes, this volume) and group living (Brewer & Caporael, this volume; van Vugt & van Lange, this volume).

These motives influence the acquisition of self-relevant information. Given that maintenance and positive self-change is adaptive, it is not surprising that individuals are particularly sensitive to information that has implications for the self. For example, humans have a nonconscious processing sensitivity for stimuli pertaining to the self, are speedier in the processing of self-relevant than self-irrelevant descriptions, and show a better memory for self- than other-relevant information (Baumeister, 1998). In addition, the self affects the processing of social information. For example, when judging others on dimensions that are central to the self, individuals process the information deeply and draw a large number of rather extreme inferences about others (Sedikides & Skowronski, 1993). Moreover, the self is often projected upon others, especially when levels of ambiguity are relatively high (Green & Sedikides, 2001), and is implicated in the choice of friends or partners (Sedikides, 2003).

Humans, however, are not mere information recipients; they are also information seekers. Early hominid survival may have depended on the type of information sought and acquired from the environment and on how this information was interpreted and used in judgment and behavior. What kind of information did our ancestors want and need to know about themselves? This is where the three classes of self-evaluation motives, valuation, learning, and homeostasis (Sedikides & Gregg, 2003; Sedikides & Strube, 1997), would seem to be quite useful. The *valuation motives* are self-protection and self-enhancement. The self-protection motive serves to filter out, negate, or discredit unfavorable self-relevant information, whereas the self-enhancement motive serves to filter in, accept, or magnify favorable self-relevant information. The *learning motives* are self-assessment and self-improvement. The self-assessment motive guides pursuit of accurate (unfavorable or favorable) self-knowledge, whereas the self-improvement motive guides pursuit of knowledge that has long-term improvement value. *Homeostatic motivation* is represented solely by self-verification. This motive guides pursuit or endorsement of self-consistent information (negative or positive).

We conceptualize the three classes of self-evaluation motives as prima facie instances of putative modular adaptations, thus assuming that they served specific adaptive purposes (Kurzban & Aktipis, this volume). In the sections below, we will elaborate on how these motives can induce cognitive, affective, and behavioral changes that are adaptive. Moreover, we propose that the motives evolved in response to individual, relational, and group adaptive problems; and that they promoted the adaptive utility of the personal self while in the long run benefiting the relational and collective selves by improving the individual's relational and group standing. Finally, once again, we posit that these motives initially emerged in the later *Homo ergaster/erectus* period.

On the Adaptiveness of Self-Evaluation Motives

Numerous adaptive benefits can accrue from the action of the *valuation motives*. Choice of tasks (e.g., hunting, alliance formation, challenge to higher-ranked conspecifics) is a prime example. Valuation motives can influence individuals to avoid tasks with a high probability of failure (and hence, a threat to the self) and to select tasks with a high probability of success (and hence a boost to the self), assuming that expected task utility or fitness effects were comparable in the two cases. It follows that maximum benefit for the self would be produced by selection of tasks that entail an optimum combination of task success and fitness payoff. Additionally, protection or boosting of the self can be achieved by the interaction of valuation motives with the representational and reflexive components, resulting in such processes as forgetting failures and remembering successes, making self-serving inferences, believing in the relative superiority of the self over others, engaging in downward social comparison, and presenting the self favorably to others.

These processes also serve affective functions: The self-protection motive contributes to self-esteem maintenance and the evasion of negative emotions (e.g., disappointment, sadness, frustration), whereas the self-enhancement motive contributes to self-esteem elevation and the experience of positive emotions (e.g., contentment, pride, happiness). These conjectures are supported by research suggesting that a relatively high level of self-esteem and positive affectivity is linked with active engagement in everyday activities, creativity and planning, an optimistic attitude, improved coping, better psychological health (e.g., lower depression, anxiety, and loneliness), and better physical health (Baumeister, Campbell, Krueger, & Vohs, 2003; Fredrickson, 2001; Taylor, Lerner, Sherman, Sage, & McDowell, 2003a, b). Also, high self-esteem and positive affectivity (e.g., extraversion, low neuroticism) can add to an individual's appeal as a mate, thus improving chances of reproductive success. Reproductive success can also be promoted by the virtue of high self-esteem and positive affectivity facilitating dyadic interactions and group-level interactions: Individuals high in self-esteem and positive affectivity are perceived as competent and resourceful, and are thus more likely to be trusted upon for positions of responsibility within the group (Buss, 1989; Hogan, Curphy, & Hogan, 1994; Kenny & Zaccaro, 1983). Consequently, high self-esteem and positive affectivity maximize chances for advancement in the group hierarchy and minimize chances for social exclusion. Both outcomes, then, contribute to reproductive success, as high group status would be associated with successful mating and the offspring of high status members would be less likely to face neglect or social exclusion.

Learning motives, with their potential to clarify and enrich the self, would also have been adaptive to early humans when they led individuals to pursue, choose, and construct tasks that are high rather than low in skill diagnosticity (Trope, 1983). Given that high diagnosticity tasks provide a definitive test of whether the organism possesses the underlying skill, they allow efficiency in later choices and time allocation decisions. For example, individuals may purposefully select tasks within particular domains (e.g., hunting, gathering, child rearing duties) that diagnostically assess their abilities to perform well in those domains. The ensuing accurate self-knowledge can be implemented in task planning, thus maximizing person–environment fit. Alternatively, if a deficiency is evident, the individual can either allocate time to alternative pursuits (e.g., shifting from child-watching to food gathering) or find ways to improve (e.g., practicing, engaging in technological innovation). Finally, individuals can utilize accurate skill knowledge to place themselves in suitable positions in the group hierarchy, thus minimizing disadvantageous conflict with conspecifics. Hence, it seems reasonable to suggest that the learning motives likely promoted reproductive fitness.

In addition, learning motives may have served critical cognitive and affective functions for group members. The self-assessment motive reduces an individual's uncertainty about self-attributes as well as aspects of the social and physical environment. Also, the self-improvement motive elevates an individual's sense of progress. This two-step benefit (i.e., reduction of uncertainty coupled with feelings of progress) contributes to personal adjustment and positive affectivity, which (as discussed earlier) facilitate reproductive fitness.

The *homeostatic motive* of self-verification stabilizes the representational aspect of the self through direction of attention to and solicitation of self-consistent feedback, biased (i.e., self-confirming) interpretation of ambiguous feedback, biased causal inferences, biased recall, and the prompting of self-corroborating behavior. Our hominid ancestors may have been prone to selecting tasks likely to confirm their notions of self-competence, a trend also observed in humans today. Also, the confirmation of self-beliefs afforded by task selection may have rendered the social environment more predictable and increased feelings of control over it, thus contributing to feelings of personal efficacy. Such feelings are highly adaptive, as they facilitate wiser decisions about energy expenditure, the setting of self-congruent goals and, more importantly, behavioral change to achieve these goals. These processes maximize outcome success and, in the long run, reproductive fitness.

Reproductive fitness could have been maximized in another way. An individual may have solicited and received confirming feedback from group members regarding social standing, role expectations, and the behavioral repertoire necessary to carry out various roles. Such feedback would help the individual to avoid the energy waste that might accompany pursuit of goals incompatible with group objectives. Moreover, such feedback may also contribute to the warding off of negative emotions (e.g., shame, guilt, embarrassment) and the promotion of positive emotions (e.g., satisfaction, self-efficacy, pride).

It is perhaps important to emphasize here that social integration is a critical feature of all primate (including, obviously, humans) societies. This reflects the fact that primate social systems are implicit social contracts in which individual members need to be willing to delay immediate personal gratification in order to achieve greater advantages in the long term through cooperating to solve the problems of day-to-day survival. There is evidence to suggest that such tasks are cognitively much more demanding than the more conventional cognitive processing of physical percepts (Kinderman, Dunbar, & Bentall, 1998). The psychological processes that underpin the sense of self may play a critical role in enabling modern humans to integrate and bond their large social groups. And, if so, they may well have played an equally important role in allowing archaic humans to do the same in the somewhat smaller social groups in which they are likely to have lived (Aiello & Dunbar, 1993). These mechanisms can thus be seen as a natural outgrowth of the "social brain hypothesis" (Dunbar, 1992, 1998).

An Integrative View of the Self-Evaluation Process

We propose that self-evaluation motives operated synergistically rather than competitively in the prehistoric environment. That is, we assume that the three classes of motives were dynamically interrelated and served complementary purposes— and continue to do so today. Our evolutionary account emphasizes the modular nature of the symbolic self and the trade-off among different modules (i.e., self-evaluation motives). Nonetheless, we postulate that the self-evaluation process is predominantly guided by the valuation motives (Sedikides & Skowronski, 2000; Sedikides & Strube, 1997; Sedikides et al., 2004). Our proposal is fully compatible with findings attesting to the universality of both valuation motivation (Brown & Kobayashi, 2002; Sedikides, Gaertner, & Toguchi, 2003; Sedikides, Gaertner, & Vevea, 2005) and self-esteem (Pyszczynski & Cox, 2004; Pyszczynski, Greenberg, Solomon, Arndt, & Schimel, 2004a, b; Sheldon, 2004).

As an example of the relevance of the valuation motives, consider the interplay between the three motive types in the context of the distinction between *candid* and *tactical* self-enhancement. Candid self-enhancement refers to flagrant attempts to increase the positivity, or decrease the negativity, of self-attributes. This type of self-enhancement is achieved either through behaviors such as brute self-aggrandization (e.g., display of one's physical prowess) or through denial of wrongdoing (e.g., as when one is caught subverting the status of dominant individuals). Such behaviors can often be directly linked to the action of valuation motives. Tactical self-enhancement, on the other hand, refers to indirect attempts to increase the positivity or decrease the negativity of the self. Tactical self-enhancement is sensitive to the social context and the balance between immediate and delayed rewards. This type of self-enhancement is often guided by the action of the learning and homeostatic motives. An example of tactical self-enhancement would be to restrain from challenging a higher-ranking conspecific or showing downright submission. However, despite the action of the learning and valuation motives in this domain, we see their action as secondary. In our view, the valuation motives generally will play a more important role in controlling the behaviors relevant to self-evaluation.

The affective consequences of the self-evaluation process likely follow a similar pattern of integration, but with the primary guiding role being played by the valuation motives. We speculate that self-enhancement increases self-esteem, self-verification induces feelings of control, self-assessment reduces uncertainty, and self-improvement instills feelings of progress. Although all of these motives are involved in the production of such feelings, we argue that control, certainty, and a sense of progress are critical to individuals because they are linked to the more basic desire for self-protection or self-enhancement.

In addition, we maintain that the self-evaluation process consists of two parts: information and action. Information refers to the generation and testing of hypotheses about the quality of the person–environment fit (e.g., "Am I strong enough to overthrow the higher-ranking group member?"). This part reflects the extent to which the individual's abilities match situational demands. The resulting data from the hypothesis-testing procedure could be used to carry out candid and, more often, tactical self-enhancement through action (e.g., coalition-building for bringing about change in the dominance hierarchy). Thus, the action component of the self-evaluation process (along with concurrent self-regulatory processes) pertains primarily to opportunistic responses to existing situations or to the strategic creation of new situations that are likely to yield beneficial outcomes or avoid harmful ones. It should be apparent from our discussion that we regard information and action as interdependent. To the extent that information about person–environment fit is veridical, likely to lead to improvement, and is self-verifying, resulting action will have a high probability of success because the individual can now make informative choices about favorable performance domains. Likewise, action success produces feedback about the validity of the behavior in question, the rate of behavioral improvement, and the verifying value of the information on which the behavior was based.

When the person–environment fit is high (i.e., when self-enhancement is carried out effectively through the information and action parts), feelings of individual self-esteem, control, certainty, and progress (as well as positive affectivity, in general) can be heightened. In our view, these self-esteem consequences are likely the most immediate outcome of the self-evaluation process. In addition to being relevant to the self, these feelings can also provide an essential gauge of the utility of the individual's actions for the group (e.g., Did the group approve of the organism? Was rejection or exclusion a possibility? Should the organism persist along the same path or redirect action, instead?) (Leary & Baumeister, 2000). In turn, the presence of these feelings is likely to increase one's mate value (Brase & Guy, 2004).

Despite the fact that heightened self-esteem can be a guide to functional behavior, it is also the case that striving for self-esteem can sometimes lead to a suboptimal adaptive response (Crocker & Park, 2004). This suboptimality can result from a discrepancy between the adaptiveness of behaviors mandated by the information and by the action components of the self-evaluation process. Although we believe that the typical state of affairs is synergy between the information and action parts of the self-evaluation process, antagonism is also a possibility. What happens under these situations?

We suggest that the activation of a particular motive depends on the trade-off between the value of veridical information and its emotional costs. On the one hand, admitting the veridicality of information that pertains to important domains (e.g., being inept at aspects of gathering or hunting tasks) can lead to serious affective consequences (e.g., depression, lethargy, malfunction). On the other hand, neglecting the relevant information through dismissal, denial, or self-deception permits the individual to function with relative efficiency (e.g., perhaps by attempting to hone alternate skills), but could also inflict irreparable damage (e.g., being perceived as a cheater and being forced to eventual social exclusion). This conflict between candid self-enhancement objectives and long-term tactical self-enhancement objectives can assume other forms. For example, willingly giving up control to a more powerful group member may seem maladaptive, because it denotes acceptance of another's superiority. However, controlled relinquishment can also be an effective or conflict-free strategy for satisfying long-term objectives such as gaining acceptance within a group (Rothbaum, Weisz, & Snyder, 1982). In such cases, a pragmatic cost–benefit analysis or motive prioritization can facilitate a balanced, successful, and, in the long term, adaptive response to a given situation.

Still, which factors influence the activation of particular motives? We argue that motive activation depends on the dynamic interplay between the self-system and the environment. For example, high certainty about a self-attribute would render additional gathering of diagnostic information inefficient. In this situation, the self-assessment motive would be dormant or deactivated, whereas the self-verification motive would become accessible and would guide behavior that is likely to confirm the self-attribute under consideration. Consequently, the individual would resist unwarranted self-knowledge changes and the integrity of the self-system would be preserved. Low self-certainty, on the other hand, could activate the self-assessment or self-improvement motive. Such activation would prompt the individual to master the contingencies necessary for informed and fruitful transactions with the environment. Regardless, the long-term demands for veridical, improving, and positively verifying information might dictate that unflattering information about the self (i.e., one's liabilities in a domain) be uncovered or disclosed in the short run.

The organism's response might also be contingent on perceptions of skill modifiability (Dunning, 1995). An individual might be predisposed to accept accurate feedback (i.e., self-assess) about a skill considered changeable and improvable through practice, but to self-protect by rejecting accurate feedback when the skill was considered unchangeable. Self-protection would be particularly likely following a prior blow to self-esteem, whereas self-assessment would be likely following a self-esteem boost (Sherman & Cohen, 2002). In addition, the organism's response might depend on the availability of cognitive resources (Swann, Hixon, Stein-Seroussi, & Gilbert, 1990). Sometimes an immediately threatening event (e.g., public provocation by another group member) may require candid self-enhancement (e.g., display of physical prowess, vocal denial of the charges, verbal attack of the offensive opponent) rather than a deliberative response (Depret & Fiske, 1993). When the external threat, though, is not pressing (e.g., planning to overthrow and replace an ineffective leader), tactical self-enhancement (e.g., a deliberate and self-presentational build up on one's ability to self-assess and self-improve) can be more appropriate than an expedient response (Cummins, 1996). Finally, social context can influence motive activation. Tactical self-enhancement (e.g., modesty) can be the more sensible alternative when one is accountable for her or his behavior to other group members (Sedikides, Herbst, Hardin, & Dardis, 2002) or when presenting the self to persons familiar with the individual's record (Tice, Butler, Muraven, & Stillwell, 1995).

Evolution and the Valuation Motives: Summary and Recapitulation

In writing and in processing these theoretical ideas, the main thrust of one's argument sometimes gets lost in the technical details of the argument. Hence, we would like to take this opportunity to recapitulate our arguments with regards to evolution and the self-motives in a more "bare bones" form. Most central to our argument is the notion that evolution favored individuals with strong valuation motives, with the other motives (learning and homeostatic) playing a role that is generally in the service of those valuation motives, not least because these ensured close integration of individuals within large, complexly organized social communities.

In particular, we propose that the action of the valuation motives conferred three major adaptive advantages. First, these motives promote the adaptiveness of an individual's self-system. These motives are crucial to effective choice behavior and success experiences that had emotional (e.g., self-esteem, self-efficacy), motivational (e.g., active engagement in daily activities, planning facilitation, persistence in the face of adversity), and physical health consequences.

Second, valuation motives improved an individual's ability to engage in social interaction. As mentioned previously (Taylor et al., 2003a, b), valuation motives are negatively associated with mental distress (e.g., depression, anxiety, neuroticism, hostility) and positively associated with both mental health (e.g., high self-esteem, optimism, happiness, feelings of mastery and agency) and physical health or prowess. Mentally and physically healthy individuals are more likely than their distressed and weak counterparts to be seen as likeable, resourceful, and interpersonally attractive. Hence, those with strong (compared to those with weak) valuation motives are considered more attractive to others and are more likely to form positive interpersonal bonds with others. Functional valuation motives, then, are likely related to an individual's perceived mate value and so contributed to their mating success.

Third, functional and active valuation motives enhance an individual's standing in the group. An agentic, mentally healthy, and interpersonally successful group member likely was perceived as someone who is deserving of the group's trust and as someone who could effectively carry out collective tasks. Trust and acceptance promote an individual's chances of moving up in the ranks of a group and of assuming a leadership role. Benefits from such a role would include increased probability of reproductive success and decreased probability of sanctions (e.g., social exclusion, bodily harm) directed either at the individual or her/his offspring.

EPILOGUE

We set out to accomplish four objectives in this chapter. We began by addressing definitional issues regarding the construct of self. We then offered an updated timeline for the evolution of *Homo sapiens*, taking into consideration recent accounts that emphasize the nonlinear and disorderly course of evolution. Next, in the context of that timeline, we discussed when the human self originated. In the course of this discussion, we challenged Leary and Buttermore's (2003) dating of self-emergence in the Upper Paleolithic era (60–50 kya) on both evidential and logical grounds, and we reviewed evidence that bolsters our previous contention that glimmerings of the human self emerged at the end of the *Homo ergaster/erectus* period. Finally, we considered the functions of the self-evaluation process in the maintenance and propagation of the self and the species, and explored how the various human motives may have worked to enhance the evolutionary functionality of this process. We hypothesized that, while there are multiple motives that work integratively in this process, these motives generally work in the service of the valuation motives.

We believe that a good number of empirically testable hypotheses can be derived from our discussion. One example is the hypothesis that valuation motives enable an individual to cope more effectively with the demanding social pressures (e.g., alliance formation, competition with rivals) imposed by the complex and flexible social world of the human species. Another hypothesis is that valuation motive strength gives individuals direct interpersonal and reproductive advantages by increasing perceived mate value. Still, a third hypothesis is that valuation motive strength is associated with higher ranking in the group and, ultimately, with smoother group functioning. These hypotheses are empirically tractable on several levels. Both behavioral studies (e.g., linking valuation motive strength to adaptive functioning) and biological studies (e.g., linking valuation motive strength to specific genes or gene abnormalities) have the potential to lead to fruitful avenues of investigation.

Another promising line of research is a systematic examination of the interplay between the executive and reflexive components of the self-system and the conferred evolutionary benefits. Although we readily acknowledge the hypersociality of the *Homo* species, we also believe that what crucially separated humans from other animals is not necessarily relational or group life per se. Rather, it is the executive and reflexive capacity to approach and avoid relationships or groups. By using this reflexive capacity in this way, an individual is capable both of harvesting the benefits of relational and group life (e.g., protection from predators, food sharing, help in habitat construction) and escaping its costs (e.g., a sudden drop in the group competitive power, reduction in group size due to unfavorable antagonistic encounters, presence of parasites in the group as discussed in Kurzban & Leary, 2001).

We welcome the conduct of such research and look forward to its results. The ideas of natural selection and evolution are powerful, and as such they can be applied in ways that are very appealing, even in the absence of data. Consequently, it is all too easy to spin alternate tales of the action of evolution in the development of the human species, and often these contradictory tales can sound equally convincing. It is because of this that empirical data testing competing evolutionary hypotheses are urgently required. Indeed, it is the empirical exploration of the ideas about the design and functions of the human capability for self that we regard as a high-priority agenda item for social psychological research.

ACKNOWLEDGMENTS

We thank Rob Kurzban for his helpful comments on an earlier draft. R. I. M. Dunbar is supported by a British Academy Research Professorship, and the Academy's support of his research is gratefully acknowledged. Correspondence concerning this chapter should be addressed to Constantine Sedikides, School of

Psychology, University of Southampton, Southampton SO17 1BJ, England, United Kingdom. Electronic mail may be sent to <cs2@soton.ac.uk>.

NOTES

1. We should note that there is some controversy as to whether Broca's area is specifically a language area (Kan & Thompson-Schill, 2004).
2. For the purposes of this discussion, we will use the umbrella term "human symbolic self" to refer to all three capacities, namely, representational, executive, and reflexive.
3. Some authors point to the importance of the location of the root of the tongue and the position of the hyoid bone in the speech production system (Nishimura, Mikami, Suzuki, & Matsuzawa, 2003).

REFERENCES

Aiello, L. C. (1996). Terrestriality, bipedalism and the origin of language. In G. Runciman, J. Maynard Smith, & R. I. M. Dunbar (Eds.), *Evolution of social behavior patterns in primates and man* (pp. 269–290). Oxford: Oxford University Press.

Aiello, L., & Dunbar, R. (1993). Neocortex size, group size and the evolution of language. *Current Anthropology, 34,* 184–193.

Aitchison, J. (1996). *The seeds of speech: Language origin and evolution.* Cambridge, UK: Cambridge University Press.

Arsuaga, J. L., Martinez, I., Gracia, A., Carretero, J. M. & Carbonell, E. (1993). Three new human skulls from the Sima de los Huesos Middle Pleistocene site in Sierra de Atapuerca, Spain. *Nature, 362,* 534–537.

Bahn, P. (1990). Motes and beams: A further response to White on the Upper Palaeolithic. *Current Anthropology, 31,* 71–76.

Barham, L. S. (2002). Systematic pigment use in the Middle Pleistocene of south-central Africa. *Current Anthropology, 43,* 181–190.

Barrett, R. A., Dunbar, R. I. M., & Lycett, J. E. (2002). *Human evolutionary psychology.* Princeton, NJ: Princeton University Press.

Baumeister, R. F. (1998). The self. In D. T. Gilbert, S. T. Fiske, & G. Lindzey (Eds.), *The handbook of social psychology* (Vol. 1, pp. 680–740). New York: Oxford University Press.

Baumeister, R. F., Campbell, J. D., Krueger, J. I., & Vohs, K. D. (2003). Does high self-esteem cause better performance, interpersonal success, happiness, or healthier lifestyles? *Psychological Science in the Public Interest, 4,* 1–44.

Bednarik, R. G. (1998). The first stirrings of creation. *UNESCO Courier, 51,* 4–10.

Bickerton, D. (1981). *Roots of language.* Ann Arbor, MI: Karoma.

Bowman, L. A., Dilley, S. R., & Keverne, E. B. (1978). Suppression of oestrogen-induced LH surges by social subordination in talapoid monkeys. *Nature, 275,* 56–58.

Brase, G. L., & Guy, E. C. (2004). The demographics of mate value and self-esteem. *Personality and Individual Differences, 36,* 471–484.

Brown, J. D., & Kobayashi, C. (2002). Self-enhancement in Japan and America. *Asian Journal of Social Psychology, 5,* 145–167.

Buss, D. M. (1989). Sex differences in human mate preferences: Evolutionary hypotheses tested in 37 cultures. *Behavioral and Brain Sciences, 12,* 1–14.

Byrne, R. W., & Whitten, A. (Eds.). (1988). *Machiavellian intelligence*. Oxford, UK: Oxford University Press.

Caporael, L. R. (2004). Bones and stones: Selection for sociality. *Journal of Cultural and Evolutionary Psychology, 2*, 195–211.

Carbonell, E., Bermudez de Castro, J. M., Arsuaga, J. L., Díez, J. C., Rosas, A., Cuenca-Bescos, G., Sala, R., Mosquera, M., et al. (1995). Lower Pleistocene hominids and artifacts from Atapuerca-TD6 (Spain). *Science, 269*, 826–832.

Clark, J. D. (1989). The origins and spread of modern humans: A broad perspective on the African evidence. In P. Mellars & C. Stringer (Eds.), *The human revolution* (pp. 566–588). Edinburgh: Edinburgh University Press.

Clark, J. D. (1995). Recent developments in human biological and cultural evolution. *South African Archaeological Bulletin, 50*, 168–174.

Clark, J. D., Beyene, Y., WoldeGabriel, G., Hart, W. K., Renne, P. R., Gilbert, H., Defleur, A., Suwa, G., Katoh, S., Ludwig, K. R., Boisserie, J. R., Asfaw, B., & White, T. D. (2003). Stratigraphic, chronological and behavioral contexts of Pleistocene *Homo sapiens* from Middle Awash, Ethiopia. *Nature, 423*, 747–752.

Corballis, M. C. (2003). From mouth to hand: Gesture, speech, and the evolution of right-handedness. *Behavioral and Brain Sciences, 26*, 199–260.

Cosmides, L. (1989). The logic of social exchange: Has natural selection shaped how humans reason? *Cognition, 31*, 187–276.

Crocker, J., & Park, L. E. (2004). The costly pursuit of self-esteem. *Psychological Bulletin, 130*, 392–414.

Cummins, D. D. (1996). Dominance hierarchies and the evolution of human reasoning. *Minds and Machines, 6*, 463–480.

Depret, E. F., & Fiske, S. T. (1993). Social cognition and power: Some cognitive consequences of social structure as a source of control deprivation. In G. Weary, F. Gleicher, & K. Marsh (Eds.), *Control motivation and social cognition* (pp. 176–202). New York: Springer.

d'Errico, F., Henshilwood, C., & Nilssen, P. (2001). An engraved bone fragment from *ca*. 70,000-year old Middle Stone Age levels at Blombos Cave, South Africa: Implications for the origin of symbolism and language. *Antiquity, 75*, 309–318.

Donald, M. (1991). *Origins of the modern mind*. Cambridge, MA: Harvard University Press.

Dunbar, R. I. M. (1984). *Reproductive decisions: An economic analysis of Gelada Baboon social strategies*. Princeton, NJ: Princeton University Press.

Dunbar, R. I. M. (1991). Functional significance of social grooming in primates. *Folia Primatologica, 57*, 121–131.

Dunbar, R. I. M. (1992). Neocortex size as a constraint on group size in primates. *Journal of Human Evolution, 22*, 469–493.

Dunbar, R. I. M. (1998). The social brain hypothesis. *Evolutionary Anthropology, 6*, 178–190.

Dunbar, R. I. M. (1999). Culture, honesty and the freeride problem. In R. I. M. Dunbar, C. Knight, & C. Power (Eds.), *The evolution of culture* (pp. 194–213). Edinburgh: Edinburgh University Press.

Dunbar, R. I. M (2003a). The social brain: Mind, language, and society in evolutionary perspective. *Annual Review of Anthropology, 32*, 163–181.

Dunbar, R. I. M. (2003b). Why are apes so smart? In P. Kappeler & M. Peirera (Eds.), *Primate life histories* (pp. 285–298). Cambridge, MA: MIT Press.

Dunning, D. (1995). Trait importance and modifiability as factors influencing self-assessment and self-enhancement motives. *Personality and Social Psychology Bulletin, 21*, 1297–1306.

Feinberg, T. E. (2001). *Altered egos: How the brain creates the self.* London: Oxford University Press.

Foley, R. A. & Lee, P. C. (1989). Finite social space, evolutionary pathways and reconstructing hominid behavior. *Science, 243,* 901–906.

Fredrickson, B. L. (2001). The role of positive emotions in positive psychology: The broaden-and-built theory of positive emotions. *American Psychologist, 56,* 218–226.

Gallup, G. G. (1997). On the rise and fall of self-conception in primates. In J. G. Snodgrass & R. L. Thompson (Eds.), *The self across psychology* (pp. 73–82). New York: New York Academy of Sciences.

Ghiglieri, M. P. (1989). Hominoid socio-biology and hominid social evolution. In P. G. Heltne & L. A. Marquardt (Eds.), *Understanding chimpanzees* (pp. 370–379). Cambridge, MA: Harvard University Press.

Gilbert, P., Price, J., & Allan, S. (1995). Social comparison, social attractiveness and evolution: How might they be related? *New ideas in psychology, 13,* 149–165.

Goren-Inbar, N., Alperson, N., Kislev, M. E., Simchoni, O., Melamed, Y., Ben-Nun, A., & Werker, E. (2004). Evidence of hominin control of fire at Gesher Benot Ya'aqov, Israel. *Science, 304,* 725–727.

Green, J. D., & Sedikides, C. (2001). When do self-schemas shape social perception?: The role of descriptive ambiguity. *Motivation and Emotion, 25,* 67–83.

Haile-Selassie, Y. (2001, July 12). Late Miocene hominids in the Middle Awash, Ethiopia. *Nature, 412,* 178–181.

Harcourt, A. H. (1988). Alliances in contest and social intelligence. In R. Byrne & A. Whitten (Eds.), *Machiavellian intelligence: Social expertise and the evolution of intellect in monkeys, apes and humans* (pp. 132–152). Oxford, England: Oxford University Press.

Henshilwood, C. S., d'Errico, F., Yates, R., Jacobs, Z., Tribolo, C., Duller, G. A. T., Mercier, N., Sealy, J. C., Valladas, H., Watts, I., & Wintle, A. (2002). Emergence of modern human behavior: Middle Stone age engravings from South Africa. *Science, 295,* 1278–1280.

Hogan, R., Curphy, G. J., & Hogan, J. (1994). What we know about leadership: Effectiveness and personality. *American Psychologist, 49,* 493–504.

Hopkins, J. (2000). Evolution, consciousness and the internality of the mind. In P. Garruthers & A. Chamberlin (Eds.), *Evolution and the human mind: Modularity, language, and meta-cognition* (pp. 276–298). Cambridge, UK: Cambridge University Press.

Jerison, H. J. (1973). *Evolution of the brain and intelligence.* New York: Academic Press.

Kan, I. P., & Thompson-Schill, S. L. (2004). Effect of name agreement on prefrontal activity during overt and covert picture naming. *Cognitive, Affective & Behavioral Neuroscience, 4,* 43–57.

Kelley, W. M., Macrae, C. N., Wyland, C. L., Caglar, S., Inati, S., & Heatherton, T. E. (2002). Finding the self?: An event-related fMRI study. *Journal of Cognitive Neuroscience, 14,* 785–794.

Kenny, D. A., & Zaccaro, S. J. (1983). An estimate of variance due to traits in leadership. *Journal of Applied Psychology, 68,* 678–685.

Kinderman, P., Dunbar, R. I. M., & Bentall, R. P (1998). Theory-minded deficits and causal attributions. *British Journal of Psychology, 89,* 191–204.

Klein, R. G. (1999). *The human career: Human biological and cultural origins.* Chicago: University of Chicago Press.

Klein, R. G., & Edgar, B. (2002). *The dawn of human culture.* New York: Wiley.

Kudo, H., & Dunbar, R. I. M. (2001). Neocortex size and social network size in primates. *Animal Behavior, 62*, 711–722.

Kuhlenbeck, H. (1973). *Central nervous system of vertebrates* (Vol. 3, Part II). New York: Arnold-Backlin-Strasse.

Kurzban, R., & Leary, M. R. (2001). Evolutionary origins of stigmatization: The functions of social exclusion. *Psychological Bulletin, 127*, 187–208.

Lahr, M. M., & Foley, R. A. (1998). Towards a theory of modern human origins: Geography, demography, and diversity in recent human evolution. *Yearbook of Physical Anthropology, 41*, 137–176.

Leary, M. R., & Baumeister, R. F. (2000). The nature and function of self-esteem: sociometer theory. In M. Zanna (Ed.), *Advances in experimental social psychology* (Vol. 32, pp. 1–62). San Diego: Academic Press.

Leary, M. R., & Buttermore, N. R. (2003). The evolution of the human self: Tracing the natural history of self-awareness. *Journal for the Theory of Social Behavior, 33*, 365–404.

Macphail, E. (1982). *Brain and intelligence in vertebrates*. Oxford, UK: Clarendon Press.

Marshack, A. (1997). The Berekhat Ram figurine: A Late Acheulian carving from the Middle East. *Antiquity, 71*, 327–337.

McBrearty, S., & Brooks, A. S. (2000). The revolution that wasn't: A new interpretation of the origin of modern human behavior. *Journal of Human Evolution, 39*, 453–563.

McHenry, H. M. (1992). How big were early hominids? *Evolutionary Anthropology, 1*, 15–19.

Mitchell, R. W. (2003). Subjectivity and self-recognition in animals. In M. R. Leary & J. P. Tangney (Eds.), *Handbook of self and identity* (pp.567–593). New York: Guilford.

Mithen, S. (2000). Paleoanthropological perspectives on the theory of mind. In S. Baron-Cohen, H. Tager-Flusberg, & D. Cohen (Eds.), *Understanding other minds* (pp. 488–502). Oxford, UK: Oxford University Press.

Nieves, J. M., & Mendoza, I. (1993). Atapuerca quien era este hombre. *Ciencia, 64–78*.

Nishimura, T., Mikami, A., Suzuki, J., & Matsuzawa, T. (2003). Descent of the larynx in chimpanzee infants. *Proceedings of the National Academy of Sciences, 100*, 6930–6933.

Parker, S. T. (1987). A sexual selection model for hominid evolution. *Human Evolution, 2*, 235–253.

Potts, R. B. (1984). Home bases and early hominids. *American Scientist, 72*, 338–347.

Pyszczynski, T., & Cox, C. (2004). Can we really do without self-esteem?: Comment on Crocker and Park (2004). *Psychological Bulletin, 130*, 425–429.

Pyszczynski, T., Greenberg, J., Solomon, S., Arndt, J., & Schimel, J. (2004a). Why do people need self-esteem?: A theoretical and empirical review. *Psychological Bulletin, 130*, 435–468.

Pyszczynski, T., Greenberg, J., Solomon, S., Arndt, J., & Schimel, J. (2004b). Converging toward an integrated theory of self-esteem: Reply to Crocker and Nuer (2004), Ryan and Deci (2004), and Leary (2004). *Psychological Bulletin, 130*, 483–488.

Quiatt, D., & Reynolds, V. (1993). *Primate behavior: Information, social knowledge, and the evolution of culture*. Cambridge: Cambridge University Press.

Rothbaum, F., Weisz, J. R., & Snyder, S. S. (1982). Changing the world and changing the self: A two-process model of perceived control. *Journal of Personality and Social Psychology, 42*, 5–37.

Scovel, T. (1998). *Psycholinguistics*. Oxford, UK: Oxford University Press.

Sedikides, C. (2003). On the status of self in social prediction: Comment on Karniol (2003). *Psychological Review, 110*, 591–594.

Sedikides, C., & Brewer, M. B. (2001). *Individual self, relational self, collective self.* Philadelphia: Psychology Press.

Sedikides, C., Gaertner, L., & Toguchi, Y. (2003). Pancultural self-enhancement. *Journal of Personality and Social Psychology, 84,* 60–70.

Sedikides, C., Gaertner, L., & Vevea, J. (2005). Pancultural self-enhancement reloaded: A meta-analytic reply to Heine(2005). *Journal of Personality and Social Psychology, 89,* 539–551.

Sedikides, C., & Gregg, A. P. (2003). Portraits of the self. In M. A. Hogg & J. Cooper (Eds.), *Sage handbook of social psychology* (pp. 110–138). London: Sage Publications.

Sedikides, C., Herbst, K. C., Hardin, D. P., & Dardis, G. J. (2002). Accountability as a deterrent to self-enhancement: The search for mechanisms. *Journal of Personality and Social Psychology, 83,* 592–605.

Sedikides, C., & Skowronski, J. J. (1993). The self in impression formation: Trait centrality and social perception. *Journal of Experimental Social Psychology, 29,* 347–357.

Sedikides, C., & Skowronski, J. A. (1997). The symbolic self in evolutionary context. *Personality and Social Psychology Review, 1,* 80–102.

Sedikides, C., & Skowronski, J. J. (2000). On the evolutionary functions of the symbolic self: The emergence of self-evaluation motives. In A. Tesser, R. Felson, & J. Suls (Eds.), *Psychological perspectives on self and identity* (pp. 91–117). Washington, DC: APA Books.

Sedikides, C., & Skowronski, J. J. (2003). Evolution of the self: Issues and prospects. In M. R. Leary & J. P. Tangney (Eds.), *Handbook of self and identity* (pp. 594–609). New York: Guilford.

Sedikides, C., Skowronski, J. J., & Gaertner, L. (2004). Self-enhancement and self-protection motivations: From the laboratory to an evolutionary context. *Journal of Cultural and Evolutionary Psychology, 2,* 61–79.

Sedikides, C., & Strube, M. J. (1997). Self-evaluation: To thine own self be good, to thine own self be sure, to thine own self be true, and to thine own self be better. *Advances in experimental social psychology* (Vol. 29, pp. 209–269). New York: Academic Press.

Sheldon, K. M. (2004). *Optimal human being: An integrated multi-level perspective.* Mahwah, NJ: Erlbaum.

Sherman, D. K., & Cohen, G. L. (2002). Accepting threatening information: Self-affirmation and the reduction of defensive biases. *Current Directions in Psychological Science, 11,* 119–123.

Skowronski, J. A., & Sedikides, C. (1999). Evolution of the symbolic self. In D. H. Rosen & M. C. Luebbert (Eds.), *Evolution of the psyche* (pp. 78–94). Westport, CT: Greenwood Publishing Croup, Inc.

Stringer, C. B., Grün, R., Schwarcz, H. P., & Goldberg, P. (1989). ESR dates for the hominid burial site of Es Skhul in Israel. *Nature, 338,* 756–758.

Swann, W. B. Jr., Hixon, J. G., Stein-Seroussi, A., & Gilbert, D. T. (1990). The fleeting gleam of praise: Cognitive processes underlying behavioral reactions to self-relevant feedback. *Journal of Personality and Social Psychology, 59,* 17–26.

Tattersall, I. (1995). *The fossil trail.* New York: Oxford University Press.

Tattersall, I. (2000). Paleoanthropology: The last half-century. *Evolutionary Anthropology, 9,* 56–62.

Taylor, S. E., Lerner, J. S., Sherman, D. K., Sage, R. M., & McDowell, N. K. (2003a). Portrait of the self-enhancer: Well adjusted and well liked or maladjusted and friendless? *Journal of Personality and Social Psychology, 84,* 165–176.

Taylor, S. E., Lerner, J. S., Sherman, D. K., Sage, R. M., & McDowell, N. K. (2003b). Are self-enhancing cognitions associated with healthy or unhealthy biological profiles? *Journal of Personality and Social Psychology, 84,* 605–615.

Tice, D. M, Butler, J. L., Muraven, M. B., & Stillwell, A. M. (1995). When modesty prevails: Differential favorability of self-presentation to friends and strangers. *Journal of Personality and Social Psychology, 69,* 1120–1138.

Tobias, P. V. (1987). The brain of *Homo habilis*: A new level of organization in cerebral evolution. *Journal of Human Evolution, 16,* 741–761.

Tooby, J., & Cosmides, L. (1996). Friendship and the Banker's paradox: Other pathways to the evolution of adaptations for altruism. In J. M. Smith, W. G. Runciman, & R. I. M. Dunbar (Eds.), *Evolution of social behavior patterns in primates and man. Proceedings of the British Academy, 88,* 119–143.

Trivers, R. L. (1971). The evolution of reciprocal altruism. *Quarterly Review of Biology, 46,* 35–57.

Trope, Y. (1983). Self-assessment in achievement behavior. In J. M. Suls & A. G. Greenwald (Eds.), *Psychological perspectives on the self* (Vol. 2, pp. 93–121). Hillsdale, NJ: Erlbaum.

Turk, D. J., Heatherton, T. F., Kelley, W. M., Funnell, M. G., Gazzaniga, M. S., & Macrae, C. N. (2002). Mike or me? Self-recognition in a split-brain patient. *Nature Neuroscience* (http:www.nature.com/natureneuroscience).

Zeller, A. (1992). Communication in the social unit. In F. D. Burton (Ed.), *Social processes and mental abilities in non-human primates: Evidence from longitudinal field studies* (pp. 61–89). Lewiston, NY: Edwin Mellen Press.

5

The Ecological Approach to Person Perception: Evolutionary Roots and Contemporary Offshoots

LESLIE A. ZEBROWITZ and JOANN MONTEPARE

A little over 20 years ago, an ecological approach to social perception was proposed to draw attention to issues overlooked in contemporary social cognition research (McArthur & Baron, 1983). These included the function of person perception to serve adaptive action, the qualities of people's faces, bodies, and voices that inform person perception, and the role of an active perceiver in extracting that information. Although evidence had documented the impact of physical qualities on a variety of social judgments, little was known about the origins of these perceptions or how they operate. In keeping with what evolutionary psychologists have dubbed the "standard social science model" view that social perceptions are social constructions, social psychologists have long assumed that the stimulus information linked to person perception is a cultural by-product and of little interest for understanding basic social cognitive processes.[1] Thus, the rare attempts that were undertaken to identify the cues that guided social perceptions were shot-gun in their approach and provided little systematic insight into the particular tangible qualities that elicited particular perceptions and why they did so. To address these questions, the ecological approach drew on Gibsonian models of object perception (e.g., Gibson, 1966, 1979; Shaw, Turvey, & Mace, 1982) that have roots in evolutionary theory. In this chapter, we discuss the tenets of the ecological approach to social perception, their ties to evolutionary psychology, and the ways in which the ecological approach extends beyond evolutionary psychology principles. We then review selected person perception research and outline a research agenda that describes core questions an ecological approach should address to deepen our understanding of person perception.

BASIC TENETS OF THE ECOLOGICAL APPROACH TO PERSON PERCEPTION

Four distinguishing tenets that characterize the ecological approach to person perception include the dictum that *perceiving is for doing*, the emphasis on identifying the *stimulus information* to which perceivers' respond, the insight that perceivers detect *behavioral affordances* in their social environment, and the articulation of factors that influence *perceivers' attunements* to these affordances. Each tenet and its evolutionary underpinnings are described below.

Perceiving is for Doing

The first tenet follows Gibson's (1979) dictum that *"perceiving is for doing."* It has two significant components. One is that a full understanding of person perception requires theory and research that incorporates a "doing"—i.e., behaving—perceiver. Evolutionary psychology likewise acknowledges the central importance of an acting perceiver, observing that "organisms that don't move, don't have brains ... the circuits of the brain are designed to generate motion—behavior—in response to information from the environment" (Cosmides & Tooby, 1997, pp. 3–4).

A second component of the ecological tenet "perceiving is for doing" is that the qualities we perceive in other people often serve an adaptive function either for the survival of the species or for the goal attainment of individuals. As such, it is assumed that person perception is typically accurate. Although evolutionary theory would agree that person perception solves adaptive problems, it differs from ecological theory in its view of adaptive function. Evolutionary psychology focuses primarily on evolutionary adaptation fulfilling the function of inclusive fitness, which is the reproductive success of an individual's genes or an individual's genetic relations (e.g., Cosmides & Tooby, 1997). Ecological theory incorporates a broader view of adaptive function. As a result, ecological theory is concerned not only with person perception mechanisms designed by natural selection, but also with those designed by idiosyncratic experiences, thereby allowing perceivers to solve unique problems faced during their individual lifetimes.

Understanding the Stimulus is Central

A second hallmark of the ecological approach is an emphasis on identifying the features of the *external stimulus environment* that inform perception. In the case of person perception, the external stimulus consists of people's tangible properties, such as appearance, movement, voice, feel, and scent. Gibson emphasized the co-evolution of perceptual systems within ecological niches and argued that understanding the nature of the stimulus information to which organisms respond will elucidate how their perceptual systems operate. Indeed, Gibson's specifications of the kinds of higher order stimulus information that inform adaptive action stimulated research that has identified neurons tuned to such information (cf. Nakayama, 1994). Evolutionary psychologists also make this point. For example,

Cosmides and Tooby (1997) note that the brain is "designed to generate behavior that is appropriate to your environmental circumstances, (p. 3)" and that "which behavior a stimulus gives rise to is a function of the neural circuitry of the organism (p. 4)." Ecological theory emphasizes the impact of the stimulus environment experienced during a perceivers' lifetime, the local ecology, as well as the nature of the stimulus environment in our evolutionary past.

In addition to emphasizing the importance of understanding the tangible properties that inform person perception, ecological theory specifies the nature of those stimuli. Gibson (1966, 1979) demonstrated that multi-modal, dynamic changes over space and time are features that provide the most useful information to perceivers in nonsocial perception, because they reveal objects' behavioral affordances (see below) as well as higher order invariant properties, such as shape and rigidity, which cannot be discerned from individual, static cues. McArthur and Baron (1983) suggested that the same would be true for person perception. Thus, the dynamic and multi-modal stimulus information that can be gleaned by an active and interactive perceiver should provide the most useful information about peoples' relatively invariant attributes (e.g., stable dispositions) and their behavioral affordances. In addition, impoverished stimulus information and a preparedness to respond to adaptively significant configurations of information are hypothesized to make predictable contributions to person perception (McArthur & Baron, 1983; Zebrowitz, 1996, 1997).

Affordances are the Objective

A third distinguishing feature of the ecological approach is an emphasis on the perception of *social affordances*. Affordances are defined by Gibson (1979, p. 127) as what the environment "offers the animal, what it provides or furnishes, either for good or ill." A more vivid explication of the concept is provided by the quotation from Koffka: "Each thing says what it is … a fruit says 'eat me'; water says 'drink me'; thunder says 'fear me'; and woman says 'love me.'" (Gibson, 1979, p. 138). Although Gibson emphasizes the objective reality of affordances, he also emphasizes their emergence from the interaction of the environment and the perceiver. A woman may afford (erotic) loving by an adult but not a child; a heterosexual man, but not a homosexual one; a secular man, but not a priest; and her spouse, but not a stranger.

The affordance concept is also found in evolutionary psychology writings, although not named as such. For instance, Cosmides and Tooby (1997) give the example of different reactions to dung by humans and dung flies. Whereas humans perceive a pile of dung as disgusting, and act on this perception, thereby avoiding contagion and disease, dung flies perceive it as delicious and also act on their perception, thereby obtaining nourishment and health. In ecological theory terms, the example illustrates the emergent nature of affordances, which depend not only on qualities of the environment but also on qualities of the perceiver.

Cosmides and Tooby's dung example illustrates how organisms' neural circuits were designed by natural selection to solve problems faced during a species' evolutionary history. Ecological theory has a broader view of the affordances to which neural circuits may be attuned, also making predictions about "acquired tastes." For example, while cheese is delectable to the French, it is disgusting to many Asians, who view it as spoiled milk. This could be an arbitrary cultural difference, whereby culturally different perceptual experiences attune individuals to different affordances. It could even be a nonarbitrary social convention, whereby cultures with a high rate of lactose intolerance have inculcated food preferences that foster the attainment of good health among individuals within those cultures. What it cannot be is a domain-specific neural circuit designed by natural selection to determine behavioral reactions to cheese. If it were, then Asian Americans would not suffer the symptoms of lactose intolerance because they would have an inherited aversion to eating dairy products.[2] Acquired tastes are also prevalent in the domain of person perception. To take one example, tatoos are beautiful in traditional Maori culture as well as some modern cultures, but reviled by most middle-class US parents of adolescents. These variations could reflect arbitrary cohort differences or they might reflect a nonarbitrary social convention, whereby cultures that need people with certain characteristics develop painful rituals that test their mettle. What they cannot reflect is a domain-specific neural circuit designed by natural selection to determine behavioral reactions to tatoos. If it were, then there would be no generation gap.

Attunements Guide Perceptions

The emergence of affordances from the interplay of perceiver and stimulus attributes is related to the fourth distinguishing tenet of the ecological approach. The detection of social affordances depends on the perceivers' *attunements*—their sensitivity to particular stimulus information. Attunements may be innate (e.g., men but not monkeys may be attuned to a woman's sexual availability). Attunements also may be educated in a process of perceptual development that varies with perceivers' behavioral capabilities (men but not boys may be attuned to a woman's sexual availability), social goals (secular men but not priests may be attuned to a woman's sexual availability), or perceptual experiences (a lover but not a stranger may be attuned to a woman's sexual availability).

The concept of attunement is implicit in evolutionary psychology's emphasis on species' differences in responses to the same stimulus. Humans are attuned to the disease-carrying affordances of dung, whereas flies are attuned to the larvae-nurturing affordances of dung. Such attunements are presumed to be innate—i.e., genetically determined—although it is acknowledged that ontogenetic events play a critical role in their development and manifestation. Ecological theory is particularly concerned with those events that can influence the development of attunements, positing an impact of perceptual experiences, social goals, or behaviors that may or may not be universal for a species. Thus, ecological theory might find it of interest to understand why some individuals perceive dung as a fuel source whereas avant garde artists have perceived it as a paint source. These individual differences in the perceived affordances of dung cannot be understood simply as the product of distal evolutionary processes that created an adaptive mechanism for responding to dung.

Strong Attunements are Overgeneralized

One of the most fruitful derivations from ecological theory is the hypothesis that innate or well-developed attunements to stimulus information can result in over-generalized and erroneous perceptions. More specifically, a set of overgeneralization hypotheses holds that the psychological qualities that are accurately revealed by the physical information that marks babies, emotion, identity, or low fitness are erroneously perceived in people whose appearance or other physical qualities resembles that of babies, a particular emotion, a particular identity, or a particular level of fitness (cf. Zebrowitz, 1996, 1997; Zebrowitz & Collins, 1997).[3] According to ecological theory, the errors yielded by such overgeneralizations occur because they are less maladaptive than those that might result from failing to respond appropriately to persons of a particular age, emotional state, identity, or health status. This postulate is consistent with error management theory posited by evolutionary psychologists (Haselton & Buss, 2000). The overgeneralization hypotheses are also consistent with the evolutionary psychology principle that neural circuits were designed by natural selection to solve problems that our ancestors faced during our species' evolutionary history. Surely, greater success at replicating one's genes through successful mating, parenting, and kin-directed activities would have accrued to those who solved the problems of distinguishing infants from adults, anger from happiness, familiar individuals from strangers, and fit individuals from unfit ones. The overgeneralization hypotheses go beyond these unequivocal person perception *adaptations* to specify what evolutionary psychology might call a set of person perception *by-products* (Buss, Haselton, Shackelford, Bleske, & Wakefield, 1998). Perceptions of people with particular facial qualities are often by-products of the evolved adaptations.

PERSON PERCEPTION RESEARCH BEARING ON ECOLOGICAL THEORY TENETS

To demonstrate what is learned about person perception within an ecological theory framework, we review research that has documented the accuracy of person perception based on tangible stimulus information, research that has elucidated the stimulus information that guides perceptions, research that has demonstrated the importance of investigating perceived affordances, and research that has documented the broad origins of perceiver attunements to particular stimulus information. This literature review is meant to be illustrative, not exhaustive.

Accurate Perceptions from Tangible Stimulus Information

Whereas previous approaches to person perception have viewed impressions of others as social constructions and focused on biases, ecological theory has directed attention to accuracy. Consistent with the assumption that perception serves an adaptive function, research has demonstrated remarkable accuracy in people's impressions of others when provided with minimal exposure to their tangible qualities, as in photographs, brief videotapes with or without a soundtrack, vocal cues in standardized statements, and movement patterns (cf. Zebrowitz & Collins, 1997). Such stimulus information enables perceivers to accurately judge a number of traits, including intelligence (e.g., Zebrowitz, Hall, Murphy, & Rhodes, 2002; Zebrowitz & Rhodes, 2004), health (e.g., Ilg, Golla, Thier, & Giese, 2004; Kalick, Zebrowitz, Langlois, & Johnson, 1998), dominance (e.g., Berry, 1991a), extraversion (e.g., Borkenau & Liebler, 1992), and sexual availability (e.g., Gangestad, Simpson, DiGeronimo, & Biek, 1992). Patterns of movement or vocal qualities also enable perceivers to accurately judge people's demographic characteristics including age (Berry, 1990; Helfrich, 1979; Montepare & Zebrowitz-McArthur, 1988), sex (Berry, 1991b; Kozlowski & Cutting, 1977; Smith, 1979), sexual orientation (Ambady, Hallahan, & Conner, 1999), and identity (Cutting & Kozlowski, 1977). Finally, "thin slices" of behavior shown in videotape segments as short as 10 seconds enable perceives to judge affordances, such as being a good teacher or doctor, and many others (cf. Ambady, Bernieri, & Richeson, 2000).[4]

Identifying the Stimulus Information

As noted earlier, the focus on constructive cognitive processes in mainstream social psychology research has traditionally ignored the external stimuli that inform person perception. A notable exception has been psychologists interested in nonverbal communication, who have generated considerable knowledge regarding the stimulus information that guides person perception.

Emotion Cues   Grounded in Darwin's (1872) suggestion that the basic expressions of emotion evolved in humans because their adaptive value for social communication promoted species survival, research on emotion perception was the first well-developed effort to pay serious attention to the stimulus information that informs perceptions. A prodigious body of research has identified specific facial components that give rise to the perception of several basic emotions, including happiness, sadness, anger, surprise, fear, and disgust (cf. Ekman, 1971; Izard, 1997). Research also has identified information in the voice (cf. Scherer, Banse, & Wallbott, 2001) and body movements (Boone & Cunningham, 1998; Montepare, Goldstein, & Clausen, 1987; Wallbott & Scherer, 1986) that communicates emotions. Research on posture and gesture has identified stimulus information that communicates general feelings of liking or disliking in addition to perceptions of more specific emotions, like joy or anger (e.g., Bull, 1987; Mehrabian, 1972; Rosenthal, Hall, Archer, DiMatteo, & Rogers, 1979). An ingenious program of research that examined primitive masks from a variety of cultures and the movement patterns of villains vs. heros in ballet has revealed that diagonality and angularity are higher order invariants that communicate anger and threat (Aronoff, Barclay, & Stevenson, 1988; Aronoff, Woike, & Hyman, 1992). Other emotion perception research has also identified dynamic stimulus information (Bassili, 1979), with some evidence that naturally occurring dynamic information can provide more effective communication of emotions than natural static expressions, as predicted by ecological theory (e.g., Frijda, 1953). Also consistent with the ecological approach, some research has demonstrated that when multi-modal information is consistent, it can yield more effective communication than single channels of stimulus information such as face or voice or body alone (DePaulo & Rosenthal, 1982).

Trait and Affordance Cues Although some early work by Secord and others emphasized the contribution of visual stimuli to person perception (e.g., Secord, Dukes, & Bevan, 1954; Secord & Muthard, 1955), it was research on the attractiveness halo effect that entered the social psychology mainstream (cf. Berscheid & Walster, 1974). This work showed that more attractive individuals are perceived to have more positive psychological qualities, including social skills, intellectual skills, dominance, and, in some cases, honesty. Consistent with the ecological assumption that perception and action are tightly coupled, more attractive individuals also benefit from more positive social outcomes. (See Eagly, Ashmore, Makhijani, & Longo, 1991; Feingold, 1992; Hatfield & Sprecher, 1986; Langlois, Kalakanis, Rubenstein, Larson, Hallam, & Smoot, 2000; Zebrowitz, 1997 for reviews.)

Whereas research on the halo effect established that attractiveness was consensually judged, little attention was initially paid to the question of what makes a person attractive. Rather, in keeping with the "standard social science model" view that social perceptions are social constructions, it was simply assumed that the stimulus information was culturally determined. However, research subsequently established that judgments of facial attractiveness generalize across diverse cultures (see Dion, 2002 for a review), and cognitive psychologists and evolutionary psychologists took up the question of what makes a person attractive and why (cf. Rhodes & Zebrowitz, 2002). Assuming that certain facial qualities are preferred because they signal high-quality mates or are closer to facial prototypes that characterize species, sex, and age, these researchers predicted and found that facial averageness, symmetry, high sexual dimorphism, youthfulness, and a pleasant expression each contribute to attractiveness (cf., Cunningham, Barbee, & Philhower, 2002; Enquist, Ghirlanda, Lundqvist, & Wachtmeister, 2002; Keating, 2002; Rhodes, Harwood, Yoshikawa, Nishitani, & McLean, 2002; Rubenstein, Langlois, & Roggman, 2002; Zebrowitz, Fellous, Mignault, & Andreoletti, 2003).

In addition to the large body of research on facial attractiveness, other work has established that vocal and body features also vary in attractiveness, with more attractive voices and bodies also producing a halo effect (e.g., Jackson & Ervin, 1992; Ryckman, Robbins, Kaczor, & Gold, 1989; Singh, 1993; Zuckerman & Driver, 1989; Zuckerman & Miyake, 1993). Articulation, resonance, monotony, and nasality are some of the vocal qualities that contribute to vocal attractiveness, while height, weight, and waist–hip-ratio are body features that make a significant contribution to body attractiveness.

Facial babyishness and facial dominance are opposite poles of a second stimulus dimension that has been shown to influence person perception. Drawing on ethological evidence that "key stimuli" elicit favorable responses to babies of many species (e.g., Lorenz, 1943) and that the response to babyish stimuli may generalize to entities other than babies (e.g., Gould, 1979; Pittenger, Shaw, & Mark, 1979), Zebrowitz and colleagues demonstrated that people with certain facial characteristics are judged as more babyfaced than their peers, with consensual judgments shown across perceiver and target age, race, and sex. They further established that facial features that differentiate real babies from adults comprise a configuration of facial qualities that make nonbabies look babyfaced—rounder and less angular faces, larger eyes, higher eyebrows, smaller nosebridges, and lower vertical placement of features, which creates a higher forehead and a shorter chin. Babyfaceness, like attractiveness, elicits predictable behaviors from perceivers, consistent with the ecological assumption that perception and action are tightly coupled (for pertinent reviews, see Keating, 2002; Montepare & Zebrowitz, 1998; Zebrowitz, 1997).

In addition to the research on babyfaceness, other work has established that age-related vocal and body features also influence person perception. Higher pitched and softer voices are judged as more childlike and are associated with more childlike psychological qualities (Montepare & Zebrowitz-McArthur, 1987); slow gaits with dragging feet and small arm swings are judged as older and are associated with low power, warmth, and sexiness (Montepare & Zebrowitz-McArthur, 1988). Gait features also predict judgments of how easy a person would be to attack (Gunns, Johnston, & Hudson, 2002; Johnston, Hudson, Richardson, & Gunns, 2004).

No theory of person perception would be complete without serious consideration of the nature of the stimulus information that guides perceivers' impressions of people. Our brief review of the influence of stimulus information on person perception has focused on effects that appear to be universal and to have evolutionary roots. However, as discussed below, stimulus information also may have different effects for different perceivers, whose attunements can vary as a function of their unique perceptual experiences, social goals, or behavioral activities. Stimuli that may elicit variable perceptions across perceivers include hair color, skin color, speech accents, gestures, glasses, clothing styles, as well as structural and dynamic qualities of face, voice, and body other than those that have been discussed. Although ecological theory acknowledges the significance of more idiosyncratic attunements, it has not yet explored them in a theoretically systematic way.

The Importance of Affordances

Traditional research on person perception has focused on judgments of people's psychological traits, which are conventionally conceptualized as consistencies in behavior across contexts and time. Considerable research has investigated "implicit personality theories," identifying the trait dimensions that play a role in person perception (e.g., Bond, 1979; McCrae & Costa, 1987; Noller, Law, & Comrey, 1987). Yet, personality traits make up only a little more than 40% of Western adults' open-ended person descriptors, and an even smaller fraction of the person descriptors in Eastern cultures (e.g., Bond & Cheung, 1983; Fiske & Cox, 1979; Miller, 1984; Shweder & Bourne, 1982). The neglected contents of social perception include concrete interpersonal interactions, such as cooperating, harming, and obliging, that may capture what ecological theory calls social affordances, the opportunities for action and interaction that people provide. The accurate detection of such behavioral opportunities has a functional value that is consistent with an evolutionary perspective.

Consistent with the assumption that perceivers are particularly interested in differentiating people in terms of their behavioral affordances, Bond (1983) found that perceivers showed consensual behavioral intentions toward people who varied on the "big five" personality dimensions, with agreeableness determining association intentions, conscientiousness influencing trust intentions, and emotional stability influencing intimacy intentions. Mignon and Mollaret (2002) also provided evidence for the centrality of behavioral affordances to person perception. In this study, perceivers were asked to judge brief videotapes of target people speaking to someone off camera. Judgments were made on 12 scales assessing the targets' behavioral dispositions (e.g., someone who yells at others) or 12 scales assessing the target's behavioral affordances (e.g., someone you would avoid provoking). Not only were judgments on the affordance scales consensual and reliable, but also targets were differentiated more by the affordance than the behavioral scales. (cf. Beauvois & Dubois, 2000; Leonova, 2004, for reviews of research on personality traits as affordances). Other evidence that people are construed in terms of their behavioral affordances is provided by studies demonstrating that people with whom one has a similar relationship (i.e., similar types of interactions) tend to be confused with one another more than people who are similar to one another on personal attributes, such as age, race, or personality traits (Fiske & Haslam, 1996).

Evolutionary theorists have suggested that species differences in perceptions can emerge from the unique combination of organisms and their particular ecological niches. Caporael's (1997) recent evolutionary based model of social cognition suggests that unique aspects of self and social identity emerged from and are sustained by human face-to-face interactions in group contexts. Ecological theory further proposes that human individual differences in person perception can emerge from the unique combination of individuals and their particular social environments. Evidence for such emergent effects is provided by research using Kenny's (1994) social relations model to investigate emotion perception accuracy. Not only were some perceivers generally more accurate in judging emotions than others and not only were the emotions of some targets more easily read than others, but also some perceiver–target dyads "clicked," yielding higher accuracy than others even when skill of the perceivers and expressers was controlled (Elfenbein, Foo, Boldry, & Tan, 2004). The perceiver–target attributes that account for this effect remain to be determined, but the results are consistent with the ecological theory assumption that affordances emerge from the interaction of unique qualities of the perceiver and environment.

The Origins of Perceiver Attunements

Ecological theory and evolutionary psychology both predict attunements that are innate (either present at birth or an inherited preparedness), and there is considerable supporting evidence. Consistent with ecological theory, research also has documented attunements that are educated through a process of perceptual development that depends on unique perceptual experiences, social goals, and behavioral activities.

Innate Attunements   Research on infants' responses to faces illustrates innate attunements. Newborns prefer looking at face-like configurations (e.g., Johnson, Dziurawiec, Ellis, & Morton, 1991), although before 2 months of age that preference may reflect a more general preference for higher stimulus density in the upper hemi-field rather than a preference for faces per se (Turati, 2004). Infants also prefer particular types of faces early in development. Specifically, they show preferential looking at faces of babies (Lasky, Klein, & Martinez, 1974; McCall & Kennedy, 1980), as well as babyfaced adults (Kramer, Zebrowitz, San Giovanni, & Sherak, 1995), and they appear to find faces of unfamiliar children less threatening than those of unfamiliar adults, even when other perceptual cues to age are held constant (Bigelow, MacLean, Wood, & Smith, 1990; Brooks & Lewis, 1976). These findings are consistent with evolutionary and ecological theory assumptions that perception serves an adaptive function, since humans who are unresponsive to faces and to age information in faces may well be at a survival disadvantage.

Infants also show a greater visual preference for faces that are more attractive, an effect that is independent of babyfaceness (Kramer et al., 1995; Langlois, Roggman, Casey, Ritter, Rieser-Danner, & Jenkins, 1987), and that generalizes across faces of varying races and ages (Langlois, Ritter, Roggman, & Vaughn, 1991; Van Duuren, Kendell-Scott, & Stark, 2003). Although an innate preference for attractiveness is consistent with evolutionary psychology predictions regarding sensitivity to facial cues for mate quality, recent research suggests that infant preferences may be better explained as a by-product of sensitivity to prototypical faces (Ramsey, Langlois, Hoss, Rubenstein, & Griffin, 2004; Rubenstein, Kalakanis, & Langlois, 1999), a mechanism that is also consistent with other perceptual by-product hypotheses (Enquist et al., 2002; Zebrowitz et al., 2003).

Infants are also attuned to facial expressions of emotion. In particular, considerable research on infants' negative reactions to a still-face (i.e., a face that suddenly adopts a neutral facial expression) has been interpreted as evidence of early sensitivity to the social communication value of facial expressions (Striano & Tomesello, 2001). Moreover, just as fear responses in adults are classically conditioned to anger faces more readily than happy ones (e.g., Lanzetta & Orr, 1980), infants as young as 5 months show a stronger startle response to noise when looking at an angry face than a happy one, indicating an attunement to the dangerous meaning of the angry face (Balaban, 1995). Other behavioral reactions to facial expressions have also revealed infants' sensitivity to their affordances (Schwartz, Izard, & Ansul, 1985; Sorce, Emde, Campos, & Klenneret, 1985). These early attunements to emotion information are consistent with evolutionary and ecological assumptions about the adaptive functions of perception, since humans who are not attuned to the signal value of emotions would be at a survival disadvantage.

Research investigating adult mate preferences provides additional support for hypothesized innate attunements to qualities that signal adaptively relevant affordances. For example, men prefer the scent of women at fertile points in their menstrual cycle as well as the scent of women with more common histocompatibility complex genes, preferences that may serve in selecting mates that afford fertility without deleterious rare alleles (Thornhill, Gangestad, Miller, Scheyd, McCollough, & Franklin, 2003). In turn, women at the fertile point in their menstrual cycle show an increased preference for facial masculinity or the scent of men with greater body bilateral symmetry, preferences that may serve in selecting potential sires who afford more genetic fitness (Rhodes, Chan, Zebrowitz, & Simmons, 2003a; Thornhill & Gangestad, 1999).

Attunements that Vary with Perceptual Experience   Evidence for an effect of perceptual experience on perceiver attunements is provided by research showing that perceivers' cultural familiarity with individuals who are expressing emotions enhances recognition of their facial expressions (Elfenbein & Ambady, 2002, 2003). These results are in keeping with what ecological theorists have called the "education of attention" (Gibson, 1966). Additional evidence is provided by the finding that people who live in cultures with a high incidence of parasites appear to have developed a stronger attunement to facial indicators of fitness, showing a stronger preference for physically attractive mates (Gangestad & Buss, 1993). Sub-cultural perceptual experiences can also influence attunements, as revealed by the finding that gay men and lesbians were more accurate than heterosexuals in judging people's sexual orientation from brief observations of their nonverbal behavior (Ambady et al., 1999). Still another example is provided by evidence supporting the Westermarck (1921) hypothesis that sexual attraction is diminished between genetically unrelated people who have been reared together (e.g., Shepher, 1971; Wolf, 1995), and that negative reactions toward incest are stronger among those who have been reared with an opposite sex individual (Lieberman, Tooby, & Cosmides, 2002). Perceptual experience with one's own face also influences person perception, with more trust exhibited toward peers who resemble oneself (DeBruine, 2002).

The effects on person perception of parasite incidence, childhood co-residence, and self-resemblance were documented by evolutionary theorists, and ecological theory provides a unifying general principle: *Perceptual experience* in these and other contexts influences the development of attunements to various affordances. Several mechanisms by which perceptual experience may have an effect on attunements have been identified, and it is worthwhile to consider the possible role of each in the development of attunements to social affordances. These mechanisms include *stimulus imprinting, attentional weighting, differentiation, prototype extraction, unitization,* and *adaptation* (cf. Goldstone, 1998).

In *stimulus imprinting*, perception becomes attuned by the development of detectors that are specialized for particular stimuli, with the detectors shaped by the impinging stimuli. For example, geese develop detectors for conspecifics based on their exposure immediately after hatching. Those whose first sight is of a human "imprint" on that person, follow it as goslings typically follow the mother goose (Lorenz, 1970). An analogous effect for sexual imprinting in the domain of person perception is provided by evidence that women's husbands facially resemble their adoptive fathers (Bereczkei, Gyuris, & Weisfeld, 2004).

In *attentional weighting*, perception becomes attuned by increasing the attention paid to perceptual features that are relevant and important. For example, after exposure to a series of faces in which some were identified as "fair" and some as "unfair," perceivers subsequently utilized the relevant feature of facial shape to categorize new faces, even though they had no conscious awareness that they were using this feature (Hill, Lewicki, Czyzewska, & Schuller, 1990). Attentional weighting can carry with it a perceptual narrowing. Whereas 6-month-old human infants were able to discriminate between faces of different monkeys as well as different humans, 9-month-olds and adults could only discriminate among human faces, an effect that parallels the developmental loss of ability to discriminate among foreign speech sounds (Pascalis, de Haan, & Nelson, 2002).

Related to attentional weighting is *differentiation*, whereby stimuli that were initially psychologically indistinguishable become separable. For example, people are more able to differentiate faces of races with which they are familiar, whereas those of an unfamiliar race tend to "all look alike" (e.g., Shapiro & Penrod, 1986).

Prototype extraction also relates to attentional weighting. Exposure to a set of stimuli increases the familiarity of a prototype of those stimuli that has not itself been viewed, but is a composite of the exposed stimuli. This mechanism has been shown to produce preferences for prototypes of a variety of stimuli, and it operates in face perception of both young infants and adults (Halberstadt & Rhodes, 2000, 2003; Rubenstein et al., 1999).

In *unitization*, perceptions that originally required detection of several parts are achieved by detecting a single unit. Research on inversion effects illustrates this process. Recognition of visual stimuli with which perceivers have considerable perceptual experience is more impaired when they are inverted than is recognition of the same stimuli by perceivers who are less highly practiced, suggesting that perceptual experience causes these stimuli to be perceived as a configural unit that is obscured by inversion (Diamond & Carey, 1986; Gauthier & Tarr, 1997; Tanaka & Gauthier, 1997). For example, recognition of own race faces, with which perceivers are highly practiced, is more impaired by inversion than is recognition of other race faces (Diamond & Carey, 1986; Rhodes, Tan, Brake, & Taylor, 1989; Sangrigoli & de Schonen, 2004).

In *adaptation*, perceptions shift following repeated exposure to a particular stimulus. Such short-term aftereffects have been documented in many different contexts, including face perception. For example, after people are adapted to male faces, a face that was previously judged to be neutral was rated as female (Kaping, Duhamel, & Webster, 2002). Such adaptation effects also lead to misperceptions of facial identity (Leopold, O'Toole, Vetter, & Blanz, 2001), and they can affect facial preferences. When adults were briefly exposed to consistent distortions of normal faces, there was an aftereffect marked by a shift toward the distorted faces in which faces looked most normal and what faces looked most attractive (Rhodes, Jeffery, Watson, Clifford, & Nakayama, 2003b).

Although person perception examples have been given to illustrate each of the foregoing mechanisms, they are actually general mechanisms for perceptual learning. Ecological theory draws attention to these processes by virtue of its concern with understanding how perceptual experience contributes to variations in perceiver attunements. Whereas the cognitive mechanisms considered by mainstream social psychology are proposed to influence how perceivers' *construct* what is perceived, these perceptual mechanisms are proposed to influence what a perceiver *detects* in a complex stimulus. In Asch's (1952) terms, cognitive mechanisms affect the judgment of the object, whereas the perceptual mechanisms affect the object of judgment—i.e., the effective stimulus information. Additional research investigating how these perceptual mechanisms operate in the domain of person perception will contribute significantly to our understanding.

Attunements that Vary with Social Goals

Consistent with the ecological approach's emphasis on proximate influences on perception, variations in social goals associated with historical events, situational factors, culture, and individual traits have all been shown to influence perceiver attunements (cf. Hilton & Darley, 1991). Historical variations in perceiver goals may account for the fact that American movie actresses with mature facial features were preferred during times of social and economic hardship, while babyfaced actresses were preferred during prosperous times (Pettijohn & Tesser, 1999). Similarly, situationally induced variations in perceiver goals may account for the finding that people preferred a more maturefaced partner when there was a threat of electric shock than when there was no threat (Pettijohn, 2000). It appears that perceivers' facial preferences track their security motivation, with higher need for security fostering sensitivity to the affordances expected from more mature-looking people.

Cultural variations in social goals may account for variations in the attractiveness halo effect. For example, perceptions of moral integrity show a stronger halo for Koreans than for Americans (Wheeler & Kim, 1997), while the reverse is true for perceptions of dominance, perhaps because the affordances of assertive people are more central to the individualist social goals of Americans, while the affordances of trustworthy people are more central to the more collectivist goals of Koreans. Whereas evolutionary psychology may account for the halo effect by positing that attractive people are accurately perceived to have traits that reflect their higher mate value, the question remains as to how to explain cultural variations in the content of the halo effect. Here one needs to invoke a proximate mechanism, such as the education of attention to attributes that have greater cultural value and that may consequently influence people's reproductive success quite apart from their genetic quality.

Individual variations in social goals, like historical, situational, and cultural variations, also have been shown to influence attunements. Dominant male perceivers show a greater preference for babyfaced women, suggesting that a higher need to control others fosters sensitivity to the desired affordances expected from babyfaced people (Hadden, & Brownlow, 1991). Other research also shows that dominant perceivers notice how assertive people are, information that is pertinent to their interpersonal goals, while dependent perceivers notice how affiliative the same individuals are, which is pertinent to their goal of eliciting approval and support in social interactions (Battistich & Aronoff, 1985). Variations in social goals may also account for the finding that people are more sensitive to how others feel about them when they are in a subordinate role as well as more sensitive to how someone of the opposite sex feels about them than someone of the same sex (Snodgrass, 1985). The finding that women who are less attractive prefer more feminized male faces (Little, Penton-Voak, Burt, & Perrett, 2002; Penton-Voak, Little, Jones, Burt, Tiddeman, & Perrett, 2003) may also be explained by variations in social goals. Insofar as less attractive women feel less capable of attracting or retaining the more fickle masculine-looking men (Gangestad & Simpson, 2000; Gray, Kahlenber, Barrett, Lipson, & Ellison, 2002), the goal of finding reciprocated affection may strengthen their attunement to the positive behavioral affordances of more feminine-looking men.

Attunements that Vary with Behavioral Activities

Although there has not been much research examining the effects of behavioral activities on attunements in person perception, there is some pertinent evidence. Hearing individuals who had experience with American Sign Language were better than hearing nonsigners at identifying facial expressions of emotion (Goldstein & Feldman, 1996), suggesting that signing and reading signs develops an attunement to visual cues to emotion. Similarly, professional actors show better decoding of affective body cues than do individuals in less physically emotive occupations, suggesting that a history of conveying feelings and intentions through bodily movement attunes perceivers to pertinent bodily cues (Rosenthal et al., 1979).

Ongoing activities also can influence attunements. A perceiver's surveillance behavior can decrease the detection of trustworthiness (Strickland, 1958), and co-operative behavior can increase the detection of co-operativeness (Kelley & Stahelski, 1970), because these activities influence the *availability* of particular stimulus information. Other perceiver behaviors may influence attunements by altering *sensitivity* to particular stimulus information. For instance, adopting a smiling facial expression can increase the perceived positivity and humor of stimuli (e.g., McArthur, Solomon, & Jaffe, 1980; Strack, Martin, & Stepper, 1988), mutual eye gaze can increase liking for the partner (Kellerman, Lewis, & Laird, 1989), and arm flexion (an approach gesture) can produce more positive evaluations as compared with arm extension (an avoidance gesture) (Cacioppo, Priester, & Berntson, 1993). There is also some evidence that imitation of facial expressions may contribute to their recognition, although a causal relationship has not been firmly established (Blairy, Herrera, & Hess, 1999; Calder, Keane, Cole, Campbell, & Young, 2000; Hess & Blairy, 2001) (cf. Laird, 1992, for related work on self-perception).

It should be noted that the relationship between action and perception is reciprocal. Not only do a perceiver's actions influence perceptual attunements, but also perception can influence action. For example, Chartrand and Bargh (1999) found that the motor behavior of participants unintentionally matched that perceived in strangers with whom they worked on a task. Relationships between behavioral activity and social perceptions are consistent with knowledge of adaptive relationships between the sensory-motor and emotion systems in the brain (e.g., Meier & Robinson, 2004), as well as with evidence that actively obtained sensory stimulation has different effects on cortical circuits than does passive stimulation (e.g., Clark, Tremblay, & Ste-Marie, 2004; Lotze, Braun, Birbaumer,

Anders, & Cohen, 2003). However, it is not always clear whether the effects of activities are mediated by changes in the information to which perceivers' are attuned or by changes in their emotional states. More research is needed to definitively establish an effect on attunements.

The Overgeneralization of Attunements

As described earlier, the ecological theory of social perception proposes that innate or well-developed attunements to stimulus information can result in overgeneralized perceptions. In particular, the psychological qualities that are accurately revealed by the physical information that marks babies, emotion, identity, or low fitness may be erroneously perceived in people whose appearance or other physical qualities resembles individuals in those categories. These overgeneralization hypotheses are logically consistent with evolutionary theory, although not explicit in its literature. More specifically, the overgeneralization effects could be framed as perceptual by-products within evolutionary psychology. Also, each overgeneralization hypothesis is grounded in an assumed adaptive mechanism that could reflect a domain-specific module, such as those proposed by evolutionary psychologists. Cross-cultural, cross-species, neural, and/or early developmental evidence is consistent with such a module for detecting babies (cf. Eibl-Eibesfeldt, 1989; Lorenz, 1943), emotions (Humphreys, Donnelly, & Riddoch, 1993; Tranel, Damasio, & Damasio, 1988; Young, Newcombe, de Haan, Small, & Hall, 1993), and identity (Bushnell, Sai, & Mullin, 1989; Field, Cohen, Garcia, & Greenberg, 198; Kendrick, da Costa, Leigh, Hinton, & Peirce, 2001; Walton, Bower, & Bower, 1992).

Babyface Overgeneralization Hypothesis   The evolutionary importance of responding appropriately to babies, such as giving protection and inhibiting aggression, has produced a strong preparedness to respond to their infantile facial qualities (Eibl-Eibesfeld, 1989; Gould, 1979; Lorenz, 1943; Todd, Mark, Shaw, & Pittenger, 1980). Considerable research supports the overgeneralization of these prepared responses to individuals whose faces merely resemble babies (cf. Montepare & Zebrowitz, 1998; Zebrowitz, 1997).

As noted above, the facial qualities that mark real babies (Enlow, 1990) also mark babyfaced individuals at other ages. Furthermore, the actual traits of babies are mirrored by impressions of and behavioral reactions to babyfaced individuals across the lifespan (Zebrowitz & Montepare, 1992), and across cultures (Zebrowitz, Montepare, & Lee, 1993). Moreover, connectionist modeling research has demonstrated that adult faces that produced greater activation of a neural network output unit trained to respond to faces of babies rather than adults were perceived as more babyfaced, warm, physically weak, naïve, and submissive, and these effects remained when attractiveness and smiling ratings were controlled (Zebrowitz et al., 2003). Finally, research investigating the actual traits of individuals who vary in babyfaceness are consistent with the claim that impressions represent an overgeneralization rather than accurate impressions. Indeed, the actual traits of babyfaced individuals often run counter to the stereotype of social, physical, and intellectual weakness. For example, research examining a large, representative sample of middle-class individuals found that more baby-faced young men are more assertive and hostile than their maturefaced peers (Zebrowitz, Collins, & Dutta, 1998), more likely to win military awards (Collins & Zebrowitz, 1995), and more intellectually competent (Zebrowitz, Andreoletti, Collins, Lee, & Blumenthal, 1998). Although we have focused here on the baby-face overgeneralization hypothesis, other research has provided evidence of broader age overgeneralization effects that involve perceptions of voices, bodies, and movement resembling individuals across the lifespan (cf. Montepare & Zebrowitz, 1998).

Emotion Overgeneralization Hypothesis   The adaptive value of responding appropriately to emotional expressions, such as avoiding an angry person and approaching a happy one, has produced a strong preparedness to respond to the tangible qualities that reveal emotions. Research has indicated that these prepared responses are overgeneralized to individuals whose facial structure resembles a particular emotional expression.

Low- as well as high-intensity angry expressions create impressions of low affiliative traits (e.g., unsociable, unfriendly, unsympathetic, sly, cold), while happy expressions create impressions of high affiliative traits (Hess, Blairy, & Kleck, 2000; Knutson, 1996). Moreover, consistent with the emotion overgeneralization hypothesis, not only do emotional expressions foster the inference of traits, but also *neutral expressions* create trait impressions. For example, some neutral expression faces create perceptions of an angry demeanor and elicit impressions of low affiliative traits; others create perceptions of a happy demeanor and elicit impressions of high affiliative traits (Montepare & Dobish, 2003).[6] Connectionist modeling research also has demonstrated that impressions of faces with neutral emotional expressions vary with their resemblance to an emotion. More specifically, neutral faces with structural dimensions that produced greater activation of a neural network output unit trained to respond to happy rather than neutral faces were perceived as higher in social warmth, health, and intelligence, and these effects held true with facial attractiveness and babyfaceness controlled (Zebrowitz, Kikuchi, & Fellous, 2004). Further research is needed to determine exactly what structural qualities in a neutral face produce resemblance to emotion expressions. Facial orientation as well as structure may foster emotion overgeneralization effects. Adults with heads tilted backward are perceived as more likely to be proud than those with heads tilted forward, who are perceived as more likely to be ashamed, mirroring the emotional states that are typically accompanied by these head gestures (Mignault & Chaudhuri, 2003).

Identity Overgeneralization Hypothesis   The evolutionary and social importance of differentiating known individuals from strangers and being wary of the latter has produced a tendency for responses to strangers to vary as a function of their resemblance to known individuals. One consequence is a "mistaken identity" effect, whereby a familiar-looking stranger is judged similarly to a known individual. In addition to explaining idiosyncratic impressions, identity overgeneralization may also contribute to negative impressions of other race individuals, who show less resemblance to known individuals.

Consistent with the ecological theory "mistaken identity effect," faces of strangers who look more familiar are perceived as more likeable and trustworthy, and these effects are independent of attractiveness, smiling, and race (Zebrowitz, Bronstad, & Lee, 2005). Research also has shown that reactions to people depend on their facial resemblance to known others. For example, people expressed a preference for the job candidate whose face more closely resembled someone who had just treated them kindly, and they avoided a stranger whose face more closely resembled someone who had just treated them irritably (Lewicki, 1985). People also expected greater fairness from a professor whose face more closely resembled the prototypical face of a set of professors known to be fair than that of a set known to be unfair, even though they had no conscious awareness of the dimension on which the faces varied (Hill et al., 1990; see Andersen & Berk, 1998 for a related discussion of transference effects). Finally, consistent with predictions regarding perceptions of other race faces, strangers whose faces are farther from the prototype of one's own racial group elicit more negative reactions. For example, high prototypical Black faces primed faster reaction times to negative nouns among White perceivers than did White faces or low prototypical Black faces (Livingston & Brewer, 2002). Also, faces with higher rated "Afrocentricism" elicited more negative trait impressions by White perceivers not only when the faces were African American, but also when they were European American (Blair, Judd, Sadler, & Jenkins, 2002). Thus, consensual impressions of racially similar vs. different strangers may be partly explained by a facial identity overgeneralization effect.

Fitness Overgeneralization Hypothesis

The evolutionary importance of recognizing individuals with disease or bad genes has produced a strong preparedness to respond to qualities that can mark low fitness. These prepared responses are overgeneralized to normal individuals whose tangible qualities resemble those who are unfit. In the case of facial qualities, this yields an anomalous face overgeneralization effect. (For related discussions, see Kurzban & Leary, 2001; Neuberg, Smith, & Asher, 2000; Park, Faulkner, & Schaller, 2003.)

Implicit in the anomalous face overgeneralization hypothesis is the "bad genes" hypothesis, which holds that certain unattractive faces signal low fitness and low mate quality (Zebrowitz & Rhodes, 2002). The "bad genes" and anomalous face overgeneralization hypotheses offer a refinement to the "good genes" hypothesis that has been offered by some evolutionary psychologists to explain facial preferences. According to the good genes hypothesis, more attractive faces signal higher mate quality, and a preference for attractiveness evolved because it enhanced reproductive success. Moreover, an assumption of a linear relationship between attractiveness or its components and genetic fitness has been implicit in the research generated by the good genes hypothesis, and there has been particular emphasis on the greater mate quality of those who are highly attractive (e.g., Buss, 1989; Thornhill & Gangestad, 1999). In contrast, the "bad genes" hypothesis argues that appearance provides an accurate index only of low genetic quality rather than a continuous index of genetic quality, and that preferences for higher attractiveness in the upper portions of the attractiveness continuum as well as the attractiveness halo effect in impressions of those faces are a perceptual by-product of an adaptive attunement to low fitness.

Recent research has supported the ecological theory hypothesis that accurate impressions of faces that signal low fitness are overgeneralized. In one study, using a representative sample of faces, low facial attractiveness, averageness, symmetry, or masculinity predicted traits indicative of low fitness, including lower than average health and intelligence, whereas high levels of these facial qualities did not predict high fitness. Nevertheless, consistent with the anomalous face overgeneralization hypothesis, intelligence and health were perceived to vary not only from low to moderate levels of attractiveness, but also from moderate to high levels (Zebrowitz & Rhodes, 2004). In another study, impressions of the health and intelligence of normal faces were predicted by the extent to which they resembled anomalous ones, as determined by connectionist modeling, and these effects could not be explained by corresponding variations in the actual health and intelligence of the normal faces (Zebrowitz et al., 2003). Greater resemblance to anomalous faces also predicted impressions of lower attractiveness, sociability, and warmth, consistent with the argument that anomalous face overgeneralization may provide an explanation for the attractiveness halo effect.

In addition to supporting the anomalous face overgeneralization hypothesis, the foregoing findings support a bad genes refinement to the good genes hypothesis that evolutionary psychologists have proposed as an explanation for facial preferences. More specifically, appearance provides an accurate index only of low genetic quality rather than a continuous index of genetic quality: unattractive faces signal low mate quality, whereas attractive faces do not signal higher mate quality than do faces that are average in attractiveness. This suggests that an eschewal of very unattractive mates would have enhanced reproductive success in our evolutionary past more than would a preference for highly attractive ones.

A RESEARCH AGENDA

Recognizing the importance of evolutionary forces, the ecological approach to person perception has motivated research questions that have received scant attention within standard social science models. At the same time, the ecological approach has raised questions about person perception that lie outside the realm of evolutionary theory. This is especially true with respect to the adaptive functions of person perception, where ecological theory calls attention to a broad range of perceived affordances, stimulus information, and attunement origins. Attention to these questions promises to deepen our understanding of person perception. Among the advances will be a contribution to the prediction of accuracy. Person perception should be more accurate when perceived affordances are assessed rather than more abstract attributes, such as personality traits, both because affordances are more likely to be specified by the tangible qualities of a person that are available in a delimited social interaction context and also because perceivers should be more attuned to properties that are functionally relevant.

Mapping Social Affordances

One question that warrants attention is whether we can identify a taxonomy of perceived social affordances analogous to the perceived traits identified in "implicit personality theories" (e.g., Bond, 1979; McCrae & Costa, 1987; Noller, Law, & Comrey, 1987). Whereas trait adjectives have been used to distill a core group of personality traits, interpersonal verbs or related gerunds may be a logical starting point for identifying a core group of social affordances (cf. Benjamin, 1974; Lorr & McNair, 1965; Wiggins, 1979). Moreover, it may be possible to incorporate such affordances into any one of several models of social interaction.

At the broadest level, affordances may be considered within Leung and Bond's (2004) culturally general set of social axioms, which are synthesized understandings of how the world works. In particular, *social cynicism* concerns the *valence* of perceived social affordances; *social complexity* concerns the *variability* of affordances; and *fate control* concerns the predictability and controllability of affordances. A taxonomy of two dozen prototypical social situations derived from theoretically distinct patterns of interdependence (Kelley, Holmes, Kerr, Reis, Rusbult, & Van Lange, 2003) may prove useful in generating the more specific content of social affordances. For example situations involving mutual behavior control provide the affordance of co-ordination. Those involving zero-sum outcomes provide the affordance of threat (Kelley, 1997). Social affordances also could be generated from social interaction models proposed by Alan Fiske (1991), Bugental (2000), and Kenrick, Li, and Butner (2003). For example, affordances such as nurturing and praising seem pertinent to the "communal sharing" interactions proposed by Fiske (1991), while dominating and complying seem pertinent to his "authority ranking" interactions. Affordances such as copulating and impregnating are pertinent to the mate choice domain proposed by Kenrick et al. (2003), and affordances such as protecting and depending upon seem pertinent to the domain of attachment (for safety purposes) proposed by Bugental (2000).

Identifying the perceived affordances that bear on the adaptive problems humans faced during their evolutionary history to insure the reproduction of their genes will contribute greatly to an understanding of the foundations of person perception. However, as the ecological framework points out, perceived affordances that bear on solutions to contemporaneous adaptive problems that may have no implications for gene replication either in the present or in the past must also be considered. Thus, research that aims to identify the set of adaptively relevant affordances should also aim to differentiate those that bear on inclusive fitness from those that bear only on contemporary adaptive success. Whatever the ultimate conceptual framework and substantive content, determining the set of significant affordances is a priority for person perception research.

Identifying the Stimulus Information

Another important area of research is to determine the stimulus information that conveys behavioral affordances and other person qualities. As discussed above, research identifying stimulus information is exemplified by evolutionary psychologists' effort to determine what stimulus qualities reveal the affordance of "good mate quality," by the present authors' efforts to determine what qualities communicate the affordance of childlike dependency and others' efforts to determine the qualities that convey the complementary affordance of dominance (e.g., Keating, 1985; Keating & Bai, 1986; Keating, Mazur, & Segall, 1981), as well as by the extensive body of research investigating nonverbal cues that communicate various emotions (e.g., Ekman, Campos, Davidson, & De Waal, 2003). In addition to identifying the stimulus information that would have been important for evolutionary adaptation, the importance of understanding the stimulus information that may have only contemporaneous adaptive value and that may have nothing to do with inclusive fitness should not be overlooked. Certainly, consequential impressions may be elicited as much by a person's style of dress as by as person's babyish appearance or angry expression.

In the quest to identify stimulus information, researchers should make use of guiding principles suggested by ecological theory. In particular, they should emphasize the greater utility of dynamic than static stimuli, multi-modal than unimodal stimuli, and stimuli that bear high resemblance to adaptively significant stimulus configurations. The directive to identify the *dynamic* stimulus information that conveys affordances can benefit from new technologies, such as motion capture (Dekeyser, Verfaillie, & Vanrie, 2002). Far more sophisticated than the "point light" methods used in the past (e.g., Berry & Misovich, 1994), motion capture methods will enable researchers to define and manipulate the complex movement patterns that characterize different social activities. Avatars in immersive virtual environments could then be programmed with such movement patterns in order to examine what they are perceived to afford (cf. Blascovich, Loomis, Beall, Swinth, Hoyt, & Bailenson, 2002; Zebrowitz, 2002). Using this methodology will also enable researchers to systematically vary movement patterns, vocal qualities, and appearance qualities in order to examine the multi-modal communication of affordances.

Mainstream research in social psychology has focused largely on the perceiver's cognitive and affective processes, paying little heed to the information provided by a stimulus person's tangible properties. The understanding of social perception and social interaction will be much advanced if we can learn what tangible properties of people communicate the whole range of affordances as well as other personal attributes.

Understanding Perceiver Attunements

A third research avenue is to determine what factors contribute to perceiver attunements. Some evolutionary psychologists have suggested that perceivers' attention is guided by functionally specialized "modules" that include an input system tuned to a particular class of stimuli whose detection serves reproductive success (cf. Wagner & Wagner, 2004). For example, evolutionary psychologists have proposed a "good mate detector" module that is attuned to stimuli such as facial averageness, symmetry, and masculinity. The wide range of adaptive functions with which ecological theory is concerned suggests that person perception often will be guided by domain general attunements rather than by various dedicated modules tuned to specific stimuli. Research in this vein has shown that, rather than a domain-specific adaptive mechanism to prefer facial averageness because it signals a good mate, there is a more general adaptive mechanism to prefer stimuli that are prototypic in the ecological niche in which the individual develops (Rhodes et al., 2003b; Rubenstein et al., 2002). Although it is a safe bet that those who look like the people who populate our world will be better mates than those who do not, the adaptive mechanism may operate simply to identify individuals who are the appropriate species, sex, and age for mating rather than within species variations in fitness (cf. Enquist et al., 2002). Other domain general attunement mechanisms derived from perceptual experience also warrant investigation in studies of person perception. As discussed earlier, these include "imprinter", "differentiater", "weighter", "unitizer", "generalizer", and "familiarity detector" (cf. Goldstone, 1998).

Ecological theory encourages research not only on perceptual experiences as a source of attunements, but also on perceiver goals and activities. Both the direct and indirect effects of these proximate variables should be taken into account. For example, behavioral activities might have a direct effect on perceiver attunements, as when manipulations of gaze duration toward one of two faces biases preferences toward the face that is looked at the most. Alternatively, behavioral activities might mediate effects of social goals, as when the manipulated goal of choosing the most attractive of two faces produces a greater shift in gaze toward the one that is ultimately chosen than does the goal of choosing the rounder of two faces (Shimojo, Simion, Shimojo, & Scheier, 2003). The net effect of the proximate causes is to produce interpersonally variable attunements as well as the species-wide inherited attunements that are the primary focus of evolutionary psychology. More research is needed to elucidate the contribution of ontogenetic events to perceiver attunements.

CONCLUSIONS

Unlike other social-psychological approaches to person perception, the ecological approach has strong roots in evolutionary theory. It posits universal, adaptive functions that run counter to what evolutionary psychologists have dubbed the "standard social science model" view that social perceptions are social constructions. This functional approach assumes that we can perceive people's behavioral affordances from their tangible properties, such as appearance, movement, voice, feel, and scent. It views such perceptions as closely coupled to action, with active perceivers achieving higher accuracy. It gives high priority to identifying the stimulus information to which perceivers' respond, and argues that erroneous perceptions can often be traced to the overgeneralization of strong adaptive attunements to particular patterns of information. It also considers various origins of perceptual attunements.

Although the ecological approach and evolutionary psychology share fundamental assumptions about social perception that have been overlooked within other social-psychological frameworks, they also each have distinctive features.

Most notably, the ecological approach calls attention to adaptive functions of person perception that lie outside the logical realm of evolutionary psychology. This generates an interest in a broader range of perceived affordances and stimulus information as well as different sources of perceptual attunements, with more attention to general mechanisms rather than the specialized modular mechanisms that have been of prime interest to evolutionary psychologists. Whereas the ecological approach did not find a wide audience when it was introduced 20 years ago in the heyday of social cognition research, we hope that the intellectual engagement that has been recently stimulated by evolutionary psychology will generate research that incorporates the tenets of its close relation, the ecological approach. Such research will deepen our understanding of person perception.

ACKNOWLEDGEMENT

Leslie A. Zebrowitz was supported in part by NIH Grant R01MH066836.

NOTES

1. It should be noted that social psychologists have more recently incorporated the ecological theory emphases on the role of an active perceiver and stimulus information in social perception (see, for example, Smith & Semin, 2004).
2. This is not to say that neural activation patterns to cheese would not differ for individuals from cultures that perceive it as disgusting and those that perceive it as delectable. However, the variations in neural activation patterns would develop with the culturally directed development of food preferences rather than guiding the development of those preferences.
3. Another overgeneralization hypothesis is "animal analogies" whereby people may be perceived to have traits that are associated with the animals that their features resemble (cf. Zebrowitz, 1997, pp. 58–61).
4. See Zebrowitz and Collins (1997) for a discussion of how tangible qualities may come to be associated with traits and affordances.
5. Research has not yet identified the basis for the perceived emotional demeanor of purportedly neutral faces. Variations in demeanor may derive from nonaffective cues such as variations in particular facial attributes or from affective cues such as past expressive habits or current traces of emotion.

REFERENCES

Ambady, N., Bernieri, F., & Richeson, J. (2000). Towards a histology of social behavior: Judgmental accuracy from thin slices of behavior. In M. P. Zanna (Ed.), *Advances in experimental social psychology* (pp. 201–272) San Diego: Academic Press.

Ambady, N., Hallahan, M., & Conner, B. (1999). Accuracy of judgments of sexual orientation from thin slices of behavior. *Journal of Personality and Social Psychology*, 77, 538–547.

Andersen, S. M., & Berk, M.S. (1998). The social-cognitive model of transference: Experiencing past relationships in the present. *Psychological Science*, 7, 109–115.

Aronoff, J., Barclay, A. M., & Stevenson, L. A. (1988). The recognition of threatening facial stimuli. *Journal of Personality & Social Psychology, 54,* 647–655.

Aronoff, J., Woike, B. A., & Hyman, L. M. (1992). Which are the stimuli in facial displays of anger and happiness? Configurational bases of emotion recognition. *Journal of Personality & Social Psychology, 62,* 1050–1066.

Asch, S. E. (1952). *Social psychology.* Englewood Cliffs, NJ: Prentice-Hall.

Balaban, M. T. (1995). Affective influences on startle in five-month-old infants: Reactions to facial expressions of emotion. *Child Development, 66,* 28–36.

Bassili, J. N. (1979). Emotion recognition: The role of facial movement and the relative importance of upper and lower areas of the face. *Journal of Personality & Social Psychology, 37,* 2049–2058.

Battistich, V. A., & Aronoff, J. (1985). Perceiver, target, and situational influences on social cognition: An interactional analysis. *Journal of Personality and Social Psychology, 49,* 788–798.

Beauvois, J. -L., & Dubois, N. (2000). Affordances in social judgment: Experimental proof of why it is a mistake to ignore how others behave towards a target and look solely at how the target behaves. *Swiss Journal of Psychology, 59*(1), 16–33.

Benjamin, L. S. (1974). Structural analysis of social behavior. *Psychological Review, 81,* 392–425.

Bereczkei, T., Gyuris, P., & Weisfeld, G. E. (2004). Sexual imprinting in human mate choice. *Proceedings of the Royal Society: Series B. Biological Sciences, 271,* 1129–1134.

Berry, D. S. (1990). What can a moving face tell us? *Journal of Personality & Social Psychology, 58,* 1004–1014.

Berry, D. S. (1991a). Child and adult sensitivity to gender information in patterns of facial motion. *Ecological Psychology, 3,* 349–366.

Berry, D. S. (1991b). Accuracy in social perception. Contributions of facial and vocal information. *Journal of Personality and Social Psychology, 61,* 298–307.

Berry, D. S., & Misovich, S J., (1994). Methodological approaches to the study of social event perception. *Personality & Social Psychology Bulletin, 20,* 139–152.

Berscheid, E., & Walster, E. (1974). Physical attractiveness. In L. Berkowitz (Ed.), *Advances in experimental social psychology* (Vol. 7, pp. 158–216). New York: Academic Press.

Bigelow, A., MacLean, J., Wood, C., & Smith, J. (1990). Infants' responses to child and adult strangers: An investigation of height and facial configuration variables. *Infant Behavior and Development, 13,* 21–32.

Blair, I. V., Judd, C. M., Sadler, M. S., & Jenkins, C. (2002). The role of Afrocentric features in person perception: Judging by features and categories. *Journal of Personality and Social Psychology, 83,* 5–25.

Blairy, S., Herrera, P., & Hess, U. (1999). Mimicry and the judgment of emotional facial expressions. *Journal of Nonverbal Behavior, 23,* 5–41.

Blascovich, J., Loomis, J., Beall, A., Swinth, K., Hoyt, C., & Bailenson, J. N. (2002). Immersive virtual environment technology as a methodological tool for social psychology. *Psychological Inquiry, 13,* 103–124.

Bond, M. H. (1979). Dimensions used in perceiving peers: Cross-cultural comparisons of Hong Kong, Japanese, American, and Filipino university students. *International Journal of Psychology, 14,* 47–56.

Bond, M. H. (1983). Linking person perception dimensions to behavioral intention dimensions: The Chinese connection. *Journal of Cross-Cultural Psychology, 14,* 41–63.

Bond, M. H., & Cheung, T. (1983). College student's spontaneous self-concept: The effect of culture among respondents in Hong Kong, Japan, and the United States. *Journal of Cross-Cultural Psychology, 14,* 153–171.

Boone, R. T., & Cunningham, J. G. (1998). Children's decoding of emotion in expressive body movement: the development of cue attunement. *Developmental Psychology, 34,* 1007–1016.

Borkenau, P., & Liebler, A. (1992). Trait inferences: Sources of validity at zero acquaintance. *Journal of Personality and Social Psychology, 62,* 645–657.

Brooks, J., & Lewis, M. (1976). Infants' responses to strangers: Midget, adult, and child. *Child Development, 47,* 323–332.

Bugental, D. B. (2000). Acquisition of the algorithms of social life: A domain-based approach. *Psychological Bulletin, 126,* 187–219.

Bull, P. E. (1987). *Posture and gesture.* Elmsford, NY: Pergamon Press.

Bushnell, I. W., Sai, F., & Mullin, J. T. (1989). Neonatal recognition of the mothers' face. *British Journal of Developmental Psychology, 7,* 3–15.

Buss, D. M. (1989). Sex differences in human mate preferences: Evolutionary hypotheses tested in 37 cultures. *Behavioural and Brain Sciences, 12,* 1–49.

Buss, D. M., Haselton, M. G., Shackelford, T. K., Bleske, A. L., & Wakefield, J. C. (1998). Adaptations, exaptations, and spandrels. *American Psychologist, 53,* 533–548.

Cacioppo, J. T., Priester, J. R., & Berntson, G. G. (1993). Rudimentary determinants of attitudes: II. Arm flexion and extension have differential effects on attitudes. *Journal of Personality & Social Psychology, 65,* 5–17.

Calder, A. J., Keane, J., Cole, J., Campbell, R., & Young, A. (2000). Facial expression recognition by people with Moebius syndrome. *Cognitive Neuropsychology (Special Issue), 17,* 73–87

Caporael, L. R. (1997). The evolution of truly social cognition: The core configurations model. *Personality and Social Psychology Review, 1,* 276–298.

Chartrand, T. L., & Bargh, J. A. (1999). The chameleon effect: The perception-behavior link and social interaction. *Journal of Personality & Social Psychology, 76,* 893–910.

Clark, S. Tremblay, F., & Ste-Marie, D., (2004). Differential modulation of corticospinal excitability during observation, mental imagery and imitation of hand actions. *Neuropsychologia, 42,* 105–112.

Collins, M., & Zebrowitz, L. A. (1995). The contributions of appearance to occupational outcomes in civilian and military settings. *Journal of Applied Social Psychology, 25,* 129–163.

Cosmides, L., & Tooby, J. (1997). *Evolutionary psychology: A primer.* Center for Evolutionary Psychology, University of California, Santa Barbara. http://www.psych.ucsb.edu/research/cep/primer.html

Cunningham, M. R., Barbee, A. P., & Philhower, C. (2002). Dimensions of facial physical attractiveness: The intersection of biology and culture. In G. Rhodes & L. A. Zebrowitz (Eds.), *Facial attractiveness: Evolutionary, cognitive, and social perspectives* (pp.193–238). Westport, CT: Ablex.

Cutting, J. E., & Kozlowski, L. T. (1977). Recognizing friends by their walk: Gait perception without familiarity cues. *Bulletin of the Psychonomic Society, 9,* 353–356.

Darwin, C. (1872). *The expression of emotion in man and animals.* Oxford, England: Appleton.

Dekeyser, M., Verfaillie, K., & Vanrie, J. (2002). Creating stimuli for the study of biological-motion perception. *Behavior Research Methods, Instruments and Computers, 34,* 375–382.

DePaulo, B., & Rosenthal, R. (1982). Diagnosing deceptive and mixed messages from verbal and nonverbal cues. *Journal of Experimental Social Psychology, 18*, 433–446.

DeBruine, L. (2002). Facial resemblance enhances trust. *Proceedings of the Royal Society of London, B, 269*, 1307–1312.

Diamond, R., & Carey, S. (1986). Why faces are and are not special: An effect of expertise. *Journal of Experimental Psychology: General, 115*, 107–117.

Dion, K. K. (2002). Cultural perspectives on facial attractiveness. In G. Rhodes & L. A. Zebrowitz (Eds.), *Facial attractiveness: Evolutionary, cognitive, and social perspectives* (pp. 239–260). Westport, CT: Ablex.

Eagly, A. H., Ashmore, R. D., Makhijani, M. G., & Longo, L. C. (1991). What is beautiful is good: A meta-analytic review of research on the physical attractiveness stereotype. *Psychological Bulletin, 110*, 109–128.

Eibl-Eibesfeldt, I. (1989). *Human ethology*. New York: Aldine de Gruyter.

Ekman P. (1971). Universals and cultural differences in facial expressions of emotion. *Nebraska symposium on motivation* (pp. 207–283). Lincoln: University of Nebraska Press.

Ekman, P., Campos, J., Davidson, R. J., & De Waal, F. (2003). *Emotions inside out*. (Vol. 1000). New York: Annals of the New York Academy of Sciences.

Elfenbein, H. A., & Ambady, N. (2002). Is there an in-group advantage in emotion recognition? *Psychological Bulletin, 128*, 243–249.

Elfenbein, H. A., & Ambady, N. (2003). When familiarity breeds accuracy: Cultural exposure and facial emotion recognition. *Journal of Personality and Social Psychology, 65*, 276–290.

Elfenbein, H. A., Foo, M. D., Boldry, J. G., & Tan, H. H. (2004). Evidence for a relationship effect in the accuracy of communicating emotion: A social relations analysis. Poster presented at the 5th Annual Meeting of the Society for Personality and Social Psychology, January 29-31,Austin, TX.

Enlow, D. H. (1990). *Facial growth*. Philadelphia: Harcourt Brace.

Enquist, M., Ghirlanda, S., Lundqvist, D., & Wachtmeister, C. A. (2002). An ethological theory of attractiveness. In G. Rhodes & L. A. Zebrowitz (Eds.), *Facial attractiveness: Evolutionary, cognitive, and social perspectives* (pp. 127–152). Westport, CT: Ablex.

Feingold, A. (1992). Good-looking people are not what we think. *Psychological Bulletin, 111*, 304–341.

Field, T. M., Cohen, D., Garcia, R., & Greenberg, R. (1984). Mother-stranger face discrimination by the newborn. *Infant Behavior & Development, 7*, 19–25.

Fiske, A. P. (1991). *Structures of social life: The four elementary forms of human relations*. New York: The Free Press.

Fiske, A. P., & Haslam, N. (1996). Social cognition is thinking about relationships. *Current Directions in Psychological Science, 5*, 143–148.

Fiske, S. T., & Cox, M. G. (1979) Person concepts: The effect of target familiarity and descriptive purpose on the process of describing others. *Journal of Personality, 47*, 136–161.

Frijda, N. H. (1953). The understanding of facial expression of emotion. *Acta Psychologica, 9*, 294–362.

Gangestad, S. W., & Simpson, J. A. (2000). The evolution of human mating: Trade-offs and strategic pluralism. *The Behavioral and Brain Sciences, 23*, 573–587.

Gangestad, S. W., & Buss, D. M. (1993). Pathogen prevalence and human mate preferences. *Ethology and Sociobiology, 14*, 89–96.

Gangestad, S. W., Simpson, J. A., DiGeronimo, K., & Biek, M. (1992). Differential accuracy in person perception across traits: Examination of a functional hypothesis. *Journal of Personality and Social Psychology, 62*, 688–698.

Gauthier, I., & Tarr, M. J. (1997). Becoming a "greeble" expert: Exploring mechanisms for face recognition. *Vision Research, 37*, 1673–1682.

Gibson, J. J. (1966). *The senses considered as perceptual systems.* Boston: Houghton Mifflin Company.

Gibson, J. J. (1979). *The ecological approach to visual perception.* Boston: Houghton Mifflin.

Goldstein, N. E., & Feldman, R. S. (1996). Knowledge of American sign language and the ability of hearing individuals to decode facial expressions of emotion. *Journal of Nonverbal Behavior, 20*, 111–122.

Goldstone, R. L. (1998). Perceptual learning. *Annual Review of Psychology, 49*, 585–612.

Gould, S. J. (1979). Mickey Mouse meets Konrad Lorenz. *Natural History, 88*, 30–36.

Gray, P. B., Kahlenber, S. M., Barrett, E. S., Lipson, S. F., & Ellison, P. T. (2002). Marriage and fatherhood are associated with lower testosterone in males. *Evolution and Human Behavior, 23*, 193–201.

Gunns, R. E., Johnston, L., & Hudson, S. M. (2002). Victim selection and kinematics. A point-light investigation of vulnerability to attack. *Journal of Nonverbal Behavior, 26*, 129–158.

Hadden, S. B., & Brownlow, S. (1991, March). *The impact of facial structure on assertiveness on dating choice.* Paper presented at the meeting of the Southeastern Psychological Association, New Orleans, LA.

Halberstadt, J., & Rhodes, G. (2000). The attractiveness of non-face averageness: Implications for an evolutionary explanation of the attractiveness of average faces. *Psychological Science, 11*, 285–289.

Halberstadt, J., & Rhodes, G. (2003). It's not just the average face that's attractive: The attractiveness of averageness in computer-manipulated birds, fish, and automobiles. *Psychonomic Bulletin & Review, 10*, 149–156.

Haselton, M. G., & Buss, D. M. (2000). Error management theory: A new perspective on biases in cross-sex mind reading. *Journal of Personality and Social Psychology, 78*, 81–91.

Hatfield, E., & Sprecher, S. (1986). *Mirror, mirror: The importance of looks in everyday life.* Albany: State University of New York Press.

Helfrich, H. (1979). Age markers in speech. In K.R. Scherer & H. Giles (Eds.), *Social markers in speech* (pp. 63–107). Cambridge: Cambridge University Press.

Hess, U., & Blairy, S. (2001). Facial mimicry and emotional contagion to dynamic emotional facial expressions and their influence on decoding accuracy. *International Journal of Psychophysiology, 40*, 129–141.

Hess, U., Blairy, S., & Kleck, R. E. (2000). The influence of facial emotion displays, gender, and ethnicity on judgments of dominance and affiliation. *Journal of Nonverbal Behavior, 24*, 265–283.

Hill, T., Lewicki, P., Czyzewska, M., & Schuller, G. (1990). The role of learned inferential encoding rules in the perception of faces: Effects of nonconscious self-perpetuation of a bias. *Journal of Experimental Social Psychology, 26*, 350–371.

Hilton, J. L., & Darley, J. M. (1991). The effects of interaction goals on person perception. In M. P. Zanna (Ed.), *Advances in experimental social psychology* (Vol. 24, pp. 235–267). San Diego, CA: Academic Press.

Humphreys, G. W., Donnelly, N., & Riddoch, M. J. (1993). Expression is computed separately from facial identity, and it is computed separately for moving and static faces: Neuropsychological evidence. *Neuropsychologia, 31*, 173–181.

Ilg, W., Golla, H. Thier, H. P., & Geise, M. A. (2004). *Influences of cerebellar diseases on gait—quantification of the spatio-temporal characteristics of walking in cerebellar patients*. Laboratory for Action Representation and Learning, Hertie Center for Clinical Brain Research. University Clinic Tubingen, Germany, unpublished manuscript.

Izard, C. E. (1997). Emotions and facial expressions: A perspective from differential emotions theory. In J. A. Russell & J. M. Fernandez-Dols (Eds.), *The psychology of facial expression* (pp. 57–77). Paris, France USA: Cambridge University Press.

Jackson, L., & Ervin, K. S. (1992). Height stereotypes of women and men: The liabilities of shortness for both sexes. *Journal of Social Psychology, 132*, 433–445.

Johnson, M. H., Dziurawiec, S., Ellis, H., & Morton, J. (1991). Newborn preferential tracking of face-like stimuli and its subsequent decline. *Cognition, 40*, 1–19.

Johnston, L., Hudson, S. M., Richardson, M. J., & Gunns, R. E. (2004). Changing kinematics as a means of reducing vulnerability to physical attack. *Journal of Applied Social Psychology, 34*, 514–537.

Kalick, S. M., Zebrowitz, L. A., Langlois, J. H., & Johnson, R. M. (1998). Does human facial attractiveness honestly advertise health? Longitudinal data on an evolutionary question. *Psychological Science, 9*, 8–13.

Kaping, D., Duhamel, P., & Webster, M. A. (2002). Adaptation to natural facial categories. *Journal of Vision, 2*, Abstract, 128a.

Keating, C. F. (1985). Human dominance signals: The primate in us. In S. L. Ellyson & J. F. Dovidio (Eds.), *Power, dominance, and nonverbal behavior* (pp. 89–108). New York: Springer.

Keating, C. F., & Bai, D. (1986). Children's attributions of social dominance from facial cues. *Child Development, 57*, 1260–1276.

Keating, C. F., Mazur, A. C., & Segall, M. H., (1981). A cross-cultural exploration of physiognomic traits of dominance and happiness. *Ethology and Sociobiology, 2*, 41–48.

Keating, C. F. (2002). Charismatic faces: Social status cues put face appeal in context. In G. Rhodes & L. A. Zebrowitz (Eds.), *Facial attractiveness: Evolutionary, cognitive, and social perspectives* (pp. 153–192). Westport, CT: Ablex.

Kellerman, J., Lewis, J., & Laird, J. D. (1989) Looking and loving: The effects of mutual gaze on feelings of romantic love. *Journal of Research in Personality, 23*, 145–161.

Kelley, H. H. (1997). The "stimulus field" for interpersonal phenomena: The source of language and thought about interpersonal events. *Personality and Social Psychology Review, 1*, 140–169.

Kelley, H. H., Holmes, J. G., Kerr, N. L., Reis, H. T., Rusbult, C. E., & Van Lange, P. A. M. (2003). *An atlas of interpersonal situations*. New York: Cambridge University Press.

Kelley, H. H., & Stahelski, A. J. (1970). Social interaction basis of cooperators' and competitors' beliefs about others. *Journal of Personality and Social Psychology, 16*, 66–91.

Kendrick, K. M., da Costa, A. P., Leigh, A. E., Hinton, M. R., & Peirce, J. W. (2001). Sheep don't forget a face. *Nature, 414*, 165–166.

Kenny, D. A. (1994). *Interpersonal perception: A social relations analysis*. New York: Guildford Press.

Kenrick, D. T., Li, N. P., & Butner, J. (2003). Dynamical evolutionary psychology: Individual decision rules and emergent social norms. *Psychological Review, 110*, 3–28.

Knutson, B. (1996). Facial expression of emotion influence interpersonal trait inferences. *Journal of Nonverbal Behavior, 20*, 165–182.

Kozlowski, L. T., & Cutting, J. E (1977). Recognizing the sex of a walker from a dynamic point-light display. *Perception and Psychophysics, 21,* 575–580.

Kramer, S., Zebrowitz, L. A., San Giovanni, J. P., & Sherak, B. (1995). Infants' preferences for attractiveness and babyfaceness. In B. G. Bardy, R. J. Bootsma, & Y. Guiard (Eds.), *Studies in perception and action III* (pp. 389–392). Hillsdale, NJ: Erlbaum.

Kurzban, R., & Leary, M. R. (2001). Evolutionary origins of stigmatization: The functions of social exclusion. *Psychological Bulletin, 127,* 187–208.

Laird, J. D. (1992). The process of emotional experience: A self-perception theory. In M. S. Clark (Ed.), *Emotion. In series: Review of personality and social psychology,* No. 13 (pp. 213–234). Thousand Oaks, CA: Sage Publications.

Langlois, J. H., Kalakanis, L., Rubenstein, A. J., Larson, A., Hallam, M., & Smoot, M. (2000). Maxims or myths of beauty? A meta-analytic and theoretical review. *Psychological Bulletin, 126,* 390–423.

Langlois, J. H., Roggman, L. A., Casey, R. J., Ritter, J. M., Reiser-Danner, L. A., & Jenkins, V. Y. (1987). Infant preferences for attractive faces: Rudiments of a stereotype? *Developmental Psychology, 23,* 363–369.

Langlois, J. H., Ritter, J. M., Roggman, L. A., & Vaughn, L. S. (1991). Facial diversity and infant preferences for attractive faces. *Developmental Psychology, 27,* 79–84.

Lanzetta, J. T., & Orr, S. P. (1980). Influence of facial expressions on the classical conditioning of fear. *Journal of Personality and Social Psychology, 39,* 1081–1087.

Lasky, R. E., Klein, R. E., & Martinez, S. (1974). Age and sex discrimination in five-and six-month-old infants. *Journal of Psychology, 88,* 317–324.

Leonova, T. (in press). L'approche écologique de la cognition sociale et son impact sur la conception des traits de personnalité. *L'Année Psychologique, 104,* 249–294.

Leopold, D. A., O'Toole, A. J., Vetter, T., & Blanz, V. (2001). Prototype-referenced shape encoding revealed by high level aftereffects. *Nature Neuroscience, 4,* 89–94.

Leung, K., & Bond, M. H. (2004). Social axioms: A model for social beliefs in multicultural perspective. In M. P. Zanna (Ed.), *Advances in experimental social psychology* (Vol. 36, pp. 119–197). San Diego,: Elsevier Academic Press.

Lewicki, P. (1985). Nonconscious biasing effects of single instances on subsequent judgments. *Journal of Personality & Social Psychology, 48,* 563–574.

Lieberman, D., Tooby, J., & Cosmides, L. (2002). Does morality have a biological basis? An empirical test of the factors governing moral sentiments relating to incest. *Proceedings of the Royal Society of London, B,* DOI 10.1098/rspb.2002.2290.

Little A. C., Penton-Voak, I. S., Burt, D. M., & Perrett, D. I. (2002). Individual differences in the perception of attractiveness: How cyclic hormonal changes and self-perceived attractiveness influence female preferences for male faces. In G. Rhodes & L. A. Zebrowitz (Eds.), *Facial attractiveness: Evolutionary, cognitive, and social perspectives* (pp. 59–90). Westport, CT: Ablex.

Livingston, R. W., & Brewer, M. B. (2002). What are we really priming? Cue-based versus category-based processing of facial stimuli. *Journal of Personality and Social Psychology, 82,* 5–18.

Lorenz, K. Z. (1943). Die angeborenen Formen Moglicher Vererbung. *Zeitschrift fur Tierpsychologie, 5,* 235–409. Cited in R. Shaw & J. Bransford (Eds.). (1977). *Perceiving, acting, and knowing: Toward an ecological psychology* (p. 125). Hillsdale, NJ: Erlbaum.

Lorenz, K. Z. (1970). Companions as factors in the bird's environment. In K. Z. Lorenz (Ed.), Studies in animal and human behaviour, (Vol. 1) (R. Martin, Trans.). Cambridge, MA: Harvard University Press. (Reprinted from *Journal of Ornithology, 83,* 137–213, 1935.)

Lorr, M., & McNair, D. (1965). Expansion of the interperson behavior circle. *Journal of Personality and Social Psychology, 2,* 823–830.

Lotze, M., Braun, C., Birbaumer, N., Anders, S., & Cohen, L. G. (2003). Motor learning elicited by voluntary drive. *Brain, 126,* 866–872.

McArthur, L. Z., & Baron, R. M. (1983). Toward an ecological theory of social perception. *Psychological Review, 90,* 215–238.

McArthur, L. Z., Solomon, M. R., & Jaffe, R. H. (1980). Weight differences in emotional responsiveness to proprioceptive and pictorial stimuli. *Journal of Personality and Social Psychology, 34,* 308319.

McCall. R. B., & Kennedy, C. B. (1980). Attention of 4-month infants to discrepancy and babyishness. *Journal of Experimental Child Psychology, 29,* 189–201.

McCrae, R. R., & Costa, P. T. Jr. (1987). Validation of the five-factor model of personality across instruments and observers. *Journal of Personality and Social Psychology, 52,* 81–90.

Mehrabian, A. (1972). *Nonverbal communication.* Oxford, England: Aldine-Atherton.

Meier, B. P., & Robinson, M. D. (2004). Why the sunny side is up: Associations between affect and vertical position. *Psychological Science, 15,* 243–247.

Mignault, A., & Chaudhuri, A. (2003). The many faces of a neutral face: Head tilt and perception of dominance and emotion. *Journal of Nonverbal Behavior, 27,* 111–132.

Mignon, A., & Mollaret, P. (2002). Applying the affordance conception of traits: A person perception study. *Personality & Social Psychology Bulletin, 28,* 1327–1334.

Miller, J. (1984). Culture and the development of everyday social explanation. *Journal of Personality & Social Psychology, 46,* 961–978.

Montepare, J. M., & Dobish, H. (2003). The contribution of emotion perceptions and their overgeneralizations to trait impressions. *Journal of Nonverbal Behavior, 27,* 237–254.

Montepare, J. M., Goldstein, S., & Clausen, A. (1987). Identification of emotions from gait information. *Journal of Nonverbal Behavior, 11,* 33–42.

Montepare, J. M., & Zebrowitz, L. A. (1998). Person perception comes of age: The salience and significance of age in social judgments. *Advances in Experimental Social Psychology, 30,* 93–161.

Montepare, J. M., & Zebrowitz-McArthur, L. (1987). Perceptions of adults with childlike voices in two cultures. *Journal of Experimental Social Psychology, 23,* 331–349.

Montepare, J. M., & Zebrowitz-McArthur, L. (1988). Impressions of people created by age related qualities of their gaits. *Journal of Personality and Social Psychology, 55,* 547–556.

Nakayama, K. (1994). James J. Gibson—An appreciation. *Psychological Review, 101,* 329–335.

Neuberg, S. L., Smith, D. M., & Asher, T. (2000). Why people stigmatize: Toward a bio-cultural framework. In T. Heathereton, R. Kleck, J. G. Hull, & M. Hebl (Eds.), *The social psychology of stigma* (pp. 31–61). New York: Guilford.

Noller, P., Law, H., & Comrey, A. L. (1987). Cattell, Comrey, and Eysenck personality factors compared: More evidence for the five robust factors? *Journal of Personality and Social Psychology, 53,* 775–782.

Park, J. H., Faulkner, J., & Schaller, M. (2003). Evolved disease-avoidance processes and contemporary anti-social behavior: Prejudicial attitudes and avoidance of people with physical disabilities. *Journal of Nonverbal Communication, 27,* 65–88.

Pascalis, O., de Haan, M., & Nelson, C. A. (2002). Is face processing species-specific during the first year of life? *Science, 296,* 1321–1323.

Penton-Voak, I. S., Little, A. C., Jones, B. C., Burt, D. M., Tiddeman, B. P., & Perrett, D. (2003). Female condition influences preferences for sexual dimorphism in faces of male humans (Homo sapiens). *Journal of Comparative Psychology, 117*, 264–271.

Pettijohn, Terry F. II, & Tesser, A., (2005). Threat and Social Choice: When Eye Size Matters. *Journal of Social Psychology, 145*, 547–570.

Pettijohn, T. F., & Tesser, A. (1999). Popularity in environmental context: Facial feature assessment of American movie actresses. *Media Psychology, 1*, 229–247.

Pittenger, J. B., Shaw, R. E., & Mark, L. S. (1979). Perceptual information for the age level of faces as a higher order invariant of growth. *Journal of Experimental Psychology: Human Perception & Performance, 5*, 478–493.

Ramsey, J. L., Langlois, J. H., Hoss, R. A., Rubenstein, A. J., & Griffin, A. M. (2004). Origins of a stereotype: Categorization of facial attractiveness by 6-month-old infants. *Developmental Science, 7*, 201–211.

Rhodes, G., Chan, J., Zebrowitz, L., & Simmons, L. W. (2003a). Does sexual dimorphism in faces signal health? *Proceedings of the Royal Society of London, Series B (Suppl.), 270*, S93–S95.

Rhodes, G., & Zebrowitz, L. A. (Eds.). (2002). *Facial attractiveness: Evolutionary, cognitive, and social perspectives.* Westport, CT: Ablex.

Rhodes, G., Harwood, K., Yoshikawa, S., Nishitani, M., & McLean, I. (2002). The attractiveness of average faces: Cross-cultural evidence and possible biological basis. In G. Rhodes & L. A. Zebrowitz (Eds.), *Facial attractiveness: Evolutionary, cognitive, and social perspectives* (pp. 35–58). Westport, CT: Ablex.

Rhodes, G., Jeffery, L., Watson, T. L., Clifford, C. W. G., & Nakayama, K. (2003b). Fitting the mind to the world: Face adaptation and attractiveness Aftereffects. *Psychological Science, 14*, 558–566.

Rhodes, G. Tan, S., Brake, S., & Taylor, K. (1989). Expertise and configural coding in face recognition. *British Journal of Psychology, 80*, 313–331.

Rosenthal, R., Hall, J. A., Archer, D., DiMatteo, M. R., & Rogers, P. L. (1979). *The PONS Test Manual: Profile of Nonverbal Sensitivity.* New York: Irvington.

Rubenstein, A. J., Kalakanis, L., & Langlois, J. H. (1999). Infant preferences for attractive faces: A cognitive explanation. *Developmental Psychology, 15*, 848–855.

Rubenstein, A. J., Langlois, J. H., & Roggman, L. A. (2002). What makes a face attractive and why: The role of averageness in defining facial beauty. In G. Rhodes & L. A. Zebrowitz (Eds.), *Facial attractiveness: Evolutionary, cognitive, and social perspectives* (pp. 1–33). Westport, CT: Ablex.

Ryckman, R. M., Robbins, M. A., Kaczor, L. M., & Gold, J. A. (1989). Male and female raters' stereotyping of male and female physiques. *Personality and Social Psychology Bulletin, 15*, 244–251.

Scarr, S. (1992). Developmental theories of the 1990s: Developmental and individual differences. *Child Development, 63*, 1–19.

Scherer, R., Banse, R., & Wallbott, H. G. (2001). Emotion inferences from vocal expression correlate across languages and cultures. *Journal of Cross-Cultural Psychology, 32*, 76—92.

Schwartz, G. M., Izard, C. E., & Ansul, S. E. (1985). The 5-month-old's ability to discriminate facial expressions of emotion. *Infant Behavior and Development, 8*, 65–77.

Secord, P. F., Dukes, W. F., & Bevan, W. (1954). Personalities in faces: I. An experiment in social perceiving. *Genetic Psychology Monographs, 49*, 231–279.

Secord, P. F., & Muthard, J. E. (1955). Personalities in faces: IV. A descriptive analysis of the perception of women's faces and the identification of physiognomic determinants. *Journal of Psychology, 39*, 269–278.

Shapiro, P. N., & Penrod, S. D. (1986). Meta-analysis of face identification studies. *Psychological Bulletin, 100,* 139–156.

Shaw, R., Turvey, M., & Mace, W. (1982). Ecological psychology: The consequences of a commitment of realism. In W. Weimer & D. Palermo (Eds.), *Cognition and symbolic processes* (Vol. 2). Hillsdale, NJ: Erlbaum.

Shepher, J. (1971). Mate selection among second generation kibbutz adolescents and adults: incest avoidance and negative imprinting. *Archives of Sexual Behavior, 1,* 293–307.

Shimojo, S., Simion, C., Shimojo, E., & Scheier, C. (2003). Gaze bias both reflects and influences preference. *Nature Neuroscience,* Published online 9 November 2003; doi:10.1038/nn1150.

Shweder, R. A., & Bourne, E. J. (1982). Does the concept of the person vary cross-culturally? In A. J. Marsella & G. M. White (Eds.), *Cultural conceptions of mental health and therapy* (pp. 97–137). London: D. Reidel.

Singh, D. (1993). Adaptive significance of female physical attractiveness: Role of waist-to-hip ratio. *Journal of Personality & Social Psychology, 65,* 293-307.

Smith, E. R., & Semin, G. R. (2004). Socially situated cognition: Cognition in its social context. In. M. P. Zanna (Ed.), *Advances in Experimental Social Psychology* (Vol. 36, pp. 57–117). San Diego: Elsevier Academic Press.

Smith, P. (1979). Sex markers in speech. In K. R. Scherer & H. Giles (Eds.), *Social markers in speech* (pp. 109–146). Cambridge: Cambridge University Press.

Snodgrass, S. (1985). Women's intuition: The effect of subordinate role in interpersonal sensitivity. *Journal of Personality and Social Psychology, 49,* 140–155.

Sorce, J. F., Emde, R. N., Campos, J. J., & Klennert, M. D. (1985). Social referencing: The infant's use of emotional signals from a friendly adult with mother present. *Developmental Psychology, 22,* 427–432.

Strack, F., Martin, L. L., & Stepper, S. (1988). Inhibiting and facilitation conditions of the human smile: A nonobstrusive test of the facial feedback hypothesis. *Journal of Personality and Social Psychology, 54,* 768–777.

Strickland, L. H. (1958). Surveillance and trust. *Journal of Personality, 26,* 200–215.

Striano, T., & Tomasello, M. (2001). Infant development: physical and social cognition. In N. J. Smelser & P. B. Baltes (Eds.), *International encyclopedia of the social & behavioral sciences* (pp. 7410–7414). Oxford: Pergamon.

Tanaka, J., & Gauthier, I. (1997). Expertise in object and face recognition. In R. L Goldstone (Ed.), *Perceptual learning* (pp. 83–125). New York: Academic Press.

Thornhill, R., & Gangestad, S. W. (1999). The scent of symmetry: A human sex pheromone that signals fitness? *Evolution & Human Behavior, 20,* 175–201.

Thornhill, R., Gangestad, S. W., Miller, R., Scheyd, G., McCollough, J. K., & Franklin, M. (2003). Major histocompatibility complex genes, symmetry, and body scent attractiveness in men and women. *Behavioral Ecology, 14,* 668–678.

Todd, J. T., Mark, L. S., Shaw, R. E., & Pittenger, J. B. (1980). The perception of human growth. *Scientific American, 242,* 106–114.

Tranel, D., Damasio, A. R., & Damasio, H. (1988). Intact recognition of facial expression, gender, and age in patients with impaired recognition of face identity. *Neurology, 38,* 690–696.

Turati, C. (2004). Why faces are not special to newborns: An alternative account of the face preference. *Current Directions, 13,* 5–8.

Van Duuren, M., Kendell-Scott, L., & Stark, N. (2003). Early aesthetic choices: Infant preferences for attractive premature infant faces. *International Journal of Behavioral Development, 2,* 212–219.

Wallbott, H. G., & Scherer, K. R. (1986). Cues and channels in emotion recognition. *Journal of Personality & Social Psychology, 51*, 690–699.

Walton, G. E., Bower, N. J., & Bower. T. G. (1992). Recognition of familiar faces by newborns. *Infant Behavior & Development, 15*, 265–269.

Wagner, W., & Wagner, G. P. (in press). Examining the modularity concept in evolutionary psychology: The level of genes, mind and culture. *Journal of Cultural and Evolutionary Psychology.*

Westermarck, E. A. (1921). *The history of human marriage* (5th ed.). London: Macmillan.

Wheeler, L., & Kim, Y. (1997). What is beautiful is culturally good: The physical attractiveness stereotype has different content in collectivistic cultures. *Personality and Social Psychology Bulletin, 23*, 795–800.

Wiggins, J. S. (1979). A psychological taxonomy of trait-descriptive terms. The interpersonal domain. *Journal of Personality and Social Psychology, 37*, 395–412.

Wolf, A. P. (1995). *Sexual attraction and childhood association: A Chinese brief for Edward Westermarck.* Stanford, CA: Stanford University Press.

Young, A. W., Newcombe, F., de Haan, E. H. F., Small, M., & Hall, D. C. (1993). Face perception after brain injury: Selective impairments affecting identity and expression. *Brain, 116*, 941–959.

Zebrowitz, L. A. (1996). Physical appearance as a basis of stereotyping. In N. MacRae, M. Hewstone, & C. Stangor (Eds.), *Foundations of stereotypes and stereotyping* (pp. 79–120). New York: Guilford Press.

Zebrowitz, L. A. (1997). *Reading faces: Window to the soul?* Boulder, CO: Westview Press.

Zebrowitz, L. A. (2002). The affordances of immersive visual environments for studying social affordances. *Psychological Inquiry, 13*, 143–145.

Zebrowitz, L. A., Andreoletti, C., Collins, M. A., Lee, S. Y., & Blumenthal, J. (1998). Bright, bad, babyfaced boys: Appearance stereotypes do not always yield self-fulfilling prophecy effects. *Journal of Personality and Social Psychology, 75*, 1300–1320.

Zebrowitz, L. A., & Bronstad, M., & Lee, H. K. (2005). *The mistaken identity effect: Positive impressions of familiar-looking strangers.* Brandeis University, Unpublished work.

Zebrowitz, L. A., & Collins, M. A. (1997) Accurate social perception at zero acquaintance: The affordances of a Gibsonian approach. *Personality and Social Psychology Review, 1*, 204–223.

Zebrowitz, L. A., Collins, M. A., & Dutta, R. (1998). Appearance and personality across the lifespan. *Personality and Social Psychology Bulletin, 24*, 736–749.

Zebrowitz, L. A., Fellous, J. M., Mignault, A., & Andreoletti, C. (2003). Trait impressions as overgeneralized responses to adaptively significant facial qualities: Evidence from connectionist modeling. *Personality and Social Psychology Review, 7*,194–215.

Zebrowitz, L. A., Hall, J. A., Murphy, N. A., & Rhodes, G. (2002). Looking smart and looking good: Facial cues to intelligence and their origins. *Personality and Social Psychology Bulletin, 28*, 238–249.

Zebrowitz, L. A., Kikuchi, M., & Fellous, J. M. (2004). The emotion overgeneralization effect: Impressions of neutral faces as a function of their structural resemblance to emotion expressions. Unpublished research. Brandeis University.

Zebrowitz, L. A. & Montepare, J. M. (1992). Impressions of babyfaced males and females across the lifespan. *Developmental Psychology, 28*, 1143–1152.

Zebrowitz, L. A., Montepare, J. M., & Lee, H. K. (1993). They don't all look alike: Individuated impressions of other racial groups. *Journal of Personality and Social Psychology, 65*, 85–101.

Zebrowitz, L. A., & Rhodes, G. (2002). Nature let a hundred flowers bloom: The multiple ways and wherefores of attractiveness. In G. Rhodes & L. A. Zebrowitz (Eds.), *Facial attractiveness: Evolutionary, cognitive, and social perspectives* (pp. 261–293). Westport, CT: Ablex.

Zebrowitz, L. A., & Rhodes, G. (2004). Sensitivity to 'bad genes' and the anomalous face overgeneralization effect: Accuracy, cue validity, and cue utilization in judging intelligence and health. *Journal of Nonverbal Behavior, 28,* 167–185.

Zuckerman, M., & Driver, R. E. (1989). What sounds beautiful is good: The vocal attractiveness stereotype. *Journal of Nonverbal Behavior, 13,* 67–82.

Zuckerman, M., & Miyake, K. (1993). The attractive voice: What makes it so? *Journal of Nonverbal Behavior, 17,* 119–135.

6

Social Functionalism and the Evolution of Emotions

DACHER KELTNER, JONATHAN HAIDT, and MICHELLE N. SHIOTA

Which of these animals is not like the others: ants, bees, naked mole rats, chimpanzees, or human beings? Each is unique in many ways, and *Homo sapiens* is certainly a remarkable organism. For our purposes, however, the outlier is actually the chimpanzee. All of the other species, including humans, are "ultrasocial" (Campbell, 1983)—they live in highly cooperative groups of hundreds or thousands of individuals with a pronounced division of labor. The insects and mole rats accomplish this miraculous degree of interdependence by a trick of genetics: They are all siblings, so from a genetic standpoint helping another is not much different from helping one's self. Humans, clearly, lack this particular motivation to cooperate. How have we managed to maintain such an extreme degree of social complexity?

How humans became an ultrasocial species is not yet fully understood, but many roads lead through the emotions. From Darwin's (1872/1965) original speculations about emotional expression, through Robert Trivers' (1971) account of the emotions that make reciprocal altruism possible, to Robert Frank's (1988) "commitment" model of moral emotions, most attempts to explain humanity's extraordinary sociality are really accounts of humanity's extraordinary emotionality. Emotions evolved because they facilitate behaviors that are adaptive for the individual (or the gene), given certain contexts. For human beings this primarily means playing the game of complex social interaction well.

In this chapter we will present a social functionalist framework for the study of emotion. We take it for granted that emotions are products of evolution (though influenced considerably by cultural learning), and we suggest that emotion-related physiological, cognitive, and motivational mechanisms are best understood in the context of the functions they serve. In the first section of this chapter we discuss the emergence and emphases of evolutionary accounts of emotion, and introduce the social functionalist approach. Emotions, from this perspective, serve survival and reproductive functions that are best understood at four levels simultaneously—intra-individual, dyadic, group, and cultural. Whereas functions at the individual level typically involve basic survival, functions at the other levels involve the facilitation of social bonding and collaboration.

In the second section, we review some of the central insights generated by a social functional approach to emotions in empirical research over the last 20 years. For example, studies have illuminated the role of emotional experience in social-moral judgments about right and wrong. New studies of emotional communication show how emotions help to coordinate social interaction. Individual differences in emotional dispositions also involve strategic expressions of emotion, in ways that reflect social functions. Thus, a social functional approach has served to guide emotion research into new and societally significant domains.

In the third section, we address the question of continuity between humans and other primates. An evolutionary approach implies a great deal of continuity between closely related species, yet we opened this paper with the claim that human beings are ultrasocial, whereas chimpanzees, our closest primate relatives, are not. We resolve this conflict by stating that the basic elements of emotionality are almost entirely conserved among humans and other primates, but that a few changes in the human mind lead to enormous differences in the emotional lives of humans. These are the very differences that make ultrasociality possible.

In the fourth section, we address one central controversy that must be resolved before an evolutionary approach to emotions can be embraced: the question of cultural variation. We conclude that the available evidence on facial expressions and emotion-specific physiology supports a universalist position (e.g., Ekman, 1992; Elfenbein & Ambady, 2002; Keltner, Gruenfeld, & Anderson 2003) at the individual and dyadic levels of analysis. However, our social functionalist approach holds that universality at the two lower levels is fully compatible with variation at the group and cultural level.

WHAT IS AN EVOLUTIONARY APPROACH TO EMOTIONS?

In 1872 Charles Darwin published *The Expression of the Emotions in Man and Animals*, a book that would have a profound impact upon both emotion research and our understanding of human origins. He wrote this book in 4 months, taking on creationist claims that humans were endowed with unique emotions setting them apart from "lower" species. To support his claims about the evolution of the human race, Darwin drew parallels between human expressions and those of other species. He offered functional arguments about the origins of particular facial displays, such as the furrowed brow, tears, and the eyebrow flash. He even queried missionaries living in other cultures about whether they had observed expressions not seen in Victorian England, to bolster his claims about the universality of emotional expressions.

Although *The Expression of the Emotions in Man and Animals* was a best seller in its day, it would be largely ignored by psychologists for nearly a century afterwards. In the early 1960s, however, several theorists revived evolutionary accounts of emotion and extended Darwin's rich observations about facial expression to controlled studies of the universality of expression (Ekman, 1972; Izard, 1977; Plutchik, 1962; Tomkins, 1962, 1963). These early evolutionary accounts were soon complemented by updated theories (Barrett & Campos, 1987; Ekman & Davidson, 1994; Tooby & Cosmides, 1990), ethological studies (e.g., Eibl-Eibesfeldt, 1989; Krebs & Davies, 1993), and philosophical analysis (Wright, 1973), which, together, have given shape to an evolutionary approach to emotion. This new evolutionist view of emotion is guided by a few general principles.

Emotions have Functions

The first thing an evolutionary approach did for the study of emotion was to help redefine what an emotion is. Emotions had been typically depicted as disruptive and debased, to be mastered by rational thought whenever possible (Calhoun & Solomon, 1984; Keltner & Gross, 1999). Among scientists, emotions were most often defined, implicitly or explicitly, in terms of specific response components—appraisal themes, action tendencies, nonverbal displays, particular subjective states or feelings, or autonomic nervous system profiles (Calhoun & Solomon, 1984). Evolutionary accounts, in contrast, define emotions in terms of functions that enable the individual to respond effectively to environmental challenges and opportunities. Anger is more than just a specific family of facial expressions or patterns of neural activation; it is a set of coordinated responses that help restore just relations. Embarrassment is more than the blush or the pronounced desire to hide; it is a form of appeasement. Emotions have the hallmarks of adaptations: They are efficient, coordinated responses that help organisms to reproduce, to protect offspring, to maintain cooperative alliances, and to avoid physical threats (Ekman, 1992; Levenson, 1999; Oatley & Jenkins, 1992; Oatley & Johnson-Laird, 1987; Simpson & Kenrick, 1998; Tooby & Cosmides, 1990).

This emphasis on function has shaped the field of emotion in several ways. It has broadened existing taxonomies of emotion, in particular directing researchers to the systematic study of several more "social" emotions such as compassion, gratitude, love, and awe (e.g., Eisenberg et al., 1989; Hazan & Shaver, 1987; Keltner & Haidt, 2003; McCullough, Kilpatrick, Emmons, & Larson, 2001). It has led appraisal researchers to engage in problem analyses for the different emotions (e.g., Tooby & Cosmides, 1990), articulating how each emotion is tailored to a prototypical challenge for survival or reproduction (e.g., Barrett & Campos, 1987; Ekman, 1992; Frijda, 1988; Keltner & Haidt, 2001; Lazarus, 1991). A functional emphasis also sheds light on an array of specific findings by linking particular components of an emotional response to particular evolutionary problems and opportunities. For example, anger is associated with enhanced distribution of blood to the hands, whereas fear involves less blood flow to the periphery (Levenson, 1992). This finding only makes sense when one considers what is needed to fight an enemy vs. escaping an attack with minimal loss of blood.

Not every instance of an emotion will reveal the functions it evolved to serve. Particular occurrences of fear, embarrassment, or anger may lead to maladaptive behavior, poorly tailored to the demands of the immediate context, and false positives (e.g., chronic shame for a disability, attachment to a security blanket) are quite common. An evolutionary approach does not demand that every emotional response be explained in terms of survival and reproductive fitness. Indeed, many evolved behaviors, functional in the appropriate context, can be elicited as a false positive by a similar but inappropriate stimulus, or can be dysfunctional in certain situations (Rose, 1998; Tomkins, 1984). Thus, it is not necessary to articulate the fitness value of human responses to kittens and puppies in order to demonstrate the evolutionary value of compassion. It is more likely that nurturant responses toward one's own young and young kin are selected for, and that biological kin recognition systems are far from perfect (Rose, 1998; Tomkins, 1984). An evolutionary approach looks for ways that, on average, emotions brought individuals reliable, specific benefits within the Environment of Evolutionary Adaptedness (EEA; Tooby & Cosmides, 1990).

Emotions Ultimately Enhance Reproductive Fitness

A second effect of an evolutionary approach has been to highlight a certain kind of answer to the question, "why do we have emotions?" The question "why?" is not exclusive to evolutionary theory—social constructivists also agree that emotions are best understood in terms of function in a given society (Oatley, 1993). From an evolutionary perspective, however, the question "why?" does not ask about the reasons a person has for a particular emotion at a specific moment in time, or even in a specific culture. Instead, evolutionary approaches ask about the systematic, beneficial consequences of emotion, in terms of enhanced survival and reproduction rates of the individual, offspring, and related kin, given the physical and social conditions of the EEA (Darwin, 1872/1965; Eibl-Eibesfeldt, 1989; Ekman, 1992; Krebs & Davies, 1993; Öhman, 1986; Plutchik, 1980; Tooby & Cosmides, 1992).

Social functionalist approaches to emotion look closely at opportunities to enhance reproductive fitness. In the last 30 years, evolutionary theorists have uncovered the profoundly social nature of human gene replication and individual survival (Cosmides & Tooby, 1992; Cronin, 1991; Eibl-Eibesfeldt, 1989; Hrdy, 1999; Sober & Wilson, 1998; de Waal, 1996). As we shall see, ultrasociality introduces a host of new opportunities and challenges for fitness, and emotions help us respond to many of these in ways that enhance reproductive success. People select mates, reproduce, raise offspring, avoid predation, gather food, and stay warm in complex, long-term relationships (Buss, 1989, 1994; Hrdy, 1999). Emotions are a critical part of developing and maintaining these bonds.

A social functional approach recognizes that certain emotions, such as fear, embarrassment, or guilt, help the individual respond adaptively to threats in the social environment. At the same time, the social functional approach helps remedy a long-standing bias in the emotion literature—the emphasis on negative emotions and inadequate specification of the emergence of positive emotions in the course of evolution (Shiota, Keltner, & John, in press). The assumption that environmental opportunities are less important than threats in determining fitness is common, but most likely a misguided assumption. The immediate costs of missing an opportunity may not be as great as the immediate costs of ignoring a threat to life and limb. Still, small differences in reproductive performance, such as those caused by differential response to opportunities, have great impact over time— fitness differentials of 1% can account for all of evolution throughout Earth's history (Ehrlich, 2000). In our more detailed analysis below, we shall see that a social functional approach to emotion identifies the evolutionary functions of several positive emotions.

Emotions Enable Social Commitments

Exactly how do emotions contribute to the array of human relationships that make up human ultrasociality? We have found a useful answer in commitment-based analyses of emotion and relationships (Frank, 1988; Gonzaga, Keltner, Londahl, & Smith, 2001, 2001; Nesse, 1990). The long-term relationships so crucial to our survival—pair bonding, parent–child bonds, cooperative alliances, group memberships—often require that individuals devote costly resources to others, and avoid self-interested behaviors that could harm social partners. Emotions help solve these commitment-related problems in two critical ways. First, emotions motivate courses of action that enhance long-term bonds, such as spousal commitment and reciprocal kindness. Emotions also serve as signals to others of long-term commitment. For example, displays of love and gratitude are reliable, sought after indicators of commitment to marital bonds and cooperative alliances, respectively.

In Table 6.1, we summarize some key social functions served by several emotions within significant relationships. In reviewing this table, it is important to keep in mind that it does not summarize all the adaptive problems humans faced in the EEA, but only some problems theorists have identified in considering emotion from an evolutionary perspective. It is also important to note that emotions most certainly have served other functions than those presented in Table 6.1. For example, anger most clearly serves important functions within reproductive relations and hierarchical relations. Compassion no doubt plays an important role in promoting cooperative relations among nonkin (e.g., Frank, 1988). The table simply lists single functions for the different emotions for illustrative purposes.

In our classification outlined in Table 6.1, emotions help to solve two kinds of social problems. On the level of intimate social interaction, evolutionary and attachment theorists have proposed that emotions address *problems of reproduction*, which include procreation and the raising of offspring to the age of reproduction (Bowlby, 1979; Shaver, Morgan, & Wu, 1996). Sexual *desire* facilitates the identification of promising sexual partners and the establishment of reproductive relations, while *love* is one component of psychological attachment between romantic partners, or pair bonding (Buss & Schmidt, 1993; Diamond, 2003; Ellis & Malamuth, 2004; Gonzaga et al., 2001; Hazan & Shaver, 1987; Shiota et al., in press). These emotions involve sensitivities to cues related to potential mate value, including beauty, fertility, chastity, social status, and character (Buss, 1994), expressive behaviors that signal interest and commitment (Frank, 1988; Gonzaga

TABLE 6.1   A Taxonomy of Opportunities and Problems, and the Functional Systems and Emotions that Solve Them

Problem	Functional Systems	Emotions	Specific Functions
Problems of Reproduction			
Finding a mate	Sex	Desire	Increase likelihood of sexual contact
	Attachment	Love	Commit to long-term bond
Keeping mate	Mate protection	Jealousy	Protect mate from rivals
Protecting offspring	attachment	Love	Increase bond between parent, offspring
	Caregiving	Compassion	Reduce distress of vulnerable individuals
Problems of Group Governance			
Cooperation	Reciprocal altruism	Gratitude	Signal, reward cooperative bond
		Guilt	Repair own transgression of reciprocity
		Anger	Motivate other to repair transgression
		Envy	Reduce unfair differences in equality
Group organization	Dominance hierarchy	Pride	Display high status
		Shame	Display reduced status
		Embarrassment	Pacify likely aggressor
		Contempt	Reduce another's status
		Awe	Endow entity greater than self with status
		Disgust	Avoidance of group members who violate cultural values

et al., 2001), and hormonal and autonomic responses that facilitate sexual behavior (Diamond, 2003). *Jealousy* motivates one to protect a mate from poaching, preserving both the mate's investment in current offspring and the opportunity to reproduce with the mate in the future (Buss & Schmidt, 1993). Love, as one component of psychological attachment, also motivates young and vulnerable offspring to stay close to protective adults. A complementary emotion, *compassion*, motivates parents to nurture and protect offspring (Shiota, Campos, Keltner, & Hertenstein, 2004).

The *problem of cooperation* lies at the heart of ultrasociality. There are many evolutionary advantages to cooperation, including reducing chance-based variance in finding food, and massive increases in productivity due to division of labor and specialization. *Gratitude* at others' altruistic acts is a signal that one recognizes the value of a benefit received and intends to repay in some form in the future (Trivers, 1971). However, unconditional cooperation is readily exploited, so humans do best when they reciprocate both cooperative and aggressive acts (Trivers, 1971). Several emotions signal when cooperative reciprocity has been violated, and motivate reparative behavior (de Waal, 1996; Frank, 1988; Nesse, 1990; Trivers, 1971). *Guilt* occurs following one's own violations of reciprocity and is expressed in apologetic, remedial behavior (Keltner & Buswell, 1996; Tangney, 1992). *Anger* motivates one to punish other individuals who have violated rules of reciprocity (Lerner, Goldberg, & Tetlock, 1998). *Envy* motivates individuals to derogate others whose favorable status is unjustified, thus preserving equal relations (Fiske, 1991).

Cooperation at the large group level requires complex distribution of labor and resources, such as food, territory, and mating opportunities; the social hierarchy provides a useful heuristic for this process (de Waal, 1986, 1988; Fiske, 1991; Keltner et al., 2003). The establishment and negotiation of status hierarchies is in part accomplished by emotions related to dominance and submission (de Waal, 1996; Öhman, 1986). *Pride* is experienced and displayed by individuals who have accomplished some socially valued task, and it projects the expectation of increased social status (Tiedens, Ellsworth, & Mesquita, 2000; Tracy & Robins, 2004). *Embarrassment* and *shame* appease dominant individuals and signal submissiveness (Keltner & Buswell, 1996; Miller & Leary, 1992). *Contempt* is defined by feelings of superiority and dominance vis-à-vis inferior others. *Awe* is experienced when one senses the presence of an entity greater than the self; it can be elicited by others who have displayed remarkable power or ability, and it endows these individuals with respect and authority (Fiske, 1991; Keltner & Haidt, 2003; Weber, 1957).

This social functional approach, rooted in recent evolutionary insights, reveals the ultrasocial nature of emotions. Once thought to be largely intrapsychic phenomena—patterns of autonomic response, or subjective experiences expressed in language—emotions are now widely studied in terms of their social functions.

The Functions of Emotions Depend on the Level of Analysis

How does one ascertain the social functions of emotions? Do all outcomes of a particular emotion speak to the social functions of that emotion? No. We have proposed that the social functions of emotions can be classified at four levels of analysis, and offered a list of the kinds of functions characteristic of each level (Keltner & Haidt, 1999; see also Averill, 1980; Frijda & Mesquita, 1994 for other approaches). Evolutionary approaches to emotion have tended to focus on the two lower levels, at which the individual or the dyad is the unit of analysis, whereas social construction approaches have tended to focus on the two higher levels, at which the group or the culture is the unit of analysis. We believe that keeping these four levels in mind is the key to reconciling the conflicting conclusions of evolutionary theorists and social constructionists. In Table 6.2, we summarize various claims about the different functions of emotion, working at these four levels of analysis. As we will try to show, the characteristics that make emotions functional at the individual and dyadic levels appear to be fairly constant across cultures, whereas the social functions of emotions at the group and cultural levels seem to be quite variable. We also

TABLE 6.2   Functions of Emotion at Four Levels of Analysis

Individual	Inform individual of problems/opportunities
	Prepare the individual for action
Dyadic	Knowledge of others' mental states
	Reward or punish prior action
	Evoke complementary or reciprocal
	behavior
Group	Define group boundaries and members
	Define group roles and identities
	Motivate collective action
Culture	Define cultural identity
	Identify norms and values
	Reify cultural ideologies and power
	structures

assume, like others (e.g., Rozin, 1996), that emotions evolved by serving adaptive functions for individuals. Once in place, these emotion-related systems and their outputs may have been recruited to serve or facilitate other higher order functions, which may or may not have been relevant to evolution.

At the individual level of analysis, researchers focus on emotion-specific changes in experience, cognition, and physiology (Clore, 1992, 1994; Clore, Gasper, & Garvin, 2001; Davidson, Pizzagalli, Nitschke, & Kalin, 2003; LeDoux, 1996; Levenson, 1992; Schwarz, 1990). At this level of analysis, emotions are thought to inform the individual about specific social events or conditions, typically those presenting a significant opportunity or threat (Campos, Campos, & Barrett, 1989; Lerner & Keltner, 2001; Lowenstein & Lerner, 2003; Schwarz, 1990). Emotions, in particular their physiological and motivational components, are also thought to prepare the individual for action in his or her best interest (e.g., Frijda, Kuipers, & ter Schure, 1989; Levenson, 1999; Russell, 1995). As one illustration, anger-related changes in sympathetic activation (Levenson, Ekman, Heider, & Friesen, 1992) and frontal activation asymmetry (Harmon-Jones, Sigelman, Bohlig, & Harmon-Jones, 2003) enable the individual to engage in aggressive, approach-related behaviors that remove sources of injustice.

At the dyadic level of analysis, the focus is on communication of emotion through facial, vocal, and postural channels (Cohn & Tronick, 1983; Ekman, 1992; Juslin & Laukka, 2003; Keltner et al., 2003; Öhman & Dimberg, 1996; Scherer, 1986; Scherer, Johnstone, & Klasmeyer, 2003). At this level of analysis, emotions help solve the "other mind" problem, communicating information about current emotions, intentions, and dispositions to conspecifics (Ekman, 1993; Fridlund, 1992; Keltner et al., 2003). Emotional communication evokes complementary and reciprocal emotions in others that help individuals respond to significant social events (Dimberg & Öhman, 1996; Keltner & Kring, 1998).

At the group level of analysis, researchers ask how emotions help collectives of interacting individuals meet their shared goals (Clark, 1990; Collins, 1990;

de Waal, 1996; Durkheim, 1912/1954). By studying role-related implications of emotions, researchers have found that emotions help define group members and negotiate group-related roles and statuses (e.g., Clark, 1990; Collins, 1990). For example, several cultures have a word that describes both a feeling, related to shame, embarrassment, and gratitude, and a deferential action directed at high status individuals ("lajya" and "hasham"; see below). The experience and display of this emotion is embedded in the recognition of one's place in a social hierarchy. The individual experience of emotion is thought to help each group member engage in collective goal-directed behavior, thereby benefiting the entire group.

At the cultural level of analysis, researchers have focused on the shaping of emotions by historical factors, and on the embedding of emotions in cultural institutions, practices, norms, and discourse (Abu-Lughod & Lutz, 1990). Emotions at this level of analysis help individuals assume cultural identities. Embarrassment (Goffman, 1967) motivates conformity and the proper playing of one's roles, while socio-moral *disgust* motivates the avoidance and shunning of people who violate key values within a culture (Rozin, Haidt, & McCauley, 2000). Emotions embedded in family conflicts, parental reactions, and socialization practices help children learn the norms and values of their culture (Bretherton, Fritz, Zahn-Waxler, & Ridgeway, 1986; Dunn & Munn, 1985; Shweder, Mahapatra, & Miller, 1987; White, 1993). Emotions interpreted through the lens of cultural values may also reify cultural ideologies and power structures (e.g., Hochschild, 1990). Much as at the group level, the selective experience and expression of emotion for certain groups justifies their position within a culture. Drawing on stereotypes of the emotions of subordinated groups, for example, Lutz (1990) has argued that cultural discourses about female emotionality relegate women to positions of subordinate status.

Emotions, then, serve different kinds of functions at each of these four levels of analysis. They inform and orient the individual, coordinate dyadic interactions, signal group identities and values, and transmit culture-related practices, identities, and ideologies. A single emotion may have multiple functions, depending on the level of analysis one considers. A brief episode of embarrassment, for example, can inform the individual of transgressions to avoid, signal others a sense of remorse for the transgression, evoking forgiveness, communicate the individual's position within a group, and convey commitments to cultural mores and standards. This multi-level analysis of the functions of emotions helps address certain problems. Most notably, conflicts between evolutionary and cultural approaches to emotion have often arisen because of arguments over the "real" function of some emotion. From a social functional approach, this is unnecessary, for emotions are expected to serve multiple functions.

Our analysis also draws attention to the ways that emotions can be put to new uses. Complex adaptations of morphology and behavior, such as bipedalism and altruism, often have been driven by multiple functions (Ehrlich, 2000). Selection does not identify a single function as the basis for preserving or eliminating a trait. Emotions that serve one function in one evolutionary context may serve a different fitness-enhancing function in a different context. The distaste humans have for noxious and potentially poisonous foods is put to use in our moral repulsion of impure actions, presumably to help group members abide by moral principles (Rozin et al., 2000). Thus, "exaptation" or "preadaptation" should always be considered as a possible explanation when multiple functions are observed for a single emotion (Ehrlich, 2000; Gould, 1991).

EMPIRICAL INSIGHTS GENERATED BY A SOCIAL-FUNCTIONAL APPROACH TO EMOTIONS

The social-functional approach to emotion has facilitated a number of substantial theoretical developments in social, personality, and clinical psychology. Over the last 20 years, emotions and their social effects have attained a central position in the explanation of several important psychological phenomena. Here we describe three examples of this development.

Emotional Experience as Social-Moral Intuition

Early studies of emotion and cognition revealed that momentary affective states could profoundly influence all sorts of judgments, even regarding objects unrelated to the elicitor of the affect (Forgas, 1995). Momentary affect has been shown to influence judgments of overall life satisfaction (Schwarz & Clore, 1983), political satisfaction, marital satisfaction, punitive judgments (Lerner et al., 1998; Weiner, Graham, & Reyna, 1997), the sense of justice (Keltner et al., 1993), attributional processes (Forgas, 1998), stereotyping (Bodenhausen, Kramer, & Susser, 1994), and perceptions of risk and certainty (Lerner & Keltner, 2001). These studies have convincingly documented that evanescent and specific emotions can guide cognitive processes to a substantial degree (Clore et al., 2001; Forgas, 1995; Schwarz, 1990).

Evolutionary accounts of emotion have helped guide the interpretation of these findings and pushed the theory one step further, contending that many emotions act as social-moral intuitions (Haidt, 2001; McCullough et al., 2001). Fast, automatic, involuntary experiences of specific emotions, imbued with motivational energy, provide gut feelings about right and wrong, virtue, one's social station, and punishment, without the need for elaborate calculation at the conscious level (Campos et al., 1989; Greene & Haidt, 2002; Haidt, 2003; Rozin et al., 2000).

Guided by this view of emotional experience, empirical studies have documented that distinct emotions map onto different domains of moral judgment. The experience of anger correlates with judgments of violated rights, disgust with violations of purity, contempt with violations of duties and obligations, and sympathy with perception of harm to others (Eisenberg et al., 1989; Haidt, 2003; Rozin, Lowery, Imada, & Haidt, 1999; Vasquez, Keltner, Ebenbach, & Banaszynski, 2001). Emotions serve as guides to specific relationships: The experience of love correlates with other measures of long-term commitment (Gonzaga et al., 2001); and the experience of embarrassment is negatively correlated with social status (Keltner, Young, Oemig, Heerey, & Monarch, 1998). Within the realm of punitive judgment, anger and sympathy are powerful determinants of preferred forms of punishment toward criminal defendants (Weiner et al., 1997), social actors (Lerner et al., 1998), and groups or nations in conflict with one's own group. Once thought to be disruptive and irrational, emotional experience is now viewed as a wellspring of social-moral intuitions. By this view, emotional experience guides moral judgment, assessments of current relationships, and preferences for punitive action in ways that contribute to the stability of the group.

Emotions Coordinate Social Interaction

Emotional expression was once viewed primarily as a readout of the individual's internal state. More recent theories, grounded in the social functional approach, have brought into focus how emotional expression coordinates social interactions—a perspective consistent with claims that communicative behaviors involved in sending messages have co-evolved with behaviors involved in receiving them (Eibl-Eibesfeldt, 1989; Hauser, 1996). Thus, one individual's emotional expression serves as a "social affordance," which evokes "prepared" responses in others (e.g., Öhman & Dimberg, 1978). Anger, for example, might have evolved to elicit fear-related responses and the inhibition of inappropriate action; distress calls might have evolved to elicit sympathetic responses in observers.

This evolutionary approach to emotional expression has facilitated several new insights into human emotional communication via facial muscle movements (Keltner et al., 2003), vocalization (Juslin & Laukka, 2003, Scherer et al., 2003), posture, and touch (Hertenstein, 2002). A first generalization to emerge from this work is that emotional expressions coordinate rapidly shifting social interactions. Emotional displays communicate information about the individual's emotional state (Ekman, 1993; Scherer, 1986), but in so doing they convey critical information about the individual's social intentions—whether to strike or flee, offer comfort or play (Fridlund, 1992). With this information, social partners can make better-informed choices about how to behave in the interaction.

Emotional expressions also communicate information about one's relational status vis-à-vis the target of the expression (Keltner, 1995; Tiedens, Ellsworth, & Mesquita, 2000). For example, emotional expressions serve as signals of commitment to important long-term relationships (see also Frank, 1988). Emotional expression conveys information about objects and events in the social environment as well (e.g., Mineka & Cook, 1993). Emotional displays evoke specific, complementary responses from observers—for example, anger evokes fear (Dimberg & Öhman, 1996), whereas distress evokes sympathy and aid (Eisenberg et al., 1989). When viewed as a unit, these exchanges of complementary emotions can enhance the stability and interdependence of the dyad. Through these processes, emotional communication helps individuals in relationships—parent and child, potential mates—respond to the demands and opportunities of their social environment. Thus, emotional expressions are basic elements of social interaction, from flirtatious exchanges to greeting rituals.

To the extent that emotional communication coordinates social interactions, individuals with deficits in the generation or perception of emotional messages should experience pronounced difficulties in social relationships. This claim, entirely in keeping with a social-functional view of emotion, has generated dozens of studies on different emotional disorders (for partial review, see Keltner & Kring, 1998). Two generalizations are emerging in this new literature on emotion and psychopathology.

First, individuals with deficits in emotional expression experience disrupted social relationships, because they provide others with less information about their mental states and fewer incentives for rewarding interactions. Thus, depressed individuals show fewer expressions of positive emotion, which produces difficulties in intimate relationships (Keltner & Kring, 1998). Depressed mothers, for example, show fewer rewarding smiles to their children, and their parent–child interactions are characterized by greater anxiety, conflict, and disorganization (Field, Healy, Goldstein, Guthertz, 1990).

Second, deficits in the perception of emotion should likewise prove problematic to relationships. For example, several studies have found that high functioning autistic children have difficulty reading the emotions of others (Heerey, Capps, & Keltner, 2003). This may in part contribute to their well-documented difficulties with close relationships.

Individual Differences in Emotion Reveal Functions of Emotion

Many individual differences in personality reflect differences in emotionality. Children vary, starting as early as 2 years of age, in how fearful, warm, or enthusiastic they are (Caspi, Bem, & Elder, 1987; Kagan, Arcus, & Snidman, 1993). Adult personality traits, most notably extraversion, agreeableness, and neuroticism, have important emotional correlates (Gross, Sutton, & Ketelaar, 1998; Larsen & Ketelaar, 1989; Watson & Clark, 1992), suggesting that emotional dispositions are a core part of personality and identity (Keltner, 2003; Malatesta, 1990).

Within a social functionalist approach, individual differences in emotion can be thought of as variation in evolutionarily significant strategies for navigating the social environment (Buss, 1987). Individual differences in emotion shape individuals' selective attention to features of complex situations, endowing them with particular, idiosyncratic meaning. Anxious individuals, for example, perceive more threat and risk in situations, whereas anger prone and cheerful individuals perceive less danger (Lerner & Keltner, 2001). Characteristic emotional experiences and displays also shape one's environment, evoking consistent responses from others and creating or closing off various kinds of opportunities for the individual. For example, people prone to positive emotional expressivity evoke more positive evaluations in others, with highly fitness-relevant implications for social and material success (Harker & Keltner, 2001). A social-functional approach to emotion allows us to propose and test specific links between dispositional experience of a given emotion and long-term life outcomes in several domains.

For example, to the extent that self-conscious emotions serve an appeasement function, prompting forgiveness in the aftermath of social transgressions and motivating adherence to group norms and morals, deficits in self-conscious emotion should relate to the tendency to fail to adhere to social and moral standards. Several recent findings lend credence to this claim. Juvenile delinquents are less likely to display embarrassment than control children in a failure-related context

(Keltner, Moffitt, & Stouthamer-Loeber, 1995). Patients with damage to the orbitofrontal cortex, who are prone to antisocial behavior, showed little embarrassment when teasing a confederate in an inappropriate fashion (Beer, Heerey, Keltner, Knight, & Scabini, 2003). In Blair's work on homicidal sociopaths, these patients showed little physiological reaction to others' appeasement displays. This may be part of a breakdown in a violence inhibition mechanism—sociopaths fail to detect and respond to others' attempts to short-circuit aggressive interactions (Blair, Jones, Clark, & Smith, 1997).

Similar evidence has been documented in studies of the lives of anger-prone individuals. Caspi, Elder, and Bem (1987) found that the tendency to express uncontrolled anger in early childhood (as assessed by parental reports of frequent, severe temper tantrums) later predicted the broader trait of ill temperedness, which showed considerable stability across the life span. Furthermore, this childhood expressive tendency predicted several negative life outcomes, including lower educational attainment, lower status jobs, lower military rank, erratic work patterns, and divorce. These studies document a spiraling pattern, where initial emotion dispositions evoke reactions from the social environment that reinforce the dispositions, leading to an expanding range of life consequences. Hypotheses about the social functions of an emotion allow us to predict what life outcomes might be associated with high or low dispositional experience of that emotion, and data regarding correlates of dispositional emotion can likewise inform theories about function (Keltner & Gross, 1999).

EMOTIONS ARE SHARED WITH OTHER PRIMATES YET HUMAN EMOTIONALITY IS UNIQUE

Anyone who owns a dog can see the emotions involved in attachment to caregivers at work in a nonprimate—distress and a cessation of play when left alone, and joy coupled with exuberant play upon one's return home. Those who work with chimpanzees and bonobos (e.g., de Waal, 1996; de Waal & Lanting, 1997) report an even greater and more differentiated emotional repertoire, with many similarities to that of human beings. While some primatologists are wary of anthropomorphizing, de Waal (1996) points out that when discussing two species as closely related as humans and chimpanzees, the default assumption should be continuity, and the burden of proof should fall on those who want to prove that human beings are unique.

We take as a premise the assumption that the foundation of human emotionality was laid down throughout the long course of mammalian and primate evolution. This premise has had tremendous impact on the methods used to study emotion, by opening the door to research with animal models (e.g., Preuschoft, 1992; Redican, 1975; Van Hooff, 1972). For example, work with rodents and primates has guided theory and research on human reward-related positive affect (e.g., Nestler, 1992; Schultz, Tremblay, & Hollerman, 2003), on the role of endogenous opiate activity in attachment to caregivers and in separation distress (e.g., Kalin, Shelton, & Barksdale, 1989),and on the neurological basis of fear (LeDoux, 1996).

Even more complex and subtle emotions, such as embarrassment, appear to have deep roots in adaptations to life in dominance hierarchies (Keltner & Buswell, 1997). Despite this overall pattern of conservation, however, a hallmark of complex systems is that small changes in structure can trigger large and wide-ranging changes in functional phenotype. In this section we describe how three specific changes unique to the human species may have given rise to drastic transformation in emotional experience.

Humans have Much Larger Frontal Cortexes than do Other Primates

The most important difference between humans and other species, providing the foundation for all other differences, is that the human brain more than doubled in size over the last 2.5 million years (Leakey, 1994). Most of this growth occurred in the frontal cortex, and one of the most expanded areas is in areas of the prefrontal cortex, the orbito-frontal and ventro-medial cortex (Brodman areas 9 and 10; see Semendeferi, Armstrong, Schleicher, Zilles, & Van Hoesen, 2001). This region of the brain is profoundly involved in the interface between higher-level cognitive processes and more primitive emotion systems. The frontal cortex is heavily implicated in mental representation, theory of mind, inhibition of behavior, and the integration of planning and memory with affective reactions (Beer et al., 2003; Rolls, 2000). Humans are able to generate emotional responses to fantasies, memories, and abstract stimulus characteristics, respond emotionally to the perceived internal states of others, modulate and re-direct dominant emotional action tendencies, and use emotion as a source of information in complex social decision-making tasks, all because of processes that appear mediated by this newly developed region of the brain.

Growth in the prefrontal cortex may have enabled development of the moral emotions, which in turn made possible human ultrasociality. In fMRI studies, increased activity in the prefrontal cortex has been observed as participants complete moral judgment tasks, particularly those that involve emotion (Greene, Sommerville, Nystrom, Darley, & Cohen, 2001), and these areas are less active in psychopaths, who lack moral emotions. When this region is damaged, patients lose the ability to integrate feeling information into their decision-making, or to take the emotional implications (to the self or others) of behaviors into account; massive impairment of professional competence and personal relationships typically follow (Damasio, 1994; for a review see Greene & Haidt, 2002).

Humans have Language

Another new cognitive ability that has shaped the way humans experience and express emotion is language. Language, combined with the frontally mediated representational abilities mentioned above, allows for the transmission of emotion in narrative processes like storytelling and gossip (Oatley, 2003). Whereas other animals can (presumably) only feel emotions linked to immediate, ongoing events, humans spend their days triggering in themselves and each other whatever emotions they desire. This process allows emotions to be exploited for group- and cultural-level social functions, as when narratives about cultural heroes are crafted to trigger admiration, gratitude, and pride, thereby strengthening group loyalties and teaching core cultural values. Recent analyses of "urban legends" show that the most successful ones, those most widely transmitted, are those that trigger stronger emotions like disgust (Heath, Bell, & Sternberg, 2001).

Language also allows emotions to be applied to novel objects. Philosophers have long observed that the intentional object of an emotion—what the emotion is about—is quite specific compared to the object of moods. Emotions such as anger or compassion are prototypically reactions to specific individuals. But human linguistic and representational capacities make it easy to think about many different entities—one's self, family, school, ethnic group, or nation—as the intentional object of almost any emotion. This more *flexible extensivity* of human emotion allows for emotions to serve functions at the group and cultural level of analysis. Love for family, and the commitment behaviors and sense of obligation the emotion produces, can be extended to love of a larger collective.

Humans have Culture

The phrase "monkey see, monkey do" is charming, but misleading. Monkeys do very little true imitation, and even chimpanzees are bad at learning by direct copying (Richerson & Boyd, 2004). It is humans, with our cumulative and ever-developing cultures, who must learn the vast majority of our behavioral repertoire by emulating conspecifics (Richerson & Boyd, 2004). Only human beings have a hunger for role models, a motivation to seek out successful individuals, get close to them, and then copy their behavior.

This need to learn brings with it an opening for a new class of emotions. Henrich and Gil-White (2001) point out that prestige in human beings is not at all like dominance in other primates, which is regulated largely by feelings of fear and submission. Human beings may be unique in having the emotion of admiration, which makes people like and look up to an exemplary person, and want to maintain proximity to that person to maximize opportunities for learning (Algoe & Haidt, 2004; Henrich & Gil-White, 2001). Human beings are probably also unique in experiencing moral elevation, a pleasurable emotional response to virtuous acts, which motivates people to emulate the actor (Haidt, 2003). These positive moral emotions are unlikely to exist in animals that do not directly copy each other's behavior.

The central role of culture in human life also means that different societies may foster very different patterns of emotional experience and communication (Ekman, 1972; Russell, 1991; Shweder & Haidt, 2000). Societies typically "hypercognize" some emotions, giving them a central role in the social structure and encouraging their experience and display, while "hypocognizing" others, de-emphasizing or actively discouraging their experience and/or display (Levy, 1984). Hypercognized emotions are represented more often and in greater detail in a society's emotion lexicon, whereas the reverse is true for hypocognized emotions (Russell, 1991). As a result of these processes, emotions with largely universal characteristics at the individual and dyadic level of analysis may show tremendous cross-cultural variation at the group and cultural levels of analysis. We discuss this distinction in greater detail in the next section.

EMOTIONS ARE BOTH UNIVERSAL AND CULTURALLY VARIABLE

The issue of culture and emotion is in some ways like an optical illusion. Looked at in one way, emotions are obviously universal. One need only read about Cain's envy of Abel, or about Buddha's descriptions of the specific effects of anger and desire upon cognition, to conclude that emotions are the same wherever you go. On the other hand, anthropologists routinely describe cultures that seem to have unique emotions and unique emotional reactions. Furthermore, many of our cultural stereotypes are, in part, claims about emotional differences between groups (e.g., hot-blooded Latins vs. stolid Scandinavians). We believe a social functionalist view can help to resolve the illusion of incompatible perspectives into a single integrated understanding. The key idea is that one must be very specific about the emotion or emotional process being addressed, and about the level of analysis on which one is focused. We offer three principles for navigating your way through the current jungle of literature on emotion.

Expect Little Variation in Links among Functional Elements at the Individual and Dyadic Levels of Analysis

At the individual level of analysis, one views emotions as ways of connecting significant environmental events with preparation for an appropriate behavioral response (Levenson, 1992). This implies consistent correlation among multiple components of emotion episodes, including appraisals of the situation, central and autonomic nervous system changes, cognitive biases, motivations, facial expressions, and other evidence of action tendencies. Facial expressions of emotion, in turn, have powerful, predictable, and specific effects on the qualities of dyadic interaction (as discussed earlier).

Most explicit cross-cultural research on emotion has examined relationships among components (e.g., appraisals, physiological changes, facial expressions) at these two lower levels of analysis. Such studies have provided strong evidence that these variables are connected in similar ways across cultures (e.g., Ekman et al., 1992; Frijda et al., 1989; Levenson et al., Mauro, Sato, & Tucker, 1992; Scherer & Walbott, 1994). The best-known research on emotion has examined how facial expressions are understood, by mapping them either to emotion words or to emotion-eliciting situations (e.g., Ekman, Friesen, & Ellsworth, 1982). These results have led many theorists to conclude that facial expressions of happiness, sadness, anger, fear, disgust, and surprise are rooted at least partly in human nature (Ekman, 1994; Elfenbein & Ambady, 2002; Haidt & Keltner, 1999), although these results are open to some alternative interpretations (Russell, 1994).

In our own study (Haidt & Keltner, 1999) we set out to test whether facial expressions and situational elicitors would be matched up similarly in India and the United States, bypassing many of the problems associated with the use of translated emotion words (Russell, 1994). We were surprised to find a very high degree of similarity, not just for the initial "Ekman 6" prototype displays (fear, anger, sadness, disgust, happiness, and surprise) but also for contempt and embarrassment expressions. We also found that, even though the Oriya language (of Eastern India) does not separate shame and embarrassment lexically, Oriya speakers in our study consistently described two different kinds of "lajya" when discussing two distinct facial expressions that Americans had labeled using these words. Two of our main conclusions from this study were that: (1) the understanding of facial expressions is perhaps the worst place to look for cultural differences; and (2) differences in the emotion lexicon across cultures may not necessarily reflect differences in emotional experience.

To the extent that cultures do appear to differ in the relationships among facial expressions, emotion language, and situational elicitors, we believe that Ekman's (1972) Neuro-Cultural Theory of facial expressions of emotion accounts well for evidence of nonuniversality. This theory proposes that an innate "Facial Action Program" guides both the display and interpretation of prototypical emotional expressions, but also includes a role for cultural "display and feeling rules" for when certain emotions are encouraged or discouraged by a particular society. This distinction works quite well, provided that the analysis is limited to the main functional components discussed above, and to the individual and dyadic levels of analysis.

Distinguish Potential from Practice

To say that the connections among emotion episode components are for the most part universal does not mean that emotions are used and experienced in similar ways around the world. Mesquita (2001) recommends distinguishing between the "potential" for experience and the "practice" of emotional experience. Potential means asking this question: If you put people in a similar testing situation, are they capable of experiencing the hypothesized linkages among emotion components? Nearly all experimental work by psychologists has tested emotion potential, and has found a general picture of similarity, nearly always above chance levels and usually far above chance.

In contrast, "practice" refers to what actually happens in people's lives. Anthropologists tell us what happens on the ground, and people's day-to-day emotional experience is often radically different across cultures. Some cultures seem to value or at least permit public expressions of anger (e.g., the Ilongot chronicled by Rosaldo, 1980), while others work hard to suppress all such expressions (e.g., the Utku Eskimos described by Briggs, 1970). In some cultures (such as ours) shame is seen as a bad emotion; it is frowned upon as a socializing tool in public schools, and people go to therapy to get free of it. In more interdependent and hierarchically structured societies there is often a hypercognized emotion, combining elements of what we call shame, embarrassment, shyness, and modesty, which is highly valued when displayed by the lower-status person in an interaction (Abu-Lughod, 1986; Doi, 1973; Menon & Shweder, 1994.). According to Mesquita, Frijda, & Scherer (1997), "people from different cultures appear to be similar in their emotion potential, especially when this potential is described at a higher level of meaning. Yet, despite the similarities in basic elements of emotional life, concrete emotional realities in different cultures may widely vary."

A corollary of the "potential vs. practice" distinction is that the emotion lexicon of a language may be informative about practice, but not necessarily about potential. Cultures do vary substantially in how they carve up the domain of emotional experience into lexically encoded categories (Heider, 1991; Russell, 1991). But do these linguistic differences imply psychological differences? The old Sapir–Whorf hypothesis (Sapir, 1921; Whorf, 1956) was exciting because it suggested that the presence or absence of a word in a language was an externally measurable sign of psychological potential. People who lacked words to distinguish kinds of snow, or blue from green, or sadness from fear, might not perceive differences between such experiences.

However, current evidence suggests that the strong version of the Sapir–Whorf hypothesis is false (Hunt & Agnoli, 1991; Oatley, 1993). As a general rule, members of a society without a word for a particular emotional state readily understand the new term, once its context is explained. As Steven Pinker says about "schadenfreude," a German emotion word with no English translation: "When English-speakers hear the word Schadenfreude for the first time, their reaction is not, 'Let me see ... Pleasure in another's misfortunes ... What could that possibly be? I cannot grasp the concept; my language and culture have not provided me with such a category.' Their reaction is, 'You mean there's a word for it? Cool!'" (Pinker, 1997, p. 367).

Expect Extensive Differences at the Group and Cultural Levels of Analysis

The key to understanding—and even predicting—cultural differences in the practice of emotion is to move to the group and cultural levels of analysis. At these levels of analysis one examines the ways that emotions help to define social identity, identify norms and values, and negotiate and reinforce power structures—processes that differ dramatically from group to group and culture to culture. Many of these differences can be traced back to economic factors, so that agricultural societies, which require a high level of cooperation, organization, and interdependence, tend to be hierarchically organized, making extensive use of what Fiske (1992) calls "authority ranking" to structure social interactions. In contrast, hunter-gatherer societies that do not engage in agriculture (Boehm, 1999), and urban cultures built around trade tend to place a greater value on individual initiative and to make greater use of what Fiske (1992) calls "equality matching" to govern trades among equals.

Different emotions are recruited to reinforce these values and relational models, which find their clearest expression in group-level interactions. For example, hierarchically organized cultures seem to make extensive use of emotions related to shame/embarrassment and respect/deference to structure group interactions (Abu-Lughod, 1986; Kitayama, Markus, & Kurokawa, 2000). Social interactions within such cultures are likely to be permeated with and guided by these feelings, such as "lajya" in Orissa, India. These emotions help to foster a high degree of obedience to superiors, conformity to sex-role expectations, and interdependence with the other members of one's family, clan, village, or other groups. In contrast, the central dynamic in egalitarian cultures is not one of respect vs. disrespect; it is vigilance against the usurpation of power or resources (Boehm, 1999). Emotions of anger and envy play a much larger role in egalitarian cultures, as they help to regulate cooperation among equals and the ever-present threat of free-riding.

CONCLUSION

Evolutionary theory has given rise to the scientific study of emotion. In this article, we have attempted to synthesize evolutionary insights concerning emotion, with an eye toward articulating new trends in the study of emotion and resolutions to questions regarding the universality and cultural variability in emotion.

In the most general sense, evolutionary approaches to emotion have led to a radical redefinition of what emotions are. For years emotions were largely thought of as intrapsychic phenomena, often disruptive or problematic in their outcomes. In contrast, an evolutionary approach highlights the functions that emotions serve for the individual, dyad and group. Evolutionary approaches trace the origins of emotions back to reproduction- and survival-related problems that defined the group living of humans. And evolutionary approaches of the past 15 years have made the case for a more general function of emotions—that they motivate survival- and reproduction-enhancing commitments to other individuals.

This general framework has revealed new insights into emotion-related processes, like experience, facial expression, and temperament. Once thought of as ineffable or beyond study, emotional experience is now thought, thanks to evolutionary insights, to play a critical role in social-moral judgments. Once largely viewed as a readout of internal states, emotion-related communication in the face, voice, and touch is now thought of in terms of how these expressive behaviors coordinate the interactions of individuals in significant relationships. And individual differences in emotions are now studied as biologically based, functional strategies that guide the individual in interacting with the environment over the course of life.

A final theme of our chapter has been to integrate the insights of evolutionary theorists, who largely focus on emotion-related processes within the individual and the dyad, and cultural approaches that focus on how emotions shape and are shaped by group- and culture-related processes, like morals, values, roles, and identity. We contend that evolution has endowed humans with emotion-related systems that solve many of the problems of social living. These aspects of emotion—expressive behavior, physiological process—have parallels in the emotion-like behaviors of other species. Yet human emotion is also unique, and shaped by language, the large cortex of the human brain, and our capacity for culture. These processes give rise to many new facets and uses of emotion, including the capacity for emotion to fold into social rituals and to become elicited by culturally specific events and objects.

Evolutionary and cultural approaches to emotion once stood in bitter opposition to one another. The synthesis of these rich traditions, however, has led to a new view of emotions, one that situates emotions at the center of human social life.

REFERENCES

Abu-Lughod, L. (1986). *Veiled sentiments*. Berkeley: University of California Press.

Abu-Lughod, L., & Lutz, C. A. (1990). *Introduction to language and the politics of emotion*. New York: Cambridge University Press.

Algoe, S., & Haidt, J. (2004). *Witnessing excellence in action: The 'other-praising' emotions of elevation, gratitude, and admiration*. Unpublished manuscript, University of Virginia.

Averill, J. R. (1980). A constructionist view of emotion. In R. Plutchik & H. Kellerman (Eds.), *Emotion: Theory, research, and experience* (pp. 305–339). New York: Academic Press.

Barrett, K. C., & Campos, J. J. (1987). Perspectives on emotional development II: A functionalist approach to emotions. In J. D. Osofsky (Ed.), *Handbook of infant development* (2nd ed., pp. 558–578). New York: Wiley.

Beer, J., Heerey, E. A., Keltner, D., Knight, R., & Scabini, D. (2003). The regulatory function of self-conscious emotion: Insights from patients with orbitofrontal damage. *Journal of Personality and Social Psychology, 85*, 594–604.

Blair, R. J .R., Jones, L., Clark, F., & Smith, M. (1997). The psychopathic individual: A lack of responsiveness to distress cues. *Psychophysiology, 34*, 192–198.

Bodenhausen, G. V., Kramer, G. P., & Süsser, K. (1994). Happiness and stereotypic thinking in social judgment. *Journal of Personality and Social Psychology, 66*(4), 621–632.

Boehm, C. (1999). *Hierarchy in the forest: The evolution of egalitarian behavior*. Cambridge, MA: Harvard University Press.

Bowlby, J. (1979). *The making and breaking of affectional bonds*. London: Tavistock.

Bretherton, I., Fritz, J., Zahn-Waxler, C., & Ridgeway, D. (1986). Learning to talk about emotions: A functionalist perspective. *Child Development, 57*, 529–548.

Briggs, J. L. (1970). *Never in anger*. Cambridge, MA: Harvard University Press.

Buss, D. (1987). Selection, evocation, and manipulation. *Journal of Personality and Social Psychology, 53*, 1214–1221.

Buss, D. M. (1989). Sex differences in human mate preferences: Evolutionary hypotheses tested in 37 cultures. *Behavioral and Brain Sciences, 12*, 1–49.

Buss, D. M. (1994). *The evolution of desire: Strategies of human mating*. New York: Basic Books.

Buss, D. M., & Schmidt, D. P. (1993). Sexual strategies theory: An evolutionary perspective on human mating. *Psychological Review, 100*, 204–232.

Calhoun, C. & Solomon, R. (1984). What is an emotion. In C. Calhoun & R. Solomon (Eds.), *Readings in philosophical psychology*. New York: Oxford University Press.

Campbell, D. T. (1983). The two distinct routes beyond kin selection to ultrasociality: Implications for the humanities and social sciences. In D. Bridgeman (Ed.), *The nature of prococial development: Theories and strategies* (pp. 11–39). New York: Academic Press.

Campos, J. J., Campos, R. G., & Barrett, K. C. (1989). Emergent themes in the study of emotional development and emotion regulation. *Developmental Psychology, 25*, 394–402.

Caspi, A., Bem, D. J., & Elder, G. (1987). Moving against the world: Life-course patterns of explosive children. *Developmental Psychology, 23*(2), 308–313.

Clark, C. (1990). Emotions and the micropolitics in everyday life: Some patterns and paradoxes of "Place". In T. D. Kemper (Ed.), *Research agendas in the sociology of emotions* (pp. 305–334). Albany, NY: State University of New York Press.

Clore, G. (1994). Why emotions are felt. In P. Ekman & R. J. Davidson (Eds.), *The nature of emotion* (pp.103–111). New York: Cambridge University.

Clore, G. L. (1992). Cognitive phenomenology: Feelings and the construction of judgment. In L. L. Martin & A. Tesser (Eds.), *The construction of social judgments* (pp. 133–163). Hillsdale, NJ: Erlbaum.

Clore, G. L., Gasper, K., & Garvin, E. (2001). Affect as information. In J. P. Forgas (Ed.), *Handbook of affect and social cognition* (pp. 121–144). Nahwah, NJ: Erlbaum.

Cronin, H. (1991). *The ant and the peacock*. New York: Cambridge University Press.

Cohn, J. F., & Tronick, E. Z. (1983). Three month old infants' reactions to simulated maternal depression. *Child Development, 54*, 185–193.

Collins, R. C. (1990). Stratification, emotional energy, and the transient emotions. In T. D. Kemper (Ed.), *Research agendas in the sociology of emotions* (pp. 27–57). Albany, NY: The State University of New York Press.

Cosmides, L., & Tooby, J. (1992). Cognitive adaptations for social exchange. In J. H. Barkow, L. Cosmides, & J. Tooby (Eds.), *The adapted mind* (pp. 163–228). New York: Oxford University Press.

Damasio, A. R. (1994). *Descartes' error: Emotion, reason, and the human brain*. New York: Free Press.

Darwin, C. (1872/1965). *The expression of the emotions in man and other animals*. Chicago: University of Chicago Press.

Davidson, R. J., Pizzagalli, D., Nitschke, J. B., & Kalin, N. H. (2003). Parsing the subcomponents of emotion and disorders: Perspectives from affective neuroscience. In R. J. Davidson, K. Scherer, & H. H. Goldsmith (Eds.), *Handbook of affective science* (pp. 8–24). New York: Oxford University Press.

de Waal, F. B. M. (1986). The integration of dominance and social bonding in primates. *Quarterly Review of Biology, 61*, 459–479.

de Waal, F. B. M. (1988). The reconciled hierarchy. In M. R. A. Chance (Ed.), *Social fabrics of the mind* (pp. 105–136). Hillsdale, NJ: Erlbaum.

de Waal, F. (1996). *Good natured: The origins of right and wrong in humans and other animals*. Cambridge, MA: Harvard University Press.

de Waal, F., & Lanting, F. (1997). *Bonobo: The forgotten ape*. Berkeley, CA: University of California Press.

Diamond, L. M. (2003). What does sexual orientation orient?: A biobehavioral model distinguishing romantic love and sexual desire. *Psychological Review, 110*(1), 173–192.

Davidson, R. J., Pizzagalli, D., Nitschke, J. B., & Kalin, N. H. (2003). Parsing the subcomponents of emotion and disorders: Perspectives from affective neuroscience. In R. J. Davidson, K. Scherer, & H. H. Goldsmith (Eds.), *Handbook of Affective Science* (pp. 8—24). New York: Oxford University Press.

Doi, T. (1973). *The anatomy of dependence*. (J. Beste, Trans.). Tokyo: Kodansha.

Dunn, J. & Munn, P. (1985). Becoming a family member: Family conflict and the development of social understanding in the second year. *Child Development, 56*, 480–492.

Durkheim, E. (1954/1912). *The elementary forms of the religious life*. (J. W. Swain, Trans.) New York: The Free Press. (Original work published 1912)

Ehrlich, P. R. (2000). *Human natures: Genes, cultures, and the human prospect*. Washington, DC: Island Press/Shearwater Books.

Eibl-Eibesfeldt, I. (1989). *Human ethology*. New York: Aldine de Gruyter.

Eisenberg, N., Fabes, R. A., Miller, P. A., Fultz, J., Shell, R., Mathy, R. M., & Reno, R. R. (1989). Relation of sympathy and distress to prosocial behavior: A multi-method study. *Journal of Personality and Social Psychology, 57*, 55–66.

Ekman, P. (1972). Universals and cultural differences in facial expressions of emotion. In J. Cole (Ed.), *Nebraska Symposium on Motivation, 1971* (pp. 207–283). Lincoln: University of Nebraska Press.

Ekman, P. (1992). Are there basic emotions? *Psychological Review, 99*, 550–553.

Ekman, P. (1993). Facial expression and Emotion. *American Psychologist, 48*, 384–392.

Ekman, P., & Davidson, R. J. (1994). *The nature of emotion*. New York: Oxford University Press.

Ekman, P., Friesen, W. V., & Ellsworth, P. C. (1982). *Emotion in the human face*. Cambridge England: Cambridge University Press.

Elfenbein, H. A., & Ambady, N. (2002). On the universality and cultural specificity of emotion recognition: A meta-analysis. *Psychological Bulletin, 128*, 203–235.

Ellis, B. J., & Malamuth, N. M. (2000). Love and anger in romantic relationships: A discrete systems model. *Journal of Personality, 68*, 525–556.

Field, T., Healy, B., Goldstein, S. & Guthertz, M. (1990). Behavior-state matching and synchrony in mother-infant interactions of nondepressed versus depressed dyads. *Developmental Psychology, 26*, 7–14.

Fiske, A. P. (1991). *Structures of social life*. New York: Free Press.

Fiske, A. P. (1992). The four elementary forms of sociality: Framework for a unified theory of social relations. *Psychological Review, 99*, 689–723.

Forgas, J. P. (1995). Mood and judgment: The affect infusion model (AIM). *Psychological Bulletin, 117*, 39–66.

Forgas, J. P. (1998). On being happy and mistaken: Mood effects on the fundamental attribution error. *Journal of Personality and Social Psychology, 75*, 318–331.

Frank, R. H. (1988). *Passions within reason: The strategic role of the emotions*. New York: W. W. Norton & Co.

Fridlund, A. J. (1992). The behavioral ecology and sociality of human faces. *Review of Personality and Social Psychology, 13*, 90–121.

Frijda, N. (1988). The laws of emotion. *American Psychologist, 43*, 349–358.

Frijda, N. H., Kuipers, P., & ter Schure, E. (1989). Relations among emotion, appraisal, and action readiness. *Journal of Personality and Social Psychology, 57*, 212–228.

Frijda, N. H., & Mesquita, B. (1994). The social roles and functions of emotions. In S. Kitayama & H. Marcus (Eds.), *Emotion and culture: Empirical studies of mutual influenced* (pp. 51–87). Washington, DC: American Psychological Association.

Goffman, E. (1959). *The presentation of self in everyday life*. Oxford, England: Doubleday.

Gonzaga, G. C., Keltner, D., Londahl, E. A., & Smith, M. D. (2001). Love and the commitment problem in romantic relationships and friendship. *Journal of Personality and Social Psychology, 81*, 247–262.

Gould, S. J. (1991). Exaptation: A crucial tool for evolutionary psychology. *Journal of Social Issues, 47*, 43–65

Greene, J., & Haidt, J. (2002). How (and where) does moral judgment work? *Trends in Cognitive Sciences, 6*, 517–523.

Greene, J. D., Sommerville, R. B., Nystrom, L. E., Darley, J. M., & Cohen, J. D. (2001). An fMRI study of emotional engagement in moral judgment. *Science, 293*, 2105–2108.

Gross, J. J., Sutton, S. K., & Ketelaar, T. (1998). Relations between affect and personality: Support for the affect-level and affective-reactivity views. *Personality and Social Psychology Bulletin, 24,* 279.

Haidt, J. (2001). The emotional dog and its rational tail: A social intuitionist approach to moral judgment. *Psychological Review, 108,* 814–834.

Haidt, J. (2003). Elevation and the positive psychology of morality. In C. L. M. Keyes & J. Haidt (Eds.), *Flourishing: Positive psychology and the life well-lived* (pp. 275–289). Washington, DC: American Psychological Association.

Haidt, J. (2003). The moral emotions. In R. J. Davidson, K. R. Scherer & H. H. Goldsmith (Eds.), *Handbook of affective sciences* (pp. 852–870). Oxford, UK: Oxford University Press.

Haidt, J., & Keltner, D. (1999). Culture and facial expression: Open-ended methods find more faces and a gradient of recognition. *Cognition and Emotion, 13,* 225–266.

Harker, L. A., & Keltner, D. (2001). Expressions of positive emotion in women's college yearbook pictures and their relationship to personality and life outcomes across adulthood. *Journal of Personality and Social Psychology, 80,* 112–124.

Harmon-Jones, E., Sigelman, J. D., Bohlig, A., & Harmon-Jones, C. (2003). Anger, coping, and frontal cortical activity: The effect of coping potential on anger-induced left frontal activity. *Cognition and Emotion, 17,* 1–24.

Hauser, M. D. (1996). *The evolution of communication.* Cambridge, MA: MIT Press.

Hazan, C., & Shaver, P. R. (1987). Romantic love conceptualized as an attachment process. *Journal of Personality and Social Psychology, 52,* 511–524.

Heath, C., Bell, C., & Sternberg, E. (2001). Emotional selection in memes: The case of urban legends. *Journal of Personality & Social Psychology, 81,* 1028–1041.

Heerey, E. A., Keltner, D., & Capps, L. M. (2003). Making sense of self-conscious emotion: Linking theory of mind and emotion in children with autism. *Emotion, 3,* 394–400.

Heider, K. G. (1991). *Landscapes of emotion: Mapping three cultures of emotion in Indonesia.* Cambridge, England: Cambridge University Press.

Henrich, J., & Gil-White, F. J. (2001). The evolution of prestige: Freely conferred status as a mechanism for enhancing the benefits of cultural transmission. *Evolution and human behavior, 22,* 1–32.

Hertenstein, M. J. (2002). Touch: Its communicative functions in infancy. *Human Development, 45,* 70–94.

Hochschild, A. R. (1990). Ideology and emotion management. In T. D. Kemper (Ed.), *Research agendas in the sociology of emotions* (pp. 117–142). Albany, NY: The State University of New York Press.

Hrdy, S. B. (1999). *Mother Nature: Maternal instincts and how they shape the human species.* New York: Ballantine.

Hunt, E., & Agnoli, F. (1991). The Whorfian hypothesis: A cognitive psychology perspective. *Psychological Review, 98,* 377–389.

Izard, C. E. (1977). *Human emotions.* New York: Plenum Press.

Juslin, P. N., & Laukka, P. (2003). Communication of emotions in vocal expression and music performance: Different channels, same code? *Psychological Bulletin, 129,* 770–814.

Kagan, J., Arcus, D., & Snidman, N., (1993). The idea of temperament: Where do we go from here? In R. Plomin & G. E. McClearn (Eds.), *Nature, nurture, and psychology.* Washington, DC: American Psychological Association.

Kalin, N. H., Shelton, S. E., & Barksdale, C. M. (1989). Behavioral and physiologic effects of CRH administered to infant primates undergoing maternal separation. *Neuropsychopharmacology, 2,* 97–104.

Keltner, D. (1995). The signs of appeasement: Evidence for the distinct displays of embarrassment, amusement, and shame. *Journal of Personality and Social Psychology, 68,* 441–454.

Keltner, D. & Buswell, B. N. (1996). Evidence for the distinctness of embarrassment, shame, and guilt: A study of recalled antecedents and facial expressions of emotion. *Cognition and Emotion, 10,* 155–171.

Keltner, D., & Buswell, B. N. (1997). Embarrassment: Its distinct form and appeasement functions. *Psychological Bulletin, 122,* 250–270.

Keltner, D., Ekman, P., Gonzaga, G. C., & Beer, J. (2003). Facial expression of emotion. In R. Davidson, K. Scherer, & H. Goldsmith (Eds.), *Handbook of Affective Science* (pp. 415–432). London: Oxford University Press.

Keltner, D., Ellsworth, P. C., & Edwards, K. (1993). Beyond simple pessimism: Effects of sadness and anger on social perception. *Journal of Personality and Social Psychology, 64,* 740–752.

Keltner, D., & Gross, J. J. (1999). Functional accounts of emotions. *Cognition and Emotion, 13,* 467–480.

Keltner, D., Gruenfeld, D. H., & Anderson, C. (2003). Power, approach, and inhibition. *Psychologial Review, 110,* 265–284.

Keltner, D., & Haidt, J. (1999). Social functions of emotions at four levels of analysis. *Cognition and Emotion, 13,* 505–521.

Keltner, D., & Haidt, J. (2001). Social functions of emotions. In T. Mayne & G. Bonanno (Eds.), *Emotions: Current issues and future directions* (pp. 192–213). New York: Guilford.

Keltner, D., & Haidt, J. (2003). Approaching awe, a moral, spiritual, and aesthetic emotion. *Cognition and Emotion, 17,* 297–314.

Keltner, D., & Kring, A. M. (1998). Emotion, social function, and psychopathology. *Review of General Psychology, 2,* 320–342.

Keltner, D., Moffitt, T., & Stouthamer-Loeber, M. (1995). Facial expressions of emotion and psychopathology in adolescent boys. *Journal of Abnormal Psychology, 104,* 644–652.

Keltner, D., Young, R. C., Oemig, C., Heerey, E., & Monarch, N. D. (1998). Teasing in hierarchical and intimate relations. *Journal of Personality and Social Psychology, 75,* 1231–1247.

Kitayama, S., Markus, H. R., & Kurokawa, M. (2000). Culture, emotion, and well-being: Good feelings in Japan and the United States. *Cognition and Emotion, 14,* 93–124.

Krebs, J. R., & Davies, N. B. (1993). *An introduction to behavioural ecology.* Oxford, UK: Blackwell.

Larsen, R. J., & Ketelaar, T. (1989). Extraversion, neuroticism, and susceptibility to positive and negative mood induction procedures. *Personality and Individual Differences, 10,* 1221–1228.

Lazarus, R. S. (1991). *Emotion and adaptation.* New York: Oxford University Press.

Leakey, R. (1994). *The origin of humankind.* New York: Basic Books.

LeDoux, J. (1996). *The emotional brain.* New York: Simon & Schuster.

Lerner, J. S., Goldberg, J. H., & Tetlock, P. E. (1998). Sober second thoughts: The effects of accountability, anger, and authoritarianism on attributions of responsibility. *Personality and Social Psychology Bulletin, 24,* 563–574.

Lerner, J. S., & Keltner, D. (2001). Fear, anger, and risk. *Journal of Personality and Social Psychology, 81*(1), 146–159.

Levenson, R. W. (1992). Autonomic nervous system differences among emotions. *Psychological Science, 3*, 23–27.

Levenson, R. W. (1999). The intrapersonal functions of emotion. *Cognition and Emotion, 13*, 481–504.

Levenson, R. W., Ekman, P., Heider, K., & Friesen, W. V. (1992). Emotion and autonomic nervous system activity in the Minangkabau of West Sumatra. *Journal of Personality and Social Psychology, 62*, 972–988.

Levy, R. I. (1984). The emotions in comparative perspective. In K. R. Scherer & P. Ekman (Eds.), *Approaches to emotion* (pp. 397–412). Hillsdale, NJ: Erlbaum.

Lowenstein, G. & Lerner, J. S. (2003). The role of affect in decision making. In R. J. Davidson, K. R. Scherer, & H. H. Goldsmith (Eds.), *Handbook of affective sciences* (pp. 619—642). New York: Oxford University Press.

Lutz, C. (1990). Engendered emotion: Gender, power, and the rhetoric of emotional control in American discourse. In C. A. Lutz & L. Abu-Lughod (Eds.), *Language and the politics of emotion* (pp. 69–91). New York: Cambridge University Press.

Malatesta, C. Z. (1990). The role of emotions in the development and organization of personality. In. R. A. Thompson (Ed.), *Nebraska symposium on motivation: Vol. 36, socioemotional development* (pp. 1–56). Lincoln: University of Nebraska Press.

Mauro, R., Sato, K., & Tucker, J. (1992). The role of appraisal in human emotions: A cross-cultural study. *Journal of Personality and Social Psychology, 62*, 301–317.

McCullough, M. C., Kilpatrick, S. D., Emmons, R. A., & Larson, D. B. (2001). Is gratitude a moral affect? *Psychological Bulletin, 127*, 249–266.

Menon, U., & Shweder, R. A. (1994). Kali's tongue: Cultural psychology, cultural consensus and the meaning of "shame" in Orissa, India. In H. Markus & S. Kitayama (Eds.), *Emotion and culture: Empirical studies of mutual influence* (pp. 241–284). Washington, DC: American Psychological Association.

Mesquita, B. (2001). Culture and emotion: Different approaches to the question. In T. J. Mayne & G. A. Bonanno (Eds.), *Emotions: Current issues and future directions. Emotions and social behavior* (pp. 214–250). New York: Guilford.

Mesquita, B., Frijda, N. H., & Scherer, K. R. (1997). Culture and emotion. In P. R. Dasen & T. S. Saraswathi (Eds.), *Handbook of cross-cultural psychology, Vol. 2: Basic processes and human development* (pp. 255–297). Boston: Allyn & Bacon.

Miller, R. S., & Leary, M. R. (1992). Social sources and interactive functions of embarrassment. In M. Clark (Ed.), *Emotion and social behavior* (pp. 322–339). New York: Sage.

Mineka, S., & Cook, M. (1993). Mechanisms involved in the observational conditioning of fear. *Journal of Experimental Psychology: General, 122*, 23–38.

Nesse, R. M. (1990). Evolutionary explanation of emotions. *Human Nature, 1*, 261–289.

Nestler, E. J. (1992). Molecular mechanisms of drug addiction. *Journal of Neuroscience, 12*, 2439–2450.

Oatley, K. (1993). Social construction in emotion. In M. Lewis & J. Haviland (Eds.), *Handbook of emotions* (pp. 342–352). New York: Guilford Press.

Oatley, K. (2003). Creative expression and communication of emotions in the visual and narrative arts. In R. J. Davidson, K. R. Scherer, & H. H. Goldsmith (Eds.), *Handbook of affective sciences* (pp. 481–502). New York: Oxford University Press.

Oatley, K., & Jenkins, J. M. (1992). Human emotions: Function and dysfunction. *Annual Review of Psychology, 43*, 55–85.

Oatley, K., & Johnson-Laird, P. N. (1987). Towards a cognitive theory of emotion. *Cognition and Emotion, 1*, 29–50.

Öhman, A. (1986). Face the beast and fear the face: Animal and social fears as prototypes for evolutionary analysis of emotions. *Psychophysiology, 23,* 123–145.

Öhman, A., & Dimberg, U. (1978). Facial expressions as conditioned stimuli for electrodermal responses: A case of "preparedness?" *Journal of Personality and Social Psychology, 36,* 1251–1258.

Pinker, S. (1997). *How the mind works.* New York: Norton.

Plutchik, R. (1962). *The emotions: Facts, theories, and a new model.* New York: Random House.

Plutchik, R. (1980). *Emotion: A psychobioevolutionary synthesis.* New York: Harper & Row.

Preuschoft, S. (1992). "Laughter" and "smile" in barbary macaques (macaca sylvanus). *Ethology, 91,* 220–236.

Redican, W. K. (1975). Facial expressions in nonhuman primates. In L. A. Rosenblum (Ed.), *Primate behavior* (pp. 103–194). New York: Academic Press.

Richerson, P. J., & Boyd, R. (2004). *Not by genes alone.* Chicago: University of Chicago Press.

Rolls, E. T. (2000). The orbitofrontal cortext and reward. *Cerebral cortex, 10,* 284–294.

Rosaldo, M. (1980). *Knowledge and passion: Ilongot notions of self and social life.* Cambridge: Cambridge University Press.

Rose, M. R. (1998). *Darwin's spectre: Evolutionary biology in the modern world.* Princeton, NJ: Princeton University Press.

Rozin, P. (1996). Towards a psychology of food and eating: From motivation to module to model to marker, morality, meaning, and metaphor. *Current Directions in Psychological Science, 5,* 18–24.

Rozin, P., Haidt, J., & McCauley, C. R. (2000). Disgust. In M. Lewis & J. M. Haviland (Eds.), *Handbook of emotions* (2nd ed., pp. 637–653). New York: Guilford Press.

Rozin, P., Lowery, L., Imada, S., & Haidt, J. (1999). The CAD triad hypothesis: A mapping between three moral emotions (contempt, anger, disgust) and three moral codes (community, autonomy, divinity). *Journal of Personality and Social Psychology, 76,* 574–586.

Russell, J. A. (1991). Culture and the categorization of emotions. *Psychological Bulletin, 110,* 426–450.

Russell, J. A. (1994). Is there universal recognition of emotion from facial expression? A review of the cross-cultural studies. *Psychological Bulletin, 115,* 102–141.

Russell, J. A. (1995). Facial expressions of emotion: What lies beyond minimal universality? *Psychological Bulletin, 118,* 379–391.

Sapir, E. (1921). *Language, an introduction to the study of speech.* New York: Harcourt, Brace and Company.

Scherer, K. R. (1986). Vocal affect expression: A review and a model for future research. *Psychological Bulletin, 99,* 143–165.

Scherer, K. R., Johnstone, T., & Klasmeyer, G. (2003). Vocal expression of emotion. In R. J. Davidson, K. R. Scherer, & H. H. Goldsmith (Eds.), *Handbook of affective science* (pp. 433–456). New York: Oxford University Press.

Scherer, K. R., & Wallbott, H. B. (1994). Evidence for universality and cultural variation of differential emotion response patterning. *Journal of Personality and Social Psychology, 66,* 310–328.

Schultz, W., Tremblay, L., & Hollerman, J. R. (2003). Changes in behavior-related neuronal activity in the striatum during learning. *Trends in Neurosciences, 26,* 321–328.

Schwarz, N. (1990). Feelings as information: Informational and motivational functions of affective states. In E. T. Higgins & R. M. Sorrentino (Eds.), *Handbook of motivation and cognition* (Vol. 2, pp. 527–561). New York: Guilford Press.

Schwarz, N., & Clore, G. L. (1983). Mood, misattribution, and judgments of well-being: Informative and directive functions of affective states. *Journal of Personality and Social Psychology, 45*, 513–523.

Semendeferi, K., Armstrong, E., Schleicher, A., Zilles, K., & Van Hoesen, G. W. (2001). Prefrontal cortex in humans and apes: A comparative study of area 10. *American Journal of Physical Anthropology, 114*, 224–241.

Shaver, P. R., Morgan, H. J., & Wu, S. (1996). Is love a "basic" emotion? *Personal Relationships, 3*, 81–96.

Shweder, R. A., & Haidt, J. (2000). The cultural psychology of the emotions: Ancient and new. In M. Lewis & J. M. Haviland-Jones (Eds.), *Handbook of emotions* (2nd ed., pp. 397–414). New York: Guilford Press.

Shweder, R. A., Mahapatra, M., & Miller, J. (1987). Culture and moral development. In J. Kagan & S. Lamb (Eds.), *The emergence of morality in young children*. Chicago: University of Chicago Press.

Shiota, M. N., Campos, B., Keltner, D., & Hertenstein, M. J. (2004). Positive Emotion and the Regulation of Interpersonal Relationships. In P. Philippot & R. S. Feldman (Eds.), *The regulation of emotion*. Mahwah, NJ: Lawrence Erlbaum.

Shiota, M. N., Keltner, D., & John, O. P. (in press). Eleven flavors of happiness: dispositional positive emotion differentiation in predicting the big five personality dimensions and psychological well-being. *Emotion*. Manuscript submitted for publication.

Simpson, J. A., & Kenrick, D. T. (1998). *Evolutionary social psychology*. Hillsdale, NJ: Lawrence Erlbaum Associates.

Sober, E., & Wilson, D. S. (1998). *Unto others: The evolution and psychology of unselfish behavior*. Cambridge, MA: Harvard University Press.

Tangney, J. P. (1992). Situational determinants of shame and guilt in young adulthood. *Personality and Social Psychology Bulletin, 18*, 199–206.

Tiedens, L. Z., Ellsworth, P. C., & Mesquita, B. (2000). Stereotypes about sentiments and status: Emotional expectations for high- and low-status group members. *Personality and Social Psychology Bulletin, 26*, 560–574.

Tomkins, S. S. (1962). *Affect, imagery, consciousness (Vol. 1, The positive affects)*. New York: Springer.

Tomkins, S. S. (1963). *Affect, imagery, consciousness (Vol. 2, The negative affects)*. New York: Springer.

Tomkins, S. S. (1984). Affect theory. In K. Scherer & P. Ekman (Eds.), *Approaches to emotion* (pp. 163–195). Hillsdale, NJ: Erlbaum.

Tooby, J., & Cosmides, L. (1990). The past explains the present: Emotional adaptations and the structure of ancestral environments. *Ethology and Sociobiology, 11*, 375–424.

Tracy, J. L., & Robins, R. W. (2004). Show your pride: Evidence for a discrete emotion expression. *Psychological Science, 15*, 94–97.

Trivers, R. L. (1971). The evolution of reciprocal altruism. *Quarterly Review of Biology, 46*, 35–57.

van Hooff, J. A. R. A. M. (1972). A comparative approach to the phylogeny of laughter and smiling. In R. A. Hinde (Ed.), *Nonverbal communication*. Cambridge: Cambridge University Press.

Vasquez, K., Keltner, D., Ebenbach, D. H., & Banaszynski, T. L. (2001). Cultural variation and similarity in moral rhetorics: Voices from the Philippines and United States. *Journal of Cross-Cultural Psychology, 32*, 93–120.

Watson, D. & Clark, L. A. (1992). On traits and temperament: General and specific factors of emotional experience and their relation to the five-factor model. *Journal of Personality, 60*, 441–476.

Weber, M. (1957). *The theory of social and economic organization*. New York: Free Press.

Weiner, B. Graham, S., & Reyna, C. (1997). An attributional examination of retributive versus utilitarian philosophies of punishment. *Social Justice Research, 10*, 431–452.

White, G. M. (1993). Emotions inside out: The anthropology of affect. In M. Lewis and J. M. Haviland (Eds.), *Handbook of emotions* (pp. 29–40). New York: Guilford.

Whorf, B. L. (1956). *Language, thought, and reality*. Cambridge, MA: Technology Press of the Massachusetts Institute of Technology.

Wright, L. (1973). Functions. *Philosophical Review, 82*, 139–168.

7

An Evolutionary Perspective on Social Identity: Revisiting Groups

MARILYNN B. BREWER and LINNDA R. CAPORAEL

*M*ost behavioral scientists today accept the basic premise that human beings are adapted for group living. Even a cursory review of the physical endowments of our species—weak, hairless, and extended infancy—makes it clear that we are not suited for survival as lone individuals, or even as small family units. Many of the evolved characteristics that have permitted humans to adapt to a wide range of physical environments, such as omnivorousness and toolmaking, create dependence on collective knowledge and cooperative information sharing. As a consequence, human beings are characterized by *obligatory interdependence* (Caporael & Brewer, 1995), and our evolutionary history is a story of coevolution of genetic endowment, social structure, and culture (Boyd & Richerson, 1985; Caporael, 2001a; Fiske, 2000; Janicki, 1998; Li, 2003).

Nevertheless, groups have not figured prominently in evolutionary psychology for several reasons. One is a long-standing prohibition on group selection, which appears to ban any discussion of the role of groups in human evolution whatsoever. Another is a long-standing, and insufficiently appreciated, commitment to self-interest as a "universal solvent" able to readily explain any apparently altruistic behavior as really self-interested. Against this background, the goal of this chapter is to reintroduce groups as an essential component in theoretical and empirical work. We begin with a discussion of group selection and multilevel evolutionary theory. We conclude that the "gene's eye" view is at the wrong level of analysis to be useful for psychologists (unless we adopt a rather close-fitting genetic determinism). Next we discuss research findings that demonstrate "ambivalent sociality" (Brewer, 1989). Human nature cannot be cast in the dichotomy of self-interest vs. altruism, the so-called central problem (Wilson, 1975) in the gene's eye view. Instead, we adopt a systems perspective (Caporael, 2001a) where the central problem is the evolution of coordination in groups. For the human case, we propose a model of coordination based on a few core group configurations. Although no evolutionary model of the past can be proved, the structure of social identity is coherent with the model, indicating that it is useful for organizing diverse research findings and pointing to further research. In the end, we briefly examine and reject, on grounds of plausibility and parsimony, the most popular explanation for in-group phenomena—intergroup warfare.

GROWING OUT OF THE GENE'S EYE VIEW: MULTILEVEL SELECTION

In the 1950s and 1960s, biologists frequently explained apparently helpful acts, such as a bird giving a warning call when a predator is spotted, as done for the good of the group or the survival of the species. In its earliest form, group selection was proposed to explain why some populations remained within the carrying capacity of their environments (Wynne-Edwards, 1962). Presumably, some members of the population would sacrifice their own reproduction to benefit the group. Stated so baldly, it is obvious that individuals who sacrifice themselves for the benefit of the group are not going to bear as many offspring as genetically self-centered defectors. Genes that caused an individual to lower her fitness by behaving "for the good of the species" would quickly disappear from the population according to Darwinian logic. G. C. William's book, *Adaptation and Natural Selection* (1966), created the gene's eye view, an extended argument against group selection and for the logic of costs and benefits to the gene. By the early 1970s, Wynne-Edwards and group selection were passionately damned; excoriating group selection in conference talks became de rigueur, proof of evolutionary orthodoxy, and required of all graduate students (Pollock, 1989).

The most familiar critiques of group selection are based on Maynard Smith's (1964) haystack model. In the model, a species of mouse colonizes haystacks in a meadow. There are two types of mice, selfish and altruistic (aggressive and timid in the original account), which can form three types of groups: all selfish groups, all altruistic groups, and mixed groups. The altruistic groups have more offspring compared to the selfish groups, so altruists are most successful. But in the mixed group, selfish mice gain the advantage of the benefits donated by the altruistic mice; their numbers in the haystack decline until only selfish mice are left. Should a mutant variant arise or migrate to an altruist haystack, the game is lost. The altruistic groups are converted into selfish groups. The only way that altruism can survive on the meadow is if there are few migrants and "infected" groups quickly go extinct. In other words, there has to be a low rate of migration and a high rate of extinction.

This way of looking at group selection was extreme and unrealistic, yet it effectively channeled discussions of group selection as individualistic economic models, as if organisms made individual choices about whether or not to group. However, from an evolutionary perspective, the tensions between levels of selection are more or less resolved in the specific phylogenetic and ecological contests in which natural selection occurs. After all, it is by virtue of species' histories and ecologies over time that mice and men differ. We believe that the original rejection of genetic group selection was well-founded but overextended. Consequently, social cognitive processes have been over-reduced to individualist factors, denying psychology access to richer evolutionary approaches.

Most animals are group-living (Pulliam & Caraco, 1984), if nothing else by virtue of the failure of kin groups to disburse. However, there is considerable variability across species in the intensity of interdependence of group-living (Avital & Jablonka, 2000; Boinski & Garber, 2000). Quite often, sociality may consist of little more than a group of opportunistic and individualistic cooperators (Norris & Schilt, 1988; Williams, 1966). A school of fish or a herd of fleet deer are aggregate groups. There may be safety in numbers, and the risks of predation might be spread out among a group of animals. As soon as the risks are reduced, the aggregate group breaks up. Some schools of fish break up under the cover of darkness. African antelopes group when they live in the open and live solitary lives in forests where hiding is easier. Individuals that form aggregates are adaptively specialized for knowing when to group and when to be solitary.

There are other kinds of groups that cannot break up. The individuals that form such groups must be part of a group in order to reproduce and survive to reproductive age. These intensely social groups organize individual efforts, communicate within the group, have tasks and roles for group members, and have definable boundaries (Brewer, 1997). In extreme cases, such as wolf packs, naked mole rats, and meerkats (a social mongoose), only a single pair of individuals in the group reproduces, somewhat like the "germ line" of the body (Avital & Jablonka, 2000). Other group members (usually relatives) may help care for the pups by feeding, guarding, and tutoring them in hunting skills. Human sociality is nowhere so extreme as to have a single breeding pair. Nevertheless, humans are obligately social, unable to survive and reproduce without a group context. A synergy between individual and group allows the group members to interact more effectively with the habitat than as lone individuals. Basically such groups cannot break up because they are organic entities.

Given the morphology and ecology of evolving hominids, the interface between hominids and their habitat must have been a group process. Finding food, defense from predation, and moving across a landscape—these matters of coping with the physical habitat—are largely group processes (Boinski & Garber, 2000). Over time, if exploiting a habitat is more successful as a coordinated group process than as an individual process, then not only would more successful groups persist, but so also would individuals better adapted to group living. The result would be a shift to cooperative groups as the selective context for uniquely human mental systems. The result of selection in groups would be the evolution of perceptual, affective, and cognitive processes that support the development and maintenance of membership in groups (Caporael, Dawes, Orbell, & van de Kragt, 1989). Without a group, the probability of reproduction and survival to reproductive age is lowered for humans.

Hierarchical Models of Human Evolution and Sociality

With the publication of Leo Buss's book, The Evolution of Individuality (1987), scientific consensus began shifting from gene-based selection models of evolution to multilevel evolutionary theories (Jablonka, 1994; Maynard Smith & Szathmáry, 1995). Buss (1987; no relation to David Buss) observed that biologists took the notion of the multicellular individual for granted. He argued that multicelluarity itself evolved through the consolidation of initially self-replicating units. A familiar example is mitochondria, cellular structures which were initially free-living units and became part of—and dependent on—replicating cells. The advantage of such consolidation would be the exploitation of the environment in a way that was otherwise unavailable to the lower-level entity. Evolutionary transitions creating new levels of selection involve both synergies and conflicts between lower and higher levels of organization. As multicellular individuals reproduce, they also reproduce the nonreproductive somatic cells. Cancer, however, can be seen as a cell line reproducing at the expense of the individual, but in the end, also at a cost to itself. Multievolutionary theory provided the needed conceptual frameworks for a new interpretation for the role of group selection in human evolution.

Hierarchical models of evolution recognize that the concept of "fit" must be conceptualized in terms of embedded structures. Genes, as one level of organization, are adapted to fit the environment of their cellular machinery; cells fit the environment of the individual organism; and individual organisms are adapted to fit the next higher level of organization within which they function. This view of adaptation and natural selection provides a new perspective on the concept of group selection as a factor in human evolution (Caporael & Brewer, 1991). With coordinated group living as the primary survival strategy of the species, the social group, in effect, provided a buffer between the individual organism and the exigencies of the physical environment. As a consequence, then, the physical environment exercises only indirect selective force on human adaptation, while the requirements of social living constitute the immediate selective environment.

Coordinating groups must meet certain structural requirements in order to exist, just as organisms must have certain structural properties in order to be viable. For community-sized groups these organizational imperatives include mobilization and coordination of individual effort, communication, internal differentiation, optimal group size, and boundary definition. The benefits to individuals of cooperative arrangements cannot be achieved unless prior conditions have been satisfied that make the behavior of other individuals predictable and coordinated. Group survival depends on successful solution to these problems of internal organization and coordination.

If individual humans cannot survive outside of groups, then the structural requirements for sustaining groups create systematic constraints on individual biological and psychological adaptations. Campbell (1974, 1990) called such constraints "downward causation" across system levels. Downward causation operates whenever structural requirements at higher levels of organization determine or shape some aspects of structure and function at lower levels (a kind of reverse reductionism). In the evolution of multicellularity, some cells "gave up" reproductive autonomy to become body cells as others eventually became reproducing gametes (Buss, 1987). Similar conflicts and opportunities are obtained for humans in the relationship between the individual and the group. Individual advantage may be curtailed at the level of the group, sometimes resulting in cooperative groups better adapted to the habitat.

Although he did not put his insight to use, even as gene-centered a theorist as E. O. Wilson (1975) himself recognized the need for multilevel theorizing when it came to human sociality:

> For the moment, suffice it to note that what is good for the individual can be destructive to the family, what preserves the family can be harsh on both the individual and the tribe to which its family belongs; what promotes the tribe can weaken the family and destroy the individual, and so on upward through the permutations of levels of organization. Counteracting selection on these different units will result in certain genes being multiplied and fixed, others lost, and combinations of still others held in static proportions. According to the present theory, some of the genes will produce emotional states that reflect the balance of counteracting selection forces at different levels (p. 4).

AMBIVALENT SOCIALITY, CORE CONFIGURATIONS, AND THEIR PSYCHOLOGICAL GLUE

Debates about human nature are often framed in terms of self-interest vs. altruism as the basis of cooperation and prosocial behavior. This framing of the debate as an either–or proposition is overly simplistic in light of the variability and context sensitivity of human social behavior. Social motives such as the need for belonging and acceptance clearly serve self-interested purposes at individual and genetic levels. Acceptance by a social group assures the individual of nurturance and aid that are essential to personal survival. But obligatory interdependence also implies that some social motives will be genuinely other-oriented as well. Since all individuals' chances for survival are affected not only by their own skills, abilities, and efforts, but also by the efforts and behaviors of others within a bounded social community, commitment to and acceptance of interdependence among all members of the social unit is a requirement of group living. Within a social community, individuals are invested in the children of other individuals—not because of genetic relatedness but because the survival of one's own offspring is dependent on the continuity of the group as a whole. Human interdependency must also have an evolutionary history that involves individual and group levels of selection. Likewise, we expect the fingerprints of this history to persist in psychological structures correlated with functional group tasks.

Ambivalent Sociality

Sociality does not imply noncontingent altruism or self-sacrifice. Humans show the capacity for variable motivation and behavior patterns contingent on the state of the environment. Recent evidence from the biology of emotions suggests that there is a meaningful distinction between selfish (i.e., self-preservation) emotions such as fear and anger, and prosocial (i.e., other-oriented) emotions, including attachment, sociability, empathy, and love. Distinct, specifiable neural systems are implicated (Buck, 1999, 2002). Social exchange is also a complex phenomenon illustrating the capacity and contingency of cooperative and altruistic behavior patterns (Van Vugt & Van Lange, this volume).

Human beings are clearly vested with self-interest, but our view of evolutionary history contends that self-interest is mitigated by identification with groups. We contend that self- and group-oriented motivations represent two separate, semiautonomous regulatory systems that hold each other in check (Brewer, 1991; Brewer & Roccas, 2001), which is to be expected from selection at both individual and group levels. Just as prices in a free market system are regulated by the independent forces of supply and demand, unbridled individual self-interest is held in check by the demands of interdependence, but at the same time, sociality is constrained by the demands of individual survival and reproduction. Since individual self-interest and collective interests do not always coincide, the necessities of group living require coordination not only between individuals but also psychologically within individuals, to meet competing demands from different levels of organization. Human social life can be characterized as a perpetual juggling act—maintaining the integrity of individual identity, interpersonal relationships, and collective interests simultaneously.

Experimental research on social dilemmas such as public goods problems and resource conservation demonstrate how individuals behave when they must choose between immediate self- and group-interest (Caporael et al., 1989; Kramer & Brewer, 1984). In these choice situations, individuals do not behave consistently selfishly or unselfishly; a great deal depends on the group context in which the decision is made. When a collective social identification is not available, individuals tend to respond to the depletion of a collective resource by increasing their own resource use, at the cost of long-term availability. However, when a symbolic collective identity has been made salient, individuals respond to a resource crisis by dramatically reducing their own resource use (Kramer & Brewer, 1984). Further, when a public goods decision is preceded by even a brief period of group discussion, the rate of cooperative choice (when decisions are made individually and anonymously) is almost 100% (R. M. Dawes, 1988; R. M. Dawes, Orbell, Simmons, & van de Kragt, 1986). This level of cooperative responding suggests that, under appropriate conditions, group welfare is just as "natural" as self-gratification as a rule for individual decision making.

Opposing Motives and the Optimal Distinctiveness Theory of Social Identity

The necessity for meeting demands of existence at the individual, interpersonal, and collective levels of organization suggests that human social life is regulated not by single social motives but by the complex effects of multiple, competing motivational systems.

Brewer's model of optimal distinctiveness (Brewer, 1991) provides one illustration of how such competing motivational systems might work. The model posits that humans are characterized by two opposing needs that govern the relationship between the self-concept and membership in social groups. The first is a need for assimilation and inclusion, a desire for belonging that motivates immersion in social groups. The second is a need for differentiation from others that operates in opposition to the need for immersion. As group membership becomes more and more inclusive, the need for inclusion is satisfied but the need for differentiation is activated; conversely, as inclusiveness decreases, the differentiation need is reduced but the need for assimilation is activated. These competing drives assure that interests at one level are not consistently sacrificed to interests at the other. According to the model, the two opposing motives produce an emergent characteristic—the capacity for social identification with distinctive groups that satisfy both needs simultaneously.

Evidence for competing social motives comes from empirical demonstrations of efforts to achieve or restore group identification when these needs are deprived. Results of experimental studies have shown that activation of the need for assimilation or the need for differentiation increases the importance of distinctive group memberships (Pickett, Silver, & Brewer, 2002b), that threat to inclusion enhances self-stereotyping on group-characteristic traits (Brewer & Pickett, 1999; Pickett, Bonner, & Coleman, 2002a), and that threat to group distinctiveness motivates overexclusion (Pickett, 1999) and intergroup differentiation (Jetten, Spears, & Manstead, 1998; Roccas & Schwartz, 1993).

The importance of the collective self is particularly evident when efforts to achieve or restore optimal group identities involve some cost to personal self-interest. This is supported by research indicating that (1) individuals often identify strongly with stigmatized groups (e.g., Crocker, Luhtanen, Blaine, & Broadnax, 1994; Simon, Glassner-Bayerl, & Stratenwerth, 1991); (2) identification with distinctive groups leads to assimilation to the in-group even when it entails loss of personal self-esteem (Brewer & Weber, 1994); (3) activation of the need for differentiation increases the value of distinctive low-status minority in-groups over high-status majority in-groups (Brewer, Manzi, & Shaw, 1993; Leonardelli, 1998); and (4) threats to inclusion or distinctiveness increase self-stereotyping even on negatively evaluated group characteristics (Branscombe & Ellemers, 1998; Pickett et al., 2002a).

The optimal distinctiveness theory was in part the product of an exercise in thinking about downward causation from the group to the individual level of analysis. The advantage of extending social interdependence and cooperation to an ever wider circle of conspecifics comes from the ability to exploit resources across an expanded territory and buffer the effects of temporary depletions or scarcities in any one local environment. But expansion comes at the cost of increased demands on obligatory sharing and regulation of reciprocal cooperation. Both the carrying capacity of physical resources and the capacity for distribution of resources, aid, and information inevitably constrain the potential size of cooperating social networks. Thus, effective social groups cannot be either too small or too large. To function, social collectives must be restricted to some optimal size—sufficiently large and inclusive to realize the advantages of extended cooperation, but sufficiently exclusive to avoid the disadvantages of spreading social interdependence too thin.

Based on this analysis of one structural requirement for group survival, we hypothesize that the conflicting benefits and costs associated with expanding group size would have shaped social motivational systems at the individual level. If humans are adapted to live in groups and depend on group effectiveness for survival, then our motivational systems should be tuned to the requirements of group effectiveness. We should be uncomfortable depending on groups that are too small to provide the benefits of shared resources but also uncomfortable if group resources are distributed too widely. A unidirectional drive for inclusion would not have been adaptive without a counteracting drive for differentiation and exclusion. Opposing motives hold each other in check, with the result that human beings are not comfortable either in isolation or in huge collectives.

The social motives postulated by optimal distinctiveness theory at the individual level create a propensity for adhering to social groups that are both bounded and distinctive. As a consequence, groups that are optimal in size are those that will elicit the greatest levels of member loyalty, conformity, and cooperation, and the fit between individual psychology and group structure is better achieved.

Interdependence at Different Levels of Organization: The Core Configuration Model

In actuality, the distinction between the individual level and social group level of organization is not a simple dichotomy. Interdependence and social coordination play out at different levels of group size and function. Caporael (1997) suggested a model for the topography of the selective environment for humans based on a consideration of tasks that are necessary for survival and reproduction and on research about group size (Binford, 2001; Hassan, 1981; Jarvenpa, 1993; Lee & DeVore, 1968). The model consists of four configurations—dyad, task group, deme (or band), and macrodeme (or macroband). A core configuration is the joint function of group size and activity. Configurations provide a context for tasks or activities that are specific to that level of organization. That is, each group configuration affords functional possibilities and coordination problems that do not exist at other levels.

Table 7.1 lists the configurations in the model, along with an approximate group size and examples of modal tasks for the configuration. The tasks listed in the table are characteristic of hunter–gatherer groups, but have analogs in present-day life. For example, dyads afford the evolution and development of

TABLE 7.1   Core Configurations of Social Groups

Configuration	Prototypic Group Size	Modal Tasks
Dyad	2	Sex; parent–child interaction
Task group	5	Foraging; hunting; working on a common task
Deme (band)	30	Workgroup coordination; migration; sharing knowledge
Macrodeme (macroband)	300	Seasonal gatherings; exchange of persons, resources, and information

Adapted from Caporael (1997).

coordinated body movements such as those used in facial imitation in the mother–infant dyad, interactional synchrony, and human sexual attraction (Perper, 1985), or the social contagion of time perception and mood (Conway, 2004). The relevance of tasks (from an evolutionary perspective) for a configuration is not the activity per se, but rather the set of social cognitive processes—afforded by the core configuration—that enable the activity. As is typical in evolutionary explanations, there is a "chicken and egg" character—neither core configurations nor their psychological correlates come first.

Details of the core configurations are available in Caporael (1997). In addition to dyads, there are task groups, demes, and macrodemes. Task group configurations afford the evolution of cognitive processes to be distributed over group members. Cognitive tasks such as perception, classification, inference, and contextually cued responses can be distributed over a group, particularly in the face of ambiguous or anomalous data from the habitat. In the hunter–gatherer group, a task group might be a hunting party interpreting signs of animal movements over a landscape. A modern example would be control tower personnel at airports interpreting signs of possible danger from ambiguous signs on a radar screen. The deme (or as anthropologists say, the band) affords a shared construction of reality or "common knowledge," as well as skills, practices, and rituals. (We use the term deme, from the Greek demos, in its original sense of a neighborhood unit rather than the biological sense of breeding population.) The deme or band is the basic economic unit, the first configuration that can be self-sustaining for survival and child rearing (but not reproduction). The deme is the staging ground for domestic life, including task-group coordination, and for cooperative alliances, which are the basis for fissioning when the community exceeds resources or is fractured by conflict.

In human evolution, the macrodeme afforded the exchange of genes, information, and resources beyond the immediate face-to-face interacting group. Among many hunter–gatherer groups, related demes met in seasonal gatherings and exchanged marriage partners, gifts, and information, and performed rituals and played competitive games. Today, scientific conferences are often seasonal meetings where information and young people are exchanged, and where the standardization and stabilization of distinctive terminology and the reaffirmation of group identity occurs. The macrodeme is the most important focus for this chapter for two reasons—representation and entitativity. The original seasonality of macrodemes implicates the representation of entitative groups beyond day-to-day engagement. That is, individual group members may change, but the group as a unit interacting with other groups persists.

Macrodemes are the prototypes for modern ethnic groups—geographically extended groups of people who do not necessarily have face-to-face relationships, but define themselves as having a common origin and share interaction norms, socialization experiences, and rituals of group identity (Gil-White, 2001; Wells, 1998). In a sense, prehistoric macrodemes freed human beings from the limits of face-to-face interaction.

There are a few general points to be made about the core configuration model. First, core configurations repeatedly assemble, in evolutionary time, in ontogeny, and in daily life. As infants develop, their increasing scope of interaction increases demands for reciprocity, skills, memory, social judgment, and so on. Second, core configurations differ in how deeply entrenched they are. Dyads are deeply entrenched; a change in their evolved functions should predict poor developmental outcomes. In contrast, macrodemes are shallowly entrenched and are relatively easy to modify. Third, humans have dramatically altered their lifestyles over the past 10 millennia, and especially in the last 300 years. Clearly the functions that evolve and develop in core configurations are capable of being extended, combined, and used in new domains. For example, a heart surgery team combines microcoordination and distributed cognition. Technology can also provide bridges between the functions of configurations. A group of 500 people given an order to march on a football field are likely to clump and straggle, but if a rousing marching song is broadcast, they can hardly avoid keeping time. Some institutions have been particularly successful in exploiting core configurations, the military being a prime example.

Relating Core Configurations and Levels of Social Identity

Recognizing that we function interdependently in social units of different size and purpose has widespread implications for theories of social influence, cooperation, social development, and even mental health. For human social life, the four levels of organization are all indispensable and not interchangeable. This means that to function effectively in the social world, individuals must possess the skills and cognitive representations needed to coordinate with others in different configurations, to move flexibly from one form of social interdependence to another as task and context require, and to establish and maintain connections with others at each level.

We suggest that the psychological glue maintaining core configurations are shifts in social identity (Caporael, 2001b). If social identity plays a central role in core configurations, then there should be evidence of "group selves" that correspond to different levels of core configuration and are connected with knowledge sharing as in distributed cognition or shared reality (Hardin & Higgins, 1996). Consistent with the core configuration model, Brewer and Gardner (1996) postulated that the *individual*, *relational*, and *collective* levels of self define distinct self-representations with different structural properties, bases of self-evaluation, and motivational concerns (see also Kashima & Hardie, 2000; Sedikides & Brewer, 2001).

The relational and collective levels of self postulated by Brewer and Gardner (1996) represent two different forms of social identification, i.e., processes by which the individual self is extended to include others as integral to the self-concept. The critical distinction between these is that relational selves are *personalized*, incorporating dyadic relationships between the self and specific close others and the extension of these relationships in the form of networks of interpersonal connections. By contrast, collective selves involve *depersonalized* relationships with others by virtue of common membership in a symbolic group. Collective identities do not require interpersonal knowledge or coordination but rely on shared symbols and cognitive representations of the group as a unit independent of personal relationships within the group.

One way to think about how social identity processes operate across the four core configurations is that the different types of group require (and engage) relational and collective identification processes to different degrees. More specifically, dyadic groups are pure relational social identities in which the specific other is incorporated in the self-unit. Some research suggests that "dyadic selves" exist as cognitive representations in which concepts of the self and other overlap (Aron, Aron, Tudor, & Nelson, 1991), as transactive memory systems (Wegner, 1986; Wegner, Raymond, & Erber, 1991), and in the coordination of bodily motion or interactional synchrony (Newbern, Dansereau, & Pitre, 1994). Interpersonal networks, such as friendship groups, also engage relational identification processes, as extensions of the basic dyadic unit.

Task groups and teams are also characterized by personalized, face-to-face interactions and no doubt elicit relational social identities within the context of specific work groups. But, unlike friendship circles, task groups also engage a degree of collective identification in the form of group goals and group achievement. Some research on team performance suggests that task group effectiveness depends both on personalized interactions and on collective representations. For instance, in an experiment on work teams Liang, Moreland, and Argote (1995) demonstrated that groups trained together (to assemble radios) outperformed groups composed of individuals trained separately to do the same task. The researchers found that group training enhanced not only recall about assembly procedures, but also specialization for remembering distinct aspects of the assembly procedure and trust in one another's knowledge about the task. Hutchins (1996) also studied teams, but in the real-life situation of navigating a large naval ship into port. Establishing the fix cycle, or position of the ship, recurs every 2 to 3 minutes. Hutchins found that no single individual is "in charge" of the performance; rather the performance emerges interactively as individuals coordinate their activities with the people "adjacent" to them, in the sense of input–output of information.

At the demic level, social selves shift from concrete-situated interaction to common bonds among individuals who do not necessarily share spatial proximity on a regular basis. Prentice, Miller, and Lightdale (1994) investigated attachment among members of campus dining clubs, which were either selective "bicker" clubs or open "sign-in" clubs. Bicker club members, who shared interpersonal bonds with each other, were attached to members of the group and showed a stronger relationship between group identification and evaluation of individual members. In contrast, sign-in eating club members were more attached to the group per se than to fellow group members. The results indicated that social identity with groups of this size can be forged at two distinct levels, one based on common bonds and interpersonal relationships, and the other based on a common or collective group identity. Moreover, most of the groups showed evidence of some mixture of both types of identification processes, though to different degrees.

By the time we reach the macrodemic level of group coordination, the relative contribution of collective identification processes exceeds that of relational identification. Although specific skills and practices are concretely situated in face-to-face groups, the psychological correlates of grouping developed at the macrodemic level can be extended to social identity with large, abstract, super-ordinate groups in the modern world—"la raza," "American," or "workers." In today's world, human beings are capable of coordination on scales far beyond the level of demes or macrodemes. Modern humans may live in cities with populations numbering in the millions. They may identify with others as parts of huge nation states. At yet higher levels of social identity, depersonalized collective selves (e.g., based on gender, national, or ethnic identity) can be an extension of the self/social identity processes with evolutionary origins in macrodeme organization.

The idea that relational and collective identification processes are combined in specific ways to define social identities corresponding to the core configurations of human social groups has yet to be empirically tested directly. However, research on social identity in organizational settings provides a context in which multiple levels of social group coordination and social identification can be observed simultaneously. As researchers in organizational behavior have noted (e.g., Ashforth & Johnson, 2001), social identities in organizations cross levels of organizational structure—from dyadic identification between workers and supervisors or peers, to social identity with work teams, to departments, to the organization as a whole. Some research on the correlates of social identity in organizations suggests that the strength of identification with groups at these different levels of the organization is not highly correlated and is predicted by different variables (e.g., Ellemers, deGilder, & vanden Heuvel, 1998; van Knippenberg & van Schie, 2000). Determining whether the antecedents of social identity at different levels (corresponding to different core configurations) may "map on" to differences in the relative importance of relational and collective identification processes at the different levels provides an interesting agenda for future research.

EVOLUTIONARY ORIGINS OF IN-GROUPS AND OUT-GROUPS

From the gene's eye view, and without access to multilevel evolutionary theory, human grouping could only be explained in terms of coalitions of self-interested cooperators who band together to dominate and exploit other groups (Alexander, 1979; Kurzban & Leary, 2001). In effect, from this perspective, in-groups emerge from intergroup conflict, and "…evolutionary scenarios that emphasize between-group competition seem more plausible than those that emphasize only within-group cooperation…" (Kurzban & Leary, 2001, p. 195). Much as biologists took individuality for granted, proponents of intergroup warfare take all the apparatus required to coordinate behavior in groups for granted.

The arguments in the previous sections make the case that there is no need to require intergroup conflict to account for in-group formation and exclusion of out-groups. In fact, in light of both paleoanthropological and archaeological evidence, it makes little sense to see conflict as the source of in-group formation. There is no reason to believe that early hominids lived under dense population conditions in which bands of people lived in close proximity with competition over local resources. Estimates of the total human population during the Middle Paleolithic are less than 1.5 million (Hassan, 1981). Group-living was well established much earlier—2.5 million years ago by human ancestors—and complex sociality evolved early among primate ancestors (Foley, 1996). Early evidence of population packing occurred around 15,000 years ago (Alexander, 1989; Stiner, 2002), too recently to have been relevant to the origins of human sociality. As Alexander himself admits, there is no evidence of intergroup conflict in early human evolutionary history (Alexander, 1989). Given the costs of intergroup fighting combined with low population density, flight rather than fight would seem to be the strategy of choice for our distant ancestors.

The idea that in-group cooperation is born of intergroup conflict is also inconsistent with contemporary research on social identity and intergroup relations (Brewer, 1999). Despite widespread belief that in-group positivity and out-group derogation are reciprocally related, empirical research demonstrates little consistent relation between the two. Indeed, results from both laboratory experiments and field studies indicate that variations in in-group positivity and social identification do not systematically correlate with degree of bias or negativity toward out-groups (Brewer, 1979; Hinkle & Brown, 1990; Kosterman & Feshbach, 1989; Struch and Schwartz, 1989). For example, in a study of the reciprocal attitudes among 30 ethnic groups in East Africa, Brewer and Campbell (1976) found that almost all of the groups exhibited systematic differential positive evaluation of the in-group over all out-groups on dimensions such as trustworthiness, obedience, friendliness, and honesty. However, the correlation between degree of positive in-group regard and social distance toward out-groups was essentially .00 across the 30 groups.

Brewer (1979) reported that most minimal group studies that assessed ratings of the in-group and out-group separately found that categorization into groups leads to enhanced in-group ratings in the absence of decreased out-group ratings. Further, the positive in-group biases exhibited in the allocation of positive resources in the minimal intergroup situation (Tajfel, Billig, Bundy, & Flament, 1971) are essentially eliminated when allocation decisions involve the distribution of negative outcomes or costs (e.g., Mummendey et al., 1992), suggesting that individuals are willing to differentially benefit the in-group compared to out-groups but are reluctant to harm out-groups more directly. In a more recent review of developmental studies on intergroup attitudes, Cameron, Alvarez, Ruble, and Fuligni (2001) similarly concluded that children tend to display a positivity bias toward their in-group, but no negativity toward the out-group.

Group boundaries and intergroup differentiation can be accounted for by the structural requirements for intragroup coordination and trust. The adaptive value of functional groups lies in interactional norms that facilitate reciprocal exchanges within the group (Gil-White, 2001; Henrich et al., 2001.) Coordination costs associated with interacting with out-groups are simply a by-product of intergroup differentiation, and this alone can account for a preference to avoid or limit contact with out-groups even in the absence of overt conflict or hostility. The heritage of our evolutionary past is not out-group hate but in-group love. Our evolutionary heritage provides new challenges in a world where global interdependence transcends the boundaries of in-group loyalties. We will need to exploit the human capacity for expansive social identity to meet the demands of modern group living. As it has done in the past, such as with the development of agriculture, warfare, and institutions that attempt to ensure justice among strangers, our species will have to reconceptualize and invent new human possibilities for ensuring identity and distinctiveness.

SUMMARY AND CONCLUSIONS

Humans are obligately social creatures, unable to reproduce and survive to reproductive age without a group. Psychologically, they are also ambivalently social, with contingent self-interested and group-oriented motives. A model of core group configurations, consistent with the hierarchical structure of biological organization, provides a systemic perspective on the evolution of human motivation, cognition, and affect. The model also coheres with research findings on human individual, relational, and collective social identities. Identity, as a psychological glue, points to understanding not only human evolution, but also how the human mind could evolve to invent new conceptions of human possibilities. The metaphoric gene's eye view, which we suggested is at the wrong level of analysis for psychology, fails to capture the nuances of human psychology or explain the remarkable inventiveness of the species.

Evolutionary psychology is currently at a delicate moment (Buller, 2005; Schmitt & Pilcher, 2004; Smith, Borgerhoff Mulder, & Hill, 2001). Darwinism has gone through cycles of rejection and reprise in the last 150 years without yet "sticking" in the human sciences. As we have repeatedly pointed out, starting in 1990 (Brewer & Caporael, 1990; Caporael & Brewer, 1990), Darwinism functions in both scientific and in social domains. In its social domain, it functions as an origin myth, explaining and justifying particular social relations, such as gender and status. That it should do so is not surprising: Neo-Darwinism's goal was to explain the same facts that nineteenth century natural theologians used as evidence for a creator (Maynard Smith, 1969). However in the human case, those "facts" were common stereotypes and folk psychological beliefs. As these are recognized and critiqued, evolutionary theory and the human sciences begin to drift apart once again.

We consider this chapter an illustration of how an evolutionary approach may be pursued in the context of scientific psychology. We have used experimental findings and considered how a simple model might explain those. Our approach is consistent with modern evolutionary ones that stress development (Gottlieb, 2002; Lickliter & Honeycutt, 2003) and niche construction (Laland, Odling-Smee, & Feldman, 2000). Some readers will notice that we have not resorted to the language of adaptation. We agree with G. C. Williams' (1966) assessment that adaptation is an onerous concept. Identifying genetically heritable adaptations about the nature of the mind is extremely difficult, particularly using traditional psychological methods (Lloyd & Feldman, 2002; Reznick & Travis, 1996). Given the substantial problems identifying adaptations and the considerable conceptual difficulties in the meaning of the term (Reeve & Sherman, 1993), we propose that the focus of evolutionary psychology is not on identifying adaptations. A more modest and robust goal would be in better understanding those links in the chain of life that recur over lifetimes, between generations, and possibly even over human evolutionary history (Caporael, 2003). For this effort, we need not only nuanced theory, but a fundamental acknowledgment that social groups have formed—and continue to be—the mind's natural environment.

REFERENCES

Alexander, R. D. (1979). Darwinism and human affairs. Seattle: University of Washington Press.

Alexander, R. D. (1989). Evolution of the human psyche. In P. Mellars & C. Stringer (Eds.), *The human revolution* (pp. 455–513). Princeton, NJ: Princeton University Press.

Aron, A., Aron, E. N., Tudor, M., & Nelson, G. (1991). Close relationships as including other in the self. *Journal of Personality and Social Psychology, 60,* 241–253.

Ashforth, B. E., & Johnson, S. A. (2001). Which hat to wear? The relative salience of multiple identities in organizational contexts. In M. Hogg and D. Terry (Eds.), *Social identity processes in organizational contexts* (pp. 31–48). Philadelphia, PA: Psychology Press.

Avital, E., & Jablonka, E. (2000). *Animal traditions: Behavioural inheritance in evolution.* New York: Cambridge University Press.

Binford, L. (2001). *Constructing frames of reference: An analytical method for archaeological theory building using hunter-gatherer and environmental data sets.* Berkeley, CA: University of California Press.

Boinski, S., & Garber, P. A. (Eds.). (2000). *On the move: How and why animals travel in groups.* Chicago: University of Chicago Press.

Boyd, R., & Richerson, P. J. (1985). *Culture and the evolutionary process.* Chicago: University of Chicago Press.

Branscombe, N. R., & Ellemers, N. (1998). Coping with group-based discrimination: Individualistic versus group-level strategies. In J. Swim & C. Stangor (Eds.), *Prejudice: The target's perspective* (pp. 243–266). New York: Academic Press.

Brewer, M. B. (1979). In-group bias in the minimal intergroup situation: A cognitive motivational analysis. *Psychological Bulletin, 86,* 307–324.

Brewer, M. B. (1989). Ambivalent sociality: the human condition. *Behavioral and Brain Sciences, 12,* 699.

Brewer, M. B. (1991). The social self: On being the same and different at the same time. *Personality and Social Psychology Bulletin, 17,* 475–482.

Brewer, M. B. (1997). On the social origins of human nature. In C. McGarty & A. Haslam (Eds.), *The message of social psychology* (pp. 54–62). Oxford: Blackwell.

Brewer, M. B. (1999). The psychology of prejudice: Ingroup love or outgroup hate? *Journal of Social Issues, 55,* 429–444.

Brewer, M. B., & Campbell, D. T. (1976). *Ethnocentrism and intergroup attitudes: East African evidence*. Beverly Hills, CA: Sage.

Brewer, M. B., & Caporael, L. R. (1990). Selfish genes versus selfish people: Sociobiology as origin myth. *Motivation and Emotion, 14,* 237–242.

Brewer, M. B., & Gardner, W. (1996). Who is this "we"? Levels of collective identity and self representation. *Journal of Personality and Social Psychology, 71,* 83–93.

Brewer, M. B., & Pickett, C. A. (1999). Distinctiveness motives as a source of the social self. In T. Tyler, R. Kramer, & O. John (Eds.), *The psychology of the social self* (pp. 71–87). Mahwah, NJ: Erlbaum.

Brewer, M. B., & Roccas, S. (2001). Individual values, social identity, and optimal distinctiveness. In C. Sedikides & M. Brewer (Eds.), *Individual self, relational self, collective self* (pp. 219–237). Philadelphia: Psychology Press.

Brewer, M. B., & Weber, J. G. (1994). Self-evaluation effects of interpersonal versus intergroup social comparison. *Journal of Personality and Social Psychology, 66,* 268–275.

Brewer, M. B., Manzi, J., & Shaw, J. (1993). In-group identification as a function of depersonalization, distinctiveness, and status. *Psychological Science, 4,* 88–92.

Buck, R. (1999). The biological affects: A typology. *Psychological Review, 106,* 301–336.

Buck, R. (2002). The genetics and biology of true love: Prosocial biological affects and the left hemisphere. *Psychological Review, 109,* 739–744.

Buller, D. J. (2005). *Adapting minds: Evolutionary psychology and the persistent quest for human nature*. Cambridge, MA: MIT Press.

Buss, L. W. (1987). *The evolution of individuality*. Princeton, NJ: Princeton University Press.

Cameron, J. A., Alvarez, J. M., Ruble, D. N., & Fuligni, A. J. (2001). Children's lay theories about ingroups and outgroups: Reconceptualizing research on prejudice. *Personality and Social Psychology Review, 5*(2), 118–128.

Campbell, D. T. (1974). "Downward causation" in hierarchically organised biological systems. In F. Ayala & T. Dobzhansky (Eds.), *Studies in the philosophy of biology* (pp. 179–186). London: Macmillan.

Campbell, D. T. (1990). Levels of organization, downward causation, and the selection-theory approach to evolutionary epistemology. In G. Greenberg & E. Tobach (Eds.), *Theories of the evolution of knowing* (pp. 1–17). Hillsdale, NJ: Erlbaum.

Caporael, L. R. (1997). The evolution of truly social cognition: The core configurations model. *Personality and Social Psychology Review, 1,* 276–298.

Caporael, L. R. (2001a). Evolutionary psychology: Toward a unifying theory and a hybrid science. *Annual Review of Psychology, 52,* 607–628.

Caporael, L. R. (2001b). Parts and wholes: The evolutionary importance of groups. In C. Sedikides & M. B. Brewer (Eds.), *Individual self, relational self, and collective self* (pp. 241–258). Philadelphia, PA: Psychology Press.

Caporael, L. R. (2003). Repeated assembly. In S. Schur & F. Rauscher (Eds.), *Alternative approaches to evolutionary psychology* (pp. 71–90). Durdrecht: Kluwer.

Caporael, L. R., & Brewer, M. B. (1990). We ARE Darwinians, and this is what the fuss is all about. *Motivation and Emotion, 14,* 287–293.

Caporael, L. R., & Brewer, M. B. (1991). Reviving evolutionary psychology: Biology meets society. *Journal of Social Issues, 47*(3), 187–195.

Caporael, L. R., & Brewer, M. B. (1995). Hierarchical evolutionary theory: There is an alternative, and it's not creationism. *Psychological Inquiry, 6,* 31–34.

Caporael, L. R., & Brewer, M. B. (2000). Metatheories, evolution, and psychology: Once more with feeling. *Psychological Inquiry, 11,* 23–26.

Caporael, L. R., Dawes, R. M., Orbell, J. M., & van de Kragt, A. J. C. (1989). Selfishness examined: Cooperation in the absence of egoistic incentives. *Behavioral and Brain Sciences, 12*, 683–739.

Conway III, L. G. (2004). Social contagion of time perception. *Journal of Experimental Social Psychology, 40*, 113–120.

Crocker, J., Luhtanen, R., Blaine, B., & Broadnax, S. (1994). Collective self-esteem and psychological well-being among White, Black, and Asian college students. *Personality and Social Psychology Bulletin, 20*, 503–513.

Dawes, R. M. (1988). *Rational choice in an uncertain world*. New York: Harcourt Brace Jovanovich.

Dawes, R. M., Orbell, J. M., Simmons, R. T., & van de Kragt, A. J. C. (1986). Organizing groups for collective actions. *American Political Science Review, 80*, 1171–1185.

Ellemers, N., deGilder, D., & vanden Heuvel, H. (1998). Career-oriented versus team-oriented commitment and behaviour at work. *Journal of Applied Psychology, 83*, 717–730.

Fiske, A. P. (2000). Complementarity theory: Why human social capacities evolved to require cultural complements. *Personality and Social Psychology Review, 4*, 76–94.

Foley, R. (1996). The adaptive legacy of human evolution: A search for the environment of evolutionary adaptedness. *Evolutionary Anthropology, 4*, 194–203.

Gil-White, F. (2001) Are ethnic groups biological "species" to the human brain? *Current Anthropology, 42*, 515–554.

Gottlieb, G. (2002). Developmental-behavioral initiation of evolutionary change. *Psychological Review, 109*, 211–218.

Hardin, C. D., & Higgins, E. T. (1996). Shared reality: How social verification makes the subjective objective. In R. M. Sorrentino & E. T. Higgins (Eds.), *Handbook of motivation and cognition. Vol. 3. The interpersonal context* (pp. 28–84). New York: Guilford Press.

Hassan, F. A. (1981). *Demographic archaeology*. New York: Academic Press.

Henrich, J., Boyd, R., Bowles, S., Camerer, C., Fehr, E., Gintis, H., et al. (2001). In search of *Homo economicus*: Experiments in 15 small-scale societies. *American Economic Review, 91*(2), 73–79.

Hinkle, S., & Brown, R. (1990). Intergroup comparisons and social identity: Some links and lacunae. In D. Abrams & M. Hogg (Eds.), *Social identity theory: Construction and critical advances* (pp. 48–70). London: Harvester Wheatsheaf.

Hutchins, E. (1996). *Cognition in the wild*. Cambridge, MA: MIT Press.

Jablonka, E. (1994). Inheritance systems and the evolution of new levels of individuality. *Journal of Theoretical Biology, 170*, 301–309.

Janicki, M. G. (1998). Evolutionary approaches to culture. In C. Crawford & D. Krebs (Eds.), *Handbook of evolutionary psychology* (pp. 163–207). Mahwah, NJ: Erlbaum.

Jarvenpa, R. (1993). Hunter-gatherer sociospatial organization and group size. *Behavioral and Brain Sciences, 16*, 712.

Jetten, J., Spears, R., & Manstead, A. S. R. (1998). Intergroup similarity and group variability: The effects of group distinctiveness on the expression of ingroup bias. *Journal of Personality and Social Psychology, 74*, 1481–1492.

Kashima, E., & Hardie, E. A. (2000). The development and validation of the Relational, Individual, and Collective Self-Aspects (RIC) Scale. *Asian Journal of Social Psychology, 3*, 19–48.

Kosterman, R., & Feshbach, S. (1989). Toward a measure of patriotic and nationalistic attitudes. *Political Psychology, 10*, 257–274.

Kramer, R. M., & Brewer, M. B. (1984). Effects of group identity on resource use in a simulated commons dilemma. *Journal of Personality and Social Psychology, 46,* 1044–1057.

Kurzban, R., & Leary, M. R. (2001). Evolutionary origins of stigmatization: The functions of social exclusion. *Psychological Bulletin, 127,* 187–208.

Laland, K. N., Odling-Smee, J., & Feldman, M. W. (2000). Niche construction, biological evolution, and cultural change. *Behavioral and Brain Science, 23,* 131–175.

Lee, R. B., & DeVore, I. (Eds.). (1968). *Man the hunter.* Chicago: Aldine.

Leonardelli, G. (1998). *The motivational underpinnings of social discrimination: A test of the self-esteem hypothesis.* Unpublished Master's thesis, Ohio State University.

Li, S.-C. (2003). Biocultural orchestration of developmental plasticity across levels: The interplay of biology and culture in shaping the mind and behavior across the life span. *Psychological Bulletin, 129,* 171–194.

Liang, D. W., Moreland, R., & Argote, L. (1995). Group versus individual training and group performance: The mediating role of transactive memory. *Personality and Social Psychology Bulletin, 21,* 384–393.

Lickliter, R., & Honeycutt, H. (2003). Developmental dynamics: Toward a biologically plausible evolutionary psychology. *Psychological Bulletin, 129,* 839–835.

Lloyd, E., & Feldman, M. W. (2002). Evolutionary psychology: The view from evolutionary biology. *Psychological Inquiry, 13,* 150–156.

Maynard Smith, J. (1964). Group selection and kin selection. *Nature, 201,* 1145–1147.

Maynard Smith, J. (1969). The status of neo-darwinism. In C. H. Waddington (Ed.), *Towards a theoretical biology* (Vol. 2, pp. 82–89). Edinburgh: Edinburgh University Press.

Maynard Smith, J., & Szathmáry, E. (1995). *The major transitions in evolution.* Oxford: W. H. Freeman.

Mummendey, A., Simon, B., Dietze, C., Grunert., M., Haeger, G., Kessler, S., Lettgen, S., & Schaferhoff, S. (1992). Categorization is not enough: Intergroup discrimination in negative outcome allocations. *Journal of Experimental Social Psychology, 28,* 125–144.

Newbern, D., Dansereau, D. F., & Pitre, U. (1994, June 29–July 3). *Ratings of synchrony in cooperative interaction predict cognitive performance.* Paper presented at the Annual Convention of the American Psychological Society, Washington, DC.

Norris, K. S., & Schilt, C. R. (1988). Cooperative societies in three-dimensional space: On the origins of aggregations, flocks, and schools, with special reference to dolphins and fish. *Ethology and Sociobiology, 9,* 149–179.

Perper, T. (1985). *Sex signals: The biology of love.* Philadelphia: ISI Press.

Pickett, C. A. (1999). *The role of assimilation and differentiation needs in the perception and categorization of ingroup and outgroup members.* Unpublished dissertation. Ohio State University.

Pickett, C. L., Bonner, B. L., & Coleman, J. M. (2002a). Motivated self-stereotyping: Heightened assimilation and differentiation needs result in increased levels of positive and negative self-stereotyping. *Journal of Personality and Social Psychology, 82,* 543–562.

Pickett, C. L., Silver, M. D., & Brewer, M. B. (2002b). The impact of assimilation and differentiation needs on perceived group importance and judgments of group size. *Personality and Social Psychology Bulletin, 28,* 546–558.

Pollock, G. B. (1989). Suspending disbelief of Wynne-Edwards and his reception. *Journal of Evolutionary Biology, 2,* 205–221.

Prentice, D., Miller, D., & Lightdale, J. (1994). Asymmetries in attachments to groups and to their members: Distinguishing between common-identity and common-bond groups. *Personality and Social Psychology Bulletin, 20,* 484–493.

Pulliam, H. R., & Caraco, T. (1984). Living in groups: Is there an optimal group size? In J. R. Krebs & N. B. Bavies (Eds.), *Behavioural ecology* (pp. 122–147). London: Blackwell.

Reeve, H. K., & Sherman, P. W. (1993). Adaptations and the goals of evolutionary research. *Quarterly Review of Biology, 68*, 1–31.

Reznick, D., & Travis, J. (1996). The empirical study of adaptation in natural populations. In M. R. Rose & G. V. Lauder (Eds.), *Adaptation* (pp. 243–289). New York: Academic Press.

Roccas, S., & Schwartz, S. (1993). Effects of intergroup similarity on intergroup relations. *European Journal of Social Psychology, 23*, 581–595.

Schmitt, D. P., & Pilcher, J. J. (2004). Evaluating evidence of psychological adaptation: How do we know one when we see one? *Psychological Science, 15*, 643–649.

Sedikides, C., & M. B. Brewer (Eds.). (2001). *Individual self, relational self, and collective self.* Philadelphia: Psychology Press.

Simon, B., Glassner-Bayerl, B., & Stratenwerth, I. (1991). Stereotyping and self-stereotyping in a natural intergroup context: The case of heterosexual and homosexual men. *Social Psychology Quarterly, 54*, 252–266.

Smith, E. A., Borgerhoff Mulder, M., & Hill, K. (2001). Controversies in the evolutionary social sciences: A guide for the perplexed. *Trends in Ecology and Evolution, 16*, 128–135.

Stiner, M. C. (2002). Carnivory, coevolution, and the geographic spread of the genus *Homo. Journal of Archeological Research, 10*, 1–63.

Struch, N., & Schwartz, S. H. (1989). Intergroup aggression: Its predictors and distinctness from in-group bias. *Journal of Personality and Social Psychology, 56*, 364–373.

Tajfel, H., Billig, M., Bundy, R., & Flament, C. (1971). Social categorization and intergroup behaviour. *European Journal of Social Psychology, 1*, 149–178.

van Knippenberg, D., & van Schie, E. (2000). Foci and correlates of organizational identification. *Journal of Occupational and Organizational Psychology, 73*, 137–147.

Wegner, D. M. (1986). Transactive memory: A contemporary analysis of the group mind. In B. Mullen & G. R. Goethals (Eds.), *Theories of group behavior* (pp. 185–208). New York: Springer.

Wegner, D. M., Raymond, P., & Erber, R. (1991). Transactive memory in close relationships. *Journal of Personality and Social Psychology, 61*, 923–929.

Wells, P. S. (1998). Identity and material culture in the later prehistory of Central Europe. *Journal of Archaeological Research, 6*, 239–298.

Williams, G. C. (1966). *Adaptation and natural selection.* Princeton, NJ: Princeton University Press.

Wilson, E. O. (1975). *Sociobiology: The new synthesis.* Cambridge, MA: Harvard University Press.

Wynne-Edwards, V. C. (1962). *Animal dispersion in relation to social behaviour.* London: Oliver and Boyd.

8

Evolutionary Bases of Prejudices

STEVEN L. NEUBERG and CATHERINE A. COTTRELL

*L*eaf through a daily newspaper, turn on the evening news, or log on to your favorite Internet news site and you will confront the ubiquity with which prejudices, discrimination, and intergroup conflict permeate everyday life. As we wrote this chapter, the news offered accounts of ethnic violence in Sudan, anti-discrimination lawsuits filed by overweight employees in the U.S., and inflammatory rhetoric spewing from French nationalists and Muslims over whether to allow students to wear religious head coverings in public school. Today, you may come across reports of Palestinians and Israelis again fighting in the Middle East, legislation proposed by nationalistic Germans to limit third-world immigration into their country, or religious conservatives and gay activists in the U.S. hurling nasty stereotype-laced barbs at one another over the issue of same-sex marriage.

Traditional social psychological perspectives on prejudice, discrimination, and intergroup conflict have focused examinations of such intergroup clashes on a number of general processes, including simple categorization, social learning, perceived competition for limited resources, and desires to enhance views of the self or one's groups (e.g., Allport, 1954; Fein & Spencer, 1997; Greenberg et al., 1990; Hamilton, 1981; Jost & Banaji, 1994; Tajfel, 1969; Tajfel & Turner, 1986). Although these approaches will continue to guide productive analysis and research, we believe that their theoretical and practical utility are limited by a focus on domain-general processes that precludes them from readily accounting for important phenomena related to issues of *content*—for the qualitatively distinct stereotypes associated with different groups, the different patterns of emotions and behaviors elicited by these groups, and the different contextual and personality factors that facilitate and inhibit these stereotypes, emotions, and actions. Why, for instance, do gay men often evoke disgust and desires to distance one's school-aged children from them, whereas Native Americans often evoke pity and desires to establish community-outreach programs for them, and African Americans often evoke fear and desires to learn new self-protection techniques? Why are those individuals concerned with contracting infectious diseases especially prejudiced against others who are physically misshapen, whereas those who view the world as a dangerous place especially prejudiced against members of ethnic outgroups? In this chapter, we review recent research on prejudice and related phenomena that have been inspired by an evolutionary framework—a framework that anticipates the phenomena that more traditional approaches struggle, even *post hoc*, to explain.

The current perspective starts from a simple supposition—that contemporary prejudices may be products of adaptations engineered by natural selection to manage the threats posed to ancestral humans by their social environments (Kurzban & Leary, 2001; Neuberg, Smith, & Asher, 2000; Schaller, Park, & Faulkner, 2003). The ancestral physical environment was harsh, and the human form of sociality—characterized by enduring, highly interdependent, cooperative alliances among small numbers of individuals—may have evolved as a means to enhance individual fitness in the face of this severity. Presumably, individuals were better able to acquire and protect critical resources (e.g., food, shelter, mates) and achieve fundamental tasks (e.g., self-protection, child rearing) by joining together in coalitions than by facing life's challenges alone (Brewer, 2001; Campbell, 1982; Richerson & Boyd, 1995). Human "ultrasociality" can thus be considered a valuable adaptation that both protects individuals from the environment's many dangers and facilitates their effective exploitation of the environment's many opportunities (Barchas, 1986; Brewer, 1997; Brewer & Caporael, 1990; Leakey, 1978).

Ultrasociality also has its fitness costs, however, as group living exposes one to individuals capable of inflicting physical harm, spreading contagious disease, free riding on one's efforts, and the like (e.g., Alexander, 1974; Dunbar, 1988). For the benefits of sociality to exceed its costs, then, mechanisms would have evolved (or existing evolved mechanisms would have been exploited) to (1) attune individuals to the features or behaviors of others that would characterize them as potential threats and (2) lead individuals to respond to these perceived threats in ways that could mitigate or eliminate them. Just as eyelids, blink reflexes, eyelashes, and tear ducts evolved to protect the eye and its important functions, prejudice and discrimination processes may have evolved to protect ultrasociality and its important functions.

The presence of evolved sociality-preserving mechanisms is not exclusive to humans; other social animals are also attuned to the kinds of dangers potentially posed by conspecifics within or outside the group and respond with behaviors apparently designed to protect themselves (and their groups) from these dangers. For instance, three-spined stickleback fish tend to avoid those that exhibit physical signs of parasitic infestation (Dugatkin, FitzGerald, & Lavoie, 1994), and chimpanzees have been observed attacking and rejecting fellow group members who come to manifest physical indications of contagious disease (e.g., polio; Goodall, 1986). Many nonhuman social creatures also act aggressively toward outsiders who attempt to infiltrate their established group (e.g., Goodall, 1986), and show evidence of stigmatizing ingroup members whose actions endanger the internal workings of the group: Chimpanzees, for instance, often reject others who violate the norm of reciprocity in food-sharing (de Waal, 1989).

Before delving deeply into our evolution-based perspective, we begin by noting the evolutionary significance of simple social categorization and stereotyping processes. The bulk of the chapter is then devoted to describing a threat-based approach to understanding prejudices, outlining some implications of this approach for altering unwarranted prejudices, and reviewing recent findings relevant to these issues.

THE BIASED NATURE OF SIMPLE SOCIAL CATEGORIZATION

Because human sociality poses risks as well as rewards, individuals are inherently selective and discriminating in their decisions about whom to pursue for friendships, romantic relationships, business associations, and such (Kurzban & Leary, 2001; Kurzban & Neuberg, 2005; Tooby & Cosmides, 1996). Sometimes we choose our friends, lovers, and business associates on the basis of our own personal experiences with them or on their public reputations as interaction partners. Often, however, we make affiliation decisions in the absence of such information, relying instead on personal features of others that merely suggest, probabilistically, their suitability as affiliation partners. This heuristic judgment process—perceiving the features of an individual, using these features to categorize him or her into a particular known group, and then drawing additional inferences about the individual based on this social categorization—is one form of stereotyping. Upon encountering on the street a person muttering to himself, one is likely to presume that he (compared to a silent passerby) is mentally ill, unpredictable, and thus to be avoided; upon meeting a previously unknown cousin from one's ancestral country, one may presume that she (compared to an unrelated stranger) will feel a sense of shared kinship and may thus be a trustworthy cooperation partner.

Questions surrounding such social categorization and stereotyping processes have generated a sizable body of valuable literature (see Brewer, 1988; Fiske & Neuberg, 1990; Hamilton & Sherman, 1994; Macrae, Stangor, & Hewstone, 1996). We note four brief points about this research that are particularly relevant to our threat-based approach to intergroup conflict.

First, an evolutionary perspective suggests that some characteristics, more than others, will define natural social categories in stereotyping processes. That is, because certain characteristics offer specific information particularly relevant to reproductive fitness, people may be especially quick to make social categorizations along these dimensions. For example, given the central role of sex in human reproduction, people ought to rapidly categorize individuals by their sex and develop reasonably articulated beliefs about males and females. Given the very different challenges and opportunities afforded by individuals of different ages, it would likewise make sense that people easily differentiate others by age and possess different sets of beliefs based on these differentiations. And given that group living is so central to individual fitness, and that humans have apparently been living as members of coalitions for millions of years, we should be quite ready to differentiate between members of coalitional ingroups versus outgroups. These hypotheses have all received strong support in the research literature (e.g., Brewer & Lui,

1989; Pendry & Macrae, 1996; Stangor, Lynch, Duan, & Glass, 1992; Taylor, Fiske, Etcoff, & Ruderman, 1978; Zárate & Smith, 1990).

Second, our threat-based evolutionary approach predicts that the most compelling, and influential, stereotypes of a particular group will be those that reflect important information about the threats and opportunities ostensibly afforded by that group. That is, we suspect that the most dominant stereotypic knowledge may be usefully framed in terms of the stable beliefs one holds about the threats and opportunities other groups are thought to offer one's own group. For example, what it means for a group to be stereotyped as "aggressive" is that their members are perceived to threaten the physical safety of one's own group; what it means for a group to be stereotyped as "lazy" is that their members are perceived to threaten the reciprocal exchange of efforts with one's own group. We discuss below several specific threats to ultrasociality (see Cottrell & Neuberg, 2005, for a somewhat more inclusive list); these threats provide a framework for predicting the content of stereotypes that are likely to dominate in people's characterizations of other groups.

Third, although many groups are characterized by both positive and negative stereotypes (Devine & Elliot, 1995; Katz & Braly, 1933; Madon et al., 2001; Niemann, Jennings, Rozelle, Baxter, & Sullivan, 1994), an evolutionary perspective suggests that, by default, beliefs about novel outgroups should lean toward being unfavorable—that is, toward being "threat-heavy"—until more textured information is gathered about them. Ingroup coalitions are characterized largely by the repeated reciprocal exchanges of material goods or efforts over time and by commitments to continue such exchanges in the future. Nearly by definition, such exchange histories and commitments do not exist across coalitional lines. Fitness considerations suggest that our stereotypes and stereotypical inferences should thus err toward characterizing outgroup coalitions and their members as being, in particular, untrustworthy and/or dangerous, which ought to propel us away from favorable interactions with them until we learn otherwise. The presence of such a negativity bias fits with the logic of Nesse's "smoke detector principle" (Nesse, 2005) and error management theory (Haselton & Buss, 2000, 2003), is articulated nicely in a thought-provoking essay by the anthropologist Robin Fox (1992), and is supported by data from the minimal intergroup and other research paradigms (e.g., Insko & Schopler, 1998; Mullen, Brown, & Smith, 1992; Tajfel, 1982).

Fourth, researchers have frequently viewed stereotyping as an irrational process that interferes with the human quest for judgmental accuracy—as an irrationality that leaves in its wake much human misery. Although there is no doubt that stereotyping processes can create problems for both perceivers and their targets, the potential benefits of stereotyping should not be dismissed too readily. Stereotyping is relatively effortless and quick—the better half of "quick and dirty." Stereotyping allows us to gain ostensibly useful knowledge about a particular individual rapidly, thereby enabling us to shift our limited attention to other potential threats and opportunities in our complex, dynamic social environments. And when stereotypical inferences have meaningful kernels of truth to them, as they often do (Lee, Jussim, & McCauley, 1995; Swim, 1994), the fitness benefits of a general inclination to stereotype others (and to act upon these stereotypes) may be greater than its fitness costs—a notion that probably explains why automatic social categorization is the default means of forming impressions of others (e.g., Brewer, 1988; Devine, 1989; Fiske & Neuberg, 1990; Macrae, Milne, & Bodenhausen, 1994). Of course, we do not deny that particular instances of stereotyping may lead to egregious errors of judgment. However, we also recognize the value of acknowledging that stereotyping, like all cognitive strategies, may be more usefully employed in some circumstances than in others. From our perspective, the speed and efficiency of stereotyping should be particularly beneficial when an individual encounters a situation in which an automatic response offers powerful fitness advantages—that is, when threats to one's personal well-being or resources, to one's group's resources, or to the integrity of one's group appear to be immediate in proximity or time.

In sum, an evolutionary approach makes some suggestions regarding what kinds of social categories and stereotypes are likely to predominate in people's minds, provides a rationale for why social stereotyping—by its very nature—is likely to be biased toward seeing unknown individuals and known outgroup members as being untrustworthy and potentially dangerous, and takes explicit note of the trade-offs inherent in social categorization and stereotyping processes.

PREJUDICES AS RESPONSES TO TANGIBLE THREATS

According to an evolutionary perspective, many prejudices, stereotypes, and discriminatory tendencies result from evolved psychological mechanisms that conferred adaptive benefits in protecting early humans against particular social threats (Kurzban & Leary, 2001; Kurzban & Neuberg, 2005; Schaller & Neuberg, 2005).

Consider the nonsocial example of a charging rhinoceros that elicits feelings of fear, thoughts of physical harm, a rush of adrenaline, and an inclination to run—all to facilitate escape from the rampaging creature. This example illustrates a general template for how humans deal with threats, one we believe is useful for understanding prejudice: Humans have evolved to become sensitive to the presence of cues that imply threats to well-being (e.g., a rapidly looming large object) and to generate in response to these cues functionally focused emotional reactions (e.g., fear) and cognitive associations (e.g., ideas of physical harm) that work together to motivate specific behaviors (e.g., running away, hiding) designed to mitigate the potential impact of the threat.

In this section, we briefly discuss some of the threats humans may be particularly attuned to, articulate the connections between these specific threats and the specific "prejudice syndromes" they engage, and review some recent empirical findings demonstrating the value of this approach. Explicit to our approach are the ideas that (1) there exist multiple, qualitatively distinct prejudice syndromes, and (2) these prejudices serve qualitatively different functions (i.e., they exist to address qualitatively distinct threats and opportunities). In this sense, prejudice syndromes may be usefully characterized as "modular"—as focused, domain-specific solutions to different recurrent problems affecting the reproductive fitness of ancestral humans (e.g., Cosmides, Tooby, & Barkow, 1992; Crawford, 1998; Tooby & Cosmides, 1990). Also explicit to our approach is that people are not prejudiced against particular groups *per se*, but rather are prejudiced against the threats that these groups are seen to pose. We elaborate on this latter point below.

Threats to Fitness and the Features that Cue Them

The ultimate desired outcome from an evolutionary perspective is to pass one's genes onto future generations. This requires that one survive to mate successfully and have one's offspring survive long enough to mate successfully as well. From this perspective, mechanisms that led our ancestors to be attuned to cues suggesting threats to their (and to their kin's) physical safety and health would have been adaptive, as threats to safety and health decrease the likelihood and opportunity for successful reproduction. Moreover, because human ancestors were fundamentally social creatures who gained great benefits from effective group action, we might expect to find mechanisms that lead humans to be attuned to threats to the resources that groups provide us—e.g., territory, property, economic standing—as well as to threats to the structures and processes that encourage effective and efficient group operations. According to the anthropological literature, effective groups tend to possess strong norms of reciprocity, trust among members, common values, authority structures for organizing individual effort and distributing group resources, mechanisms for socializing members, and the like (e.g., Brown, 1991). Individuals should thus be especially attuned to potential threats to reciprocity, trust, value systems, authority structures, socialization processes, and so on (Neuberg et al., 2000).

These threats are qualitatively distinct, and thus will often be cued by qualitatively distinct features (see Table 8.1 for several illustrative examples). Cues signaling a potential threat of physical injury include those that suggest a capacity to do harm (e.g., large size, presence of a weapon), a current intention to do harm (e.g., rapid approach, angry facial expression), and an increased probability of a future inclination to do harm (e.g., maleness, outgroup-identifying features such as physiognomy, clothing, language, skin color). Cues suggesting threats to health include those highly diagnostic of the presence of contagious pathogens (e.g., fluid secretions, skin lesions), those implicated heuristically by the more general tendency for diseased individuals to exhibit physical or behavioral abnormalities (e.g., facial scars, nonworking limbs, etc.; Kurzban & Leary, 2001; Park, Faulkner, & Schaller, 2003; Schaller et al., 2003), those suggesting behaviors that bring one into contact with contaminated materials (e.g., anal sex), and those suggesting a lack of "decontamination" behaviors (e.g., dirtiness). Potential threats to group integrity may be cued by features that, for example, imply an inability to contribute to group efforts (e.g., those suggesting physical or mental disability) or an unwillingness to do so (e.g., membership in another coalition, facial morphologies suggestive of untrustworthiness; Yamagishi, Tanida, Mishima, Shimoma, & Kanazawa, 2003; Zebrowitz, Voinescu, & Collins, 1996).

TABLE 8.1   An Illustrative Set of Prejudices, the Perceived Intergroup Threats that Elicit Them, and Variables that Moderate Them

Perceived Threat to Ingroup	Example Cues to Threat	Primary Prejudice Syndrome Elicited by Threat	Example Moderating Variables
Threat to physical safety	Large size, quick approach, angry facial expression, maleness	Fear and safety-preserving behaviors	Ambient darkness, belief in a dangerous world
Threat to physical health	Physical malformations, lack of cleanliness, foreign food preparation customs	Disgust and health-protecting behaviors	Physical contact, perceived vulnerability to disease
Threat to reciprocity relations	Unfamiliarity, mental or physical disability, untrustworthy appearance (i.e.,"crooked-face")	Anger and avoidance of exchange opportunities	Economic stress, belief in "protestant work ethic"

Ancestral humans with inclinations to attend to and be subsequently wary of individuals exhibiting cues suggesting that they posed physical safety, health, or group integrity threats would have reduced their exposure to these threats and thereby would have reproduced more successfully than their counterparts lacking these inclinations. Over time, the human population would have increasingly come to possess these inclinations, such that even in modern times these mechanisms would influence our reactions to others.

It is important to make several points here. First, as illustrated with the above examples, different cues signal different threats. As such, the ability to *differentiate* among threats and their cues will be critical to the effectiveness of any functional system that must operate within a complex environment, which we shall see below.

Second, although there likely exist evolved sensitivities to some particular features—the strongest candidates to us would appear to include cross-cultural, cross-species cues suggesting threats to physical safety (e.g., rapid approach, large size, unfamiliarity) and health (e.g., unusual bodily discharges, erratic limb movements)—many cues gain their meaning via an innate capacity to learn especially quickly those features, within local environments, that predict potential threats (Öhman & Mineka, 2001).

For instance, it seems quite clear that there exists no evolved racial prejudice *per se*, as contact with members of different races is too recent a development to have biologically evolved (Kurzban, Tooby, & Cosmides, 2001). What likely has evolved, however, is a psychology that is (1) sensitive to the threats potentially posed by coalitional outgroups (which have existed for millions of years), (2) knowledgeable about the general classes of cues that imply membership in coalitional outgroups (e.g., language, physiognomy, cultural customs), and (3) inclined to learn the specific features within the local environment that cue membership in specific outgroups (Kurzban et al., 2001; Schaller et al., 2003). In the United

States, skin color and racial physiognomy are cues to coalitional groups in conflict with one another, and thus individuals learn to classify others on these dimensions; in other societies, coalitional conflict rests on other distinctions (e.g., tribal affiliation), and thus people there learn to classify others on the basis of features such as language or dress. Thus, although cursory characterizations suggest that very different prejudices exist in these different cultures, a more thorough analysis reveals that these cultures share a common, evolved coalitional psychology—one sensitive to the kinds of information likely to reveal threatening coalitional outgroups and inclined to learn from the local culture the features useful for identifying their members. Norenzayan and Heine (2005; Norenzayan, Schaller, & Heine, this volume) provide thoughtful discussions of the linkages between evolved adaptations and cultural influences as they create and constrain contemporary social behavior.

Finally, the links between perceived features and presumed threat are merely probabilistic. Although large, rapidly approaching men may indeed often pose very real physical dangers, and individuals with open sores and coughs may indeed be more effective vectors of contagious disease, such individuals, instead, could be approaching to provide aid or could be suffering from a noncontagious malady, respectively. The heuristic nature of the cue-threat link is highlighted by the sometimes clearly irrational nature of these links. For instance, because cues implying health threats derive from the tendency for diseased individuals to exhibit physical or behavioral abnormalities, threat-based reactions are also directed toward individuals with facial scars, missing limbs, obesity, and other physical disfigurements—even when such individuals are explicitly known not to be carrying a contagious disease (Park et al., 2003; Zebrowitz & Collins, 1997).

Prejudice Syndromes

We suggest that humans (and other social animals) evolved a complement of "prejudice syndromes"—integrated suites of emotional reactions, stereotypical expectations, and discriminatory inclinations—designed to minimize the set of threats often posed by sociality (Schaller & Neuberg, 2005).

Emotions are central to any functional system, as they (1) alert the individual to the presence of circumstances that threaten or profit important goals and (2) organize and coordinate psychological action (attention, inferences, behavioral inclinations) so that we might respond more effectively to events related to survival and success (e.g., Carver & Scheier, 1990; Cosmides & Tooby, 2000; Ekman, 1999; Nesse, 1990; Plutchik, 1980, 2003; Simon, 1967; Tooby & Cosmides, 1990). Note that there is a functional specificity to the emotional system: Different emotions are evoked by different threatening events (e.g., Frijda, 1986; Izard, 1991; Plutchik, 1980; Roseman, Wiest, & Swartz, 1994; Tomkins, 1963). The threat to physical safety like that posed by the rushing rhinoceros immediately elicits fear—and not anger, disgust, sadness, guilt, or pity. Moreover, each emotion is associated with its own specific configuration of physiological, cognitive, and behavioral tendencies that operate together to facilitate resolution of the threat. The fear elicited by the rapidly looming rhino directs our attention toward escape and prepares us via its associated "symptoms"—the rush of adrenaline, the flow of blood toward large muscles, etc.—to attempt a get-away.

The emotion systems that constitute the core of prejudice syndromes—most prominently, the fear, anger, and disgust systems—serve fundamental, nonsocial functions for humans (e.g., predator avoidance, protection of offspring, avoidance of rotting meat) and exist in nonsocial and minimally social animals that have much longer evolutionary histories than humans (e.g., Izard, 1978; Öhman, 1993; Rozin, Haidt, & McCauley, 1993); these emotional systems did not evolve as a means of addressing problems inherent in ultrasociality. Natural selection, however, frequently exploits existing adaptations for alternative purposes. Because of the long history of human ultrasociality, these evolved emotion systems likely became exploited to help humans protect valuable group resources and maintain the integrity of critical social structures and processes. Thus, just as an anticipated threat of a charging beast evokes fear and its associated cognitions and behavioral inclinations, an anticipated threat of an attack on one's coalition by members of another coalition should do the same; just as an attempt by a scavenging animal to steal hard-won food would evoke something like anger in pre-ultrasocial ancestors, so too might the attempted theft of a valuable group resource evoke anger in their ultrasocial descendants. Somewhat more complex is the exploitation of pre-existing disgust mechanisms—which likely initially evolved to solve the nonsocial problem of unwittingly ingesting pathogen-contaminated materials—to also serve social functions related to not just physical but also moral contamination (Haidt, Rozin, McCauley, & Imada, 1997; Rozin, Lowery, & Ebert, 1994; Keltner, Haidt, & Shiota, this volume).

Recent findings strongly support the idea of functional prejudice syndromes. In a series of studies (e.g., Cottrell & Neuberg, 2004; Cottrell & Neuberg, 2005; Neuberg & Cottrell, 2002), we have assessed European Americans' threat perceptions, prejudice, emotional reactions, and behavioral inclinations toward a wide range of racial, ethnic, national, religious, ideological, and sexual orientation groups. First, as one might expect, different groups often evoke quite different patterns of threat perceptions—a finding underappreciated by traditional realistic threat models, which have not formally differentiated among qualitatively distinct tangible threats (LeVine & Campbell, 1972; Sherif, 1966; Stephan & Renfro, 2002).

More important, different patterns of threat are associated with different, and functionally appropriate, patterns of elicited emotions and behavioral inclinations. For example, within our undergraduate European American population, African Americans and Mexican Americans elicit perceptions of greater threat to physical safety, greater amounts of reported fear, and reports of enhanced inclinations to engage in safety-preserving behaviors such as carrying a means of self-defense, learning new self-defense strategies, and voting to increase police patrols. Fundamentalist Christians and feminist activists are seen to pose threats to values and personal freedoms, elicit emotion profiles characterized by relatively high levels of moral disgust and anger, and evoke enhanced inclinations to perform value- and freedom-defending behaviors such as removing children from classrooms in which fundamentalist Christians and feminist activists are teaching, preventing children from reading books or watching television shows about them, and protesting appointments of such individuals to government committees that make social policies and laws. Gay men are seen to pose greater threats to health (presumably because of the heuristic association between anal intercourse and HIV), elicit relatively high levels of physical disgust, and evoke enhanced inclinations to carry out health-protecting behaviors such as getting more frequent medical checkups, avoiding a water fountain or restroom if it has just been used by a gay man, and washing one's hands after contact with such individuals. As hypothesized, different threats are associated with different prejudice syndromes.

Moreover, after statistically controlling for the specific threats ostensibly posed by the different groups, the nature of the groups themselves predicts little of our participants' emotional reactions (Cottrell & Neuberg, 2005). The reverse is not the case, however; specific threats continue to powerfully predict emotional reactions even after controlling for the groups. It seems, then, that people may not be prejudiced against particular groups *per se*, but rather may be prejudiced against the specific constellations of threats apparently posed by these groups. This is a subtle, but important, distinction. It suggests a continuity between social prejudices and the more fundamental (and nonsocial) evolved mechanisms that link particular threats to particular emotions and behavioral inclinations. It helps explain why particular prejudices against some groups have changed over time, and, for some (e.g., many 19th and early 20th century immigrant groups to the US), have essentially disappeared: The threats ostensibly posed by a particular group either changed or faded away. And, related to this last point, it suggests an approach to prejudice reduction that is more textured than typically proposed: Change the particular perceived threats, and the particular prejudices change. We explore this last point in more detail below.

The above findings, and others like them, capture people's perceptions of emotional reactions elicited by, and behavioral inclinations toward, *known* groups, meaning that our findings linking threats to emotions to behavioral inclinations are correlational. The functional hypothesis, though, is causal: Threats perceived to be posed by a group should *cause* the experience of threat-relevant emotions, which should activate or strengthen threat-relevant behavioral inclinations. In a recent experiment, we led participants to believe that particular ethnic groups from Central Europe were immigrating in increasing numbers to our local metropolitan area. In reality, these groups were fictitious, enabling us to manipulate via bogus United Nations documents the particular threats—e.g., to physical safety, health, values—these groups would ostensibly pose to our local community. In a similar experiment, we led our participants to believe that individuals with exotic, understudied diseases would be moving to a research center on campus; as in the other study, we manipulated the threats these individuals ostensibly posed to the local collegiate community. In both studies, we measured participants' emotional reactions to these groups and their behavioral inclinations toward them. Results were largely consistent with predictions (Wilbur, Shapiro, & Neuberg, 2005). As one example, immigrants presented as posing physical safety threats evoked from our participants enhanced fear and reports that they would more often "look over their shoulders" and would be more likely to purchase a means of self-defense. Moreover, in this example and others, the effect of the manipulated threat on behavioral inclinations was mediated by the functionally related emotion. Findings such as these reveal that the linkages between perceived threats and emotional and behavioral reactions are indeed causal.

The concept of functional prejudice syndromes adds both texture and depth to an understanding of prejudice and discrimination. The conventional view of negative prejudice holds that it is an unfavorable feeling toward a group and its members (e.g., Allport, 1954; Fiske, 1998). This conceptualization of prejudice, as a general attitude or simple evaluation, has long dominated the research literature and has been the point of departure for most theoretical and empirical approaches designed to explicate prejudice's origins, operations, and implications. This view ignores, however, the complexity of the actual emotional reactions people have to other groups (e.g., Brewer & Alexander, 2002; Dijker, 1987; Esses, Haddock, & Zanna, 1993; Fiske, Cuddy, Glick, & Xu, 2002; Mackie, Devos, & Smith, 2000). An evolutionary approach anticipates this complexity, as it presumes that different groups should elicit qualitatively different prejudices to the extent that they are perceived to pose qualitatively different threats. Moreover, one implication of this evolutionary approach is that conventional methods of measuring prejudice—as simple favorable versus unfavorable attitudes, employing direct or indirect "feeling thermometers" of various sorts (e.g., Bobo & Kluegel, 1993; Greenwald, McGhee, & Schwartz, 1998)—can mask the presence of these qualitatively different prejudices. Indeed, numerous cases within our data sets reveal that groups that elicit the same levels of negative prejudice using conventional measures actually elicit quite different patterns of discrete emotions (Cottrell & Neuberg, 2005). Given that different emotional patterns emerge from different patterns of threat and motivate different patterns of behavior, as our data show, employing attitude-based conceptualizations and operationalizations of prejudice can only hinder the development of coherent prejudice theory and the design of successful prejudice-reducing interventions.

In sum, consistent with an evolutionary approach, these and other recent findings (e.g., Schaller et al., 2003; Schaller, Park, & Mueller, 2003) make clear that people react with specific, threat-focused responses—prejudice syndromes—to groups they view as threatening.

Specific Vulnerabilities Amplify Specific Prejudices

Evolved responses are functionally flexible: They are sensitive to contextual information that heuristically suggests their relevance and cost–benefit value (e.g., Conway & Schaller, 2002; Gangestad & Simpson, 2000; Kenrick, Li, & Butner, 2003; Schaller et al., 2003). To say that fear is an evolved response is not to say we are always fearful. Rather, it is to say that we become fearful when circumstances—situational or internal—imply the presence of some threat to physical safety. *If* one feels vulnerable to a particular threat, *then* the evolved responses specific to that threat will be engaged. For example, ambient darkness, which suggests one's vulnerability to danger and harm, tends to increase the magnitude of the acoustic startle reflex (Grillon, Pellowski, Merikangas, & Davis, 1997). Similarly, previous attacks by predators lower the threshold at which prey identify subsequent events as being dangerous (Nesse, 2005). Thus, if prejudice syndromes are indeed responses to specific threats, as we have suggested, they ought to be triggered more easily, and experienced more intensely, in some (specific) situations (i.e., those that suggest a vulnerability to the target-relevant threat) and for some (specific) individuals (i.e., those who have a low threshold for perceiving—accurately or not—the target-relevant threat).

For example, in situations that activate a concern for physical safety, and for people who are chronically concerned about physical safety, prejudice syndromes characterized by a prominent fear component—such as those elicited by African Americans in our university and national samples—should emerge more readily and powerfully. Consider, then, a recent experiment by Schaller et al. (2003). Nonblack students, who had previously completed a scale assessing chronic concerns about physical safety (Belief in a Dangerous World, BDW; Altemeyer, 1988), rated white men and black men on characteristics relevant to physical safety threat (e.g., hostility) and irrelevant to such a threat (e.g., ignorance) in a room that was either well lit or totally darkened. In ancestral times especially, ambient darkness would have been a valid indicator of one's vulnerability to physical attack, so much so that a psychological inclination toward being fearful in the dark would likely have been selected for. As a consequence, even today, people should nonetheless exhibit a physical safety concern when plunged into darkness. The darkened laboratory room was thus viewed by the researchers as a situational activator of self-protective concern.

Neither room darkness nor dispositional vulnerability influenced ratings of the two groups on the threat-irrelevant traits. However, consistent with the idea that felt vulnerability ought to enhance the prominence of functionally relevant prejudice syndromes, participants who both scored high on the BDW and had been plunged into darkness judged the black men as particularly hostile and untrustworthy. Note the textured, functional specificity of this effect: Individuals who felt dispositionally less vulnerable to harm did not display this stereotypical bias against black men; individuals in a nonthreatening situation (i.e., the well-lit room) did not exhibit this bias against the black men; this bias did not extend to evaluations of black men on unfavorable stereotypical, but nonthreatening, traits; and even those who both possessed a dispositional vulnerability to physical threat and were confronted by a fear-provoking situation did not exhibit such a bias toward nonblack targets.

A set of studies by Jon Maner and his colleagues (Maner et al., 2005) makes a similar point. In one experiment, European American participants were exposed to a film designed to elicit self-protection concerns (versus a control film), and subsequently judged the emotions putatively displayed on the (objectively neutrally expressive) faces of briefly presented male and female African American (outgroup) and European American (ingroup) targets. The researchers' hypothesis was guided by a functional logic—that individuals concerned with self-protection would be especially biased toward seeing indicators of threat in those most believed to pose the possibility of threatening one's physical safety. Consistent with this reasoning, participants were especially likely to perceive anger (a signal of impending safety threat) on the faces of the outgroup, African American males (i.e., those stereotypically believed to have the strongest inclination to threaten physical safety). Note, again, the functional specificity of the effect: Inferences of anger were not made to European American (male or female) or to African American female faces; the inference of emotion to the African American male faces was limited to anger, and did not extend to even other high arousal negative emotions (i.e., fear); and the attributions of anger to African American male faces did not occur in the nonthreatening control condition.

Consider a second threat domain. As discussed above, one of the costs posed by sociality is the enhanced risk of catching diseases from others. Indeed, the perception of this health threat underlies, at least partially, the stigmatization of people known to carry contagious diseases (e.g., Crandall & Moriarty, 1995). Given the risk-averse nature of evolved threat-avoidance mechanisms, however, an evolutionary approach also suggests that people may stigmatize even those who are healthy but nonetheless possess cues that merely *suggest* the presence of contagious disease (Kurzban & Leary, 2001; Schaller et al., 2003). As we noted above, these cues could include any salient morphological abnormality—what Goffman (1963) referred to as "abominations of body"—as contagious pathogens have often-enough across evolutionary time been revealed via their effects on observable features of body (e.g., Rhodes, Zebrowitz, Clark, Kalick, Hightower, & McKay, 2001). Thus, physical abnormalities are likely to automatically activate disease-relevant emotions (e.g., disgust) and cognitions (e.g., implicit associations between target persons and the concept of disease) that motivate behavioral avoidance. And just as enhancing one's vulnerability to physical safety threat amplifies the emergence of a fear-based prejudice syndrome, an enhanced vulnerability to a health threat should amplify the emergence of a disgust-based prejudice syndrome.

Again, research by Schaller and his colleagues is instructive. Participants in one study implicitly associated physically disabled individuals with disease—even when informed that the disability was caused by disease-irrelevant *accidents*—and this association was stronger for those who dispositionally viewed themselves as being highly vulnerable to contagious disease (e.g., they thought they caught colds easily; Park et al., 2003). In another study, participants who reported being vulnerable to disease also reported holding stronger negative prejudices against obese individuals, and participants who had recently been exposed to a slide show depicting images of contagious pathogens and diseases were especially likely to implicitly associate the specific concept of disease, but not the more general concept of unpleasantness, with fat people (but not thin people; Park, Schaller, & Crandall, 2005).

Related research capitalizes on the idea that subjectively foreign people are also likely to be heuristically associated with disease. In times long past, individuals from outside one's own coalition were more likely than ingroup members to carry pathogens for which ingroup members had not yet developed immunities. Subjective foreignness would thus have been a useful (albeit imperfect) indicator of contagion risk, and thus a psychological sensitivity to (and wariness of) foreignness may have been selected for, such that even in contemporary times people—especially those dispositionally concerned with their vulnerability to disease—would see foreign individuals as threats to health and react to them with negative (disgust-based) prejudice.

In one set of studies, participants who were chronically concerned about contracting disease were more likely to implicitly associate unfamiliar, but not familiar, immigrant groups with danger, and those who had recently viewed a slide show depicting images of contagious germs and bacteria were especially likely to respond with negative evaluations of unfamiliar, but not familiar, immigrant groups (Faulkner, Schaller, Park, & Duncan, 2004). In other research, pregnant women in the first trimester—when both mother and fetus are most vulnerable to disease and infection—reported intensified negative feelings toward foreign students living in the U.S., relative to those reported by women in later trimesters (Navarrete, Fessler, & Eng, 2005).

We see, then, that an approach to prejudice emerging from an evolutionary perspective not only accurately predicts the presence of multiple, highly articulated prejudice syndromes, each functionally elicited by specific threats, but it also successfully suggests factors—personal and situational—that should amplify or inhibit the emergence of each syndrome and thereby alter reactions to different groups. It is useful to note that the moderating variables just discussed—e.g., ambient darkness, perceived vulnerability to contagious diseases, pregnancy status—lie well outside the theoretical architecture of nonevolutionary approaches to understanding stereotyping and prejudice. The textured, patterned results of the studies reported here, as well as others, follow quite clearly from an evolutionary-based functional analysis; they are difficult to explain with other, more traditional, theoretical approaches to prejudice.

IMPLICATIONS FOR INTERVENTION

The threat-based approach to prejudice—in which specific cues lead to specific perceptions of threat, which themselves lead to functionally-relevant prejudice syndromes and which are moderated by functionally-relevant contextual factors—suggests various strategies for reducing discriminatory treatment of others.

First, our model presumes that people are concerned about specific threats—related to physical safety, health, and the processes and structures that make ingroups valuable for their members—and that these threats are activated by the perception of specific cues. To the extent, then, that members of often-stigmatized groups fail to display such cues, or that perceivers' attention is drawn away from them, stigmatization should be reduced. Consider, for example, that plastic surgery to repair facial disfigurements reduces avoidant reactions to individuals born with, or who later acquire, such features (Berscheid & Gangestad, 1982; U.S. Department of Health and Human Services, 2000). This strategy of stigma reduction is explicitly employed by the philanthropic organization, Smile Train, which provides surgery to mend the visually unappealing cleft lips and palates in poor children. As their literature states, these surgeries create "a second chance at life" and give these children "[their] future back"—a future absent of social rejection and its tangible consequences (www.smiletrain.org). Similarly, the U.S. Food and Drug Administration recently approved an injectable substance, Sculptra, to plump out the sunken cheeks and deep pockets that result from facial wasting associated with AIDS and its treatment. Although the facial wasting itself poses no direct health threat, and the substance has no medicinal purposes, the FDA commissioner stressed that its value stemmed from the fact that "[negative] change in facial appearance is one of the emotionally devastating and stigmatizing side effects of HIV/AIDS and the drugs used to treat it" (U.S. Food and Drug Administration, 2004).

One might consider other applications of this general strategy as well. For instance, all else being equal, might it be that immigrants who choose to learn and to speak publicly the language of their new country, and to exchange their native cultural practices for the practices of their new home, will appear less "foreign" and thus elicit less prejudice? Such interventions emerge straightforwardly from our analysis, and indeed will appear intuitively obvious to some: Eliminate the cues that heuristically imply threat and one eliminates the prejudice. It is perhaps surprising, then, that this general strategy appears infrequently in formal intervention programs designed to reduce prejudices and discrimination. The underutilization of this strategy in actual prejudice-reduction interventions likely stems from the theoretical architectures upon which many interventions are based: Because these theoretical approaches do not assign a primary causal role to specific threats and their associated heuristic cues, there would appear to be little reason to alter such cues. This rationale—misguided from our perspective—would appear to characterize many of the interventions based on the logics of contact and recategorization processes, and those based on the idea that prejudice is motivated primarily by ego- or social-identity defense.[1]

Second, interventions may reduce discrimination by weakening the link between such cues and their associated threats. Educational efforts and personal contact may, over time, weaken these links in cases where there exists no significant kernel of truth—as in the obesity/contagious-disease associations discussed earlier. In some cases, however, such a kernel does exist (Lee et al., 1995), sometimes due to the very fact of discrimination itself. For instance, to the extent that immigrant or ethnic minority groups experience much lower standards of living, they may indeed exhibit higher levels of criminal activity and contagious disease. Programs at the level of public policy and social services that enhance, for example, legitimate employment opportunities and access to health care may thus do more than just enhance the economic and tangible welfare of those less well off; they should also reduce the extent to which such groups are targeted for prejudice.

Third, interventions may also be designed to break the link between perceived threats and their automatically associated prejudice syndromes. We note, however, that this may be an especially difficult approach, as some of these threat–prejudice links may be innate whereas others may be learned very easily and quickly when young (Öhman & Mineka, 2001). We suggest that strategies appreciating the psychology of habituation may show some promise at this stage of the prejudice process: Just as health care practitioners, with successful expo-sure over time, may experience lessened disgust when encountering the bodily fluids and severe physical abnormalities of some of their patients, and just as well-seasoned, successful soldiers may experience less extreme fear in battle than their less seasoned counterparts, so too may heavily exposed social perceivers come to experience less intense prejudice syndromes when perceiving the threats posed by particular groups. Note that this strategy adds important texture to the solutions proposed by the more general contact hypothesis (Miller & Brewer, 1984; Pettigrew & Tropp, 2000; Stephan & Stephan, 1996), as it suggests that *particular* experiences will be required to mitigate the prejudice syndromes created by *particular* perceived threats. Indeed, it raises the possibility that interventions based on contact might be significantly strengthened by applying some of the ideas inherent in the behavioral exposure therapies that clinicians employ to combat particular phobias (e.g., Marks & Tobena, 1990).

Moreover, even in the absence of eliminating automatic threat–prejudice links, it should be possible to supplement initially activated prejudice syndromes with reactions that are more favorable. For instance, even though many individu-als react initially with disgust to those who are physically malformed, people often learn to supplement these reactions with more thoughtful, favorable emotional responses, such as admiration or sympathy.

Fourth, as this perspective and others suggest, interventions may also be designed to interrupt the link between activated prejudice syndromes and mani-fested discriminatory behavior. Indeed, for both internal reasons (e.g., those relat-ed to consciously held values that discrimination is immoral) and external reasons (e.g., those related to perceived costs of social censure and punishment), people often do control the expression of their prejudiced reactions (e.g., Crandall & Eshleman, 2003; Devine, 1989; Monteith, Ashburn-Nardo, Voils, & Czopp, 2002). Note, however, that our evolutionary approach suggests that motivations to inhib-it prejudiced reactions are likely to weaken as the perceived threat strengthens and becomes more tangibly immediate.

Finally, and most important, the recognition that there exist psychologically distinct prejudices, and that these prejudices are cued by different features and facilitated and mitigated by qualitatively different variables, forces the recognition that *different interventions will be required to fight different prejudices*. To be effective, an intervention will need to target a specific threat and the prejudice syndrome elicited by that threat. Thus, one should not presume that an interven-tion designed to successfully reduce the fear directed at African American men would also reduce the resentment directed at welfare recipients or the disgust elicited by gay men. For example, our framework suggests that by altering indi-viduals' felt vulnerabilities and acute sensitivities to specific threats, we will alter their prejudices against specific groups (but not others), and in very specific ways. For instance, leading people to believe that violent crime in general is on a down-swing should reduce the fear-tinged prejudices directed at African Americans, but will have little effect on prejudices against the physically handicapped; whereas, leading people to believe that contagious illnesses are being successfully combat-ed by new drugs should reduce the disgust-tinged prejudices against physically handicapped individuals, but will have little effect on prejudices against African Americans.

Moreover, interventions will likely need to be sensitive to the different origins that apparently similar prejudices may have for different perceivers. For example, antipathy toward an immigrant group could be based on perceived threats to safety for some perceivers but on threats to economic security or health for others. In addition, given that perceivers differ in their chronic sensitivities to different threats, and that different threats may be acutely prominent in communities at different times (e.g., because of economic downturns, crime waves, etc.), successful interventions will likely be those tailored to the threats most salient at the time in the minds of the targeted audience.

This is not to say that currently popular means of prejudice reduction, such as creating contact between members of prejudiced and stigmatized groups (Miller & Brewer, 1984; Pettigrew & Tropp, 2000; Stephan & Stephan, 1996), cannot be effective. It is to say, however, that such approaches are likely to benefit greatly from an explicit consideration of those threats potentially perceived within the contact situation and broader context. For instance, one might be wary of attempting to reduce the fear felt by whites toward blacks by bringing the two groups together at nighttime (given that darkness invigorates the perception of physical safety threat), of attempting to reduce the disgust felt by individuals toward those stigmatized for having malformed bodies by beginning the contact experience with physically immediate positioning and gestures (e.g., handshakes or hugs), or of beginning an intergroup dialogue between a longstanding local group and new foreign immigrants by pointing out all the novel customs and practices the new group will bring to the community. The current evolutionary approach, with its functional focus on qualitatively distinct threats, prejudice syndromes, and moderating circumstances, makes clear that intervention strategies will be most successful when they are highly tuned to the specific prejudices they are meant to fight.

It is useful here to make one more point. We have focused thus far on the idea that different cues activate different threats, which is often the case. It is also true, however, that some cues may imply multiple threats. For instance, features that suggest "foreign" outgroup status—distinctive physical appearance, language, dress, food preparation customs, and social interaction habits—may imply threats of physical injury, disease, and also various threats to group resources and integrity. We suspect that it is the multiple threats implied by foreign outgroup status that account for the special difficulty encountered by those hoping to mitigate interethnic prejudices and conflict.

CONCLUSIONS

Researchers have been empirically studying prejudice for well over 70 years, and much of value has been learned from a variety of perspectives. The bulk of theorizing and empirical work has focused on issues of process—of how we obtain our stereotypes and prejudices (e.g., socialization by parents), of the circumstances in which we decide to derogate others (e.g., when our self-esteem or social identity has been recently threatened by failure), of when available stereotypes are most readily applied to individual group members (e.g., when the perceiver is under cognitive load), etc. These process approaches share in common an inattention to issues of content: Many stereotypes may indeed be influenced by social learning—but *why* are people in a local community taught that members of a new immigrant group have specific characteristics A, B, and C, but not characteristics D, E, and F, and *why* do the stereotypes and prejudices directed at some groups (e.g., the physically malformed) seem to be similar across cultures, across time, and even across related social species? As a second example, if we derogate others to feel good about ourselves or about our group (e.g., Fein & Spencer, 1997), why do we put down members of ethnically foreign immigrant groups and gay men but not individuals who cook food for a living? After all, if we are just seeking to boost ourselves, with minimum creativity virtually *any* group could do. Finally, how can such approaches, and others sharing their process orientation, account for why people experience various, qualitatively distinct forms of prejudice—e.g., fear- versus anger- versus disgust-based—and for why different groups elicit some forms of prejudice more than others? The simple answer is that they cannot: The process approaches just do not have built into their theoretical architectures the means for addressing issues of content.

In contrast, our evolutionary approach is designed to do just that. One feature of a good theory is that it generates novel hypotheses subsequently supported by new research. Although the application of evolutionary theory to issues of prejudice is recent, the research reviewed here demonstrates that an evolutionary approach is performing strongly on this count. Because of this evolutionary approach, we now have a much better understanding of the diversity of qualitatively distinct prejudices that exist, the characteristics that elicit them, and the kinds of factors—personal and contextual—that facilitate and inhibit their prominence and expression. Because of this approach, the view of "prejudice" as a monolithic construct, straightforwardly measured via simple assessments of attitude, has been severely challenged. Because of this approach, simple conceptualizations of discrimination in terms of "approach versus avoidance" seem untenable. Because of this approach, the psychology of disease avoidance now has an important role in understanding a wide range of prejudices. Because of this approach, person and contextual variables conceptually irrelevant to traditional theories of prejudice (e.g., personal vulnerability to disease, ambient darkness, pregnancy status) are recognized for the impact they have on the moderation of particular prejudice syndromes.

Our enthusiasm for this evolutionary approach should not be misinterpreted as a call to supplant more traditional approaches for understanding prejudice and related phenomena. Rather, the multiple approaches should be viewed less as alternatives and more as complements, with the logical implication being that a broader goal for the field should be a considered, thoughtful attempt at conceptual integration. If 70 years of research has taught us anything, it is that prejudice is a difficult nut to crack. We hope that this brief overview of an evolutionary approach has not only revealed something of its great promise, but also interests others in joining us to further explore its potential.

NOTES

1. We wonder whether a second reason for the relative infrequency of the "cue-change" strategy in established intervention programs may relate less to the structure of formal guiding theory and more to the values and ideologies of those of us interested in reducing prejudices and discrimination. The strategy of reducing prejudice by reducing the threat-implying cues displayed by those targeted for prejudice implies—correctly—that stigmatized targets sometimes have a degree of control over the extent and manner in which they are discriminated against. This, however, is a politically and ethically contentious implication, as it appears to suggest that the victimized themselves are to blame for their stigmatization (although this does not logically follow from the premise), and that they thus might reasonably be held responsible for mitigating the unfavorable ways in which they are treated (although this, too, does not logically follow). Moreover, we suspect the cue-change strategy comes across as inconsistent with the idea that people ought to be accepting (or, at minimum, tolerant) of diversity in ethnicity, physical appearance, religious belief, sexual orientation, etc.; with this value of diversity as context, the suggestion that individuals who are "different" might alter themselves or change their public actions seems patently unfair and immoral.

    Of course, our evolutionary approach itself is technically agnostic with respect to the issues of who should be responsible for mitigating inappropriate prejudices or whether diversity is to be valued. It thus makes, in an unflinching manner, a straightforward point that many flinching practitioners do not fully utilize—that because observable cues heuristically associated with threat play an important role in evoking prejudices and discrimination, the altering of these observable cues can provide one avenue for mitigating them.

REFERENCES

Alexander, R. D. (1974). The evolution of social behavior. *Annual Review of Ecology and Systematics, 4,* 325–384.

Allport, G. W. (1954). *The nature of prejudice.* Cambridge, MA: Addison-Wesley.

Altemeyer, B. (1988). *Enemies of freedom.* San Francisco: Jossey-Bass.

Barchas, P. (1986). A sociophysiological orientation to small groups. In E. Lawler (Ed.), *Advances in group processes* (Vol. 3, pp. 209–246). Greenwich, CT: JAI Press.

Berscheid, E., & Gangestad, S. (1982). The social psychology of facial physical attractiveness. *Clinics in Plastic Surgery, 9,* 289–296.

Bobo, L., & Kluegel, J. R. (1993). Opposition to race-targeting: Self-interest, stratification ideology, or racial attitudes? *American Sociological Review, 58,* 443–464.

Brewer, M. B. (1988). A dual process model of impression formation. *Advances in Social Cognition, 1,* 1–36.

Brewer, M. B. (1997). On the social origins of human nature. In C. McGarty & S. A. Haslam (Eds.), *The message of social psychology: Perspectives on mind in society* (pp. 54–62). Cambridge, MA: Blackwell.

Brewer, M. B. (2001). Ingroup identification and intergroup conflict: When does ingroup love become outgroup hate? In R. Ashmore, L. Jussim, & D. Wilder (Eds.), *Social identity, intergroup conflict, and conflict reduction* (pp. 17–41). New York: Oxford University Press.

Brewer, M. B., & Alexander, M. G. (2002). Intergroup emotions and images. In D. M. Mackie & E. R. Smith (Eds.), *From prejudice to intergroup relations: Differentiated reactions to social groups* (pp. 209–225). New York: Psychology Press.

Brewer, M. B., & Caporael, L. R. (1990). Selfish genes vs. selfish people: Sociobiology as origin myth. *Motivation and Emotion, 14,* 237–242.

Brewer, M. B., & Lui L. L. (1989). The primacy of age and sex in the structure of person categories. *Social Cognition, 7,* 262–274.

Brown, D. E. (1991). *Human universals.* New York: McGraw-Hill.

Campbell, D. T. (1982). Legal and primary-group social controls. *Journal of Social and Biological Structures, 5,* 431–438.

Carver, C. S., & Scheier, M. F. (1990). Origins and functions of positive and negative affect: A control-process view. *Psychological Review, 97,* 19–35.

Conway, L. G. III, & Schaller, M. (2002). On the verifiability of evolutionary psychological theories: An analysis of the psychology of scientific persuasion. *Personality and Social Psychology Review, 6,* 152–166.

Cosmides, L., & Tooby, J. (2000). Evolutionary psychology and the emotions. In M. Lewis & J. M. Haviland-Jones (Eds.), *Handbook of emotions* (pp. 91–115). New York: Guilford Press.

Cosmides, L., Tooby, J., & Barkow, J. H. (1992). Introduction: Evolutionary psychology and conceptual integration. In J. H. Barkow, L. Cosmides, & J. Tooby (Eds.), *The adapted mind* (pp. 3–18). New York: Oxford University Press.

Cottrell, C. A., & Neuberg, S. L. (2004, January). *From threat to emotion to action: A sociofunctional analysis of intergroup interactions.* Paper presented at the annual meeting of the Society for Personality and Social Psychology, Austin, Texas.

Cottrell, C. A., & Neuberg, S. L. (2005). Different emotional reactions to different groups: A sociofunctional threat-based approach to 'prejudice.' *Journal of Personality and Social Psychology, 88,* 770–789.

Crandall, C. S., & Eshleman, A. (2003). A justification-suppression model of the expression and experience of prejudice. *Psychological Bulletin, 129,* 414–446.

Crandall, C. S., & Moriarty, D. (1995). Physical illness stigma and social rejection. *British Journal of Social Psychology, 34,* 67–86.

Crawford, C. (1998). The theory of evolution in the study of human behavior: An introduction and overview. In C. Crawford & D. L. Krebs (Eds.), *Handbook of evolutionary psychology: Issues, ideas, and applications* (pp. 3–42). Mahwah, NJ: Lawrence Erlbaum Associates.

de Waal, F. B. M. (1989). Food sharing and reciprocal obligations among chimpanzees. *Journal of Human Evolution, 18,* 433–459.

Devine, P. G. (1989). Stereotypes and prejudice: Their automatic and controlled components. *Journal of Personality and Social Psychology, 56,* 5–18.

Devine, P. G., & Elliot, A. J. (1995). Are racial stereotypes really fading? The Princeton trilogy revisited. *Personality and Social Psychology Bulletin, 11,* 1139–1150.

Dijker, A. J. (1987). Emotional reactions to ethnic minorities. *European Journal of Social Psychology, 17,* 305–325.

Dugatkin, L. A., FitzGerald, G. J., & Lavoie, J. (1994). Juvenile three-spined sticklebacks avoid parasitized conspecifics. *Environmental Biology of Fishes, 39,* 215–218.

Dunbar, R. I. M. (1988). *Primate social systems.* Ithaca, NY: Cornell University Press.

Ekman, P. (1999). Basic emotions. In T. Dalgleish & M. Power (Eds.), *The handbook of cognition and emotion* (pp. 45–60). Sussex, UK: Wiley.

Esses, V. M., Haddock, G., & Zanna, M. P. (1993). Values, stereotypes, and emotions as determinants of intergroup attitudes. In D. M. Mackie & D. L. Hamilton (Eds.), *Affect, cognition, and stereotyping: Interactive processes in group perception* (pp. 137–166). San Diego, CA: Academic Press.

Faulkner, J., Schaller, M., Park, J. H., & Duncan, L. A. (2004). Evolved disease-avoidance mechanisms and contemporary xenophobic attitudes. *Group Processes and Intergroup Relations, 7*, 333–353.

Fein, S., & Spencer, S. J. (1997). Prejudice as self-image maintenance: Affirming the self through derogating others. *Journal of Personality and Social Psychology, 73*, 31–44.

Fiske, S. T. (1998). Stereotyping, prejudice, and discrimination. In D. T. Gilbert, S. T. Fiske, & G. Lindzey (Eds.), *Handbook of social psychology* (Vol. 2, pp. 357–414). Boston, MA: McGraw-Hill.

Fiske, S. T., Cuddy, A. J., Glick, P., & Xu, J. (2002). A model of (often mixed) stereotype content: Competence and warmth respectively follow from perceived status and competition. *Journal of Personality and Social Psychology, 82*, 878–902.

Fiske, S. T., & Neuberg, S. L. (1990). A continuum of impression formation, from category-based to individuating processes: Influences of information and motivation on attention and interpretation. In M. P. Zanna (Ed.), *Advances in experimental social psychology* (Vol. 23, pp. 1–74). New York: Academic Press.

Fox, R. (1992). Prejudice and the unfinished mind: A new look at an old failing. *Psychological Inquiry, 3*, 137–152.

Frijda, N. H. (1986). *The emotions.* Cambridge, UK: Cambridge University Press.

Gangestad, S. W., & Simpson, J. A. (2000). On the evolutionary psychology of human mating: Trade-offs and strategic pluralism. *Behavioral and Brain Sciences, 23*, 573–587.

Goffman, E. (1963). *Stigma: Notes on the management of the spoiled identity.* New York: Simon & Schuster.

Goodall, J. (1986). Social rejection, exclusion, and shunning among the Gombe chimpanzees. *Ethology and Sociobiology, 7*, 227–236.

Greenberg, J., Pyszczynski, T., Solomon, S., Rosenblatt, A., Veeder, M., Kirkland, S., & Lyon, D. (1990). Evidence for terror management theory II: The effects of mortality salience on reactions to those who threaten or bolster the cultural worldview. *Journal of Personality and Social Psychology, 58*, 308–318.

Greenwald, A. G., McGhee, D. E., & Schwartz, J. K. L. (1998). Measuring individual differences in implicit cognition: The implicit association test. *Journal of Personality and Social Psychology, 74*, 1464–1480.

Grillon, C., Pellowski, M., Merikangas, K. R., & Davis, M. (1997). Darkness facilitates acoustic startle reflex in humans. *Biological Psychiatry, 42*, 453–460.

Haidt, J., Rozin, P., McCauley, C. R., & Imada, S. (1997). Body, psyche, and culture: The relationship between disgust and morality. *Psychology and Developing Societies, 9*, 107–131.

Hamilton, D. L. (1981). *Cognitive processes in stereotyping and intergroup behavior.* Hillsdale, NJ: Erlbaum.

Hamilton, D. L., & Sherman, J. W. (1994). Stereotypes. In R. S. Wyer Jr. & T. K. Srull (Eds.), *Handbook of social cognition* (2nd ed., Vol. 2, pp. 1–68). Hillsdale, NJ: Erlbaum.

Haselton M. G., & Buss, D. M. (2000). Error management theory: A new perspective on biases in cross-sex mind reading. *Journal of Personality and Social Psychology, 78*, 81–91.

Haselton, M. G., & Buss, D. M. (2003). Biases in social judgment: Design flaws or design features? In J. Forgas, K. Williams, & B. von Hippel (Eds.), *Responding to the social world: Implicit and explicit processes in social judgments and decisions* (pp. 21–43). New York: Cambridge.

Insko, C. A., & Schopler, J. (1998). Differential distruct of groups and individuals. In C. Sedikides, J. Schopler, & C. A. Insko (Eds.), *Intergroup cognition and intergroup behavior* (pp. 75–108). Mahwah, NJ: Erlbaum.

Izard, C. E. (1978). *Human emotions.* New York: Plenum Press.

Izard, C. E. (1991). *The psychology of emotions.* New York: Plenum Press.

Jost, J. T., & Banaji, M. R. (1994). The role of stereotyping in system-justification and the production of false consciousness. *British Journal of Social Psychology, 33,* 1–27.

Katz, D., & Braly, K. (1933). Racial stereotypes of one hundred college students. *Journal of Abnormal and Social Psychology, 28,* 280–290.

Kenrick, D. T., Li, N. P., & Butner, J. (2003). Dynamical evolutionary psychology: Individual decision rules and emergent social norms. *Psychological Review, 110,* 3–28.

Kurzban, R., & Leary, M. R. (2001). Evolutionary origins of stigmatization: The functions of social exclusion. *Psychological Bulletin, 127,* 187–208.

Kurzban, R., & Neuberg, S. L. (2005). Managing ingroup and outgroup relationships. In D. Buss (Ed.), *Handbook of evolutionary psychology* (pp. 653–675). New York: Wiley.

Kurzban, R., Tooby, J., & Cosmides, L. (2001). Can race be erased? Coalitional computation and social categorization. *Proceedings of the National Academy of Sciences, 98,* 15387–15392.

Leakey, R. E. (1978). *People of the lake: Mankind and its beginnings.* New York: Avon.

Lee, Y. T., Jussim, L., & McCauley, C. (Eds.). (1995). *Stereotype accuracy: Toward appreciating group differences.* Washington, DC: The American Psychological Association.

LeVine, R. A., & Campbell, D. T. (1972). *Ethnocentrism: Theories of conflict, ethnic attitudes and group behavior.* New York: Wiley.

Mackie, D. M., Devos, T., & Smith, E. R. (2000). Intergroup emotions: Explaining offensive action tendencies in an intergroup context. *Journal of Personality and Social Psychology, 79,* 602–616.

Macrae, C. N., Milne, A. B., & Bodenhausen, G. V. (1994). Stereotypes as energy-saving devices: A peek inside the cognitive toolbox. *Journal of Personality and Social Psychology, 66,* 37–47.

Macrae, C. N., Stangor, C., & Hewstone, M. (Eds.). (1996). *Stereotypes and stereotyping.* New York: Guilford Press.

Madon, S., Guyll, M., Aboufadel, K., Montiel, E., Smith, A., Palumbo, P., & Jussim, J. (2001). Ethnic and national stereotypes: The Princeton trilogy revisited and revised. *Personality and Social Psychology Bulletin, 27,* 996–1010.

Maner, J. K., Kenrick, D. T., Becker, D. V., Robertson, T., Hofer, B., Delton, A. W., Neuberg, S. L., Butner, J., & Schaller, M. (2005). Functional projection: How fundamental social motives can bias interpersonal perception. *Journal of Personality and Social Psychology, 88,* 63–78.

Marks, I. M., & Tobena, A. (1990). Learning and unlearning fear: A clinical and evolutionary perspective. *Neuroscience and Biobehavioral Reviews, 14,* 365–384.

Miller, N., & Brewer, M. B. (1984). *Groups in contact: The psychology of desegregation.* New York: Academic Press.

Monteith, M. J., Ashburn-Nardo, L., Voils, C. I., & Czopp, A. M. (2002). Putting the brakes on prejudice: On the development and operation of cues for control. *Journal of Personality and Social Psychology, 83,* 1029–1050.

Mullen, B., Brown, R., & Smith, C. (1992). Ingroup bias as a function of salience, relevance, and status: An integration. *European Journal of Social Psychology, 22*, 103–122.

Navarrete, C. D., Fessler, D. M. T., & Eng, S. J. (2005). Disease-avoidance and intergroup bias: The effects of disgust sensitivity and pregnancy on ethnocentric attitudes. University of California, Los Angeles. Manuscript submitted for publication.

Nesse, R. M. (1990). Evolutionary explanations of emotions. *Human Nature, 1*, 261–289.

Nesse, R. M. (2005). Natural selection and the regulation of defenses: A signal detection analysis of the smoke detector principle. *Evolution and Human Behavior, 26*, 88–105.

Neuberg, S. L., & Cottrell, C. A. (2002). Intergroup emotions: A sociofunctional approach. In D. M. Mackie & E. R. Smith (Eds.), *From prejudice to intergroup relations: Differentiated reactions to social groups* (pp. 265–283). New York: Psychology Press.

Neuberg, S. L., Smith, D. M., & Asher, T. (2000). Why people stigmatize: Toward a socio-functional framework. In T. F. Heatherton, R. E. Kleck, M. R. Hebl, & J. G. Hull (Eds.), *The social psychology of stigma* (pp. 31–61). New York: Guilford.

Niemann, Y. F., Jennings, L., Rozelle, R. M., Baxter, J. C., & Sullivan, E. (1994). Use of free response and cluster analysis to determine stereotypes of eight groups. *Personality and Social Psychology Bulletin, 20*, 379–390.

Norenzayan, A., & Heine, S. J. (2005). Psychological universals: What are they and how can we know? *Psychological Bulletin, 131*, 763–784.

Öhman, A. (1993). Fear and anxiety as emotional phenomena: Clinical phenomenology, evolutionary perspectives, and information processing mechanisms. In M. Lewis & J. M. Haviland (Eds.), *Handbook of emotions* (pp. 511–536). New York: Guilford.

Öhman, A., & Mineka, S. (2001). Fears, phobias, and preparedness: Toward an evolved module of fear and fear learning. *Psychological Review, 108*, 483–522.

Park, J. H., Faulkner, J., & Schaller, M. (2003). Evolved disease-avoidance processes and contemporary anti-social behavior: Prejudicial attitudes and avoidance of people with disabilities. *Journal of Nonverbal Behavior, 27*, 65–87.

Park, J. H., Schaller, M., & Crandall, C. S. (2005). Obesity as a heuristic cue connoting contagion: Perceived vulnerability to disease promotes anti-fat attitudes. University of British Columbia. Manuscript submitted for publication.

Pendry, L. F., & Macrae, C. N. (1996). What the disinterested perceiver overlooks: Goal-directed social categorization. *Personality and Social Psychology Bulletin, 22*, 249–256.

Pettigrew, T. F., & Tropp, L. R. (2000). Does intergroup contact reduce prejudice? Recent meta-analytic findings. In S. Oskamp (Ed.), *Reducing prejudice and discrimination: The Claremont symposium* (pp. 93–114). Mahwah, NJ: Erlbaum.

Plutchik, R. (1980). *Emotion: A psychoevolutionary synthesis*. New York: Harper and Row.

Plutchik, R. (2003). *Emotions and life: Perspectives from psychology, biology, and evolution*. Washington, DC: American Psychological Association.

Rhodes, G., Zebrowitz, L. A., Clark, A., Kalick, S. M., Hightower, A., & McKay, R. (2001). Do facial averageness and symmetry signal health? *Evolution and Human Behavior, 22*, 31–46.

Richerson, P., & Boyd, R. (1995, January). *The evolution of human hypersociality*. Paper for Ringberg Castle Symposium on Ideology, Warfare and Indoctrinability, Ringberg, Germany.

Roseman, I. J., Wiest, C., & Swartz, T. S. (1994). Phenomenology, behaviors, and goals differentiate discrete emotions. *Journal of Personality and Social Psychology, 67*, 206–221.

Rozin, P., Haidt, J., & McCauley, C. R. (1993). Disgust. In M. Lewis & J. M. Haviland (Eds.), *Handbook of emotions* (pp. 575–594). New York: Guilford.

Rozin, P., Lowery, L., & Ebert, R. (1994). Varieties of disgust faces and the structure of disgust. *Journal of Personality & Social Psychology, 66,* 870–881.

Schaller, M., & Neuberg, S. L. (2005). The nature in prejudice(s). Arizona State University. Manuscript submitted for publication.

Schaller, M., Park, J. H., & Faulkner, J. (2003). Prehistoric dangers and contemporary prejudices. *European Review of Social Psychology, 14,* 105–137.

Schaller, M., Park, J. H., & Mueller, A. (2003). Fear of the dark: Interactive effects of beliefs about danger and ambient darkness on ethnic stereotypes. *Personality and Social Psychology Bulletin, 29,* 637–649.

Sherif, M. (1966). *In common predicament: Social psychology of intergroup conflict and cooperation.* Boston: Houghton-Mifflin.

Simon, H. A. (1967). Motivational and emotional controls of cognition. *Psychological Review, 74,* 29–39.

Stangor, C., Lynch, L., Duan, C., & Glass, B. (1992). Categorization of individuals on the basis of multiple social features. *Journal of Personality & Social Psychology, 62,* 207–218.

Stephan, W. G., & Renfro, C. L. (2002). The role of threat in intergroup relations. In D. M. Mackie & E. R. Smith (Eds.), *From prejudice to intergroup emotions: Differentiated reactions to social groups* (pp. 191–207). New York: Psychology Press.

Stephan, W. G., & Stephan, C. W. (1996). *Intergroup relations.* Chicago: Brown and Benchmark.

Swim, J. K. (1994). Perceived versus meta-analytic effect sizes: An assessment of the accuracy of gender stereotypes. *Journal of Personality and Social Psychology, 66,* 21–36.

Tajfel, H. (1969). Cognitive aspects of prejudice. *Journal of Social Issues, 25,* 79–97.

Tajfel, H. (1982). Social psychology of intergroup relations. *Annual Review of Psychology, 33,* 1–39.

Tajfel, H., & Turner, J. C. (1986). An integrative theory of intergroup conflict. In S. Worchel & W. Austin (Eds.), *Psychology of intergroup relations* (pp. 2–24). Chicago: Nelson-Hall.

Taylor, S. E., Fiske, S. T., Etcoff, N. L., & Ruderman, A. J. (1978). Categorical and contextual bases of person memory and stereotyping. *Journal of Personality & Social Psychology, 36,* 778–793.

Tomkins, S. S. (1963). *Affect, imagery, consciousness: Vol. 2. The negative affects.* New York: Springer.

Tooby, J., & Cosmides, L. (1990). The past explains the present: Emotional adaptations and the structure of ancestral environments. *Ethology and Sociobiology, 11,* 375–424.

Tooby, J., & Cosmides, L. (1996). Friendship and the Banker's Paradox: Other pathways to the evolution of adaptations for altruism. In W. G. Runciman, J. Maynard Smith, & R. I. M. Dunbar (Eds.), *Evolution of Social Behaviour Patterns in Primates and Man. Proceedings of the British Academy, 88,* 119–143.

U.S. Department of Health and Human Services. (2000). *Oral health in America: A report of the surgeon general—Executive summary.* Rockville, MD: U.S. Department of Health and Human Services, National Institutes of Dental and Craniofacial Research, National Institutes of Health.

U.S. Food and Drug Administration. (2004, August 3). *FDA approves Sculptra for HIV patients.* Retrieved from http://www.fda.gov/bbs/topics/news/2004/NEW01100.html

Wilbur, C. J., Shapiro, J. R., & Neuberg, S. L. (2005). From specific threats to specific prejudices: Causal evidence. University of Western Ontario. Manuscript in preparation.

Yamagishi, T., Tanida, S., Mishima, R., Shimoma, E., & Kanazawa, S. (2003). You can judge a book by its cover: Evidence that cheaters may look different than cooperators. *Evolution and Human Behavior, 24,* 290–301.

Zárate, M. A. & Smith, E. R. (1990). Person categorization and stereotyping. *Social Cognition, 8,* 161–185.

Zebrowitz, L. A., & Collins, M. A. (1997). Accurate social perception at zero acquaintance: The affordances of a Gibsonian approach. *Personality and Social Psychology Review, 1,* 203–222.

Zebrowitz, L. A., Voinescu, L., & Collins, M. A. (1996). "Wide eyed" and "crooked-faced": Determinants of perceived and real honesty across the life span. *Personality and Social Psychology Bulletin, 22,* 1258–1269.

9

Accuracy and Bias in Romantic Relationships: An Evolutionary and Social Psychological Analysis

GARTH J. O. FLETCHER, JEFFRY A. SIMPSON, and ALICE D. BOYES

*T*he study of accuracy and bias in social judgment and person perception has had a long and tumultuous history in the psychological sciences. Research examining accuracy in personality judgments was alive and well from the 1920s to the 1950s. The publication of a devastating methodological critique by Cronbach (1955), however, brought this area of research to an abrupt halt. In the aftermath of Cronbach's seminal article, research on social judgment and person perception within social psychology shifted to discerning how social perception processes operate, accompanied by a sublime indifference to the validity or truth of associated lay judgments (Funder, 1995).

By the 1980s, agnosticism about the validity of social judgments and perceptions had given way to bold claims that human social cognition was inherently flawed, biased, or even irrational (Nisbett & Ross, 1980). A flood of research investigating various kinds of errors and biases in social perception seemed to show that people fall prey to a wide array of perceptual and inferential biases, ranging from the fundamental attribution error, to the false consensus effect, to the confirmation bias, to various self-referential and self-serving biases, to name but a few (see Krueger & Funder, 2004). As Fiske and Taylor (1984) lamented at that time, "Instead of a naïve scientist entering the environment in search of the truth, we find the rather unflattering picture of a charlatan trying to make the data come out in a manner most advantageous to his or her already held theories." (p. 88)

This bleak view of the rationality of social judgments and perceptions has, however, been seriously challenged during the past two decades (for reviews, see Fletcher, 1995; Krueger & Funder, 2004). And, one of the principal arenas in which this debate has raged has been the field of interpersonal relationships. The simple-minded question—are lay judgments biased or inaccurate?—has given way to a burgeoning body of research exploring the conditions under which individuals display accurate or biased (usually enhancing, but also negative biases) judgments of romantic partners and relationships.

For the most part social psychologists have remained content with examining the proximal cognitive processes involved in making accurate or biased judgments. Although there is nothing wrong with adopting this focus, it addresses questions at only one level of conceptual analysis (proximate causation) and ignores important questions and issues at other levels of analysis (i.e., ontogeny, phylogeny, and ultimate causation; see Sherman, 1988). Thus, a principal feature missing from contemporary research dealing with bias and accuracy is a comprehensive theoretical perspective that predicts and explains the *specific* conditions under which people should be more accurate or more biased in their interpersonal judgments. In this chapter, we argue that certain evolutionary principles can help provide just such an overarching theoretical framework. Our approach is based on the proposition that the study of bias and accuracy in close relationships—particularly romantic relationships—holds special significance from an evolutionary perspective. The reason is straightforward—romantic relationships are directly linked to mating and sometimes parenting, both of which were centrally associated with reproductive-fitness outcomes in evolutionary history.

We introduce the chapter by describing a central paradox of love and intimacy: namely, love seems at once blind and also firmly rooted in reality. Love sometimes seems to motivate people to be overly optimistic in their judgments and decisions, occasionally to the point of irrationality. On the other hand, love (and associated high levels of intimacy) may at times motivate people to arrive at accurate judgments and decisions, derived from a more solid and secure knowledge base. For example, falling head over heels in love in the course of a holiday romance may motivate Stephen to agonize over his options, and to find out more about his partner, before making subsequent life-changing decisions (e.g., throwing up his well-paid job and moving to another country).

We attempt to reconcile this apparent inconsistency and describe how evolutionary thinking can help explain and integrate a host of seemingly disparate empirical findings on human mating perceptions, judgments, and decisions. After discussing the distinction between bias and accuracy, we discuss two fundamental motives that have been studied extensively in the field of interpersonal relationships—the desire to make *accurate* decisions/judgments, and the desire to make *enhancing* (positively biased) decisions/judgments.

Following this treatment, we present a model grounded in evolutionary principles and reasoning. The model claims that these two motivational sets comprise adaptations, which have evolved to be expressed conditionally depending on the social and environmental circumstances. They are the product of evolutionary forces because (we argue) their usage has increased the likelihood that individuals attained or maintained fitness-enhancing outcomes (e.g., finding and sustaining good, stable mating relationships with partners who had the ability to provide high levels of investment) and/or decreased the likelihood that individuals experienced fitness-decreasing outcomes (e.g., inappropriate mates who provided poor parental investment). Our model explains and integrates several perplexing findings from research in romantic relationships, it generates some novel predictions, and highlights new research directions.

IS LOVE BLIND OR ACCURATE?

The study of bias and accuracy in romantic relationships provides an exemplary forum in which to test the operation of two major motivational models concerned with the motives for accuracy or enhancement (Simpson, Fletcher, & Campbell, 2001). In essence, the "love is blind" thesis claims that love generates positively biased and Pollyannaish views of close partners and relationships. Thus, unless people view their relationships through rose-colored glasses, individuals will find it difficult, if not impossible, to make decisions that involve serious long-term commitments or the maintenance of happiness. Relationship happiness (and associated personal well-being) and the maintenance of illusions, thus, go hand in hand (Murray, 2001).

A plausible prima facie case, however, can also be made for the "accuracy" model. This model proposes that individuals should typically be motivated to view and understand their partners and relationships accurately, and that a firm grasp on reality is required for healthy personal and relationship functioning. Moreover, the way in which primary relationships are central to well-being, which is used to support the "love is blind" model, can also be pressed into service in support of the "accuracy" model. Given that close relationships can produce both long-term happiness and misery, then individuals should be powerfully motivated to be vigilant and to use their cognitive and social talents to the full in determining the truth value of their attributions. For example, determining whether a potential or current romantic partner is dishonest and conniving or honest and well-meaning has enormous implications for the future well-being of both the individual and the relationship.

Both models are plausible and both are supported by empirical evidence (for reviews, see Fletcher, 2002; Gagne & Lydon, 2004; Murray, 2001). Murray and her colleagues, for example, have provided support for two central propositions. First, individuals often repel doubts that might corrode commitment and trust by reconstructing or restructuring their relationship-specific theories, narratives, and beliefs. Second, as love's blinkers grow stronger and more opaque, individuals tend to idealize their partners more, exaggerate similarities between themselves and their partners, and subsequently develop happier, more stable relationships (see Murray, 2001).

The accuracy model, on the other hand, also has empirical support. Individuals who perceive that their partners and relationships are wonderful are not necessarily building castles in the air. Rather, such evaluations are typically anchored in the objective realities of relationships, which are observable by outsiders and that reliably predict their future course (Fletcher, 2002). Individuals who evaluate their partners and relationships more positively, for instance, tend to discuss relationship problems in a more constructive fashion than do those who perceive their partners and relationships in less glowing terms (Fletcher &

Thomas, 2000). Romantic partners also share similar relationship evaluations (e.g., Campbell, Simpson, Kashy, & Fletcher, 2001), and the negativity of joint relationship evaluations is one of the best predictors of dissolution in both dating and married couples (Karney & Bradbury, 1995).

We are left, then, with an apparent paradox. On the one hand, individuals tend to perceive and evaluate their romantic partners and relationships in enhancing, overly optimistic ways. However, they also perceive and evaluate their partners/relationships in an accurate, reality-based manner. Love seems to both blind and to possess a firm grasp of reality. We attempt to resolve this paradox in the remainder of the chapter.

BIAS AND ACCURACY IN ROMANTIC RELATIONSHIPS

Consider the following example (adapted from Fletcher, 2002), which is pictured in Table 9.1. Using 1-7 Likert-type scales (where 1 = not at all like my partner and 7 = very much like my partner), Mary rates her current partner (Stephen) as highly sensitive (7), very warm (6), very sexy (6), and moderately ambitious (5). For the sake of this exercise, also assume that we have another set of valid benchmark ratings of Stephen that we will assume, for the sake of the argument, represent *perfectly* valid and accurate ratings. These additional ratings happen to be sensitive (6), warm (5), sexy (5), and ambitious (4). Comparing the two sets of ratings, Mary is positively biased but accurate. That is, the mean level of Mary's judgments (6) is one unit higher than the mean of the valid benchmark ratings (5), yet she is accurately tracking relative levels across the different traits ($r = 1.0$). If, however, Mary gave ratings of 6, 7, 5, and 6, respectively, this would reflect the same level of positivity bias, but no accuracy. In this second scenario, the mean level of her judgments is once again one unit higher than the mean of the benchmark ratings, but she is no longer accurately tracking levels across the different traits ($r = .00$). Mary might also be both unbiased and positively inaccurate (e.g.,

TABLE 9.1   How Accurate and Biased is Mary?

	Stephen's Actual Personality	Mary's Perceptions of Stephen			
		High Accuracy, No Bias	High Accuracy, High Bias	Low Accuracy, High Bias	Low Accuracy, No Bias
Sensitive	6	6	7	6	3
Warm	5	5	6	7	3
Sexy	5	5	6	5	7
Ambitious	4	4	5	6	7
Total	20	20	24	24	20
Correlation: perceptions vs. reality		1.0	1.0	0.00	−0.71

a rating pattern such as 3, 3, 7, and 7). In this third scenario, Mary's mean level of judgments is equal to the mean of the benchmark ratings (5), but she is tracking the different traits quite inaccurately ($r = -.71$).

Note that in this example we have assumed that we have perfectly accurate benchmark ratings of Stephen with which to compare Mary's ratings against. In the real world of research, of course, we do not possess such gold-plated guarantees of the validity or accuracy of such benchmark ratings. Nevertheless, this example shows clearly that positivity bias and accuracy can be relatively independent. This example also raises the possibility that judgments of individuals can be both positively biased and accurate, perhaps possessing the best of both worlds. It also raises a question concerning what variables bias and accuracy might differentially predict and why. We deal with this literature below. But first, we discuss a very different conception of bias that has been the subject of much research and fierce dispute in the general cognitive and social psychological literature, but also surfaces in the relationship domain: namely, bias as conceptualized and measured in terms of the way in which pre-existent knowledge structures influence other judgments or memory processes.[1]

There may appear to be something unsettlingly irrational about the way in which people seem to ignore or reinterpret data when clinging to their most cherished implicit relationship theories, expectancies, and beliefs. This is particularly true in close relationships. A sizable amount of research has confirmed that individuals involved in happier and more stable romantic relationships (1) frequently exaggerate the degree to which they are similar to their partners (Murray, Holmes, Bellavia, Griffin, & Dolderman, 2002), (2) retrospectively embellish their memories of being happy at earlier points in their relationships (Karney & Frye, 2002), (3) exaggerate the positive qualities of their partners (Murray, Holmes, & Griffin, 1996a) and the degree to which their partners resemble their ideal partners (Murray, Holmes, & Griffin, 1996b), (4) view their partners as better than themselves (Gagne & Lydon, 2003), and (5) see their relationships as superior to other relationships (Fowers, Lyons, Montel, & Shaked, 2001; Van Lange & Rusbult, 1995).

Demonstrations of these theory-guided biases, however, do not show that people are irrational or blind to the truth. Approaching the world in a completely open-minded and atheoretical manner would reveal an overwhelming morass of information that would render causal understandings nearly impossible. Just as scientists develop theories to explain or interpret data, weigh the outcomes, and then conduct Bayesian-like calculations (Fletcher, 1996), lay persons must also make important judgments under conditions of uncertainty that demand consideration of both incoming data *and* pre-existent theories or beliefs. For example, if Susan is asked to judge how similar she is to John on certain personality dimensions, she is likely to do so by accessing her implicit theories and models of people in general, her partner and relationship-specific theories and models, and any potentially diagnostic information that she has at hand. If she has a happy relationship with John, and believes that greater similarity portends a more successful relationship, this is likely to (quite rationally) generate biased judgments of John in the direction of greater self-partner similarity. Thus, theory-guided judgments, be they scientific or implicit, are bound to be biased.[2]

Within social psychology, studies of judgmental accuracy have typically examined relations between judgments made by individuals and external criteria or benchmark variables. These external criteria/variables have included self-reported perceptions by relationship partners (e.g., Thomas & Fletcher, 2003), perceptions of observers of the relationship (e.g., Collins & Feeney, 2000), observer ratings of behavioral interactions (Simpson, Orina, & Ickes, 2003) or (using longitudinal designs) memories or predictions that can be matched with self-reports gathered either previously or later (e.g., Sprecher, 1999). For the most part, these studies have revealed quite respectable levels of accuracy obtained by the judges (usually in the $r = .20$ to $.60$ range).

One important subset of studies has compared the accuracy of observers (i.e., people who know one or both relationships partners well) to relationship insiders (i.e., the relationship partners themselves). The results of these studies have been mixed. MacDonald and Ross (1999), for example, found that college students made more positive but less accurate predictions about the longevity of their current dating relationships than either their roommates or their dating partners' parents. Thomas and Fletcher (2003) used a mind-reading paradigm in which long-term dating couples initially engaged in a problem-solving discussion. After the discussion, each individual reported the private thoughts and feelings that she/he had during the discussion. Each individual then tried to infer the thoughts and feelings of his/her partner during the discussion as accurately as possible. Mind-reading accuracy (i.e., empathic accuracy) was assessed by having raters compare the thought/feeling inferences of each individual against the actual thoughts and feelings reported by his/her partner. Relationship insiders (i.e., partners) were significantly more accurate than either the close friends of each couple or total strangers (who also viewed the videotaped discussions and completed exactly the same tasks).

As reviewed earlier, a commonly replicated finding shows that more positively biased partner and relationship perceptions are associated with greater relationship satisfaction. However, studies examining the link between accuracy and relationship satisfaction have reported a more inconsistent pattern of findings, with weak or null findings often reported (e.g., Acitelli, Kenny, & Weiner, 2001; Ickes & Simpson, 2001; Murray et al., 1996a, 1996b; Thomas & Fletcher, 2003).

Recent studies, however, indicate that certain variables may moderate the accuracy-satisfaction link. In Thomas and Fletcher's (2003) mind-reading study, for example, among partners involved in longer-term relationships more accurate partner mind-reading predicted greater relationship satisfaction. Among those involved in shorter-term relationships, on the other hand, more accurate partner mind-reading actually predicted *less* satisfaction. This study tested and discounted several plausible alternate explanations for this effect, including the possible impact of assumed similarity, shared cognitive focus, the extent to which private thoughts and feelings were openly disclosed during the discussion, and the diagnosticity of the behaviors displayed during the discussion. Thomas and Fletcher speculated that the problem-solving discussions might have been more threatening to individuals involved in newer relationships, which could have generated more defensiveness and, therefore, less accurate partner mind reading.

Studies that have assessed both bias and accuracy are particularly illuminating because they use the same samples and typically the same variables to measure each construct. Murray et al. (2002), for example, found that women who are more egocentric (i.e., who view their partners as more similar to themselves than is warranted) tended to understand their partners more accurately. Sprecher (1999) found that, over time, individuals involved in dating relationships retrospectively rated their earlier levels of love and satisfaction as being on a higher upward trajectory over time than in fact was the case. For example, those individuals who had level trajectories of satisfaction over time tended to recall that they had steadily improved. Nevertheless, the sample overall quite accurately retrospectively tracked and reported *relative* increases or decreases in love and satisfaction over past periods in their relationships.

In a prior section, we speculated that individuals can theoretically posses the best of both worlds and be simultaneously both positively biased and accurate. These results show that our speculations were correct.

The Quest for Truth vs. the Need for Positivity

One way of reconciling the "love is blind" and the "accuracy" models is to propose that both are valid, but under different circumstances or in different social contexts. The existence of threatening events or threatening relationship interactions, for example, may increase the accessibility and importance of positivity-seeking or relationship-maintenance goals, thereby subverting truth-seeking, accuracy goals (see Ickes & Simpson, 2001). We will detail later the way in which these two goals might influence the levels of positivity bias and accuracy of judgments in relationship settings. For now, we will establish the role and importance of these two goals by examining some recent related research.

The first demonstration of this proposition was in a study of empathic accuracy (mind reading) in dating couples. Simpson, Ickes, and Blackstone (1995) had dating partners rate and discuss slides of either highly attractive or unattractive members of the opposite-sex with their dating partners. To heighten the general level of threat, the slides ostensibly were of individuals on campus in a "dating pool" who wanted to meet and date new people. The rating and discussion interactions were videotaped. The partners were then led to separate rooms where each person watched their interaction and listed all of their private thoughts and feelings during the rating-and-discussion task. Following this, each individual tried to infer his/her partner's private thoughts and feelings as accurately as possible while viewing the videotape a second time. The results revealed that partners who were closer (i.e., more interdependent) and who discussed and rated highly attractive others were more inaccurate at reading their partners' private thoughts and feelings than were individuals involved in less close relationships or who discussed and rated unattractive others.

On the other hand, when individuals must make evaluations or decisions about important relationship-relevant events, especially those that entail escalations of commitment, the accessibility and power of truth-seeking goals should become ascendant, suppressing the motive to enhance the partner/relationship. Gagne and Lydon (2004) have tested these notions by experimentally manipulating deliberative (pre-decisional) and implemental (post-decisional) mindsets. In one study (Gagne & Lydon, 2001, Study 3), dating partners were asked to either describe the pros and cons of an undecided relationship project (e.g., should they live together) or to describe how they planned to achieve/implement a project to which they were already committed (e.g., finding an apartment). Partners who were induced into a rational, even-handed, deliberative frame of mind made more accurate predictions about how long their relationships would last (compared to how long they did eventually last) than did partners who made the same predictions while in a positivity-seeking or relationship-maintenance, implemental mindset.

The issue of whether these two competing mind-sets (truth seeking vs. positivity seeking) are categorical constructs, and the extent to which they are independent or operate in a hydraulic fashion, are open empirical questions. However, we suspect that they probably operate as relatively independent dimensions, as shown in Figure 9.1. Our reasons are twofold. First, as previously described, judgmental bias and accuracy are potentially quite independent. Second, it is easy to come up with plausible relationship examples that exemplify the four categories defined by the two dimensions (see Figure 9.1).

Consider the following four examples, moving clockwise round the figure and starting in the top-right quadrant. (1) Gary has invested substantial money and time in his relationship with Mary, and they have lived together for 2 years. He is trying to decide whether he should ask her to marry him. Gary is strongly motivated to

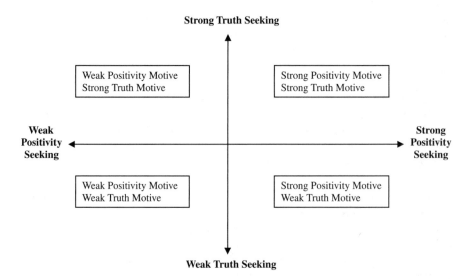

FIGURE 9.1   Four possible combinations of bias and accuracy in relationship judgments, defined according to two motivational dimensions.

enhance his relationship judgments, but he also is intent on making accurate predictions and judgments. (2) Gary has been married for 6 months, and he is very happy. His wife (Mary) cooks him an unappetizing meal (an unusual occurrence). He wants to maintain his positive views of his wife (e.g., he accepts her explanation that the recipe was bad), but he takes her attribution at face value and is not motivated to think about the causes in an in-depth fashion. (3) Gary has been on the prowl in a bar. He is drunk, it is late, and he unexpectedly receives an offer of sexual activity from one of the few single women. Gary does not really notice or care about Mary's personality. (4) Gary is speed dating; he has 10 minute interviews with 15 women, and has to pick between one and three women to go out with on extended dates. Gary is motivated to ascertain the facts and make realistic attributions in assessing each woman's potential mate value, but he is not motivated to exaggerate the positive qualities of the women (at least not before he makes his final decision).

ENTER EVOLUTIONARY PSYCHOLOGY

Progress has been made toward discovering the proximal psychological processes that are responsible for generating biased and accurate perceptions, evaluations, and judgments in romantic relationships. Much less remains known, however, about the ultimate-level evolutionary forces that might have shaped the proximal-level processes and effects reviewed above. In this section, we describe how certain evolutionary ideas and principles can clarify when individuals should be more accurate or more biased, especially when making interpersonally relevant evaluations or judgments. We then describe a proximal-level model of bias and accuracy that is built on this theoretical scaffolding.

An Evolutionary Prolegomenon

In the vast majority of mammalian species, males are promiscuous and contribute little more than sperm to their mates. Most mammalian females, by comparison, invest heavily and often exclusively in caring for and rearing offspring (Trivers, 1985). In roughly 4% of mammals, however, males and females emotionally bond and have sustained, socially monogamous mateships (Trivers, 1985). In such species, males invest and assist in rearing offspring in some manner (e.g., by protecting young against predators, finding food, building nests or shelters). Among mammals, human males display perhaps the highest levels of investment.

Humans also possess mammalian neurophysiological mechanisms that support and sustain emotional bonds to specific persons, particularly children and long-term mates. The hormonal systems that produce strong feelings of attachment and emotional bonding involve oxytocin and vasopressin, two similar neuropeptides (Insel, 2000). A common argument is that evolutionary processes have lifted and reworked the ancient mechanisms that promote mother–infant bonding in mammals to promote pair-bonding between humans (see Diamond, 2004; Insel, 2000). Consistent with this viewpoint, the few mammalian species in which males *do* bond and invest in offspring (e.g., humans, prairie voles) have rich networks of oxytocin receptors in the brain. In contrast, species in which males are more promiscuous and less likely to invest in offspring (e.g., montane voles, rats) have relatively few oxytocin receptors (Insel, 2000).

It is not enough to sire children for genes to survive. The evolutionary function of emotional bonding for men is likely to involve the way in which increased time and investment devoted to needy offspring should (on average) have increased the offspring's chances of surviving into adulthood, thus passing on their fathers' genes. This line of reasoning is especially plausible with respect to humans, given the prolonged period of time that humans spend as neophytes and the extensive teaching and learning that is required to equip children with the skills necessary to promote their own reproductive fitness. In the currency of reproductive fitness, therefore, biparental care may have been critical in the evolutionary history of humans, and emotional bonding with mates should have played a key role in facilitating paternal investment.

This evolutionary thesis, however, can be used to support both sides of the accuracy vs. enhancement debate. Consider the "love is blind" perspective. Love's cognitive blinkers might represent an evolutionary mechanism designed to increase commitment and keep parents together long enough to give their offspring an improved chance at survival beyond puberty (Frank, 1988; Mellen, 1981). According to this account, love provides the intimate relationship mind with a positive and over-optimistic default setting. From an evolutionary perspective, however, the human mind should (also) have been molded to discern critical truths and realities in the social world, particularly in situations where the costs of being wrong would be likely to have harmed reproductive fitness, and this is certainly true in some relationship contexts (see Haselton & Buss, 2000). Indeed, the proposition that evolution has sculpted the intimate relationship mind to routinely remain blind to the truth in fitness-relevant relationship contexts seems odd if not bizarre.

As we have demonstrated, individuals can produce partner and relationship evaluations that are simultaneously biased and accurate, and such outcomes may be commonplace. This apparent contradiction, however, becomes less paradoxical when one incorporates ultimate-level evolutionary thinking. Evolutionary approaches can offer both theoretical integration *and* novel predictions with respect to many of the proximal-level accuracy and enhancement findings described above. In what follows, we borrow principles from an evolutionary-based conditional strategies approach to understanding mating in humans, known as the Strategic Pluralism Model (Gangestad & Simpson, 2000). This model postulates that humans have evolved to pursue conditional mating strategies in which two sets of mate attributes were systematically "traded off"—attributes signaling that a partner will be a good, investing mate/parent, and attributes signaling that a mate's fitness could be transmitted genetically to future offspring.

The Evolution of Flexible Mating Strategies: A Conditional Strategies Approach

Gangestad and Simpson (2000) have proposed that humans should have evolved flexible mating strategies that were—and probably still are—sensitive to local environmental ecologies. According to their Strategic Pluralism Model (Gangestad & Simpson, 2000), good genes sexual selection and good parenting sexual selection may have jointly operated to generate some of the variation and contextual effects associated with the deployment of short- and long-term mating tactics witnessed in both sexes. Given the strong and sustained demands of biparental care during evolutionary history, men and women should both have been selected to enact long-term mating tactics and invest heavily in offspring. Both sexes, however, should also have evolved to enact ecologically contingent or "conditional" mating strategies, allocating some effort to short-term and extra-pair mating in certain conditions.

More specifically, women may have evolved to trade-off valid evidence of the genetic fitness of potential mates (e.g., their health, attractiveness, and/or vitality) for evidence of their ability and willingness to invest in the relationship and possible offspring (e.g., their capacity for status/resources and/or their willingness to be warm, loyal, and trustworthy). The specific mating tactics and preferences that women adopted, however, should have been contingent on the nature and quality of their local environment. If the local environment was harsh and demanded biparental care, women should have placed relatively greater weight on the investment potential of prospective mates (e.g., their status/resources and/or their warmth/trustworthiness) and less emphasis on potential indicators of genetic fitness (e.g., their health, attractiveness, and/or vitality). As a result, a larger proportion of women should have adopted long-term mating tactics. If, on the other hand, the local environment was prevalent with pathogens or signaled the importance of channeling genetic fitness to offspring, women should have placed relatively greater weight on indicators of genetic fitness in prospective mates (e.g., their health, attractiveness, and/or vitality). In such environments, a larger proportion of women should have been willing to engage in selective short-term or extra-pair matings allowing them to reap genetic benefits from such men at the possible risk of losing parental investment from their primary mates.

The Strategic Pluralism Model also predicts that if most women expected or wanted greater paternal investment, most men (especially those who may have been less genetically fit) should have offered greater and perhaps more exclusive parental investment, allocating more of their time and effort to long-term mating tactics and considerable parental investment. Under these conditions, variance in men's mating success should have reduced, chiefly because a larger proportion of men should have mated successfully. If, however, women's demand for genetic benefits increased, some men (especially those who possessed possible benefits) could have dedicated greater effort to short-term or extra-pair mating tactics, thereby increasing variance in the mating success of men. In all likelihood, however, only a small proportion of men should have been able to enact short-term mating tactics successfully, independent of the local environmental factors to which women were responding.

Several of the basic predictions derived from the Strategic Pluralism Model have been supported (see Gangestad & Simpson, 2000 for an extensive review). Moreover, recent tests of the model have confirmed that women are more attracted to men who display cues likely to be associated with better fitness, but only when women evaluate such men as potential short-term mates and only when they are ovulating (that is, only during the phase of their reproductive cycles when they are most likely to obtain the benefits of the "good genes" from such men; see Gangestad, Simpson, Cousins, Garver-Apgar, & Christensen, 2004). In addition, individuals in different regions of the world appear to adopt short- and long-term mating strategies facultatively in response to local environmental demands and pressures, just as the model anticipates (Schmitt, 2005). Furthermore, women tend to place special value on the physical attractiveness of potential extra-pair mates (see Scheib, 2001).

Other research has also documented that men and women in many different cultures tend to focus on similar features and attributes when evaluating long-term mates (see Buss, 1989; Schmitt, 2005). For both genders, the most-valued mate features tend to be intelligence, warmth/kindness, and trustworthiness worldwide. Physical attractiveness, good health, and vitality are also important to both genders. However, they are valued slightly more by men than by women (Buss, 1989), particularly in cultures that have greater gender inequality (Eagly & Wood, 1999). These physical features, however, tend to be rated as less important than warmth/kindness and trustworthiness by most women and men.

The possession of (or ability to acquire) status and resources is also rated as important by both genders, but significantly more so by women than men (Buss, 1989). Once again, however, this gender difference is attenuated in cultures or regions with greater gender equality (Eagly & Wood, 1999). When making distinctions between necessities and luxuries in potential mates, men demand sufficient levels of physical attractiveness as necessary features in mates, women demand sufficient levels of status and resources, and both genders demand sufficient levels of kindness/warmth and intelligence (Li, Bailey, Kenrick, & Linsenmeier, 2002).

Consistent with the Strategic Pluralism Model, factor analytic studies indicate that most mate attributes cluster into three major categories: attractiveness/vitality, warmth/trustworthiness, and status/resources (Fletcher, Simpson, Thomas, & Giles, 1999; Fletcher, Tither, O'Loughlin, Friesen, & Overall, 2004). Considering that the mate attributes in these studies were taken from open-ended protocols generated by participants themselves, these categories are likely to reflect the primary dimensions on which people base their mate-selection decisions (rather than merely existing in the minds of evolutionary psychologists).

Testing predictions from the Ideal Standards Model (Simpson et al., 2001), Fletcher, Simpson, and their colleagues have established that these three categories are used not only to select mates, but also to evaluate the quality of current partners and relationships (Campbell et al., 2001; Fletcher et al., 1999; Fletcher, Simpson, & Thomas, 2000) and to regulate and modify negative features of the self or the partner in ongoing relationships (Overall, Fletcher, & Simpson, in press). This body of research has revealed, for example, that the larger the discrepancy between an individual's ideal standards and his or her perceptions of the current partner on each of the mate-choice dimensions, (1) the more negatively she/he rates the current relationship, (2) the more likely the relationship will dissolve, and (3) the more the individual will strive to change his/her partner's negative attributes.

Why are these categories—warmth/trustworthiness, attractiveness/vitality, and status/resources—so central in mate selection and retention? Most social psychological approaches are indifferent to this question. Evolutionary approaches, however, are not. Depending on the nature and demands of local environments, differential attention to these dimensions might have enhanced reproductive fitness in our evolutionary past by orienting people toward diagnostic evidence of a potential or a current mate's investment potential and "good genes." In certain situations, high levels of warmth/kindness and trustworthiness, for instance, should have provided honest advertisements of a mate's capacity to be a good long-term mate and parent. This should have been particularly true when a mate displayed high levels of warmth/kindness and trustworthiness in situations that were potentially costly, detrimental, or dangerous to him or her (e.g., trust diagnostic situations: see Simpson, in press). Mates who continue to exhibit steadfast trust and confidence in their partners even when doing so might leave them open to exploitation, for example, could be construed by their partners as providing valid evidence of the mate's long-term relationship potential.

The possession of status and resources, or the unrelenting drive to obtain them, should have signaled the ability and/or potential for a mate to invest heavily in the relationship and any offspring. Attractiveness and vitality also might have served as one indirect marker of "good genes," signaling fertility in women and/or genetically based health qualities in either gender (cf. Gangestad & Simpson, 2000). There is mounting evidence for each of these postulates, including the claim that greater attractiveness/vitality was probably tied to greater reproductive success during evolutionary history (Gangestad & Simpson, 2000; Jones, Little, Penton-Voak, Tiddeman, Burt, & Perrett, 2001; but see Rhodes & Zebrowitz, 2001, for some alternate views).

Also consistent with a conditional mating strategies approach, several theoretically meaningful moderating variables appear to govern the choices and evaluations that people make when evaluating potential or current mates. First, gender moderates the importance that men and women place on the three mate-selection categories. According to parental investment theory (Trivers, 1972), the gender that initially invests more in offspring ought to be choosier and more discriminating when evaluating mates. Given that women initially invest more than men in terms of gestation, giving birth, and lactation, and can produce fewer children during their lifetimes, most women should rate mate-selection criteria related to good investment as more important than criteria associated with good genes. Indeed, women do rate a mate's status/resources and warmth/trustworthiness as more important than men do, whereas men typically rate physical attractiveness as more important than women do (for reviews, see Buss, 1999; Fletcher, 2002).

Second, mating histories and perceptions of self-perceived mate value should partially determine the weight placed on specific mate-value qualities in both potential and current mates. In line with this proposition, the more positively an individual perceives his/her own mate value on a given mate dimension (e.g., attractiveness/vitality), the higher the mate-criteria standards that she/he sets for prospective and current romantic partners on that specific dimension (see Fletcher, 2002). This may partially explain why assortative mating effects are typically so pronounced.

Third, mate selection goals shift in predictable ways in short- vs. long-term mating contexts. Mate-selection criteria for a good long-term mate and parent, for instance, are rated as less important in short-term romantic relationships than in long-term relationships, with the sole exception of attractiveness/vitality (Buss & Schmitt, 1993; Fletcher & Simpson, 2000). Although most men have lower minimal partner standards than most women for engaging in short-term sexual liaisons (Regan, 1998), consistent with a conditional strategies approach, both genders tend to place equal or greater emphasis on physical attractiveness in short-term partners and relationships compared to long-term relationships (Fletcher et al., 2004; Sprecher & Regan, 2002). For women, these findings make sense from an evolutionary standpoint because attractiveness/vitality is one marker of a male's good genes, and the primary gain for women from brief affairs is good genes from the male. These findings also make evolutionary sense for men, especially when one considers that both youth and attractive body shape in women correlate positively with their degree of fertility and, hence, their current reproductive status (see Fletcher 2002; Kenrick & Keefe, 1992).

A Model Predicting Positivity Bias and Accuracy in Romantic Relationships

Guided by social psychological and evolutionary evidence, theory, and reasoning, our model offers some unique predictions about when positivity bias or accuracy should be most likely to occur in romantic relationship contexts. Predictions generated by our model are depicted in Table 9.2. We make two simplifying assumptions to reduce the complexity of the model. In particular, we have portrayed long- and short-term relationships as being discrete categories (rather than continuously distributed dimensions), and we have done the same for the two motives (truth seeking and positivity seeking). The model includes only two quadrants of the four shown in Figure 9.1: the top-left quadrant (truth-seeking motive) and the bottom-right quadrant (positivity-seeking motive). The model makes

TABLE 9.2   A Model Showing Predicted Amounts of Positive Bias and Accuracy, Based on an Evolutionary Conditional Strategies Model of Mate Selection

| | Truth-Seeking Motive | | Positivity-Seeking Motive | |
	Bias	Accuracy	Bias	Accuracy
Long-Term Relationships				
Warmth/trustworthiness	++	+++++	+++++	++
Attractiveness/vitality	++	+++++	+++++	++
Status/resources	++	+++++	+++++	++
Short-Term Relationships				
Warmth/trustworthiness	+	+++	+++	+
Attractiveness/vitality	++	+++++	+++++	++
Status/resources	+	+++	+++	+

Note: The number of + signs represents the strength of each predicted effect within each category.

three major sets of predictions. We discuss each set in turn, followed by a discussion of the roles played by individual differences and gender.

The Interaction between Positivity Bias vs. Accuracy and Truth Seeking vs. Positivity Seeking

For both long- and short-term relationships, the model predicts that truth-seeking motives should depress positive bias and enhance accuracy, whereas the positivity-seeking motive should enhance bias and suppress accuracy. What factors might encourage people to adopt either motivational stance?

First, it seems likely that the stage of the relationship should be an important factor given the potential costs and benefits involved (see Haselton & Funder, this volume). All relationships, either long- or short term, eventually reach critical decision points that have important implications for an individual's reproductive fitness. These include choosing a good mate, deciding to have sex, deciding whether to become involved in an exclusive relationship, to have children, to get married, and to leave a current mate for a new one. In such circumstances, the level of mutual commitment may be uncertain, but the decisions that are made could have profound and lasting affects on both personal well-being and reproductive fitness. During our evolutionary past, making intelligent and informed assessments in such contexts should, on average, have enhanced reproductive fitness. Accordingly, these circumstances should have encouraged truth-seeking motives rather than merely trying to feel good about partners and relationships.

Second, after major commitment decisions have been made, the need to view both the relationship and the partner in a positive light should generally become more important. In this context, positive biases may help to justify and cement the relationship, which in turn should have encouraged individuals to achieve fitness-enhancing goals and actions, such as meeting the needs of one's mate and sustaining the long-term emotional bonds and commitment required for raising children successfully.

Third, levels of accuracy and positivity bias should vary as a function of local environmental conditions. If individuals find themselves in environments in which pathogens and disease are prevalent, for instance, they should be more motivated to assess the attractiveness/vitality (i.e., the long-term health) of prospective and current mates accurately. On the other hand, if individuals find themselves in environments in which biparental care is virtually mandatory for children to survive and be raised to reproductive age, they should be more motivated to assess a current or potential mate's ability and willingness to provide resources accurately (Gangestad & Simpson, 2000). Thus, the levels of accuracy vs. enhancement may also hinge on the nature of local ecologies.

Differences between Short- and Long-term Relationships

According to the model, levels of positivity bias and accuracy may be somewhat weaker for short-term than for long-term relationships, principally because both motivational sets should operate more strongly in long-term relationships. Why do we make this claim? First, long-term relationships typically should have had more important long-term reproductive fitness implications than short-term relationships. Second, the costs associated with making bad judgments or relationship dissolution are generally not as serious for casual affairs or for dating relationships compared to long-term relationships (e.g., marriage). All these factors should conspire to make the predicted patterns of accuracy and positivity bias effects slightly stronger in long- than in short-term relationships.

The Odd Case of Attractiveness/Vitality

The major exception to our prior claims concerns attractiveness/vitality. As we have already described, research has documented that both women and men rate attractiveness and sexuality as important—or perhaps more important—in short-term relationships than in long-term relationships (e.g., Fletcher et al., 2004). From an evolutionary angle, this makes sense especially for women when one considers that, in short-term relationships, men often contribute little more than their genes to potential children. With regard to perceptions of attractiveness/vitality, therefore, people might be motivated to display both greater positivity bias *and* accuracy, at least relative to the two other mate-selection categories.

Gender and Individual Differences

According to our model, the role of gender and individual differences in the importance that individuals place on different mate-selection categories (within each gender) should produce the main effects within each cell. For example, people who place greater emphasis on attractiveness/vitality when evaluating and choosing mates should be more accurate at judging attractiveness/vitality when in a truth-seeking mode than persons who place less importance on attractiveness/vitality and who are also in a truth-seeking mode. However, individuals who place more weight on attractiveness/vitality ought to become more positively biased in related judgments when their relationships enter maintenance stages or when mundane decisions are being made.

Gender differences may also influence the pattern of outcomes in view of the fact that the sexes tend to place differential importance on certain mate-selection categories. Women, for example, may be more accurate than men when judging the degree to which their romantic partners are genuinely warm, kind, loyal, and ambitious. Indeed, evidence suggests that women *are* more accurate than men at making these judgments, at least in long-term relationship contexts (Fletcher, 2002).

Research by Haselton and Buss (2000) reveals characteristic sex differences in levels of bias; namely, men tend to perceive or exaggerate levels of sexual interest in potential mates, whereas women tend to underestimate levels of men's desire for commitment in courtship settings. They predicted (and explained) these findings by postulating adaptive cognitive mechanisms for men not to miss any opportunity for sex, and for women to avoid developing sexual relationships with untrustworthy men.

A Broader View of the Model

This model has several nice features. It neatly resolves the "love is blind" vs. "love is wise" paradox. It is consistent with and integrates extant empirical findings relevant to bias and accuracy in romantic relationships. It incorporates theoretically meaningful moderating variables. It suggests how local environmental factors and circumstances might accentuate the importance of accuracy or positive bias with respect to specific mate-selection categories. And it suggests how and why motivations regarding accuracy vs. enhancement of partners and relationships vary across the three major mate-selection categories.

Although the model remains speculative, research has supported a few of its core tenets. For example, research supports the assumption that this model identifies the most important categories that people routinely apply when evaluating their romantic partners and relationships: warmth/trustworthiness, attractiveness/vitality, and status/resources (Fletcher et al., 1999). Preliminary evidence also supports a central postulate of the model, namely that positive bias and accuracy operate *within* each judgment domain rather than in terms of global judgments across domains. For example, confirmatory factor analyses have shown that for ideal importance ratings (in both long- and short-term contexts), individual differences function within each mate criterion category, not merely across categories in terms of overall desired standards (see Fletcher et al., 2004).

Moreover, Boyes and Fletcher (2004) have reported evidence of substantial positive bias in a sample of dating partners involved in long-term relationships for all three mate-selection categories (warmth/trustworthiness, attractiveness/vitality, and status/resources), with more positive bias predicting greater relationship satisfaction. Moderate levels of accuracy were also found for partner attributions, but accuracy was not related to relationship satisfaction (a common finding described previously). Nevertheless, individuals who attributed more importance to specific mate-evaluation categories tended to be more accurate in those domains.

Our model also implies that some reinterpretation of prior research on accuracy and positive bias might be necessary. Much of the research conducted by Murray and her colleagues, for example, has measured bias and accuracy in long-term relationships using global personality traits that primarily measure attributes aligned with the warmth/trustworthiness category. Thus, one cannot necessarily presume that these previous findings will generalize to short-term relationship contexts or to the mate-selection attributes represented in the attractiveness/vitality and the status/resources categories.

Finally, Neff and Karney (2002) have claimed that global judgments of a relationship partner tend to be more accurately attributed than specific traits, but that global traits are often more positively biased than specific traits. Although this is a plausible hypothesis, specificity vs. globality was confounded with the relevance to relationship or mate evaluations in that work. Attractive, successful, and understanding, for example, were counted as global attributions, whereas patient, organized, athletic ability, and tidiness were defined as specific attributions. A recent study by Gill and Swann (2004) also confirmed that traits deemed as more relevant to intimate relationships tend to be judged more accurately than those perceived as less relevant.

CONCLUSIONS

In closing, the model that we have advanced is grounded in the proposition that love can be blinkered yet also wedded to reality, primarily because it is a product of evolutionary forces designed to achieve two distinct goals in the service of enhancing reproductive fitness. These two goals, in turn, have been translated into two powerful motivations. On the one hand, individuals should be motivated to choose partners and relationships judiciously and to arrive at accurate partner and relationship assessments. On the other hand, they should be motivated to see their partners and relationships in the best possible light in order to maintain established bonds critical to raising offspring successfully.

Admittedly, our model remains both speculative and partial. For example, it does not deal specifically with the role of emotional arousal, and it simplifies some key distinctions that are bound to be more complex than we have indicated. Moreover, we remain uncertain about the exact nature and level of evolutionary adaptations involved in our model. It may be, for example, that the levels of bias and accuracy in relationships are produced as a function of basic evolutionary adaptations that underlie love, attachment, and mate-selection processes.

At the same time, the model also has some unique strengths. For instance, it directly addresses a distinction that has been badly blurred in psychology—bias and accuracy—and it attempts to explain and predict the precise conditions under which most people can be more accurate or more biased when making certain relationship-relevant judgments. We hope that our treatment is a good exemplar of the way in which evolutionary reasoning and social psychology models can work together to produce a more innovative and fruitful account of the intimate relationship mind.

NOTES

1. This concept of bias should also be distinguished from the terms positive and negative bias used in error management theory (see Haselton & Nettle, 2006). This approach is based on a signal detection model, in which a positive bias implies that the individual is likely to form a belief that is true (when it is false), and a negative bias implies that an individual is likely to form a belief that is false (when it is true). Thus, in this model, bias is more or less equated with accuracy, and the terms "positive" and "negative" should not be interpreted as equivalent to evaluative valence.

2. The question of how much weight should be given to prior theory, and how much to data, is a problem for all of science. Indeed, it is one of the central issues in the philosophy of science and methodology. This issue is not easily resolvable, but it is clear that strictly probabilistic models (such as Bayes' theorem) do not solve the problem (see Fletcher, 1995).

REFERENCES

Acitelli, L. K., Kenny, D. A., & Weiner, D. (2001). The importance of similarity and understanding of partners' marital ideals to relationship satisfaction. *Personal Relationships, 8,* 167–185.

Boyes, A. D., & Fletcher, G. J. O. (2004). *Bias and accuracy in intimate relationships in perceptions of mate value.* Paper presented at the Society of Personality and Social Psychology, Austin, TX.

Buss, D. M. (1989). Sex differences in human mate preferences: Evolutionary hypotheses tested in 37 cultures. *Behavioral and Brain Sciences, 12,* 1–49.

Buss, D. M. (1999). *Evolutionary psychology: The new science of the mind.* Boston: Allyn & Bacon.

Buss, D. M., & Schmitt, D. P. (1993). Sexual strategies theory: An evolutionary perspective on human mating. *Psychological Review, 100,* 204–232.

Campbell, L., Simpson, J. A., Kashy, D. A., & Fletcher, G. J. O. (2001). Ideal standards, the self, and flexibility of ideals in close relationships. *Personality and Social Psychology Bulletin, 27,* 447–462.

Collins, N. L., & Feeney, B. C. (2000). A safe haven: An attachment theory perspective on support seeking and caregiving in intimate relationships. *Journal of Personality and Social Psychology, 78,* 1053–1073.

Cronbach, L. (1955). Processes affecting scores on "understanding of others" and "assumed similarity". *Psychological Bulletin, 52,* 177–193.

Diamond, L. M. (2004). Emerging perspectives on distinctions between romantic love and sexual desire. *Current Directions in Psychological Science, 13,* 116–119.

Eagly, A. H., & Wood, W. (1999). The origins of sex differences in human behavior: Evolved dispositions versus social roles. *American Psychologist, 54,* 408–423.

Fiske, S. T., & Taylor, S. E. (1984). *Social cognition.* Reading, MA: Addison-Wesley.

Fletcher, G. (1995). *The scientific credibility of folk psychology.* Hillsdale, NJ: Erlbaum.

Fletcher, G. (2002). *The new science of intimate relationships.* Malden, MA: Blackwell.

Fletcher, G. J. O. (1996). Realism versus relativism in psychology. *American Journal of Psychology, 109,* 409–429.

Fletcher, G. J. O., & Simpson, J. A. (2000). Ideal standards in close relationships: Their structure and functions. *Current Directions in Psychological Science, 9,* 102–105.

Fletcher, G. J. O., Simpson, J. A., & Thomas, G. (2000). The measurement of perceived relationship quality components: A confirmatory factor analytic approach. *Personality and Social Psychology Bulletin, 26,* 340–354.

Fletcher, G. J. O., Simpson, J. A., Thomas, G., & Giles, L. (1999). Ideals in intimate relationships. *Journal of Personality and Social Psychology, 76,* 72–89.

Fletcher, G. J. O., & Thomas, G. (2000). Behavior and on-line cognition in marital interaction. *Personal Relationships, 7,* 111–130.

Fletcher, G. J. O., Tither, J. M., O'Loughlin, C., Friesen, M., & Overall, N. (2004). Warm and homely or cold and beautiful? Sex differences in trading off traits in mate selection. *Personality and Social Psychology Bulletin, 30,* 659–672.

Fowers, B. J., Lyons, E., Montel, K. H., & Shaked, N. (2001). Positive illusions about marriage among married and single individuals. *Journal of Family Psychology, 15,* 95–109.

Frank, R. H. (1988). *Passions within reason.* New York: Norton.

Funder, D. C. (1995). On the accuracy of personality judgment: A realistic approach. *Psychological Review, 102,* 652–670.

Gagne, F. M., & Lydon, J. E. (2001). Mind-set and close relationships: When bias leads to (in)accurate predictions. *Journal of Personality and Social Psychology, 81,* 85–96.

Gagne, F. M., & Lydon, J. E. (2003). Identification and the commitment shift: Accounting for gender differences in relationship illusions. *Personality and Social Psychology Bulletin, 29*, 907–919.

Gagne, F. M., & Lydon, J. E. (2004). Bias and accuracy in close relationships: An integrative review. *Personality and Social Psychology Review, 8*, 322–338.

Gangestad, S. W., & Simpson, J. A. (2000). The evolution of human mating: Trade-offs and strategic pluralism. *Behavioral & Brain Sciences, 23*, 573–644.

Gangestad, S. W., Simpson, J. A., Cousins, A. J., Garver-Apgar, C. E., & Christensen, P. N. (2004). Women's preferences for male behavioral displays change across the menstrual cycle. *Psychological Science, 15*, 203–207.

Gill, M. J., & Swann, W. B. (2004). On what it means to know someone: A matter of pragmatics. *Journal of Personality & Social Psychology, 86*, 405–418.

Haselton, M. G., & Buss, D. M. (2000). Error management theory: A new perspective on biases in cross-sex mind reading. *Journal of Personality and Social Psychology, 78*, 81–91.

Haselton, M. G., & Nettle, D. (2006). The paranoid optimist: An integrative evolutionary model of cognitive biases. *Personality and Social Psychology Review, 10*, 47–66.

Ickes, W., & Simpson, J.A. (2001). Motivational aspects of empathic accuracy. In G. J. O. Fletcher & M. S. Clark (Eds.), *Blackwell handbook of social psychology: Interpersonal processes* (pp. 229–250). Malden, MA: Blackwell.

Insel, T. R. (2000). Toward a neurobiology of attachment. *Review of General Psychology, 4*, 176–185.

Jones, B. C., Little, A. C., Penton-Voak, I. S., Tiddeman, B. P., Burt, D. M., & Perrett, D. I. (2001). Facial symmetry and judgments of apparent health—Support for a "good genes" explanation of the attractiveness-symmetry relationship. *Evolution and Human Behavior, 22*, 417–429.

Karney, B. R., & Bradbury, T. N. (1995). The longitudinal course of marital quality and stability: A review of theory, methods, and research. *Psychological Bulletin, 118*, 3–34.

Karney, B. R., & Frye, N. E. (2002). "But we've been getting better lately": Comparing prospective and retrospective views of relationship development. *Journal of Personality and Social Psychology, 82*, 222–238.

Kenrick, D. T., & Keefe, R. C. (1992). Age preferences in mates reflect sex differences in reproductive strategies. *Behavioral and Brain Sciences, 15*, 75–133.

Krueger, J. I., & Funder, D. C. (2004). Towards a balanced social psychology: Causes, consequences and cures for the problem-seeking approach to social behavior and cognition. *Behavioral and Brain Sciences, 27*, 313–376.

Li, N. P., Bailey, J. M., Kenrick, D. T., & Linsenmeier, J. A. W. (2002). The necessities and luxuries of mate preferences: Testing the tradeoffs. *Journal of Personality and Social Psychology, 82*, 947–955.

MacDonald, T. K., & Ross, M. (1999). Assessing the accuracy of predictions about dating relationships: How and why do lovers' predictions differ from those made by observers? *Personality and Social Psychology Bulletin, 25*, 1417–1429.

Mellen, S. L. W. (1981). *The evolution of love.* New York: Freeman.

Murray, S. L. (2001). Seeking a sense of conviction. In G. J. O. Fletcher & M. S. Clark (Eds.), *Blackwell handbook of social psychology: Interpersonal processes* (pp.107–126). Malden, MA: Blackwell.

Murray, S. L., Holmes, J. G., Bellavia, G., Griffin, D. W., & Dolderman, D. (2002). Kindred spirits? The benefits of egocentrism in close relationships. *Journal of Personality and Social Psychology, 82*, 563–581.

Murray, S. L., Holmes, J. G., & Griffin, D. W. (1996a). The benefits of positive illusions: Idealization and the construction of satisfaction in close relationships. *Journal of Personality and Social Psychology, 70*, 79–98.

Murray, S. L., Holmes, J. G., & Griffin, D. W. (1996b). The self-fulfilling nature of positive illusions in romantic relationships: Love is not blind, but prescient. *Journal of Personality and Social Psychology, 71*, 1155–1180.

Neff, L. A., & Karney, B. R. (2002). Judgments of a relationship partner: Specific accuracy but global enhancement. *Journal of Personality, 70*, 1079–1112.

Nisbett, R. E., & Ross, L. (1980). *Human inference: Strategies and shortcomings of social judgment.* Englewood Cliffs, NJ: Prentice-Hall.

Overall, N. C., Fletcher, G. J. O., & Simpson, J. A. (in press). Why do people try to change their intimate relationships? The regulation function of ideal standards. *Journal of Personality and Social Psychology.*

Regan, P. C. (1998). Minimum mate selection standards as a function of perceived mate value, relationship context, and sex. *Journal of Psychology and Human Sexuality, 10*, 53–73.

Rhodes, G., & Zebrowitz, L. A. (Eds.). (2001). *Facial attractiveness: Evolutionary, cognitive, and social perspectives.* Westport, CT: Ablex.

Scheib, J. E. (2001). Context-specific mate choice criteria: Women's trade-offs in the contexts of long-term and extra-pair mateships. *Personal Relationships, 8*, 371–389.

Schmitt, D. P. (2005). Sociosexuality from Argentina to Zimbabwe: A 48-nation study of sex, culture, and strategies of human mating. *Behavioral and Brain Sciences, 28*, 247–311.

Sherman, P. W. (1988). The levels of analysis. *Animal Behavior, 36*, 616–619.

Simpson, J. A. (in press). Foundations of interpersonal trust. In A. W. Kruglanski & E. T. Higgins (Eds.), *Social psychology: Handbook of basic principles* (2nd ed.). New York: Guilford.

Simpson, J. A., Fletcher, G. J. O., & Campbell, L. (2001). The structure and function of ideal standards in close relationships. In G. J. O. Fletcher & M. S. Clark (Eds.), *Blackwell handbook of social psychology: Interpersonal processes* (pp. 86–106). Malden, MA: Blackwell.

Simpson, J. A., Ickes, W., & Blackstone, T. (1995). When the head protects the heart: Empathic accuracy in dating relationships. *Journal of Personality and Social Psychology, 69*, 629–641.

Simpson, J. A., Orina, M. M., & Ickes, W. (2003). When accuracy hurts and when it helps: A test of the empathic accuracy model in marital interactions. *Journal of Personality and Social Psychology, 85*, 881–893.

Sprecher, S. (1999). "I love you more today than yesterday": Romantic partners' perceptions of changes in love and related affect over time. *Journal of Personality and Social Psychology, 76*, 46–53.

Sprecher, S., & Regan, P. C. (2002). Liking some things (in some people) more than others: Partner preferences in romantic relationships and friends. *Journal of Social and Personal Relationships, 19*, 463–481.

Thomas, G., & Fletcher, G. J. O. (2003). Mind-reading accuracy in intimate relationships: Assessing the roles of the relationship, the target, and the judge. *Journal of Personality and Social Psychology, 85*, 1079–1094.

Trivers, R. (1985). *Social evolution.* Menlo Park, CA: Benjamin/Cummings.

Trivers, R. L. (1972). Parental investment and sexual selection. In B. Campbell (Ed.), *Sexual selection and the descent of man, 1871–1971* (pp. 136–79). Chicago: Aldine.

Van Lange, P. A. M., & Rusbult, C. E. (1995). My relationship is better than—and not as bad as—yours is: The perception of superiority in close relationships. *Personality and Social Psychology Bulletin, 21*, 32–44.

10

Evolution, Relationships, and Health: The Social Shaping Hypothesis

SHELLEY E. TAYLOR and GIAN C. GONZAGA

*D*ealing with environmental stressors such as predators, aggressive rivals, and the divergent interests of conspecifics is one of the primary evolutionary challenges faced by all creatures. In this respect, nature has often been ingenious in its solutions: thick skin, sharp teeth, quick reflexes, and even camouflage. Humans, like many other primate species, have adapted group living and deep investment in social bonds as a primary solution to the problems of survival and reproduction (Caporeal, 1997; Dunbar, 1998). This observation has long been acknowledged in both evolutionary biology and evolutionary psychology but until recently, few scholars have recognized how important social relationships are for managing stress, for health, and for longevity. Recent converging evidence from biology and psychology reveals the manifold benefits of social relationships.

Social relationships are vital resources for managing the demands of the environment. Suggestive evidence for this assertion is provided by the fact that social isolation is associated with a heightened risk of disease and early mortality in both animals and humans (Cacioppo & Hawkley, 2003; House, Landis, & Umberson, 1988). Thus, the absence of social ties is toxic for health. Social relationships themselves can have dramatic and long-lasting effects on biological functioning and health as well. A harsh social environment characterized by cold, conflictual, or neglectful interactions is associated with a high risk of prolonged illness and early mortality, whereas warm and supportive relationships have long-term benefits for health and longevity. Social support, common to these latter relations, is the perception or experience that one is loved and cared for by others, esteemed and valued, and part of a social network of mutual assistance and obligations (Wills, 1991). The impact of social support on health equals or exceeds that of well-established predictors of health outcomes, including smoking and lipid levels.

THE SOCIAL SHAPING HYPOTHESIS

In this chapter, we begin by proposing a general model of how social relationships may influence biopsychosocial functioning and health, which we call the *social shaping* hypothesis. Social shaping refers to how social relationships modulate an individual's psychological, biological, social, and behavioral responses to stressful events and circumstances. These effects, as we will show, can be both short- and long-term and can have effects on biological, emotional, and social functioning. Social shaping is based on the idea that humans have evolved in such a way that a person's social relationships help to shape and regulate that person's stress responses. To this end, we suggest that social shaping serves three primary functions.

First, relationships can serve a calibration function. Specifically, relationships help to shape the stress systems that respond to threats in the environment. As we will show, caregiving relationships, particularly those early in life, especially serve this function. Beginning at birth, the quality of caregiving can permanently affect an infant's biological, emotional, and social responses to stressful conditions across the life span. These effects can occur at the level of gene expression, they can exert permanent organizational effects on biological responses to stress, and they ultimately predict longevity and the likelihood of a broad array of illnesses.

The second function is regulation. That is, social relationships help to regulate stress responses during daily interaction by influencing the magnitude of stress responses. This more proximal function interacts with the more distal calibration just described such that individuals' responses to stress depend both on how their systems (physiological and psychological) developed early in life and how their current relationships moderate their biopsychosocial responses to threat. Relationships can increase tension and exaggerate stress response or buffer an individual against the deleterious biological effects of stress.

Finally, relationships serve an information function, transmitting important knowledge about the environment to relationship partners. This information function may be direct, as when one person warns another about an impending threat. It may also be indirect, in that relationships themselves are affected by highly stressful conditions, often deteriorating in threatening times. For example, the lower a person's socioeconomic status (SES), the more he or she is exposed to a broad array of day-to-day hassles and threats (e.g., Adler, Boyce, Chesney, Cohen, Folkman, & Syme, 1994; Adler, Marmot, & McEwen, 2000); rancorous social relationships of all kinds are often the consequence of such environmental stress. Spousal abuse, divorce rates, child abuse, and other indicators of social strain, such as homicide or assault, all show moderate social class gradients (see Taylor, 2002 for a review). More focused investigations also reveal how stress in one domain of life, such as work, spills over into other life arenas, such as family life (see Taylor, 2002 for a review). Thus, social relations provide information by acting as a barometer of how stressful the environment is.

We first detail the biological mechanisms whereby stress adversely affects health and note how social relationships may reduce or augment those biological responses. Then we develop the rationale for the social shaping hypothesis and review evidence for it. In so doing, we focus especially on three types of relationships and how they each illustrate the functions of social shaping. We then detail the important effects relationships have on health and survival. We first turn to the parent–child relationship, especially the mother–child relationship, and show how the nature of this early relationship can calibrate the biological stress response of the offspring, and what implications this has for health across a lifetime and, perhaps, into the next generation. Second, we review research showing that the male–female pair-bond can affect the stress responses of the individuals in the relationship. Finally, we discuss how same-sex ties influence responses to stress by providing important information about the challenges and opportunities of an individual's immediate environment.

HOW STRESS CAN AFFECT HEALTH

The impact of social relationships on biological and psychological functioning is heavily mediated by stress responses. The human response to stress implicates several interacting systems. The amygdala is responsive to novel conditions or signs of potential danger in the environment. Together with the other areas in the brain (the anterior cingulate cortex may be implicated, for example), it sends signals to the hypothalamus, which engages stress responses in the sympathetic nervous system (SNS) and the hypothalamic pituitary adrenal (HPA) axis. These systems are responsible for the release of hormones that mobilize the organism to fight or flee in response to stress.

The actions of the SNS are mediated primarily by the catecholamines norepinephrine and epinephrine, which exert effects on adrenergic receptors in target tissues to produce, among other changes, increases in heart rate and blood pressure, dilation of the airways, and enhanced availability of glucose and fatty acids for energy. These coordinated responses facilitate short-term mobilization of an organism's resources for the rapid, intense physical activity involved in the "fight-or-flight" response.

The HPA axis also plays a central role in managing threat. Corticotropin-releasing hormone (CRH), produced in the para-ventricular nuclei (PVN) of the hypothalamus, stimulates the secretion of adrenocorticotropic hormone (ACTH) by the anterior pituitary, resulting in the release of glucocorticoids. The primary glucocorticoid in humans is cortisol, and corticosterone in animals. Glucocorticoids serve an important function at low basal levels by permitting or restoring processes that prime homeostatic defense mechanisms (Munck & Naray-Fejes-Toth, 1994). This integrated pattern of HPA axis activation modulates a wide range of somatic functions including energy release, immune activity, mental activity, growth, and reproductive function. At low basal levels, glucocortiocoids promote mental and physical health as well as normal development.

However, larger, more frequent, and more long-lasting increases in glucocorticoids, as occurring in chronically or recurrently stressful environments, can compromise health. A hyperresponsive HPA axis influences the development of hypertension and cardiovascular disease, immune suppression, hyperinsulimia, and insulin resistance, enhancing risk for diabetes. Glucocorticoids are also implicated in age-related decreases in immune competence and cognitive functioning. Hyperactivity of the HPA axis is also thought to contribute to anxiety disorders and depression, as well as to growth retardation and developmental delay. As this analysis suggests, the HPA axis interacts with other systems, including the autonomic nervous system and the immune system, such that changes in HPA axis functioning will affect these and other systems as well.

Thus, coordinated stress responses can assume the form of hypervigilance, intense biological stress responses (SNS and HPA axis), strong emotional reactions such as anxiety, and social reactions such as clinging, aggression, or withdrawal. Such fast-acting hair-trigger responses are adaptive for coping with immediate threats. Alternatively, through feedback from the prefrontal cortex, stress responses may be moderated and down-regulated. That is, the realization that a threat is not as severe as it first appeared or that one has the resources to cope with it, including social resources, lessens these stress responses.

The long-term effects of social relationships on health and longevity are mediated, in part, by the prevalence and intensity of these stress responses. With chronic or recurrent activation, the functioning of these stress systems may be compromised, as physiological systems change to meet the recurring demands of a stressful environment. Constant or recurrent exposure to stressful circumstances can lead to alterations in SNS functioning and HPA axis responses to stress and potentially to disruptions in other systems such as immunologic, dopaminergic, and serotonergic functioning (McEwen, 1998). Deficiencies in the ability to mount a parasympathetic system (PNS) response to stress may be affected as well (see Repetti, Taylor, & Seeman, 2002 for a review). Through these processes, repeated social challenges can ultimately disrupt homeostatic processes that are central to the maintenance of health. The consequences may be cascading, potentially irreversible effects that can lead to stress-related physical and emotional disorders.[1] Conversely, supportive social relationships can be protective against these sorts of changes by preventing a stress response altogether in situations that are not particularly threatening or that are merely novel, by muting the strength of biological stress responses, and/or by promoting faster recovery of these system from the effects of stress. Social support may exert its regulatory effects on biological functioning, in part, via the prefrontal cortical pathway noted above, in that even mere awareness that one has social support available can lead to less intense responses to stress and/or faster recovery from stress.

Having described the social shaping hypothesis in general terms and its biological underpinnings, we next consider specific evidence for it. To illustrate the regulatory role of social relationships in an individual's biological, emotional, and social functioning, we examine specific social relationships, beginning with child–parent ties, with a special emphasis on how these relationships may calibrate an offspring's stress response.

PARENT–CHILD BOND

The parent–child bond has long been recognized as vital to survival. However, that recognition has not led to substantial research regarding the ways in which such bonds are protective. Although the importance of the idealized bond of closeness and warmth between parent and child, especially mother and child, is widely acknowledged, the mother–child relationship is studied as much for its rifts and deviations (e.g., infanticide) as for the vital functions it provides (see, for example, Hrdy, 1999). In the following section, we discuss ways in which the mother–infant bond is vital for the developing offspring, with particular focus on how these early relationships may calibrate physiological responses to stress. In theory, these comments apply to father–infant relations as well, in that human parenting is marked by substantial paternal investment relative to other species, but more of the relevant literature has focused on the mother–infant bond.

The often-cited survival functions of the maternal–infant bond include protection from harm, feeding through nursing, and provision of care during childhood, especially during illness or injury. Adopting an evolutionary health psychology perspective reveals that the functions of the maternal–infant bond are far broader. Across multiple encounters with her offspring, the mother's behavior toward her offspring conveys information about the stressfulness of the external environment, sending signals to her infant, which in turn affect the infant's development of psychological and biological responses to stress.

These powerful effects have been especially well documented in animal studies. For example, Meaney and associates (Francis, Diorio, Liu, & Meaney, 1999; Liu et al., 1997) studied the impact of maternal nurturance on offspring responses to stress. They employed a paradigm in which infant rats are separated from the mother for a brief period and subsequently returned to the cage. The maternal response to being reunited is typically to begin vigorous licking and grooming and arched-back nursing of the returned offspring. The immediate effect of these maternal behaviors is to reduce corticosterone responses and sympathetic activity in offspring and mother alike. But the long-term effects of maternal nurturance are important as well. Offspring who are the recipients of this nurturant attention also get lifelong protection against stress. Specifically, as adults, rat pups who had been the recipients of warm maternal care in this paradigm had reduced plasma ACTH and corticosterone responses to acute stress, increased hippocampal glucocorticoid receptor messenger RNA expression, enhanced glucocorticoid feedback sensitivity, and decreased levels of hypothalamic CRH messenger RNA, all factors that reflect a better regulated and more efficient HPA axis stress response. As they matured, the offspring also showed more open-field exploration, suggesting that they were experiencing less anxiety in novel situations. As adults, they were less likely to show age-related onset of HPA axis dysregulation in response to challenge and were less likely to exhibit age-related cognitive deficits. As noted, some of these effects were evident at the level of gene expression.

We interpret these findings to indicate that maternal nurturance or its absence acts as a signal to the offspring as to how stress responses should develop. When maternal responses are nurturant, reflective of a benign environment, the HPA axis of offspring operates efficiently and returns to baseline quickly following a stressful encounter; and these effects can persist across the offspring's life span. The offspring show fewer signs of anxiety, less HPA axis activity in response to stress, and fewer signs of compromised HPA axis functioning in adulthood. In contrast, rats from species that are low lickers and groomers or who, for other reasons, do not receive this warm, nurturant activity (as through experimental manipulations) have what amount to hair-trigger HPA axis responses to stress. They are quick to show signs of anxiety and slow to explore new environments; their corticosterone responses to stressful conditions are strong and persistent, and over the long term they experience the accumulated damage that Meaney and colleagues documented in adulthood. Thus, these studies provide important evidence that maternal behavior actively shapes the offspring's biological and socioemotional responses to potentially stressful or merely novel situations across the life span.

If this reasoning is correct, then one would expect to see evidence that variations in stressful circumstances in the environment are reflected in maternal behavior. Rosenblum, Coplan, Friedman, Bassoff, Gorman, and Andrews (1994) manipulated the environments in which mother macaque monkeys raised their offspring by altering how easy or difficult it was for them to find food. The purpose of the study was to see if harsh or difficult conditions influenced the mother's caregiving toward her infants and to examine how the infants' development was affected as a result. In one environment, food was readily available and the mother monkeys were attentive to their offspring whose development proceeded normally. In a second environment, finding food required more effort but the mothers still raised their offspring with attentiveness, and normal development of the offspring ensued. In the third environment, however, food was sometimes plentiful and sometimes not, and under these "variable foraging" conditions the mothers became harsh and inconsistent in their mothering.

The offspring of the variable foraging mothers showed clear alterations in their life-long biological, emotional, and social responses to stress. As infants, they exhibited sustained clinging to the mother, low levels of social play and exploration, and high levels of affective disturbance. In adulthood, they had more extreme HPA axis responses to stress, and they were fearful and socially maladept as well. They had more dominance struggles and lower levels of grooming, suggesting long-term deficits in social behavior. Variable foraging was also related to elevated levels of serotonin and dopamine metabolite concentrations (Coplan et al., 1998), suggesting some disruption in these systems as well. The authors concluded that when mothers are psychologically unavailable to their infants, due to ongoing stress in the environment, the resulting attachments will be less secure, normal emotional and social development will be disrupted, and psychopathology will more likely develop (Rosenblum & Paully, 1984; see also Coplan et al., 1996). The important role that early nurturance plays in normal growth and socioemotional development is now well documented in animal studies.

This work is significant, in part, because the environments in which the mothers raised their offspring were manipulated, thus demonstrating the causal importance of the stressful social environment in maternal nurturance. Studies that cross-foster offspring to caregivers high or low in nurturance illustrate the remaining piece of this causal pathway, and show how caregiving style can alter the phenotypic expression of genetically based temperamental differences. For example, Suomi (1997) assigned rhesus monkeys selectively bred for differences in temperamental reactivity to foster mothers who were either unusually nurturant or within the normal range of mothering. Highly reactive infants cross-fostered to normal mothers exhibited deficits in social behavior and in adulthood tended to drop and remain low in the dominance hierarchy (Suomi, 1991). Reactive infants cross-fostered to highly nurturant females, in contrast, showed higher levels of social skills, and in adulthood they were more likely to rise to the top of the dominance hierarchy. When highly reactive female offspring became mothers themselves, they adopted the maternal style of their foster mothers, independent of their own reactivity profile (Suomi, 1987). Studies like these demonstrate the behavioral intergenerational transfer of nurturance and its centrality to the development of emotional and social skills (see also Francis et al., 1999). Studies like these also demonstrate how rapidly these major changes in stress-responsive biological systems can occur and how enduring their effects can be.

In humans, attachment is a marker for the maternal–infant bond, and attachment is implicated in the relation of early family environment to emotional, social, and biological responses to health. Early in childhood, attachment style is typically assessed by a child's response to the strange situation (Ainsworth, Blehar, Waters, & Wall, 1978). In the strange situation, a young child (generally 12–18 months) is put in a novel environment and then goes through a series of separations and reunions with a parent, usually the mother, both in the presence of a stranger or alone. Children who are distressed while separated but easily soothed by the return of the parent are considered to have a secure attachment style. Children who either show little distress while the parent is absent, or who greatly protest during the absence of the parent and are not easily soothed when the parent returns, are considered to have an insecure attachment style. In several studies, insecurely attached infants who participated in a strange situation task had higher cortisol responses than securely attached infants (Gunnar, Brodersen, Nachmias, Buss, & Rigatuso, 1996; Nachmias, Gunnar, Mangelsdorf, Parritz, & Buss, 1996; Spangler & Grossman, 1993). Studying children receiving well-baby examinations, Gunnar and her associates found that securely attached children were less likely to show elevated cortisol responses to normal stressors such as inoculations than less securely attached children (Gunnar, Brodersen, Krueger, & Rugatuso, 1996). As was true in the animal model of Suomi (1991), the protective effects of secure attachment were especially evident for socially fearful or inhibited children (see also Hart, Gunnar, & Cicchetti, 1996; Levine and Weiner, 1988).

In a related work, Repetti et al. (2002) examined the emotional, social, and biological impact of growing up in a family lacking in nurturance and characterized instead by overt conflict and aggression, by a cold and unaffectionate interaction style, or by neglect. In a review of several hundred studies, they concluded that offspring from these "risky" families have gaps in their emotional and social regulatory skills and show heightened sympathetic and HPA axis responses to stress. In an empirical investigation, Taylor, Lerner, Sage, Lehman, and Seeman (2004) found that a stressful environment in early childhood (operationalized as low SES) promoted these risky family characteristics and their consequences: The offspring from risky families were more likely to experience symptoms of depression and anxiety, they showed gaps in social support, they had elevated cortisol responses to stress, and their self-rated health was poor; in males, heart rate and blood pressure responses to stress were elevated.

Findings consistent with this reasoning were also reported by Fellitti and colleagues (Felitti et al., 1998), who related early family environment characteristics to health outcomes in adulthood. In a study of 13,494 adults, they found a strong, graded relationship between exposure to abuse and household dysfunction during childhood and risk for a broad array of adult health outcomes, including heart disease, some cancers, chronic lung disease, skeletal fractures, liver disease, depressive episodes, and whether a suicide had ever been attempted. As in the animal studies, some of these family dynamics may derive from shared genetic inheritance, but evidence suggests that environmental factors are implicated as well (Cadoret, Yates, Troughton, Woodworth, & Stewart, 1995).

As noted in both the animal and human studies just reviewed, emotional and social functioning as well as biological functioning are critically involved in these pathways (Repetti et al., 2002). Children from risky families appear to lack certain emotion regulation skills. For example, they do not do well at recognizing their own emotions, recognizing the emotional states of others, and managing their emotional responses to social situations. As evolutionary psychologists have noted, the ability to send and receive emotional cues about the nature of the environment is a vital survival skill, so much so that some of these processes may be universal or near-universal across cultures (Ekman, 1972, 1992). But children from risky families instead exhibit high levels of internalizing symptoms (social withdrawal and anxiety) or externalizing symptoms (aggression and hyperactivity) in response to potentially stressful circumstances. In other words, they show signs of a hair-trigger flight-or-fight response to situations that are interpreted by others as normal or, at least, as less stressful.

Risky family environments also produce offspring lacking in social competence (Repetti et al., 2002). Researchers who have documented this relation often go into the home to observe the child's family environment and then obtain ratings from teachers and peers regarding the target child's social competence. Risky family environments can produce children who exhibit a range of socially inappropriate behaviors, leading to the result that they are not well liked. In some cases, the child may be highly aggressive, and in other cases, socially withdrawn (Repetti et al., 2002). These findings, too, are suggestive of an exaggerated fight-or-flight response to social situations. These poor social skills may also represent risk factors for disease later in life, because people with deficits in social skills may have difficulty attracting and maintaining social relationships, with the result that their ability to gain social support may be compromised.

To summarize, then, the parent–child bond, especially the mother–child bond, appears to function not only to ensure the immediate survival of offspring, but also to act as a general signal to the offspring's developing affective, social, and biological systems as to how stressful the environment will be and what responses will be needed to meet its demands. Children from non-nurturant families respond to novel and potentially stressful circumstances with more reactive biological responses to stress, including autonomic reactivity and HPA axis reactivity; they exhibit deficits in the abilities to send and read emotional cues from others; and their social skills reveal gaps and impairments. In essence, fight-or-flight responses to stress on all three levels (biological, emotional, and social) are ratcheted up in those whose early relationships are low in nurturance. Children who grow up in highly nurturant families instead show more muted biological responses to novel or potentially stressful circumstances; they greet novel environments with more enthusiasm and exploration; they show fewer signs of aggression or withdrawal (fight-or-flight) in response to potentially stressful circumstances; and their emotional and social skills are better developed. The fact that evidence from related animal models so closely parallels the findings in humans suggests substantial cross-species commonalities in the functions of these early bonds.

There are some important implications of the calibration function of early social relationships. The first is that a parent may shape a child's stress response to be adaptive in the short term, but in ways that forecast long-term costs. This observation has some theoretical precedence. It has been proposed that different attachment styles (secure, anxious, and ambivalent) are all adaptive to the rearing environment (Belsky, Steinberg, & Draper, 1991), but sometimes at the cost of long-term social and emotional functioning. This issue leads to some provocative questions. What happens when an individual's circumstances change? For example, will changing from a difficult and unpredictable environment to one that is safe and predictable alter an individual's stress responses? It may be possible to alter one's stress responses, but the likelihood of substantial change would seem to depend on a number of conditions: (1) that there is a fundamental shift in the stressfulness of the environment; (2) that there is a change in the individual's social relationships that reflects the changing circumstances; and (3) that the individual has relatively little experience with the pre-existing environment. Thus, we would expect that alterations in biological stress responses in a direction more beneficial for long-term health will be more likely if a person moved from a dangerous neighborhood to a safe one, married an emotionally stable spouse, and was still relatively young, rather than moving to a slightly safer neighborhood, with an existing spouse, and lived in the dangerous neighborhood for most of his/her life. We take up the question of short-term benefits and long-term costs at more length in our conclusions.

A second implication of the calibration function can be drawn: Recent research has shown that the early attachment relationship can provide a prototype model of attachment that continues to influence behavior into late adolescence and early adulthood (Fraley, 2002) and theoretically throughout the lifetime (Bowlby, 1973, 1980). Moreover, attachment style can be transmitted across generations (mothers who are insecure tend to have insecure infants and mothers who are secure tend to have secure infants) (e.g., Suomi, 1991; van Ijzendoorn, 1995). Thus, early relationships in humans, like those in other animal species, may not only modulate an individual's own stress response for a lifetime, but also affect adult attachment status, parenting ability, and the stress responses of offspring.[2]

PAIR-BONDING

Analyses of pair relationships in evolutionary biology and evolutionary psychology have focused heavily on factors that go into mate selection, because of its relevance to sexual selection. However, a growing body of work also shows the significance of the pair bond for health and survival. Just as the parent–child bond shapes the biological, social, and affective functioning of offspring, especially in response to stress, intimate relationships including the marital bond affect these systems in ways that influence health and longevity. In this next section, we focus on the ways in which pair-bonds may regulate the moment-to-moment stress responses of each partner and what implications this process may have for health.

Research on adult attachment shows how individuals engage intimate partners to help regulate their response to stressful circumstances. Drawing on the writings of Bowlby (1973, 1980) and research on caregiver–offspring attachment, adult relationship researchers have proposed that adult romantic relationships can also be conceptualized from an attachment perspective (e.g, Hazan & Shaver, 1987).[3] In this perspective, individuals who have a secure attachment style believe that intimate partners are reliable sources of support in stressful times. In contrast, individuals who have an insecure attachment style (either anxious ambivalent or avoidant) believe that intimate partners will be relatively unreliable sources of support during stressful times. An important implication is that adult attachment guides how individuals use partners to regulate behavioral and physiological responses during stressful situations. Moreover, adult attachment also affects how individuals provide care to partners who are facing stressful situations. Thus, the attachment system, which is rooted in our evolutionary past, affects the way individuals interpret and communicate information about the stressfulness of the environment and also has implications for how intimate partners may draw on each other to help regulate their responses to acute stressors.

Studies have investigated how adult attachment affects individuals' seeking and provision of support to each other in the face of stress. In one study, women anticipated participating in a stressful laboratory task. Those who had a secure attachment style were more likely to seek support from their partners, but only when they felt anxious about the impending task. Male partners who had a secure attachment style were more likely to provide support, but only when their partners showed more anxiety about the impending task. Insecurely attached women and men showed the opposite pattern, seeking and providing support respectively when the women were less anxious rather than more anxious (Simpson, Rholes, & Nelligan, 1992). In another study, men anticipated participating in a stressful laboratory task. Female partners who had a secure attachment style were more likely to give support if their partners sought it than women who had an insecure attachment style (Simpson, Rholes, Orina, & Grich, 2002). These effects have also been replicated with a real-world stressor (one's partner getting on an airplane to leave) (Fraley & Shaver, 1998).

Attachment also affects how romantic partners provide care for each other during stressful times. Specifically, Feeney and Collins (2001) showed that individuals with an insecure attachment style are relatively poor at providing care when their partner is facing a stressful situation; in contrast, individuals with a secure attachment style are better at calibrating the amount of care they need to provide to meet the needs of their partner (Collins & Feeney, 2000; Feeney & Collins, 2001). Thus, the adult attachment system affects the way individuals interpret information about the stressfulness of the environment, determines whether individuals use intimate partners to regulate their own responses to stressful situations, and affects how partners regulate the responses of a distressed partner. Those who have a secure attachment style are better at eliciting and using support from their partner when needed and at providing care for intimate partners in ways that match the demands of stressful circumstances.

Adult attachment may also affect the ways in which individuals use relationship partners to manage their physiological responses to stress. Carpenter and Kirkpatrick (1996) found that women with an insecure attachment style had an elevated heart rate and blood pressure response to a stressful task when their partner was present, relative to when their partner was not present and relative to women with secure attachment styles. In another study, Feeney and Kirkpatrick (1996) investigated the effect of partner separation and attachment on heart rate and blood pressure responses to a stressful laboratory task in women. When the partner was absent during the first half of the stressor (and present during the second half), women with anxious and avoidant attachment styles had exaggerated heart rate and blood pressure before, during, and after the stressor, but this was not the case when the partner was present during the first part of the stressor (and left during the second half of the stressor). This pattern suggests that individuals who have insecure attachment styles are especially sensitive to their partner being absent when a stressful event first occurs.

The implication of this work is that women with insecure attachment styles may find their romantic partners to be a liability during time of stress. These women have greater blood pressure and heart rate reactivity when the partner is present during a stressful event, especially if the partner was absent at the start of the stressor and later arrived, relative to when the partner was absent throughout the stressful event. This response is not found in women with secure attachment styles. (Note that women with secure attachment styles do not necessarily benefit physiologically from the presence of a partner; they merely do not suffer the same costs that women with insecure attachment styles suffer.)

Consistent with these conjectures, people in poor-quality marriages have a higher likelihood of illness, they report more physical symptoms, they experience a poorer long-term prognosis if they are ill, and they experience a longer recovery from illness (see Kiecolt-Glaser & Newton, 2001 for a review). Among other findings, low marital quality has been tied to higher blood pressure and heart rate responses to stress, increased likelihood of cancer, adverse changes in rheumatoid arthritis disease, heightened risk of death among those already diagnosed with cancer, and a broad array of disabilities. These relations are typically stronger for women than men. An epidemiological study of marriage and mortality in Sweden showed that both men and women who were divorced, separated, or widowed were at increased mortality risk (Hemstrom, 1996).

As these findings imply, the marital bond has been heavily studied in the context of stress and coping, because it is both a major source of social support for most adults and a major source of chronic strain for many.[4] Like the mother–child bond, marital quality reflects and conveys information about the stressfulness of the external environment. For example, SES (a marker for environmental stress) is significantly related to an increased likelihood of divorce and spousal abuse. Men may disproportionately be the stress carriers in these relations. For example, work spillover effects, whereby stress at work spills over into more conflictual interactions with family, have been demonstrated primarily in studies of men (see Taylor, 2002 for a review). In addition, Repetti (1997) found that stressful work-days promoted fight (i.e., conflict) or flight (i.e., withdrawal) behavior in married men, but the same relations were not found for married women.

The significance of marital quality for health is undeniable. Generally, marriage acts as a tie that benefits physical and mental health, much as the early caregiving relationship does. These effects are especially pronounced for men. Married men have a 250% lower mortality rate, compared to single age-matched, SES-matched unmarried men. Marriage is only modestly related to age at mortality for women. Traditionally, this difference has been attributed to the fact that men's single lifestyles are more health compromising than women's and married men's are (e.g., Umberson, 1987). For example, single men practice poorer health habits than married men do, and they are more likely to abuse substances, such as alcohol and drugs, that can be associated with a heightened risk of disease or accidental death; single men's lifestyles are more likely to involve risky activities (such as risky sports and heightened risk of vehicular accidents), and they have a higher frequency of aggressive encounters that may lead to health-compromising or fatal consequences. There are marked parallels in other primate species, in which unattached males are vulnerable to attack by conspecifics or predators and to infection and disease. For example, unattached male primates are more likely to have parasitic infections, because they are less likely to be groomed by others, whereas males with social attachments are groomed more frequently with resulting health benefits. Thus, the male–female bond appears to foster a healthy lifestyle for males and to have survival advantages for males as a result.

Gender differences in social support may contribute to the beneficial effects of marriage on men's health. Men report that they get their social support primarily from their partner, relative to other potential sources of support, such as men friends, relatives, and children. Women, however, seek and obtain social support from a broad array of contacts, especially female friends and relatives, and report that they turn to their spouse less than to other sources of social support (see Taylor, 2002 for a review). Consequently the health benefits of social support through marriage are more likely to accrue to men than to women who, even when single, may have a broader array of social supportive relationships available to them.

Men and women have different patterns of autonomic and HPA axis reactivity to events in marriage that may affect their health and longevity differently. For example, for men, home acts as a safety signal; when men return home after a workday, their autonomic arousal shows a marked decline. The autonomic arousal of married women, however, remains elevated long into the evening (e.g., Frankenhaeuser, 1993; Frankenhaeuser et al., 1989; Goldstein, Shapiro, Chicz-DeMet, & Guthrie, 1999), perhaps because traditionally women's roles have extended throughout the day, rather than being demarcated by a specific period of activity. Having a partner is a source of comfort and support for men in times of stress, but not to the same degree for women. For example, empirical investigations of responses to laboratory challenges show that men's biological stress responses are lower when their partner is present (Kiecolt-Glaser & Newton,

2001). In fact, merely thinking about their partner reduces men's biological stress responses to laboratory challenges (Broadwell & Light, 1999). These benefits are not found for women, whose biological stress responses are often stronger when their partner is present (Kiecolt-Glaser & Newton, 2001) and who show no stress-buffering effect of thinking about their partner (Broadwell & Light, 1999). Patterns of reactivity to marital conflict also vary between the genders. In studies assessing autonomic and HPA axis responses to laboratory-induced marital conflict, men often show little or no change in heart rate, blood pressure, and other indicators of stress. Women, in contrast, show strong autonomic and HPA axis responses to marital conflict (see Kiecolt-Glaser & Newton, 2001 for a review).

To summarize, when considering the protective impact of the pair-bond on health, there is a confluence of influences to be considered, some of which may cancel each other out. Specifically, when men draw on social support for coping with stress, they typically turn to their partners. The benefits, in terms of muted biological responses to stress and health, are now well established. Moreover, even the negative effects of conflictual interactions with their partner have a lesser impact on men. The additional fact that home functions as a safety signal for men may also be significant in the strong protective relation of marriage on men's health.

In the case of women, however, married women experience elevations in stress responses for a longer part of the day. Women seek social support disproportionately from friends and relatives and are somewhat less likely to turn to their partners. In response to marital conflict, they show stronger autonomic and HPA axis responses than men do. Consequently, the health advantages that might accrue to women from the social support of marriage appear to be attenuated by these mitigating factors, such that women gain only modest health benefits from marriage. Nonetheless, the pair-bond, like the parent–child relationship, is informed by the stressfulness of the environment and subsequently shapes biological responses to stress, with long-term outcomes for health. The patterns show considerable differentiation by gender, however.

SAME-SEX TIES

Gender differences in patterns of social support point to the importance of studying friendship as a bond that may be health protective as well. As an object of investigation, same-sex ties have not received the attention they are due, either in evolutionary psychology or in health psychology. In this section, we describe ways in which these social ties may shape biological and socioemotional functioning, especially in stressful conditions, with special emphasis on how these ties provide valuable information about the stressfulness of the environment.

The study of men's bonds with each other has been heavily influenced by several early accounts of male collectivities, notably Lionel Tiger's (1969) *Men in Groups*, Karl Lorenz's (1966) *On Aggression*, and Robert Ardrey's (1961) *African Genesis*. The template for understanding men's relations with each other has come from studying primate species and accordingly scientists have noticed and emphasized these commonalities, particularly hierarchies, coalition formation, and aggression. The image of men's groups that is conveyed by these volumes and that has guided many anthropological accounts of men's ties with other men is that male aggression, fueled by testosterone, underlies many of men's interactions with each other. These accounts suggest that the ability to rise to the top of a hierarchy, pursue goals single-mindedly, and even engage in warfare may be attributed to the interpersonal challenges that men pose for each other. Historically, groups of men have taken on survival-related tasks for the social group, including hunting, defense, and war. When a group is organized around a vital task, a hierarchy with a clear dominance structure and established coalitions is beneficial, because it provides a chain of command for structured, coordinated action.

The struggle for dominance and the use of aggression to get it are present in men's groups, but recent analyses of both primate species and humans suggest that, rather than fostering aggression, the dominance hierarchies that are characteristic of boys' and men's groups often contain, control, and marginalize aggression instead. Contrary to earlier stereotypes, men who rise to the top of male hierarchies are not typically those who are most aggressive but rather those with socioemotional skills, the ability to work with others to form coalitions and relationships, and the skills to lure, appease, and cajole and marginalize those who violate norms and rules (Taylor, 2002). In essence, those who can get others to play by the social rules are most likely to rise to the top of a hierarchy.

Although aggression is high when dominance hierarchies are unstable, once a hierarchy is established, aggression is rarer and typically plays only a modest role in maintaining the social structure. Spontaneous submission, grooming, alliances, and active intervention by high-status males smoothes over much of the incipient conflict that could otherwise arise. In his studies of olive baboons, Sapolsky (1998) recounts how those who rise to the top of a dominance hierarchy typically have skills for reconciliation, reassurance, and appeasement for restoring social relations. Similarly, Goodall (1986) reported how alpha males maintain control through savvy skill and gentle bullying, often stopping fights by sitting between quarreling parties to keep them from renewing their conflict. Thus, evidence suggests that well-controlled responses to stress and socioemotional skills lead to success in negotiating adult life, among at least some primate species.

Just as maternal nurturance can underlie the development of socioemotional skills, experience with male peers is thought to be vital to the refinement of these skills among males as well. Consider the ubiquitous rough-and-tumble play of male humans and many animal species. At one time, researchers believed that play-fighting in males constituted practice for adult combat. However, the evidence now suggests that play-fighting is distinctly different from combat and that the two activities involve little overlap in skills. Rather, play appears to help animals distinguish play-fighting from true aggression (e.g., Pellis & Pellis, 1998). Although this knowledge is not necessarily critical in childhood, it can assume substantial importance as animals become sexually mature and stronger and begin competing for mates and for dominance in a social group (Pellis & Pellis, 1996). In a test of this hypothesis, Koolhaas and colleagues (Van den Berg, Hol, Van Ree, Spruijt, Everts, & Koolhaas, 1999) raised young male rats without contact with male peers, and then compared their behavior in adulthood with that of male rats who had grown up with the normal rough-and-tumble play of the male peer group. The rats without play experiences were less likely to deal effectively with both friendly and aggressive encounters from other males and adults. Thus, rather than practice in aggression, the rough-and-tumble play characteristic of young males of many species instead appears to teach young males how to manage it.

The picture that is emerging of male–male relationships, then, is that, much as mother–infant relations shape the parameters of emotional, social, and biological responses to novelty and stress, male–male encounters continue to refine a male's skills for detecting threatening vs. nonthreatening circumstances and for responding appropriately to them. Thus, male–male relationships may convey information about the nature of the environment and provide guidelines for addressing its social demands.

Male–male bonds also influence biological functioning, in part, by regulating hormones such as testosterone and serotonin. Testosterone naturally increases when men compete, as they do in struggles for dominance. Once dominance struggles have ended, the higher-status males typically have higher levels of testosterone than the lower-status males, which may promote reproductive success. Serotonin also appears to be significant in dominance struggles and aggression. In a study demonstrating this point, Raleigh and colleagues (Raleigh, McGuire, Brammer, Pollack, & Yuwiler, 1991) created small groups of vervet monkeys, each with three adult males and three adult females and offspring. After a dominance hierarchy had been established, they removed the dominant male from the group and then selected one of the two remaining subordinate males and injected him with a drug that either enhanced or diminished serotonergic activity. In every case, the monkey that was treated with the serotonin enhancer became the dominant monkey, whereas the monkey who received a drug that diminished serotonergic functioning dropped in status (i.e., his male cage-mate became dominant). Interestingly, the impact of serotonin on dominance was socially mediated. Specifically, injection with a serotonin enhancer led to more prosocial activity and more acceptance by the females in the group, whereas treatment that diminished serotonergic activity led to quarrelsome, irritable, aggressive behavior in the males that alienated the group's females. In short, socioemotional skills determined which monkeys moved into leadership positions, and serotonin played a regulatory role in these social processes.

There are clear implications of these processes for health. In his studies of olive baboons, for example, Sapolsky (1998) found that on every hormone and physiological measure he studied, subordinate baboons looked worse than dominant baboons. For example, they had higher levels of resting stress hormones, more sluggish stress responses, lower levels of HDL cholesterol (high levels of HDL are an indicator of good health), and fewer T cells, suggesting a poorly functioning immune system. As noted, these effects are mirrored in human hierarchies, in the robust relationships between SES and health outcomes. Health statistics uniformly show that lower-status men are more likely to die of homicide, suicide, complications from assaults and wounds, and premature chronic disease than any other segment of the population. In summary, then, male–male relations clearly shape biological, emotional, and social functioning in ways that reflect the stressfulness of the environment, affect responses to stress, and have long-term implications for health.

What of female ties to each other? Women form bonds with other women, but these bonds have been less studied than those of men, in part because they tend to be more informal and flexible. However, like the parent–infant bond and the pair-bond, females' relationships with each other are responsive to the stressfulness of the external environment. Taylor and colleagues (Taylor, 2002; Taylor, Klein, Lewis, Gruenewald, Gurung, & Updegraff, 2000) maintain that women's ties follow from an evolutionary heritage that selected for female friendship, because female "befriending" acts as an organized system for coping with stress by women. Specifically, the need for food, safety, the care of children, and comfort in the face of stress have been met by these ties.

Women's and men's friendship patterns are reliably different. Throughout life, women seek more close friends than men do. Beginning in early childhood, girls develop more intimate friendships than boys do. Although in adulthood, men's networks are larger, primarily because they are more likely to be employed and to participate in political and social activities, women continue to maintain large numbers of informal ties.

The inclination of women to bond together may have biological origins that are evident in animal species as well. For example, McClintock found that when too few individual cages necessitated housing her female Norway rats together in groups of about five, the rats lived 40% longer than when they were housed alone (McClintock, 1998). Male rats, in contrast, live longer if they live in proximity to each other, but not in the same cage, which tends to promote male–male aggression.

Women's networks form an inner core of social life that may be barely visible in nonstressful times, but these bonds become more prominent under conditions of stress. Often the bonds are based on kinship with mothers, sisters, aunts, and children, and other times they are based on friendship. The needs they meet are fundamental for survival: getting food, caring for children, protecting against violence, and regulating stress responses. All of these tasks involve the transmission of important information, such as where to best find food, how to soothe a crying infant, what places are dangerous, and the like. Turning to the group in times of stress is beneficial to both men and women, of course. But the particular importance of the social group for women in times of stress may stem from the fact that it has traditionally fallen to women to provide safety for herself and her offspring, a task that is especially benefited by alliances with a social group (Taylor, 2002).

Female primates, including humans, typically need to gather food for themselves and their offspring, and female friends and relatives help them with these tasks. Primatologist Richard Wrangham (1980) suggests that female friendships may have evolved primarily to manage food collection and distribution, with females sharing information about where the food is, harvesting food collectively, and driving off rival groups (see Taylor, 2002).

Childcare is also a vital function performed primarily through female–female associations. In some primate species, females trade off childcare with kin, friends, or younger female "baby-sitters," so that their time is freed up to forage for food. Infant sharing of this kind has been reliably related to health outcomes (Hrdy, 1999). When care of infants is shared among females (both human and primates), the offspring grow faster, whether it is because their mothers are freer to forage for food, because their sitters feed them, or both. Not incidentally, these "baby-sitting" arrangements act as childcare training for younger females (Keverne, Nevison, & Martel, 1999). McKenna (1981) estimates that among some primate species, allomothering, that is, taking care of others' infants, may constitute up to 50% of the caregiving an infant receives. Among humans, childcare appears to have resided with the biological mother in most societies, including hunter–gatherer societies as well as current-day ones (Corter & Fleming, 1990; Hrdy, 1999). But allomothering is ubiquitous among humans as well. The preferred form of childcare is care by a female relative. Present statistics suggest that upwards of 97% of childcare workers are women, and 85% of teenage baby-sitters are female (Taylor, 2002).

Bonds among females appear to reliably strengthen and become more coordinated in times of stress. Several primate studies (see De Waal, 1996) have found that under conditions of stress or threat, even in species in which female–female bonds are typically weak, those bonds may strengthen to meet challenges. For example, female chimpanzees do not typically have strong bonds with each other, but in the captive environment they are more likely to bond together to protect themselves against abusive males (De Waal, 1996).

As this point suggests, bonds with other females also provide protection from potential predators. In early history, mothers attempting to protect both themselves and their children from predators would have needed help from others. Although a protective male is likely to have provided some of that assistance, the fact that women spent much of their lives apart from men and are involved in different tasks meant that men would not have been a constant source of protection. Moreover, men themselves are often the primary predators of women. Murphy and Murphy (1974) have described how, among the Mundurucu of Brazil, women travel in groups because of their vulnerability to unwanted intercourse. A study of domestic violence in Papua, New Guinea found levels of wife beating as high as 97% in some provinces (Counts, 1990). However, in two provinces the rate was very low. Anthropologist William Mitchell (1990) argues that women in these two communities formed bonds both with their own kin and with female friends that acted as deterrents against male aggression. Parallel evidence suggests that when females are isolated from each other, they experience greater vulnerability to abuse. For example, Wolf (1975) studied young Chinese brides and documented the risk of physical abuse they experienced upon marrying, because custom dictated that they move away from family and friends to live near their husbands' families.

If the necessity of female bonds under stress is as great as just maintained, there should be evidence that females draw on social support more than men do in times of stress. Indeed, this is the case. Although the margin by which women seek social support under stress more than men (and girls more than boys) is small, it is extremely robust. The overwhelming majority of studies show that women are more likely to seek social support for coping with stress (e.g., Tamres, Janicki, & Helgeson, 2002.). Field studies of particular stressful circumstances suggest that networks of women often arise spontaneously to meet survival needs. For example, in poor communities (Newman, 1999) or in communities under intense stress (such as Eastern Europe following the fall of communism), networks of women develop to help with the provision of food, childcare, shelter, and other necessities (see Taylor, 2002).

Do these relationships have effects on health? Throughout the world, women live longer than men.[5] Although not all the reasons underlying this difference are known, gender differences in social ties and stress responses appear to be implicated. As noted, men are more likely to respond to stress with behavioral indications of fight (such as aggression) or flight (social withdrawal or substance abuse); women are more likely to respond to stress with processes we have characterized as "tend-and-befriend" (Taylor, 2002; Taylor et al., 2000), that is, tending to offspring in times of stress and drawing on the social group, especially other women, for managing stressful events. Thus, part of the gender difference in age at mortality may be explained by men's greater propensity to experience stress-related problems marked by fight-or-flight, such as homicide, suicide, assault, substance abuse, and early heart disease. Women, in contrast, may enjoy some protection from the fact that they draw on social support for managing stress more than men do, and indeed, some evidence suggests that women experience more health benefits in response to social support than men do (Schwarzer & Leppin, 1989). Thus, the social ties that women enjoy with other women clearly merit investigation as a potentially significant predictor of women's health and longevity. It may be that some component of the large difference in age at mortality between women and men is accounted for by the friendships that women create with other women.

To summarize, ties among women are typically informal and flexible, and they may have been selected for because they helped to provide nourishment for families and safety for women and children. Women who affiliated with each other were better able to fend off threats than those who did not, thereby ensuring their own survival and enhancing the likelihood that their children would survive as well.

GIVING HELP AND SOCIAL SUPPORT

We have reviewed substantial evidence for social shaping, namely the phenomenon that a person's social relationships reflect the stressfulness of the environment and actively craft his or her biological, emotional, and social responses to stress. Whereas rancorous relationships promote stress reactions that are strong and easily engaged, socially supportive relations keep stress responses at a more modest level and/or reduce them more rapidly when they occur. In the long term, these effects of relationships have a substantial impact on health. The clear regulatory functions that social support serves suggest that these supportive processes would not be left to chance, but would rather be selected for, in the evolutionary sense. But what induces people to provide help to each other? What processes ensure that the regulatory functions that social support provides will be met?

Within evolutionary biology, this debate has often centered around the apparent paradox of altruism: What induces people to give help, provide sustenance, and meet the needs of others when these actions can potentially compromise personal resources and safety? Altruistic behavior has long been a thorny issue for evolutionary biology and evolutionary psychology. Implicitly, the assumption underlying much of the debate has been that getting help from others is a good thing, but giving it is costly (Hamilton, 1963; Trivers, 1971). This assumption has carried over into the literature addressing social support and health. The argument maintains that when a person provides social support for another, it taxes his or her resources, time, and attention. As such, the implicit understanding within the social support literature has been that there are few, if any, benefits to providing social support for others and a broad array of potential costs.

This argument is unquestionably valid at extreme levels of help-giving. An important source of evidence for this conclusion has been studies of caregivers. Research uniformly suggests that intense caregiving is associated with deleterious effects on health (see Taylor, 2002 for a review). But generalizing from caregiver studies to situations of help-giving more generally may be risky. Caregiver studies usually look at extreme situations involving labor-intensive disorders. These studies also focus disproportionately on elderly caregivers who are at risk for the exacerbation of immune-related disorders. Thus, although caregiver studies have been valuable in identifying the impact of social strain on immune functioning and health, these experiences may not be representative of the effects of support provision on immune function and health.

Recent research by Brown and associates (Brown, Nesse, Vinokur, & Smith, 2003) has examined the relative contributions of providing vs. receiving social support to mortality in older adults. They found that death was significantly less likely for individuals who *provided* support to others. Indeed, in this study, receiving social support had no impact on mortality, when providing support was statistically controlled. (These effects were significant only for females, although the trend was in the same direction for males.) On the surface, such results are startling because they run contrary to so much thinking about social support and altruism more generally. How are they to be understood?

The implications of findings like these are just emerging, but they are likely to be profound. They suggest there has been a bias in the literature regarding providing support to others. Giving support may not be inherently biologically costly. When people give support to others, they may simultaneously be receiving psychological and biological benefits. Mothers reunited with offspring following a stressful period, whether in animal studies or studies of working women, have lower stress responses; that is, tending is stress-reducing for mothers. When men and women turn to each other or to friends for support, they are typically both giving and receiving support at the same time. Although clearly at very taxing levels of support-giving this relationship breaks down, giving support to others appears to be associated with psychological benefits and with benefits for health. Nor are the benefits of giving support confined to current human social conditions. Help-giving at moderate levels appears to be associated with processes underlying resistance to infection, recovery from illness, and wound-healing, all of which would have been vital during humans' early history. As such, the paradox of altruism would seem to be lessened.

CONCLUSIONS

We have reviewed a broad array of evidence for social shaping, that is, the idea that social relationships: (1) provide information about and reflect the stressfulness of the environment; (2) are implicated in the development of biological stress regulatory systems; and (3) influence the magnitude of biological, emotional, and social responses during stressful episodes with consequent effects on health. Rancorous and conflictual social relationships of all kinds often result from stressful conditions and increase the likelihood of recurrent or prolonged stress responses, most notably in the autonomic system and the HPA axis. As was noted in the research on "risky families," evidence from animal and human studies suggests that these encounters can have permanent organizational effects on emotional, social, and biological responses to stress. The health-compromising effects of elevated, recurrent, protracted, or chronic responses to stress are increasingly well documented, as stress has been tied to a broad array of adverse health conditions. For example, early onset of chronic diseases such as heart disease, hypertension, and Type 2 Diabetes and exacerbation of immune-related disorders have been tied to protracted stress responses (McEwen & Lasley, 2002).

Accordingly, one may well ask, what would be potentially adaptive about these long-term effects of problematic social relationships on stress responses, given their uniform association with poor health? Are there functions to be discerned from these processes or are they merely an unfortunate by-product of rancorous social ties? The significance of an overactive or recurrent stress response for long-term health outcomes such as chronic diseases is now well known, but at the time that these processes evolved, few people lived long enough to experience their long-term costs. Rather, having a hair-trigger response to potentially stressful circumstances undoubtedly had substantial adaptive value for survival. The autonomic nervous system and the HPA axis together mobilize an individual for fight-or-flight as an efficient and effective means for warding off many stressors, such as attack by potential predators or conspecifics. Rancorous or stressful social relationships appear to act as signals that the environment is a threatening one, and that having finely tuned, highly keyed, quick-acting, and long-lasting stress responses will be protective. This process is most evident in research regarding the mother–offspring relationship, explored in animal and human studies, but it is also evident in adult social relationships as well.

By contrast, warm, supportive, and soothing social relationships promote many of the opposite effects. Warm and friendly relations act as signals that the environment is a benign one. The slow-acting or modest stress responses that are associated with this support may well be appropriate for environments marked by sufficient resources to meet the needs of all group members. Among other functions, they appear to promote exploratory and novelty-seeking behavior. In benign environments, there would be few, if any, costs to having a shorter-term, better-modulated stress response with rapid recovery. But the quality of a relationship may become an especially powerful predictor of long-term health during times of stress. For example, although an inconsistent or harsh parent will calibrate a child's stress response to a difficult rearing environment, a parent who remains consistent and sensitive in caring for their offspring under stressful circumstances will help a child develop more flexible resources to deal with stressors, possibly leading to better long-term health outcomes (see Maunder & Hunter, 2001). In romantic relationships, those who have secure attachment styles are better able to use a partner's support and allocate support to a partner in the face of a stressor. In same-sex ties, those who are best able to promote smooth social functioning in the face of conflict or stress reap the most social and health benefits. While under dire circumstances, having a bad relationship may be better than having no relationships at all, the balance of the data suggests that stressful circumstances, for the most part, bring the importance of the quality of a relationship for long-term health and well-being into sharp relief.

In our current lives, which are often busy and marked by chronic stressors, the maladaptive nature of overactive and recurring stress responses is abundantly clear. We no longer need to make use of the rapid and dramatic physiological, neuroendocrine, and emotional changes that result from the perception of threat, because most of our chronic stressors are psychological in nature, rather than the physical threats with which our ancestors needed to cope. Consequently, these systems that were so adaptive in our prehistory are now associated with the deleterious health consequences that ultimately kill most of us. As such, the beneficial side of social bonds, whether the parent–child relation, the pair-bond, or friendship, remain the most health-protective resource that humans possess.

ACKNOWLEDGMENT

The National Science Foundation (SBR 9905157) and the National Institute of Mental Health (MH 056880) provided support for the preparation of this manuscript.

NOTES

1. McEwen (McEwen and Stellar, 1993; McEwen, 1998) suggests that recurrent or chronic exposure to stress may interact with genetic predispositions, leading to cascading, potentially irreversible effects on susceptibility to stress, biological markers of the cumulative adverse effects of stress, and stress-related physical and mental disorders. He argues that this accumulating "allostatic load" leads to accelerated aging, which over the long-term may increase risk for chronic hypertension, slower cardiovascular recovery from stress, hippocampal atrophy and accompanying cognitive dysfunction, signs of dysregulation of the HPA axis, dysregulation of the PNS, and dysregulation of serotonergic functioning among other deleterious biological changes (see McEwen, 1998; Seeman, Berkman, Gulanski, Robbins, Greenspan, Charpentier, & Rowe, 1995; Seeman, Singer, Rowe, Horwitz, & McEwen, 1997, for reviews).

2. This is not to say that these patterns are completely set. Attachment researchers have proposed that individuals with harsh backgrounds can become responsive and warm parents and therefore not pass their childhood attachment style to their children, a phenomenon termed "earned security" (see Phelps, Belsky, & Crnic, 1998; Pearson, Cohn, Cowan, & Cowan, 1994).

3. Although researchers and theoreticians have drawn from Bowlby's original work as inspiration for research into both caregiver–offspring and adult romantic attachment, it is still an open question as to how these systems relate to each other. Although there is some evidence that memories of caregiver–offspring relationships covary in predictable ways with adult romantic relationships (e.g.,

Hazan & Shaver, 1994), there is less work investigating how attachment measures from the two traditions of research relate to each other. Research tends to show positive, but modest, correlations (see Bartholomew & Shaver, 1998). There is also little work relating attachment as measured early in childhood to later attachment to adult romantic partners.

4. In our examination of pair-bonding, we look primarily at the heterosexual marital bond, because most of the relevant research has involved heterosexual married couples. The potentially protective effects of gay and lesbian relationships on partner health has not been sufficiently well studied to discern their health-protective effects, but one would anticipate that many of the benefits that accrue in heterosexual relationships would be found in same-sex relationships as well.

5. The degree to which this is true varies substantially. In countries where women die in childbirth in heavy numbers or are not permitted access to health care, the margin is slim or reversed.

REFERENCES

Adler, N., Boyce, T., Chesney, M., Cohen, S., Folkman, S., & Syme, L. (1994). Socioeconomic inequalities in health: No easy solution. *Journal of the American Medical Association, 49*, 3140–3145.

Adler, N., Marmot, M., & McEwen B. (2000). *Socioeconomic status and health in industrial nations: Social, psychological, and biological pathways* (pp. 210–225). New York: New York Academy of Sciences.

Ainsworth, M. D. S., Blehar, M. C., Waters, E., & Wall, S. (1978). *Patterns of attachment: Psychological study of the strange situation*. Hillsdale, NJ: Erlbaum.

Ardrey, R. (1961). *African genesis: A personal investigation into the animal origins and nature of man*. London: Collins.

Bartholomew, K., & Shaver, P. R. (1998). Methods of assessing adult attachment: Do they converge? In J. A. Simpson & W. S. Rholes (Eds.), *Attachment theory and close relationships* (pp. 25–45). The Guilford Press: New York.

Belsky, J., Steinberg, L., & Draper, P. (1991). Childhood experience, interpersonal development, and reproductive strategy: An evolutionary theory of socialization. *Child Development, 62*, 647–670

Bowlby, J. (1973). *Attachment and loss. Vol 2: Separation, anxiety, and anger*. New York: Basic Books.

Bowlby, J. (1980). *Attachment and loss. Vol 3: Loss*. New York: Basic Books.

Broadwell, S. D., & Light, K. C. (1999). Family support and cardiovascular responses in married couples during conflict and other interactions. *International Journal of Behavioral Medicine, 6*, 40–63.

Brown, S. L., Nesse, R. M., Vinokur, A. D., & Smith, D. M. (2003). Providing social support may be more beneficial than receiving it: Results from a prospective study of mortality. *Psychological Science, 14*, 320–327.

Cacioppo, J. T., & Hawkley, L. C. (2003). Social isolation and health, with an emphasis on underlying mechanisms. *Perspectives in Biology and Medicine, 46*, 39–52.

Cadoret, R. J., Yates, W. R., Troughton, E., Woodworth, G., & Stewart, M. A. (1995). Genetic-environmental interaction in the genesis of aggressivity and conduct disorders. *Archives of General Psychiatry, 52*, 916–924.

Caporeal, L. R. (1997). The evolution of truly social cognition: The core configuration model. *Personality and Social Psychology Review, 1*, 276–298.

Carpenter, E. M., & Kirkpatrick, L. A. (1996). Attachment style and presence of a romantic partner as moderators of psychophysiological responses to a stressful laboratory situation. *Personal Relationships, 3,* 351–367.

Collins, N. L., & Feeney, B. C. (2000). A safe haven: An attachment theory perspective on support-seeking and caregiving in adult romantic relationships. *Journal of Personality and Social Psychology, 78,* 1053–1073.

Coplan, J. D., Andrews, M. W., Rosenblum, L. A., Owens, M. J., Friedman, S., Gorman, J. M., & Nemeroff, C. B. (1996). Persistent elevations of cerebrospinal fluid concentrations of corticotropin-releasing factor in adult nonhuman primates exposed to early life stressors: Implications for the pathophysiology of mood and anxiety disorders. *Proceedings of the National Academy of Sciences, 93,* 1619–1623.

Coplan, J. D., Troust, R. C., Owens, M. J., Cooper, T. B., Gorman, J. M., Nemeroff, C. B., & Rosenblum, L. A. (1998). Cerebrospinal fluid concentrations of somatostatin and biogenic amines in grown primates reared by mothers exposed to manipulated forging conditions. *Archives of General Psychiatry, 55,* 473–477.

Corter, C. M., & Fleming, A. S. (1990). Maternal responsiveness in humans: Emotional, cognitive, and biological factors. *Advances in the Study of Behavior, 19,* 83–136.

Counts, R. L. (1990). Domestic violence in Oceania: Introduction. *Pacific Studies, 12,* 1–5.

De Waal, F. (1996). *Good natured: The origins of right and wrong in humans and other animals.* Cambridge, MA: Harvard University Press.

Dunbar, R. (1998). The social brain hypothesis. *Evolutionary Anthropology, 6,* 178–190.

Ekman, P. (1972). Universals and cultural differences in facial expressions of emotion. In J. K. Cole (Ed.), *Nebraska symposium on motivation, 1971* (pp. 207–283). Lincoln: University of Nebraska Press.

Ekman, P. (1992). Are there basic emotions? *Psychological Review, 99,* 550–553.

Feeney, B. C., & Collins, N. L. (2001). Predictors of caregiving in adult intimate relationships: An attachment theoretical perspective. *Journal of Personality and Social Psychology, 80,* 972–994.

Feeney, B. C., & Kirkpatrick, L. A., (1996). Effects of adult attachment and presence of romantic partners on physiological responses to stress. *Journal of Personality and Social Psychology, 70,* 255–270.

Felitti, V. J., Anda, R. F., Nordenberg, D., Williamson, D. F., Spitz, A. M., Edwards, V., Koss, M. P., & Marks, J. S. (1998). Relationship of childhood abuse and household dysfunction to many of the leading causes of death in adults. *American Journal of Preventive Medicine, 14,* 245–258.

Fraley, R. C. (2002). Attachment stability from infancy to adulthood: Meta-analysis and dynamic modeling of developmental mechanisms. *Personality and Social Psychology Review, 6,* 123–151.

Fraley, R. C., & Shaver, P. R. (1998). Airport separations: A naturalistic study of adult attachment dynamics in separating couples. *Journal of Personality and Social Psychology, 75,* 1198–1212.

Francis, D., Diorio, J., Liu, D., & Meaney, M. (1999). Nongenomic transmission across generations of maternal behavior and stress responses in the rat. *Science, 286,* 1155–1158.

Frankenhaeuser, M. (1993, February 22–25). *On the psychobiology of working life.* International Conference on Work and Health.

Frankenhaeuser, M., Lundberg, M., Fredrikson, M., Melin, B., Tuomisto, M., Myrsten, A., Hedman, M., Bergman-Losman, B., & Wallin L. (1989). Stress on and off the job as related to sex and occupational status in white-collar workers. *Journal of Organizational Behavior, 10,* 321–346.

Goldstein, I., Shapiro, D., Chicz-DeMet, A., & Guthrie, D. (1999). Ambulatory blood pressure, heart rate, and neuroendocrine responses in women nurses during work and off work days. *Psychosomatic Medicine, 61,* 387–396.

Goodall, J. (1986). *The chimpanzees of Gombe: Patterns of behavior.* Cambridge: Belknap Press of Harvard University Press.

Gunnar, M. R., Brodersen, L., Krueger, K., & Rigatuso, J. (1996). Dampening of adrenocortical responses during infancy: Normative changes and individual differences. *Child Development, 67,* 877–889.

Gunnar, M. R., Brodersen, L., Nachmias, M., Buss, K., & Rigatuso, J. (1996). Stress reactivity and attachment security. *Developmental Psychobiology, 29,* 191–204.

Hamilton, W. D. (1963). The evolution of altruistic behavior. *The American Naturalist, 97,* 354–356.

Hart, J., Gunnar, M., & Cicchetti, D. (1996). Altered neuroendocrine activity in maltreated children related to symptoms of depression. *Development and Psychopathology, 8,* 201–214.

Hazan, C., & Shaver, P. R., (1987). Romantic love conceptualized as an attachment process. *Journal of Personality and Social Psychology, 52,* 511–524.

Hazan, C., & Shaver, P. R., (1994). Attachment as an organizational framework for research on close relationships. *Psychological Inquiry, 5,* 1–22.

Hemstrom, O. (1996). Is marriage dissolution linked to differences in mortality risk for men and women? *Journal of Marriage and the Family, 58,* 366–378.

House, J. S., Landis, K. R., & Umberson, D. (1988). Social relationships and health. *Science, 241,* 540–545.

Hrdy, S. B. (1999). *Mother nature: A history of mothers, infants, and natural selection.* New York: Pantheon Books.

Keverne, E. B., Nevison, C. M., & Martel, F. L. (1999). Early learning and the social bond. In C. S. Carter, I. I. Lederhendler, & B. Kirkpatrick (Eds.), *The integrative neurobiology of affiliation* (pp. 263–274). Cambridge, MA: MIT Press.

Kiecolt-Glaser, J. K., & Newton, T. L. (2001). Marriage and health: His and hers. *Psychological Bulletin, 127,* 472–503.

Levine, S., & Wiener, S. G. (1988). Psychoendocrine aspects of mother-infant relationships in nonhuman primates. *Psychoneuroimmunology, 13,* 143–154.

Liu, D., Diorio, J., Tannenbaum, B., Caldji, C., Francis, D., Freedman, A., Sharma, S., Pearson, D., Plotsky, P. M., & Meaney, M. J. (1997). Maternal care, hippocampal glucocorticoid receptors, and hypothalamic-pituitary-adrenal responses to stress. *Science, 277,* 1659–1662.

Lorenz, K. (1966). *On aggression* (M. K. Wilson, Trans.). New York: Harcourt, Brace and World.

Maunder, R. G., & Hunter, J. J. (2001). Attachment and psychosomatic medicine: Developmental contributions to stress and disease. *Psychosomatic Medicine, 63,* 556–567.

McClintock, M. (1998, May 6). Personal communication.

McEwen, B. S. (1998). Protective and damaging effects of stress mediators. *New England Journal of Medicine, 338,* 171–179.

McEwen, B. S., & Lasley, E. N. (2002). *The end of stress as we know it.* Washington DC: National Academies Press.

McEwen, B. S., & Stellar, E. (1993). Stress and the individual: Mechanisms leading to disease. *Archives of Internal Medicine, 53,* 2093–2101.

McKenna, J. J. (1981). The primate infant caregiving behavior: Origins, consequences and variability with emphasis on the common Indian Langur monkey. In D. J. Gubernick & P. H. Klopfer (Eds.), *Parental care in mammals*. New York: Plenum.

Mitchell, W. E. (1990). Why Wape men don't beat their wives: Constraints toward domestic tranquility in a New Guinea society. *Pacific Studies, 13*(3), 141–150.

Munck, A., & Naray-Fejes-Toth, A. (1994). Glucocorticoids and stress: Permissive and suppressive actions. *Academic Science, 746*, 115–133.

Murphy, Y., & Murphy, R. (1974). *Women of the forest*. New York: Columbia University Press.

Nachmias, M., Gunnar, M. R., Mangelsdorf, S., Parritz, R. H., & Buss, K. (1996). Behavioral inhibition and stress reactivity: The moderating role of attachment security. *Child Development, 67*, 508–522.

Newman, K. (1999). *No shame in my game: The working poor in the inner city*. New York: Alfred Knopf/Russell Sage Foundation.

Pearson, J. L., Cohn, D. A., Cowan, P. A., & Cowan, C. P. (1994). Earned- and continuous-security in adult attachment: Relation to depressive symptomatology and parenting style. *Development and Psychopathology, 6*, 359–373.

Pellis, S. M., & Pellis, V. C. (1996). On knowing it's only play: The role of play signals in play fighting. *Aggression and Violent Behavior, 1*, 249–268.

Pellis, S. M., & Pellis, V. C. (1998). Play fighting of rats in comparative perspective: A schema for neurobehavioral analyses. *Neuroscience and Biobehavioral Reviews, 23*, 87–101.

Phelps, J. L., Belsky, J., & Crnic, K. (1998). Earned security, daily stress, and parenting: A comparison of five alternative models. *Development and Psychopathology, 10*, 21–38.

Raleigh, M. J., McGuire, M. T., Brammer, G. L., Pollack, D. B., & Yuwiler, A. (1991). Serotonergic mechanisms promote dominance acquisition in adult male vervet monkeys. *Brain Research, 559*, 181–190.

Repetti, R. L. (1997, April). *The effects of daily job stress on parent behavior with preadolescents*. Paper presented at the biennial meeting of the Society for Research in Child Development, Washington D C.

Repetti, R. L., Taylor, S. E., & Seeman, T. E. (2002). Risky families: Family social environments and the mental and physical health of offspring. *Psychological Bulletin, 128*, 330–366.

Rosenblum, L. A., Coplan, J. D., Friedman, S., Bassoff, T., Gorman, J. M., & Andrews, M. W. (1994). Adverse early experiences affect noradrenergic and serotonergic functioning in adult primates. *Biological Psychiatry, 35*, 221–227.

Rosenblum, L. A., & Paully, G. S. (1984). The effects of varying environmental demands on maternal and infant behavior. *Child Development, 55*, 305–314.

Sapolsky, R. M. (1998). *Why zebras don't get ulcers: An updated guide to stress, stress-related disease, and coping*. New York: W. H. Freeman.

Schwarzer, R., & Leppin, A. (1989). Social support and health: A meta-analysis. *Psychology and Health, 3*, 1–15.

Seeman, T. E., Berkman, L. F., Gulanski, B. I., Robbins, R. J., Greenspan, S. L., Charpentier, P. A., & Rowe, J. W. (1995). Self-esteem and neuroendocrine response to challenge: MacArthur studies of successful aging. *Journal of Psychosomatic Research, 39*, 69–84.

Seeman, T. E., Singer, B. H., Rowe, J. W., Horwitz, R. I., & McEwen, B. S. (1997). Price of adaptation — allostatic load and its health consequences. *Archives of Internal Medicine, 157*, 2259–2268.

Simpson, J. A., Rholes, W. S., & Nelligan, J. S. (1992). Support seeking and support giving within couples in an anxiety-provoking situation: The role of attachment styles. *Journal of Personality and Social Psychology, 62,* 434–446.

Simpson, J. A., Rholes, W. S., Orina, M. M., & Grich, J. (2002). Working models of attachment, support giving, and support seeking in a stressful situation. *Personality and Social Psychology Bulletin, 28,* 598–608.

Spangler, G., & Grossmann, K. E., (1993). Biobehavioral organization in securely and insecurely attached infants. *Child Development, 64,* 1439–1450.

Suomi, S. J. (1987). Genetic and maternal contributions to individual differences in rhesus monkey biobehavioral development. In N. A. Krasnagor, E. M. Blass, M. A. Hofer, & W. P. Smotherman (Eds.), *Perinatal development: A psychobiological perspective* (pp. 397–420). New York: Academic Press.

Suomi, S. J. (1991). Up-tight and laid-back monkeys: Individual differences in the response to social challenges. In S. Brauth, W. Hall, & R. Dooling (Eds.), *Plasticity of development* (pp. 27–56). Cambridge, MA: MIT Press.

Suomi, S. J. (1997). Early determinants of behavior: Evidence from primate studies. *British Medical Bulletin, 53,* 170–184.

Tamres, L., Janicki, D., & Helgeson, V. S. (2002). Sex differences in coping behavior: A meta-analytic review. *Personality and Social Psychology Review, 6,* 2–30.

Taylor, S. E. (2002). *The tending instinct: Women, men, and the biology of our relationships.* New York: Holt.

Taylor, S. E., Klein, L. C., Lewis, B. P., Gruenewald, T. L., Gurung, R. A. R., & Updegraff, J. A. (2000). Biobehavioral responses to stress in females: Tend-and-befriend, not fight-or- flight. *Psychological Review, 107,* 411–429.

Taylor, S. E., Lerner, J. S., Sage, R. M., Lehman, B. J., & Seeman, T. E. (2004). Early environment, emotions, responses to stress, and health. Special Issue on Personality and Health. *Journal of Personality, 72,* 1365–1393.

Tiger, L. (1969). *Men in Groups.* New York: Vintage Books.

Trivers, R. L. (1971). The evolution of reciprocal altruism. *Quarterly Review of Biology, 45,* 35–37.

Umberson, D. (1987). Family status and health behaviors: Social control as a dimension of social integration. *Journal of Health and Social Behavior, 28,* 306–319.

Van den Berg, C. L., Hol, T., Van Ree, J. M., Spruijt, B. M., Everts, H., & Koolhaas, J. M. (1999). Play is indispensable for adequate development of coping with social challenges in rats. *Developmental Psychobiology, 34,* 129–138.

van Ijzendoorn, M. (1995). Adult attachment representations, parental responsiveness, and infant attachment: A meta-analysis on the predictive validity of the adult attachment interview. *Psychological Bulletin, 117,* 387–403.

Wills, T. A. (1991). Social support and interpersonal relationships. In M. S. Clark (Ed.), *Prosocial behavior* (pp. 265–289). Newbury Park, CA: Sage.

Wolf, M. (1975). Women and suicide in China. In M. Wolf & R. Witke (Eds.), *Women in Chinese society.* Stanford: Stanford University Press.

Wrangham, R. W. (1980). An ecological model of female-bonded primate groups. *Behaviour, 75,* 262–300.

11

The Altruism Puzzle: Psychological Adaptations for Prosocial Behavior

MARK VAN VUGT and PAUL A. M. VAN LANGE

With those animals which were benefited by living in close association, the individuals which took the greatest pleasure in society would best escape various dangers, while those that cared least for their comrades, and lived solitary, would perish in greater numbers. (Charles Darwin in *The Descent of Man*, 1871, p. 105)

H *umans are social animals* is an often stated phrase, but what exactly does it mean? We are certainly not as solitary as some mammals, such as sharks, foxes, and cats, whose sociability does not stretch far beyond mating engagements (Wilson, 1975). Humans are together for a variety of additional reasons, including joint parental care, territorial and group defense, trade, and the provision of scarce goods like food and shelter (Kenrick, Li, & Butner, 2003; Van Vugt, 1998). At first sight, human sociability pales in comparison with that of bees, ants, and termites that are known to routinely sacrifice their lives to defend their colonies. Self-sacrifice in social insects, however, only occurs within family groups where genetic interests are strongly overlapping (Wilson, 1975). In contrast, humans have an unrivalled capacity to sacrifice themselves for individuals that are not closely related, sometimes in large social groups (Fehr & Fischbacher, 2003; Wilson, 2002).

Examples are abound. Humans invest time and effort in helping the needy within their community and make frequent anonymous donations to charities (Van Lange, Van Vugt, Bekkers, Schuyt, & Schippers, 2006; Van Vugt, Snyder, Tyler, & Biel, 2000). They come to each other's aid in natural disasters (Van Vugt, 2001; Van Vugt & Samuelson, 1999). They respond to appeals to sacrifice themselves for their nation in wartime (Stern, 1995). And, they put their lives at risk by aiding complete strangers in emergency situations (Becker & Eagly, 2004).

The tendency to benefit others—not closely related—at the expense of oneself, which we refer to here as altruism or prosocial behavior, is one of the major puzzles in the behavioral sciences.[1] For many decades, biologists, economists, and psychologists alike have been telling their audiences that humans are fundamentally selfish: When faced with two behavioral options, individuals will choose the alternative that yields the best immediate personal payoffs. But, as the above examples illustrate, this picture is incomplete at best in explaining human social behavior. We need to rethink the validity of the self-interest model in light of the evidence for the ubiquity of examples of altruism and prosocial behavior in human society.

In this chapter, we pursue this goal in several steps. We first present the archetypical social decision situation that humans have faced throughout evolutionary history, the social dilemma, and explain how this over time may have shaped a prosocial tendency in humans. Second, we discuss two broad evolutionary theories of prosocial behavior, and focus our attention on a simple, yet powerful psychological mechanism of social exchange that can account for a broad range of phenomena that have been observed in social psychological research on altruism and prosocial behavior. The wealth of data supports an adaptationist perspective on social exchange (Cosmides & Tooby, 1992; Schmitt & Pilcher, 2004). Throughout human evolutionary history, the benefits of social exchange were so substantial that it increased the relative fitness of those engaging in altruistic interactions, thus enabling this capacity to spread through the population. But, as we shall see, the potential fitness costs associated with making a risky prosocial move were such that it would only be elicited under well-defined social conditions. The main purpose of this chapter is to identify the social psychological conditions that made the evolution of altruism possible and allowed humans to "adapt" to their (natural and social) environments.

SOCIAL DILEMMAS

Perhaps nothing can illustrate the significance of altruism better than the example of the Prisoner's Dilemma Game (PDG). The PDG represents a broad class of social decision situations, also known as social dilemmas, in which there is a conflict between an individual's self-interest and his or her shared interests with other individuals. The assumptions behind the game are relatively straightforward (Dawes, 1980; Van Vugt, 1998):

1. Each individual is better off acting in their immediate self-interest; yet,
2. If all individuals act according to their self-interest, then everyone will be worse off.

Broadly speaking, any situation in which you are tempted to do something, but know it would be a grave mistake if everybody acted like you, is likely to be a social dilemma. Take the example of two students, Ann and James, who share a house together. Each of them would be better off if they relied upon the other to clean the house (assuming that for most cleaning is a pain). Yet, if neither of them makes an effort to clean the house, the house becomes a mess and they will both be worse off.

The interdependence structure of this example can be presented in an outcome matrix, like the one in Figure 11.1. The altruistic or cooperative choice (C-choice) in this example stands for cleaning the house, whereas the defecting choice (D-choice) stands for not cleaning the house. If Ann cleans the house by herself, but James does nothing, the outcomes for James are very good (say 10 on a personal-satisfaction scale), but they are poor for Ann (say 0). In game-theoretical terms, James gets the free rider's payoff, whereas Ann earns the sucker's payoff (Komorita & Parks, 1994). In contrast, if James cleans by himself, but Ann does nothing, then the outcomes for Ann are good (10), but for James they are bad (0)— here Ann is the free rider or "cheater" and James is the "sucker." If Ann and James share the cleaning, the outcomes for both of them are moderately good (say 5 each), which is not as good as when the other person does all the cleaning. Yet, and here lies the crux of the social dilemma, if neither Ann nor James cleans the house, their outcomes will be relatively poor (say 2 each), which is worse than their outcomes had they both shared the cleaning (5 each).

What makes the social dilemma paradigm so powerful is that the key properties of the conflict between self-interest and collective interest that underlies the dilemma can be easily extended to situations (1) in which the consequences of noncooperative behavior are much more severe, and (2) there are larger groups of individuals involved. As an example, in a legendary article "Tragedy of the Commons," the late Garrett Hardin (1968) addressed the preservation of common pasture grounds in 17th and 18th century England. The story describes how a collection of herdsmen raise their cattle on a public pasture (known as the Commons). According to Hardin, the tragedy starts once one herdsman realizes that he is better off adding a piece to his herd. His profits in terms of meat and wool increase, so he argues, whereas the losses of adding a cow or sheep (e.g., grazing space) are negligible, because they will be shared with all herdsmen. As all herdsmen come to the same conclusion at some point—there is no a priori reason why they will not—it all ends in disaster as the Commons is being overgrazed. As Hardin (p. 1244) puts it dramatically "Freedom in the Commons will bring ruin to all."

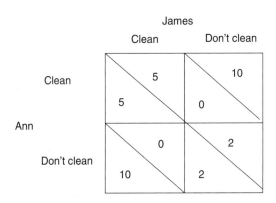

FIGURE 11.1 An example of a Prisoner's Dilemma Game: keeping the house tidy, whereby "Clean" is the cooperative choice and "Don't clean" the defective choice.

This parable could easily lead to a wrong conclusion. Social dilemmas often do not end in collective disaster when they are played out in the real world, especially when individuals can "enlarge the shadow of the [their] future" (Axelrod, 1984, p. 126). Historical evidence shows, for example, that most commons grounds in England and other countries were, in fact, managed very well by local communities (Gardner & Stern, 1996; Ostrom, 1990)—many commons still exist to this day. Even the Cold War, which inspired so much research into social dilemmas, ended peacefully. In addition, findings from experimental social dilemma research involving repeated interactions between strangers suggest that the vast majority of interactions result in mutual cooperation (De Cremer & Van Vugt, 1999; Komorita & Parks, 1994). Finally (and perhaps the most devastating for the self-interest model), even if there is no expectation of future interaction between complete strangers in the laboratory, still around 40–60% of people make an altruistic move (Caporael, Dawes, Orbell, & Vandekragt, 1989; Fehr & Fishbacher, 2003; Van Lange, 1999).

The validity of the self-interest model is also undermined by a simple thought experiment. In the house-sharing example, if neither James nor Ann makes an effort to clean the house, their situation simply becomes unbearable over time. If James does all the cleaning, but Ann systematically refuses, the relationship between the two will deteriorate over time and James will leave the house, forcing Ann to look for a new room mate to exploit, who will then also leave until there is no one who wants to share a house with Ann. Thus, the most likely outcome over time is that Ann will go some way in sharing the cleaning duties with James.[2]

Thus, the notion that people often act altruistically in social dilemmas is suggested by historical, experimental, and anecdotal evidence. Once people are aware that their interests are at least partly overlapping, and that they have some sense of a shared future, they will often act benevolently toward each other (cf. Axelrod, 1984).

THE EVOLUTIONARY APPROACH

So, what are the ultimate, evolutionary origins of the rich patterns of prosocial behavior that we find in human society? Addressing the evolutionary question is important, for at least *three* reasons. First, it may strengthen the validity of social psychological theories of altruism and prosocial behavior (as well as other puzzling human social behaviors) by providing a fuller and richer account of the phenomenon. In this regard, it is important to note that the evolutionary approach complements rather than competes with social psychological analyses of altruism and cooperation. It looks at the question of altruism at a different level of analysis.

Social psychologists are generally interested in studying proximal explanations for altruism, trying to establish which factors decrease or increase the likelihood of altruism toward others through empirical research (the "how" question). In contrast, evolutionary theorists are interested primarily in the ultimate functions of altruism (the "why" question), trying to figure out whether this type of behavior could have been selected for in human evolutionary history—the adaptation question (Schmitt & Pilcher, 2004).

To give an example, social psychological research on empathy—defined in terms of feelings of sympathy, compassion, tenderness, and the like—examines the conditions under which individuals may become altruistically motivated by benefiting another person as an end in itself (e.g., Batson, 1998; Batson, Duncan, Ackerman, Buckley, & Birch, 1981). Evolutionary psychologists look for evidence to suggest that empathy is a psychological adaptation that has emerged through natural selection, such that individuals who possessed the capacity to empathize with others were more successful in propagating their genes into the next generation than individuals without this capacity. Combining the proximate and ultimate levels of analysis can obviously provide a much richer perspective on the origins of altruism than any singular approach can. Unfortunately, many researchers tend to confuse these levels of analysis in their work, failing to make a distinction between proximate and ultimate explanations for social behavior (cf. Barrett, Dunbar, & Lycett, 2002).

Second, addressing the evolutionary question may help to resolve particular contradictions and controversies in social psychological research on altruism. For example, it sheds light on the debate whether empathy derives from selfish or unselfish motivations (Batson, Sager, Garst, Kang, Rubchinsky, & Dawson, 1997; Cialdini, Brown, Lewis, Luce, & Neuberg, 1997). The evolutionary perspective makes clear that these views may not be as incompatible as they seem. Rather than looking at empathy from the perspective of the individual actor, one could look at it from the perspective of the actor's genes (Dawkins, 1976). From the perspective of the gene, it makes sense that, under specific circumstances, such as when empathy is aroused, individuals act prosocially toward specific others. So, selfishness at the gene level does not automatically result in selfish behavior at the level of the organism.

Third, an evolutionary perspective facilitates social psychological research on altruism by generating a plethora of new research questions, hypotheses and analyses. These new developments may bridge fields and even disciplines, thereby serving the cumulative function of knowledge. For instance, an evolutionary perspective suggests that altruism cannot be sustained without some form of discrimination between recipients—the costs of altruism are simply too high to be ignored. Thus, the human psychological system is likely to possess particular "protection" mechanisms that act as brakes on altruism. One likely mechanism is the ability to detect and avoid free riders or cheaters, those who try to exploit the benevolence of others. On the basis of psychological research, informed by an evolutionary perspective, there is now growing support for the presence of a cheater-detection system in the human psyche, but much further research is needed to bolster this claim (Cosmides & Tooby, 1992).

HUMAN EVOLUTION AND THE ALTRUISM PUZZLE

So, what do we know about human evolutionary history that may shed light on the selfishness vs. altruism debate? Most experts agree that the roots of human social behavior lie far back in the Pleistocene, a period that started a couple of million years ago and continued until the agricultural revolution, some 10,000 years ago (Barrett et al., 2002; Boyd & Richerson, 1985; Dunbar, 1993). There can be little doubt that this interval, which encompasses about 95% of human history, has left deep traces in the human body and psyche. During this period, humans lived predominately in relatively small and stable nomadic hunter–gatherer groups, with high degrees of mutual dependence and kinship, and relatively minor status and power differences between individuals. Group living provided our hominid ancestors with numerous benefits for survival and reproduction, such as communal childcare, protection against predators, and food sharing, but it also introduced various specific problems that needed to be solved to reap the benefits of group living. Experts agree that many of the more basic problems were, in fact, archetypical social dilemmas (Fehr & Fischbacher, 2003; Kenrick et al., 2003).[3]

To illustrate, in order to survive in harsh climates, it was essential for our ancestors to obtain a daily nutritious diet of fruits and meat. The daily provision of meat, in particular, was not guaranteed, however, because the returns of hunting were likely to be variable. Furthermore, meat came in packages that were often too large to consume by one family. Hence, there would be days with a food surplus and days with a food shortage. This would open up the possibility to engage in altruistic exchanges, whereby individuals (or families) would share their food with others that were less lucky on that particular day (Hawkes, 1993). These recipients would return this favor at a later day. This resembles the PDG that we sketched in Figure 11.1, which can promote group cooperation, but leaves an individual open to exploitation from cheaters.

Social dilemmas would have been everywhere in traditional hunter–gatherer societies, not just in food sharing, but also in cooperative hunting, territorial group defense, and the communal care for children. Therefore, it is not at all unlikely that across millions of years humans have evolved specific psychological and behavioral adaptations to cope with social dilemmas (Nesse, 2001). The benefits of group living, or the costs of solitary living, were simply too large to be ignored. An obvious adaptation that would greatly facilitate group living for any individual would be the emergence of some degree of altruism, targeted toward specific others under specific circumstances.

On the face of it, however, altruism provides a major puzzle for Darwin's theory of evolution. Evolutionary theory assumes that individuals who possess particular traits and behaviors that produce survival and reproductive benefits leave more offspring than individuals without such characteristics. And, to the extent that these traits and behaviors are inheritable, they will spread through a population. Yet, how can altruism, a behavior that enhances the welfare of others at the cost of the individual, enhance the individual's reproductive success? Darwin struggled with this question, but failed to come up with a satisfactory answer.

Only in the past few decades have evolutionary scientists come up with various plausible evolutionary scenarios for altruism. Unlike Darwin who believed that individuals, or sometimes even groups, were the units of natural selection, these scientists argued that the basic selection unit is the gene and that our bodies are merely "vehicles for the transmission of genes" (Dawkins, 1976). This gene-eyed perspective of human nature opens up the possibility that, under certain specific conditions, altruistic tendencies can be adaptive. Which are these theories? And, more important for the present argument, to what extent are they able to account for altruism toward those that are not closely related?

Kin-Selection Theory

According to Hamilton's (1964) theory of kin selection, individuals can promote their own genetic future by making sacrifices on behalf of others who carry copies of their genes. The kin-selection model predicts that individuals engage in altruistic sacrifices on behalf of close relatives, such as offspring, more than distant relatives, such as cousins, and more toward distant relatives than toward genetic strangers. Yet, altruistic behavior only emerges if the costs for the helper are lower than the benefits for the recipient multiplied by the degree of relatedness between the two individuals, which is known as *Hamilton's formula*:

$$rB > C$$

where r represents the degree of relatedness, B the benefit to recipient, and C the cost to helper.

There is considerable support for the kin-selection hypothesis of altruism among human samples. For example, Burnstein, Crandall, and Kitayama (1994) found in a number of scenario studies that intended helping increased with genetic relatedness, and, consistent with the kin-selection model, this relationship was particularly strong in life–death situations, such as entering a burning building to save another person's life (see also Neyer & Lang, 2003). Furthermore, a survey among female residents in Los Angeles found that, in times of need, close relatives were a greater source of help than were unrelated individuals (Essock-Vitale & McGuire, 1985).

There is no doubt that the kin-selection model accounts for a considerable portion of sacrifice in our everyday lives (as readers with young children will appreciate), but can it also account for prosocial acts toward individuals that are not closely related, which is so uniquely human? Genetic relatedness declines extremely quickly if we go beyond the nuclear family, so the answer should be negative.

However, an intriguing possibility is that, because humans spent most of their history in small, kin-based groups, no perfect mechanism has evolved for discriminating between kin and non-kin, as this was not particularly necessary within these conditions. Therefore, humans rely on heuristic but imperfect kinship rules as the basis for altruism. Physical similarity, similarity in attitudes or culture, and geographical proximity could potentially all be used as kinship cues. Although these cues are fallible to denote kinship in modern society, they may have been effective throughout much of evolutionary history. This "big mistake" hypothesis for altruism has received some skepticism from evolutionary scientists (Boyd & Richerson, 1985), but initial tests have produced some hopeful results.

For example, there is evidence that fathers favor children that look more like them (Burch & Gallup, 2000). Also, adults report greater willingness to assist unrelated children who have similar facial features (DeBruine, 2004), and they are more likely to help someone who shares their name or speaks the same dialect

(Barrett et al., 2002). Even something as remote as attitude similarity can apparently elicit a kinship cue. In an ingenious social cognition experiment, Park and Schaller (2005) showed that participants subconsciously linked a target person believed to hold similar attitudes to themselves with word stimuli denoting kinship (e.g., family). Further research is needed to investigate the importance of other possible kinship cues, such as proximity and shared personality traits, and their consequences in terms of prosocial behavior toward strangers.

Social Exchange Theory

Kin selection may have paved the way for a second, and perhaps more powerful mechanism for altruism toward genetic strangers, social exchange. Once the capacity for altruism toward kin had evolved, it became possible to bestow small benefits on those that were around, but were non-kin (Barrett et al., 2002). Unlike kin altruism, however, this system would have been based on a mechanism of social exchange.

Social Exchange Between Individuals
The theory of reciprocal altruism (Trivers, 1971) holds that individuals sometimes act benevolently toward others in the expectation of a reciprocal act of kindness in the future. Examples of reciprocity can be found in most social mammals. The blood sharing among vampire bats and the formation of fighting coalitions among chimpanzees are often cited as examples (de Waal, 1996; Wilkinson, 1984). Yet, there is no species in which reciprocity is as common, as varied, and highly developed as among humans. Humans trade in nearly everything that is of value, from food and weapons to information and sex. Furthermore, exchanges can be paid out in a different currency (e.g., sex for money). In this regard, it is perhaps better to use the more generic term of social exchange for this type of altruism rather than reciprocity (cf. Cosmides & Tooby, 1992).[4]

Social Exchange Within Groups
In humans, social exchanges are not necessarily restricted to two individuals, but they frequently occur within larger social networks (Alexander, 1987). Generalized exchange networks involve situations where individuals, who act benevolently toward others, do not necessarily expect a return from the recipients themselves but from a third party. For example, an individual A may share his food with individual B, and upon seeing this a third individual C may share his food with A. One of the reasons this system works is that by acting altruistically, individuals develop a positive *reputation* within their group, which increases their attractiveness as potential exchange partners (Alexander, 1987; cf. costly signaling theory; McAndrew, 2002).

Yet, there is another intriguing possibility for the evolution of prosocial behavior in larger groups, something which Darwin himself recognized in *The Descent of Man*:

> A tribe including many members who, from possessing in high degree the spirit of patriotism, fidelity, obedience, courage, and sympathy, were always ready to aid one another, and to sacrifice themselves for the common good, would be victorious over most other tribes, and this would be natural selection.

According to this argument, which is often referred to as group selection or multilevel selection (Campbell, 1975; McAndrew, 2002; Wilson, 2002), acting prosocially toward members of your in-group may be beneficial to you as it can ensure that your group is victorious over other groups in an intergroup competition. Although within the group altruists fare worse than cheaters, groups with many altruists fare better than groups with many cheaters, giving altruists indirect benefits via group selection. The evolution of altruism (and other social traits) may thus be possible via selection at the level of the group rather than the individual. However, this model only works if (1) the between-group selection pressures are stronger than the within-group selection pressures (i.e., intergroup competition overrides intragroup competition), (2) groups frequently disband and individuals have the opportunity to choose with whom they interact, and (3) in- and out-group members can be easily distinguished—these conditions are likely to uphold for humans (Wilson, 2002).

Brakes on Social Exchange   The evolution of social exchange required the presence of various social, structural, and biological conditions that acted as brakes on social exchange to reduce the risks of exploitation by an exchange partner (Cosmides & Tooby, 1992; Trivers, 1971). For example, individuals must interact repeatedly with the same individuals, and there must be many opportunities for social exchange during the lifetime of these individuals. Humans' long lifetimes and the presence of small and stable groups during much of evolutionary history would have favored these conditions. In addition, for social exchange to evolve, the human psychological system needs to be equipped with a number of different auxiliary mechanisms. These psychological mechanisms should protect individuals against the risks of exploitation by the recipients of their prosocial acts, and they are likely to have co-evolved alongside the social exchange mechanism to enable individuals to reap the benefits of social exchange.

What should an evolved psychological system for social exchange look like and what evidence can we find in the social psychological literature on altruism and prosocial behavior for the existence of these psychological mechanisms? Previously, evolutionary psychologists have been primarily interested in the cognitive adaptations underlying social exchange (e.g., computational and memory abilities; Cosmides & Tooby, 1992). Here, we are primarily concerned with the social and motivational adaptations that gave rise to social exchange. In the next section, we discuss several key properties of an evolved social psychological system of social exchange that, we believe, have allowed humans to reap the benefits of altruistic interactions.

AN EVOLVED SOCIAL PSYCHOLOGY OF ALTRUISM AND PROSOCIAL BEHAVIOR

The theory of social exchange makes a number of powerful predictions about an evolved social psychology of prosocial behavior: Who should we help, why should we help, and when should we help? Below, we review the evidence for several of these hypotheses.

Trust

To reap the benefits of social exchange, there must be a psychological mechanism in place that protects individuals from engaging in interactions with poor exchange partners, i.e., individuals who are either unwilling or unable to reciprocate. One such mechanism should enable individuals to detect free riders and avoid interacting with them, which is also known as a *cheater-detection system* (Cosmides & Tooby, 1992). If individuals are unable to distinguish between potential cooperators and free riders, and interact with both types of people indiscriminately then a social exchange system cannot evolve over time because it is too costly for the individual. There are a number of socio-cognitive capacities that are needed to enable individuals to make decisions about whom they are going to interact with, for example, the ability to recognize many different individuals, and remember the history of interactions with these individuals (cf. cheater-detection system). Ultimately, these revolve around the notion of *trust* —a belief in the trustworthiness and honesty of others (Holmes & Rempel, 1989; Komorita & Parks, 1994; Yamagishi, 1986).

The social psychological literature is quite clear about the benefits of trust. For example, relationships characterized by high-level trust appear to be more rewarding, enjoyable, and stable over time (Simpson, Gangestad, & Lerma, 1990). Trust also enhances benevolent actions. For example, close relationship partners are more likely to make sacrifices for one another—by giving up leisure time to care for each other—if they expect their partners to do the same for them (Wieselquist, Rusbult, Foster, & Agnew, 1999). Similarly, employees who trust their employers to treat them well are more likely to help out their organization in times of need (Tyler & Smith, 1998). Finally, individuals are more prepared to make sacrifices for their group if they expect other members to do the same (De Cremer & Van Vugt, 1999; Kramer & Brewer, 1984).

Given the importance of trust for social exchange, it is not all that surprising that humans are fairly good at making decisions about who they can trust or not. To illustrate, after a brief encounter with another student, individuals were able to predict with 75% accuracy whether that person would cooperate or defect in a Prisoner's Dilemma (Frank, 1988). Nevertheless, individuals do sometimes make errors of judgment, but if they find out that they are being cheated upon, they retaliate swiftly and aggressively (Fehr & Fishbacher, 2003; Trivers, 1971) or terminate the relationship altogether (Van Vugt & Hart, 2004).

Negativity Effect

In a related vein, the evolution of social exchange would be facilitated if individuals would attend more strongly to negative impressions than positive impressions about potential exchange partners. A false negative—believing that someone is a cooperator who, in reality, is a defector—is more detrimental to the welfare of the altruist than a false positive believing that someone is a defector who, in reality, is a cooperator. Hence, we should expect humans to show a bias toward negative rather than positive personality information, especially information about the morality of an exchange partner. Furthermore, the negativity bias should be particularly pronounced when the prosocial act is highly costly (e.g., lending a large sum of money).

These predictions are, by and large, supported by the social psychological literature on person perception (Baumeister, Bratslavsky, Finkenauer, & Vohs, 2001; Reeder & Brewer, 1979; Taylor, 1991). The negativity effect (sometimes also referred to as negativity bias) refers to the phenomenon whereby, relative to positive person information, negative person information elicits more physiological arousal, draws greater attention, and exerts greater impact on judgments and impressions as well as behaviors. Several explanatory mechanisms underlying the negativity effect have been advanced, including neurological mechanisms (e.g., the brain seeks to reduce or suppress all deviations from hedonic neutrality), and several range-frequency explanations (e.g., the novel, the infrequent, and the unexpected draws more attention; Taylor, 1991). At an ultimate, evolutionary level, this bias can be explained by the fact that in social exchange dilemmas it is vital to tell the cooperators from the cheaters, and avoid interacting with the latter category of individuals.

A nice illustration of the negativity bias comes from research on sex differences in reading the intentions of potential mates. Because the costs of a sexual encounter with an unreliable mate are much higher for females than for males, Haselton & Buss (2000) argued that it would be in a woman's interest to underestimate the commitment of men in order to avoid a false negative (mistaking a cheater for a cooperator). Their results confirmed this prediction, thus supporting our evolutionary argument about the adaptive benefits of judgment biases in targeting prosocial behavior.

Commitment and Loyalty

Altruism based on social exchange can only evolve if individuals themselves are not too opportunistic in entering and leaving reciprocal relationships. The capacity for commitment, defined in terms of strong desire to continue the relationship, long-term orientation, and feelings of attachment may have evolved for the purpose of relationship maintenance. Commitment, sometimes also referred to as loyalty, improves the functioning of a social exchange system by mechanisms that are conceptually linked to altruism and prosocial behavior, and therefore can be viewed as a psychological adaptation for social exchange (Nesse, 2001; Rusbult & Van Lange, 2003; Van Vugt & Hart, 2004).

For example, commitment enables individuals to maintain an exchange relationship that was rewarding in the past, but for some reason is not quite as rewarding now. Commitment thus gives exchange partners a little bit of credit in reciprocating the investments that an individual has made in the relationship. These investments would, of course, be lost if individuals were to leave relationships impulsively. Commitment would also serve as a signal to the other party that the relationship is likely to endure, despite the temporary decline, which makes altruistic exchanges between partners further possible (Rusbult, 1983). Finally, there may be indirect benefits to expressions of commitment. Showing commitment may enhance the reputation of an individual in the eyes of a third party, and may therefore make the individual a more attractive exchange partner in the future (Frank, 1988).

It may come as little surprise that commitment is the main predictor of satisfaction and stability in close relationships (Rusbult, 1983) and in groups (Van Vugt & Hart, 2004). It is also predictive of cognitive and behavioral activities to maintain relationships, such as derogating or driving away tempting alternatives (Johnson & Rusbult, 1989). Furthermore, commitment enhances positive illusions about the relationship, serving the belief that their own relationship is better than—and not as bad as—others' relationships (Murray, Holmes, & Griffin, 1996; Rusbult, Van Lange, Wildschut, Yovetich, & Verette, 2000; Van Lange & Rusbult, 1995). Perhaps most importantly, loyalty and commitment promote tendencies toward altruism and cooperation, such as willingness to sacrifice, engaging in extra-role behaviors in teams and organizations, and responding constructively (rather than destructively) to another's destructive behavior (Rusbult, 1983).

Forgiveness

To evolve, a system of social exchange would have to be sufficiently flexible to deal with minor deviations from strict reciprocity. In the social dilemma literature, social exchange is often conceptualized in terms of a tit-for-tat strategy (mimicking the partner's choice). Whereas tit-for-tat has been shown to promote altruistic exchanges, more so than unconditionally altruistic or defective strategies (Axelrod, 1984), it has an important limitation. This limitation derives from the fact that tit-for-tat becomes trapped in a cycle of noncooperative interaction, once a noncooperative choice is made—accidental or nonaccidental. The only way out of this so-called echo effect (or negative reciprocity) is that one individual initiates a unilateral, risky altruistic move.

Forgiveness (responding altruistically to a partner's noncooperative choice) is an important psychological mechanism that may keep social exchange going in such situations. Thus, we believe that human tendencies to be forgiving may have evolved for this particular purpose. Computer simulations and laboratory studies on social dilemmas have both shown that forgiveness overcomes the detrimental effects of unintended errors in non-cooperation (Bendor, Kramer, & Stout, 1991; Van Lange, Ouwerkerk, & Tazelaar, 2002). Similarly, there is evidence from close relationship research that acts of forgiveness facilitate the stability and satisfaction of close relationships through tendencies related to prosocial behavior (Fincham, 2000; Karremans, Van Lange, Ouwerkerk, & Kluwer, 2003; McCullough, Worthington, & Rachal, 1997).

Without some degree of forgiveness it is hard to imagine how individuals could continue to reap the benefits from social exchange, especially in situations when intentions cannot be perfectly communicated—which is often true in social dilemmas in everyday life (e.g., arriving late for a meeting because of an unforeseen traffic jam; accidentally saying the wrong thing). The act of forgiving is probably so important for the functioning of groups that it is one of the cornerstones of almost every society, religious or nonreligious (Wilson, 2002)—see social norms.

Social Emotions

Empathy The evolution of social exchange would greatly benefit from the existence of a psychological system that enables individuals to quickly assess if and how much another person requires aid. If this is true, then humans should be sensitive to any cues that yield information about the cost and benefits of helping so that altruists know how much help is required and recipients know how much they should reciprocate. People are indeed very attuned to the costs and benefits of altruism (Penner, Piliavin, Dovidio, & Schroeder, 2005). But, it is often a complex calculation and the ability to put oneself in another person's shoes or "perspective taking"—a main component of empathy—can be viewed as a heuristic rule for making a calculated decision. Furthermore, empathy should be stronger the greater the victim's need, because this increases the potential benefit of helping the victim and therefore their gratitude.

There is substantial evidence that empathy promotes altruism toward complete strangers (e.g., Batson, 1987; Batson et al., 1981). Empathy increases helping, even if there are substantial costs in money, time, and effort associated with the helping act (Batson et al., 1981, 1997). In contrast, needy people are much less likely to receive aid in the absence of empathic concern. Although some critics argue that empathy is really a selfish emotion—based on a merger between the images of the self and the other (Cialdini et al., 1997)—there is no denying the fact that strong feelings of empathy can give rise to altruism toward complete strangers.

Then, why are individuals selective in who they empathize with? According to Batson et al.'s (1981, 1997) experiments, individuals empathize more with people who are similar to them. One evolutionary explanation for this finding may be that helpers have less difficulty in assessing the amount of aid victims need if they are similar to themselves. Another intriguing possibility, however, is that people are more likely to help similar people, because similarity may be used as a cue for kinship—the big mistake hypothesis (Park & Schaller, 2005). Thus, helping a similar (i.e., kin) person would be less costly because it contributes indirectly to their individual fitness—via the kin-selection route. Whether empathy as an adaptation is ultimately shaped by kinship psychology or social exchange psychology remains to be seen, but there can be little doubt about the role of this prosocial emotion in regulating helping behavior.

Other Emotions The benefits of social exchange are so substantial that we would expect prosocial behavior to be evoked not just by empathy, but also by a range of other emotions. For example, the experience of a self-conscious emotion, like *guilt*, in response to one's own cheating makes individuals less likely to transgress next time, thereby maintaining the quality of their exchange relationship (Haidt, 2001). Guilt should also increase altruism. Research on the negative state-relief hypothesis (Cialdini & Futz, 1990) provides support for this claim.

Similar benevolent acts are expected if people experience other self-conscious emotions, such as shame and embarrassment, for failing to reciprocate. In contrast, emotions that people experience in reaction to free riders, such as *anger, contempt,* and *envy*—the so-called other-condemning emotions (Haidt, 2001)—should result in a decline in prosocial behavior. These are testable propositions.

Social Norms

So far, we have reviewed evidence for the existence of psychological adaptations that can explain the emergence of prosocial behavior at the dyadic level, such as empathy and trust. This is perhaps an easier task than trying to understand prosocial behavior within larger groups where the problem of cheaters is likely to be much greater. For example, why would people contribute to team performance, why would they volunteer for a job, or pay their taxes if they fear that there will be people who free ride on their sacrifices (Van Vugt et al., 2000)? Earlier, we have offered two evolutionary models for understanding prosocial behavior in large groups, (1) reputations (Alexander, 1987) and (2) group selection (Wilson, 2002). Both are likely to have played a role in shaping prosocial tendencies in humans. Altruism at the group level, however, could have evolved only under a narrow set of social and structural conditions. Once these were in place, individuals could reap the benefits from investing in larger groups.

For most of history, humans lived in relatively small and stable groups (Barrett et al., 2002). This condition opens up the possibility for the evolution of social exchange on the group level, in addition to the interpersonal level. Group-based altruism (based on generalized exchange) can be beneficial particularly in cooperative situations with highly uncertain payoffs that involve more than two individuals (e.g., hunting large game, group defense). The evolution of generalized social exchange would not be possible without the support of *social norms* to regulate cooperative exchanges between the individual and the group. Thus, social norms may have found a place in human society as a way to promote cooperation and deter free riding in large groups.

Norms about *fairness* and *morality* are examples. They regulate social exchanges between members of groups and are designed to promote group harmony and ensure that everyone gets what they deserve, whatever that may be (Tyler & Smith, 1998). Justice is so strongly engrained within the human psychological system that we are prepared to punish cheaters, even if they have not done us any harm personally—moralistic aggression (Fehr & Fischbacher, 2003; Van Vugt & Chang, 2006; de Waal, 1996).

There is much evidence for the importance and prevalence of these moral norms in human societies (Krebs & Janicki, 2002). Most societies have *decency norms* in place to promote cooperation and coordination between individuals, for example, not interrupting a conversation, giving up seats to elderly people, and acknowledging the receipt of a gift. Societies also have *obedience norms* (e.g., respecting your parents) and *solidarity norms* in place (e.g. defending your country), which help to foster group cohesion. Most societies also work on the basis of strict *fairness rules* that promote altruistic exchanges by prescribing how scarce resources and goods ought to be divided between the group members. For example, it is universally accepted that wealthy individuals in a group should contribute more to the common good than the poor—in modern society this principle is enforced through a progressive tax system.

Failure to adhere to these moral and fairness norms often evokes strong expressions of anger, rage, condemnation, and sometimes even revenge (cf. retributive justice; Tyler & Smith, 1998). Social disapproval, ostracism, prison sentences, and death penalties are but a few examples of the widespread tendency in human societies to engage in cheater punishment (Van Vugt & Chang, 2006).

Group Identification and Xenophobia

Social exchange within groups could only come about if there was a mechanism in place that allowed groups to create, preserve, and adhere to group boundaries to serve as a guide to whom prosocial activities should be directed. Hence, it would have been vital to know who is an in-group member and who is an out-group member. This is especially important in intergroup competitions in which helping a person from a rival group would harms one's own group, which is likely to have been the situation during much of human history (Alexander, 1987; Van Vugt & Hart, 2004). Thus, we would expect humans to have evolved capacities to attend very carefully to information about group memberships (Campbell, 1975), and form deep emotional attachments to in-groups (in-group identification) as well as strong resentments against out-groups (xenophobia).

There is a considerable body of social psychological research to confirm the existence of intergroup bias. Individuals are much more likely to act altruistically toward in-group members rather than outgroup members even when group categorization is based on a completely random event, like the flip of a coin (Tajfel & Turner, 1986), and the categorization cuts across friendship groups (Sherif & Sherif, 1953). In addition, humans have a propensity to identify themselves quickly and spontaneously as group members rather than as unique individuals (Brewer, 1979). Group identification promotes self-sacrificial behaviors for the benefit of groups, for example, in a resource crisis or intergroup conflict (De Cremer & Van Vugt, 1999; Kramer & Brewer, 1984). Group identification also creates a strong sense of individual loyalty toward groups, which further enhances group-based altruism (Levine & Moreland, 2002; Van Vugt & Hart, 2004).

Group Size

Generalized social exchange systems must have evolved in conjunction with adaptations to regulate the size of groups. Obviously, the larger the group the more difficult it becomes to detect free riders. Yet, larger groups also yield better protection against predators and rival groups (Alexander, 1987). Hence, we would expect humans to have the capacity to create flexible group arrangements in response to different types of environmental threats and opportunities (e.g., fission–fusion societies; Barrett et al., 2002). For example, in in-group settings in which the costs of free riding are huge, such as in highly interdependent work teams, we would expect individuals to have a preference for keeping group sizes relatively small.

There is a good deal of evidence suggesting that people prefer to work in smaller groups of five to eight people. This "dinner-party" size has been observed by anthropologists studying interactions, exchange, and culture in tribes, organizational psychologists studying teams and self-organizing groups, and game theorists analyzing the mathematics of interpersonal decisions (Gallucci, Van Lange, & Ouwerkerk, 2004). Social dilemma researchers, too, have observed that cooperation declines with increasing group size, and that such decline sets in when groups constitute more than eight individuals (Liebrand, 1984).

Several interesting and plausible psychological explanations have been advanced to account for the group size effect in social dilemmas. For example, anonymity increases with group size, whereas perceptions of personal efficacy (e.g., the feeling of making a difference) and feelings of personal responsibility or identity tend to decrease with group size. Also, a series of computer simulations of social dilemmas have shown that small groups do very well in terms of maintaining cooperation. Moreover, individuals spontaneously form groups of sizes that are not much larger than five (Gallucci et al., 2004). Thus, one could argue that group formation decisions may ultimately (and at least partially) be rooted in adaptations for social exchange.

Group Stability

The theory of social exchange would also predict that humans have an evolved psychology for group stability—keeping the group together. The costs of altruism are such that individuals are unlikely to engage in cooperative exchanges within groups if they are not confident that the group will stay together for a while in order for individuals to get a return from their investment. Hence, individuals should be sensitive to information about the duration of their group membership. Moreover, once they have invested in a group, they should want to engage in activities to keep the group together, and react negatively to forces that undermine group integrity.

There is some evidence to suggest that individuals carefully attend to cues about the longevity of group membership. For example, individuals cooperate more in groups with a fixed membership than in groups with a fluid membership, primarily because they trust each other more (Van Vugt, Hart, & Chang, 2006). In addition, individuals often defect on the last trial of a social dilemma—thus, when the termination of the group is eminent (cf. endgame effect; Murnighan & Roth, 1983). Finally, group members often treat newcomers with some distrust, and they do not immediately accept them as full members (Moreland & Levine, 1982).

The social psychological literature is also quite clear about a link between investment size and loyalty—a powerful mechanism to keep groups together. The more individuals invest in their group or relationship, the more committed they are to maintain it, thereby foregoing attractive exit options (Rusbult, 1983; Van Vugt & Hart, 2004). Furthermore, the loss of a group member—a threat to group stability—often evokes strong negative reactions from current members. Current members often treat departing members with some disdain, presumably out of fear that they may set an example to others. And, leavers are especially disliked if they join a rival group (Levine & Moreland, 2002; Van Vugt & Chang, 2006). Finally, the departure of a member often gives rise to ceremonial activities to strengthen the bonds of the group (e.g., farewell parties, funerals; Moreland & Levine, 1982). Thus, it is perhaps not too far-fetched to argue that prosocial behavior systems rely upon a broad range of activities that humans display, which may have been designed for keeping large groups together (Wilson, 2002).

Individual Differences in Altruism and Prosocial Behavior

Research has found considerable individual differences in prosocial inclination. Altruism, for example, is more prevalent among individuals who score consistently higher on scales of agreeableness, prosocial values, trust, communal orientation, collectivism, and moral development (e.g., Clark & Mills, 1979; Penner et al., 2005; Triandis, 1994; Van Lange, Otten, De Bruin, & Joireman, 1997; Van Vugt, Meertens, & Van Lange, 1995; Yamagishi, 1986). On a measure of social value orientation, usually around 60% individuals can be classified as individuals who are primarily concerned with maximizing mutual gains (i.e., prosocials), while 30% are primarily concerned with maximizing absolute personal gains (i.e., individualists), and 5–10% with maximizing relative personal gains (i.e., competitors). Together these latter two orientations are sometimes referred to as proselfs (Van Lange & Kuhlman, 1994). How does this fit with an adaptationist perspective on social exchange and prosocial behavior?

First, social-value orientation is a better predictor of behavior in one-shot dilemmas than in repeated dilemmas. In repeated social dilemmas, behavior is also importantly influenced by the strategy of the partner (McClintock & Liebrand, 1988; Van Lange, 1999). Both results are in agreement with an evolutionary theory of social exchange. It is not surprising that many individuals would start with an altruistic move on their first encounter with a stranger—provided that the act of benevolence is not too costly—because generosity builds trust (Van Lange et al., 2002).

Then why do some people defect on their first choice? We believe that differences in prosocial behavior, at least in part, arise from early interaction experiences and childhood environments that channel an individual's development toward pursuing different adaptive strategies (Penner et al., 2005). For example, analyzing the family background of a large sample of individuals, one of us found that prosocials, relative to proselfs, came from families with more siblings, particularly sisters, and they also had a more secure attachment style (Van Lange et al., 1997). Also, prosocials were less likely to be first-borns. It might be interesting for further research to look into other developmental differences shaping altruistic orientations, such as age differences between siblings, children, and family stability (Sulloway, 1996).

Furthermore, it is possible that social value orientations are affected by present social circumstances that activate either a cooperative or competitive strategy. For example, in a relatively stable working environment it pays to cooperate with someone on a first encounter as you may meet that same person again. In contrast, in settings characterized by many short-term exchanges with strangers, like in the car-sale or estate-agency business, it may pay to cheat every now and then. In the same way, cross-cultural differences in altruism (Triandis, 1994) may be traced back to differences in the stability of the social environment, which may favor a particular behavioral strategy. For example, encountering an extended family member is more likely to happen in a collectivistic culture than in an individualistic culture, and it therefore pays not to cheat so as to avoid damaging one's reputation (Moghaddam, 1998).

Finally, it is possible that individual differences in altruism can be sustained, to some extent, through *frequency-dependent selection* (Mealey, 1995). This is particularly relevant for the competitive orientation, which is found among only 5–10% of the population. As long as the frequency of individuals who constantly cheat is sufficiently small, this strategy may be sustained in a population, because the costs of fully eradicating this strategy are higher than the damage it does. Once this strategy spreads through a population, however, the benefits of cheating decrease because there would be more pressure on the evolution of protective mechanisms to detect and punish cheaters.

Thus, the existence of individual differences in altruism is compatible with an evolutionary theory of social exchange if we assume that social exchange is an inherently flexible system sensitive to environmental cues. Interactions between childhood and adulthood experiences as well as minor variations in genetic material probably determine whether individuals approach social dilemmas with more selfish or selfless intentions. Yet, such minor personality differences can have profound effects on the outcomes of any social exchange, as shown in prisoner's dilemma research (Kelley & Stahelski, 1970).

THE INDIVIDUAL WITHIN SOCIETY

Humans are Social Animals

This is a true, but incomplete statement. Unlike members of other social species, humans have evolved a unique capacity to act prosocially toward genetic strangers, sometimes in very large groups. To explain the rich patterns of altruism and prosocial behavior, in this chapter we have gone back to the ancestral world of the Pleistocene where humans spent 95% of their history living in highly interdependent nomadic hunter–gatherer bands, presumably of around 50–200 individuals (Barrett et al., 2002). To reap the numerous benefits of group life (e.g., group defense, food sharing), our ancestors had to come up with various cooperative solutions to a range of social dilemmas that they encountered on a daily basis (Kenrick et al., 2003; Van Vugt, 1998).

Given the necessity of group living, it is not unlikely that, through evolutionary time, humans evolved a specific psychological and behavioral system that enables them to solve such dilemmas. An example of such a system is *social exchange*, which makes it possible for humans to engage in altruistic exchanges with other individuals in dyads or larger groups. We have reviewed the social psychological literature on altruism and cooperation for evidence that humans possess an evolved psychology of social exchange. This review has highlighted a range of social psychological adaptations that could have been in place to make social exchanges between individuals and within groups possible. Trust, forgiveness, empathy, social norms, group identification, and group stability are but a few examples of such social psychological mechanisms, which protect altruistic individuals, at least to some extent, against the dangers of cheating and free riding.

The Function of Society

Before closing, we wish to address a final peculiarity of human social behavior, the ability to cooperate in extremely large social units, sometimes comprising millions of individuals working together—as in the example of nation states or mass social movements (Van Vugt et al., 2000). Can an evolved psychology of social exchange, which is rooted in adaptations for small group interaction, account for this? For various reasons, we believe it can.

First, one should realize that these large social units consist of many levels of groupings that are hierarchically linked. For example, a country is divided into regions, which in turn are divided into cities, city areas, streets, and so forth. Because of the interrelations between these levels, what seems to be an altruistic act on the level of society (e.g., engaging in water conservation) may, in fact, be motivated by the fear of social sanctions within a much smaller community (Van Vugt, 2001).

Second, the pressures on humans for operating in flexible social exchange units have made it possible for humans to form emotional attachments with social groups in addition to forging interpersonal bonds. The capacity for group identification may have resulted from this selection pressure. Once the capacity is there, it can be easily extended to social organizations on a much larger scale, such as identifying with one's local football team, the members of one's social class or country.

Third, humans possess a unique mechanism of information exchange, language, which makes it possible to identify cheaters and free riders more effectively, and on a much larger scale than for other social animals. Computer simulations show that if individuals can exchange information about free riders then it becomes much harder for free riders to invade a population of cooperators (Enquist & Leimar, 1993). Reputational concerns mushroom if individuals have the opportunity to gossip about each other (Dunbar, 1993). Social dilemma research also shows that cooperation rates in larger groups increase dramatically when individuals have the opportunity to talk to each other (Dawes, McTavish, & Shaklee, 1977). In this regard, it is not surprising that some theorists have argued that the language capacity and a large brain size, in general, evolved for the specific purpose of fostering cooperation within large groups (i.e., the social brain hypothesis; Dunbar, 1993).

Finally, large-scale cooperation can be sustained in the presence of moral norms, another unique feature of the human psyche (but see de Waal, 1996). In small groups, altruists can punish cheaters by themselves, however, in large groups the altruists must rely on others to do the sanctioning for them. Selection pressures on increasing group size—possibly for the purpose of improving group defense against either predators or rival groups (Alexander, 1987; Barrett et al., 2002)—may have created pressures to evolve a moral system whereby penalties were not just imposed on cheaters but also on individuals who failed to punish cheaters (Fehr & Fishbacher, 2003). Such moral norms, which are in today's society conveyed through the state or the church ("Thou shall not steal"), can be an effective means of sustaining prosocial behavior on societal scale (Wilson, 2002).

CONCLUSION

This chapter outlined an evolutionary perspective on human altruism and prosocial behavior. We argued that prosocial tendencies have evolved (at least in part) to reap the benefits of social exchanges in order to adapt to social dilemmas and related conflicts between the interests of two or more individuals. We have specified a range of conditions under which an evolved psychology of prosocial behavior (based on social exchange) could emerge and reviewed the social psychological literature for evidence. Research on a range of interpersonal processes (e.g., empathy, negativity effects, and forgiveness) and group processes (e.g., group identification and xenophobia) is generally consistent with hypotheses derived from an evolutionary theory of social exchange.

This chapter suggests (at least to us) that the search for social psychological adaptations underlying altruism and prosocial behavior is a worthwhile enterprise. We hope that the readers of this chapter will take up the challenge to conduct further research on altruism, which connects social psychological and evolutionary perspectives. Only then will we move toward a more complete understanding of one of the great puzzles of human behavior, altruism.

ACKNOWLEDGMENT

The first author was supported by a grant from the Leverhulme Trust Foundation (F/00180/L).

NOTES

1. The social psychological literature draws a distinction between altruism and prosocial behavior (Batson, 1998; Penner et al., 2005). Prosocial behavior refers to any kind of action that benefits others and is motivated by a variety of interpersonal motives, including pursuit of various self-rewards. In contrast, altruism refers to the underlying motivation to increase the welfare of others. In this chapter, we will use these terms interchangeably, because we are primarily interested in understanding actions in which there is an underlying *intention* to help others. If that is not the case, there is not much interesting to be explained. For example, a pedestrian on a zebra crossing who accidentally steps in front of a car, thereby injuring himself, but

saving another person's life is helping the other person. But this is not a case of altruism, and therefore requires no theoretical explanation. Only if the pedestrian steps in front of the car *for the purpose* of saving the other's life are we dealing with a case of altruism, which needs to be explained.

2. This example is reminiscent of the well-known hawks and doves example in the evolutionary biological literature, where over time the outcomes of peaceful interactions between doves exceed the outcomes of repeated interactions between hawks and doves, or hawk–hawk interactions (Maynard-Smith & Price, 1973).

3. This is not to deny that there were no other social problems than social dilemmas in the ancestral world. Numerous important social problems revolve around coordination (e.g., leader–follower problems) or competition (e.g., status and dominance). Undoubtedly, these problems have also shaped the human psychological system. But they are unlikely candidates for the emergence of altruism.

4. This theory should not be confused with exchange theories that were once popular within the social sciences (Homans, 1950). These theories advocated the self-interest model by arguing that social interactions are rational exchanges whereby individuals attempt to minimize the costs and maximize the rewards of their interaction. Such theories have a hard time explaining spontaneous help toward strangers in emergency situations. In contrast, by adopting a selfish-gene model, an evolutionary-based theory of social exchange can explain why individuals sometimes relinquish their immediate interests to help a needy stranger.

REFERENCES

Alexander, R. D. (1987). *The biology of moral systems.* Hawthorne: De Gruyter.

Axelrod, R. (1984). *The evolution of cooperation.* New York: Basic Books.

Barrett, L., Dunbar, R., & Lycett, J. (2002). *Human evolutionary psychology.* Basingstoke: Palgrave.

Batson, C. D. (1998). Altruism and prosocial behavior. In D. Gilbert, S. Fiske, & G. Lindzey (Eds.), *Handbook of social psychology* (pp. 282–316). New York: McGraw-Hill.

Batson, C. D., Duncan, B. D., Ackerman, P., Buckley, T., & Birch, K. (1981). Is empathic emotion a source of altruistic motivation? *Journal of Personality and Social Psychology, 40,* 290–302.

Batson, C. D., Sager, K., Garst, E., Kang, M., Rubchinsky, K., & Dawson, K. (1997). Is empathy-induced helping due to self-other merging? *Journal of Personality and Social Psychology, 73,* 495–509.

Baumeister, R. F., Bratslavsky, E., Finkernauer, C., & Vohs, K. D. (2001). Bad is stronger than good. *Review of General Psychology, 5,* 323–370.

Becker, S., & Eagly, A. H. (2004). The heroism of women and men. *American Psychologist, 59,* 163–178.

Bendor, J., Kramer, R. M., & Stout, S. (1991). When in doubt... cooperation in a noisy prisoner's dilemma. *Journal of Conflict Resolution, 35,* 691–719.

Brewer, M. B. (1979). In group bias in the minimal group paradigm: A cognitive-motivational analysis. *Psychological Bulletin, 86,* 307–324.

Boyd, R., & Richerson, P. J. (1985). *Culture and the evolutionary process.* Chicago: University of Chicago Press.

Burch, R. L., & Gallup, G. G. (2000). Perceptions of paternal resemblance predict family violence. *Evolution and Human Behavior, 21,* 429–435.

Burnstein, E., Crandall, C., & Kitayama, S. (1994). Some neo-Darwinian decision rules for altruism: Weighing cues for inclusive fitness as a function of the biological importance of the decision. *Journal of Personality and Social Psychology, 67,* 773–789.

Campbell, D. T. (1975). On the conflicts between biological and social evolution and between psychology and moral tradition. *American Psychologist, 30,* 1103–1126.

Caporael, L., Dawes, R. M., Orbell, J., & Vandekragt, A. J. (1989). Selfishness examined. *Behavioral and Brain Sciences, 12,* 683–739.

Cialdini, R. B., & Fultz, J. (1990). Interpreting the negative mood-helping literature via mega analysis: A contrary view. *Psychological Bulletin, 107,* 210–214.

Cialdini, R. B., Brown, S. L., Lewis, B. P., Luce, C., & Neuberg, S. L. (1997). Reinterpreting the empathy-altruism relationship: When one into one equals oneness. *Journal of Personality and Social Psychology, 73,* 481–494.

Clark, M. S., & Mills, J. (1979). Interpersonal attraction in exchange and communal relationships. *Journal of Personality and Social Psychology, 37,* 12–24.

Cosmides, L., & Tooby, J. (1992). Cognitive adaptations for social exchange. In J. Barkow et al., *The adapted mind: Evolutionary psychology and the generation of culture* (pp. 163–28). New York: Oxford University Press.

Darwin, C. (1871). *The descent of man.* London: Murray.

Dawes, R. M. (1980). Social dilemmas. *Annual Review of Psychology, 31,* 169193.

Dawes, R. M., McTavish, J., & Shaklee, H. (1977). Behavior, communication, and assumptions about other people's behavior in a commons dilemma situation. *Journal of Personality and Social Psychology, 35,* 1–11.

Dawkins, R. (1976). *The selfish gene.* Oxford: Oxford University Press.

DeBruine, L. M. (2004). Resemblance to self increases the appeal of child faces to both men and women. *Evolution and Human Behavior, 25,* 142–154.

De Cremer, D., & Van Vugt, M. (1999). Social identification effects in social dilemmas: A transformation of motives. *European Journal of Social Psychology, 29,* 871–893.

Dunbar, R. M. (1993). The co-evolution of neo-cortical size, group size and language in humans. *Behavioral and Brain Sciences, 16,* 681–735.

Enquist, M., & Leimar, O. (1993). The evolution of cooperation in mobile organisms. *Animal Behavior, 45,* 747–757.

Essock-Vitale, S. M., & McGuire, M. T. (1985). Women's lives viewed from an evolutionary perspective. II. Patterns of helping. *Ethology and Sociobiology, 6,* 155–173.

Fehr, E., & Fischbacher, U. (2003). The nature of human altruism. *Nature, 425,* 785–791.

Fincham, F. D. (2000). The kiss of the porcupines: from attributing responsibility to forgiving. *Personal Relationships, 7,* 1–23.

Frank, R. (1988). *Passions within reason.* New York: Norton.

Gallucci, M., Van Lange, P. A. M., & Ouwerkerk, J. (2004). *The evolution of small groups.* Unpublished manuscript, Free University, Amsterdam.

Gardner, G. T., & Stern, P. C. (1996). *Environmental problems and human behavior.* New York: Allyn & Bacon.

Haidt, J. (2001). The emotional dog and its rational tail: A social intuitionist approach to moral judgment. *Psychological Review, 108,* 814–834.

Hamilton, W. D. (1964). The genetical evolution of social behavior, I, II. *Journal of Theoretical Biology, 7,* 1–52.

Hardin, G. (1968). The tragedy of the commons. *Science, 162,* 1243–1248.

Haselton, M. G., & Buss, D. M. (2000). Error management theory: A new perspective on biases in cross-sex mind reading. *Journal of Personality and Social Psychology, 78,* 81–91.

Hawkes, K. (1993). Why hunter–gatherers work: An ancient version of the problem of public goods. *Current Anthropology, 34*, 341–361.

Holmes, J. G., & Rempel, J. K. (1989). Trust in close relationships. In C. Hendrick (Ed.), *Review of personality and social psychology* (Vol. 10, pp. 187–220). London: Sage.

Homans, G. (1950). *The human group.* London: Routledge.

Johnson, D. J., & Rusbult, C. E. (1989). Resisting temptation: Devaluation of alternative partners as a means of maintaining commitment in close relationships. *Journal of Personality and Social Psychology, 57*, 967–980.

Karremans, J. C., Van Lange, P. A. M., Ouwerkerk, J., & Kluwer, E. S. (2003). When forgiving enhances psychological well-being: The role of interpersonal commitment. *Journal of Personality and Social Psychology, 84*, 1011–1026.

Kelley, H. H., & Stahelski, A. J. (1970). Social interaction basis of cooperators' and competitors' beliefs about others. *Journal of Personality and Social Psychology, 16*, 66–91.

Kenrick, D., Li, N. P., & Butner, J. (2003). Dynamical evolutionary psychology: Individual decision rules and emergent social norms. *Psychological Review, 110*, 3–28.

Komorita, S. S., & Parks, C. D. (1994). *Social dilemmas.* Dubuque, IA: Brown & Benchmark.

Kramer, R. M., & Brewer, M. B. (1984). Effects of group identity on resource use in a simulated commons dilemma. *Journal of Personality and Social Psychology, 46*, 1044–1057.

Krebs, D. & Janicki, M. (2002). Biological foundations of moral norms. In M. Schaller, & C. Crandall (Eds.), *Psychological foundations of culture.* Hillsdale, NJ: Erlbaum.

Levine, J. L., & Moreland, R. (2002). Group reactions to loyalty and disloyalty. In E. Lawler, & S. Thye (Eds.), *Group cohesion, trust, and solidarity* (Advances in group processes, Vol. 19, pp. 203–228). Amsterdam: Elsevier Science.

Liebrand, W. B. G. (1984). The effects of social motives communication and group size on behavior in an *n*-person multi-stage mixed motive game. *European Journal of Social Psychology, 14*, 239–264.

Maynard-Smith, J., & Price, G. (1973). The logic of animal conflict. *Nature, 246*, 15–18.

McAndrew, F. T. (2002). New evolutionary perspectives on altruism: Multi-level selection and costly signaling theories. *Current Directions in Psychological Science, 11*, 79–82.

McClintock, C., & Liebrand, W. B. G. (1988). Role of interdependence structure, individual value orientation, and another's strategy on social decision-making: A transformational analysis. *Journal of Personality and Social Psychology, 55*, 396–409.

McCullough, M. E., Worthington, E. L., Jr., & Rachal, K. C. (1997). Interpersonal forgiving in close relationships. *Journal of Personality and Social Psychology, 73*, 321–336.

Mealey, L. (1995). The sociobiology of sociopathy: An integrated evolutionary model. *Behavioral and Brain Sciences, 18*, 523–599.

Moghaddam, F. M. (1998). *Social psychology: Exploring universals across cultures.* New York: W. H. Freeman.

Moreland, R. L., & Levine, J. M. (1982). Socialization in small groups: Temporal changes in individual-group relations. In L. Berkowitz (Ed.), *Advances in experimental social psychology* (Vol. 15, pp. 137–192). New York: Academic Press.

Murnighan, J. K., & Roth, A. E. (1983). Expecting continued play in Prisoner's Dilemma games: A test of several models. *Journal of Conflict Resolution, 27*, 279–300.

Murray, S. L., Holmes, J. G., & Griffin, D. (1996). The benefits of positive illusions: Idealization and the construction of satisfaction in close relationships. *Journal of Personality and Social Psychology, 70*, 79–98.

Nesse, R. M. (2001). *Evolution and the capacity for commitment.* New York: Russell Sage Foundation.

Neyer, F. J., & Lang, F. R. (2003). Blood is thicker than water: Kinship orientation across adulthood. *Journal of Personality and Social Psychology, 84,* 310–321.

Ostrom, E. (1990). *Governing the commons.* New York: Cambridge University Press.

Park, J. H., & Schaller, M. (2005). Does attitude similarity serve as a heuristic cue for kinship? Evidence of an implicit cognitive association. *Evolution and Human Behavior, 26,* 158–170.

Penner, L., Piliavin, J., Dovidio, J., & Schroeder, D. (2005). Prosocial behavior: Multilevel perspectives. *Annual Review of Psychology, 56,* 365–392.

Reeder, G., & Brewer, M. B. (1979). A schematic model of dispositional attribution in interpersonal perception. *Psychological Review, 86,* 61–79.

Rusbult, C. E. (1983). A longitudinal test of the investment model: The development (and deterioration) of satisfaction and commitment in heterosexual involvements. *Journal of Personality and Social Psychology, 45,* 101–117.

Rusbult, C. E., & Van Lange, P. A. M. (2003). Interdependence, interaction, and relationships. *Annual Review of Psychology, 54,* 351–375.

Rusbult, C. E., Van Lange, P. A. M., Wildschut, T., Yovetich, N. A., & Verette, J. (2000). Perceived superiority in close relationships: Why it exists and persists. *Journal of Personality and Social Psychology, 79,* 521–545.

Schmitt, D. P., & Pilcher, J. J. (2004). Evaluating evidence of psychological adaptation. *Psychological Science, 15,* 643–649.

Sherif, M., & Sherif, C. W. (1953). *Groups in harmony and tension.* New York: Harper Row.

Simpson, J. A., Gangestad, S. W., & Lerma, M. (1990). Perception of physical attractiveness: Mechanisms involved in the maintenance of romantic relationships. *Journal of Personality and Social Psychology, 59,* 1192–1201.

Stern, P. C. (1995). Why do people sacrifice for their nations? *Political Psychology, 16,* 217–235.

Sulloway, F. (1996). *Born to rebel.* New York: Pantheon.

Tajfel, H., & Turner, J. C. (1986). The social identity theory of intergroup behavior. In S. Worchel & W. Austin (Eds.), *Psychology of intergroup relations* (pp. 7–24). Chicago: Nelson-Hall.

Taylor, S. E. (1991). Asymmetrical effects of positive and negative events: The mobilization-minimization hypothesis. *Psychological Bulletin, 110,* 67–85.

Triandis, H. C. (1994). *Culture and social behavior.* New York: McGraw-Hill.

Trivers, R. L. (1971). The evolution of reciprocal altruism. *Quarterly Review of Biology, 46,* 35–57.

Tyler, T., & Smith, H. (1998). Social justice and social movements. In D. Gilbert, S. Fiske, & G. Lindzey (Eds.), *Handbook of social psychology* (pp. 595–632). New York: McGraw-Hill.

Van Lange, P. A. M. (1999). The pursuit of joint outcomes and equality in outcomes: An integrative model of social value orientation. *Journal of Personality and Social Psychology, 77,* 337–349.

Van Lange, P. A. M., & Kuhlman, D. M. (1994). Social value orientations and impressions of partner's honesty and intelligence: A test of the might versus morality effect. *Journal of Personality and Social Psychology, 67,* 126–141.

Van Lange, P. A. M., & Rusbult, C. E. (1995). My relationship is better than—and not as bad as—yours is: The perception of superiority in close relationships. *Personality and Social Psychology Bulletin, 21,* 32–44.

Van Lange, P. A. M., Otten, W., De Bruin, E. M. N., & Joireman, J. A. (1997). Development of prosocial, individualistic, and competitive orientations: Theory and preliminary evidence. *Journal of Personality and Social Psychology*, *73*, 733–746.

Van Lange, P. A. M., Ouwerkerk, J., & Tazelaar, M. (2002). How to overcome the detrimental effects of noise in social interaction: The benefits of generosity. *Journal of Personality and Social Psychology*, *82*, 768–780.

Van Lange, P. A. M., Van Vugt, M., & Bekkers, R, Schuyt, T., & Schippers, M. (2006). *From experimental games to real life: The ecological validity of social value orientation*. Unpublished Manuscript, Free University of Amsterdam.

Van Vugt, M. (1998). The conflicts of modern society. *The Psychologist*, *5*, 289–292.

Van Vugt, M. (2001). Community identification moderating the impact of financial incentives in a natural social dilemma. *Personality and Social Psychology Bulletin*, *27*, 1440–1449.

Van Vugt, M., & Chang, K. S. (2006). *Group reactions to loyal and disloyal high status members*. Unpublished manuscript, University of Kent .

Van Vugt, M., & Hart, C. M. (2004). Social identity as social glue: The origins of group loyalty. *Journal of Personality and Social Psychology*, *86*, 585–598.

Van Vugt, M., & Samuelson, C. D. (1999). The impact of metering in a natural resource crisis: A social dilemma analysis. *Personality and Social Psychology Bulletin*, *25*, 731–745.

Van Vugt, M., Hart, C. M., & Chang (2006). *Stability in social dilemmas*. Unpublished manuscript, University of Kent.

Van Vugt, M., Jepson, S. F., Hart, C. M., & De Cremer, D. (2004). Autocraticleadership in social dilemmas: A threat to group stability. *Journal of Experimental Social Psychology*, *40*, 1–13.

Van Vugt, M., Meertens, R. M., & Van Lange, P. A. M. (1995). Car versus public transportation? The role of social value orientations in a real-life social dilemma. *Journal of Applied Social Psychology*, *25*, 258–278.

Van Vugt, M., Snyder, M., Tyler, T., & Biel, A. (2000) *Cooperation in modern society: Promoting the welfare of communities, states, and organizations*. London, UK: Routledge.

de Waal., F. (1996). *Good natured: The origins of right and wrong in humans and other animals*. Cambridge, MA: Harvard University Press.

Wieselquist, J., Rusbult, C. E., Foster, G. A., & Agnew, C. R. (1999). Commitment, prorelationship behavior, and trust in close relationships. *Journal of Personality and Social Psychology*, *77*, 942–966.

Wilkinson, G. S. (1984). Reciprocal food sharing in the vampire bat. *Nature*, *308*, 181–184.

Wilson, D. S. (2002). *Darwin's Cathedral: Evolution, religion, and the nature of society*. Chicago: The University of Chicago Press.

Wilson, E. O. (1975). *Sociobiology: the new synthesis*. Cambridge, MA: Harvard University Press.

Yamagishi, T. (1986). The structural goal/expectation theory of cooperation in social dilemmas. In E. Lawler (Ed.), *Advances in group processes* (Vol. 3, pp. 51–87). Greenwich, CT: JAI Press.

12

The Evolution of Aggression

DAVID M. BUSS and JOSHUA D. DUNTLEY

Out of the more than 10 million animal species that exist, and out of the 4000 mammals that exist, only two species have been documented to form intense coordinated coalitions that raid neighboring territories for the purpose of killing conspecifics. These two species are chimpanzees and humans (Wrangham & Peterson, 1996).

Humans, like chimpanzees, form aggressive, male-bonded coalitions where members support each other in a mutual quest to aggress against others. Human history is filled with records of group-on-group warfare—the Spartans and Athenians, the crusades, the Hatfields and McCoys, the Palestinians and the Israelis, and the Tutsis and the Hutus of Rwanda. Across cultures, men commonly bond with one another to attack other groups or to defend their own group against attack. Humans and chimpanzees share this unique pattern of aggression with each other and with no other terrestrial species (Wrangham & Peterson, 1996). There is a key difference, however, in the way that scientists explain aggression perpetrated by chimps and the aggressive behavior of humans. In the case of chimpanzees, there is resounding agreement that their aggressive behavior is the designed output of context-specific adaptations. In explaining human aggression, social scientists are often quick to marginalize the causal role of evolution, or else mention but fail to adequately consider it (e.g., Baumeister & Vohs, 2004; Staub, 2004; Zimbardo, 2004).

As a result, the field of psychology lacks a complete understanding of questions like: Where does human aggression come from? Has evolution by natural selection fashioned specialized adaptations to inflict costs on other individuals? Have these evolutionary forces acted upon males and females equally, sculpting identical aggressive psychologies?

THEORIES OF AGGRESSION

Contemporary psychological theories of aggression often invoke general learning mechanisms combined with explanations specifying the plagues of modern living—violence in movies and TV, teachings in Western society, the purchase of toy weapons by parents for their children (Berkowitz, 1993). By watching aggressive models on TV, for example, children are said to acquire aggressive dispositions through observational learning (Berkowitz, 1993; Eron, 1982; Huesmann & Eron, 1986). Although these factors undoubtedly play a causal role in the development of aggression, they run aground as *complete* explanations when confronted with the historical and cross-cultural records.

They have trouble in explaining the bioarchaeological findings, which reveal a long history of human violence thousands of years before the invention of guns or TV, or even the rise of Western civilization (see Buss, 2005, for a review of this evidence). Fifty-nine human skeletons, for example, were recently found in a cemetery at Gebel Sahaba in Egyptian Nubia, dating from the Late Paleolithic, between 12 and 14,000 years ago. More than 40% contained embedded stone projectiles. Many had multiple wounds. The majority of injuries appear on male skeletons. Most wounds pierced the left sides of the crania and rib cages, suggesting right-handed killers who attacked while their victims faced them. This is merely one among dozens of discoveries from the bioarcheological record that provide conclusive evidence of humans killing other humans over deep time (Buss, 2005; Larsen, 1997).

Traditional theories of aggression that invoke the plagues of modern living also have trouble in explaining the prevalence of violence among traditional societies that are uninfluenced by Western civilization and entirely lack the exposure to TV (e.g., Chagnon, 1983). Among the Yanomamö of Venezuela, for example, 30% of males die at the hands of other humans, either from within their local tribe or as a result of wars with neighboring tribes (Chagnon, 1988). Although the Yanomamö may be unusually violent as a group, rates of homicide are commonly high among traditional societies, such as the Gebusi of West Africa (Keeley, 1996), the Ache of Paraguay (Hill & Hurtado, 1996) and the Tiwi of Northern Australia (Hart & Pilling, 1960). Even among the relatively peaceful !Kung San of Africa, homicide rates exceed those in the cities of Detroit and Los Angeles (Daly & Wilson, 1988). A deeper set of explanatory principles is needed to understand patterns of aggression in men and women, one that does not rely primarily on modern phenomena such as violence on TV, the mass media, Western society, toys, over-crowding, or the alienation of modern living.

Most social psychology textbooks typically contain chapters on aggression that examine various explanations for its occurrence (e.g., Myers, 1995; Sabini, 1992). Among the explanations considered, one usually finds a section on the "instinct theory of aggression," usually attributed to Freud and the ethologist Konrad Lorenz. The section is selected to represent a class of "biological explanations." According to these accounts, aggressive energy is said to be an instinctual drive that builds up until it explodes. It may be "released" by external stimuli, but its continuous internal production guarantees that it will be "pushed out" one way or another.

This depiction of instinct theory is usually dismissed with dispatch. According to Myers (1995), for example, "the idea that aggression is an instinct collapsed as the list of supposed human instincts grew to include nearly every conceivable human behavior ... what the social scientists had tried to do was to explain social behavior by naming it" (p. 438). The second argument for dismissal is that "instinct theory ... fails to account for the variation in aggressiveness, from person to person and culture to culture" (Myers, 1995, p. 439). According to this argument, "biological" represents those things that are invariant, and so evidence of cultural or individual variability requires "non-biological" explanations.

Berkowitz (1993) provides a more detailed critique. He dismisses the instinct conception on the following grounds: (1) scientists have not discovered any reservoirs of aggressive energy in the brain or rest of body; (2) research rarely reveals spontaneous aggression, but commonly finds that aggressive behavior occurs in response to external stimuli; and (3) there are different types of aggression, not a single type. Following these dismissals, textbook writers proceed to spend the bulk of their coverage on theories of aggression that invoke environmental conditions, such as observational learning as a result of media exposure to violence (for a notable exception, see Kenrick, Neuberg, & Cialdini, 2005).

Perhaps the dismissal of biological explanations was too hasty. During the domination of learning theory, which reigned over psychology for the bulk of the last century, biological explanations were commonly ridiculed. The dichotomies drawn between instincts and learning, biology and environment, or nature and nature, however, are now known to be misleading and logically incoherent (Tooby & Cosmides, 1992). These dichotomies obscure more than they reveal. A primary benefit of an evolutionary model of human aggression is that it is truly integrative. It does not deny the importance of environmental influences. Rather, evolutionary psychology gives us the conceptual tools to understand precisely how and why certain environmental factors affect the psychological adaptations that produce aggression.

The fact that humans show such behavioral flexibility and context-sensitivity is certainly enough evidence to discard notions of inflexible aggressive instincts invariably getting "pushed out" into behavior regardless of circumstances. But neither are humans passive receptacles for environmental forces, unformed lumps of clay until molded by reinforcement contingencies. A more complex model is needed—a model anchored in evolutionary psychology.

AGGRESSION AS AN EVOLVED SOLUTION TO ADAPTIVE PROBLEMS

An evolutionary psychological perspective does not yield just one hypothesis about the origins of aggression or any other behavioral phenomenon. Within evolutionary psychology, several hypotheses are sometimes proposed and put into scientific competition with each other. Below we detail several adaptive problems for which aggression is hypothesized to be an evolved solution (see also Buss & Shackelford, 1997). We argue that humans have evolved complex situationally contingent adaptations to inflict costs on other humans in order to solve an array of diverse adaptive problems.

Appropriate the Resources of Others

Humans, perhaps more than any other species, stockpile resources that historically have been valuable for survival and reproduction. These include fertile land and access to fresh water, food, tools, and weapons. There are many means of gaining access to the valuable resources held by others, such as engaging in social exchange, stealing, or trickery. Aggression is also a highly effective means of co-opting the resources of others.

Aggression to appropriate resources can occur at the individual or group level. At the individual level, one can use physical force to take resources from others. Modern-day forms include bullies at school who take lunch-money, books, leather jackets, or designer sneakers from other children (Olweus, 1978). Childhood aggression is commonly about resources, such as toys and territory (Campbell, 1993). Adult forms include muggings and beatings as a means to forcibly extract money or other goods from others. The *threat* of aggression may be enough to secure resources from others, as when a child gives up his lunch money to prevent being beaten or a small-store owner gives mobsters money for "protection" to prevent his or her business from being ransacked.

People, particularly men, often form coalitions for the purposes of forcibly co-opting the resources of others. Among the Yanomamö, for example, male coalitions raid neighboring tribes and forcibly take food and reproductive-aged women (Chagnon, 1983). Throughout human recorded history, warfare has been used to co-opt the land possessed by others, and to the victors go the spoils. Selection has favored aggressive strategies when the benefits, on average, outweighed the costs in the currency of fitness. Thus, one hypothesis of the origins of aggression is to acquire reproductively relevant resources.

Defend against Attack

The presence of aggressive conspecifics poses a serious adaptive problem for would-be victims—they stand to lose valuable resources that are co-opted by the aggressors. In addition, victims may suffer injury or death, impeding both survival and reproduction. Victims of aggression may also lose in the currency of status and reputation. The loss of face or honor that results from being abused with impunity can lead to further abuse by others, who may select victims in part based on the ease with which they can be exploited or their unwillingness to retaliate.

Aggression, therefore, can be used to defend against attack. It can help to prevent one's resources from being forcibly taken and cultivate a reputation that deters other would-be aggressors. And aggression can be used to prevent the loss of status and honor that would otherwise follow from being victimized with impunity. Defense against attack, in summary, is a second adaptive problem for which aggression evolved as a solution.

Inflict Costs on Intrasexual Rivals

A third adaptive problem is posed by same-sex rivals who are vying for access to the same resources. One such resource consists of access to valuable members of the opposite sex. The image of the beach bully kicking sand in the face of a weaker man and walking away with the man's girlfriend is a stereotyped notion of intrasexual competition, but the underlying logic it conveys is powerful.

Aggression to inflict costs on rivals can range from verbal barbs to beatings and killings. Both men and women derogate their same-sex rivals, impugning their status and reputation to make the rivals less desirable to members of the other sex (Buss & Dedden, 1990). At the other end of the spectrum, men sometimes kill their same-sex rivals in duels. Bar fights that start as trivial altercations sometimes escalate to the point of death (Daly & Wilson, 1988). And men sometimes kill other men discovered to have had sex with their wives or girlfriends (Daly & Wilson, 1988).

Since evolution operates according to design differences that contribute to differential success at reproductive competition, a cost inflicted on a rival often can translate into a benefit for the perpetrator. According to this third evolutionary hypothesis, a key function of verbal and physical aggression is to inflict costs on same-sex rivals.

Ascend Dominance Hierarchies

Aggression, in some contexts, functions to increase one's status or power within existing social hierarchies. Among the Ache of Paraguay and the Yanomamö of Venezuela, for example, men engage in ritual club fights with other men. Men who have survived many club fights are admired and feared, and so attain status and power as a result of their successful aggression (Chagnon, 1983; Hill & Hurtado, 1996). Modern societies have ritualized aggression in the form of boxing matches, for example, where the victor experiences status elevation and the loser status loss.

Men who expose themselves to danger in warfare to kill enemies are regarded as brave and courageous, and consequently experience an elevation in their status within the group (Chagnon, 1983; Hill & Hurtado, 1996). Within street gangs, men who display ferocity in their beatings of fellow or rival gang members experience status elevation (Campbell, 1993).

The hypothesis that physical aggression sometimes serves the adaptive function of status elevation does not imply that this strategy works in all groups. Aggression within many groups may result in a status decrement. A professor who punched another professor at a faculty meeting or while teaching a class, for example, would almost certainly experience a decline in status.

Dissuade Romantic Partners from Infidelity

A fifth hypothesis is that aggression and the threat of aggression function to deter long-term mates from sexual infidelity. Much empirical evidence suggests that male sexual jealousy is the leading cause or precipitating context of spousal battering (Daly, Wilson, & Weghorst, 1982). Studies of battered women, for example, document that in the majority of cases, women cite extreme jealousy on the part of their husbands or boyfriends as the key factor leading to their abuse (Dobash

& Dobash, 1984). As repugnant as this may be, some men may beat their wives to deter them from consorting with other men. One method by which this is hypothesized to occur is through women's self-esteem (Buss, 2005). If self-esteem functions, in part, to track a person's mate value (Kirkpatrick & Ellis, 2001), getting beaten may lower a woman's self-esteem and hence self-perceived mate value, creating the belief that she would be unable to find a more desirable mate than the one she currently has.

Regain Former Mates

A sixth evolutionary hypothesis is that aggression and the threat of aggression are part of strategies designed to reacquire mates who have broken off a romantic relationship. On the surface, the use of aggression to attract a former mate may seem counterintuitive. But aggression and the threat of aggression in these contexts could be used as a strategy of negative reinforcement, where aggression is a negative reinforcer that is removed when a relationship is established. The object of the aggression—the desired or former mate—is encouraged to establish a romantic relationship with the aggressor in order to avoid the costs of being a victim of aggression. Indeed, one of the functions of stalking is to regain mates who have defected (Duntley & Buss, 2006). When a man's romantic partner has left the relationship, stalking her inflicts a cost for any attempt she makes to mate with other men, while simultaneously deterring other men from approaching her.

Obtain Sexual Access to the Otherwise Inaccessible

A seventh potential function of aggression is to obtain sexual access to women who are otherwise unwilling (Malamuth, 2005). Sexual aggression ranges from touching a woman's body without her permission, to using threats, to physically forcing a woman to have sex against her will (Buss, 1989). The rates of sexual aggression among humans, in fact, are alarmingly high. Some estimate that as many as 14–25% of women have been forced into unwanted sex at some point in their lives (e.g., Paton & Mannison, 1995). Some species are known to have adaptations to rape, such as scorpion flies and orangutans. One hypothesis is that humans have also evolved adaptations to rape (Thornhill & Palmer, 2000). Our reading of the research suggests that, at present, there is no compelling evidence that humans have evolved adaptations to rape (Buss, 2003; see Symons, 1979; for a similar assessment). Nonetheless, absence of evidence is not evidence of absence.

Whether rape is caused by adaptations specifically designed for forced intercourse, or alternatively is a byproduct of adaptations designed for other functions, evolved psychological mechanisms for aggression almost certainly play a critical role. Once the capacity for aggression evolved within the human repertoire, for example, it could be co-opted to solve adaptive problems that differ from those for which it was originally designed. Obtaining sexual access from unwilling women might be one of those adaptive problems.

AGGRESSION AS A CONTEXT-CONTINGENT STRATEGY

This account of seven pivotal adaptive problems is undoubtedly incomplete; aggression probably is directed toward solving other adaptive problems as well. The key point is that aggression is not a unitary, monolithic, or context-blind strategy. Rather, aggression is likely to be highly context-specific, triggered primarily in circumstances that resemble those in which our ancestors confronted specific adaptive problems and reaped particular benefits.

Consider the use of spousal battering to solve the adaptive problem of a partner's potential infidelity. This adaptive problem is more likely to be confronted by men who are lower in relative mate value than their wives, for example, or who experience a decrement (e.g., loss of a job) in the resources that women value (Buss, 2003). Under these conditions, the probability that a woman might commit infidelity or defect from the relationship altogether is likely to be higher, and so the adaptive problem is confronted more severely. Men in these conditions are predicted to be more aggressive than men whose partners are less likely to commit infidelity or to defect from the relationship.

Adaptive benefits must be evaluated within the context of the costs of carrying out an aggressive strategy. Our use of the terms cost and benefit refer to the effects that a particular strategy had on the fitness of individuals over evolutionary time. Costs led to decreases in fitness and benefits led to fitness increases. Aggression, by definition, inflicts costs on others, and those others cannot be expected to absorb the costs passively or with indifference: "Lethal retribution is an ancient and cross-culturally universal recourse for those subjected to abuse" (Daly & Wilson, 1988, p. 226). One of the most robust findings in aggression research is that aggression tends to cause retaliatory aggression (Berkowitz, 1993; Buss, 1961). This can sometimes lead to escalating cycles of aggression and counter-aggression, as in the fabled family feud between the Hatfields and McCoys (Waller, 1993).

One critical context for costs pertains to the reputational consequences of aggression. Cultures and sub-cultures differ in whether aggression enhances or depresses status. Among "cultures of honor," for example, failure to aggress when insulted can lead to status loss (Nisbett, 1993). A daughter who has brought shame upon the family name by engaging in premarital sex, for example, may be killed as an "honorable" solution to the family's resultant status loss (Daly & Wilson, 1988). The failure to kill a dishonorable daughter may result in a substantial decrease in status in these cultures.

Another dimension of cost is the ability and willingness of the victim to retaliate. Among school children, bullies typically select victims or "whipping boys" who cannot or will not retaliate (Olweus, 1978). Similarly, the husband of a woman whose four strapping brothers and powerful father live nearby will think twice before beating her for flirting with someone else. The presence of extended kin, therefore, is one context of cost that should moderate the manifestation of spousal violence. Recent empirical evidence supports this prediction. In a study of domestic violence in Madrid, Spain, it was found that women with higher densities of genetic kin both inside and outside Madrid experienced lower levels of domestic violence (Figueredo, 1995). A higher density of genetic kin within Madrid appears to have exerted a larger protective effect than kin outside Madrid, suggesting the importance of kin's proximity.

The key point is that an evolutionary psychological perspective predicts that evolved mechanisms will be designed to be sensitive to context, not the rigid invariant expression of aggression depicted in earlier instinct theories. Thus, findings of variability in aggression across contexts, cultures, and individuals in no way falsifies particular evolutionary hypotheses. Indeed, context-sensitivity of mechanisms proposed to produce aggression is a critical lever for testing evolutionary hypotheses.

Earlier researchers in this area concluded that variability simultaneously falsified "biological" theories and confirmed "learning" theories. Evolutionary psychology jettisons this false dichotomy by proposing a specific interactionist model—aggression as evoked by particular adaptive problems confronted in particular cost–benefit contexts. In principle, the mechanisms producing aggression could remain dormant for the entire life of an individual. If a problem ancestrally solvable by aggression is not encountered, cognitive adaptations to produce aggressive behavior will not be activated. Aggression, on this account, is based on evolved psychological mechanisms, but is not rigid or invariant and does not get "pushed out" regardless of circumstances.

WHY ARE MEN TYPICALLY MORE PHYSICALLY AGGRESSIVE THAN WOMEN?

In a sample of homicides committed in Chicago from 1965 through 1980, 86% were committed by men (Daly & Wilson, 1988). Of these, 80% of the victims were also men. Although the exact percentages vary from culture to culture, cross-cultural homicide statistics reveal strikingly similar findings. In all cultures studied to date, men are overwhelmingly more often the killers and their victims are mostly other men. Any reasonably complete theory of aggression must provide an explanation for both facts—why men engage in violent forms of aggression so much more often than women and why other men are most often their victims.

An evolutionary model of intrasexual competition provides the foundation for such an explanation. It starts with the theory of parental investment and sexual selection. In species in which females invest more heavily in offspring than males, females are a valuable limiting resource on male reproduction. Male reproduction is constrained not by their ability to survive, but by their ability to gain sexual access to the high-investing females.

The sex difference in minimum obligatory parental investment (e.g., mammalian females bear the burdens of internal fertilization, placentation, and gestation) means that males can sire more offspring than females. Stated differently, the ceiling on reproduction is much higher for males than for females. This difference leads to differences in the variances in reproduction between the sexes. The differences between the haves and have-nots, therefore, are greater for males than for females.

The greater the variance in reproduction, the more selection favors riskier strategies (including intrasexual competition) within the sex that shows high variance. In an extreme case, such as the elephant seals off the coast of Northern California, 5% of the males sire 85% of all offspring produced in a breeding season (Le Boeuf & Reiter, 1988). Species that show higher variance in the reproduction of one sex compared to the other tend to be highly sexually dimorphic across a variety of physical characteristics. The more intense the effective polygyny, the more dimorphic the sexes are in size and form (Trivers, 1985). There is no reason to believe that the same principle would not apply to sex differences in corresponding cognitive mechanisms.

Effective polygyny means that some males gain more than their "fair share" of copulations, while other males are shut out entirely, banished from contributing to the ancestry of future generations. Such a system leads to more ferocious competition within the high-variance sex. In essence, polygyny selects for risky strategies, including those that lead to violent combat with rivals and those that lead to increased risk-taking to acquire the resources needed to attract members of the high-investing sex. Members of one's own sex are primary competitors for valuable members of the opposite sex.

Violence can occur at the top as well as the bottom of the hierarchy. Given an equal sex ratio, for each man who monopolizes two women, another man is consigned to bachelorhood (Daly & Wilson, 1996). For those facing reproductive oblivion, a risky, aggressive strategy may represent a last resort. The homicide data reveal that men who are poor and unmarried are more likely to kill than their more affluent, married counterparts (Wilson & Daly, 1985). In short, there are two sides to the use of aggression in competitive contexts marked by some degree of polygyny: (1) aggression by a male to "win big," thereby gaining access to multiple mates, and (2) aggression to avoid total reproductive failure by being shut out of mating altogether.

To understand why men would take large risks in mating contexts, let us consider an analogy: Foraging for food. Consider an animal that is able to secure a foraging territory that provides just enough food to stay alive, but insufficient food to breed. Outside this territory are risks, such as predators that may prey upon the animal if the animal leaves its home territory. In this situation, the only males who succeed in breeding are those willing to take risks to venture outside of their secure territory to get food. Some will be killed by predators, of course, and that is why venturing outside is risky. But some will manage to avoid predators, secure additional food, and thereby successfully breed. Those who fail to take the risks to venture outside their territory will fail to breed entirely. This situation selects for risk-taking as a strategy for breeding. Selection in this context acts as a sieve, filtering out those who fail to take risks. Those who play it safe will not leave descendents.

As Daly and Wilson (1988) note, "sexual dimorphism and violent male–male competition are ancient and enduring elements of our human evolutionary history" (p. 143). Current levels of sexual dimorphism among humans are roughly the same as those of our ancestors living 50,000 years ago. Male–male combat among humans, as among other sexually dimorphic mammals, is a leading cause of injury and death among males.

Modern humans have inherited the psychological mechanisms that led to ancestral success. This is not to imply that men have a conscious or unconscious desire to increase their reproductive success. Nor is it meant to imply that men have an "aggression instinct" in the sense of some pent-up energy that must be released. Rather, men have inherited from their ancestors psychological mechanisms sensitive to contexts in which aggression probabilistically leads to the successful solution of particular adaptive problems.

This account provides a parsimonious explanation for the two facts revealed in the cross-cultural homicide record. Males are more often the perpetrators of violence because they are the products of a long history of mild but sustained effective polygyny characterized by risky strategies of intrasexual competition for access to the high-investing sex. The fact that men die on average seven years earlier than women is but one of the many markers of this aggressive intrasexual strategy (Trivers, 1985).

Men are the victims of aggression far more than women because men are in competition primarily with other men. It is other men who form the primary sources of strategic interference, other men who impede access to resources needed to attract women, and other men who try to block their access to women. To the victors go the spoils. The losers remain mateless and sustain injury or even early death.

Women also engage in aggression, and their victims are also typically members of their own sex. The forms of aggression committed by women, however, are typically less florid, less violent, and hence less risky than those committed by men—facts accounted for by the theory of parental investment and sexual selection (see Campbell, 1995, 2002). In studies of verbal aggression through derogation of competitors, for example, women slander their rivals by impugning their physical appearance and hence reproductive value (Buss & Dedden, 1990; Campbell, 1993).

Not only are the functions of aggression in different contexts distinct, the kinds of costs that different forms of aggression inflict are unique. Sexual aggression may deprive women of their preferred mate, subject them to physical harm and reputational damage, and expose them to sexually transmitted diseases. Physical aggression can inflict injuries to body and reputation. And homicide brings the life of another individual to an end. Arguably no other form of aggression has captured the attention of the public and researchers more than murder.

DO HUMANS HAVE EVOLVED HOMICIDE ADAPTATIONS?

"Then she said that since she came back in April she had fucked this other man about ten times. I told her how can you talk love and marriage and you been fucking with this other man. I was really mad. I went into the kitchen and got the knife. I went back to our room and said were you serious when you told me that. She said yes. We fought on the bed, I was stabbing her and her grandfather came up and tried to take the knife out of my hand. I told him to go and call the cops for me. I don't know why I killed the woman, I loved her" (Carlson, 1984, p. 9).

Roughly 1 in 15,000 people is murdered in the United States each year (Stolinsky & Stolinsky, 2000). On first glance, this seems like a fairly rare event. But computed over a 75-year lifespan, this equates to a 1 in 200 chance of being murdered at some point during an individual lifetime (Ghiglieri, 1999). In 1999, homicide ranked 14th among the leading causes of death for men and women of all ages (Centers for Disease Control, 2002). But for men between the ages of 15 and 35, it was the second leading cause of death. For black men between 15 and 35, homicide was the leading cause of death.

Homicide rates in the United States are much higher than in many industrialized nations, exceeding those in the United Kingdom and Japan by a factor of 10; exceeding those in France, Austria, Sweden, and Germany by a factor of 9; and exceeding the rates in Canada, Italy, Portugal, Korea, and Belgium by a factor of 5. But the homicide rates in many other countries are equivalent to or exceed those in the United States (United Nations, 1998). The lifetime likelihood of being murdered in Venezuela and Moldova is 1 in 90, twice that of the United States. In Estonia and Puerto Rico, the likelihood is 1 in 60, three times that of the United States. And in Colombia and South Africa, the likelihood is better than 1 in 20 that a person will die at the hands of a murderer, more than 10 times the lifetime homicide risk in the United States. Even among those nations that currently exhibit low homicide rates, a lack of murder is not a consistent part of their history. Historical evidence suggests that the relative absence of homicide in some countries is a recent invention (e.g., Ruff, 2001; Dower & George, 1995).

Within-culture rates of homicide typically do not include casualties of warfare or genocide. In addition, the murder rates in these nations would undoubtedly be much higher were it not for emergency medical interventions that were not available to our ancestors for most of our evolutionary history. This is precisely the point made by a recent "Ambulance-Homicide Theory." Researchers found that faster ambulances and better emergency room care were significantly responsible for the decrease in homicide rates over the last three decades in the United States. In fact, it has been estimated that there would be 30,000 to 50,000 additional murders in the United States each year—tripling, quadrupling, or more the current homicide rate—without the advances in emergency-care technology that have occurred during the last 30 years (Harris, Thomas, Fisher, & Hirsch, 2002).

Mainstream social scientists often explain the sex differences in homicide rates within the United States by invoking "culture-specific gender norms" (e.g., Berkowitz, 1993). This theory encounters an empirical problem: The sex difference is found in *every culture* across the globe for which homicide statistics are available (Daly & Wilson, 1988). Theories that invoke local cultural norms obviously cannot satisfactorily explain a universal human pattern.

Actual homicides are statistically rare, and thus difficult to study. For every homicide that is actually committed, however, there may be dozens or hundreds of *thoughts* or *fantasies* that individuals entertain about killing another human being. Consider this homicidal fantasy reported by a male undergraduate: "I wanted to kill my old girlfriend. She lives in (another city) and I was just wondering if I could get away with it. I thought about the (price of) airfare and how I might set up an alibi. I also thought about how I would kill her in order to make it look like a robbery. I actually thought about it for about a week and never did come up with anything" (Kenrick & Sheets, 1993, p. 15). This man did not kill his girlfriend. But the recurrence of thoughts about homicide opens up a window for investigation into the psychology of murder.

The evolutionary psychologists Doug Kenrick and Virgil Sheets have capitalized on this opportunity. They conducted two studies on a total of 760 undergraduates. The methods were simple. They asked subjects to provide demographic information, including age and sex, and then to describe the last time they had thoughts about killing someone. They inquired about the circumstances that triggered the violent thoughts as well as the content of those thoughts: "who you wanted to kill, how you imagined doing it, etc" (Kenrick & Sheets, 1993, p. 6). They queried subjects about the frequency of fantasies, the specific relationship with the person they thought of killing, and whether the fantasy had been triggered by a physical attack, a public humiliation, or any of a list of other triggers.

The two studies revealed similar results, so we will focus only on the second study, which was larger and more detailed in scope. First, more men (79%) than women (58%) reported experiencing at least one homicidal fantasy. Second, 38% of the men, but only 18% of the women, reported having had several homicidal fantasies. And third, men's fantasies tended to last longer than women's fantasies. Most women (61%) reported that their homicidal thoughts typically lasted only a few seconds. Most men reported that their homicidal thoughts lasted a few minutes, with 18% reporting that their fantasies lasted a few hours or longer. These findings support the hypothesis that men are psychologically more disposed to homicide than women—a finding also supported by statistics of actual homicides.

Sex differences were also apparent in the triggers of homicidal thoughts. Men were more likely to have homicidal thoughts than women in response to a personal threat (71% vs. 52%), the fact that someone stole something from them (57% vs. 42%), a desire to know what it is like to kill (32% vs. 8%), a conflict over money (27% vs. 10%), and a public humiliation (59% vs. 45%). Men and women differed in the targets of their homicidal fantasies. Men were more likely to fantasize about killing a stranger (53% vs. 33%), a national leader (34% vs. 17%), a boss (35% vs. 21%), and a roommate (34% vs. 23%).

The logic of inclusive fitness theory predicts greater conflicts between children and their stepparents than between children and their genetic parents, and the homicidal fantasy evidence bears this out. Of those who had lived with a stepparent, fully 44% reported fantasies about killing them. And among those who lived for longer than six years with a stepparent, an even larger number—59%—reported such homicidal fantasies. In contrast, the figures for killing a mother or father were lower—31% and 25%, respectively.

How can these findings be explained from an evolutionary perspective? There are two distinct avenues of explanation. The one adopted by Kenrick and Sheets (1993), and also by Daly and Wilson (1988), may be called the "byproduct hypothesis." According to this hypothesis, murder is the byproduct of psychological mechanisms that evolved for their nonlethal consequences. For example, males have evolved a psychological propensity for violence as a means of coercive control and eliminating sources of conflict. This propensity typically results in threats of violence or sub-lethal violence as the behavioral output. Occasionally, however, there is a "slip" in the brinkmanship, such that the violence accidentally bubbles over into a homicide: "There is brinkmanship in any such contest, and the homicides by spouses of either sex may be considered slips in this dangerous game" (Daly & Wilson, 1988). The same slips may occur in other forms of homicide, such as male–male homicide.

An alternative is "Homicide Adaptation Theory" (Buss & Duntley, 2006). According to this theory, humans, and especially men, have evolved specific psychological mechanisms that steer them toward the murder of conspecifics under certain, predictable circumstances such as warfare, intrasexual rivalry, or spousal infidelity or defection. Humans presumably have homicidal fantasies as one component of these evolved homicide adaptations. In many circumstances, the costs of killing are evaluated to be too great—in all societies, a person risks the wrath of kin and punishment from other interested members of the group (Daly & Wilson, 1988). These costs are weighted and deter many from killing. The hypothesis is not that men have a "killer instinct" whereby they are impelled to kill regardless of circumstances. Rather, we are proposing that acts of killing are one part of the behavioral output of evolved homicide mechanisms triggered by specific contextual inputs. The presence of these inputs indicates an adaptive problem for which homicide was ancestrally a solution that, on average, led to greater levels of survival and reproduction than competing behavioral strategies. Homicide is only one among many possible solutions for any given adaptive problem. Whether homicide or some other strategy is adopted depends on cost–benefit calculations made by evolved mechanisms designed to weigh the likely outcomes of competing strategies. Most of the time, after all of the costs and benefits associated with committing homicide are considered, nonlethal measures will be adopted instead. Buss and Duntley (2006) hypothesize that, in ancestral environments, homicide would only have been an effective solution to rare, very specific adaptive problems.

According to Homicide Adaptation Theory, murder should not be considered as just the extreme end of a continuum of violence. It is an evolutionarily unique and powerful strategy (Buss, 2005; Buss & Duntley, 2006; Duntley, 2005; Duntley & Buss, 2005). Killing a conspecific leads to the absolute end of direct competition between two individuals. The person who is killed can no longer compete with his killer. A murdered competitor can no longer directly influence the environment or social context that he shared with his murderer. The unique outcomes of homicide would have created equally unique selection pressures to shape human psychology specifically for contexts of homicide (Buss & Duntley, 2006; Duntley & Buss, 2005).

Different ancestral problems required different specific solutions. We propose that there are *multiple*, different psychological adaptations for homicide, each of which is devoted to the solution of different kinds of adaptive problems. The problems incumbent in committing infanticide, for example, are quite different from those that need to be solved in contexts of warfare. As a result, psychological design for infanticide is hypothesized to be distinct from psychological design for warfare. Similarly, psychological design for mate homicide in men is distinct from psychological design for mate killing in women. Some information processing mechanisms are undoubtedly shared between the different adaptations for homicide and with adaptations for the solution of other domains of adaptive problems. Selection would favor the sharing of subroutines performing the same function over reinventing them anew for each psychological adaptation. However, we argue that any given adaptation for homicide has at least one design feature that is distinct from other adaptations.

Nature of Psychological Mechanisms for Homicide

We hypothesize that there were specific combinations of adaptive problems individuals recurrently faced in the evolutionary past that would have been best solved by killing. Selection would have favored individuals who possessed psychological adaptations that reliably led to the production of murderous behavior when they faced such contexts. The best solution to most adaptive problem contexts faced by our ancestors did not involve homicide. However, the potential fitness gains accomplished by the use of murder to solve a small, specific set of adaptive problems would have selected for psychological adaptations to kill.

We hypothesize that psychological mechanisms for homicide function to steer an individual in the direction of adaptive behaviors that reliably result in the death of another individual. This is accomplished through a variety of affective, motivational, and computational systems that narrow in on murder as the solution to adaptive problems. The adaptive problems to which we are referring are fluid, unfolding and changing over time. As time passes and other individuals pursue adaptive strategies, the nature of adaptive problems changes. And the solution to one set of adaptive problems may reliably create others. It is the reliable unfolding of adaptive problems that shaped psychological adaptations in humans over evolutionary time, including those that end others' lives.

The adaptive problems homicide is capable of solving, the range of behaviors capable of killing specific conspecifics, and the consequences of the homicide combine to create the selection pressures that shaped adaptations for murder. A large number of distinct adaptive problems are potentially solvable by homicide. We hypothesize that psychological adaptations for homicide are correspondingly numerous and distinct. Different adaptive problems were ancestrally solvable by murdering a cheating mate, for example, than by killing a disabled newborn. The range of behaviors capable of ending the lives of each of these people is largely nonoverlapping. Different levels of force are required to strangle an infant and an adult. There is different risk of the killer being injured in each case. The majority of the consequences of each kind of homicide are also distinct. An infant poses less danger to the killer than an adult. Different categories of adaptive problems are potentially solvable through the murder of infants and adults. Different reputational consequences also follow from each kind of homicide. The differences between each kind of killing illustrate the very large chasm in the selection pressures that shaped psychological adaptations for each kind of murder. These differences would have shaped corresponding differences in the adaptations' functional design.

Just as there are likely differences in the psychological adaptations that lead to murder as the solution to different adaptive problems, there are also probable similarities in the function of many, if not all, homicide mechanisms. What follows is a brief outline of some of the evolved functional components of human murder adaptations (for a more complete treatment, see Buss & Duntley, 2006).

Sensitive to Adaptive Problems Solvable by Homicide

It would not be adaptive for homicide adaptations to be activated invariantly across contexts, just as it would not be adaptive for a person to actively experience a fear of snakes if there were no snakes nearby. Because committing homicide frequently involves the risk of incurring significant costs, such as being punished or killed by the victim's kin and social allies, one design feature of adaptations for murder is that they should only become activated when an individual faces problems with extremely high fitness consequences ancestrally solvable by killing a conspecific. We hypothesize that such contexts include threats to the lives of self or kin, the loss of a valuable mate, the loss of valuable territory or resources, and the loss of status and reputation.

Catalog Homicide-Relevant Information

A second hypothesized design feature of adaptations for murder is the cataloging of homicide-relevant information present in the local environment. Such information includes: specific methods of killing and the location of tools for murder available in local environments, the lethality of each method, and the particular reputational consequences of killing in solution to different adaptive problems. Other mechanisms are hypothesized to simultaneously keep track of the particular costs and benefits of each method of killing. This information would be used to calibrate murder adaptations to favor some available murder strategies over others.

Estimate Formidability of Victims

One danger of murdering another person is the risk of being physically injured in the process. To address this problem, we hypothesize that selection fashioned mechanisms to factor the physical formidability of the victim into decisions about which among available methods would be most effective at killing the person. Similar mechanisms would also estimate the formidability of the kin and social allies of the intended victim, providing information about the ability to fend off retribution from them and control the resources that may be acquired through killing.

Forecast Likely Consequences of Murder

The range of outcomes of killing in solution to each adaptive problem is hypothesized to be as recurrent over our evolutionary history as the specific contexts leading to murder. This would have provided selection pressure for mechanisms capable of forecasting the likely future consequences of murder, such as the reputational consequences of the homicide and the probability and type of retribution likely to be pursued by the kin and social allies of the victim.

Cognitively Simulate Killing

Symons (1979) argues that sexual fantasies evolved to deal with rare, complex problems. His argument is based on the premise that a function of ideation is to help solve the adaptive problems. Even if only a small fraction of sexual fantasies lead to an actual sexual encounter, the fantasies themselves are still functional, low-cost preparations for events with potentially high fitness consequences. It is the high fitness consequences of sexual behavior that selected for the production of fantasies about sex. Similarly, we argue that the high fitness consequences of homicide selected for specific, directed thoughts of murder.

We hypothesize that elaborate fantasies about killing are not required in every context in order to effectively produce homicidal behavior. The problems a new mother needs to solve in order to commit infanticide, for example, are very small in number and simple in nature. Newborns are helpless to defend themselves and are physiologically fragile. Their deaths can be produced with greater haste, with less planning, and can be more easily blamed on causes other than murder. We hypothesize that the so-called "shaken baby syndrome" is the result of activation of adaptations for infanticide. It is a frequently occurring behavior in adults who become frustrated with the costs inflicted on them by a squalling infant. Parents who shake their babies often report that they only did it to try to quiet their children down. The behavior also reliably leads to infant death from traumatic brain injuries (Geddes et al., 2003). The killing of healthy, adult rivals, on the other hand, is relatively more difficult to complete and would benefit from the additional computational power of scenario building. Adults will actively fight back against a killer. Substantially more force is required to bring about rivals' violent deaths. It is also more difficult to make the violent death of a rival look like something other than a homicide, which may lead the genetic relatives and social allies of a murdered rival to seek revenge on the killer.

A number of problems need to be addressed in order for a cognitive system to support homicidal ideations. First, psychological mechanisms must activate scenario building and focus it on homicide as the solution to an adaptive problem or problems. We hypothesize that homicidal ideation, like actual murders, will be more likely to occur when the elimination of another individual contributes to the solution of numerous adaptive problems simultaneously. The more problems killing solves, the more likely someone will end up dead. Consistent with Symons's logic about sexual fantasies, thoughts of murder occur in response to rare, complex sets of circumstances for which the devotion of greater cognitive resources is required to evaluate the efficacy of and possibly implement a homicidal strategy.

Once ideation is activated and focused to explore a homicidal strategy, specific content must be provided to move the scenario forward. Not any nor all kinds of content would be appropriate for a murder fantasy. We hypothesize that mechanisms evolved specifically to direct scenario building for homicide. These mechanisms select and organize inputs, and introduce them into homicidal fantasies across time. "Decisions" about what input to introduce and when are based on the ancestral frequency and fitness consequences of similar scenarios calibrated by experience acquired during ontogeny. We hypothesize that not one, but many homicidal scenarios may be constructed, guided by psychological mechanisms that organize and reorganize the introduction of inputs over time to explore the range of possible contingencies and outcomes of a plan to kill. In sum, mechanisms are hypothesized to vary the kind of information introduced and the timing of the introduction of specific variables across multiple, distinct incarnations of a plan for murder. Homicide mechanisms are also hypothesized to change the values of the individual variables that are introduced.

We hypothesize that specific mechanisms evolved to forecast the likely future costs and benefits of each specific behavior leading to a homicide. These forecasts are based on two factors: would-be killers' fantasized future representations of themselves (FFK for fantasized future killer) and features of the fantasized future environment (FFE) relevant to a plan for murder. Some features of both the FFK and FFE are essentially unchanging, such as a person's height and the force of gravity, and would be constants in calculations of the likely outcomes of a homicidal strategy. Other features are more variable. We hypothesize that mechanisms evolved to produce estimates of the values of variable features of the FFK and FFE in which a strategy of homicide may be adopted.

Each variable feature is likely variable only within a specific range of values, often functionally represented in terms of a normal distribution. For example, the formidability of intended murder victims is likely to vary predictably within a fairly narrow range. Estimates could be based on such factors as their size, age, and observations of their behavior. These estimates are hypothesized to be integrated into calculations of the likely future effectiveness of a particular plan for murder.

Uncertainty

An important factor hypothesized to increase the complexity of using murder as part of a strategy to solve adaptive problems is uncertainty. Varying degrees of uncertainty pervade every aspect of adaptive problems solvable by homicide. There is uncertainty about the reliability of the environmental cues that activate adaptations for homicide. For example, is a rival having clandestine sexual encounters with a person's mate or are the two of them just friends who enjoy each other's company? Uncertainty also surrounds the estimates of variables entered into calculations of every aspect of a homicide scenario—from how much physical force a particular weapon will require to end someone's life, to how vigorously the victim will fight back, to how easily the murder could be covered up, to how likely genetic relatives of the victim will be to seek revenge. Seeking out additional information is one strategy to decrease uncertainty. A person can test the strength of social alliances, the lethality of a weapon, or learn the daily routines of intended victims to discover when they are most vulnerable. Meticulous planning of every detail of a murder informed by additional information may also make killers' minds more certain of the outcome of their plans. Some degree of uncertainty, however, always remains.

As a homicidal strategy actually unfolds over time, some aspects of a situation may occur in ways that were not anticipated. This can happen for at least three reasons. First, incorrect knowledge may be entered into the calculations that are the underpinnings of plans for murder. Assumptions may be made about the formidability of a victim, for example, based on their size, weight, and observations made of them in limited contexts. If the victim earned a black belt in martial arts years before observations were made, then information about his or her formidability would be in error and some methods of killing the person would be less likely to be effective. Second, unanticipated events may confound a plan to kill. For example, a victim may unexpectedly bump into a friend while jogging in the evening, an activity the victim usually does alone. The presence of the victim's friend may be enough to derail plans for the victim's murder. Finally, killers may fail to enter a relevant piece of information into their homicidal plans. A murder may be planned for night, for example, after the victim is asleep. Killers may not consider how much the darkness would cripple their ability to navigate in the victim's home.

It is important to understand how uncertainty can limit the power of homicide scenario building for at least two reasons. First, it suggests that cognitive adaptations for murder must have evolved ways of dealing with the different kinds of uncertainty. Second, it illustrates how errors in plans to kill that stem from problems of uncertainty can derail an attempt at homicide and effectively save a victim's life. In many contexts, we propose that the psychology of would-be killers is not absolutely committed to ending the life of another person rather than doing something else, even if they have a complete plan for murder and have begun implementing that plan. Other intervening factors can redirect a killer's homicidal strategy to nonlethal alternatives at any point in time until their victim is dead.

Clearly, killing people is not the only strategy capable of solving the adaptive problems that can be solved by murder. We propose that mechanisms evolved to weigh the costs and benefits of homicide relative to alternative strategies for the solution of adaptive problems. The process of creating elaborate homicidal scenarios, of developing a plan to end another person's life, we argue, most often leads people to evaluate that the costs of killing are too high and the benefits too low to actually commit murder.

When a homicidal strategy is evaluated to be too costly, we hypothesize that evolved mechanisms to inhibit killing steer an individual away from lethal behaviors. Such mechanisms include: emotional charging that makes thoughts or behaviors leading to homicide feel aversive, the diversion of attention to other, nonlethal strategies, and focused scenario-building dedicated to specific nonlethal alternatives. In rare instances when a course of action involving conspecific killing is evaluated to be the best among alternative strategies, however, we propose that specific evolved mechanisms motivate murder. These mechanisms include: blindness to nonlethal alternatives to homicide, the suspension of empathy or sympathy for the victim, emotional charging capable of producing murderous behaviors, and endocrinological rewards for the exploration and implementation of behaviors capable of killing.

The Power of Scenario Building

It is important not to overestimate the power of unguided scenario building in producing homicidal behavior or any behavior. There is no empirical basis to broadly assert that all behaviors, including homicide, can be accounted for by human ability to cognitively simulate events and "figure things out." Without restrictions on the kinds of information that qualify as relevant inputs and the range of behavioral strategies capable of solving problems, the process of scenario building would succumb to combinatorial explosion (Tooby & Cosmides, 1992), rendering it functionless and a massive waste of cognitive resources. A complete theory of scenario building needs to specify the function of people's fantasies, explain why people fantasize about some things and not others, explain where information inputs to the scenarios come from and why they are used instead of other inputs, explain how cognitive simulations are developed over time, and explain the specific relationship between thoughts of future events and future behaviors. Simply positing that people "learn" how to figure things out is not an adequate explanation without a complete account of how learning takes place, why some things are learned and others are not, and why the building of some scenarios—such as homicidal ideations—persists among people for whom killing likely would never be the most adaptive strategy.

In our arguments, we propose that cognitive simulations require specific inputs to define and guide the situation under consideration that are linked to specific behavioral outputs. We propose that selection operated to define these aspects of scenario building. Over our evolutionary history, individuals who possessed and utilized an evolved menu of inputs that predefined and guided cognitive simulations would have been at an advantage over those with no such guidance. As selection operated on scenario building, it would have favored some menus of inputs, some directions for the unfolding of scenarios, and some consequent behaviors over others. Although cognitive simulations may indeed help to figure things out, they do not do so blindly. The foundation of their content was shaped by the experiences of our ancestors.

Two competing evolutionary hypotheses of killing—the "byproduct hypothesis" and "Homicide Adaptation Theory"—have not yet been pitted against each other in empirical tests. The high prevalence of homicidal fantasies, the predictability of the circumstances that trigger them, the evidence on sex differences, and the premeditated quality of many homicides, however, do not accord well with the byproduct hypothesis. Additionally, advocates of the byproduct hypothesis have failed to specify precisely which mechanisms homicide is a byproduct of, or how these mechanisms reliably malfunction to produce homicide in fairly predictable circumstances. Homicide Adaptation Theory, in contrast, is quite clear about the hypothesized functions of psychological mechanisms that lead to murder. Research designed to test these competing evolutionary hypotheses is underway. Within the next decade, we can expect a resolution of the debate about whether humans have evolved specific homicide mechanisms.

CONCLUSIONS

From the perspective of evolutionary psychology, aggression is not a singular or unitary phenomenon. Rather, it represents a collection of strategies that are manifest under highly specific contextual conditions. The mechanisms underlying aggression have emerged, on this account, as solutions, albeit repugnant ones, to a host of distinct adaptive problems, such as resource procurement, intrasexual competition, hierarchy negotiation, and mate retention.

From an evolutionary perspective, variability in aggression—between the sexes, across individuals, over the lifespan, and across cultures—is predicted. This contrasts markedly from earlier instinct theories in which aggression was presumed to be manifest invariantly, "pushed out" in all people one way or another. It also contrasts with domain-general learning accounts by hypothesizing specific, dedicated psychological mechanisms that have evolved over thousands of generations in response to particular social adaptive problems. Simultaneously, however, an evolutionary perspective illustrates the point that documented variability does not imply that biology is irrelevant. An evolutionary psychological perspective is truly interactionist—it specifies a set of causal conditions in which particular features of the perpetrator, victim, social context, and adaptive problem are likely to evoke aggression as a strategic solution.

An evolutionary perspective suggests at least seven classes of benefits that would have accrued to ancestors who used an aggressive strategy: Appropriating the resources of others, defending oneself and kin against attack, inflicting costs on intrasexual rivals, negotiating status and power hierarchies, deterring long-term mates from infidelity or defection, aiding in the reacquisition of mates, and acquiring sexual access to otherwise inaccessible individuals.

Sound evolutionary arguments predict that aggression is likely to emerge more strongly among men, with both aggressors and victims being men. Given a mating system with some degree of polygyny, selection will favor "risky tactics" among men both to gain sexual access to more women than their "fair share" and to avoid being excluded from mating entirely. The empirical evidence provides strong support that most physical aggression is perpetrated by men and most of the victims are men.

Evolutionary psychologists have advanced two contrasting hypotheses designed to explain the evolution of killing other human beings. The first hypothesis suggests that killings are nonadaptive or maladaptive byproducts of adaptations designed to use nonlethal violence and the threat of violence as a means of coercively controlling other human beings. The second hypothesis suggests that humans, especially men, have evolved specific homicide adaptations that are designed to motivate killing other humans under specific circumstances when the benefits outweigh the costs. The high prevalence of homicidal fantasies, the predictability of the circumstances that trigger them, the evidence on sex differences, and the premeditated quality of many homicides all seem to support Homicide Adaptation Theory (Duntley & Buss, 2005), although further research is needed to pit predictions from the two theories against each other directly.

An evolutionary psychological perspective on human aggression contains many limitations. This perspective currently cannot account, for example, for why three men confronted with a wife's infidelity will result in a beating in one case, a homicide in the second case, and getting drunk in the third case. It currently cannot account for why some cultures, such as the Yanomamö, seem to require male violence to attain a position of status, whereas in other cultures aggression leads to irreparable reputational damage. The current evolutionary psychological account of aggression is limited in these and many other respects.

Even at this preliminary stage of inquiry, however, an evolutionary psychological account of aggression has heuristic value, suggesting particular lines of investigation not examined by other approaches. It can account parsimoniously for a host of otherwise inexplicable findings, such as the universally greater prevalence of aggression by men against other men, the ubiquity of male sexual jealousy as a cause of spousal violence and spousal homicide, and the identification of step parenting as a causal context putting children at risk of aggression. As such, an evolutionary psychological account brings us one step closer to understanding why humans everywhere inflict violent costs on other humans.

ACKNOWLEDGMENTS

The authors thank Doug Kenrick, Mark Schaller, and Jeff Simpson for helpful comments on an earlier draft of this chapter.

REFERENCES

Baumeister, R. F., & Vohs, K. D. (2004). Four roots of evil. In A. G. Miller (Ed.) *The social psychology of good and evil*. New York: Guilford.

Berkowitz, L. (1993). *Aggression: Its causes, consequences, and control*. New York: McGraw-Hill.

Buss, A. H. (1961). *The psychology of aggression*. New York: Wiley.

Buss, D. M. (1989). Conflict between the sexes: Strategic interference and the evocation of anger and upset. *Journal of Personality and Social Psychology, 56*, 735–747.

Buss, D. M. (2003). *The evolution of desire: Strategies of human mating* (Rev. ed.). New York: Basic Books.

Buss, D. M. (2005). *The murderer next door: Why the mind is designed to kill*. New York: Penguin.

Buss, D. M., & Dedden, L. A. (1990). Derogation of competitors. *Journal of Social and Personal Relationships, 7*, 395–422.

Buss, D. M., & Duntley, J. D. (2006). *Homicide adaptation theory*. Manuscript submitted for publication.

Buss, D. M., & Shackelford, T. K. (1997). Human aggression in evolutionary psychological perspective. *Clinical Psychology Review, 17*, 605–619.

Campbell, A. (1993). *Men, women, and aggression*. New York: Basic Books.

Campbell, A. (1995). A few good men: Evolutionary psychology and female adolescent aggression. *Ethology and Sociobiology, 16*, 99–123.

Campbell, A. (2002). *A mind of her own: The evolutionary psychology of women*. Oxford: Oxford University Press.

Centers for Disease Control and Prevention National Center for Injury Prevention and Control. (2002). http://webapp.cdc.gov/sasweb/ncipc/leadcaus10.html

Chagnon, N. (1983). *Yanomamö: The fierce people* (3rd ed.). New York: Holt, Rinehart, & Winston.

Chagnon, N. (1988). Life histories, blood revenge, and warfare in a tribal population. *Science*, *239*, 985–992.

Daly, M., & Wilson, M. (1988). *Homicide*. Hawthorne, NY: Aldine.

Daly, M., & Wilson, M. (1996). Evolutionary psychology and marital conflict: The relevance of stepchildren. In D. M. Buss & N. Malamuth (Eds.), *Sex, power, conflict: Evolutionary and feminist perspectives* (pp. 9–28). New York: Oxford University Press.

Daly, M., Wilson, M., & Weghorst, S. J. (1982). Male sexual jealousy. *Ethology and Sociobiology*, *3*, 11–27.

Dobash, R. E., & Dobash, R. P. (1984). The nature and antecedents of violent events. *British Journal of Criminology*, *24*, 269–288.

Dower, J. W., & George, T. S. (1995). *Japanese history and culture from ancient to modern times*. Princeton, NJ: Markus Wiener.

Duntley, J. D. (2005). Adaptations to dangers from humans. In D. M. Buss (Ed.), *The handbook of evolutionary psychology*. New York: Wiley.

Duntley, J. D., & Buss, D. M. (2005). The plausibility of adaptations for homicide. In P. Carruthers, S. Laurence, & S. Stich (Eds.), *The structure of the innate mind*. New York: Oxford University Press.

Duntley, J. D., & Buss, D. M. (2006). *The evolutionary psychology of stalking*. Department of Psychology, University of Texas. Manuscript in preparation.

Eron, L. D. (1982). Parent–child interaction, television violence, and aggression of children. *American Psychologist*, *37*, 197–211.

Figueredo, A. J. (1995). Preliminary report: Family deterrence of domestic violence in Spain. Department of Psychology, University of Arizona.

Geddes, J. F., Tasker, R. C., Hackshaw, A. K., Nickols, C. D., Adams, G. G., Whitwell, H. L., & Scheimberg, I. (2003). Dural hemorrhage in non-traumatic infant deaths: Does it explain the bleeding in 'shaken baby syndrome'? *Neuropathology & Applied Neurobiology*, *29*, 14–22.

Ghiglieri, M. P. (1999). *The dark side of man: Tracing the origins of violence*. Reading, MA: Perseus Books.

Harris, A. R., Thomas, S. H., Fisher, G. A., & Hirsch, D. J. (2002). Murder and medicine. *Homicide Studies*, *6*, 128–166.

Hart, C. W., & Pilling, A. R. (1960). *The Tiwi of North Australia*. New York: Hart, Rinehart, & Winston.

Hill, K., & Hurtado, A. M. (1996). *Ache life history*. New York: Aldine De Gruyter.

Hill, R. (1945). Campus values in mate selection. *Journal of Home Economics*, *37*, 554–558.

Huesmann, L. R., & Eron, L. D. (1986). *Television and the aggressive child: A cross-national comparison*. Hillsdale, NJ: Lawrence Erlbaum Associates.

Keeley, L. H. (1996). *War before civilization*. New York: Oxford University Press.

Kenrick, D. T., Neuberg, S. L., & Cialdini, R. B. (2005). *Social psychology: Unraveling the mystery*. New York: Allyn & Bacon.

Kenrick, D. T. & Sheets, V (1993). Homicidal fantasies. *Ethology and Sociobiology*, *14*, 231–246.

Kirkpatrick, L. A., & Ellis, B. J. (2001). An evolutionary-psychological approach to self-esteem: Multiple domains and multiple functions. In M. Clark & G. Fletcher (Eds.), *The Blackwell handbook in social psychology: Vol. 2. Interpersonal processes* (pp. 411–436). Oxford, England: Blackwell.

Larsen, C. L. (1997). *Bioarcheology: Interpreting behavior from the human skeleton*. Cambridge: Cambridge University Press.

Le Boeuf, B. J., & Reiter, J. (1988). Lifetime reproductive success in northern elephant seals. In T. H. Clutton-Brock (Ed.), *Reproductive success* (pp. 344–362). Chicago: University of Chicago Press.

Malamuth, N. (2005). Sexual coercion. In D. M. Buss (Ed.), *The handbook of evolutionary psychology*. New York: Wiley.

Myers, D. G. (1995). *Social psychology* (5th ed.). New York: McGraw-Hill.

Nisbett, R. E. (1993). Violence and U.S. regional culture. *American Psychologist, 48,* 441–449.

Olweus, D. (1978). *Aggression in schools*. New York: Wiley.

Paton, W., & Mannison, M. (1995). Sexual coercion in high school dating. *Sex Roles, 33,* 447–457.

Ruff, J. R. (2001). *Violence in early modern Europe 1500–1800*. Boston: Cambridge University Press.

Sabini, J. (1992). *Social psychology* (2nd ed.). New York: Norton.

Staub, E. (2004). Basic human needs, altruism, and aggression. In A. G. Miller (Ed.), *The social psychology of good and evil*. New York: Guilford.

Stolinsky, S. A., & Stolinsky, D. C. (2000). Homicide and suicide rates do not covary. *The Journal of Trauma, Injury, Infection, and Critical Care, 48,* 1168–1169.

Symons, D. (1979). *The evolution of human sexuality*. New York: Oxford University Press.

Thornhill, R., & Palmer, C. (2000). *A natural history of rape: Biological bases of sexual coercion*. Cambridge, MA: MIT Press.

Tooby, J., & Cosmides, L. (1992). Psychological foundations of culture. In J. Barkow, L. Cosmides, & J. Tooby (Eds.), *The adapted mind* (pp. 19–136). New York: Oxford University Press.

Trivers, R. (1985). *Social evolution*. Menlo Park, CA: The Benjamin/Cummings Publishing Company.

United Nations. (1998). *United Nations 1996 demographic yearbook*. New York: United Nations.

Waller, A. L. (1993). The Hatfield–McCoy feud. In W. Graebner (Ed.), *True stories from the American past* (pp. 35–54). New York: McGraw-Hill.

Wilson, M., & Daly, M. (1985). Competitiveness, risk-taking, and violence: The young male syndrome. *Ethology and Sociobiology, 6,* 59–73.

Wrangham, R., & Peterson, D. (1996). *Demonic males*. Boston: Houghton Mifflin.

Zimbardo, P. G. (2004). A situationist perspective on the psychology of evil: Understanding how good people are transformed into perpetrators. In A. G. Miller (Ed.), *The social psychology of good and evil*. New York: Guildford.

13

Evolutionary Social Influence

JILL M. SUNDIE, ROBERT B. CIALDINI, VLADAS GRISKEVICIUS, and DOUGLAS T. KENRICK

*A*ttempts to influence the behavior of others are ubiquitous among social animals. Whining dogs, crying babies, monkeys with outstretched hands, and salespeople offering free lunches to potential clients are all attempting to shift another's energy and resources toward them and away from other activities. Some such influence attempts succeed, others fail, and still others elicit more anger than compliance. A complex set of navigational rules governs the continual give-and-take of influence appeals in social animals. How does an individual maximize the personal gains of group living, such as sharing food or protection from threats, while minimizing the costs that come from deferring to higher-status others or participating in group defense? And how does one group member convince others to make sacrifices for his or her benefit, without pushing so far as to violate group norms and warrant rejection?

Social psychologists have devoted a great deal of research to understanding human social influence processes. We will argue that research on social influence could be enriched by incorporating several evolutionary principles, and that evolutionary psychology could in turn be profitably expanded by examining social influence principles in an adaptationist light. A central argument will be that different social relationships are associated with different influence goals; one wants different things from a parent, a mate, a friend, an underling, a superior, and an out-group stranger. Different tactics will vary in success depending on the nature of the relationship between the target (the person who has the influence attempt directed at him or her) and the agent (the person making the influence attempt). We will consider different influence goals associated with different domains of social life, and examine a set of six principles of social influence through an adaptationist lens. We will also consider how an evolutionary perspective may offer some new insights about how and when these principles of social influence will be differentially effective, and when their use will be seen as especially illegitimate. Although there is empirical support for some of the hypotheses we present here, most of the implications of an evolutionary approach to social influence remain to be tested.

GENERAL PRINCIPLES PEOPLE USE TO INFLUENCE ONE ANOTHER

After observing real-world influence techniques and reviewing related empirical research, Cialdini (2001) outlined six principles of social influence: reciprocity (people feel obligated to comply to those who give them gifts), liking (people say yes to those they like), scarcity (people differentially value something that is scarce or dwindling in availability), social proof (people look to the behavior of similar others when they are unsure how to behave), authority (people follow the advice of experts and those in power), and commitment and consistency (people behave consistently with their commitments). The person who is a target of one or more of these influence approaches is presumed to comply with an influence agent's request, or not, using these principles as a simple set of heuristics (e.g., Is this request coming from an authority? Are others responding favorably? Did I previously commit to do this?). Below, we begin by reviewing some relevant evolutionary theoretical constructs, and then connect certain of these constructs to each principle of social influence.

DOMAIN SPECIFICITY AND MECHANISM FLEXIBILITY

Evolutionary approaches to behavior assume that the brain solves social problems by executing problem-specific psychological mechanisms that were shaped by the processes of natural selection (e.g., Cosmides & Tooby, 1992). This view challenges traditional assumptions that the range of human thought and behavior can be understood with the application of one or two broad and unqualified domain-general principles (such as "do what feels good" or "maximize reproductive fitness"). The modularity assumption is founded in part on the assumption that selection favors relatively efficient solutions to recurrent problems faced by animals living in specialized niches, and that focused solutions are more efficient than broad, nonspecific ones. Considerations of engineering efficiency dictate that the brain includes a diverse set of tools for solving different social problems, just as a mechanic requires very different and specialized tools for jacking up a car, removing lug nuts, adjusting spark plugs, and appraising the chemical content of tailpipe emissions. Supporting this assumption, broad-ranging evidence indicates that human learning and cognition operate according to different rules, using different neural architectures and programs, in processing information about words, faces, tastes, poisonous insects, loud noises in the dark, and so on (Kenrick, Sadalla, & Keefe, 1998; Sherry & Schacter, 1987). Applied to social influence, this modular approach suggests that people may pay attention to, remember, and weigh information differently in deciding how to respond to influence attempts when different social goals are active. This implies that solutions to the problem of gaining compliance from a potential dating partner, for example, might differ considerably from those involved in gaining compliance from one's parents or convincing unrelated group members to defer to your leadership.

DECISION HEURISTICS IN EVOLUTIONARY PERSPECTIVE

The study of decision heuristics has typically been conducted with primary focus on either: (1) heuristics as built-in *biases* in judgment, which can regularly produce decision *errors* or irrational choices (e.g., Kahneman, Slovic, & Tversky, 1982; Nisbett & Ross, 1980) or (2) heuristics as efficient and accurate solutions to recurring and complex social and environmental problems, which result in solutions that are, on average, quick and accurate (e.g., Gigerenzer & Selten, 2001; Gigerenzer & Todd, 1999). Adopting the latter view of simple decision rules, Gigerenzer and his colleagues have proposed that humans evolved what they call an "adaptive toolbox" of heuristics. This toolbox is presumed to contain a large number of evolved, domain-specific heuristics, including "lower-order" basic cognitive building blocks, such as perception and memory, as well as "higher-order" heuristics that may employ emotions, norms, and imitation. We suggest that different influence tactics are components of a *social* adaptive toolbox, and that using these different tactics helps individuals to effectively negotiate the balance of selfish and prosocial motives within the group. By using a tactic such as citing an authority, offering a gift, or mentioning a common friend, influence agents (i.e., those attempting to influence the behavior of another) make salient to their targets specific features of the situation or their relationship[1] that will be likely to engage the desired heuristic response. While these request tactics can be used to cheat a target when applied outside of their normal social context (i.e., the context within which the use of the heuristic evolved), the general tendency to comply with such requests would likely have been a successful strategy for maintaining mutually beneficial social relationships, on average. The sense of obligation to reciprocate a gift, the tendency to value scarce items relatively more, and the desire to say "yes" to people we like all have plausible evolutionary underpinnings. Like all tools, however, each of these principles and our responses to them will be implemented selectively, depending on the social task at hand.

SOCIAL DOMAINS: POSING PERSISTENT PROBLEMS OF INFLUENCE

We have elsewhere suggested that humans universally confront persistent problems in a set of broad social domains: forming social coalitions, gaining and maintaining status, protecting oneself and valued others from threats, finding mates, maintaining romantic bonds, and caring for family members (e.g., Kenrick, Li, & Butner, 2003). Each social domain poses a unique set of recurring problems that our ancestors would have had to solve in order to survive and reproduce. The different goal states associated with each domain can be activated either by internal thought processes or environmental inputs. Once activated, these goal states direct cognitive and physiological resources toward advancement in that particular domain. For example, either thinking deeply about a recent romantic experience or encountering an attractive potential romantic partner can serve to activate a mating-related goal. When a particular goal is active, cognitive processes such as attention will be differentially focused on goal-relevant stimuli. Evidence suggests that in mate selection, as well as other domains, attention may be directed toward different kinds of stimuli for men and women. Sex differences have also been shown to exist for judgments about, and memory for, goal-relevant stimuli (Haselton & Buss, 2000; Maner et al., 2003).

Activating one of the six broad social goals may facilitate or inhibit the subsequent activation of other goals (Martindale, 1980, 1991; Tipper, 1992). For example, if a man's mate selection goals are active, he may be attuned to threats or opportunities related to his status (which is linked to a man's mating success). In contrast, the activation of self-protection goals due to immediate threats to one's physical safety will likely inhibit the activation of goals in other domains such as status or mate retention. For each active goal state, there is a need to negotiate a relevant set of social relationships in order to reach one's objectives. Each of the social domains can be slightly reframed as involving recurring problems of social influence, as outlined in Table 13.1.

A large body of literature on person and situation factors in social influence processes has helped identify and better predict the conditions under which the six social influence principles, and their associated tactics and techniques, will be more or less successful. Yet, very little attention has been devoted to what role evolutionarily relevant variables might play in influence processes. To take a simple example, consider the principle of reciprocity (i.e., people will generally feel obligated to reciprocate a favor or a concession). Although it is regarded as a universal principle (Brown, 1991; Gouldner, 1960), the extent and content of reciprocal exchange actually varies considerably depending on the social domain within which one is exchanging resources. For example, parents caring for their children do not expect reciprocation of benefits in the same way as do friends exchanging gifts, and the rules of exchange between men and women during courtship likely differ from those between higher- and lower-status individuals in a work group (Fiske, 1992; Foa & Foa, 1976; Kenrick & Trost, 1989; Mills & Clark, 2001). In the following section, we will consider how and why these constraints on reciprocity operate, and will also explore domain-specific constraints on the use and effectiveness of liking, social proof, scarcity, authority, and commitment and consistency. As outlined in Table 13.2, we will ask for each principle: What function has this principle likely served in human social groups? And what is the normal social context for its operation (i.e., when and with whom is it normally used)?

USING TWO DIFFERENT EVOLUTIONARY LENSES TO EXAMINE THE INFLUENCE PRINCIPLES

Throughout our discussion of the six influence principles, we will outline testable hypotheses generated from an evolutionary perspective. Each hypothesis was formulated by taking one of two possible points of view: (1) that the effectiveness of a given social influence principle in gaining compliance will depend on the *type*

TABLE 13.1 Six Broad Domains of Social Life and Examples of Intrinsic Social Influence Problems

Social Domain	Domain-Specific Problem to be Solved	Domain-Specific Social Influence Problem	Relevant Evolved Decision Constraint
Coalition formation	Forming and maintaining reciprocal and cooperative alliances (to achieve goals that require coordination)	Assure others you will not cheat them in future interactions, and that you are a worthy ally	Cooperation is more likely among those who (1) are close relatives, and (2) have reciprocally shared resources in the past
Status	Acquiring prestige and power over one's in-group members	Convince other group members to defer to you, and to award you differential power within the group	Cost/benefit ratio of striving for status more favorable for males because females emphasize male status in choosing mates
Self-protection	Protecting oneself and valued others (e.g., kin) from threats	Convince out-group members that aggression toward one's in-group would be costly	Male out-group members heuristically associated with threat; males more involved in intra- and intergroup exchanges of threats
Mate selection	Finding eligible, desirable mates and securing those relationships	Convince a desirable member of the opposite sex to begin a romantic relationship	Men biased to overestimate female sexual interest; women biased to underestimate levels of male commitment
Mate retention	Investing in existing mating relationships in ways that lead to retention of desired relationships over time	Convince one's mate to remain committed to the relationship (i.e., get married, work through post-marital conflicts)	Women inclined to break bond if partner compromises resources, or if a high-status alternative is available; men inclined to break bond if a partner is sexually unfaithful, or if there are physically attractive alternatives available
Parental care	Investing resources in ways that promote the lifetime reproductive potential of one's offspring, and the offspring of one's kin	Persuade one's parents to share time and other resources with you, instead of your siblings	Familial provision of resources and care will follow the order: self > sibling's own offspring > step-children

of relationship between the agent (influencer) and the target (influencee) or (2) that the effectiveness of a given social influence principle will depend on whether the *target's active goal state* is a good match with what is communicated during an influence attempt.

Focusing first on the type of relationship, we propose that shared genes between close relatives, or shared reproductive interests between romantic partners and their extended families, have important implications for the dynamics of social influence within these relationships. We also expect these unique relationship types to be characterized by *different* social influence dynamics than other types of relationships, such as those between unrelated friends or coworkers. Some social relationships are leveraged more than others to achieve each specific goal outlined in Table 13.1. For example, coalition formation requires that people expand beyond their kin-based social networks to form mutually beneficial relationships with unrelated individuals, often by appealing to shared interests or goals. While these shared interests with nonrelatives are not reproductively based, they can have indirect effects on reproductive success by affecting things such as the composition and ordering of status hierarchies over time, and the allocation of vital economic resources. Where we believe there are interesting predictions to be made about the effect of these different relationship types on social influence processes, we have outlined them below.

The second way we apply the organizing structure of the broad social domains (Table 13.1) to social influence research is by considering how certain active goal states translate into a propensity to comply with certain kinds of influence attempts. As we will describe in more detail in the following sections, we propose that certain influence principles are better matches with certain active goal states. For example, a person with an active coalition formation goal should be more susceptible to signals that an influence agent wants to form a relationship with him or her.

RECIPROCITY

A commonly used influence tactic involves providing favors or concessions to others, in the hope that they reciprocate when you later request a favor or concession. Reciprocity operates on three types of social obligation: To *give* to those you wish to establish or maintain good relations with, to *receive* or accept what is offered to you, and to *repay* those who have given to you in the past (Mauss, 1954). More generally, reciprocity can aid in facilitating within-group cooperation. Some tasks cannot be accomplished by individuals alone—hunting often involves teamwork, as does moving large objects, or building a hut. The constraints on human reciprocity were likely fine-tuned when humans lived in small, close-knit groups; the universal nature of reciprocity norms implies that the origins of this social arrangement reach back far into humans' evolutionary history. However, most research on this tactic has been conducted between strangers in a laboratory setting, or by naturalistic observation of techniques designed for success in one-time stranger-to-stranger interactions. Taking a broader adaptationist perspective on reciprocity tactics, we will consider how evolutionary constructs such as reciprocal altruism, inclusive fitness, and differential parental investment can enhance our understanding of how this tactic functions within *familiar* social relationships. We will also discuss how those evolutionary constructs help to illuminate important similarities and differences between these more intimate influence processes and social influence between strangers.

Reciprocal altruism plausibly evolved within social groups as a risk-reduction strategy to deal with highly unpredictable environments. By forming alliances with nonrelatives, individuals could further extend their potential resource base, and spread their risk of failing to attain a scarce resource in any given day, or week, over a larger number of individuals (see Table 13.2). The Ache, a group of foraging tribes in South America, reduce nutritional uncertainty through reciprocal meat sharing (Kaplan & Hill, 1985a). Meat is a scarce resource that Ache hunters spend a great deal of time pursuing, but with only intermittent success. When a hunter does bring in a catch, he distributes the proceeds evenly among the members of his group. Because no one hunter, even a highly skilled one, can count on

TABLE 13.2   Proposed Functional Basis and Normal Social Context of Each Influence Tactic

Influence Principle	Functional Basis	When and With Whom: Normal Social Context
Reciprocity	Sharing resources over time helps ensure survival by pooling risk, thereby reducing individual variance in resource acquisition	Reciprocate with non-kin in-group members, and with potential romantic partners, to demonstrate a willingness to form a relationship or to secure indebtedness
Liking	Saying "yes" to those we like enhances trust and alliances with those individuals	Say "yes" to friends (similar others), and potential mates (attractive others)
Social proof	• Imitating popular choices takes advantage of others' experience and knowledge, especially when one confronts a novel problem. • Conforming to local norms helps group processes flow smoothly	• Follow other in-group members for normative social behaviors when personally novel problems are encountered, and when it is necessary to coordinate group activities • Follow in-group peers for mate choice
Scarcity	• Overreacting to scarcity can motivate one to gather more of a disappearing valuable resource, and to avoid the downside risk of resource variance • Acquiring scarce resources can enhance positive differentiation from in-group competitors for mates or status	• Move quickly to take advantage of limited opportunities popular with similar others • For males, choose scarce goods to enhance intrasexual competition within a mating pool
Authority	Following the advice of those with wisdom and experience increases likelihood of making correct decisions	• Follow advice from others known to have expertise and trustworthiness • Defer within one's group, although young males may have an incentive to reject an authority to display status
Commitment and consistency	Sticking to one's commitments inspires others to see one as trustworthy and reliable	Behave consistently with in-group members, particularly with distant relatives and non-kin group members such as friends, potential romantic partners, and current mates

catching enough prey to feed himself and his family in any given week, this reciprocal arrangement helps all group members, even the superior hunters from time to time.

A consideration of the crucial role reciprocal relationships played in helping our ancestors maintain necessities such as food and shelter (see also Betzig & Turke, 1986) may help us to understand why normative pressure to comply with reciprocity-based tactics is so strong, and why violators of reciprocal agreements are often socially sanctioned. People wary of forming reciprocal relationships are perceived negatively in social settings (Cotterell, Eisenberger, & Speicher, 1992) and are subject to various forms of social rejection, or in more extreme cases, outright expulsion from their group. Because of this potentially high personal cost, individuals are wise to fulfill their reciprocal obligations to trusted in-group members, and actively respond to requests employing reciprocity-based tactics.

The specific rules of exchange, and the resources traded, differ across kin-based relationships and other types of social relationships; a pattern illuminated by the theory of inclusive fitness. Hamilton (1964) demonstrated how cooperation can be enhanced via genetic relatedness and shared reproductive interests of the individuals involved. The resources a brother receives may enhance his reproductive potential directly, but his nonrecipient sister also benefits indirectly by an amount discounted by the siblings' degree of genetic similarity (here, approximately 50%). Because the sister shares genes with her brother, any offspring her brother produces will also carry some of her own genetic material, contributing to the representation of her genes in future generations. In this way, genetic relatives have powerful incentives for sharing and cooperating that are not based on a tit-for-tat system of reciprocal exchange. Therefore, reciprocity tactics should not be necessary to elicit cooperation from close relatives. It is more likely that these tactics serve to solve the problem of how to influence nonrelatives.

Consistent with this notion, Fiske (1992) notes that resources are often allocated among close kin based on need (i.e., via communal sharing), rather than by social rank, history of past favors, or market pricing. Researchers Clark and Mills (Clark & Mills, 1979, 1993; Mills & Clark, 2001) also distinguish between *exchange* and *communal* social relationships. In their framework, an individual in a communal relationship is chronically concerned with the relationship partner's welfare, and provides resources to him or her based upon need, or a desire to express that concern. This arrangement stands in contrast to the exchange relationship, where resources are provided to the relationship partner only if the provider can reasonably expect that something specific will be provided in return. Like Fiske, Clark and Mills (1979) have argued that family relationships are highly likely to follow communal norms for exchange. The evolutionary perspective holds that inclusive fitness is a driving force in creating communalism in close kin relationships.

Viewed through the lens of inclusive fitness, people are expected to make additional, finer distinctions within their kin groups based on degrees of genetic relatedness or the extent of shared reproductive interests, and these distinctions would be expected to result in different behaviors (Burnstein, Crandall, & Kitayama, 1994). While close kin may consider their relationships with one another as communal in nature, some relationships may be more communal than others, meaning that some relationships will take priority over others (Mills & Clark, 2001). A parent may consider the needs of his child, for example, to trump the needs of his uncle. Even though his uncle may have contributed many more resources to him in the past than his child has, a larger proportion of genetic overlap with the child, all else equal, would favor the child as recipient contrary to what reciprocity rules would suggest.

While inclusive fitness has implications for whom to prioritize in the sharing of resources, it also has implications for how much tolerance one should have for relatives who fail to reciprocate. By tolerance, we mean that future cooperative behavior, or sharing of resources, will continue even in the face of reciprocity transgressions. We expect that the thresholds for tolerance of *failures* to reciprocate will be significantly higher in relationships between close kin than distant kin, because of the difference in the contribution of those relatives to the individuals' inclusive fitness. Similarly, relationships between close kin should be characterized by higher levels of tolerance than relationships between unrelated friends. Clark and Mills' finding that people in communal relationships allocate resources based on need and not based on expected returns, and Fiske's notion that kin tend to engage in communal sharing, provide support for these hypotheses.

When inclusive fitness is factored in, reciprocity-based influence tactics are expected to be most effective in affecting the behavior of nonrelatives—for whom no fundamental (i.e., inclusive fitness) basis for cooperative exchange exists. A special case within the set of non-kin social relationships, however, is the romantic relationship. While genetic overlap is not the basis of a cooperative bond between romantic partners, the shared reproductive interests of the partners have important implications for the partners' respective inclusive fitness. Below, we consider the unique resources exchanged by men and women in the context of romantic partnerships, and discuss the role the reciprocity principle may play in furthering mate selection and mate retention goals (refer to Table 13.1).

The rules of reciprocity and the resources exchanged within the mate selection and mate retention domains follow patterns consistent with Trivers' (1972) theory of differential parental investment (see also Kenrick & Trost, 1989). When mate selection goals are active, cognitions about potential partners are presumably guided, to some degree, by the search for a good bargain in the exchange of the individuals' own reproductive resources for those uniquely provided by the opposite sex. Men and women often choose to form long-term reciprocal relationships with romantic partners who agree to exchange these different reproductive resources exclusively with them. Ancestral humans who failed to attend (consciously or unconsciously) to the gains from trading these reproductive resources would have experienced lower reproductive success relative to their contemporaries, and may have failed to reproduce altogether.

In this reproductive exchange, men and women are expected to be influenced by different features of, and different behaviors of, potential and existing mates. Women offer biological resources necessary for a nine month internal gestation, and provide continued direct investment for months or years in feeding and other infant care. The biological investment needed for a male to produce offspring, on the other hand, is relatively small (the theoretical minimum being the time and energy it takes to engage in a single act of intercourse). This difference in the minimum investment required to produce offspring predicts a variety of behavioral sex differences. For example, women are relatively more resistant than men to engaging in uncommitted sex (Clark & Hatfield, 1989), and have higher minimum standards for acceptable sexual partners (Kenrick, Groth, Trost, & Sadalla, 1993; Kenrick, Sadalla, Groth, & Trost, 1990; Regan, 1998). Women also prefer to begin having sex later in a romantic relationship than men do (Buss & Schmidt, 1993), and tend to underestimate men's commitment to their relationships (Haselton & Buss, 2000). During courtship men employ a variety of reciprocity-based tactics (e.g., providing gifts of valued resources) to encourage potential mates to form romantic reciprocal relationships with them, and evidence suggests that one of several motivations for women to engage in short-term mating is to access present or future resources for themselves and their offspring (Hrdy, 1999). Gifts from men to women may be attempts to instill a longer-term sexual obligation—men, for example, report liking an available woman less if she immediately reciprocates a favor he does for her, or gift he gives her (Clark & Mills, 1979).

Once a mate is secured, maintaining the relationship (see Table 13.1, mate retention domain) involves, to some extent, monitoring the ongoing gains from trading these divergent reproductive resources. The highly interdependent nature of romantic partners' reproductive success creates incentives to cooperate and share that are highly similar to those among close kin. However, while people cannot replace their genetic relatives with more desirable others, they can replace their romantic partners. If either party in a romantic relationship becomes dissatisfied, he or she can pursue other romantic alternatives. Violations of the exclusive reciprocal exchange of men's and women's unique reproductive resources (e.g., a woman refusing sexual access and/or engaging in extra-pair sex, a man diverting economic resources to another woman) are perceived as particularly grave offenses, and are common grounds for relationship dissolution across a wide range of cultures (Betzig, 1989; Buss, Larsen, Westen, & Semmelroth, 1992). In this way, romantic relationships are akin in some fundamental ways to reciprocal relationships with nonrelatives, where perceived long-term inequities in exchange (and particularly in the case of reproductively relevant resources) will often lead to severance of the current relationship and to the pursuit of better alternatives.

LIKING

Another technique that influence agents commonly use is to attempt to induce their targets to like them. We are more inclined to comply with another's request when we like the requester, or when we feel flattered by the requester's behavior. Liking is commonly enhanced by feelings of similarity and familiarity between the agent and the target, and by requester attractiveness. For example, a salesperson may seek to uncover common interests (e.g., golf, grandchildren, or driving the same kind of car) with a prospective buyer, and raise these topics during a sales interaction. Liking tactics can be used to communicate that a reciprocal relationship (or the potential for one) exists between the individuals involved. It makes sense to say "yes" to those we enjoy affiliating with, or wish to form social relationships with.

Because genetic relatives already have powerful inclusive fitness incentives for cooperation, the liking principle is expected to have a greater impact on compliance in non-kin interactions, such as between friends or potential romantic partners. Because there are different behavioral constraints for the domains of coalition formation and mate selection, different influence techniques are expected to be effective depending on which goal is currently active. We want different things from people we feel similar to, but to whom we are not romantically attracted, than from people to whom we are romantically attracted. Attractive others may be considered as potential mates while similar and familiar others are candidates for platonic reciprocal relationships. Therefore, we separately consider below the liking-based tactics within the coalition formation and mate selection domains (see Table 13.1).

First we will consider the influence techniques that enhance liking of the agent by the target through the use of similarity appeals. Professed similarity between the target and the agent (e.g., "No kidding, my father also grew up in Pittsburgh!") plausibly serves as a cue to in-group membership, and the favorable associations that accompany it. Castelli, Vanzetto, Sherman, and Arcuri (2001) found support for such a role of in-group vs. out-group distinctions in persuasion by demonstrating that targets more readily conform to a person who has used stereotype-consistent descriptions of a common out-group ("Did you hear the one about the social constructionist and the Mafia don?"). Another recent study suggests that perceived attitude similarity between oneself and a stranger can automatically activate kinship cognitions, inducing a person to behave prosocially toward that similar other (Park & Schaller, 2005).

An agent who highlights shared interests and other similarities, and smiles warmly at the target, for example, may be welcomed as an in-group member by the target. This position provides advantages to the agent in gaining compliance with favors requested. There may be some situations in which a target is particularly concerned with creating and expanding his or her social networks, and under such conditions the power of similarity-based liking tactics should be further enhanced. We would expect that targets with active coalitional goals (e.g., a first-year graduate student attending a conference, or a person who has just relocated to a new neighborhood) should be more susceptible than average to similarity-based influence attempts, particularly if the influence agents involved are potentially valuable alliance partners.

While similarity may serve as a proxy for kinship or in-group membership, and be leveraged to gain compliance, attractiveness is the persuasion currency of most value in the mating domains. Because of the constraints imposed on mate selection processes by differential parental investment, as discussed above, men's and women's cognitive processes about mating-relevant criteria diverge. Because of the different resources men and women contribute to the reproductive process, men place a relatively higher value on physical attractiveness (a cue to fertility-related biological resources), while women place more weight on ability to provide indirect economic resources and particularly so for a potential long-term mate. Men have a very high ceiling on the number of offspring they can produce over a lifetime (perhaps hundreds) via multiple sexual partners. For women, there is a biological limit on lifetime production of offspring, and any casual sexual encounter can result in a high-cost, long-term investment. Therefore, women tend to be choosier about their sexual partners and less inclined toward casual sex than men (Kenrick et al., 1990, 1993).

Natural selection has shaped the cognitive processes of all humans to minimize errors in judgment associated with high personal fitness costs, a key assumption of error management theory (Haselton & Buss, 2000). It is more costly for a man to err by failing to detect sexual receptiveness in a woman (representing access to her valuable biological resources), for example, and more costly for a woman to err by overestimating a man's commitment to her (representing provision of valuable indirect economic resources). Actions that signify liking include touching the target on the arm, smiling repeatedly, complimenting the target, etc. These actions overlap with the set of behaviors that men report (when they observe a woman initiating those behaviors toward a man) as signals that a woman is sexually interested in her male interaction partner. Women infer significantly less sexual interest on the part of the same woman when observing the identical interchange.

This research suggests that some aspects of liking-based influence attempts may not be perceived identically by men and women. The effectiveness of liking tactics, such as touching a target on the arm, may be influenced by the sex and physical attractiveness of the agent and target involved, and the target's present openness to mating opportunities. If mating goals are active for a target, liking-based influence tactics delivered by an attractive opposite-sex agent may be particularly successful, compared to those delivered by an unattractive or same-sex agent. And in general, we would expect targets that are not receptive to short-term mating opportunities (or have nonmating-related goals active) to be less responsive to such influence attempts.

SCARCITY

Another commonly used influence tactic plays upon people's motivation to obtain resources perceived to be scarce or dwindling in supply. Scarcity information seems to function as a signal of relative value, and enhances a resource's desirability. Interpersonally, influence agents make use of the scarcity principle by communicating that benefits they are offering to their targets are very popular ("these time-share units are going fast"), time restricted ("the sale on this sofa lasts this weekend only"), or inherently limited in supply ("only a lucky few will get these rent-controlled apartments"). When scarcity information is delivered by a trusted source, it serves as an accurate value cue. Individuals can capitalize on social learning by being attuned to information that implies local desirability, particularly via the "going fast" type of scarcity. When the availability of necessary resources is highly variable, scarcity information of the "going fast" and time-limited varieties can motivate efforts to obtain what remains of the disappearing resource, and prevent or minimize associated losses.

Scarcity information might serve to trigger loss aversion—the tendency for people to be more distressed when facing potential losses than they feel rewarded by equivalent gains on the same dimension (e.g., Kahneman, Knetsch, & Thaler, 1986). Such a response could contribute to enhanced resource valuations as people become willing to "pay more" to avoid those possible losses. One argument for human tendencies toward loss aversion in decision-making is that in subsistence environments, such as the ones in which humans evolved, the downside risk of resource variance is of greater concern because of the dire negative consequences (e.g., starvation and illness) than the upside of resource variance is beneficial (Lumsden & Wilson, 1981, p. 90). The ability to store bounties of excess food, for example, is often not an option for those living in traditional societies (e.g., Betzig & Turke, 1986; Kaplan & Hill, 1985a). While group cooperation and sharing can mitigate the downside risk for a given group member, as in the reciprocal meat-sharing among the Ache, it cannot overcome natural fluctuations in levels of the resources themselves (fewer game animals in times of drought, for example). Under such conditions, the potential costs of *failing* to respond to scarcity information about crucial resources are likely to be higher than the costs of increasing acquisition effort in response to a false signal. Such a cost structure may have led individuals to heuristically connect scarcity with value.

But what if the scarce resource is not a necessity, and therefore does not have the same negative implications for risk to health and welfare? Are preferences for certain luxuries, as opposed to necessities, also susceptible to scarcity tactics? If so, what function might be served by a heuristic response to information that these luxury resources are scarce? Research on the mating rituals of bowerbirds suggests a possible answer. Male satin bowerbirds spend much time and effort during mating season constructing a large circular wreath-like structure designed to impress the females of the species, and thereby aid in securing mates. Males decorate their twig-based constructions with whatever scarce items they can collect (or steal from competitors' bowers), including shells, flowers, and colorful feathers (Borgia & Gore, 1986). Female bowerbirds choose their mates in part by how elaborately decorated the bower is (the structure serves no functional purpose for either the male or female after mating takes place), and so males compete with one another to display the most interesting and unique structure as this translates directly into enhanced reproductive success (Coleman, Patricelli, & Borgia, 2004). Male bowerbirds must be attuned to rare or scarce decorative items in the environment, as these will serve to positively differentiate them as mates from the competition. Is it possible that some scarce resources also serve such a purpose for humans? Below, we consider the argument that unique, scarce resources provide a rare opportunity to get a "leg up" on the competition.

When individuals seek to climb group status hierarchies, or try to woo potential mates, they must provide some observable evidence of their quality relative to the competition. The display of honest signals of mate quality (e.g., Zahavi & Zahavi, 1997) has been widely documented in animal species, and is governed by the process of sexual selection. Whether one is competing against same-sex group members for status, or trying to impress opposite sex potential mates, positively differentiating oneself from the competition is the key. Instead of triggering a loss prevention response, scarcity information about nonessential resources relevant to the status and mate selection domains (see Table 13.1) may signal an opportunity for positive differentiation. This should be particularly true when acquiring these scarce resources involves extensive effort, or requires some unique talent that other group members have difficulty imitating (Miller, 2000). To illustrate, Ache men vary in their talent for hunting, and so successful hunters share more of the meat they bring in than they can ever hope to gain in return. As one might expect, successful hunters receive other kinds of social rewards for their ability to obtain these locally scarce resources: Specifically, superior hunters have greater access to mates (have more affairs), and also have more children that survive to reproductive age (Kaplan & Hill, 1985b). Such payoffs in status and mating domains may provide incentives to exert more effort to acquire scarce desirable resources.

Based on the status and mating-related rewards afforded to those who are successful in positively differentiating themselves, we are able to make some predictions about when scarcity influence tactics will be differentially successful. Here we focus on scarcity information about limited supply (which offers an opportunity to differentiate oneself), as opposed to the "going fast" type of scarcity (which implies widespread consumption). When influence targets have status goals active (see Table 13.1), their valuations of desirable resources should be more sensitive to information that those resources are rare or difficult to obtain. We expect a similar susceptibility to limited-supply scarcity among *male* influence targets with active mate selection or mate retention goals (see Table 13.1), particularly when possession of the scarce resource is meaningfully tied to some important mate selection criteria employed by local women. A man trying to impress a date with his desirability, for example, might react negatively on discovering that two other new BMW sedans have parked next to his in the restaurant parking lot. By contrast a man concerned with protecting his child would not be expected to react negatively on discovering that two of his neighbors also have expensive Brittax infant safety seats in their new Volvo station wagons. Much as positive differentiation makes one more noticeable and attractive as a potential mate, it may also make one more attractive as an alliance partner. Possessing scarce information, items, or other resources may also enhance one's value as a coalition member. We therefore expect that targets' valuations of resources will be particularly sensitive to limited-supply information when coalition formation goals are active (see Table 13.1), and when the resource is particularly desirable to the group with which he or she wishes to affiliate.

SOCIAL PROOF

Another influence principle involves social proof; when people are uncertain how to behave in a given situation, they will tend to look to others around them to help them decide (Sherif, 1936; Wooten & Reed, 1998). In its normal social context, the principle of social proof also allows individuals to capitalize on social learning. If one is uncertain which response is appropriate in a social situation, and others around you have already made their choices, presumably they have more information or experience than you do in those circumstances. Within a trusted in-group, where individuals have many shared interests and interdependent outcomes, looking to others makes sense and would typically result in the correct decision.

There are numerous benefits of matching the most common local behavior in human groups. Henrich and Boyd (1998) have used computer simulations to demonstrate how selection often favors such conformity, particularly under conditions likely to be confronted by human groups. Taking a well-worn path through an unknown stretch of jungle is less likely to land one in a swamp or at the bottom of a cliff, for example, and throwing a boomerang, casting a fishing line, or setting a trap the way the locals do is more likely to result in dinner than free-styling it. Furthermore, many group activities require some conformity to a common collective decision (e.g., where to build the next campsite, how to cast the fishing net, etc.).

Consistent with the expectation that social proof is more powerful when it comes from in-group members, similarity between the target and another group member has been shown to enhance the likelihood that the group members' behavior will be incorporated into a target's own choices (Abrams, Wetherell, Cochrane, Hogg, & Turner, 1990; Burn, 1991; Schultz, 1999). Similarity may function as a proxy for in-group membership or activate kinship cognitions, as suggested above, and enhance a target's confidence that the group members' behavior is the normative choice in that context.

From an evolutionary perspective, social proof can be a useful heuristic to apply if the benefits from increased group coordination or accuracy in social judgment are not outweighed by costs in other social domains, such as gaining and maintaining status (see Table 13.1). According to a meta-analysis of gender effects in conformity, there is a general tendency for women to conform more readily than men (Eagly & Carli, 1981). Subsequent research demonstrated that this sex difference was pronounced when the pressure to conform was manifest in public, and where information delivered by the members of a group differed from the private opinions or judgments of the targets. In public, men exhibited a resistance to persuasion, whereas women demonstrated similar levels of conformity in public and in private (Eagly, Wood, & Fishbaugh, 1981). Baumeister and Sommer (1997) suggested that this tendency toward nonconformity among men in public might not be motivated by a need to assert their independence, as Eagly et al. (1981) suggested, but by their desire to be accepted by the group in a very specific light—as leaders. Worldwide, men are more likely to seek and obtain positions of leadership and political power (e.g., Inter-Parliamentary Union, 2004). This pattern is consistent with expectations based on sexual selection and differential parental investment, which highlight the differential reproductive benefits to males demonstrating social dominance. Together, these findings suggest that the costs of conforming to the views of one's group are not the same for men and women; that for male targets, conformity might be perceived as challenging their relative position in the group's status hierarchy.

From an evolutionary perspective, there are more severe reproductive consequences for men who fail to carefully attend to issues of relative status within their groups. Males toward the bottom of the status hierarchy are considered less desirable by women, particularly as long-term partners, across many diverse cultures (Buss, 2004, pp. 114–115). Although conformity based on social proof can lead to more accurate judgments, the informational benefits may be offset by reputation costs. We therefore predict that when mating or status goals (see Table 13.1) are activated for males, they will exhibit more resistance to social proof in public settings.[2] Resistance to conformity should be greater when local social norms emphasize individual achievement over group welfare, or when males in a group differ widely in their reproductive potential.

In the domains of mate selection and retention (see Table 13.1), being attuned to cues to valuable assets and the willingness to continue to share those assets with one's current partner become key adaptive problems to be solved. When there is uncertainty about a potential mate's value, as is the case when not all cues to mate value are equally observable, social proof may help a person make more accurate judgments of targets' mate value. For example, females may be able to quickly conclude that a given male has value as a potential mate because he displays evidence of a large resource base relative to his competitors (e.g., expensive home and leadership position in his group), but it may be more difficult to assess his willingness to share those resources faithfully with a relationship partner. Women attempting to estimate the likelihood of resource *investment* by a potential mate, for example, might consult others for their opinions in hopes of making a more accurate assessment.

There are documented examples of the application of social proof during mate choice among certain animal species. For instance, Höglund, Alatalo, Gibson, and Lundberg (1995) found that female black grouse were more likely to choose a particular male as a mate if they had witnessed that male copulating with an experimentally planted female dummy on his territory. In another set of studies conducted with guppies, Dugatkin (2000) demonstrated that when controlling for male attractiveness, female guppies preferred to mate with the male they had previously observed mating with a female model. In other words, when the relative quality of two male guppies was difficult to distinguish (under conditions of uncertainty), the heuristic of social proof kicked in. Social proof also appears to play a role in reducing uncertainty in the mate selection processes of humans. Graziano and his colleagues (Graziano, Jensen-Campbell, Shebilske, & Lundgren, 1993) found that women's private assessments of men's physical attractiveness and desirability as dating partners were significantly different when they viewed other women's ratings of the male targets' physical attractiveness and personality. In particular, negative information was given more weight than positive information, suggesting that reliance on social proof in this context is related to reducing the costs of choosing incorrectly. This effect was sex-specific; men's assessments of women were not affected by negative ratings given by other men. When there is imperfect diagnostic information concerning potential mates (i.e., uncertainty), women appear to rely on the judgments of other women as a benchmark (see also Kenrick & Gutierres, 1980).

Social proof may also play a role in calibrating adaptive decision rules to the local social ecology. In the mating domain there is evidence that one's sexual strategy, whether monogamous or promiscuous, is influenced by what others in the local mating pool are doing. Buunk and Bakker (1995) found that the likelihood of engaging in extra-pair sexual relations was significantly influenced by descriptive norms (many of my friends are doing it), over and above any effects of injunctive norms for the behavior (important others would consider it acceptable). Males, as the sex investing less in the reproductive process, are somewhat more responsive to social proof information that having multiple sexual partners is locally acceptable, whereas females, the sex investing more, are somewhat more resistant to social proof information regarding promiscuity (Kenrick et al., 2003). Kenrick et al. (2003) used simulations to demonstrate how minor random variations in the location of men and women adopting sex-typical decision rules (about whether to mate in a restricted or unrestricted manner) could lead neighborhoods to converge over time into completely monogamous or promiscuous environments. Different patterns emerged as men and women were influenced to change from a preferred sexual strategy when a local majority played the opposite strategy. Although men's and women's decision rules (as reported by college students) were not dramatically different, local variations in playing by either the male or female rules result in neighborhood-wide changes being much larger than the initially small differences in men's and women's strategies. These simulations provide a useful illustration of how individual decision-rules that evolved via sexual selection and differential parental investment can compound into the emergence of powerful and self-organizing social norms.

AUTHORITY

Another powerful influence principle is authority, or heuristic deference to another individual's opinions and recommendations when they are perceived as being either an expert on a particular topic, or a generally trustworthy individual (Cialdini, 2001). A person is more likely to defer to authorities when he or she lacks the experience to make an informed decision, and when the outcome of the choice is critical. In its normal social context, deference to an authority's expertise allows individuals to capitalize on the social learning of others, and to profit from division of expertise within the group. Reliance on an expert makes sense when the goal is to make an accurate and efficient decision, and when there is a correct answer.

Authority can also be based upon characteristics not linked to informational expertise, such as physical size. Evidence suggests that leaders, such as corporation executives and heads of state, are often chosen based upon the seemingly irrelevant characteristic of height (Simonton, 1994). Conversely, perceivers see the same individual as taller when he is presented as having a relatively higher status rank (e.g., a professor as opposed to a graduate student). The link between physical size and authority seems to make little sense in the modern world, and it is often lamented as an irrational aspect of leader choice. Furthermore, men are more likely to be chosen as leaders than are women, despite the lack of evidence that men actually make more effective leaders (Eagly, Karau, &

Makhijani, 1995). Men are more frequently chosen as political leaders worldwide (Inter-Parliamentary Union, 2004), and were the traditional chiefs in tribal society (Daly & Wilson, 1983).

An evolutionary perspective can help explain why height and gender are perceived as important criteria in choosing leaders (even if that perception does not fit with demands of modern corporations or political decision-making groups). In the ancestral environment, large males may have been more effective in negotiating intergroup conflict. Males are, compared to females, also more likely to compete for positions of status, owing to differential parental investment and sexual selection (Kenrick, Trost, & Sundie, 2004). In species in which females make higher investment in offspring, males tend to mature later, grow physically larger, and engage in relatively more intrasexual competition—all characteristics of *Homo sapiens* (Geary, 2000). Further, among humans, intergroup fighting is and has always been common. Human males are, compared to females, more likely to be involved in such intergroup dominance competition (Sidanius, Levin, Liu, & Pratto, 2000). Males across societies are likely to seek status via roles such as policemen and soldiers, and females tend, on average, not to be as involved in these arenas (Pratto, Stallworth, Sidanius, & Siers, 1997).

A consideration of the universal sex difference in the occupancy of various forms of status leads to questions about the role of sex as a moderating variable in influence behaviors. Consider the classic demonstration of the power of authority in social influence—Milgram's (1974) experiments on obedience to authority. In the best-known studies, the authority figures, the participants, and the victims were all males. A very simple hypothesis would be that males who are ordering violence against other males are more likely to be obeyed than when females are either the authorities or the victims. Abundant research does in fact demonstrate that members of both sexes are more likely to aggress against males than against females (Daly & Wilson, 1988). In most of this classic aggression research, the authority figure (experimenter) was likely to be a male. We are not aware of studies in which the gender of each of the roles were systematically varied, or of studies in which the attractiveness of female victims was varied, but interesting interactions would be expected given our above reasoning.

Another interesting set of questions following this line of reasoning would ask about the physical size of the authority figure. We would predict that larger experimenters will generate more obedience, but only when they are males. It would similarly be of interest to examine physical size as a moderating factor in studies involving less direct social pressure, i.e., in studies of compliance (where participants receive requests rather than orders) and conformity (where neither requests nor orders are involved).

We noted at several points above that different influence tactics might be differentially effective when participants are in certain motivational states as opposed to others. We would expect that activation of different social goals would have similar differential effects on the power of physical size as an influence factor. For example, people who are made to feel self-protective following a fear manipulation ought to be more responsive to a large male authority figure than people for whom say parental care or mate retention are activated (see Table 13.1). A manipulation of status concerns would likewise be expected to make physical size a salient cue, again particularly when the authority figure was a male. However, in this case, the effects might be different for male and female participants. We would expect male participants concerned about their status to be especially likely to resist influence attempts by a physically large male, whereas this would not be expected for female participants.

COMMITMENT AND CONSISTENCY

The final influence tactic we consider is based on people's tendency to follow a course of action if they have previously made a commitment to that course. As noted earlier, cooperative alliances have been a powerful factor in human evolution. By relying on one another, our ancestors could accomplish tasks they would have been unable to accomplish alone, such as hunting large mammals, sharing food in times of variable nutrient availability, building shelters, and protecting themselves against hostile out-groups. To carry out such group tasks, group members had to be able to count on one another to stick to important commitments (such as showing up for a group hunt or meeting up at a certain location in 2 day's time). Cottrell, Neuberg, and Li (2005) demonstrated that when people seek various types of coalition partners, being trustworthy tops the list of desirable attributes.

Perhaps owing to the importance of being perceived as reliable and trustworthy, people generally hold to the rule "stick to your commitments" in a simple and heuristic manner (Cialdini, 2001). An influence agent may leverage this heuristic in numerous ways. For example, the agent attempting to gain compliance with a large request may first attempt to get that target to comply with a much smaller request: a commitment and consistency-based tactic called the *foot-in-the-door*. Once the target has committed to supporting a cause in some small way, such as putting a 3-in. square sign in their front yard advocating safe driving, he or she is significantly more inclined to agree to more substantial follow-up requests, such as replacing the unobtrusive sign with a large, unattractive billboard (Freedman & Fraser, 1966). Once the homeowners had publicly committed to the cause, and began to see themselves as advocates of safe driving, pressures to comply with cause-related requests loomed large.

A number of classic social psychological theories have addressed the motivation to act consistently (e.g., Festinger's cognitive dissonance theory, 1957; Heider's balance theory, 1958). According to dissonance theory, for example, people have a strong intrinsic motivation to view themselves as consistent, and this motivation is powerful enough to lead to a number of counterintuitive and sometimes self-destructive behaviors. For example, dissonance researchers examining "insufficient justification" have argued that people will often increase their commitment to a course of action after being exposed to evidence that their commitment is poorly justified. In a classic participant-observational study, Festinger and his colleagues joined a group of people (called the "Seekers") who had committed themselves to the view that a great cataclysm would occur on earth on a particular date, and that they alone would be borne away on a flying saucer. After the specified date came and went without a cataclysm or a visiting flying saucer, several members of the Seekers enhanced their commitment to the group's beliefs. Along similar lines, several studies demonstrated that people who had undergone a severe initiation were more committed to their group afterwards than control participants who had not experienced similar abuse (Aronson & Mills, 1959; Gerard & Mathewson, 1966). Dissonance theory suggests that this increased commitment to the group justifies (i.e., reduces the dissonance associated with) volunteering for membership in a group that routinely engages in abuse of its members.

From an adaptationist perspective, we doubt very much that people are frequently inclined to place a high value on cognitive consistency *per se*, especially if that consistency comes at a cost to social and material resources. People may well be generally motivated to appear consistent to others, and this heuristic tendency may occasionally result in seemingly behavioral irrationalities. However, we would expect that such tendencies are much more likely to be manifested around questions involving unverifiable beliefs or social reality rather than physical reality. When there is a clear correct answer that can be validated against physical reality, it seems likely that people will override their motivation to want to reduce "cognitive dissonance" in favor of reducing the loss of good resources after bad. Indeed, one key detail of the story of the Seekers that often fails to make it into social psychologists' lectures about cognitive dissonance is that most of the group members became less, rather than more, committed to the groups' beliefs after their central prophecy failed.

We would hypothesize that any tendency to act consistently with one's commitments will ultimately be driven not by motives that begin and end in the person's head, but by the adaptive social consequences of acting consistently or inconsistently. Thus consistency motivation should vary depending on which commitments are made and to whom, and on who is watching. For instance, people should be more likely to increase their commitment to a group after painful or humiliating initiations only when that group affords the initiates significant social and/or reproductive benefits, and when the initiates perceive that few, if any, viable alternatives are available.

Insufficient justification findings might be extrapolated to romantic relationships to suggest that people will sometimes become more committed to partners who treat them relatively poorly, as opposed to relatively well. Thus, evidence that one's partner had engaged in a minor infidelity might be expected to enhance one's commitment to a partner (especially if one had already committed resources and energy to the relationship, and made a public commitment). We would suggest that this pattern of "dissonance reduction" is very unlikely to occur for males, who risk investing resources in offspring who are not their own if they remain with a sexually unfaithful partner. On the other hand, a dissonance-like pattern might occasionally occur for females, but for different reasons—another woman's interest in a man does not raise the risk that a woman will unknowingly raise another woman's offspring, so single sexual infidelities do not constitute as great a potential reproductive liability. Further, most human societies have been somewhat polygynous, and evidence that other women find a man attractive may actually increase his perceived mate value. As discussed earlier, there is some evidence that women's judgments of a man's attractiveness are relatively more affected by other women's judgments (compared to the effect of other men's judgments on one another; Graziano et al., 1993). This is not to suggest that women will generally find infidelities grounds for increasing their feelings of commitment and relationship satisfaction. Indeed women are just as angry and jealous over infidelities as are men (e.g., Sagarin & Guadagno, 2004). Affairs can threaten, or directly result in losses of resources provided by women's mates. However, we would argue that any counterintuitive prediction that people will become more committed to unfaithful partners will surely not hold for males, and if ever found for females will be the product of processes other than the motivation to achieve cognitive consistency.

In general, we would hypothesize that people will be more susceptible to commitment and consistency tactics when their coalition formation goals are active (see Table 13.1), particularly if the influence agent is a member of a group the target finds particularly desirable. The pressure to appear consistent should also be enhanced when dealing with potential romantic partners, who are likely making assessments of a possible mate's trustworthiness and reliability.

HOW WE CAN BE CHEATED

Any of the six influence principles we have covered can be employed deceptively to gain compliance from an unwitting target. In this section, we outline how we think an evolutionary perspective can contribute to our understanding about why such deception succeeds. We will also offer a perspective on the countermeasures people employ to combat such deceptive practices. First we will consider how people's tendency to categorize others in social interactions makes individuals susceptible to being cheated.

In or Out: In-Group and Out-Group Distinctions in Social Influence

The tendency to make distinctions between in-group and out-group members is universal (Pinker, 2002). Experimental evidence suggests that targets are quickly encoded as belonging, or not belonging, to the in-group, and that the resulting categorization influences subsequent cognitive processing about that person (Maner et al., 2003). Strangers or out-group members are generally not afforded any implicit trust. However, when a stranger sends signals ordinarily associated with commitment and the desire for a long-term social relationship during an influence attempt (perhaps during a sales pitch), these signals are sometimes sufficient to evoke a desired heuristic compliance response. What are these signals? Offering gifts, favors, or concessions, and in certain instances displaying cues to sexual interest, can all serve to communicate a desire to be included in the target's in-group. Displaying cues to similarity, as noted above, may serve to activate kinship cognitions (a special type of in-group cognitions) that then predispose targets to cooperate. We propose that the tendency to categorize others quickly as in-group or out-group members enhances susceptibility to being cheated by agents using influence principles deceptively, and provide some examples for specific influence principles below.

It usually makes sense to comply with in-group members' requests, because the opportunity for mutually beneficial exchange in the future can outweigh any present costs. In the case of the reciprocity principle, even offers of very inexpensive gifts such as a can of Coke (Regan, 1971) or a flower (Cialdini, 2001) can be sufficient to significantly raise compliance rates with a donation request that follows. This implies that people are quite sensitive to such overtures, and that the economic value of what is offered may be far less important than the act of offering itself. We suggest that such overtures can serve to shift the target's perceptions of the influence agent (albeit unconsciously) toward in-group membership, and thereby engage responses normally appropriate for dealing with trusted in-group members. For example, with in-group members, reciprocity norms dictate that one is obligated to *receive* and *repay*. Unscrupulous influence agents take advantage of this heuristic response to cues of in-group membership, and extend gifts to targets simply to increase the chances of gaining subsequent compliance with their request.

The deceptive use of reciprocity tactics is further fueled by the lack of costs to offset the benefits expected by unscrupulous agents employing these techniques. Recall that the costs of violating reciprocity norms, for example, are social in nature and at worst result in expulsion from the group and all its benefits. A compliance professional who is a stranger to his or her target in a modern urban environment often has little or no interest in becoming a member of that target's in-group, and therefore does not face the normal costs associated with using influence tactics deceptively. In fact, in one-time interactions with unfamiliar others, influence agents can often expect net benefits from applying liking or reciprocity tactics dishonestly—they can gain targets' compliance in the short-run, and then disappear before any long-term costs come to bear.

Influence agents may also feign various overlapping interests in hopes of increasing their chances of success in gaining compliance from a target. An agent may insincerely compliment a target, point out false shared interests or values, or attempt to capitalize on his or her physical attractiveness by showering positive attention on an influence target. Such actions communicate liking, which characterizes close relationships such as friendships, but also can serve as an effective manipulation tool for unethical agents to advance their own objectives. As noted above, manipulations of liking based on similarity can activate kinship cognitions (Park & Schaller, 2005). Once in-group cognitions, or more specifically kinship cognitions, are activated for an influence target, conditions become ripe for cheating and exploitation by unscrupulous agents.

Compliance professionals can also take advantage of our heuristic responses to social proof information, particularly when their targets are uncertain about which choice is correct. Social proof does not require that a group be present for the target to observe directly—information about the previous choices of others in similar circumstances can also be effective. Reflections of social proof, such as "over 1 million sold" or "75% of Democrats support…" can serve as evidence that the choice makes sense for the target too. Such evidence is given more weight to the extent that a target perceives the "other people" to be similar to him or her on a problem-relevant dimension. To the extent that perceived similarity is a proxy for in-group membership, it will add to the power of the social proof because people often trust that what is beneficial for other in-group members will also be good for them.

In-group vs. out-group distinctions may also affect the operation of the authority and commitment and consistency principles. Authority is based on expertise and trustworthiness assessments, and so unscrupulous influence agents convincingly displaying false symbols of in-group or kin-group membership with a target should be perceived as more trustworthy, enhancing that agent's authority status. This enhanced credibility can then presumably be leveraged to gain the targets' deference and compliance.

Influence professionals have developed a host of deceptive tactics based on people's motivation to appear consistent and stick to their commitments, ranging from inducements to "sign on the dotted line," to more elaborate tactics. For example, the "low ball" technique involves getting a customer to commit to buying a commodity at a certain price, and then to change the deal to the advantage of the influence agent (Cialdini, Cacioppo, Bassett, & Miller, 1978). As traditionally used by car salespersons, the customer agrees to buy a car at a certain price (say, $20,000), and after several minutes the salesperson returns from the manager's office with a downtrodden look, saying "the manager agreed to sell it for that price, but for that price we can't include the CD player and upgraded speakers you wanted." After having committed themselves to closing the deal, customers frequently comply despite the change in what they are getting for their money, or end up agreeing to pay more than the agreed upon price to add additional options, such as the stereo system in the example above. After making such deals under such pressure, customers may feel cheated, as evidenced by the fact that many states have passed laws requiring several days "cooling off" period during which customers can recant on unfavorable transactions. Because people are likely to be more concerned with self-presentation when among in-group members, influence agents who can activate in-group or kinship cognitions for a target based on false cues should also be more successful in employing consistency-based tactics. Targets should feel more pressure to be consistent if these in-group cognitions are active at the time that the agent makes his or her request.

I Won't be Fooled Again

How might individuals react to deceptive influence attempts, or think about them retrospectively when they are duped into complying? While reciprocity motivation can be powerful in cementing mutually beneficial social relationships, it can also induce strong negative emotional responses (e.g., shame, regret, anger, or a desire for revenge) when used deceptively. Gintis, Bowles, Boyd, & Fehr (2003) propose that human social behavior is governed by *strong* reciprocity—a tendency, on the positive side, to be more generous with others than is economically rational, and, on the negative side, to incur great costs to punish cheaters, even when there is no reasonable belief that the costs will be recouped. The willingness to sacrifice additional resources to punish a cheater (who has taken away resources already) suggests that there is social value in being regarded by others as someone "not to be cheated." Such vigilante justice for reciprocity cheaters may well be guided by a psychological mechanism specifically designed to detect cheaters on reciprocal social contracts, and motivate action accordingly.

Cosmides and Tooby (1992) outlined the capabilities a cheating detection mechanism would encompass, and have provided experimental evidence in support of its existence. People are good at solving normally difficult logical problems if those problems are framed in terms of possible violations of a social contract, and this enhanced facility at thinking about possible cheaters is found cross-culturally (Sugiyama, Tooby, & Cosmides, 2002). It is plausible that the negative emotions associated with being socially cheated serve to motivate the infliction of costs upon the deceptive agent (Cosmides & Tooby, 2000). The influence agent responsible might be classified as a cheater and out-group member, punished, or barred from future involvement, depending on the severity of the offense. The presence of specialized reasoning in humans for uncovering cheaters on social contracts implies that at least some social cheating was a regular feature of the ancestral environment, and that capabilities for detection and adequate response contributed to the reproductive success of our ancestors.

Humans are not the only species that fall prey to unscrupulous influence attempts, such as false cues to similarity and familiarity. Mimicry and the false signaling of group membership are employed by a wide variety of animals, insects, and plants to further their own self-interests in survival and reproduction (see Alcock, 2001 for a review). For example, female cuckoos regularly parasitize other bird species by placing their eggs in an unwitting host's nest while it is away. Apparently unequipped to distinguish a cuckoo's egg from her own, the host incubates the egg and even provides food and protection to the cuckoo chick along with its own genetic hatchlings. Because of the reproductive costs imposed on the host by such a system of exploitation, the host species may develop defenses against the deception. This may include an enhanced capability to detect physical differences between the cuckoos' eggs and the host's own eggs, if the costs of developing those features do not exceed the benefits. The result is a kind of host–parasite arms race (Dawkins, 1982), where via differential reproduction the parasite also develops countermeasures to the host species' enhanced deception-detection capabilities. For example, in geographic regions where the cuckoo has been exploiting a host for many generations, cuckoo eggs have changed in color to match the hosts' eggs quite closely, thereby making discrimination more difficult (Underwood & Sealy, 2002).

The relationship between the cuckoo and its host serves as a metaphor for the relationship between human influence agents and their targets. While influence agents can take advantage of liking tactics to gain compliance, for example, influence targets are likely equipped with deception-detection capabilities such as the cheating detection mechanism and the inclination toward costly revenge noted above. Such capabilities can be developed more rapidly than the speed of natural selection, since people can also presumably learn, over the course of repeated influence interactions, what the signs of deception are and be attentive to their presence. Hence, they may become better at detecting deception attempts by opportunistic influence agents over time. Such learning also occurs in other species. In passerine birds, for example, experimental evidence suggest that younger females' nests are more likely to be parasitized by nearby cuckoos in part because they are less likely to recognize the parasitic eggs than are the older females of the species (Grim, 2002).

What are the outcomes for human agents that choose to engage in deceptive practices? When deception becomes clear to the target in retrospect, the tactic employed should cease to work as well in future interactions between that agent and target. The person duped may take steps to avoid future contact with this individual, and may spread negative word-of-mouth about the influence agent to others. In this case, damage to the agent's social reputation is the likely result. Even when deception is not uncovered, deceptive tactics that only benefit the agent will often result in poor outcomes for the target. Those poor outcomes may also serve to deter future interaction with the agent involved (Cialdini, 1999).

CONCLUSIONS

We propose that research on social influence could be enhanced by considering more deeply the evolutionary context for which the various tactics were designed. An evolutionary perspective offers powerful theories such as inclusive fitness and sexual selection that could be used to generate unique hypotheses about social influence. These theories counsel a greater focus on research exploring influence within various kinds of familiar relationships, such as kin relationships, romantic partnerships, and friendships, where the exchange of resources is continually guided by mutual influence over time (e.g., Oriña, Wood, & Simpson, 2002). Within these relationships, features of the bond between two individuals, whether it be liking based on similar interests, shared reproductive interests between long-term romantic partners, or shared genes between kin, may fundamentally affect the costs and benefits associated with compliance, and the relative success of the various tactics designed to achieve it. Likewise, people's responses to the perception that they have been cheated by an influence agent may heavily depend on the type of relationship between the influence agent and the target, with more tolerance expected toward kin, little or no tolerance expected toward strangers, and varying degrees of tolerance expected toward other kinds of relationship partners such as friends and romantic partners.

Much of the focus in previous social influence research has been on interactions between strangers, and how the various influence principles can be exploited by unscrupulous agents (and how people might protect themselves from such agents). Consequently, the six major influence tactics have been framed as sources of error in social decision-making—focusing on how compliance with such tactics commonly results in irrevocable costs. We think it is crucial to consider that influence tactics are a part of the evolved social adaptive toolbox, and normally work to promote long-term beneficial exchange relations between individuals over time. From an evolutionary perspective, we can re-examine the deceptive use of these tactics by taking into account that in the social conditions faced by our distant human ancestors, the chance of being exploited by an unscrupulous stranger was likely lower than it is in today's modern world, and that the defenses we have developed to deal with social cheaters in ancestral times may not always be well-suited for punishing deceptive agents of influence today. By considering how influence tactics are designed to serve fundamental social goals such as gaining and maintaining status, building coalitions, and winning over potential mates, we can obtain new insights about how those tactics are sometimes exploited in modern environments.

NOTES

1. This is expected to hold true whether the relationship implied by the behavior of the agent is authentic or not (i.e., the influence agent may be attempting to deceive the influence target).
2. In research, since the writing of this chapter, we have found empirical support for this hypothesis (see Griskevicius, Goldstein, Mortensen, Cialdini, & Kenrick, in press).

REFERENCES

Abrams, D., Wetherell, M., Cochrane, S., Hogg, M. A., & Turner, J. C. (1990). Knowing what to think by knowing who you are: Self-categorization and the nature of norm formation, conformity and group polarization. *British Journal of Social Psychology*, 29, 97–119.

Alcock, J. (2001). *Animal behavior: An evolutionary approach*. Sunderland, MA: Sinauer Assoc.

Aronson, E., & Mills, J. (1959). The effect of severity of initiation on liking for a group. *Journal of Abnormal and Social Psychology*, 59, 177–181.

Baumeister, R. F., & Sommer, K. L. (1997). What do men want? Gender differences in two spheres of belongingness. *Psychological Bulletin*, 122, 38–44.

Betzig, L. (1989). Causes of conjugal dissolution: A cross-cultural study. *Current Anthropology*, 30, 654–676.

Betzig L. L., & Turke, P. W. (1986). Food sharing on Ifaluk. *Current Anthropology*, 27, 397–400.

Borgia, G., & Gore, M. (1986). Feather stealing in the satin bowerbird (*Plitonorhynchus violaceus*): Male competition and the quality of display. *Animal Behaviour*, 34, 727–738.

Brown, D. E. (1991). *Human universals*. New York: McGraw-Hill.

Burn, S. W. (1991). Social psychology and the stimulation of recycling behaviors: The block leader approach. *Journal of Applied Psychology*, 21, 611–629.

Burnstein, E., Crandall, C., & Kitayama, S. (1994). Some neo-Darwinian decision rules for altruism: Weighing cues for inclusive fitness as a function of the biological importance of the decision. *Journal of Personality and Social Psychology*, 67, 773–789.

Buss, D. M. (2004). *Evolutionary psychology: The new science of the mind* (2nd ed.). Boston: Pearson.

Buss, D. M., Larsen, R. J., Westen, D., & Semmelroth, J. (1992). Sex differences in jealousy: Evolution, physiology, and psychology. *Psychological Science, 3,* 251–255.

Buss, D. M., & Schmitt, D. P. (1993). Sexual strategies theory: An evolutionary perspective on human mating. *Psychological Review, 100,* 204–232.

Buunk, B. P., & Bakker, A. B. (1995). Extradyadic sex: The role of descriptive and injunctive norms. *The Journal of Sex Research, 32,* 313–318.

Castelli, L., Vanzetto, K., Sherman, S. J., & Arcuri, L. (2001). The explicit and implicit perception of in-group members who use stereotypes: Blatant rejection but subtle conformity. *Journal of Experimental Social Psychology, 37,* 419–426.

Cialdini, R. B. (1999). Of tricks and tumors: Some little-recognized costs of dishonest use of effective social influence. *Psychology & Marketing, 16,* 91–98.

Cialdini, R. B. (2001). *Influence: Science and practice* (4th ed.). Boston: Allyn & Bacon.

Cialdini, R. B., Cacioppo, J. T., Bassett, R., & Miller, J. A. (1978). Low-ball procedure for producing compliance: Commitment then cost. *Journal of Personality and Social Psychology, 36,* 463–476.

Clark, R. D., & Hatfield, E. (1989). Gender differences in receptivity to sexual offers. *Journal of Psychology & Human Sexuality, 2,* 39–55.

Clark, M. S., & Mills, J. (1979). Interpersonal attraction in communal and exchange relationships. *Journal of Personality and Social Psychology, 37,* 12–24.

Clark, M. S., & Mills, J. (1993). The difference between communal and exchange relationships: What it is and is not. *Personality and Social Psychology Bulletin, 19,* 684–691.

Coleman, S. W., Patricelli, G. L., & Borgia, G. (2004). Variable female preferences drive complex male displays. *Nature, 428,* 742–745.

Cosmides, L., & Tooby, J. (1992). Cognitive adaptations for social exchange. In J. H. Barkow, L. Cosmides, & J. Tooby (Eds.), *The adapted mind: Evolutionary psychology and the generation of culture* (pp. 163–228). London: Oxford University Press.

Cosmides, L., & Tooby, J. (2000). Evolutionary psychology and the emotions. In M. Lewis & J. M. Haviland-Jones (Eds.), *Handbook of emotions* (pp. 91–115). New York: The Guilford Press.

Cotterell, N., Eisenberger, R., & Speicher, H. (1992). Inhibiting effects of reciprocation wariness on interpersonal relationships. *Journal of Personality and Social Psychology, 62,* 658–668.

Cottrell, C. A., Neuberg, S. L., & Li, N. P. (2005). What do people desire in others? A sociofunctional perspective on the importance of different valued characteristics. Manuscript submitted for publication.

Daly, M., & Wilson, M. (1983). *Sex, evolution and behavior.* Belmont, CA: Wadsworth.

Daly, M., & Wilson, M. (1988). *Homocide.* New York: Aldine deGruyter.

Dawkins, R. (1982). *The extended phenotype: The gene as the unit of selection.* Oxford: Oxford University Press.

Dugatkin, L. A. (2000). *The imitation factor: Evolution beyond the gene.* New York: Free Press.

Eagly, A. H., & Carli, L. L. (1981). Sex of researchers and sex-types communications as determinants of sex differences in influencability: A meta-analysis of social influence studies. *Psychological Bulletin, 90,* 1–20.

Eagly, A. H., Karau, S. J., & Makhijani, M. G. (1995). Gender and the effectiveness of leaders: A meta-analysis. *Psychological Bulletin, 117,* 125–145.

Eagly, A. H., Wood, W., & Fishbaugh, L. (1981). Sex differences in conformity: Surveillance by the group as a determinant of male nonconformity. *Journal of Personality and Social Psychology, 40,* 384–394.

Festinger, L. (1957). *A theory of cognitive dissonance*. Stanford, CA: Stanford University Press.

Fiske, A. P. (1992). The four elementary forms of sociality: Framework for a unified theory of social relations. *Psychological Review, 99*, 689–723.

Foa, E. B., & Foa, U. G. (1976). Resource theory of social exchange. In J. W. Thibaut, J. Spence, & R. C. Carson (Eds.), *Contemporary topics in social psychology*. Morristown, NJ: General Learning Press.

Freedman, J. L., & Fraser, S. C. (1966). Compliance without pressure: The foot-in-the-door technique. *Journal of Personality and Social Psychology, 4*, 195–203.

Geary, D. C. (2000). Evolution and proximate expression of human paternal investment. *Psychological Bulletin, 126*, 55–77.

Gerard, H. B., & Mathewson, G. C. (1966). The effects of severity of initiation on liking for a group: A replication. *Journal of Experimental Social Psychology, 2*, 278–287.

Gigerenzer, G., & Selten, R. (Eds.). (2001). *Bounded rationality: The adaptive toolbox*. Cambridge, MA: The MIT Press.

Gigerenzer, G., & Todd, P. M. (Eds.). (1999). *Simple heuristics that make us smart*. London: Oxford University Press.

Gintis, H., Bowles, S., Boyd, R., & Fehr, E. (2003). Explaining altruistic behavior in humans. *Evolution and Human Behavior, 24*, 153–172.

Gouldner, A. W. (1960). The norm of reciprocity: A preliminary statement. *American Sociological Review, 25*, 161–178.

Graziano, W. G., Jensen-Campbell, L. A., Shebilske, L. J., & Lundgren, S. R. (1993). Social influence, sex differences, and judgments of beauty: Putting the interpersonal back in interpersonal attraction. *Journal of Personality and Social Psychology, 65*, 522–531.

Grim, T. (2002). Why is mimicry in cuckoo eggs sometimes so poor? *Journal of Avian Biology, 33*, 302–305.

Griskevicius, V., Goldstein, N. J., Mortensen, C. R., Cialdini, R. B., & Kenrick, D. T. (in press). Going along versus going alone: When fundamental motives facilitate strategic (non) conformity. *Journal of Personality and Social Psychology*.

Hamilton, W. D. (1964). The genetic evolution of social behavior. *Journal of Theoretical Biology, 7*, 1–52.

Haselton, M. G., & Buss, D. M. (2000). Error management theory: A new perspective on biases in cross-sex mind reading. *Journal of Personality and Social Psychology, 78*, 81–91.

Heider, F. (1958). *The psychology of interpersonal relations*. Hillsdale, NJ: Lawrence Erlbaum Associates, Inc.

Henrich, J., & Boyd, R. (1998). The evolution of conformist transmission and the emergence of between-group differences. *Evolution and Human Behavior, 19*, 215–241.

Höglund, J., Alatalo, R. V., Gibson, R. M., & Lundberg, A. (1995). Mate-choice copying in black grouse. *Animal Behaviour, 49*, 1627–1633.

Hrdy, S. B. (1999). *Mother nature*. New York: Random House.

Inter-Parliamentary Union. (2004). *Women in national parliaments*. Retrieved January 13, 2005, from http://www.ipu.org/wmn-e/classif.ht.

Kahneman, D., Knetsch, J., & Thaler, R. (1986). Fairness and the assumptions of economics. *Journal of Business, 59*, S285–S300.

Kahneman, D., Slovic, P., & Tversky, A. (Eds.). (1982). *Judgment under uncertainty: Heuristics and biases*. New York: Cambridge University Press.

Kaplan, H., & Hill, K. (1985a). Food sharing among Ache foragers: Tests of explanatory hypotheses. *Current Anthropology, 26*, 223–246.

Kaplan, H., & Hill, K. (1985b). Hunting ability and reproductive success among male ache foragers: Preliminary results. *Current Anthropology, 26*, 131–133.

Kenrick, D. T., Groth, G. E., Trost, M. R., & Sadalla, E. K. (1993). Integrating evolutionary and social exchange perspectives on relationship: Effects of gender, self-appraisal, and involvement level on mate selection criteria. *Journal of Personality and Social Psychology, 64*, 951–969.

Kenrick, D. T., & Gutierres, S. E. (1980). Contrast effects and judgments of physical attractiveness: When beauty becomes a social problem. *Journal of Personality and Social Psychology, 38*, 131–140.

Kenrick, D. T., Li, N. P., & Butner, J. (2003). Dynamical evolutionary psychology: Individual decision rules and emergent social norms. *Psychological Review, 110*, 3–28.

Kenrick, D. T., Sadalla, E. K., Groth, G., & Trost, M. R. (1990). Evolution, traits, and the stages of human courtship: Qualifying the parental investment model. *Journal of Personality, 58*, 97–116.

Kenrick, D. T., Sadalla, E. K., & Keefe, R. C. (1998). Evolutionary cognitive psychology: The missing heart of modern cognitive science. In C. Crawford & D. L. Krebs (Eds.), *Handbook of evolutionary psychology* (pp. 485–514). Hillsdale, NJ: Erlbaum.

Kenrick, D. T., & Trost, M. R. (1989). A reproductive exchange model of heterosexual relationships: Putting proximate economics in ultimate perspective. In C. Hendrick (Ed.), *Review of personality & social psychology* (Vol. 10). Newbury Park, CA: Sage.

Kenrick, D. T., Trost, M. R., & Sundie, J. M. (2004). Sex-roles as adaptations: An evolutionary perspective on gender differences and similarities. In A. H. Eagly, A. E. Beall, & R. J. Sternberg (Eds.), *The psychology of gender*. New York: The Guilford Press.

Lumsden, C. J., & Wilson, E. O. (1981). *Genes, mind, & culture: The coevolutionary process*. Cambridge, MA: Harvard University Press.

Maner, J. K., Kenrick, D. T., Becker, D. V., Delton, A. W., Hofer, B., Wilbur, C. J., & Neuberg, S. L. (2003). Sexually selected cognition: Beauty captures the mind of the beholder. *Journal of Personality and Social Psychology, 85*, 1107–1120.

Martindale, C. (1980). Subselves. In L. Wheeler (Ed.), *Review of personality & social psychology*. Beverly Hills, CA: Sage.

Martindale, C. (1991). *Cognitive psychology: A neural-network approach*. Pacific Grove, CA: Brooks/Cole.

Mauss, M. (1954). *The gift* (I. G. Cunison, Trans.). London: Cohen and West.

Milgram, S. (1974). *Obedience to authority: An experimental view*. New York: Harper & Row.

Miller, G. (2000). *The mating mind: How sexual choice shaped the evolution of human nature*. New York: Random House.

Mills, J., & Clark, M. S. (2001). Viewing close romantic relationships as communal relationships: Implications for maintenance and enhancement. In J. Harvey & A. Wenzel (Eds.), *Close romantic relationships: Maintenance and enhancement* (pp. 13–25). Mahwah, NJ: Lawrence Erlbaum Associates, Inc.

Nisbett, R., & Ross, L. (1980). *Human inference: Strategies and shortcomings of social judgment*. Englewood Cliffs, NJ: Prentice-Hall.

Oriña, M. M., Wood, W., & Simpson, J. A. (2002). Strategies of influence in close relationships. *Journal of Experimental Social Psychology, 38*, 459–472.

Park, J. H., & Schaller, M. (2005). Does attitude similarity serve as a heuristic cue for kinship? Evidence of an implicit cognitive association. *Evolution and Human Behavior, 26*, 158–170.

Pinker, S. (2002). *The blank slate: The modern denial of human nature.* New York: Viking.

Pratto, F., Stallworth, L. M., Sidanius, J., & Siers, B. (1997). The gender gap in occupational role attainment: A social dominance approach. *Journal of Personality and Social Psychology, 72*, 37–53.

Regan, R. T. (1971). Effects of a favor on liking and compliance. *Journal of Experimental Social Psychology, 7*, 627–639.

Regan, P. C. (1998). What if you can't get what you want? Willingness to compromise ideal mate selection standards as a function of sex, mate value, and relationship context. *Personality and Social Psychology Bulletin, 24*, 1294–1303.

Sagarin, B. S., & Guadagno, R. E. (2004) Sex differences in the contexts of extreme jealousy. *Personal Relationships, 11*, 319–328.

Schultz, P. W. (1999). Changing behavior with normative feedback interventions: A field experiment on curbside recycling. *Basic & Applied Social Psychology, 21*, 25–36.

Sherif, M. (1936). *The psychology of norms.* New York: Harper.

Sherry, D. F., & Shachter, D. L. (1987). The evolution of multiple memory systems. *Psychological Review, 94*, 439–454.

Sidanius, J., Levin, S., Liu, J., & Pratto, F. (2000). Social dominance orientation, anti-egalitarianism and the political psychology of gender: An extension and cross-cultural replication. *European Journal of Social Psychology, 30*, 41–67.

Simonton, D. K. (1994). Greatness: *Who makes history and why.* New York: The Guilford Press.

Sugiyama, L. S., Tooby, J., & Cosmides, L. (2002). Cross-cultural evidence of cognitive adaptations for social exchange among the Shiwiar of Ecuadorian Amazonia. *Proceedings of the National Academy of Sciences, 99*, 11537–11542.

Tipper, S. P. (1992). Selection for action: The role of inhibitory mechanisms. *Current Directions in Psychological Science, 1*, 105–109.

Trivers, R. L. (1972). Parental investment and sexual selection. In B. Campbell (Ed.), *Sexual selection and the descent of man 1871–1971* (pp. 136–179). Chicago: Aldine.

Underwood, T. J., & Sealy, S. G. (2002). Adaptive significance of egg coloration. In D. C. Deeming (Ed.), *Avian incubation: Behaviour, environment and evolution.* Oxford: Oxford University Press.

Wooten, D. B., & Reed II, A. (1998). Informational influence and the ambiguity of product experience: Order effects on the weighing of evidence. *Journal of Consumer Psychology, 7*, 79–99.

Zahavi, A., & Zahavi, A. (1997). *The handicap principle: A missing piece of Darwin's puzzle.* New York: Oxford University Press.

14

Groups as Adaptive Devices: Human Docility and Group Aggregation Mechanisms in Evolutionary Context

TATSUYA KAMEDA and R. SCOTT TINDALE

Camp 10 Ms. above the river Plate
Monday, July the 23rd, 1804—

a fair morning—Sent out a party of 5 men to look to timber for Ores two other parties to hunt at 11 oClock Sent, G. Drewyer & Peter Crusett ½ Indn. to the Otteaus Village about 18 ms. West of our Camp, to invite the Chiefs & principal men of that nation to come & talk with us &. &., also the *panis* if they Should meet with any of that nation (also on the S. Side of the Plate 30 ms. higher up) (at this Season of the year all the Indians in this quater are in the Plains hunting the Buffalow from Some Signs Seen by our hunter and the Praries being on fire in the derection of the Village induce a belief that the Nation have returned to get green Corn) raised a flag Staff put out Some provisions which got wet in the french Perogue to Sun & Dry—I commenced Coppying may map of the river to Send to the Presdt. of US. by the Return of a pty of Soldiers, from Illinois five Deer Killed— one man a bad riseing on his left breast. Wind from the N. W. [By William Clark, Co-captain of the Corps of Discovery (Nebraska edition of the Lewis and Clark journals edited by Gary E. Moulton. All errors are original.)]

T he text above is an excerpt from the journals of William Clark, who co-captained, with Meriwether Lewis, the expedition of the American West 1804 through 1806 (Moulton, 2003). President Thomas Jefferson ordered them to organize a corps to travel up the Missouri River to the Rocky Mountains and westward along possible river routes to the Pacific Ocean. Their 3-year journey with 33 crew members, later known as the Corps of Discovery, in totally unexplored territories provides vivid examples of recurrent adaptive tasks that groups encounter in unsophisticated natural environments. As evident in the quotation above, included in those adaptive tasks are securing food and fuel resources, finding shelters, acquiring knowledge about geography, animals, and plants, guarding against predators and enemies, possibly making allies with out-groups, and so on.

Although parallels between such modern, Holocene natural environments and the Pleistocene Environment of Evolutionary Adaptiveness (EEA) are at best speculative (cf. Potts, 1996; Richerson & Boyd, 2000), there is no doubt that humans have used (and will continue to use) groups to manage many adaptive tasks in our lives. Groups have been one of the most frequently used adaptive devices throughout hominid evolution and in modern human histories as well. Given this, social psychologists would be well served by revisiting various group behaviors and group phenomena from an evolutionary and adaptationist perspective, which in turn may provide for a common conceptual ground with evolutionary biologists interested in human social behaviors.

In this chapter, we aim to illustrate this approach, revisiting some of the core intra-group processes and group aggregation mechanisms in the light of adaptation. The adaptationist approach that we endorse in this chapter entails first specifying recurrent survival problems in our everyday, viz., ecologically representative, group settings. Then, it tries to disentangle specific design features of our cognitive and behavioral solutions, viz., strategies and heuristics, to those problems that enhance the fitness of individuals within the groups. As in the expedition by the Corps of Discovery, the lands awaiting us are largely unexplored. We hope that, along the way, we will also discover (or rediscover) many interesting themes and eventually find a new route to the conceptually refined "evolutionary social psychology of groups" (Kameda & Hastie, 2004; Krueger & Funder, 2004).

OUR WORKING MAP

A journey without a map can be quite dangerous, especially because the endeavor we will undertake is highly exploratory. Fortunately, our predecessors left us with a useful working map.

Efficiency in Group Performance as a Central Adaptive Question

As exemplified in the quotation from the journals of Captain Clark, group performance in recurrent adaptive tasks, such as hunting prey, gathering resources, finding shelter, monitoring against predators and enemies, and so on, directly determines the fitness of individuals within the groups. Questions concerning efficiency in collective performance are thus of central theoretical significance for understanding how humans, as fundamentally social species, achieve adaptations (Boyd & Richerson, 1985; Dunbar, 1992; Wilson & Sober, 1994). In a seminal work in the field of group psychology, Ivan Steiner (1972) provided a useful conceptual framework for studying group performance, although he did not explicitly link his framework to adaptation.

Steiner argued that, in order to evaluate a group's productivity, some performance baseline is needed for comparison. By positing a baseline for the group's optimal level of production under the assumption of some idealized coordination/combination of member resources, we can tell how well actual groups perform compared to the optimal baseline, figuring out empirically and theoretically potential causes that determine the actual group outcomes. In other words, such a baseline can serve as a heuristic device to help group research (Kerr, MacCoun, & Kramer, 1996; Kerr & Tindale, 2004).

One potential performance baseline frequently used in group research is the productivity level of the group's most competent member (Davis, 1969; Lorge & Solomon, 1955). For example, much of the early group research focused on intellectual tasks called "Eureka" tasks. As exemplified by some mathematical problems in the modern settings, an Eureka problem has a correct answer which is so intuitively compelling that, once someone offers it in a group, the group immediately recognizes its correctness. Thus, one normative baseline expected for a group is given by the performance level of the group's best member (or someone leading the group intellectually). Given our ordinary beliefs (e.g., "groups yield synergy", "two heads are better than one", and "the best and brightest serves as a group leader"), a group should yield performance that exceeds or at least is comparable to its most competent member's solo productivity. However, previous research has consistently found that usually groups not only fail to exceed such a baseline, but also often fall short of it. Such underperformance is rather counterintuitive, and has naturally been a major focus of small group research (e.g., Hill, 1982; Laughlin, 1999; Laughlin & Ellis, 1986; see Kerr & Tindale, 2004, for a recent comprehensive review).

Process Losses

To understand the gap between actual group performance and the productivity baseline, Steiner (1972) coined a term, *process losses*. Steiner argued that inefficiencies inherent in social processes are responsible for the group's failure to achieve "synergy," or even the performance level of its best member. Steiner (1972) also argued that process losses stem from one of two sources: *coordination* and *motivation* problems.

Coordination problems refer to difficulties in orchestrating members' various resources (knowledge, skills, and expertise) properly in a group setting. For example, if a member with poor eyesight were mistakenly assigned the role of lookout in the Corps of Discovery, then the group should be at serious risk. In many actual situations, however, members' expertise and skills are not directly observable, potentially leading to coordination failures. How to coordinate members' mental as well as physical resources is a key determinant of effective group performance.

On the other hand, motivation problems refer to members' loss of motivation in a group setting. The best-known example in social psychology is the social-loafing phenomenon, where members decrease individual inputs when their rewards are made contingent on pooled group performance (Latané, Williams, & Harkins, 1979). For example, if acquired resources are equally shared in groups (as is hunted meat in many hunter–gatherer societies; Kaplan & Hill, 1985), then members might well exploit others' efforts while avoiding to incur risks in foraging in the wild environment (cf. Kameda, Takezawa, & Hastie, 2003).Given that such a free-riding opportunity is inevitably inherent in many collective-action situations (Kerr & Stanfel, 1993; Olson, 1965), securing members' contributions toward a common goal is another key determinant of group performance.

We believe that Steiner's (1972) classic classifications of process losses will serve as a useful working map for our journey. In the following, we will revisit the coordination problems and the motivation problems from an evolutionary and adaptationist perspective. Along the way, we may observe that some of the group phenomena or biases that were originally thought to be problematic are not so problematic in light of adaptation. Some of them may be by-products or even manifestations of adaptive cognitive and behavioral mechanisms in ecologically representative settings (Gigerenzer & Selten, 2001).

In any event, this is only a rough conjecture at this point. Not wasting words, we have to record truthfully what we will discover (or rediscover) along the way onto our working map.

COORDINATION PROBLEMS

How to coordinate members' resources is a key to effective group performance. Indeed, classic studies in group problem-solving showed that unstructured group interaction often fails to deploy the right members at the right time. For example, Davis and Restle (1963; Restle & Davis, 1962), who studied logical reasoning by ad hoc (i.e., temporary) groups, found that group interaction was better approximated by an "egalitarian model" than by an "hierarchical model"; rather than a member on the right track leading the discussion, all members participated almost equally in the group discussion. When the group task is of an intellectual Eureka type, such a process often leads to inefficient outcomes, although the consensus process per se may look highly "democratic." Likewise, in jury deliberation (another ad hoc group), jurors often compete for status. For the first few hours of deliberation, some jurors "show-off" their toughness for the purpose of establishing their prestige in the group, while sacrificing factual discussions about the case (see Hastie, Penrod, & Pennington, 1983 for the most comprehensive jury study to date). Sociologists have developed a framework to study how such a "power and prestige order" may develop in interacting groups (Ridgeway & Walker, 1995). These observations suggest that proper coordination of members' resources constitutes a major challenge for the functioning of groups. The question, then, is how to solve this problem?

One obvious solution may be establishing effective leadership. Competent leaders (such as Captains Lewis and Clark) may solve the coordination problems properly. Yet, competence may have to be demonstrated first for the person to be regarded as a leader in the group, making the issue somewhat circular; how is a person with good coordination ability selected as a leader in the group?—a second-order coordination problem.

Or, is the establishing of leadership the only way to solve the coordination problems? Besides the use of leadership, there may be some "wisdom of the group" that people adopt naturally, similar to the adaptive heuristics discussed in the literature of individual judgment and decision-making. Researchers identified various "fast and frugal" heuristics whereby individuals can make adaptive judgments and decisions quickly, while substantially saving computation costs (e.g., Payne, Bettman, & Johnson, 1993; Gigerenzer, Todd, & the ABC Research Group, 1999). Some group-level heuristics, comparable to these individual heuristics, may exist that circumvent coordination problems. As candidates for such group-level adaptive shortcuts, we will focus on two social psychological phenomena here—use of "meta knowledge" (Cannon-Bowers, Salas, & Converse, 1993), and operation of "social-sharedness biases" (Tindale & Kameda, 2000) in group interaction.

Meta Knowledge

Meta knowledge, in the present context, refers to knowledge that one or more members have concerning the group as compared to members' knowledge about the task per se. For example, knowledge of who knows what, who possesses which skills, which members fulfill specific roles, etc. would all be considered meta knowledge about the group. This knowledge could be shared among all the members, or known by only some of the members. Recent research has shown that such meta knowledge can be an extremely important component of effective group performance (Cannon-Bowers et al., 1993; Hinsz, 1995; Stewart & Stasser, 1995; Tindale, Kameda, & Hinsz, 2003). In particular, allowing this information to be shared among all the members enhances group performance (Helmreich, 1997; Rentsch & Hall, 1994). Training groups so that group members both realize and understand the roles played by other members has been shown to increase performance in cockpit crews (Helmreich, 1997) and surgical teams (Helmreich & Schaefer, 1994).

Transactive Memory   One of the areas of meta knowledge in groups that has received a fair amount of attention is "transactive memory" (Wegner, 1987). Wegner argued that groups can store and process more information than individuals because they can share the responsibility of knowledge storage. However, in order to retrieve the information efficiently, a shared knowledge system must exist identifying who in the group knows what—a transactive memory system. Once such a system exists, each individual member only needs to store information for which they are responsible, easing the memory load on each member but increasing the total amount of information available to the group—cognitive division of labor.

A number of studies have shown that groups with a transactive memory system can outperform those without one (Hollingshead, 1998; Wegner, Erber, & Raymond, 1991). However, there is also evidence that such systems begin to form quite quickly through normal group interaction (Moreland, Argote, & Krishnan, 1998). Moreland et al. compared the performance of three-person groups trained as a group in assembling transistor radios to those groups whose members were trained in the task individually. The training period was only 30 minutes, yet groups trained as a group outperformed those where the members were trained individually. In addition, measures of shared knowledge of the task and differential expertise were shown to mediate the effects of the training manipulation. Thus, in only 30 minutes, groups had begun to develop a useful transactive memory system.

Statistical Cues About Relative Expertise   There are also a number of statistical cues present in normal group interaction that group members could use to infer knowledge and expertise (Littlepage, Schmidt, Whisler, & Frost, 1995). Littlepage et al. found that member confidence and talkativeness both determined perceived expertise, though their relationship to actual expertise was rather tentative. Littlepage and Mueller (1997) also found that resorting to reason as an influence tactic led experts to be perceived as such and to be more influential.

Another statistical property that seems to be important in expertise perceptions is cognitive centrality (Kameda, Ohtsubo, & Takezawa, 1997). Kameda et al. found that a member having a large amount of information that is also shared by others (i.e., cognitive centrality) led others to see him/her as more expert and leader-like. Such perceptions also led the cognitively central person to be more influential. Other task-specific factors (e.g., age for knowledge of history, physical fitness for physically demanding tasks, etc.) probably also play a role in appropriate situations (cf. Ridgeway & Walker, 1995). Exactly which cues are used in which situations is yet to be systematically addressed. Nevertheless, group members do seem generally to be adept at using ecologically valid cues to locate their more skilled or knowledgeable members (Littlepage et al., 1995).

Our Gossiping Mind: A Possible Social Engine for Sustaining Valid Meta Knowledge

To summarize, these observations suggest that meta knowledge, along with the use of ecologically valid statistical cues, often helps normal groups to deploy the right members for the right roles. Then, how and to what extent is proper meta knowledge developed, updated, and shared in those groups? We speculate that gossips or other "social broadcasting" mechanisms may play a key part in these processes. In a recent review article, Dunbar (2004) suggested that approximately two thirds of our freely forming conversation time is devoted to social topics, most of which can be given the generic label, gossip. Dunbar argues that gossip originally served a bonding function in social groups, which had its evolutionary origin in social grooming among primates. It also seems likely that such gossiping facilitates exchanging of information about other members' "personalities," constantly updating the shared meta knowledge in groups.

This thinking suggests an interesting hypothesis. There are some data suggesting that gossiping covers more diverse topics and is more frequent among women than men (see Jarvenpa & Brumbach (1988) for observations about a hunter–gatherer society; Parquette & Underwood (1999) for data about American adolescents). If this is indeed the case, women may play key roles in updating and sharing of transactive memory (Wegner, 1987). For example, compared to normal mixed-sex groups, artificial groups composed only of men may suffer from coordination problems more severely. Indeed, the Clark journals indicate that, in the early phase of their journey, status competition in the men-dominant Corps of Discovery sometimes led to serious failures in group coordination.

According to traditional social psychological accounts, these problems arise mainly because men are poorer at handling the "socioemotional" aspects of group performance, compared to women (cf. Wood, 1987). In contrast, the evolutionary reasoning suggests a more "cognitive" explanation: The problem may be caused by an overall decrease in quality and amount of gossiping in men-dominant groups. Social network analysis comparing information flows in mixed-sex groups and men-only groups may illuminate a critical route for development of valid meta knowledge in groups. In any event, given our nature as a gossiping animal, cultural transmission (Boyd & Richerson, 1985) of meta knowledge seems to be a desirable byproduct in normal groups.

Social Sharedness

We have seen that meta knowledge, which seems to be sustained via various cultural transmission mechanisms including gossiping (Boyd & Richerson, 1985; Dunbar, 2004), provides one key solution to the coordination problems in normal groups. In this section, we discuss "social-sharedness biases" (Tindale & Kameda, 2000) as another key mechanism to cope with coordination problems, especially when groups make important decisions.

Robustness of Group Decision-Making Anthropologists suggest that group decision-making is perhaps one of the most-frequently used adaptive devices by humans, not only in modern industrialized societies, but also in traditional tribal societies. For example, Boehm (1996) reviewed ethnographic data about group decision-making in various tribal societies, including Mae Enga in New Guinea. The ethnography showed that, when making important decisions (e.g., whether to raid an adjacent tribe to solve land disputes), Mae Enga usually held meetings composed of adult men. "Big man" (the most powerful man in the tribe) typically serves as a chairperson of the meeting rather than a dictatorial authority.

With these ethnographic anecdotes in mind, let us first review briefly the experimental research on group decision-making. A recent social psychological conceptualization of group decision-making has viewed groups as information-processing systems (Hinsz, Tindale, & Vollrath, 1997). A central component of understanding how group-level information processing is distinguishable from individual-level information processing is "social sharedness" (Kameda, Tindale, & Davis, 2003). Social sharedness involves the notion that many relevant components of a decision task can be shared to greater or lesser degrees by the members of a group. Most importantly, the greater the degree of "sharedness," the greater the impact that component will have on the group processes and decision outcomes, which may be given the generic label, "social-sharedness biases"

(Tindale & Kameda, 2000). Much of the research literature on group decision-making can be seen as reflecting this basic phenomenon. Previous research has shown that social sharedness operates robustly at three different levels, viz., preference, information, and task representation.

Shared Preferences   Probably the most well-validated aspect of social sharedness involves *shared preferences* (Davis, 1982; Kameda et al., 2003). In situations where no single-decision option can be proven to be superior on its own, groups often resolve differences among member preferences through majority or plurality type processes (Kameda et al., 2003; Tindale, 1993). By definition, majority/plurality processes favor the preference that is most shared among the group members. Such rules have been formalized in many circumstances (e.g., legal or corporate situations), but they also tend to emerge from normal group consensus processes (Davis, 1982). Research on groups for many different decision tasks in many different decision environments (including non-Western cultures) has found robust operations of majority/plurality processes (see Kameda et al., 2003 for review).

Shared Information   Preferences are not the only aspect of group decision-making where social sharedness has been found. Another well-researched demonstration of the bias has involved *shared information* in groups (Stasser & Titus, 1985; Wittenbaum & Stasser, 1996). In attempting to isolate the effects of informational vs. normative social influence, Stasser and Titus (1985) created laboratory situations where group members initially shared some information but each member also possessed some unique or nonredundant information in the group. By carefully distributing the information, Stasser and his colleagues contrived situations where the entire set of information available to a group designated one alternative as objectively superior if pooled successfully during discussion; however, the information that was initially shared by all members favored a different alternative. This set-up is called the "hidden-profile paradigm" because the superior alternative is hidden in the skewed information distribution. Stasser et al. found that groups usually failed to pool all the information; instead, they spent far more time discussing the shared as opposed to the unique information, choosing the inferior alternative favored by the shared information. This effect has now been replicated dozens of times in many different decision domains (Gigone & Hastie, 1993; Larson, Foster-Fishman, & Keys, 1994).

Shared-Task Representations   Another form of the social sharedness, identified by Tindale, Smith, Steiner, Filkins, and Sheffey (1996), involves *shared task representations*. Shared task representations are "any task/situation relevant concept, norm, perspective, or cognitive process that is shared by most or all of the group members" (Tindale et al., 1996, p. 84). They argue that whenever a shared task representation exists, alternatives consistent with it are easier to defend, which leads to asymmetries in the consensus processes (see Laughlin & Ellis, 1986, for asymmetric "truth-wins" social processes in groups working on mathematical problems supported by shared algebraic axioms). Tindale et al. (1996) found asymmetries for a number of judgment and decision tasks where shared heuristic strategies (Kahneman, Slovic, & Tversky, 1982) lead groups to favor responses consistent with the heuristics. Similar effects have been found for shared norms of defendant protection in mock jury deliberation (MacCoun & Kerr, 1988).

Revisiting the Social-Sharedness "Biases" from an Adaptationist Perspective

The aforementioned research suggests that, when proper meta knowledge is not readily available in a focal-task situation, groups usually resort to or are guided by the "social-sharedness biases." Socially shared preference, information, and task representations tend to dominate social processes and determine final group outcomes (see Tindale et al., 2003; Tindale & Kameda, 2000 for recent reviews).

Admittedly, most previous research that identified these group phenomena was not carried out from the evolutionary and adaptationist perspective. However, given their robustness, these "biases" may be conceptualized as evolved adaptive mechanisms that enhance our average fitness in the group. In the following, we specifically focus on three such phenomena: conformity bias (e.g., Asch, 1951; Latané & L'Herrou, 1996; Latané & Wolf, 1981), majoritarian group decision-making (e.g., Davis, 1973; Kameda et al., 2003; Stasser, Kerr, & Davis, 1989a), and dominant role of shared information (e.g., Stasser & Titus, 2003). We revisit potential functions served by these "biases," considering how they can function as "fast and frugal" decision heuristics (Gigerenzer et al., 1999) and may circumvent the coordination problems in groups.

Conformity Bias   In the social psychological literature, conformity to the majority occasionally has been characterized as a "morally undesirable" phenomenon (cf. Krueger & Funder, 2004). In studies from Asch's (1951) classic work through its criticism by Moscovici (1976), majority opinions have often been portrayed as wrong, distorting physical realities severely (Asch, 1951), or obsessed with outdated, conservative views (Moscovici, 1976); thus conforming to those incorrect majorities is not justified (cf. Martin & Hewstone, 2003). Likewise, in the growing literature on what economists call "herd" behavior (Anderson & Holt, 1997; Banerjee, 1992; Bikhchandani, Hirshleifer, & Welch, 1992), a spiral tendency in financial markets, viz., conforming to each other's behavior in a panic-striking manner, is often a catchy example of the phenomenon (e.g., Eguíluz & Zimmerman, 2000).

However, these images of majority influence as a misguiding force may be seriously misguided itself in the adaptationist sense. If the majority of the population held adaptively unfit cognitive/behavioral traits, they would be selected against, allowing minority mutants with more fit traits to proliferate in the population. Then, over time, the population will be occupied with the new majorities with the fit traits. In other words, evolutionarily speaking, it is much more likely that, on average, the population is composed of fit majorities than is composed of unfit majorities, which makes the conformity bias to the majority highly adaptive (Boyd & Richerson, 1985). Notice that, if a cognitive/behavioral trait achieves good performance *on average*, it is often evolvable; the perfect error-free criterion, though occasionally adopted in social psychology (Krueger & Funder, 2004), is not an adequate criterion for evolvability of a trait. In this sense, conformity to the majority position can be seen as a fast and frugal heuristic (Gigerenzer et al., 1999, 2001) that serves our adaptation quite efficiently.

Henrich and Boyd (1998), and Kameda and Nakanishi (2002, 2003) extended these ideas further by evolutionary computer simulations and by a series of experiments. They showed that conformity bias is theoretically evolvable *even in a more challenging environment*, viz., in a temporally fluctuating environment.

Recent studies on ice cores and ocean sediments suggest that the Pleistocene EEA was an environment with frequent climate fluctuations on submillennial time scales (cf. Potts, 1996; Richerson & Boyd, 2000). Notice that, in such a nonstationary, fluctuating environment, a population can be momentarily composed of *incorrect* majorities owing to the temporal environmental drift. If the adaptive environment has recently changed (e.g., climate change), the population is momentarily composed of majorities with outdated, unfit traits.

Nevertheless, Henrich and Boyd (1998) and Kameda and Nakanishi (2002, 2003) showed theoretically that conformity bias to majorities is still evolvable. Even if the adaptive environment may fluctuate over time (as was the case in Pleistocene EEA), conformity bias enables us to choose an appropriate behavior in the environment most of the time, without incurring much computation cost; individuals with conformity bias show greater fit on average than those without one. The economists working on herd behavior have also reached the same conclusion. They argue that the behavior itself originates from rational (adaptive) Bayesian calculation under uncertainty, although it *sometimes* could yield the incorrect panic-like chain reactions in a group (Anderson & Holt, 1997; Banerjee, 1992; Bikhchandani et al., 1992).

These theoretical analyses strongly suggest that the net-benefit criterion (focusing on average merit), rather than an error-free criterion (focusing on perfect functioning), favors the evolvability of conformity bias under uncertainty (cf. Festinger, 1954). As ecological evidence for this assertion, it is noteworthy that many "lower" animals that live in groups also possess conforming tendencies, including some fish, birds, and herbivores (cf. Heyes & Galef, 1996).

Majoritarian Group Decision-Making

Essentially, the same argument applies to one of the most robust findings in group research—that group consensus is often guided by majority/plurality processes. Although groups do not necessarily take a formal vote, their decisions are well predicted by consensus processes guided by majority/plurality opinions at the outset of interaction (Davis, 1973; Stasser, Kerr, & Davis, 1980; see Kameda et al., 2003 for recent reviews).

Recently, several researchers have revisited adaptive efficiencies of group decision-making by majority/plurality rule directly. Sorkin and his colleagues (Sorkin, Hays, & West, 2001; Sorkin, West, & Robinson, 1998) approached this issue using a signal-detection approach. They showed, both empirically and analytically, that majority processes tend to maximize group performance in situations where ideal preference-weighting schemes are not available—i.e., the members lack meta knowledge about relative expertise on the task.

Using Monte-Carlo simulations and behavioral experiments, Hastie & Kameda (2005) showed that majority/plurality rules tend to produce high levels of decision performance (as well as other desirable social-choice features: cf. Arrow, 1963; Mueller, 1989) with very little cost in terms of cognitive computation efforts. They argue that, compared to the conformity bias operating at the individual level, majoritarian decision-making serves as an even quicker and statistically more reliable aggregation mechanism at the group level. Hastie and Kameda (2005) speculate that, because of the adaptive efficiencies, majority norms may have evolved in many cultures, including hunter–gatherer societies (Boehm, 1996), as fast and frugal decision heuristic.

Interestingly, nonhuman animals living in groups also show majority-like group aggregation processes when they choose sites for foraging, nesting, and so on (honeybees: Seeley & Burhman, 1999; baboons and red deer: Conradt & Roper, 2003). These observations provide further evidence for the robustness of majority/plurality rules in ecologically representative settings. In passing, Captain Clark used the majority rule to decide where to set his winter camp when exploring the Northwest Territory in 1805. Everyone in the expedition, including servants and native guides, had an equal vote in the majority rule decision. This social choice procedure may have been adaptive as well as fitting the democratic ideals he cited in his journals (Moulton, 2003), given that no workable meta knowledge was available in this unfamiliar environment.

Dominant Role of Shared Information

As reviewed earlier, group discussion tends to be dominated by shared information (e.g., Stasser & Stewart, 1992; Stasser, Talyor, & Hanna, 1989b; Stasser & Titus, 1985, 1987). Socially shared information is more likely to be attended to and even preferred (Wittenbaum, Hubbell, & Zuckerman, 1999) by members than is unshared information. Stasser views these group tendencies as problematic because they preclude groups from discovering "hidden profiles." When information is distributed among members in a skewed manner where a superior alternative is hidden, group tendencies to focus on shared information can yield inefficient group outcomes (see Stasser & Titus, 2003 for recent comprehensive review). This argument per se is well taken, but how robust is the hidden-profile phenomenon in ecologically representative environments?

The difficulty of discovering hidden profiles is heightened when members have no meta knowledge about who knows what (Stewart & Stasser, 1995). In normal groups, however, people typically have meta knowledge, such as the aforementioned transactive memory (Wegner, 1987). Even in ad hoc task groups such as juries or project teams, we often form expectations about other people's knowledge or expertise based on their professions, ages, sexes, etc. (Ridgeway & Walker, 1995). Although not perfect, these cognitive shortcuts provide some valid clues about who is likely to know what, potentially helping groups discover hidden profiles most of the time.

In some cases, it is nevertheless true that members could lack meta knowledge completely, engaging in adaptive tasks as equal status members without division of roles. As in the Clark journals, this is particularly true when groups are placed in an unfamiliar setting, exploring the local environment for adaptation. How serious is the hidden-profile problem in such a situation? Metaphorically, this is like a situation where randomly placed sensors collect environmental information in a mutually independent manner. It is easy to see that, in those settings, skewed information–distribution against a superior alternative (e.g., a good hunting site) is unlikely to occur; given mutually independent information search, a hidden profile could occur, but with an extremely small probability. Furthermore, shared information is often statistically more reliable (law of large numbers) than unshared information under such a circumstance (Kerr & Tindale, 2004; Tindale & Kameda, 2000). Thus, social mechanisms that place larger weights on shared as opposed to unshared information are adaptively beneficial on average, although they sometimes could yield errors. In this sense, the aforementioned "cognitive centrality effect," where members who share information with most others can exert greater social influence independently of their majority/minority preference status (Kameda et al., 1997), may be seen as another fast and frugal heuristic under uncertainty. By endowing an expert power to such members, groups can reach statistically reliable decisions (by law of large numbers) efficiently most of the time.

Modifying Our Working Map

Let us recapitulate what we have discovered (or rediscovered) so far for including in our working map. Meta knowledge, along with the use of somewhat valid statistical cues, usually provides efficient solutions to many coordination problems in normal groups. When proper meta knowledge is not available, then the social-sharedness biases often come to govern group interactions.

The three social-sharedness "biases" examined in some detail in this section serve a common adaptive function: They reduce the uncertainty involved in perceptions of the external world by capitalizing on *consensus* at various levels, cognitively and behaviorally. More specifically, conformity bias allows us to acquire fit behaviors efficiently in a current environment, even when the environment is nonstationary and fluctuates over time (Henrich & Boyd, 1998; Kameda & Nakanishi, 2002, 2003). Majoritarian group decision-making cancels out random errors in individual judgments and preferences, just as a sample mean provides an unbiased estimate about the population mean in statistics (Hastie & Kameda, 2005). Socially shared information is more likely to be statistically valid and reliable than is unshared information.

As evident in the earlier quotation from the Clark journals, holding valid environmental perceptions is an essential component of many survival tasks (e.g., identifying a good foraging site, knowing right geographical directions, and finding a safe shelter). In this sense, all these biases may be regarded as built-in adaptive tools that allow us to handle the *statistical uncertainty* inevitable in our perceptions of an unsophisticated natural environment. They may yield erroneous outcomes in some artificial cases where information/preference distributions are highly biased (e.g., contrived "hidden-profile" situation, Asch's incorrect majorities), but enhance our fitness on average in ecologically representative settings, while efficiently bypassing the coordination problems in group performance.[1]

MOTIVATION PROBLEMS

We continue our journey of (re)discovery to the next territory on our working map. Motivation problems have been a major research agenda in group psychology (Steiner, 1972). Researchers have identified various conditions that determine people's motivations in group settings, viz., factors yielding motivation losses (or social loafing: Latané et al., 1979) and factors yielding motivation gains (e.g., Kerr, 2001; Williams & Karau, 1991; Witte, 1989). Since excellent reviews are already available on this issue (Levine & Moreland, 1990; Sheppard, 1993; Williams, Harkins, & Karau, 2003), we do not repeat them here. Instead, we revisit the motivation problems specifically from a game-theoretic perspective. We argue that what behavioral ecologists call a "producer–scrounger" phenomenon (Giraldeau & Caraco, 2000; Kameda & Hastie, 2006) may underlie various motivation problems in groups, and speculate their implications for evolutionary adaptation.

Motivation Losses and Motivation Gains

First, let us briefly summarize several key findings about motivation problems. Since the early work by Ringelmann in the 1880s, numerous studies have examined people's motivation in group settings.

Motivation Losses   A robust finding in these settings is social loafing, the phenomenon that members decrease their effort-levels when their inputs are pooled into a collective group performance. The best known example is a classic study by Latané et al. (1979), who coined the term "social loafing" to describe the motivation losses in group settings. In this study, college students were asked to shout and clap as loudly as possible, both individually and in a group setting. Exerting clever experimental controls, these researchers were able to show that a large portion of decrement in group performance was attributable to reduced individual effort, rather than to coordination losses (Steiner, 1972). Numerous studies thereafter replicated the basic finding, employing a wide variety of cognitive and motor tasks (see Williams et al., 2003 for review).

Motivation Gains   Although still smaller in numbers, recent work began to focus on the other side of the coin, motivation gains, where members increase efforts when with others. Two phenomena have been demonstrated empirically, social compensation effect (Williams & Karau, 1991) and the Köhler effect (Hertel, Kerr, & Messé, 2000; Stroebe, Diehl, & Abakoumkin, 1996; Witte, 1989). Social compensation emerges when individuals work harder on a collective task in order to compensate for the expected poor performance of other group members (Williams et al., 2003). The Köhler effect, a closely related phenomenon, occurs when less-able members of groups increase their efforts when working at conjunctive tasks (where the poorest performance alone determines the group outcome: Steiner, 1972).

Riddle So, we have two sets of phenomena, motivation losses and motivation gains. How can we reconcile these seemingly contradictory findings in an integrative framework? Several researchers have challenged this riddle.

Karau and Williams (1993) argue that expectancy-value theories provide a useful framework to integrate the phenomena (see also Sheppard, 1993). This model suggests that individuals are motivated to work hard on a collective task only to the extent that they expect their inputs are instrumental in achieving group outcomes that they value personally. In group situations where individual inputs are pooled in an additive manner to determine final group outcomes (Steiner, 1972), each individual effort is instrumentally not so meaningful, leading to social loafing (i.e., free riding on other members' efforts). However, when one's input is critical to achieve desired group outcome, motivation gains, such as social compensation and the Köhler effect, are obtained.

We believe that the expectancy-value framework is a useful first step to understand the motivation problems in an integrative manner. To pursue this perspective further, we believe that it is necessary to conceptualize the notion of "instrumentality" (Karau & Williams, 1993) more formally. Karau and Williams (1993) defined instrumental behavior rather loosely, as behavior that achieves group outcomes that *an individual values personally*. From an evolutionary and adaptationist perspective, however, we must be more specific about how a given behavior increases one's *fitness*, rather than generally claiming that the behavior promotes the individual's attainment of some proximal (psychological) goal.

Toward this end, we introduce a game-theoretic framework, arguing that many motivation problems may be better understood as manifestations of the "producer–scrounger" equilibrium (Giraldeau & Caraco, 2000; Kameda & Hastie, 2006).

Game Theoretic Framework: A Quick Primer

Before going further, let us briefly explain a game theoretic framework. Perhaps the best-known game among social psychologists is the social dilemma game where individuals have two behavioral strategies, to cooperate or defect, in a collective-action situation (cf. van Vugt & van Lange, this volume). Among real-world examples included in this game category are provision of public goods (e.g., public-broadcasting service, parks), consumption of natural resources (e.g., air, fish), and so on. In many such cases, defection or free riding (e.g., not contributing to PBS) is more profitable than cooperation, making the efficient provision of public goods, controlled consumption of natural resources, etc. quite difficult (Hardin, 1968; Olson, 1965).

Dominant Strategy and Equilibrium As illustrated in the social dilemma game, we can formulate various interdependent structures existent among individuals as games. Such formalization allows us to examine how each of the strategies in the game performs against other strategies, in terms of net profit. A strategy that outperforms other strategies unilaterally in profit is called a *dominant strategy*. If we draw an analogy to biological evolution ("evolutionary games": Maynard Smith, 1982; Gintis, 2000), organisms with the dominant strategy gradually proliferate (producing many offspring), finally dominating the population. Such a stable collective state is called an (evolutionarily stable) equilibrium in that the strategy dominates while preventing for any other mutant strategies to intrude into the population (see Kameda et al. (2003) for a social psychological application of evolutionary games to development of social norms).

In some other games, like the producer–scrounger game that we will discuss below, several different strategies may coexist at the equilibrium, just as different subspecies coexist in natural environments in a stable manner. More precisely, those strategies make equal profit at the equilibrium, so none of them can dominate the others. This type of equilibrium is called *mixed equilibrium* in that several different strategies are mixed in the population.

Producer–Scrounger Game

Now, let us return to the original path in our journey. We had been at the entrance of the new territory, wondering why seemingly contradictory motivation phenomena (losses and gains) are observed in group performance. We will challenge this riddle from a game-theoretic perspective.

Trade-off Relations Inherent in Different Survival Tasks Social species living in groups share many adaptive problems with humans, such as foraging resources, finding shelters, and guarding against predators/enemies. These situations are essentially identical to the situations that the Corps of Discovery faced 200 years ago. Behavioral ecology (Krebs & Davies, 1993, 1997), the study of animal behaviors in their natural habitats, thus provides many useful insights for understanding how humans may solve these adaptive problems.

For illustration, let us consider group vigilance against predators. According to behavioral ecological models, the lives of many animal species are divided between foraging for food and avoiding predations by other animals (cf. Krebs & Davies, 1993, 1997). These two activities are often mutually excusive—extra effort in one reduces the effort available to the other. Therefore, when an animal forages for food, it must divide its time and attention between feeding and being vigilant for predators. Needless to say, such a trade-off applies to humans as well.

The behavioral ecology literature suggests that many animals' behaviors under the trade-off may be approximated by a cost–benefit model (e.g., Lima, Valone, & Caraco, 1985). Laboratory experiments as well as field observations of many species (e.g., rodents, birds) suggest that, if the animals live *solitary* lives, individual optimization models essentially approximate their allocation decisions. The times allotted for being vigilant and feeding yield approximately a maximum joint fitness to the individuals most of the time (Houston, McNamara, & Hutchinson, 1993).

Complications that Arise in Groups   On the other hand, if animals live in groups, like humans, game-theoretic aspects complicate the allocation decisions (Pulliam, Pyke, & Caraco, 1982). Often, social foragers can enjoy "aggregation economies" or benefit of grouping, compared to solitary foragers. In a group, there are many eyes searching for predators (engaging in risk monitoring activity). Thus, each animal can spend more time feeding, engaging in "intake" activity.

However, exactly these features yield an incentive for free riding. "If many others are already on watch, why should I bother? Let others guard us from risk while I'm eating 100% of the time." Giraldeau and Caraco (2000) named generically such an interdependent structure (including the vigilance-foraging situation) a *producer–scrounger game*. In the producer–scrounger game, if there are many "producers" of *public or collective goods* that are beneficial to others as well as self (e.g., contributing to collective vigilance by engaging in the monitoring of predators), each individual is better off starting to exploit others' efforts (e.g., eating 100% of the times). However, if there are many "scroungers" (on another's monitoring efforts), each individual is better off starting to produce (e.g., being vigilant). For instance, if no one around serves as a sentinel, gain from one's own risk monitoring exceeds its cost (making sure you will not be eaten is better than eating).

Emergence of Mixed Equilibrium   Notice that, different from the social dilemma game (cf. van Vugt & van Lange, this volume), defection is *not* a dominant strategy in the producer–scrounger game. The net profit of one strategy is not fixed (i.e., neither strategy is a dominant strategy), but is dependent on the frequency of the other strategy in a group. That is, if there are too many players with one strategy, each individual is better off starting to adopt the other strategy; increase in the frequency of one strategy in a group makes that strategy less profitable, while making the other strategy more profitable.

Since the two strategies are mutually constrained in terms of profitability, we can expect a mixed equilibrium to eventually emerge in the group (Gintis, 2000; Maynard Smith, 1982). At equilibrium, the group reaches a stable state where producers and scroungers coexist. In a context of foraging under risk, the group is composed of two types of individuals in a stable manner, those who engage mainly in risk monitoring at the expense of foraging, and those who exploit others' monitoring efforts and mostly concentrate on foraging (Kameda & Tamura, in press).[2]

Motivation Problems Revisited from a Game-Theoretic Perspective

Note that, in the above game-theoretic formulation, each individual cooperates (i.e., producing collective goods such as serving as a guard) if and only if cooperation is *instrumental* for the individual's (*not* the group's) fitness. More formally, one cooperates if the cost of cooperation (e.g., giving up feeding) is less than the benefit of cooperation (e.g., avoiding predation)—when the act of cooperation pays off. Depending on the result of cost–benefit analysis, individuals may work hard toward the group goal (motivation gains) or simply loaf around (motivation losses). And, most importantly, the instrumentality of one's input per se hinges on how other group members behave. If there are many producers in a group, individuals are better off starting to scrounge, while if there are too many scroungers, individuals are better off starting to produce. The result is a mixed equilibrium where producers and scroungers coexist in the group in a stable manner (see Kameda & Hastie, 2006 for a more comprehensive discussion).

Thus, we can formalize "instrumentality" of one's input (Karau & Williams, 1993) unambiguously by the notion of producer–scrounger game. There have been several empirical studies (mostly from our own laboratory) that examined the usefulness of these ideas to explain human behaviors in group settings.

Collective Vigilance Against Predators or Enemies

Kameda and Tamura (in press) tested the aforementioned feeding-vigilance trade-off directly. They implemented a collective foraging situation under risk in a laboratory. Six individuals participated as a group in the experiment. The individuals faced the feeding-vigilance trade-off, viz., earning experimental reward (money) by solving individually as many calculation problems as possible while guarding against a common risk that their accumulated reward could be deprived. Kameda and Tamura (in press) recorded how often each individual in a group served as a sentinel against the common risk. The results confirmed their predictions. Over time, the group became divided between producers who engaged in costly risk monitoring and scroungers on those monitoring efforts, eventually approaching the game-theoretic equilibrium.

Free Riding in Social/Cultural Learning

In another study, Kameda and Nakanishi (2002, 2003) tested the producer–scrounger phenomenon in a social/cultural learning context. As argued earlier, social/cultural learning is an effective way to reduce uncertainty about the environment, helping individuals adopt an adaptive behavior cheaply. Individual learning by trial and error is often costly. However, it is exactly this feature that may yield an incentive to free ride. If many others engage in costly individual learning, each individual is better off skipping the individual learning and free riding (scrounging) on others' learning outcomes.

Note that such a free-rider problem poses almost no serious adaptive consequence if the environment is stationary; if someone in the group engages in individual learning just once, the single learning conveys all the necessary information for the entire group. However, if the adaptive environment is fluctuating (Henrich & Boyd, 1998; Potts, 1996; Richerson & Boyd, 2000), periodic updating about the environmental knowledge via individual learning is critical. This poses a producer–scrounger dilemma.

On the basis of these notions, Kameda and Nakanishi (2002, 2003) implemented a nonstationary, fluctuating adaptive environment in a laboratory. The results clearly supported their predictions. Over time, the group became divided between "information producers" who engage in the costly individual learning and "information scroungers" who just rely on others, eventually approaching the mixed equilibrium.

Modifying Our Working Map Again

Although these studies did not address traditional group-performance settings directly (but see Kameda, Tsukasaki, & Hastie, 2006, for a description of how this phenomenon functions in group decision-making), we strongly believe that the notion of producer–scrounger equilibrium may be critical to integrate various social psychological findings about motivation problems in groups.

To recapitulate, "instrumentality" (Karau & Williams, 1993) of one's input in a group setting hinges on how other group members behave. If there are many producers in a group, individuals are better off starting to scrounge, while if there are too many scroungers, individuals are better off starting to produce. As a consequence, we have a mixed equilibrium where producers and scroungers coexist in a stable manner—as we often experience in our own everyday lives. In other words, both motivation losses and motivation gains in groups may be captured under *a single game-theoretic framework* where the notion of instrumentality is formally definable (cf. Kameda & Hastie, 2006).

CONCLUSION

We have explored two territories related to group performance in our journey of (re)discovery. We started out with a working map based on Steiner's (1972) classic classification about process losses, viz., coordination problems and motivation problems. What have we been able to add to our working map by this journey?

First, some of the group phenomena or biases that were originally thought to be problematic may not be so problematic in the light of evolutionary adaptation. When the net-benefit criterion, rather than the error-free criterion, is adopted (Gigerenzer et al., 1999; Hastie & Rasinski, 1987; Kameda & Hastie, 2004; Krueger & Funder, 2004), many of the group "biases" may now be seen as by-products or manifestations of adaptive cognitive and behavioral mechanisms in ecologically representative settings. Among those are various social-sharedness effects, such as conformity, majoritarian group decision-making, and the dominant impact of shared information/knowledge. These "biases" help groups to circumvent coordination problems (Steiner, 1972) without sacrificing adaptive efficiencies, by capitalizing on consensus at various levels (Festinger, 1954). We conjecture that other group "biases," which we were not able to cover in this journey, may also be endowed a totally new status in the light of adaptation.

Second, various motivation problems (losses and gains) may be understood as a manifestation of the producer–scrounger phenomenon. Individuals are neither automatic cooperators nor defectors who always behave in the same manner, but determine whether to produce or scrounge by a cost–benefit analysis. That is, they act "instrumentally," if we use the terminology of Karau and Williams (1993), depending on how others behave in a group. As a result, producers and scroungers may coexist in many real-world human groups, as often found in avian species (Giraldeau & Caraco, 2000) and in other taxa (cf. Krebs & Davies, 1993, 1997). Interestingly, Kameda and Nakanishi (2003) showed, both theoretically and empirically, that despite the producer–scrounger problem group life can still yield better mean outcomes (i.e., fitness) than solitary lifestyle. Although free riding is unavoidable in groups, groups can still yield "aggregation economies" compared to solitary individuals.

Finally, our journey may have some implications for what is called group-level selection. Because of our unique reliance on groups (e.g., group decision-making and problem-solving) and our peculiarly "groupy" psychological characteristics (e.g., docility to social norms: Simon, 1990), some evolutionary theorists argue that group-level selection (selection between groups) may indeed have played a substantive role in hominid evolution. Natural selection may have operated at the group level as well as at the (conventionally assumed) individual level in hominid evolution, yielding "ultrasocial" human traits (Boyd & Richerson, 1985; Fehr & Henrich, 2003; Sober & Wilson, 1998; Wilson & Sober, 1994).

The plausibility of group-level selection is currently the topic of vigorous debate in evolutionary biology (see a special issue of *American Naturalist*, 1997 Supplement, Vol. 150, Issue 1), and is sometimes even regarded as "heretical" in evolutionary biology. However, we believe that we should not discard this notion hastily when we think about human evolution. Group phenomena we have observed in the first half of this chapter, viz., human docility (or conformity) to majority social norms, dominant roles of shared knowledge, group decision-making, and so on, reduce within-group phenotypic (i.e., behavioral) variances, whereas they enhance between-group variances (Boyd & Richerson, 1985). All these mechanisms facilitate individuals belonging to the same groups to behave in a similar manner. In other words, these "groupy" human traits (which, as we saw in previous sections of this chapter, have adaptive grounds at the *individual* level) enhance the chance of group-level selection substantively, compared to species living solitary lives. Thus, the group-level selection may not only be logically possible but also plausible in human evolution.

This is the end of our journal. Although we have tried to record our (re)discoveries along the journey as truthfully as possible onto our working map, we are afraid that some of them may have been misplaced. We wait for future work to correct those errors. Also, we must admit that our working map is still sporadic. We hope that our map, although incomplete by far, will serve as a useful milestone for other explorers in these and adjacent new territories, and that many observers will also join us in this truly exciting endeavor, which is an ever evolving journey.

ACKNOWLEDGMENTS

This work chapter was supported by the Grant-in-Aid for Scientific Research 14310048 from the Ministry of Education, Culture, Sports, Science and Technology of Japan to the first author, and by Grant #SES 0136332 from the National Science Foundation to the second author. We are grateful to Mark Schaller, Douglas Kenrick, Reid Hastie, Yoshuke Ohtsubo, Daisuke Nakanishi, Taiki Takahashi, Ryo Tamura, Takafumi Tsukasaki, and Daisuke Nakama for their helpful comments on an earlier version of this manuscript.

NOTES

1. Solving statistical uncertainty is critical for reasons other than holding valid environmental perception. For example, high statistical uncertainty in food-provision (e.g., uncertainty in meat supply) is a recurrent adaptive problem in many hunter–gather societies. Kaplan and Hill (1985) argued that a communal-sharing norm, a norm that designates uncertain resources as common property to be shared, is a collective solution to this problem. Using an "evolutionary game analysis" (Gintis, 2000; Maynard Smith, 1982, see the next section), Kameda, Takezawa, and Hastie (2003) showed that such a norm is indeed evolvable as a consequence of individual-level fitness maximization under statistical uncertainty. They also showed empirically that our modern minds are sensitive to uncertainty information, as exemplified by "psychology of windfall gains" (Kameda, Takezawa, Tindale, & Smith, 2002).

2. This situation is similar to a "Hawk–Dove game" (Maynard Smith & Price, 1973) where two players (e.g., animals) are in conflict over a valuable resource. In the original Hawk–Dove game, two strategies are defined. The "hawk" strategy is to escalate battle until injured or the opponent retreats. The "dove" strategy is to display hostility but retreat before injured if the opponent escalates. Different from the prisoner's dilemma (social dilemma) game, there is no dominant strategy in the Hawk–Dove game. Net payoff to one strategy is dependent on the frequency of the other strategy in the group. A mixed equilibrium emerges eventually, where the Hawks and the Doves coexist in the population in a stable manner (see Gintis, 2000; Maynard Smith, 1982 for details).

REFERENCES

Anderson, L. R., & Holt, C. A. (1997). Information cascades in the laboratory. *American Economic Review*, 87, 847–862.

Arrow, K. J. (1963). *Social choices and individual values* (2nd ed.). New Haven, CT: Yale University Press.

Asch, S. (1951). Effects of group pressure upon the modification and distortion of judgment. In H. Guetzkow (Ed.), *Groups, leadership and men*. Pittsburgh: Carnegie Press.

Banerjee, A. V. (1992). A simple model of herd behavior. *Quarterly Journal of Economics*, 107, 797–817.

Bikhchandani, S., Hirshleifer, D., & Welch, I. (1992). A theory of fads, fashion, custom, and cultural change as informational cascades. *Journal of Political Economy*, 100, 992–1026.

Boehm, C. (1996). Emergency decisions, cultural-selection mechanics, and group selection. *Current Anthropology*, 37, 763–793.

Boyd, R., & Richerson, P. J. (1985). *Culture and the evolutionary process*. Chicago: University of Chicago Press.

Cannon-Bowers, J. A., Salas, E., & Converse, S. A. (1993). Shared mental models in team decision making. In N. J. Castellan (Ed.), *Individual and group decision making: Current Issues* (pp. 221–246). Hillsdale, NJ: Lawrence Erlbaum.

Conradt, L., & Roper, T. J. (2003). Group decision-making in animals. *Nature*, 421, 155–158.

Davis, J. H. (1969). *Group performance*. Reading, MA: Addison-Wesley.

Davis, J. H. (1973). Group decision and social interaction: A theory of social decision schemes. *Psychological Review*, 80, 97–125.

Davis, J. H. (1982). Social interaction as a combinatorial process in group decision. In H. Brandstatter, J. H. Davis, & G. Stocker-Kreichgauer (Eds.), *Group decision making* (pp. 27–58). London: Academic Press.

Davis, J. H., & Restle, F. (1963). The analysis of problems and prediction of group problem solving. *Journal of Abnormal and Social Psychology, 66,* 103–116.

Dunbar, R. I. M. (1992). Neocortex size as a constraint on group size in primates. *Journal of Human Evolution, 20,* 469–493.

Dunbar, R. I. M. (2004). Gossip in evolutionary perspective. *Review of General Psychology, 8,* 100–110.

Eguíluz, V. M., & Zimmerman, M. G. (2000). Transmission of information and herd behavior: An application to financial markets. *Physical Review Letters, 85,* 5659–5662.

Fehr, E., & Henrich, J. (2003). Is strong reciprocity a maladaptation? On the evolutionary foundations of human altruism. In P. Hammerstein (Ed.), *The genetic and cultural evolution of cooperation.* Cambridge, MA: MIT Press.

Festinger, L. (1954). A theory of social comparison processes. *Human Relations, 7,* 117–140.

Gigerenzer, G., & Selten, R. (Eds.). (2001). *Bounded rationality: The adaptive toolbox.* Cambridge, MA: MIT Press.

Gigerenzer, G., Todd, P. M., & the ABC Research Group. (1999). *Simple heuristics that make us smart.* New York: Oxford University Press.

Gigone, D., & Hastie, R. (1993). The common knowledge effect: Information sharing and group judgment. *Journal of Personality and Social Psychology, 65,* 959–974.

Gintis, H. (2000). *Game theory evolving: A problem-centered introduction to modeling strategic behavior.* Princeton, NJ: Princeton University Press.

Giraldeau, L. -A., & Caraco, T. (2000). *Social foraging theory.* Princeton, NJ: Princeton University Press.

Hardin, G. (1968). The tragedy of the commons. *Science, 162,* 1243–1248.

Hastie, R., & Kameda, T. (2005). *The robust beauty of the majority rule. Psychological Review, 112,* 494–508.

Hastie, R., Penrod, S. D., & Pennington, N. (1983). *Inside the jury.* Cambridge, MA: Harvard University Press.

Hastie, R., & Rasinski, K. A. (1987). The concept of accuracy in social judgment. In D. Bar-Tal & A. Kruglanski (Eds.), *The social psychology of knowledge* (pp. 193–208). New York: Cambridge University Press.

Helmreich, R. L. (1997). Managing human error in aviation. *Scientific American, 276,* 62–67.

Helmreich, R. L., & Schaefer, H. G. (1994). Team performance in the operating room. In M. N. Bogner (Ed.), *Human error in medicine* (pp. 123–141). Hillsdale, NJ: Lawrence Erlbaum.

Henrich, J., & Boyd, R. (1998). The evolution of conformist transmission and the emergence of between-group differences. *Evolution and Human Behavior, 19,* 215–241.

Hertel, G., Kerr, N. L., & Messé, L. A. (2000). Motivation gains in groups: Paradigmatic and theoretical advances on the Köhler effect. *Journal of Personality and Social Psychology, 79,* 580–601.

Heyes, C. M., & Galef, B. G. Jr., (Eds.). (1996). *Social learning in animals: The roots of culture.* San Diego, CA: Academic Press.

Hill, G. W. (1982). Group versus individual performance: Are $N+1$ heads better than one? *Psychological Bulletin, 91,* 517–539.

Hinsz, V. B. (1995). Mental models of groups as social systems: Considerations of specification and assessment. *Small Group Research, 26,* 200–233.

Hinsz, V. B., Tindale, R. S., & Vollrath, D. A. (1997). The emerging conception of groups as information processors. *Psychological Bulletin, 121,* 43–64.

Hollingshead, A. (1998). Retrieval process in transactive memory systems. *Journal of Personality and Social Psychology, 74*, 659–671.

Houston, A. I., McNamara, J. M., & Hutchinson, J. M. (1993). General results concerning the trade-off between gaining energy and avoiding predation. *Philosophical Transactions of the Royal Society of London, Series B, 341*, 375–397.

Jarvenpa, R., & Brumbach, H. (1988). Socio-spatial organization and decision-making processes: Observations from the Chipewyan. *American Anthropologist, 90*, 598–618.

Kahneman, D., Slovic, P., & Tversky, A. (Eds.). (1982). *Judgment under uncertainty: Heuristics and biases.* Cambridge, UK: Cambridge University Press.

Kameda, T., & Hastie, R. (2004). Building an even better conceptual foundation: Commentary on Krueger & Funder (2004). *Behavioral and Brain Sciences, 27*, 345–346.

Kameda, T., & Hastie, R. (2006). "Producer-scrounger equilibrium" in social groups. Manuscript in preparation.

Kameda, T., & Nakanishi, D. (2002). Cost-benefit analysis of social/cultural learning in a non-stationary uncertain environment: An evolutionary simulation and an experiment with human subjects. *Evolution and Human Behavior, 23*, 373–393.

Kameda, T., & Nakanishi, D. (2003). Does social/cultural learning increase human adaptability? Rogers's question revisited. *Evolution and Human Behavior, 24*, 242–260.

Kameda, T., Ohtsubo, Y., & Takezawa, M. (1997). Centrality in socio-cognitive network and social influence: An illustration in a group decision making context. *Journal of Personality and Social Psychology, 73*, 296–309.

Kameda, T., Takezawa, M., & Hastie, R. (2003). The logic of social sharing: An evolutionary game analysis of adaptive norm development. *Personality and Social Psychology Review, 7*, 2–19.

Kameda, T., Takezawa, M., Tindale, R. S., & Smith, C. (2002). Social sharing and risk reduction: Exploring a computational algorithm for the psychology of windfall gains. *Evolution and Human Behavior, 23*, 11–33.

Kameda, T., & Tamura, R. (in press). "To eat or not to be eaten?": Collective risk-monitoring in groups. *Journal of Experimental Social Psychology.*

Kameda, T., Tindale, R. S., & Davis, J. H. (2003). Cognitions, preferences, and social sharedness: Past, present, and future directions in group decision making. In S. L. Schneider & J. Shanteau (Eds.), *Emerging perspectives on judgment and decision research* (pp. 215–240). Cambridge, UK: Cambridge University Press.

Kameda, T., Tsukasaki, T., & Hastie, R. (2006). *Democracy under uncertainty: Adaptive robustness of group decision-making beyond voter's paradox.* Manuscript in preparation.

Kaplan, H., & Hill, K. (1985). Food sharing among ache foragers: Tests of evolutionary hypotheses. *Current Anthropology, 26*, 223–246.

Karau, S. J., & Williams, K. D. (1993). Social loafing: A meta-analytic review and theoretical integration. *Journal of Personality and Social Psychology, 65*, 681–706.

Kerr, N. L. (2001). Motivation gains in performance groups: aspects and prospects. In J. Forgas & K. Williams (Eds.), *The social mind: Cognitive and motivational aspects of interpersonal behavior* (pp. 350–370). New York: Cambridge University Press.

Kerr, N. L., MacCoun, R., & Kramer, G. P. (1999). Bias in judgment: Comparing individuals and groups. *Psychological Review, 103*, 687–719.

Kerr, N. L., & Stanfel, J. A. (1993). Role schemata and member motivation in task groups. *Personality and Social Psychology Bulletin, 19*, 432–442.

Kerr, N. L., & Tindale, R. S. (2004). Group performance and decision making. *Annual Review of Psychology, 55*, 623–655.

Krebs, J. R., & Davies, N. B. (1993). *An introduction to behavioural ecology* (3rd ed.). Oxford: Blackwell.

Krebs, J. R., & Davies, N. B. (1997). *Behavioural ecology: An evolutionary approach* (4th ed.). Oxford: Blackwell.

Krueger, J. I., & Funder, D. C. (2004). Towards a balanced social psychology: Causes, consequences and cures for the problem-seeking approach to social behavior and cognition. *Behavioral and Brain Sciences, 27,* 313–327.

Larson, J. R., Jr., Foster-Fishman, P. G., & Keys, C. B. (1994). Discussion of shared and unshared information in decision-making groups. *Journal of Personality and Social Psychology, 67,* 446–461.

Latané, B., & L'Herrou, T. (1996). Spatial clustering in the Conformity Game: Dynamical social impact in electronic groups. *Journal of Personality and Social Psychology, 70,* 1218–1230.

Latané, B., Williams, K., & Harkins, S. (1979). Many hands make light the work: The causes and consequences of social loafing. *Journal of Personality and Social Psychology, 37,* 822–832.

Latané, B., & Wolf, S. (1981). The social impact of majorities and minorities. *Psychological Review, 88,* 438–453.

Laughlin, P. R. (1999). Collective induction: Twelve postulates. *Organizational Behavior and Human Decision Processes, 80,* 50–69.

Laughlin, P. R., & Ellis, A. L. (1986). Demonstrability and social combination processes on mathematical intellective tasks. *Journal of Experimental Social Psychology, 22,* 177–189.

Levine, J. M., & Moreland, R. L. (1990). Progress in small group research. *Annual Review of Psychology, 41,* 585–634.

Lima, S., Valone, T. J., & Caraco, T. (1985). Foraging-efficiency–predation-risk tradeoff in the gray squirrel. *Animal Behavior, 33,* 155–165.

Littlepage, G. E., & Mueller, A. L. (1997). Recognition and utilization of expertise in problem-solving groups: Expert characteristics and behavior. *Group Dynamics, 1,* 324–328.

Littlepage, G. E., Schmidt, G. W., Whisler, E. W., & Frost, A. G. (1995). An input–process–output analysis of influence and performance in problem solving groups. *Journal of Personality and Social Psychology, 69,* 877–889.

Lorge, I., & Solomon, H. (1955). Two models of group behavior in the solution of eureka-type problems. *Psychmetrica, 20,* 139–148.

MacCoun, R., & Kerr, N. L. (1988). Asymmetric influence in mock jury deliberations: Juror's bias for leniency. *Journal of Personality and Social Psychology, 54,* 21–33.

Martin, R., & Hewstone, M. (2003). Social-influence processes of control and change: Conformity, obedience to authority, and innovation. In M. A. Hogg & J. Cooper (Eds.), *Sage handbook of social psychology* (pp. 347–366). London: Sage.

Maynard Smith, J. (1982). *Evolution and the theory of games.* Cambridge, England: Cambridge University Press.

Maynard Smith, J., & Price, G. R. (1973). The logic of animal conflict. *Nature, 246,* 15–18.

Moreland, R. L., Argote, L., & Krishnan, R. (1998). Training people to work in groups. In R. S. Tindale, J. E. Edwards, L. Heath, E. J. Posavac, F. B. Bryant, E. Henderson-King, Y. Suarez-Balcazar, & J. Myers (Eds.), *Social psychological applications to social issues: Applications of theory and research on groups.* (Vol. 4, pp. 37–60). New York: Plenum Press.

Moscovici, S. (1976). *Social influence and social change.* New York: Academic Press.

Moulton, G. E. (Ed.). (2003). *The definitive journals of Lewis & Clark.* Lincoln, NE: University of Nebraska Press.

Mueller, D. C. (1989). *Public choice II*. New York: Cambridge University Press.

Olson, M. (1965). *The logic of collective action: Public goods and the theory of groups*. Cambridge, MA: Harvard University Press.

Parquette, J., & Underwood, M. (1999). Gender differences in young adolescents' experiences of peer victimization: Social and physical aggression. *Merrill–Palmer Quarterly, 45*, 242–265.

Payne, J. W., Bettman, J. R., & Johnson, E. J. (1993). *The adaptive decision maker*. Cambridge, UK: Cambridge University Press.

Potts, R. B. (1996). *Humanity's descent*. New York: Avon Books.

Pulliam, H. R., Pyke, G. H., & Caraco, T. (1982). The scanning behavior of juncos: A game-theoretical approach. *Journal of Theoretical Biology, 95*, 89–103.

Rentsch, J. R., & Hall, R. J. (1994). Members of great teams think alike: A model of team effectiveness and schema similarity among team members. *Advances in Interdisciplinary Studies of Work Teams, 1*, 223–261.

Restle, F., & Davis, J. H. (1962). Success and speed of problem solving by individuals and groups. *Psychological Review, 69*, 520–536.

Richerson, P. J., & Boyd, R. (2000). Built for speed: Pleistocene climate variation and the origin of human culture. In F. Tonneau & N. S. Thompson (Eds.), *Perspectives in ethology (vol.13): Evolution, culture, and behavior* (pp. 1–45). New York: Kluwer Academic.

Ridgeway, C. L., & Walker, H. A. (1995). Status structures. In K. S. Cook, G. A. Fine, & J. S. House (Eds.), *Sociological perspectives on social psychology* (pp. 281–310). Needham Heights, MA: Allyn and Bacon.

Seeley, T. D., & Burhman, S. C. (1999). Group decision making in swarms of honey bees. *Behavioral Ecology and Sociobiology, 45*, 19–31.

Sheppard, J. A. (1993). Productivity loss in performance groups: A motivation analysis. *Psychological Bulletin, 113*, 67–81.

Simon, H. A. (1990). A mechanism for social selection and successful altruism. *Science, 250*, 1665–1668.

Sober, E., & Wilson, D. S. (1998). *Unto others: The evolution and psychology of unselfish behavior*. Cambridge, MA: Harvard University Press.

Sorkin, R. D., Hays, C., & West, R. (2001). Signal-detection analysis of group decision making. *Psychological Review, 108*, 183–203.

Sorkin, R. D., West, R., & Robison, D. E. (1998). Group performance depends on the majority rule. *Psychological Science, 9*, 456–463.

Stasser, G., Kerr, N. L., & Davis, J. H. (1980). Influence processes in decision-making groups. In P. B. Paulus (Ed.), *Psychology of group influence* (pp. 431–477). Hillsdale, NJ: Erlbaum.

Stasser, G., Kerr, N. L., and Davis, J. H. (1989a). Influence processes and consensus models in decision-making groups. In P. B. Paulus (Ed.), *Psychology of group influence* (2nd ed., pp. 279–326). Hillsdale, NJ: Erlbaum.

Stasser, G., & Stewart, D. D. (1992). Discovery of hidden profiles by decision-making groups: Solving a problem vs. making a judgment. *Journal of Personality and Social Psychology, 63*, 426–434.

Stasser, G., Taylor, L. A., & Hanna, C. (1989b). Information sampling in structured and unstructured discussions of three- and six-person groups. *Journal of Personality and Social Psychology, 57*, 67–68.

Stasser, G., & Titus, W. (1985). Pooling of unshared information in group decision making: Biased information sampling during discussion. *Journal of Personality and Social Psychology, 48*, 1467–1478.

Stasser, G., & Titus, W. (1987). Effects of information load and percentage of shared information on the dissemination of unshared information during group discussion. *Journal of Personality and Social Psychology, 53,* 81–93.

Stasser, G., & Titus, W. (2003). Hidden profile: A brief history. *Psychological Inquiry, 14,* 304–313.

Steiner, I. D. (1972). *Group processes and productivity.* New York: Academic Press.

Stewart, D. D., & Stasser, G. (1995). Expert role assignment and information sampling during collective recall and decision making. *Journal of Personality and Social Psychology, 69,* 619–628.

Stroebe, W., Diehl, W., & Abakoumkin, G. (1996). Social compensation and the Köhler effect: Toward a theoretical explanation of motivation gains in group productivity. In E. H. Witte & J. H. Davis (Eds.), *Understanding group behavior (Vol. 2): Small group processes and interpersonal relations* (pp. 37–65). Mahwah, NJ: Erlbaum.

Tindale, R. S. (1993). Decision errors made by individuals and groups. In N. Castellan, Jr., (Ed.), *Individual and group decision making: Current issues* (pp. 109–124). Hillsdale, NJ: Lawrence Erlbaum.

Tindale, R. S., & Kameda, T. (2000). "Social sharedness" as a unifying theme for information processing in groups. *Group Processes and Intergroup Relations, 3,* 123–140.

Tindale, R. S., Kameda, T., & Hinsz, V. (2003). Group decision making: Review and integration. In M. A. Hogg & J. Cooper (Eds.), *Sage handbook of social psychology* (pp. 381–403). London: Sage.

Tindale, R. S., Smith, C. M., Thomas, L. S., Filkins, J., & Sheffey, S. (1996). Shared representations and asymmetric social influence processes in small groups. In E. Witte, & J. H. Davis (Eds.), *Understanding group behavior: Consensual action by small groups* (Vol. 1, pp. 81–103). Mahwah, NJ: Lawrence Erlbaum.

van Vugt, M. & van Lange, P. (2006). The origins of cooperation. In M. Schaller, J. Simpson, & D. Kenrick (Eds.), *Evolution and social psychology.* New York: Psychology Press.

Wegner, D. M. (1987). Transactive memory: A contemporary analysis of the group mind. In B. Mullen & G. R. Goethals (Eds.), *Theories of group behavior* (pp. 185–208). New York: Springer.

Wegner, D. M., Erber, R., & Raymond, P. (1991). Transactive memory in close relationships. *Journal of Personality and Social Psychology, 61,* 923–929.

Williams, K. D., Harkins, S. G., & Karau, S. J. (2003). Social performance. In M. A. Hogg & J. Cooper (Eds.), *Sage handbook of social psychology* (pp. 327–346). London: Sage.

Williams, K. D., & Karau, S. J. (1991). Social loafing and social compensation: The effects of expectations of co-worker performance. *Journal of Personality and Social Psychology, 61,* 570–581.

Wilson, D. S., & Sober, E. (1994). Reintroducing group selection to the human behavioral sciences. *Behavioral and Brain Sciences, 17,* 585–654.

Witte, E. H. (1989). Koehler rediscovered: The anti-Ringelmann effect. *European Journal of Social Psychology, 19,* 147–154.

Wittenbaum, G. M., Hubbell, A. P., & Zuckerman, C. (1999). Mutual enhancement: Toward an understanding of collective preference for shared information. *Journal of Personality and Social Psychology, 77,* 967–978.

Wittenbaum, G. M., & Stasser, G. (1996). Management of information in small groups. In J. L. Nye & A. M. Brower (Eds.), *What's social about social cognition* (pp. 3–28). Thousand Oaks, CA: Sage.

Wood, W. (1987). Meta-analytic review of sex differences in group performance. *Psychological Bulletin, 102,* 53–71.

15

Evolution and Culture

ARA NORENZAYAN, MARK SCHALLER,
and STEVEN J. HEINE

*H*uman mental capacities, including the capacities for culture, are the product of biological evolution. Human mental capacities in turn develop in, draw from, and operate within richly structured cultural environments. These two uncontroversial truisms are often seen as competing, mutually exclusive statements about human psychology. But they are not. Not only are these two perspectives compatible, they are in fact mutually necessary for a thorough scientific understanding of psychological processes on the one hand, and human cultures on the other.

This chapter has two goals. One goal is to discuss how an evolutionarily informed social psychology contributes to a basic understanding of culture and how it emerges in human populations. To accomplish that goal, one must first explain how culture is afforded by individual-level psychological capacities that operate in the context of social interactions. Therefore, we describe how basic evolved psychological capacities, such as imitation, conformity, and communication, make culture possible. In addition, one must explain why some beliefs and behaviors become and remain cultural—widely distributed across a population—whereas others do not. (Why, for example, are beliefs in ghosts, spirits, and gods so popular across human populations, but beliefs in zombies are not?) We describe how basic mechanisms of social cognition, social motivation, and social interaction influence the extent to which specific beliefs and behavioral expectations are successfully transmitted within a population, thus creating and sustaining cultures with specific predictable normative contents.

The second goal of this chapter is to discuss the central role of cross-cultural research in addressing a question of fundamental importance to evolutionary social psychology: To what extent are psychological mechanisms universal across human populations? Any evolutionarily informed theory of psychological processes implies some degree of universality. But any meaningful test of this universality assumption requires rigorous attention to the fact of cross-cultural differences, and to the causes of those cross-cultural differences. Cultural diversity offers substantial obstacles—and unique opportunities—for any evolutionary approach to social psychology. We elaborate on these obstacles and opportunities in the later half of this chapter.

EVOLVED PSYCHOLOGICAL FOUNDATIONS OF CULTURE

In much of the empirical literature on culture and psychology, culture is treated as known. We know that cultures exist, and we can describe the specific kinds of collectively shared beliefs, rituals, and other norms that define different cultures. The questions of primary interest to cultural psychologists have been the impact of those cultural variables on individuals' thoughts and actions (for reviews, see Fiske, Kitayama, Markus, & Nisbett, 1998; Markus & Kitayama, 1991; Nisbett, Peng, Choi, & Norenzayan, 2001; Nisbett & Norenzayan, 2002).

Of course, culture is itself something that must be explained. Why does culture exist at all? Why are cultures generally defined by specific distribution of some norms, rather than others? Why, amid all the options available within any single human group, do some kinds of belief and behavior become culturally popular while others never catch on? These and other important questions about culture demand that we treat culture—and the specific norms that define culture—as consequences as well as causes of human cognition and behavior (Kameda, Takezawa, & Hastie, 2003; Lehman, Chiu, & Schaller, 2004; Schaller & Crandall, 2004).

Humans are not just group-living social animals. They are also cultural animals. Humans, more than any other species, have the special capacity to preserve behavioral modifications and inventions initiated by group members, by transmitting them horizontally across group members, and vertically across generations (Boyd & Richerson, 1985; Cavalli-Sforza & Feldman, 1981; Heyes & Galef, 1996; Sperber, 1990, 1996; Tomasello, Kruger, & Ratner, 1993). For example, once a new and useful food-gathering technique is discovered by some individuals, humans have the capacity to preserve and improve upon the new skill through social, rather than biological transmission. Many theorists have suggested that the cognitive and behavioral capacities that make human culture possible—complex communication skills, social learning mechanisms, identification with a social group, and biased processing of information that favors in-group members and prestigious individuals—evolved because of the adaptive benefits that they offered to individuals (Boyd & Richerson, 1985; Henrich & Boyd, 1998; Henrich & Gil-White, 2001; Richerson & Boyd, 2005; Tomasello, 1999; Tomasello et al., 1993). Individual survival and reproduction was facilitated by participation within certain kinds of coordinated group activity where behavioral changes could be retained and perpetuated within the group. Thus it is likely that psychological mechanisms promoting these sorts of coordinated group actions evolved in humans (Richerson & Boyd, 2005). Several chapters in this book (Brewer & Caporael, this volume; Van Vugt & Van Lange, this volume) review many of these specific arguments, and so we will not belabor them here. The summary point is simply this: There are very likely specific evolved psychological mechanisms within social groups for the emergence of the sort of coordinated group activity that is minimally necessary for human culture to exist.

Human cultures are more than just well-coordinated social groups; they are well-coordinated social groups in which the individuals share massive amounts of common goals, desires, values, beliefs, and other forms of knowledge. Cultures are defined not just by the fact that individuals within those cultures share many kinds of knowledge, but also by the specific kinds of knowledge that they find important to share. Cultures consist of specific prohibitions and taboos, specific moral "rights" and "wrongs," specific supernatural beliefs, specific themes in literature and art, and so on. Although cross-cultural research often draws attention to the differences between cultures (e.g., different supernatural agents appear in different religious traditions), this body of literature also reveals striking similarities in the basic contours of any culture (e.g., most if not all religions revolve around one or more supernatural agents that share striking cognitive similarities across cultures). Indeed, thorough reviews of the ethnographic record have revealed hundreds of universal patterns and norms across the full spectrum of human cultures (Brown, 1991). What accounts for the similarities underlying different belief systems? One set of answers is provided by evolutionary analyses of human cognition and social behavior.

Collective Consequences of Common Cognitive and Motivational Architecture

Many defining elements of human culture may be aggregate by-products of evolved cognitive and motivational mechanisms (Tooby & Cosmides, 1992). The universal cultural prohibition against incest offers one example. The thought of incest typically elicits disgust, an affective reaction that would have served the adaptive function of discouraging genetically nonoptimal sexual couplings (Lieberman, Tooby, & Cosmides, 2003). If indeed there evolved a tendency for the idea of incest to trigger disgust, a consensually held moral aversion to incest can be viewed simply as a by-product of the underlying evolutionary process. Moreover, within a species that also has a sophisticated capacity to communicate and persuade, it is possible that these individual-level disgust reactions will become reinforced at the cultural level as well, in the form of laws and other institutionalized codes of conduct. As a result, most if not all cultures will likely develop and propagate mechanisms such as taboos against incest.

Similar analyses can be applied to other elements of morality within human cultures. It has been argued that specific cognitive capacities evolved that allow individuals to be especially adept at identifying others who violate expectations of reciprocity and fair social exchange (e.g., Sugiyama, Tooby, & Cosmides, 2002; see also Van Vugt & Van Lange, this volume). As a consequence, most cultures have developed norms and rules that govern social exchange processes. The failure to follow these rules is often treated as a moral transgression, and there typically exist institutionalized means of punishing these transgressions. Children are socialized to internalize behaviors that reinforce the cognitive mechanisms for social exchange. These complex systems of cultural norms may reflect an inevitable collective consequence of a cognitive architecture that evolved in response to selection pressures associated with the benefits, and risks of social exchange (Tooby & Cosmides, 1992). Thus, learned cultural processes serve as external reinforcements to already existing naturally selected tendencies in humans. More broadly, a number of theorists have argued that a wide range of moral norms— including norms governing obedience, reciprocity, caregiving, group solidarity, and social responsibility—may be inevitable aggregate by-products of psychological mechanisms that evolved in response to specific kinds of adaptive problems (Krebs & Janicki, 2004).

In addition to moral norms, other kinds of cultural norms too may reflect evolved tendencies to engage in certain patterns of thought or action. Consider the role of beliefs about in-groups and out-groups in creating and maintaining cultural identity. An important part of any culture is the popularly shared belief that "we" have certain desirable characteristics that are distinct from the characteristics of people in other cultures. A variety of evolutionary analyses—some of which focus on adaptive behavior within in-groups (e.g., Brewer, 1999; Brewer & Caporael, this volume) and some of which focus on adaptive reactions to outgroup members (e.g., Schaller, Faulkner, Park, Neuberg, & Kenrick, 2004; see Neuberg & Cottrell, this volume)—imply that these culturally normative belief systems may be aggregate by-products of evolved cognitive mechanisms.

Similar analyses can be applied even to cultural artifacts—art, music, literature, and mythology. Several theorists (e.g., Dissanayake, 1992; Miller, 1999, 2000) have argued that the production of art, and themes represented within art, is driven by fundamental evolutionary pressures. Aesthetic preferences in various domains appear to be linked to evolved constraints on perceptual systems. People enjoy visual art that reflects adaptive ways of interacting with physical landscapes (Orians & Heerwagen, 1992). More generally, the specific patterns and themes evident in the arts and crafts of any culture may stem, in part, from commonly shared evolved preferences for certain kinds of sensory experiences. Popular forms of cultural mythology may also be constrained by evolved aspects of human cognition. Several analyses have shown that mythic tales—including both religious myths and secular folktales—tend to be more memorable if they include a few, but not too many, "magical" elements (e.g., Norenzayan & Atran, 2004). These kinds of mythic tales are, therefore, more likely to persist in the collective memory across all individuals within any cultural population. In general, it appears that specific features of evolved cognitive mechanisms can exert an influence on the specific kinds of artifacts that are likely to become and remain defining features of a culture.

This approach to understanding the origins of culture—as a population-level consequence or by-product of evolved psychological mechanisms—has been applied most strenuously to that part of human culture that is perhaps most prototypical: religion.

In every society known to anthropologists, there is evidence for the following: (1) beliefs in supernatural agents (e.g., gods, ghosts, jinns, ancestor spirits); (2) the supernatural agents demand costly sacrifice (hard-to-fake public expressions of commitment in time and resources); and (3) the supernatural agents manage existential anxieties, such as those triggered by death, hopelessness, and loss of meaning. The ritualized coordination of these three elements yields "religion" (Atran, 2002; Atran & Norenzayan, 2004; Norenzayan & Atran, 2004). Thus, widespread religious beliefs and rituals can be understood as population-level manifestations of the "evolutionary landscape" that shape the individual cognitive and motivational tendencies such as the tendency to anthropomorphize or impute agency onto the natural world, or the motivational tendency to engage in hard-to-fake expressions of commitment to one's group. In recent years, a growing body of research has been examining the cognitive, motivational, and communicative processes that give rise to cultural and religious beliefs (Atran, 2002; Barrett, 2000; Boyer, 1992, 1994, 2003; Norenzayan & Hansen, 2006).

For example, there is abundant empirical research on the cognitive factors that constrain the cultural success of supernatural beliefs. One starting point in these analyses is the observation that spirits and other supernatural concepts found in culturally successful narratives (such as religious mythologies) have properties that are partially, but not entirely, counterintuitive (Boyer, 1994). Spirits may be invisible or may pass through solid objects, but otherwise they possess the intuitive properties of ordinary intentional agents. Supernatural agents may have supernatural abilities of perception, but they also obey many of the mundane laws of folk physics and folk biology (e.g., they get hungry; they cannot occupy more than one physical location at a time). Indeed, it appears that people assume a substantial set of intuitive properties even for beings that are putatively supernatural. Controlled experiments indicate that people spontaneously anthropomorphize God in their reasoning—attributing human-like traits such as consciousness and intentionality—even if doing so contradicts their stated theological beliefs (Barrett & Keil, 1996). The attribution of anthropomorphic traits is such a hypersensitive cognitive tendency that it is extended even to inanimate objects, such as faces in clouds, voices in the wind, and talking mountains (Guthrie, 1993). Mythical and religious traditions all over the world make ample use of such images, and as a result, belief in fantastic intentional beings (ghosts, spirits, and jinns) is culturally more contagious than belief in fantastic beings devoid of mental states, such as zombies (Atran, 2002; Boyer, 1994).

Other research indicates that culturally successful materials favor minimal rather than large violations of ontological expectations. In a content analysis of Ovid's *Metamorphoses*, Kelly and Keil (1985) found that the ontological transformations experienced by the characters followed a distinct pattern: The number of transformations of one ontological category to other ontological categories decreased as the distance between the two categories increased. Thus, it was far more likely for a conscious being to be transformed into an animal, than a conscious being to be transformed into an inanimate object. Transformations that occur across wide swaths of ontological distance may be just too counterintuitive to be psychologically appealing. If indeed minimally counterintuitive concepts are cognitively optimal, they should enjoy a cognitive advantage in memory. They should also enjoy a transmission advantage in communication. Recent studies have supported both conclusions (see Barrett & Nyhoff, 2001; Boyer & Ramble, 2001).

Cognitive processes operate not only at the level of individual supernatural beliefs (e.g., belief in ghosts), but at the level of narratives as well (e.g., the Hindu Vedas depicting creation stories, or the folktale of the *Little Red Riding Hood*). Norenzayan, Atran, Faulkner, and Schaller (in press) speculated that minimally counterintuitive narratives are the most likely to be culturally successful, because they enjoy a recall advantage relative to narrative templates that are massively counterintuitive or to those with no supernatural content. Counterintuitive narrative elements attract attention, and evoke a sense of magic or mystery, and therefore may encourage further cognitive processing that aids recall of these narrative structures. But only if these counterintuitive elements are connected to a meaningful set of everyday expectations can these narratives be readily represented, rehearsed, and transmitted to others. Consistent with this idea, Norenzayan et al. (in press) found that a few (but not too many) counterintuitive elements in a narrative facilitated both long-term recall and cultural success. For instance, in an analysis of actual folktales (those collected by the Grimm Brothers), minimally counterintuitive folktales were found to be especially culturally successful.

This line of research offers just one example of a broader phenomenon. To the extent that ideas, beliefs, and other knowledge structures correspond to specific kinds of cognitive templates, they are more likely to be culturally successful over time (Berger & Heath, 2005).

Cognition, Communication, and Evolved Constraints on Socially Constructed Culture

Culture is not merely an additive by-product of mutually interacting but independent human brains clumped together in time or space. Culture is a social construction, sculpted by mutually influencing individuals occupying a particular time or space. People communicate, and in doing so, they influence each other. While the ability to communicate may not have evolved specifically to serve a cultural function, the consequences of communication on culture are profound. Research informed by dynamic social impact theory reveals that simple acts of interpersonal communication inevitably, over time, shape the basic contours of culture (Harton & Bourgeois, 2004; Latané, 1996). Other research reveals that mere acts of communication predictably influence beliefs about the groups with which we identify—thus shaping important socially shared perceptions of what "our" culture is like (Kashima & Kostopoulos, 2004). These and other lines of work (e.g., Boster, 1991; Sperber, 1990) highlight the fundamental role that acts of interpersonal communication play in the social construction of culture.

But people do not communicate about just anything, and they do not influence each other randomly. The social construction of culture is importantly constrained by individual thoughts, desires, and decisions. Thus, cultural-level phenomena are predictably constrained and afforded by the evolutionary mechanisms that shape those thoughts, desires, and decisions.

Evolved constraints on socially constructed cultural norms are illustrated by the results of research that investigate the selective communication of beliefs, stories, and other kinds of knowledge structures. What specific kinds of things do people actually talk about, and what are the eventual consequences for popular culture? Several lines of work answer that question with results showing that (1) people are likely to talk about those things that reflect evolutionarily adaptive mechanisms, and therefore (2) these particular things—rather than others—are likely to become and remain culturally popular.

One line of work examines the social transmission and consequent popularity of trait-based group stereotypes. People are more highly motivated to talk about some kinds of personality traits than others, and those traits that are more "communicable" are more likely to persist in popular stereotypes of salient ethnic groups. For example, traits that are especially communicable were also especially persistent in popular stereotypes of African-Americans throughout the 20th century (Schaller, Conway, & Tanchuk, 2002). But what makes a trait especially communicable? Here is where the role of evolved motivational systems can come into play. One evolved motivational system pertains to sociality itself—the need to belong and the desire to be an accepted member of a social group (Baumeister & Leary, 1995; Brewer & Caporael, this volume). In order to satisfy this need, we are typically motivated to present ourselves in a socially acceptable manner to others. This self-presentational concern manifests itself in strategic decisions about interpersonal communication (e.g., we strategically express certain opinions or avoid certain topics of conversation with others). Drawing on this logic, Schaller and Conway (1999) tested the hypothesis that this belongingness motive influences decisions to communicate about certain kinds of stereotypic traits rather than others, and that these strategic communication decisions consequently influence the contents of emerging socially shared stereotypic beliefs. Empirical results supported the hypothesis. Other motivational concerns—such as self-protection—may be even more evolutionarily fundamental. Schaller et al. (2004) report preliminary evidence showing that personality traits that most clearly connote potential threat (e.g., "hostile") or lack of threat (e.g., "honest") tend to be more communicable, and that these threat-relevant traits have also been especially persistent in popular stereotypes of African-Americans.

Evolved motivational systems, such as those pertaining to self-protection, tend to be linked to distinct emotional responses, such as fear and disgust (see Keltner, Haidt, & Shiota, this volume). Knowledge structures that elicit these functional emotions may be especially communicable, and therefore especially likely to become culturally popular and persistent. This line of reasoning has been supported by studies on the transmission and popularity of "urban legends" (Heath, Bell, & Sternberg, 2001). Contemporary folklorists have collected hundreds of these apocryphal tales, and there is considerable variability in the extent to which urban legends are popularly known. Most never catch on widely and so cannot be considered to be integral parts of any culture. But some do catch on (such as the enduring myth—entirely debunked by actual research—about the risk of razor blades in Halloween apples). They capture individuals' attention, people feel compelled to share these stories with others, and so they become enduring parts of popular culture. Heath et al. (2001) found that urban legends are more communicable, and more likely to be popular, if they more strongly elicit the evolved self-protective emotion of disgust.

These examples focus on specific kinds of cultural knowledge structures (stereotypes and legends) that people explicitly talk about with one another. But evolutionary constraints on the social construction of culture are not limited to just these kinds of norms. Recent work by Kenrick, Li, and Butner (2003) reveals how evolved cognitive architecture can guide the social construction of cultural norms governing mating behavior.

Every culture is marked by specific rituals, institutions, and other norms pertaining to mating behavior. In some cultures polygamy is prevalent; in others it is forbidden. In most cultures, norms encourage long-term "restricted" mating, but in some cultures, short-term "unrestricted" mating is far more common. Drawing jointly on insights from evolutionary psychology and dynamic systems models, Kenrick et al. (2003) show how these cultural norms can be understood as a product of a dynamic process of implicit interpersonal negotiation, the eventual outcomes of which are constrained by evolved decision rules.

Because of the evolutionary pressures imposed by differential parental investment, there is an average tendency for men to be more inclined toward unrestricted mating and women toward more restrictive mating. But actual mating behavior is flexible, and is responsive to aspects of the immediate context—such as individuals' perceptions about the extent to which others (especially potential mates) prefer a restricted vs. unrestricted approach to mating. The style of mating adopted by any pair of mates is therefore the product of a sort of implicit negotiation, informed not only by the preferences of the two individuals within the pair, but also by the preferences of other potential mates in the local geographical vicinity. This creates a dynamic process in which small amounts of variation in local sex ratios and mating preferences can exert a substantial impact on the mating norms that emerge across a population. The results of this process are such that there emerges a tendency for most (but not all) heterosexual populations to develop norms promoting restricted mating relationships. On the other hand, the same dynamic process predicts a greater tendency toward unrestricted mating norms within male homosexual populations. More generally, broad patterns of cross-cultural similarity, punctuated by certain specific kinds of cross-cultural difference, can be predicted from the operation of dynamic social influence processes that are constrained by evolved decision rules (Kenrick et al., 2003).

Thus, even though many aspects of culture are socially constructed through interpersonal acts of social influence, this social construction process is fundamentally shaped by the evolved cognitive architecture of those individuals who—often unwittingly—do the constructing.

PSYCHOLOGICAL UNIVERSALS ACROSS CULTURES

It is clear that an evolutionary perspective on social psychology can contribute to the scientific understanding of what culture is and how it emerges and stabilizes in human populations. It is less clear, perhaps, that evolutionary social psychology can benefit from a cross-cultural perspective. One specific benefit is that rigorous cross-cultural analyses of social psychological processes are essential to conclusions about the evolved basis of those processes.

Evolutionary psychology rests on the idea that many mental processes have been naturally selected to solve the adaptive tasks faced by ancestral populations. It follows from this assumption that there exists some universally shared repertoire of core psychological mechanisms. It is an important scientific goal to discover and document evidence of these alleged human universals across cultures (Buss, 2001; Schmitt & Pilcher, 2004). Unfortunately, the documentation of universals has been a neglected topic of inquiry within psychology in general, and within social psychology in particular. To address this problem, Norenzayan and Heine (2005) recently articulated a conceptual framework that can facilitate research into human universals. Here, we summarize some of the observations and implications derived from this framework.

Most social psychologists would agree that, at some level, members of the human species share universal conceptual and motivational mechanisms that interact with cultural contexts in important ways—some set of psychological building blocks without which cultures and cultural learning would be impossible. Similarly, most social psychologists would agree that, at some level, cultural contexts are implicated in psychological processes, and as a result give rise to cultural variation. Indeed, some appreciation of human universals and cultural diversity is necessary in order to make sense of the vast theoretical and empirical literature of social psychology. However, the challenge in considering universals within a context of cultural diversity is to target an appropriate level of analysis to make sense of them. At too abstract a level, universals are too diffuse to be of significant empirical import (Geertz, 1973). At too concrete a level, however, it is unlikely that many universals will be identified. The key is to articulate the optimal level of abstraction that renders potential universals useful in research, general enough to occur, yet tangible enough to have psychological authenticity.

Psychology's narrow empirical base, focused primarily on Western, middle-class, secular, college-educated populations, is an obvious and daunting obstacle to the discovery of genuine psychological universals (for recent discussions of this problem, see Medin & Atran, 2004; Norenzayan & Heine, 2005; Rozin, 2001; Sears, 1986). A phenomenon identified at, say, a mid-western US university does not inform whether that phenomenon exists elsewhere in a different human population. Perhaps the same phenomenon is present elsewhere, but simply remains undocumented. Or perhaps it exists elsewhere in a somewhat different form. Or perhaps it is largely absent. One important rationale for cross-cultural research, then, is that systematic empirical observation across cultures is an essential and necessary means of disentangling the culture-specific from the universal.

If we fail to engage in such cross-cultural research (or fail to attend closely to its results), then we all fall prey too easily to a pernicious sort of culture blindness, in which we wrongly assume the universality of some culture-specific manifestation of a deeper underlying universal, and fail to discover that deeper universal itself. Alternatively, it is possible that some psychological processes are cultural inventions, and do not reflect any apparent evolved basis whatsoever. Either way, this is a serious liability for any scientist who wishes to draw accurate conclusions about the evolutionary (and thus at some level universal) bases of psychological phenomena.

Consider, for example, the debate over the universality of marriage from the anthropological literature (e.g., Goody, 1977; Levi-Strauss, 1969). If defined as a form of institutionalized arrangement for men and women to form a long-term mating relationship that facilitates the conception and caring of offspring, then marriage is universal across human cultures (Brown, 1991). However, at the level of particular cultural instantiations, we see a wide variety of marital arrangements around the world (e.g., arranged monogamy, voluntary serial monogamy, polygyny, fraternal polyandry, endogamy, and exogamy). If we are interested in articulating the evolutionary origins of marriage it is crucial that we are targeting the appropriate level of analysis. An evolutionary account of, say, serial monogamy is unlikely to be persuasive, given that exclusively monogamous relations are uncommon in many cultures. In contrast, an evolutionary account of marriage that is defined in the more abstract way (described above) would—given its universal presence in societies—rest on much firmer ground.

For a psychological example, consider the question of whether a need for positive self-regard is a psychological universal. The idea that people are motivated to seek and maintain a positive self-view is a foundational assumption of many theories in psychology (e.g., Allport, 1955; James, 1950/1890; Taylor & Brown, 1988). Thus, the question of whether a need for positive self-regard is universal is an important one. A perusal of the evidence for positive self-regard across cultures, however, underscores the importance of being explicit about the level of abstraction that one is considering. One way to consider the question of whether people are motivated to have positive self-regard is to conceive of positive self-regard as *self-enhancement*—operationalized as the tendency to dwell on and elaborate positive information about the self, relative to the tendency to dwell on and elaborate information about one's weaknesses (e.g., Heine, 2005a; Taylor & Brown, 1988). At this more specific level of abstraction there is a great deal of cultural variability. For instance, comparisons of East Asians and Westerners reveal pronounced cross-cultural differences in dispositional measures of positive self-concept, self-serving biases, and reactions to success and failure feedback (Heine, Lehman, Markus, & Kitayama, 1999). One recent meta-analysis comparing self-enhancement tendencies among East Asians and Westerners revealed cross-cultural differences with an average effect size of $d = .85$ (Heine & Hamamura, 2005). Whereas there is abundant evidence for self-enhancement among Westerners (average $d = .86$), evidence for self-enhancement among East Asians living in East Asia is strikingly lacking (average $d = -.02$). This relative absence of self-enhancement among East Asians does not appear to be due to experimental artifacts (see Heine, 2003, 2005a; Heine et al., 1999; for a dissenting view see Brown & Kobayashi, 2002). In contrast to the pursuit of self-esteem that is so commonly documented among individuals in Western cultures, East Asians appear to be more concerned with securing "face"; and rather than engaging in strategic self-enhancement, East Asians are more concerned with self-improvement (Heine, 2005b; Heine et al., 1999).

These and other similar findings certainly cast doubt on the universality of a motive for self-enhancement or positive self-regard (Heine et al., 1999). This is worth keeping in mind when evaluating the plausibility of theories that propose an evolved basis for self-esteem. Barkow (1989) proposed that self-esteem was selected to serve as a gauge of subtle changes of the individual's status within dominance hierarchies. Leary and colleagues (Leary, Tambor, Terdal, & Downs, 1995) argued that self-esteem is an adaptation that functions as an indicator to detect when our social relationships with others were vulnerable. Terror management theory (Pyszczynski, Greenberg, & Solomon, 2004) maintains that self-esteem emerged as an adaptation that serves to stave off the debilitating existential anxieties that come from fears of mortality. These different perspectives on the origins of self-esteem can be interpreted in different ways. If interpreted as theories specifying evolutionary origins of some general mechanism that makes self-evaluation possible, without specifying the psychological forms that this mechanism takes, then perhaps these theories are not directly tested by cross-cultural differences in self-enhancement. But if these theories are interpreted—as they often are—as specifying evolutionary origins for a need for positive self-esteem, then the cross-cultural evidence is both pertinent and problematic. At minimum, a plausible evolutionary account cannot be inconsistent with the cross-cultural data. Ideally, it should not simply be mute on the matter either. A truly compelling evolutionary explanation for self-enhancement should explain why this phenomenon appears more strongly in some cultures than in others, and needs to embed this explanation within a set of processes that are genuinely universal.

That last statement is the key; a compelling evolutionary account must identify evolved mechanisms at a level of conceptual abstraction for which there is evidence of universality. For instance, rather than focusing on a motive for positive self-regard, it might be more plausible to focus on a deeper motive to "be a good self"—that is, to strive to be the kind of person who is viewed as appropriate, good, and significant in one's culture (e.g., Crocker & Park, 2004; D'Andrade, 1984; Heine et al., 1999; Kluckhohn, 1962). Within Western, individualistic cultures, self-enhancement and self-promotion may well be useful means toward being a good self, but not so among East Asians. Instead, in collectivistic East Asian cultures, self-improvement and saving face may be much more useful means of obtaining the same universal goal (Heine, 2003, 2005b; Heine et al., 1999). Thus it is the need to be a good self—and not the need for positive self-regard—that is the more plausible psychological universal. Evolutionary theories of self-concept might sensibly be targeted at this level of abstraction (see Heine, Proulx, & Vohs, in press).

The same logic can be applied to a variety of other social psychological phenomena. Consider racism, for example. Although race-based prejudice has been a staple of the social psychological literature for decades and represents a paradigmatic case of intergroup prejudice, it would be a conceptual mistake to articulate evolutionary theories that focus on racism, per se. While race is a sociologically important construct in contemporary Western cultures, it is largely irrelevant to social life in many other human populations (and is highly unlikely to have been relevant in ancestral populations). The paradigmatic prejudices in other cultures are based on entirely different kinds of categorical distinctions (language, religion, family lineage, and so forth). Therefore, to understand the evolutionary roots of racism, one must focus on a level of conceptual abstraction that is deeper than race, and that encompasses these other kinds of categorical distinctions as well—and is more truly universal. Theories that focus on subjective impressions of foreignness, for instance, or on coalitional group membership are more likely to have merit as evolutionary explanations (e.g., Hirschfeld, 1996; Kurzban, Tooby, & Cosmides, 2001; Schaller, Park, & Faulkner, 2003).

As these examples illustrate, the existence of naturally selected psychological processes does not preclude the possibility that these adaptations are expressed in different forms in different populations. The human brain evolved to learn from and be responsive to the physical environment (Kenrick, Ackerman, & Ledlow, 2003, Moore, 2004). Similarly, it evolved to function in social groups and to be responsive to the workings of other minds in the local social environment (e.g., Dunbar, 1992; Tomasello et al., 1993). Consequently, psychological adaptations are best conceptualized as context-contingent decision rules that are sensitive to local variation in local ecologies and social geometries (Cohen, 2001; Kenrick et al., 2003). We rarely encounter evolved psychological processes at the universal level directly; they typically appear to us in context-specific, culturally instantiated forms. In some cases, the instantiations are not so diverse and the universal phenomena are easily discerned (e.g., preferences for sweet and fatty foods [Rozin, 1976]; sex differences in violence [Daly & Wilson, 1988]). In other cases, however, the instantiations are so varied that the underlying universals do not lend themselves to easy observation (Heine et al., 1999; Markus & Kitayama, 1991; Nisbett et al., 2001; Shweder, Much, Mahapatra, & Park, 1997). Nevertheless, it is only by assessing cultural diversity—and taking those cultural differences seriously—that we can distinguish between specific instantiations and true universals.

In order to draw sensible conceptual conclusions about what is universal and what is not, one must also make distinctions between different levels of universals that are meaningful for psychological analysis. Norenzayan and Heine (2005) recently developed a framework that offers a useful scheme for drawing conclusions about, and formulating theories of, cross-cultural differences and human universals.

Levels of Psychological Universals

Norenzayan and Heine (2005) proposed three levels of psychological universals and one case of nonuniversal that can be observed cross-culturally. This model rests on a powerful analogy of the mind as a *toolbox* (Cole, 1996; Piaget, 1952; Resnick, 1994; Stich, 1990; Vygotsky, 1978). Psychological processes, including cognitive structures, emotions, and motivations, can be thought of as tools for behavior. Just as the handyman's specialized toolbox is utilized to construct, repair, add, and transform, the mental toolbox is accessed to solve the myriad problems of everyday life. In a world joined together by nails, a hammer is a more useful tool than a wrench. In a world held together by nuts and bolts, a wrench is a more useful tool than a hammer. To the extent that the worlds in which people inhabit are different (or are believed to be so), there emerge different affordances that elicit the use of different tools.

This perspective leads us to ask three questions about the comparability of psychological tools across cultures (see Figure 15.1). First, are the tools in the cognitive toolboxes—the cognitive availability of these mental processes—the same or different across cultures? Second, even if the repertoire of tools is the same, do people rely on the same or different tools to solve a given problem? Third, even if the tools are the same, and the same tools are used to solve a given problem, is the tool accessed with the same facility or frequency? The answers to these three questions suggest four degrees of universality: (1) *nonuniversals* (different tools altogether); (2) *existential universals* (same tool, but differential functions or uses); (3) *functional universals* (same tool and same function, but differential accessibilities); and (4) *accessibility universals* (same tool, use, and degree of accessibility).

Specific patterns of cross-cultural evidence imply the existence of specific kinds of universals. If there is no evidence of cross-cultural differences at all—that is, a particular phenomenon emerges with a similar effect size across cultures—this implies that the phenomenon falls in the category of an accessibility universal. An example is the cognitive ability to estimate quantity approximately. This analog "number sense" is insensitive to exactitude, and is shared by humans and

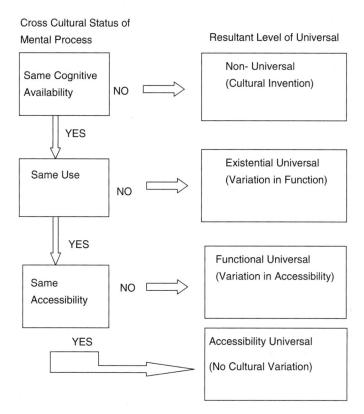

FIGURE 15.1 Decision flowchart indicating different levels of psychological universals.

higher primates alike (Dehaene, 1997). Recent evidence indicates that this ability operates in the same way among English speakers who employ an elaborate counting system, as well as among a preliterate culture (the Piraha of Amazonia) who employ a very simple counting system that does not differentiate between specific quantities greater than two (Gordon, 2004).

The phenomenon is demoted to a functional universal, however, if the shape of the relationship between the variables is the same across cultures, but the effect sizes differ systematically and predictably. A possible candidate for a functional universal is the tendency to make internal attributions for behavior. Empirical evidence indicates that this tendency does emerge cross-culturally, but is generally weaker in non-Western societies (Choi, Nisbett, & Norenzayan, 1999; Norenzayan & Nisbett, 2000).

In contrast, if qualitatively distinct patterns of findings emerge in different cultures (e.g., a relation between variables that is observed in one culture entirely disappears or reverses in other cultures), then the phenomenon fails the test of a functional universal. A case in point is self-enhancing and self-critical motivations for success and failure (see Heine, 2005b for a discussion). In a series of experiments, Heine and his colleagues found that success feedback (relative to failure feedback) led to more persistence later on that same purported creativity task among self-enhancing Americans. The reverse was true for self-critical Japanese, who persisted longer after failure. This indicates that the relationship between intrinsic motivation and experiences with success and failure are functionally different across cultures.

This kind of evidential pattern does not necessarily indicate that a particular psychological phenomenon is actually absent from the psychological repertoires in some cultures; it may instead reflect the relative dominance of alternative psychological strategies that exist in those cultures. If so, the phenomenon would be considered an existential universal. In such cases, the next step would be to consider more carefully whether the phenomenon does indeed exist in the psychological repertoires across cultures, even if its functional use differs; if evidence indicates that it does not, then the phenomenon cannot be considered a universal at any level. Such a case can be made, for example, for the cognitive ability to count. Counting beyond two is a form of numerical thinking that appears to be contingent on a culturally available counting system (Gordon, 2004; see Norenzayan & Heine, 2005, for further discussion).

Levels of Universals in Theory Development

Evolutionary psychological theories can gain generality and empirical focus if they are calibrated to account for the observed level of universality in the cross-cultural evidence. As an illustration, consider Buss's (1989) cross-cultural survey of gender differences in mate preferences. Consistent with hypotheses derived from sexual selection theory, Buss predicted and found that in virtually all cultures men valued physical attractiveness and pre-marital chastity more than women, whereas women valued status and good financial prospects more than men. Buss concluded that these preferences are evolved psychological universals. However, Buss also found considerable cross-cultural variation in the size of these gender differences. For example, the gender difference in valuing good financial prospects was twice as large in Nigeria as in Belgium. There was also robust cross-cultural variation in the desirability of chastity, ranging from virtually no gender difference at all in Sweden, to substantial gender differences in other countries. In fact, the overall results indicated that the respondents' culture was a stronger predictor of their mate preferences (for all traits considered) than gender. Eagly and Wood (1999) reanalyzed Buss' data and demonstrated that the size of the gender differences varied systematically as a function of measures of gender inequality in each culture, such that the gender effect increased with more gender inequality. Eagly and Wood concluded that the results are consistent with social structural theories of gender differences.

These explanations are not mutually exclusive, and indeed can be complementary. That gender effects were found consistently across cultures, despite variation in their size, supports the conclusion that the gender differences in mate preferences (predicted by Buss's evolutionary analysis) are functional universals. On the other hand, the fact that the size of these differences varies across cultures indicates that they fail the test of an accessibility universal, and supports the conclusion that these gender differences—even if rooted in evolved psychological universals—are responsive to local cultural conditions.

One does not need to accept the specific framework proposed by Norenzayan and Heine in order to appreciate the broader point: Evolutionarily derived theories of social psychological phenomena can gain clarity and precision if they account for universality and variation at different conceptual levels. Theoretical debates can be sharpened, and perhaps even resolved, by specifying the particular level at which a psychological universal is alleged to occur.

Universality, Cultural Variability, and the Argument for Innateness

Universality is an important consideration for determining whether psychological phenomena are explainable in terms of innate structures. However, arguing for universality is distinct from arguing for innateness. There are at least three distinct reasons why some psychological phenomena might be universal across cultures:

1. It may result from innate, naturally selected psychological tendencies that emerge everywhere in the same ontogenetic sequence (such as language acquisition; Pinker & Bloom, 1992).
2. It may be a cultural by-product of naturally selected tendencies (such as religion; Atran & Norenzayan, 2004).
3. It may reflect independent cultural invention, or cultural diffusion of some learned response that serves the same useful purpose everywhere—what Dennett (1995, p. 486) refers to as "good tricks" (such as counting systems, calendars, writing, trading, and cognitions and behaviors associated with these inventions).

Thus, universality is encouraging but not conclusive evidence for the innateness of a psychological process. Any argument for the innateness of a process has to make a compelling case that the process is unlikely to have achieved universality due to repeated independent invention, or due to widespread cultural propagation.

On the other hand, cultural variability emerges for several possible reasons: (1) differential distribution of psychological traits due to cultural learning mechanisms such as mimicry, conformity, and instruction (e.g., Boyd & Richerson, 1985; Markus & Kitayama, 1991; Nisbett et al., 2001); (2) the same innate but flexible psychological tendency expressing itself differently in response to varied ecological conditions, such as when different forms of marriage emerge in response to variation in resource scarcity (e.g., Kenrick et al., 2003; Tooby & Cosmides, 1992); and (3) differential distribution of gene frequencies across different cultural populations. There is considerable theoretical and empirical support for the first two explanations for cultural variation. Here we examine briefly the plausibility of the third possibility.

Research in behavioral genetics reveals that many psychological traits and tendencies are substantially heritable (e.g., Plomin, Owen, & McGuffin, 1994; Roy, Neale, & Kendler, 1995; Turkheimer, 2000). Furthermore, findings from the Human Diversity Genome project identify a number of genes that systematically vary across human populations (e.g., Cavalli-Sforza & Cavalli-Sforza, 1995), including genes associated with distinct blood groups (Landsteiner, 1901), lactose intolerance (Flatz, 1987), and resistance to malaria (Allison, 1954). Might there also be systematic population variance in those genes that underlie social psychological phenomena?

If group-level psychological differences are associated with group-level genetic differences, selection pressures must have diverged in different populations. Cavalli-Sforza and Cavalli-Sforza (1995) argue that we should see the greatest differential selection pressures on traits that have had powerful consequences on fitness and that occurred consistently over long periods of time, such as those related to thermal regulation, pathogen resistance, and diet. This is unlikely to be the case with most psychological traits and tendencies. Most large-scale societal changes that separate cultures today—with the possible exception of the agricultural revolution that occurred in some societies 10,000 years ago—have very short time frames that preclude the impact of culturally differential selective pressures on the gene pool.

Perhaps the best way to empirically address the question of whether variation in genes or in cultural practices underlies cross-cultural differences in psychological processes is to contrast groups such that race is held constant but cultural context is varied. Immigrants and their descendants provide practical samples that afford this investigation. Empirical results consistently show that immigrants and their descendants exhibit psychological processes intermediate to their ancestors who remained in their heritage culture, and their compatriots in their host culture—evidence consistent with a truly cultural, rather than genetic, explanation for cross-cultural differences. For example, Asian-Americans exhibit psychological tendencies intermediate to those of Asians in Asia and Americans of European descent (e.g., Kitayama, Markus, Matsumoto, & Norasakkunkit, 1997;

Norenzayan, Smith, Kim, & Nisbett, 2002); if anything, Asian-Americans more closely resemble European Americans (Heine & Hamamura, 2005). Furthermore, the longer the people of Asian descent have been in North America, the more similar their psychological tendencies resemble those of European Americans, to the point that third-generation Asian-Canadians are indistinguishable from Canadians of other cultural backgrounds (Heine & Lehman, 2004; McCrae, Yik, Trapnell, Bond, & Paulhus, 1998). At present we know of no compelling empirical evidence to suggest an innate basis of the cross-cultural differences that have been identified in social psychological studies, although a more thorough set of psychological traits would have to be investigated before any final conclusion can be reached.

Toward a Culturally Informed Evolutionary Psychology

The past quarter century has witnessed not just the burgeoning importance of evolutionary inquiry as a means of generating important psychological discoveries, it has also witnessed the burgeoning importance of cross-cultural inquiries into psychological phenomena as well. Lurking within both perspectives is a fundamental concern with psychological universals. Cultural psychologists typically do not assume universality, at least usually not at the level of the phenomenon under investigation. Rather, they actively seek to test—and often reject—presumptions of universality. The result is a body of evidence that reveals remarkable variability even in psychological processes that had been tacitly assumed to be "basic," "fundamental," or otherwise universal (e.g., Heine et al., 1999; Nisbett et al., 2001). This evidence has provided both a challenge to existing psychological theories, and a stimulus for the development of newer, more sophisticated theories of human psychology (e.g., Choi et al., 1999; Kenrick et al., 2003; Medin & Atran, 2004). Just as importantly, perhaps, cultural psychology provides a set of methodologies and tools that can be used in the service of any investigation that requires sensitivity to questions about what is universal and what is not.

As we have discussed, these questions are fundamental to evolutionary psychology. Evolutionary approaches to human behavior have inspired some of the most wide-ranging cross-cultural studies in the social psychological literature (e.g., Buss, 1989; Daly & Wilson, 1988; Ekman, Sorenson, & Friesen, 1969; Kenrick & Keefe, 1992), and an increasing number of evolutionary psychologists are now availing themselves of cross-cultural methods in fruitful ways. Some of these studies provide important evidence showing that psychological phenomena previously documented in Western cultures also emerge in cultures that more closely reflect the subsistence nature of ancestral hunter–gatherer populations (e.g., German & Barrett, 2005; Sugiyama et al., 2002). Other studies employ samples from a wide variety of world cultures, and so provide unique opportunities to test and recalibrate tacit assumptions about universality (e.g., Schmitt et al., 2003).

Still other studies exploit existing knowledge about local ecologies to deduce and test evolutionary hypotheses that explicitly imply cross-cultural differences. For example, according to one evolutionary perspective on interpersonal attraction, subjective judgments about physical attractiveness are influenced by the perception of morphological features that covary with disease resistance and long-term health outcomes; and because of this, attractiveness is a desirable feature in a mate. If so, it follows that individuals should be especially likely to value physical attractiveness as a mate-selection criterion under ecological conditions in which the threat of disease is especially high. Consistent with this hypothesis, Gangestad and Buss (1993) found that a greater priority is placed on a mate's physical attractiveness within cultures that historically have faced greater threats from parasitic diseases. This kind of study highlights yet one more way in which cross-cultural inquiry, focused on ecological variation, can be used to test theories within the realm of evolutionary social psychology.

CONCLUSION

Human social cognition and behavior has been substantially shaped by a long history of biological evolution, and continues to be substantially shaped by culture. Humans are endowed with a host of naturally selected cognitive and motivational tendencies that had fitness consequences in the ancestral environment. Among these tendencies is a set of powerful cognitive capacities that allow for mimicry, conformity, and social learning, thus ensuring that behavioral changes will be culturally transmitted and stabilized at rates much faster than genetic transmission would allow. The complex interactions between biology and culture are still poorly understood, and difficult to figure out. But it is worth trying, as these interactions hold the key to the full story of human nature. Many of the sophisticated attempts to conceptualize these interactions (e.g., Boyd & Richerson, 1985; Lumsden & Wilson, 1981; Tomasello, 1999; Sperber, 1996; see Janicki & Krebs, 1998 for a review) are central to social psychological inquiry. A social psychology that is sensitive to both evolutionary universals and cross-cultural differences has much to offer to the community of scientists seeking to solve these puzzles. Social psychological inquiry can help us discover the cognitive and motivational capacities that make culture possible. It can help us reconstruct the subtle psychological mechanisms through which some beliefs, but not others, achieve cultural success—thus contributing to predictable patterns of cultural similarity and diversity. Cross-cultural studies are central to this project. Only through cross-cultural comparisons can we discover the true universal nature of our species. And only through these comparisons can we describe the many ways by which evolved psychological structures give rise to, and then interact with the astonishing range of human potentials that we observe in the world around us.

REFERENCES

Allison, A. C. (1954). The distribution of the sickel-cell trait in East Africa and elsewhere, and its apparent relationship to the incidence of subtertian malaria. *Transactions of the Royal Society of Tropical Medicine and Hygeine, 48,* 312–318.

Allport, G. W. (1955). *Becoming.* New Haven: Yale University Press.

Atran, S. (2002). *In gods we trust: The evolutionary landscape of religion.* Oxford: Oxford University Press.

Atran, S., & Norenzayan, A. (2004). Religion's evolutionary landscape: Counterintuition, commitment, compassion, communion. *Behavioral and Brain Sciences, 27*(6), 713–777.

Barkow, J. H. (1989). *Darwin, sex, and status: Biosocial approaches to mind and culture.* Toronto: University of Toronto Press.

Barrett, J. L. (2000) Exploring the natural foundations of religion. *Trends in Cognitive Science, 4,* 29–34.

Barrett, J. L., & Keil, F. (1996). Conceptualizing a non-natural entity: Anthropomorphism in god concepts. *Cognitive Psychology, 31,* 219–247.

Barrett, J. L., & Nyhof, M. A. (2001). Spreading nonnatural concepts: The role of intuitive conceptual structures in memory and transmission of cultural materials. *Journal of Cognition and Culture, 1,* 69–100.

Baumeister, R. F., & Leary, M. R. (1995). The need to belong: Desire for interpersonal attachments as a fundamental human motivation. *Psychological Bulletin, 117,* 497–529.

Berger, J. A., & Heath, C. (2005). Idea habitats: How the prevalence of environmental cues influences the success of ideas. *Cognitive Science, 29,* 195–221.

Boster, J. S. (1991). The information economy model applied to biological similarity judgment. In L. B. Resnick, J. M. Levine, & S. D. Teasley (Eds.), *Perspectives on socially shared cognition* (pp. 203–225). Washington, DC: American Psychological Association.

Boyd, R., & Richerson, P. J. (1985). *Culture and the evolutionary process.* Chicago: University of Chicago Press.

Boyer, P. (1992). Explaining religious ideas: Outline of a cognitive approach. *Numen, 39,* 27–57.

Boyer, P. (1994). *The naturalness of religious ideas.* Berkeley: University of California Press.Boyer, P. (2003). Religious thought and behaviour as by-products of brain function. *Trends in Cognitive Sciences, 7,* 119–124.

Boyer, P., & Ramble, C. (2001). Cognitive templates for religious concepts: Cross-cultural evidence for recall of counter-intuitive representations. *Cognitive Science, 25,* 535–564.

Brewer, M. B. (1999). The psychology of prejudice: Ingroup love or outgroup hate? *Journal of Social Issues, 55,* 429–444.

Brown, D. E. (1991). *Human universals.* New York: McGraw-Hill.

Brown, J. D., & Kobayashi, C. (2002). Self-enhancement in Japan and America. *Asian Journal of Social Psychology, 5,* 145–168.

Buss, D. M. (1989). Sex differences in human mate preferences: Evolutionary hypotheses tested in 37 cultures. *Behavioral and Brain Sciences, 12,* 1–49.

Buss, D. M. (2001). Human nature and culture: An evolutionary psychological perspective. *Journal of Personality, 69,* 955–978.

Cavalli-Sforza, L. L., & Cavalli-Sforza, F. (1995). *The great human diasporas: The history of diversity and evolution.* Reading, MA: Perseus Books.

Cavalli-Sforza, L. L., & Feldman, M. W. (1981). *Cultural transmission and evolution.* Princeton, NJ: Princeton University Press.

Choi, I., Nisbett, R. E., & Norenzayan, A. (1999). Causal attribution across cultures: Variation and universality. *Psychological Bulletin, 125,* 47–63.

Cohen, D. (2001). Cultural variation: Considerations and implications. *Psychological Bulletin, 127,* 451–471.

Cole, M. (1996). *Cultural psychology: A once and future discipline.* Cambridge: Belknap Press.

Crocker, J., & Park, L. E. (2004). The costly pursuit of self-esteem. *Psychological Bulletin, 130*, 392–414.

Daly, M., & Wilson, M. (1988). *Homicide*. New York: Aldine de Gruyter.

D'Andrade, R. (1984). Cultural meaning systems. In R. A. Shweder & R. A. Levine (Eds.), *Culture theory; Essays on mind, self, and emotion* (pp. 88–119). Cambridge, UK: Cambridge University Press.

Dehaene, S. (1997). *The number sense: How the mind creates mathematics*. Oxford: Oxford University Press.

Dennett, D. C. (1995). *Darwin's dangerous idea: Evolution and the meanings of life*. New York: Simon and Schuster.

Dissanayake, E. (1992). *Homo aestheticus: Where art comes from and why*. New York: Free Press.

Dunbar, R. I. M. (1992). Neocortex size as a constraint on group size in primates. *Journal of Human Evolution, 20*, 469–493.

Eagly, A. H., & Wood, W. (1999). The origins of sex differences in human behavior: Evolved dispositions versus social roles. *American Psychologist, 54*, 408–423.

Ekman, P., Sorenson, E. R. & Friesen, W. V. (1969). Pan-cultural elements in facial displays of emotions. *Science, 164*, 86–88.

Fiske, A. P., Kitayama, S., Markus, H. R., & Nisbett, R. E. (1998). The cultural matrix of social psychology. In D. T. Gilbert, S. T. Fiske, & G. Lindzey (Eds.), *Handbook of social psychology* (4th ed., pp. 915–981). Boston: McGraw-Hill.

Flatz, G. (1987). Genetics of lactose digestion in humans. *Advances in Human Genetics, 16*, 1–77.

Gangestad, S. W., & Buss, D. M. (1993). Pathogen prevalence and human mate preferences. *Ethology and Sociobiology, 14*, 89–96.

Geertz, C. (1973). The growth of culture and the evolution of mind. In C. Geertz, *The interpretation of cultures* (pp. 55–87). New York: Basic Books.

German, T. P., & Barrett, H. C. (2005). Functional fixedness in a technologically sparse culture. *Psychological Science, 16*, 1–5.

Goody, J. R. (1977). *Production and reproduction: A comparative study of the domestic domain*. Cambridge: Cambridge University Press.

Gordon, P. (2004). Numerical cognition without words: Evidence from Amazonia. *Science, 306*, 496–499.

Guthrie, S. E. (1993). *Faces in the clouds*. New York: Oxford University Press.

Harton, H. C., & Bourgeois, M. J. (2004). Cultural elements emerge from dynamic social impact. In M. Schaller & C. S. Crandall (Eds.), *The psychological foundations of culture* (pp. 41–75). Mahwah, NJ: Lawrence Erlbaum Associates, Inc.

Heath, C., Bell, C., & Sternberg, E. (2001). Emotional selection in memes: The case of urban legends. *Journal of Personality and Social Psychology, 81*, 1028–1041.

Heine, S. J. (2003). Self-enhancement in Japan? A reply to Brown and Kobayashi. *Asian Journal of Social Psychology, 6*, 75–84.

Heine, S. J. (2005a). Where is the evidence for pancultural self-enhancement? A reply to Sedikides, Gaertner, & Toguchi. *Journal of Personality and Social Psychology, 89*, 531–538.

Heine, S. J. (2005b). Constructing good selves in Japan and North America. In R. M. Sorrentino, D. Cohen, J. M. Olson, and M. P. Zanna (Eds.), *Culture and social behavior: The tenth Ontario symposium* (pp. 115–143). Hillsdale, NJ: Lawrence Erlbaum Associates, Inc.

Heine, S. J., & Hamamura, T. (2005). *In search of East Asian self-enhancement*. University of British Columbia, Manuscript submitted for publication.

Heine, S. J., & Lehman, D. R. (2004). Move the body, change the self: Acculturative effects on the self-concept. In M. Schaller & C. Crandall (Eds.), *Psychological foundations of culture* (pp. 305–331). Mahwah, NJ: Lawrence Erlbaum Associates, Inc.

Heine, S. J., Lehman, D. R., Markus, H. R., & Kitayama, S. (1999). Is there a universal need for positive self-regard? *Psychological Review, 106,* 766–794.

Heine, S. J., Proulx, T., & Vohs, K. D. (in press). Meaning maintenance model: On the coherence of human motivations. *Personality and Social Psychology Review.*

Henrich, J., & Boyd, R. (1998). The evolution of conformist transmission and between-group differences. *Evolution and Human Behavior, 19,* 215–242.

Henrich, J., & Gil-White, F. J. (2001). The evolution of prestige: Freely conferred deference as a mechanism for enhancing the benefits of cultural transmission. *Evolution and Human Behavior, 22,* 165–196.

Heyes, C. M., & Galef, B. G., Jr. (1996). *Social learning and imitation: The roots of culture.* New York: Academic Press.

Hirschfeld, L. A. (1996). *Race in the making: Cognition, culture, and the child's construction of human kinds.* Cambridge, MA: MIT Press.

James, W. (1950/1890). *The principles of psychology.* New York: Dover Publications.

Janicki, M. G., & Krebs, D. L. (1998). Evolutionary approaches to culture. In C. Crawford & D. L. Krebs (Eds.), *Handbook of evolutionary psychology: Ideas, issues, and applications* (pp. 163–207). Mahwah, NJ: Lawrence Erlbaum Associates, Inc.

Kameda, T., Takezawa, M., & Hastie, R. (2003). The logic of social sharing: An evolutionary game analysis of adaptive norm development. *Personality and Social Psychology Review, 7,* 2–19.

Kashima, Y., & Kostopoulos, J. (2004). Cultural dynamics of stereotyping: Interpersonal communication may inadvertently help maintaining auto-stereotype too. *Cahiers de Psychologie Cognitive, 22,* 445–461.

Kelly, M. H., & Keil, F. (1985). The more things change: Metamorphoses and conceptual structure. *Cognitive Science, 9,* 403–416.

Kenrick, D. T., Ackerman, J., & Ledlow, S. (2003). Evolutionary social psychology: Adaptive predispositions and human culture. In J. DeLamater (Ed.), *Handbook of social psychology* (pp. 103–124). New York: Kluwer-Plenum.

Kenrick, D. T., & Keefe, R. C. (1992). Age preferences in mates reflect sex differences in human reproductive strategies. *Behavioral and Brain Sciences, 15,* 75–133.

Kenrick, D. T., Li, N. P., & Butner, J. (2003). Dynamical evolutionary psychology: Individual decision-rules and emergent social norms. *Psychological Review, 110,* 3–28.

Kitayama, S., Markus, H. R., Matsumoto, H., & Norasakkunkit, V. (1997). Individual and collective processes in the construction of the self: Self-enhancement in the United States and self-criticism in Japan. *Journal of Personality and Social Psychology, 72,* 1245–1267.

Kluckhohn, C. (1962). *Culture and behavior.* New York: Free Press of Glencoe.

Krebs, D., & Janicki, M. (2004). Biological foundations of moral norms. In M. Schaller & C. S. Crandall (Eds.), *The psychological foundations of culture* (pp. 125–148). Mahwah, NJ: Lawrence Erlbaum Associates, Inc.

Kurzban, R., Tooby, J., & Cosmides, J. (2001). Can race be erased? Coalitional computation and social categorization. *Proceedings of the National Academy of Sciences, 98,* 15387–15392.

Landsteiner, K. (1901). Uber agglutinationserscheinungen normalen menschlichen. *Wiener Klin. Wochenschr, 14,* 1132–1134.

Latané, B. 1996. Dynamic social impact: The creation of culture by communication. *Journal of Communication, 46*(4), 13–25.

Leary, M. R., Tambor, E. S., Terdal, S. K., & Downs, D. L. (1995). Self-esteem as an interpersonal monitor: The sociometer hypothesis. *Journal of Personality and Social Psychology, 68*, 518–530.

Lehman, D. R., Chiu, C.-Y., & Schaller, M. (2004). Psychology and culture. *Annual Review of Psychology, 55*, 689–714.

Levi-Strauss, C. (1969). *The elementary structures of kinship*. Boston: Bacon Press.

Lieberman, D., Tooby, J., & Cosmides, L. (2003). Does morality have a biological basis? An empirical test of the factors governing moral sentiments regarding incest. *Proceedings of the Royal Society B, 270*, 819–826.

Lumsden, C. J., & Wilson, E. O. (1981). *Genes, mind, and culture: The coevolutionary process*. Cambridge, MA: Harvard University Press.

Markus, H. R., & Kitayama, S. (1991). Culture and the self: Implications for cognition, emotion and motivation. *Psychological Review, 98*, 224–253.

McCrae, R. R., Yik, M. S. M., Trapnell, P. D., Bond, M. H., & Paulhus, D. L. (1998). Interpreting personality profiles across cultures: Bilingual, acculturation, and peer rating studies of Chinese undergraduates. *Journal of Personality and Social Psychology, 74*, 1041–1055.

Medin, D. L., & Atran. S. (2004). The native mind: Biological categorization, reasoning and decision making in development and across cultures. *Psychological Review, 111*, 960–983.

Miller, G. F. (1999). Sexual selection for cultural displays. In R. Dunbar, C. Knight, & C. Power (Eds.), *The evolution of culture* (pp. 71–91). Edinburgh, UK: Edinburgh University Press.

Miller, G. F. (2000). Evolution of human music through sexual selection. In N. L. Wallin, B. Merker, & S. Brown (Eds.), *The origins of music* (pp. 329–360). Cambridge, MA: MIT Press.

Moore, B. R. (2004). The evolution of learning. *Biological Review, 79*, 301–335.

Nisbett, R. E., & Norenzayan, A. (2002). Culture and cognition. In H. Pashler & D. L. Medin (Eds.), *Stevens' handbook of experimental psychology: Cognition* (3rd ed., Vol. 2, pp. 561–597). New York: Wiley.

Nisbett, R. E., Peng, K., Choi, I., & Norenzayan, A. (2001). Culture and systems of thought: Holistic vs. analytic cognition. *Psychological Review, 108*, 291–310.

Norenzayan, A., & Atran, S. (2004). Cognitive and emotional processes in the cultural transmission of natural and nonnatural beliefs. In M. Schaller & C. S. Crandall (Eds.), *The psychological foundations of culture* (pp. 149–169). Mahwah, NJ: Lawrence Erlbaum Associates, Inc.

Norenzayan, A., Atran, S., Faulkner, J., & Schaller, M. (in press). Memory and mystery: The cultural selection of minimally counterintuitive narratives. *Cognitive Science*.

Norenzayan, A., & Hansen, I. G. (2006). Belief in supernatural agents in the face of death. *Personality and Social Psychology Bulletin, 32*, 174–187.

Norenzayan, A., & Heine, S. J. (2005). Psychological universals across cultures: What are they and how do we know? *Psychological Bulletin, 131*, 763–784.

Norenzayan, A., & Nisbett, R. E. (2000). Culture and causal cognition. *Current Directions in Psychological Science, 9*, 132–135.

Norenzayan, A., Smith, E. E., Kim, B., & Nisbett, R. E. (2002). Cultural preferences for formal versus intuitive reasoning. *Cognitive Science, 26*, 653–684.

Orians, G. H., & Heerwagen, J. H. (1992). Evolved responses to landscapes. In J. H. Barkow, L. Cosmides, & J. Tooby (Eds.), *The adapted mind: Evolutionary psychology and the generation of culture* (pp. 555–579). New York: Oxford University Press.

Piaget, J. (1952). *The origins of intelligence in the child*. New York: Norton.

Pinker, S., & Bloom, P. (1992). Natural language and natural selection. In J. H. Barkow, L. Cosmides, & J. Tooby (Eds.), *The adapted mind: Evolutionary psychology and the generation of culture* (pp. 451–494). Oxford: Oxford University Press.

Plomin, R., Owen, M. J., & McGuffin, P. (1994). The genetic basis of complex human behaviors. *Science, 264,* 1733–1739.

Pyszczynski, T., Greenberg, J., & Solomon, S. (2004). Why do people need self-esteem? A theoretical and empirical review. *Psychological Bulletin, 130,* 435–468.

Resnick, L. B. (1994). Situated rationalism: Biological and social preparation for learning. In L. A. Hirschfeld & S. A. Gelman (Eds.), *Mapping the mind: Domain specificity in cognition and culture* (pp. 474–494). Cambridge, UK: Cambridge University Press.

Richerson, P. J., & Boyd, R. (2005). *Not by genes alone: How culture transformed human evolution.* Chicago: University of Chicago Press.

Roy, M., Neale, M. C. & Kendler, K. S. (1995). The genetic epidemiology of self-esteem. *British Journal of Psychiatry, 166,* 813–820.

Rozin, P. (1976). Psychological and cultural determinants of food choice. In T. Silverstone (Ed.), *Appetite and food intake* (pp. 286–312). Berlin, Germany: Dahlem Konferenzen.

Rozin, P. (2001). Social psychology and science: Some lessons from Solomon Asch. *Personality & Social Psychology Review, 5,* 2–14.

Schaller, M., & Conway, L. G., III (1999). Influence of impression-management goals on the emerging contents of group stereotypes: Support for a social evolutionary process. *Personality and Social Psychology Bulletin, 25,* 819–833.

Schaller, M., Conway, L. G., III, & Tanchuk, T. L. (2002). Selective pressures on the once and future contents of ethnic stereotypes: Effects of the communicability of traits. *Journal of Personality and Social Psychology, 82,* 861–877.

Schaller, M., & Crandall, C. S. (2004). *The psychological foundations of culture.* Mahwah, NJ: Lawrence Erlbaum Associates, Inc.

Schaller, M., Faulkner, J., Park, J. H., Neuberg, S. L., & Kenrick, D. T. (2004). Impressions of danger influence impressions of people: An evolutionary perspective on individual and collective cognition. *Journal of Cultural and Evolutionary Psychology, 2,* 231–247.

Schaller, M., Park, J. H., & Faulkner, J. (2003). Prehistoric dangers and contemporary prejudices. *European Review of Social Psychology, 14,* 105–137.

Schmitt, D. P. and 118 members of the International Sexuality Description Project. (2003). Universal sex differences in the desire for sexual variety: Tests from 52 nations, 6 continents, and 13 islands. *Journal of Personality and Social Psychology, 85,* 85–104.

Schmitt, D. P., & Pilcher, J. J. (2004). Evaluating evidence of psychological adaptation: How do we know one when we see one? *Psychological Science, 15,* 643–649.

Sears, D. O. (1986). College sophomores in the laboratory: Influences of a narrow data base on social psychology's view of human nature. *Journal of Personality and Social Psychology, 51,* 515–530.

Shweder, R. A., Much, N. C., Mahapatra, M., & Park, L. (1997). The "big three" of morality (autonomy, community, divinity) and the "big three" explanations of suffering. In A. M. Brandt & P. Rozin (Eds.), *Morality and health* (pp. 119–169). New York: Routledge.

Sperber, D. (1990). The epidemiology of beliefs. In C. Fraser & G. Gaskell (Eds.), *The social psychological study of widespread beliefs* (pp. 25–44). Oxford, UK: Clarendon Press.

Sperber, D. (1996). *Explaining culture: A naturalistic approach.* Cambridge, MA: Blackwell.

Stich, S. (1990). *The fragmentation of reason*. Cambridge, MA: MIT Press.

Sugiyama, L. S., Tooby, J., & Cosmides, L. (2002). Cross-cultural evidence of cognitive adaptations for social exchange among the Shiwiar of Ecuadorian Amazonia. *Proceedings of the National Academy of Sciences, 99*, 11537–11542.

Taylor, S. E., & Brown, J. D. (1988). Illusion and well-being: A social psychological perspective on mental health. *Psychological Bulletin, 103*, 193–210.

Tomasello, M. (1999). *The cultural origins of human cognition*. Cambridge, MA: Harvard University Press.

Tomasello, M., Kruger, A. C., & Ratner, H. H. (1993). Cultural learning. *Behavioral and Brain Sciences, 16*, 495–552.

Tooby, J., & Cosmides, L. (1992). The psychological foundations of culture. In J. H. Barkow, L. Cosmides, & J. Tooby (Eds.), *The adapted mind: Evolutionary psychology and the generation of culture* (pp. 19–136). New York: Oxford University Press.

Turkheimer, E. (2000). Three laws of behavior genetics and what they mean. *Current Directions in Psychological Science, 5*, 160–164.

Vygotsky, L. S. (1978). *Mind in society: The development of higher psychological processes*. Cambridge: Harvard University Press.

Author Index

Abakoumkin, G., 329
Abbey, A., 23
Abrams, D., 301
Abu-Lughod, L., 123, 131, 132
Acitelli, L. K., 194
Ackerman, J., 354
Ackerman, P., 241
Adler, N., 212
Adolphs, R., 29
Agnew, C. R., 246
Agnoli, F., 132
Aiello, L. C., 60, 62, 64, 66, 70
Ainsworth, M. D. S., 217
Aitchison, J., 64
Aktipis, C. A., 3, 5, 9, 23, 24, 43, 47, 49, 67
Alatalo, R. V., 302
Alcock, J., 2, 310
Alexander, M. G., 173
Alexander, R. D., 154, 155, 164, 244, 250, 251, 256
Algoe, S., 129
Allan, S., 55
Allen, K., 44
Allison, A. C., 358
Allport, G. W., 26, 163, 173, 352
Altemeyer, B., 174
Alvarez, J. M., 30, 155
Ambady, N., 26, 28, 86, 91, 116, 130
Anders, S., 95
Andersen, S. M., 97
Anderson, C., 116
Anderson, L. R., 325, 326
Andreoletti, C., 87, 96
Andrews, M. W., 216
Andrews, P. W., 18
Ansul, S. E., 90
Archer, D., 86
Archer, J., 5
Arcuri, L., 297
Arcus, D., 126
Ardon, A. M., 44
Ardrey, R., 223
Argote, L., 153, 321
Armstrong, E., 128
Arndt, J., 70
Aron, A., 153
Aron, E. N., 153
Aronoff, J., 86, 93
Aronson, E., 48, 306

Arrow, K. J., 327
Arsuaga, J. L., 66
Asch, S. E., 93, 325
Ashburn-Nardo, L., 178
Asher, T., 97, 164
Ashforth, B. E., 154
Ashmore, R. D., 87
Atran, S., 346, 347, 348, 351, 357, 359
Averill, J. R., 121
Avital, E., 145
Axelrod, R., 6, 240, 248

Bahn, P., 55
Bai, D., 100
Bailenson, J. N., 100
Bailey, J. M., 5, 200
Bakker, A. B., 303
Balaban, M. T., 90
Banaji, M. R., 7, 163
Banaszynski, T. L., 124
Banerjee, A. V., 325, 326
Banse, R., 86
Barbee, A. P., 87
Barchas, P., 164
Barclay, A. M., 86
Bargh, J. A., 94
Barham, L. S., 65
Barkow, J. H., 168, 353
Barksdale, C. M., 127
Baron, R. M., 81, 83
Baron-Cohen, S., 29, 42
Barrett, E. S., 94
Barrett, H. C., 5, 16, 27, 40, 41, 359
Barrett, J. L., 347
Barrett, K. C., 117, 122
Barrett, L., 60, 241, 242, 244, 250, 251, 254, 256
Bartholomew, K., 232
Bassett, R., 309
Bassili, J. N., 86
Bassoff, T., 216
Batson, C. D., 241, 249, 256
Battistich, V. A., 93
Baumeister, R. F., 16, 39, 47, 48, 67, 68, 71, 247, 263, 301, 349
Baxter, J. C., 166
Beall, A., 100
Bearhs, J. O., 44
Beauvois, J.-L., 89

Becker, D. V., 9
Becker, S., 237
Bednarik, R. G., 65
Beer, J., 127, 128
Bekkers, R., 237
Bell, C., 129, 349
Bellavia, G., 193
Belsky, J., 219
Bem, D. J., 126, 127
Bendor, J., 248
Benjamin, L. S., 99
Bentall, R. P., 69
Bereczkei, T., 91
Berger, J. A., 348
Berk, M. S., 97
Berkman, L. F., 231
Berkowitz, L., 264, 265, 269, 273
Bernieri, F. J., 26, 86
Berntson, G. G., 94
Berry, D. S., 86, 100
Berscheid, E., 87, 176
Bettman, J. R., 321
Betzig, L., 294, 296, 299
Bevan, W., 87
Bickerton, D., 64
Biek, M., 30, 86
Biel, A., 237
Bigelow, A., 90
Bikhchandani, S., 325, 326
Billig, M., 155
Binford, L., 150
Birbaumer, N., 94
Birch, K., 241
Blackstone, T., 195
Blaine, B., 149
Blair, I. V., 97
Blair, R. J. R., 127
Blairy, S., 94, 96
Blakeslee, S., 44, 45, 49
Blanz, V., 92
Blascovich, J., 100
Blehar, M. C., 217
Bleske, A. L. 4, 85
Bloom, P., 357
Blumenthal, J., 96
Blythe, P., 16
Bobo, L., 173
Bodenhausen, G. V., 124
Boehm, C., 132, 133, 323, 327
Bohlig, A., 122
Boinski, S., 145
Boldry, J. G., 89
Bolger, N., 30
Bond, M. H., 88, 89, 99, 359
Bonner, B. L., 149
Boone, R. T., 86

Borgerhoff Mulder, M., 156
Borgia, G., 299
Borkenau, P., 86
Boster, J. S., 348
Bourgeois, M. J., 348
Bourne, E. J., 88
Bower, N. J., 95
Bower, T. G., 95
Bowlby, J., 119, 219, 220
Bowles, S., 309
Bowman, L. A., 62
Boyce, T., 212
Boyd, R., 6, 129, 143, 164, 242, 243, 301, 309, 318, 323, 326, 328, 333, 335, 344, 358, 360
Boyer, P., 347
Boyes, A. D. 2, 39, 67, 205
Bradbury, T. N., 192
Brake, S., 92
Braly, K., 166
Brammer, G. L., 225
Branscombe, N. R., 149
Brase, G. L., 71
Bratslavsky, E., 247
Braun, C., 94
Breckler, S. J., 47
Bretherton, I., 123
Brewer, M. B., 3, 4, 6, 48, 57, 67, 97, 143, 145, 146, 148, 149, 152, 155, 156, 164, 165, 173, 178, 179, 246, 247, 251, 344, 346, 349
Briggs, J. L., 131
Broadnax, S., 149
Broadwell, S. D., 223
Brodersen, L., 217
Bronstad, M., 97
Brooks, A. S., 66
Brooks, J., 90
Brown, D. E., 168, 290, 345, 352
Brown, J. D., 24, 47, 49, 70, 352
Brown, R., 155, 166
Brown, S. L., 229, 241
Brownlow, S., 93
Brumbach, H., 322
Buck, R., 147
Buckley, T., 241
Bugental, D. B., 8, 99
Buhrman, S. C., 327
Bull, P. E., 86
Buller, D. J., 156
Bundy, R., 155
Burch, R. L., 243
Burn, S. W., 301
Burnstein, E., 5, 243, 294
Burt, D. M., 94, 201
Bushnell, I. W., 95
Buss, A. H., 269

Buss, D. M., 2, 4, 5, 6, 8, 16, 18, 23, 24, 30, 41, 68, 85, 91, 97, 118, 119, 120, 126, 166, 198, 200, 201, 202, 204, 247, 264, 265, 266, 268, 269, 272, 275, 277, 282, 290, 296, 298, 302, 351, 356, 359, 360
Buss, K., 217
Buss, L. W., 145, 146
Buswell, B. N., 121, 128
Butler, J. L., 72
Butner, J., 9, 99, 173, 237, 289, 350
Buttermore, N. R., 55, 57, 60, 61, 62, 65, 66, 73
Buunk, B. P., 303
Byrne, R. W., 60, 63

Cacioppo, J. T., 94, 211, 309
Cadoret, R. J., 218
Caglar, S., 64
Cairnes, K. J., 47
Calder, A. J., 94
Calhoun, C., 117
Cameron, J. A., 155
Campbell, A., 266, 267, 272
Campbell, D. T., 115, 146, 155, 164, 171, 245, 251
Campbell, J. D., 47, 68
Campbell, L., 3, 191, 192, 200
Campbell, R., 94
Campos, B., 120
Campos, J. J., 90, 100, 117, 122, 124
Campos, R. G., 122
Cannon-Bowers, J. A., 321
Caporael, L. R., 3, 6, 57, 58, 67, 89, 143, 145, 146, 148, 150, 151, 152, 156, 157, 164, 211, 240, 344, 346, 349
Capps, L. M., 126
Caraco, T., 145, 329, 330, 331, 332, 334
Carbonell, E., 66
Cardena, E., 44
Carey, S., 92
Carli, L. L., 301
Carlsmith, J. M., 47
Carpenter, E. M., 221
Carretero, J. M., 66
Carruthers, P., 40
Carver, C. S., 170
Case, T. I., 16
Casey, R. J., 90
Caspi, A., 126, 127
Castelli, L., 297
Cavalli-Sforza, F., 358
Cavalli-Sforza, L. L., 344, 358
Chagnon, N., 15, 264, 266, 267
Chambers, J. R., 17
Chan, J., 91
Chang, K. S., 250, 252, 253
Charpentier, P. A., 231

Chartrand, T. L., 94
Chaudhuri, A., 96
Chesney, M., 212
Cheung, C. K. T., 16
Cheung, T., 88
Chicz-DeMet, A., 222
Chiu, C.-Y., 344
Choi, I., 344, 356, 359
Choi, W., 16
Christensen, P. N., 200
Cialdini, R. B., 3, 241, 249, 265, 288, 303, 305, 308, 309, 311
Cicchetti, D., 217
Clark, A., 175
Clark, C., 122, 123
Clark, F., 127
Clark, J. D., 65, 66
Clark, L. A., 126
Clark, M. S., 253, 290, 294, 295, 296
Clark, R. D., 296
Clark, S., 94
Clausen, A., 86
Clifford, C. W. G., 92
Clore, G. L., 122, 124
Cochrane, S., 301
Cohen, D., 95, 354
Cohen, G. L., 72
Cohen, J. D., 128
Cohen, L. G., 95
Cohen, S., 212
Cohn, D. A., 231
Cohn, J. F., 122
Cole, J., 94
Cole, M., 354
Coleman, J. M., 149
Coleman, S. W., 299
Collins, B. E., 47
Collins, M. A., 85, 86, 96, 102, 168, 170
Collins, N. L., 194, 220
Collins, R. C., 122, 123
Coltheart, M., 40
Comrey, A. L., 88, 99
Conner, B., 28, 86
Conradt, L., 327
Converse, S. A., 321
Conway, L. G., III, 3, 151, 173, 349
Cook, M., 125
Cooper, J., 48
Coplan, J. D., 216
Corballis, M. C., 64
Corter, C. M., 227
Cosmides, L., 5, 16, 18, 19, 20, 28, 29, 39, 40, 41, 42, 43, 46, 47, 63, 82, 83, 91, 117, 118, 165, 168, 169, 170, 238, 241, 244, 245, 246, 265, 281, 288, 310, 345, 346, 354, 358
Costa, P. T., 30, 88, 99

Cotterell, N., 294
Cottrell, C. A., 3, 6, 7, 8, 166, 171, 172, 173, 305, 346
Counts, R. L., 227
Cousins, A. J., 200
Cowan, C. P., 231
Cowan, P. A., 231
Cox, C., 70
Cox, M. G., 88
Crandall, C. S., 5, 17, 24, 31, 175, 178, 243, 294, 344
Crawford, C., 168
Crnic, K., 231
Crocker, J., 71, 149, 353
Cronbach, L., 189
Cronin, H., 118
Cuddy, A. J., 173
Cummins, D. D., 72
Cunniff, C., 28
Cunningham, J. G., 86
Cunningham, M. R., 87
Curphy, G. J., 68
Cutting, J. E., 86
Czerlinksi, J., 18, 22
Czopp, A. M., 178
Czyzewska, M., 92

da Costa, A. P., 95
Daly, M., 2, 5, 264, 267, 269, 270, 271, 273, 274, 275, 304, 354, 359
Damasio, A. R., 95, 128
Damasio, H., 29, 95
D'Andrade, R., 353
Dansereau, D. F., 153
Dardis, G. J., 72
Darley, J. M., 128
Darwin, C., 4, 15, 86, 115, 118, 237
Davidson, R. J., 100, 117, 122
Davies, N. B., 117, 118, 331, 334
Davis, J. H., 319, 320, 323, 324, 325, 326
Davis, M., 174
Dawes, R. M., 145, 148, 238, 240, 255
Dawkins, R., 241, 242, 310
Dawson, K., 241
De Bruin, E. M. N., 253
De Cremer, D., 240, 246, 251
de Haan, E. H. F., 92
de Haan, M., 95
de Schonen, S., 92
De Waal, F., 100, 118, 121, 123, 127, 164, 227, 244, 250, 255
DeBruine, L. M., 5, 91, 243
Dedden, L. A., 267, 272
deGilder, D., 154
Dehaene, S., 356
Dekeyser, M., 100

Demos, R., 48
Dennett, D. C., 357
Denton, K., 22
DePaulo, B., 87
Depret, E. F., 72
d'Errico, F., 65
Devine, P. G., 166, 178
Devore, I., 15, 16, 150
Devos, T., 173
Diamond, L. M., 119, 120, 197
Diamond, R., 92
Diehl, M., 329
DiGeronimo, K., 30, 86
Dijker, A. J., 173
Dilley, S. R., 62
DiMatteo, M. R., 86
Dimberg, U., 122, 125
Dion, K. K., 87
Diorio, J., 215
Dissanayake, E., 346
Dobash, R. E., 267
Dobash, R. P., 267
Dobish, H., 96
Doi, T., 131
Dolderman, D., 193
Donald, M., 60
Donnelly, N., 95
Dovidio, J. F., 249
Dower, J. W., 273
Downs, D. L., 353
Draper, P., 219
Driver, R. E., 87
Duan, C., 166
Dubois, N., 89
Dugatkin, L. A., 164, 302
Duhamel, P., 92
Dukes, W. F., 87
Dunbar, R. I. M., 3, 60, 62, 63, 64, 66, 69, 70, 164, 211, 241, 242, 255, 318, 322, 323, 354
Duncan, B. D., 241
Duncan, L. A., 176
Dunn, J., 123
Dunning, D., 72
Duntley, J. D., 2, 5, 6, 8, 268, 275, 277, 282
Durkheim, E., 123
Dutta, R., 96
Dyck, R. v., 44
Dziurawiec, S., 90

Eagly, A. H., 87, 200, 237, 301, 303, 357
Ebel, R. L., 1
Ebenbach, D. H., 124
Ebert, J. P., 7
Ebert, R., 171
Eder, R. A., 29, 30
Edgar, B., 57, 59

Eguiluz, V. M., 325
Ehrlich, P. R., 123, 124
Eibl-Eibesfeldt, I., 95, 117, 118, 125
Eisenberg, N., 117, 124, 125
Eisenberger, N. I., 16
Eisenberger, R., 294
Ekman, P., 15, 86, 100, 116, 117, 118, 122, 125,
   129, 130, 131, 170, 218, 359
Elder, G., 126, 127
Elfenbein, H. A., 89, 91, 116, 130
Ellemers, N., 149, 154
Elliot, A. J., 166
Ellis, A. L., 319, 324
Ellis, B. J., 4, 6, 119, 268
Ellis, H., 90
Ellison, P. T., 94
Ellsworth, P. C., 121, 125, 130
Ellsworth, P. E., 30
Elzinga, B. M., 44
Emde, R. N., 90
Emler, N. P., 8
Emmons, R. A., 117
Eng, S. J., 176
Enquist, M., 87, 90, 100, 255
Erber, R., 153, 321
Eron, L. D., 264
Ervin, K. S., 87
Eshleman, A., 178
Esses, V. M., 173
Essock-Vitale, S. M., 243
Etcoff, N. L., 166
Everts, H., 224

Faulkner, J., 7, 24, 97, 164, 168, 176, 346, 348,
   354
Fazio, R. H., 48
Feeney, B. C., 194, 220, 221
Fehr, E., 237, 240, 242, 246, 250, 256, 309, 335
Fein, S., 163, 180
Feinberg, T. E., 64
Feingold, A., 87
Feldman, M. W., 156, 157, 344
Feldman, R. S., 94
Felitti, V. L., 218
Fellous, J. M., 87, 96
Feshbach, S., 155
Fessler, D. M. T., 176
Festinger, L., 42, 46, 47, 48, 305, 326, 334
Fiddick, L., 20
Fiedler, E. R., 27
Fiedler, K., 19
Field, T. M., 95
Field, T., 126
Figueredo, A. J., 270
Filkins, J., 324
Fincham, F. D., 248

Fink, B., 27
Finkenauer, C., 247
Fischbacher, U., 237, 240, 242, 246, 250, 256
Fishbaugh, L., 301
Fisher, G. A., 273
Fiske, A. P., 89, 99, 121, 132, 143, 290, 294,
   344
Fiske, S. T., 17, 72, 88, 165, 166, 173, 189
FitzGerald, G. J., 164
Flament, C., 155
Flatz, G., 358
Fleming, A. S., 227
Fletcher, G. J. O., 2, 5, 8, 39, 67, 189, 191, 192,
   193, 194, 200, 201, 202, 204, 205, 206
Flowers, B. J., 193
Foa, E. B., 290
Foa, U. G., 290
Fodor, J., 27, 40, 41, 45
Foley, R. A., 57, 60
Foley, R., 155
Folkman, S., 212
Foo, M. D., 89
Forgas, J. P., 124
Forsyth, D. R., 47
Foster, G. A., 246
Foster-Fishman, P. G., 324
Fox, R., 166
Fraley, R. C., 219, 220
Francis, D., 215, 217
Frank, R. H., 115, 119, 121, 125, 198, 246, 248
Frankenhauser, M., 222
Franklin, M., 27, 91
Fraser, S. C., 305
Fredrickson, B. L., 68
Freedman, J. L., 305
Fridlund, A. J., 122, 125
Friedman, J. N. W., 26
Friedman, S., 216
Friesen, M., 200
Friesen, W. V., 122, 130, 359
Frijda, N. H., 86, 117, 121, 122, 130, 131, 170
Fritz, J., 123
Frost, A. G., 322
Frye, N. E., 193
Fuligni, A. J., 155
Fultz, J., 249
Funder, D. C., 3, 5, 16, 17, 18, 20, 21, 23, 25,
   26, 30, 189, 203, 318, 325, 326, 334
Funnell, M. G., 64

Gaertner, L., 57, 70
Gagne, F. M., 191, 193, 196
Galef, B. G., Jr., 326, 344
Gallistel, C. R., 45
Gallucci, M., 252
Gallup, G. G., 60, 243

Gangestad, S. W., 5, 27, 30, 86, 91, 94, 97, 173, 176, 198, 199, 200, 201, 203, 246, 360
Garber, P. A., 145
Garcia, A., 66
Garcia, R., 95
Gardner, G. T., 240
Gardner, W., 152
Garst, E., 241
Garver-Apgar, C. E., 200
Garvin, E., 122
Gasper, K., 122
Gauthier, I., 92
Gazzaniga, M. S., 43, 64
Geary, D. C., 5, 304
Geddes, J. F., 278
Gee, T., 44
Geertz, C., 351
Geise, M. A., 86
Gelman, S. A., 29, 30
George, T. S., 273
Gerard, H. B., 306
German, T. P., 359
Ghiglieri, M. P., 63, 273
Ghirlanda, S., 87
Ghiselin, M. T., 41, 43
Gibson, J. J., 41, 81, 82, 83, 91
Gibson, R. M., 302
Gigerenzer, G., 18, 19, 21, 22, 40, 44, 289, 320, 321, 325, 326, 334
Gigone, D., 324
Gilbert, D. T., 72
Gilbert, P., 55
Giles, L., 200
Gill, M. J., 205
Gilovich, T., 17, 21
Gil-White, F. J., 129, 151, 155, 344
Gintis, H., 309, 331, 332, 336
Giraldeau, L.-A., 329, 330, 332, 334
Glass, B., 166
Glassner-Bayerl, B., 149
Gleaves, D. H., 44
Glick, P., 173
Goffman, E., 123
Gold, J. A., 87
Goldberg, J. H., 121
Goldberg, P., 66
Goldstein, D. G., 22
Goldstein, I., 222
Goldstein, N. E., 94
Goldstein, S., 86, 126
Goldstone, R. L., 91, 100
Golla, H., 86
Gonsalkorale, K., 5
Gonzaga, G. C., 2, 5, 119, 124
Goodall, J., 164, 224

Goody, J. R., 352
Gordon, P., 356
Gore, M., 299
Goren-Inbar, N., 59
Gottlieb, G., 156
Gould, S. J., 87, 95, 124
Gouldner, A. W., 290
Govan, C. L., 16
Graham, S., 124
Grammer, K., 27
Gray, P. B., 94
Graziano, W. G., 302, 307
Green, J. D., 67
Greenberg, J., 70, 163, 353
Greenberg, R., 95
Greene, J. D., 124, 128
Greenspan, S. L., 231
Greenwald, A. G., 46, 47, 173
Gregg, A. P., 46, 48, 67
Grich, J., 220
Griffin, A. M., 90
Griffin, D. W., 17, 193, 248
Grillon, C., 174
Grim, T., 311
Griskevicius, V., 3
Gross, J. J., 117, 126, 127
Grossman, K. E., 217
Groth, G., 296
Gruenewald, T. L., 226
Gruenfeld, D. H., 116
Grun, R., 65
Guadagno, R. E., 307
Gulanski, B. I., 231
Gunnar, M. R., 217
Gunns, R. E., 88
Gur, R. C., 42, 45, 49
Gurung, R. A. R., 226
Guthertz, M., 126
Guthrie, D., 222
Guthrie, S. E., 347
Gutierres, S. E., 302
Guy, E. C., 71
Gyuris, P., 91

Hadden, S. B., 93
Haddock, G., 173
Hagel, R., 27
Haidt, J., 3, 7, 39, 48, 117, 121, 123, 124, 129, 130, 171, 249, 250, 349
Haile-Selassie, Y., 58
Halberstadt, J., 92
Hall, D. C., 95
Hall, J. A., 86
Hall, R. J., 321
Hallahan, M., 28, 86

Hallam, M., 87
Hamamura, T., 352, 359
Hamilton, D. L., 163, 165
Hamilton, W. D., 228, 243, 294
Hanna, C., 327
Hansen, I. G., 347
Harcourt, A. H., 63
Hardie, E. A., 152
Hardin, C. D., 152
Hardin, D. P., 72
Hardin, G., 239, 330
Harker, L. A., 126
Harkins, S., 319, 329
Harmon-Jones, C., 122
Harmon-Jones, E., 48, 122
Harris, A. R., 273
Hart, C. M., 246, 247, 248, 251, 252
Hart, C. W., 264
Hart, J., 217
Harton, H. C., 348
Harwood, K., 87
Haselton, M. G., 3, 4, 5, 18, 23, 24, 41, 85, 166, 198, 203, 204, 206, 247, 290, 296, 298
Haslam, N., 89
Hassan, F. A., 150, 155
Hastie, R., 318, 320, 324, 327, 328, 329, 330, 333, 334, 336, 344
Hastorf, A. H., 30
Hatfield, E., 87, 296
Hauser, M. D., 41, 125
Hawkes, K., 242
Hawkley, L. C., 211
Hays, C., 326
Hazen, C., 117, 119, 220, 232
Healy, B., 126
Heath, C., 129, 348, 349
Heatherton, T. F., 64
Heberlein, A. S., 29
Heerey, E. A., 124, 126, 127
Heerwagen, J. H., 346
Heider, F., 15, 305
Heider, K. G., 122, 132
Heine, S. J., 3, 7, 47, 170, 351, 352, 353, 354, 356, 359
Helfrich, H., 86
Helgeson, V. S., 227
Helmreich, R. L., 47, 321
Hemstrom, O., 221
Henrich, J., 129, 155, 301, 326, 328, 333, 335, 344
Henshilwood, C., 65
Herbst, K. C., 72
Hermer, L., 45
Hernandez, E., 44
Herrera, P., 94

Hertel, G., 329
Hertenstein, M. J., 120, 125
Hertwig, R., 18, 19
Hess, U., 94, 96
Hewstone, M., 165, 325
Heyes, C. M., 326, 344
Heyman, G. D., 29, 30
Higgins, E. T., 4, 152
Hightower, A., 175
Hill, G. W., 319
Hill, K., 156, 264, 267, 293, 299, 300, 319, 336
Hill, T., 92
Hinkle, S., 155
Hinsz, V. B., 321, 323
Hinton, M. R., 95
Hirsch, D. J., 273
Hirschfeld, L. A., 354
Hirshleifer, D., 325
Hixon, J. G., 72
Hoffrage, U., 19, 44
Hogan, J., 68
Hogan, R. T., 8, 68
Hogg, M. A., 301
Hoglund, J., 302
Hol, T., 224
Hollerman, J. R., 127
Hollingshead, A., 321
Holmes, J. G., 99, 193, 246, 248
Holt, C. A., 325, 326
Homans, G., 257
Honeycutt, H., 156
Hopkins, J., 60
Hoss, R. A., 90
House, J. S., 211
Houston, A. I., 331
Hoyt, C., 100
Hrdy, S., 15, 118, 215, 226, 227, 296
Hubbell, A. P., 327
Hudson, S. M., 88
Huesmann, L. R., 264
Humphreys, G. W., 95
Hunt, E., 132
Hunter, J. J., 230
Hurtado, A. M., 264, 267
Hutchins, E., 153
Hutchinson, J. M., 331
Hyman, L. M., 86

Ickes, W., 194, 195
Ilg, W., 86
Imada, S., 124, 171
Inati, S., 64
Insel, T. R., 197, 198
Insko, C. A., 166
Izard, C. E., 86, 90, 117, 170, 171

Jablonka, E., 145
Jackson, L., 87
Jaffe, R. H., 94
James, W., 16, 352
Janicki, D., 227
Janicki, M. G., 143, 250, 346, 360
Jarvenpa, R., 150, 322
Jeffery, L., 92
Jenkins, C., 97
Jenkins, J. M., 117
Jenkins, V. Y., 90
Jennings, L., 166
Jensen-Campbell, L. A., 302
Jerison, H. J., 59, 60
Jetten, J., 149
John, O. P., 118
Johnson, D. L., 248
Johnson, E. J., 321
Johnson, L., 86
Johnson, M. H., 90
Johnson, S. A., 154
Johnson-Laird, P. N., 20, 117
Johnston, L., 88
Johnston, V. S., 27
Johnstone, T., 122
Joireman, J. A., 253
Jones, B. C., 94, 201
Jones, E. E., 47, 48
Jones, L., 127
Jost, J. T., 163
Judd, C. M., 97
Juslin, P. N., 122, 125
Jussim, L., 166

Kaczor, L. M., 87
Kagen, J., 126
Kahlenber, S. M., 94
Kahneman, D., 17, 18, 19, 21, 289, 299, 325
Kalakanis, L., 87, 90
Kalick, S. M., 86, 175
Kalin, N. H., 122, 127
Kameda, T., 3, 6, 318, 320, 321, 322, 323, 324,
    325, 326, 327, 328, 329, 330, 331, 332, 333,
    334, 336, 344
Kan, I. P., 75
Kang, M., 241
Kanizawa, S., 27, 168
Kaping, D., 92
Kaplan, H., 293, 299, 300, 319, 336
Karau, S. J., 303, 329, 330, 333, 334
Karney, B. R., 192, 193, 205
Karremans, J. C., 248
Kashima, E., 152
Kashima, Y., 348
Kashy, D. A., 192

Katz, D., 166
Katzko, M. W., 49
Keane, J., 94
Keating, C. F., 87, 88, 100
Keefe, R. C., 202, 288, 359
Keeley, L. H., 264
Keil, F., 347
Kellerman, J., 94
Kelley, H. H., 94, 99, 254
Kelley, W. M., 64
Kelly, M. H., 347
Keltner, D., 3, 7, 39, 116, 117, 118, 119, 120,
    121, 122, 124, 125, 126, 127, 128, 130, 171,
    349
Kendell-Scott, L., 90
Kendler, K. S., 358
Kendrick, K. M., 95
Kennedy, C. B., 90
Kenny, D. A., 68, 89, 194
Kenrick, D. T., 2, 3, 5, 7, 9, 10, 22, 25, 99, 117,
    118, 173, 200, 202, 237, 242, 254, 265, 274,
    288, 289, 290, 295, 296, 298, 302, 303, 304,
    346, 350, 354, 358, 359
Kerr, N. L., 99, 319, 320, 325, 326, 328, 329
Ketelaar, T., 4, 6, 126
Keverne, E. B., 62, 227
Keys, C. B., 324
Kickuchi, M., 96
Kiecolt-Glaser, J. K., 221, 222, 223
Kilpatrick, S. D., 117
Kim, B., 359
Kim, Y., 93
Kinderman, P., 69
Kirkpatrick, L. A., 221, 268
Kitayama, S., 5, 47, 132, 243, 294, 344, 352,
    354, 358
Klasmeyer, G., 122
Kleck, R. E., 96
Klein, L. C., 226
Klein, R. E., 90
Klein, R. G., 57, 59, 66
Klein, S. B., 44
Klennert, M. D., 90
Kluckhohn, C., 353
Kluegel, J. R., 173
Kluwer, E. S., 248
Knetsch, J., 299
Knight, R. T., 29
Knight, R., 127
Knutson, B., 96
Kobayashi, C., 70, 352
Komorita, S. S., 239, 240, 246
Koolhaas, J. M., 224
Kosterman, R., 155
Kostopoulos, J., 348

Kozlowski, L. T., 86
Kramer, G. P., 124, 319
Kramer, R. M., 148, 246, 248, 251
Kramer, S., 90
Krebs, D. L., 22, 143, 250, 346, 360
Krebs, J. R., 117, 118, 331, 334
Kring, A. M., 122, 126
Krishnan, R., 321
Kroll, N., 29
Krueger, J. I., 16, 18, 20, 68, 189, 318, 325, 326, 334
Krueger, K., 217
Kruger, A. C., 344
Kruglanski, A. W., 4
Kudo, H., 63
Kuhlenbeck, H., 62
Kuhlman, D. M., 253
Kuipers, P., 122
Kurokawa, M., 132
Kurzban, R., 3, 5, 6, 9, 23, 24, 40, 43, 47, 49, 67, 74, 97, 154, 164, 165, 167, 168, 169, 175, 354
Kyl-Heku, L. M., 16

Laham, S., 5
Lahr, M. M., 57
Laird, J. D., 94
Lakatos, I., 3
Laland, K. N., 156
Landis, K. R., 211
Landsteiner, K., 358
Lang, F. R., 243
Langlois, J. H., 86, 87, 90
Lanting, F., 127
Lanzetta, J. T., 90
Larsen, C. L., 264
Larson, A., 87
Larson, D. B., 117
Larson, J. R., Jr., 324
Larson, R. J., 126, 296
Laskey, R. E., 90
Lasley, E. N., 230
Latane, B., 319, 325, 329, 348
Laughlin, P. R., 319, 324
Laukka, P., 122, 125
Lavoie, J., 164
Law, H., 88, 99
Lazarus, R. S., 117
Le Boeuf, B. J., 271
Leakey, R. E., 128, 164
Leary, M. R., 16, 24, 47, 49, 55, 57, 60, 61, 62, 65, 66, 71, 73, 74, 97, 121, 154, 164, 165, 167, 168, 175, 349, 353
Ledlow, S., 354
LeDoux, J. E., 43, 122, 127

Lee, H. K., 95, 97
Lee, P. C., 60
Lee, R. B., 150
Lee, S. Y., 96
Lee, Y. T., 166, 177
Legrenzi, M. S., 20
Legrenzi, P., 20
Lehman, B. J., 217
Lehman, D. R., 47, 344, 352, 359
Leigh, A. E., 95
Leimar, O., 255
Leonardelli, G., 149
Leonova, T., 89
Leopold, D. A., 92
Leppin, A., 228
Lerma, M., 246
Lerner, J. S., 68, 121, 122, 124, 125, 126, 217
Leung, K., 99
Levenson, R. W., 117, 122, 130
Levin, S., 304
Levine, J. M., 251, 252, 253, 329
LeVine, R. A., 171
Levine, S., 217
Levi-Strauss, C., 352
Levy, R. I., 129
Lewicki, P., 92, 97
Lewis, B. P., 226, 241
Lewis, J., 94
Lewis, M., 90
L'Herrou, T., 325
Li, N. P., 5, 9, 99, 173, 200, 237, 289, 305, 350
Li, S.-C., 43
Liang, D. W., 153
Lickliter, R., 156
Lieberman, D., 91, 345
Lieberman, M. D., 16
Liebler, A., 86
Liebrand, W. B. G., 252, 253
Light, K. C., 223
Lightdale, J., 153
Lima, S., 331
Lindsey, S., 19
Linsenmeier, J. A., 5, 200
Lipson, S. F., 94
Little, A. C., 94, 201
Littlepage, G. E., 322
Liu, D., 215
Liu, J., 304
Livingston, R. W., 97
Lloyd, E., 157
Londahl, E. A., 119
Longo, L. C., 87
Loomis, J., 100
Lopes, L. L., 17, 21

Lorenz, K. Z., 87, 91, 95, 223
Lorge, I., 319
Lorr, M., 99
Lotze, M., 94
Lowenstein, G., 122
Lowery, L., 124, 171
Luce, C., 241
Luhtanen, R., 149
Lui, L. L., 165
Lumsden, C. J., 299, 360
Lundberg, A., 302
Lundgren, S. R., 302
Lundqvist, D., 87
Lutz, C. A., 123
Lycett, J., 60, 241
Lydon, J. E., 191, 193, 196
Lynch, L., 166
Lynch, M., 48
Lyons, E., 193

MacCoun, R., 319, 325
MacDonald, T. K., 194
Mace, W., 81
Mackie, D. M., 173
Maclean, J., 90
Macphail, E., 62
Macrae, C. N., 64, 165, 166
Madon, S., 166
Mahapatra, M., 123, 354
Makhijani, M. G., 87, 303
Malamuth, N. M., 119, 268
Malatesta, C. Z., 126
Maner, J. K., 5, 7, 9, 22, 23, 24, 174, 290, 307
Mangelsdorf, S., 217
Mannison, M., 268
Manstead, A. S. R., 149
Manzi, J., 149
Mark, L. S., 87, 95
Marks, I. M., 178
Markus, H., 6, 39, 47, 132, 344, 352, 354, 358
Marmot, M., 212
Marr, D., 40
Marshack, A., 65
Martel, F. L., 227
Martignon, L., 18, 22
Martin, L. L., 94
Martin, R., 325
Martindale, C., 290
Martinez, I., 66
Martinez, S., 90
Mashima, R., 27
Mathewson, G. C., 306
Matsumoto, H., 358
Matsunaga, A., 29
Matsuzawa, T., 64, 75

Maunder, R. G., 230
Mauro, R., 130
Mauss, M., 292
Maynard Smith, J., 144, 145, 156, 257, 331, 332, 336
Mazur, A. C., 100
McAndrew, F. T., 244, 245
McArthur, L. Z., 81, 83, 94
McBrearty, S., 66
McCall, R. B., 90
McCauley, C. R., 123, 166, 171
McClintock, C., 253
McClintock, M., 226
McCollough, J. K., 91
McCrae, R. R., 30, 88, 99, 359
McCullough, M. C., 117, 124
McCullough, M. E., 248
McDowell, N. K., 68
McEwen, B. S., 212, 214, 230, 231
McGhee, D. E., 173
McGuffin, P., 358
McGuire, M. T., 225, 243
McHenry, H. M., 64
McKay, R., 175
McKenna, J. J., 227
McLean, I., 87
McNair, D., 99
McNally, J. J., 42
McNamera, J. M., 331
McTavish, J., 255
Mealey, L., 254
Meaney, M., 215
Medin, D. L., 351, 359
Meertens, R. M., 253
Mehrabian, A., 86
Meier, B. P., 94
Mellen, S. L. W., 198
Mellers, J., 19
Mendoza, I., 66
Menon, U., 131
Merikangas, K. R., 174
Mesquita, B., 121, 125, 131
Messe, L. A., 329
Mignault, A., 87, 96
Mignon, A., 89
Mikami, A., 64, 75
Milgram, S. 304
Miller, D. T., 153
Miller, G. F., 16, 300, 346
Miller, J. A., 309
Miller, J., 88, 123
Miller, N., 178, 179
Miller, R. S., 47, 121
Miller, R., 91
Mills, J., 48, 253, 290, 294, 295, 296, 306

Mineka, S., 3, 7, 125, 169, 177
Minsky, M., 48, 49
Mishima, R., 27, 168
Misovich, S. J., 100
Mitchell, R. W., 56
Mitchell, W. E., 227
Mithen, S., 60, 65
Miyake, K., 87
Moffitt, T., 127
Moghaddam, F. M., 254
Mollaret, P., 89
Monarch, N. D., 124
Monteith, M. J., 178
Montel, K. H., 193
Montepare, J., 3, 6, 7, 86, 88, 95, 96
Moore, B. R., 354
Moreland, R. L., 153, 251, 252, 253,
    321, 329
Morgan, H. J., 119
Moriarty, D., 175
Morton, J., 90
Moscovici, S., 325
Moulton, G. E., 317, 327
Much, N. C., 354
Mueller, A. L., 322
Mueller, A., 24, 173
Mueller, D. C., 327
Mullen, B., 166
Mullin, J. T., 95
Mummendey, A., 155
Munck, A., 213
Munn, P., 123
Muraven, M. B., 72
Murnighan, J. K., 252
Murphy, N. A., 86
Murphy, R., 227
Murphy, Y., 227
Murray, S. L., 191, 193, 194, 195, 248
Muthard, J. E., 87
Myers, D. G., 264, 265

Nachmias, M., 217
Nakanishi, D., 326, 328, 333, 334
Nakayama, K., 82, 92
Naray-Fejes-Toth, A., 213
Navarrete, C. D., 176
Neale, M. C., 358
Neff, L. A., 205
Nelligan, J. S., 220
Nelson, C. A., 92
Nelson, G., 153
Nesse, R. M., 5, 24, 119, 121, 166, 170, 174,
    229, 242, 247
Nestler, E. J., 127
Nettle, D., 18, 23, 24, 206

Neuberg, S. L., 3, 6, 7, 8, 97, 164, 165, 166, 167,
    168, 170, 171, 172, 173, 241, 265, 305, 346
Neuhoff, J. G., 18, 23
Nevison, C. M., 227
Newbern, D., 153
Newcombe, F., 95
Newman, K., 227
Newton, T. L., 221, 222, 223
Neyer, F. J., 243
Niemann, Y. F., 166
Nieves, J. M., 66
Nilssen, P., 65
Nisbett, R. E., 189, 269, 289, 344, 354, 356,
    358, 359
Nishimura, T., 64, 75
Nishitani, M., 87
Nitschke, J. B., 122
Noller, P., 88, 99
Norasakkunkit, V., 358
Norenzayan, A., 3, 7, 170, 344, 346, 347, 348,
    351, 354, 356, 357, 359
Norris, K. S., 145
Nyhoff, M. A., 347
Nystrom, L. E., 128

Oatley, K., 117, 118, 128, 132
Odling-Smee, J., 156
Oemig, C., 124
Öhman, A., 3, 7, 118, 121, 122, 125, 169, 171,
    177
Ohtsubo, Y., 322
O'Laughlin, C., 200
Olson, M., 320, 330
Olsson, A., 7
Oltmanns, T. F., 26
Olweus, D., 266, 269
Orbell, J. M., 145, 148, 240
Orians, G. H., 346
Orina, M. M., 194, 220, 311
Orr, S. P., 90
Ostrom, E., 240
O'Toole, A. J., 92
Otten, W., 253
Ouwerkerk, J., 248, 252
Overall, N., 200
Owen, M. J., 358

Palmer, C., 268
Park, J. H., 5, 7, 24, 97, 164, 168, 170, 173,
    175, 176, 244, 249, 297, 308, 346, 354
Park, L. E., 71, 353
Park, L., 354
Parker, S. T., 63
Parks, C. D., 239, 240, 246
Parquette, J., 322

Parritz, R. H., 217
Pascalis, O., 92
Paton, W., 268
Patricelli, G. L., 299
Paulhus, D. L., 359
Paulley, G. S., 216
Payne, J. W., 321
Pearson, A., 29
Pearson, J. L., 231
Pellis, S. M., 224
Pellis, V. C., 224
Pellowski, M., 174
Pendry, L. F., 166
Peng, K., 344
Penner, L. A., 249, 253, 256
Pennington, N., 320
Penrod, S. D., 92, 320
Penton-Voak, I. S., 27, 94, 201
Pereyra, L., 20
Perper, T., 151
Perrett, D. I., 27, 94, 201
Peterson, D., 263
Pettigrew, T. F., 178, 179
Pettijohn, T. F., 93
Phaf, R. H., 44
Phelps, E. A., 7
Phelps, J. L., 231
Piaget, J., 354
Pickett, C. L., 149
Pierce, J. W., 95
Pilcher, J. J., 3, 156, 238, 240, 351
Piliavin, J. A., 249
Pillhower, C., 87
Pilling, A. R., 264
Pinker, S., 15, 27, 28, 43, 46, 49, 132, 307, 357
Pitre, U., 153
Pittenger, J. B., 87, 95
Pittman, T. S., 47
Pizzagalli, D., 122
Plomin, R., 358
Plutchik, R., 117, 118, 170
Pollack, D. B., 225
Pollock, G. B., 144
Potts, R. B., 59, 318, 326, 333
Powell, R. A., 44
Pratto, F., 304
Prentice, D., 153
Preuschoft, S., 127
Price, G. R., 257, 336
Price, J., 55
Priester, J. R., 94
Pronin, E., 17
Proulx, T., 353
Pulliam, H. R., 145, 332
Pyke, G. H., 332
Pyszczynski, T., 70, 353

Quiatt, D., 56

Rachal, K. C., 248
Raleigh, M. J., 225
Ramachandran, V. S., 44, 45, 49
Ramble, C., 347
Ramsey, J. L., 90
Rasinski, K. A., 334
Ratner, H. H., 344
Raymond, P., 153, 321
Redican, W. K., 127
Reed, A., 300
Reeder, G., 247
Reeve, H. K., 157
Regan, P. C., 202, 296
Regan, R. T., 308
Reis, H. T., 99
Reiter, J., 271
Rempel, J. K., 246
Renfro, C. L., 171
Rentsch, J. R., 321
Repetti, R. L., 214, 217, 218, 222
Resnick, L. B., 354
Restak, R. M., 44, 49
Restle, F., 320
Reyna, C., 124
Reynolds, V., 56
Reznick, D., 157
Rhodes, G., 86, 87, 91, 92, 97, 98, 101, 175, 201
Rholes, W. S., 220
Richardson, M. J., 88
Richerson, P. J., 6, 129, 143, 164, 242, 243, 318, 323, 326, 333, 335, 344, 358, 360
Richeson, J. A., 26, 86
Riddock, M. J., 95
Ridgeway, C. L., 320, 322, 327
Ridgeway, D., 123
Rieser-Danner, L. A., 90
Rigatuso, J., 217
Ritter, J. M., 90
Robbins, M. A., 87
Robbins, R. J., 231
Robins, R. W., 121
Robinson, D. E., 326
Robinson, M. D., 94
Roccas, S., 148, 149
Rogers, P. L., 86
Roggman, L. A., 87, 90
Rolls, E. T., 128
Roney, C. J. R., 46
Roper, T. J., 327
Rorty, A. O., 39
Rosaldo, M., 131
Rose, M. R., 118
Roseman, I. J., 170

Rosenberg, S., 39
Rosenblum, L. A., 216
Rosenthal, R., 28, 86, 87, 94
Ross, L., 17, 189, 289
Ross, M., 194
Roth, A. E., 252
Rothbaum, F., 72
Rowe, J. W., 231
Roy, M., 358
Rozelle, R. M., 166
Rozin, P., 39, 122, 123, 124, 171, 351, 354
Rubchinsky, K., 241
Rubenstein, A. J., 87, 90, 92, 101
Ruble, D. N., 30, 155
Ruderman, A. J., 166
Ruff, J. R., 273
Rusbult, C. E., 99, 193, 246, 247, 248, 252
Russell, J. A., 122, 129, 130, 131, 132
Rutherford, M. D., 29
Ryckman, R. M., 87

Sabini, J., 264
Sackeim, H. A., 42, 45, 49
Sadalla, E. K., 2, 288, 296
Sadler, M. S., 97
Sagarin, B. S., 307
Sage, R. M., 68, 217
Sager, K., 241
Sai, F., 95
Salas, E., 321
Salmon, C., 5
Samuelson, C. D., 237
San Giovanni, J. P., 90
Sangrigoli, S., 92
Sapir, E., 132
Sapolsky, R. M., 224, 225
Sato, K., 130
Saxby, R. R., 29
Scabini, D., 127
Schacter, D. L., 288
Schaefer, H. G., 321
Schaller, M., 3, 4, 5, 7, 24, 97, 164, 167, 168,
    169, 170, 173, 174, 175, 176, 244, 249, 297,
    308, 344, 346, 348, 349, 354
Scheib, J. E., 200
Scheier, C., 101
Scheier, M. F., 170
Scherer, K. R., 122, 125, 130, 131
Scherer, R., 86
Scheyd, G., 91
Schilt, C. R., 145
Schimel, J., 70
Schippers, M., 237
Schleicher, A., 128
Schlenker, B. R., 47
Schmidt, G. W., 322

Schmitt, D. P., 3, 5, 23, 119, 120, 156, 200, 202,
    238, 240, 296, 351, 359
Schneider, D. J., 30
Schoeneman, T. J., 47
Schopler, J., 166
Schroeder, D. A., 249
Schuller, G., 92
Schultz, P. W., 301
Schultz, W., 127
Schuyt, T., 237
Schwarcz, H. P., 66
Schwartz, G. M., 90
Schwartz, J. K. L., 173
Schwartz, S. H., 155
Schwartz, S., 149
Schwarz, N., 122, 124
Schwarzer, R., 228
Scovel, T., 64
Sealy, S. G., 310
Sears, D. O., 351
Secord, P. F., 87
Sedikides, C., 3, 7, 8, 9, 46, 48, 55, 56, 57, 61,
    62, 67, 70, 72, 152
Seeley, T. D., 327
Seeman, T. E., 214, 217, 231
Segal, M. H., 100
Selten, R., 289, 320
Semendeferi, K., 128
Semin, G. R., 102
Semmelroth, J., 296
Shackelford, T. K., 4, 85, 265
Shaked, N., 193
Shaklee, H., 255
Shapiro, D., 20, 222
Shapiro, J. R., 172
Shapiro, P. N., 92
Shaver, P. R., 117, 119, 220, 232
Shaw, J., 149
Shaw, R. E., 87, 95
Shaw, R., 81
Shebilske, L. J., 302
Sheets, V., 274
Sheffey, S., 324
Sheldon, K. M., 70
Shelton, S. E., 127
Shepher, J., 91
Sheppard, J. A., 329, 330
Sherak, B., 90
Sherif, C. W., 251
Sherif, M., 171, 251, 300
Sherman, D. K., 68, 72
Sherman, J. W., 165
Sherman, P. W., 157, 190
Sherman, S. J., 297
Sherry, D. F., 288
Shimojo, E., 101

Shimojo, S., 101
Shimoma, E., 27, 168
Shiota, M. N., 3, 7, 39, 118, 119, 120, 171, 349
Shrauger, J. S., 47
Shweder, R. A., 88, 123, 129, 131, 354
Sidanius, J., 6, 304
Siers, B., 304
Sigelman, J. D., 122
Silver, M. D., 149
Simion, C., 101
Simmel, M., 16
Simmons, L. W., 91
Simmons, R. T., 148
Simon, B., 149
Simon, H. A., 20, 21, 170, 335
Simonton, D. K., 303
Simpson, J. A., 2, 3, 5, 10, 27, 30, 39, 67, 86,
   94, 117, 173, 189, 191, 192, 194, 195, 198,
   199, 200, 201, 202, 203, 220, 246, 311
Singer, B. H., 231
Singh, D., 87
Skinner, B. F., 1
Skowronski, J. J., 3, 55, 56, 57, 61, 62, 67, 70
Slovic, P., 289, 325
Small, M., 95
Smith, C. M., 324, 336
Smith, C., 166
Smith, D. M., 97, 164, 229
Smith, E. A., 156
Smith, E. E., 359
Smith, E. R., 102, 166, 173
Smith, H., 246, 250, 251
Smith, J., 90
Smith, M. D., 119
Smith, M., 127
Smith, P., 86
Smoot, M., 87
Snidman, N., 126
Snodgrass, S., 94
Snyder, M., 237
Snyder, S. S., 72
Sober, E., 118, 318, 335
Solomon, H., 319
Solomon, M. R., 94
Solomon, R., 117
Solomon, S., 70, 353
Sommer, K. L., 16, 301
Sommerville, R. B., 128
Sorce, J. F., 90
Sorenson, E. R., 359
Sorkin, R. D., 326
Sorrentino, R. M., 46
Spangler, G., 217
Spanos, N. P., 44
Spears, R., 149
Speicher, H., 294

Spelke, E. S., 45
Spencer, S. J., 48, 163, 180
Sperber, D., 40, 42, 45, 47, 49, 344, 348, 360
Sprecher, S., 87, 194, 195, 202
Spruijt, B. M., 224
Stahelski, A. J., 94, 254
Stallworth, L. M., 304
Stanfel, J. A., 320
Stangor, C., 165, 166
Stark, N., 90
Stasser, G., 321, 324, 325, 326, 327
Staub, E., 263
Steele, C. M., 48
Steinberg, L., 219
Steiner, I. D., 318, 319, 320, 329, 330, 334
Stein-Seroussi, A., 72
Stellar, E., 231
Ste-Marie, D., 94
Stephan, C. W., 178, 179
Stephan, W. G., 171, 178, 179
Stepper, S., 94
Stern, P. C., 237, 240
Sternberg, E., 129, 349
Stevenson, L. A., 86
Stewart, D. D., 321, 327
Stewart, M. A., 218
Stich, S., 354
Stillwell, A. M., 72
Stiner, M. C., 155
Stolinsky, D. C., 271
Stolinsky, S. A., 271
Stone, V. E., 29
Stout, S., 248
Stouthamer-Loeber, M., 127
Strack, F., 94
Stratenwerth, I., 149
Striano, T., 90
Strickland, L. H., 94
Stringer, C. B., 65
Stroebe, W., 329
Strube, M. J., 67, 70
Struch, N., 155
Sugiyama, L. S., 310, 345, 359
Suh, E. M., 30
Sullivan, E., 166
Sulloway, F., 253
Sundie, J. M., 3, 5, 304
Suomi, S. J., 216, 217, 219
Surbey, M. K., 42
Susser, K., 124
Sutton, S. K., 126
Suzuki, J., 64, 75
Swann, W. B., Jr., 47, 48, 72, 205
Swartz, T. S., 170
Swim, J. K., 166
Swinth, K., 100

Syme, L., 212
Symons, D., 16, 39, 268, 278
Szathmary, E., 145

Tajfel, H., 155, 163, 166, 251
Takezawa, M., 320, 322, 336, 344
Tambor, E. S., 353
Tamres, L., 227
Tamura, R., 332, 333
Tan, H. H., 89
Tan, S., 92
Tanaka, J., 92
Tanchuk, T. L., 349
Tangney, J. P., 121
Tanida, S., 27, 168
Tarr, M. J., 92
Tattersall, I., 57, 66
Taylor, K., 92
Taylor, L. A., 327
Taylor, S. E., 2, 5, 17, 24, 49, 68, 73, 166, 189,
     212, 214, 217, 222, 224, 226, 227, 228, 229,
     247, 352
Tazelaar, M., 248
Temblay, L., 127
ter Schure, E., 122
Terdal, S. K., 353
Tesser, A., 47, 93
Tetlock, P. E., 121
Thagard, P., 3
Thaler, R., 299
Thier, H. P., 86
Thomas, G., 192, 194, 200
Thomas, L. S., 324
Thomas, S. H., 273
Thompson-Schill, S. L., 75
Thornhill, R., 91, 97, 268
Tice, D. M., 47, 48, 72
Tiddeman, B. P., 94, 201
Tiedens, L. Z., 121, 125
Tiger, L., 223
Tindale, R. S., 3, 6, 319, 321, 323, 324, 325,
     328, 336
Tipper, S. P., 290
Tither, J. M., 200
Titus, W., 324, 325, 327
Tobena, A., 178
Tobias, P. V., 59
Todd, J. T., 95
Todd, P. M., 16, 18, 289, 321
Toguchi, Y., 70
Tomasello, M., 90, 344, 354, 360
Tomkins, S. S., 117, 118, 170
Tooby, J., 5, 15, 16, 18, 19, 20, 28, 29, 39, 40,
     41, 42, 43, 46, 47, 63, 82, 83, 91, 117, 118,
     165, 168, 169, 170, 238, 241, 244, 245, 246,
     265, 281, 288, 310, 345, 346, 354, 358

Tracy, J. L., 121
Tranel, D., 29, 95
Trapnell, P. D., 359
Travis, J., 157
Tremblay, F., 94
Triandis, H. C., 30, 253, 254
Trivers, R. L., 4, 23, 63, 115, 121, 197, 201,
     228, 244, 245, 246, 271, 272, 295
Tronick, E. Z., 122
Trope, Y., 46, 68
Tropp, L. R., 178, 179
Trost, M. R., 5, 290, 295, 296, 304
Troughton, E., 218
Tsukasaki, T., 334
Tucker, J., 130
Tudor, M., 153
Turati, C., 90
Turk, D. J., 64
Turke, P. W., 294, 299
Turkheimer, E., 27, 358
Turner, J. C., 163, 251, 301
Turner, R. H., 48
Turvey, M., 81
Tversky, A., 18, 19, 21, 289, 325
Tyler, T., 237, 246, 250, 251

Uleman, J. S., 28
Umberson, D., 211, 222
Underwood, M., 322
Underwood, T. J., 310
Updegraff, J. A., 226

Valone, T. J., 331
van de Kragt, A. J. C., 145, 148, 240
Van den Berg, C. L., 224
Van Duuren, M., 90
Van Hoesen, G. W., 128
Van Hooff, J. A. R. A. M., 127
van Ijzendoorn, M., 219
van Knippenberg, D., 154
Van Lange, P. A. M., 2, 6, 39, 67, 99, 148, 193,
     237, 240, 247, 248, 252, 253, 330, 332, 344,
     345
Van Ree, J. M., 224
van Schie, E., 154
Van Vugt, M., 2, 6, 39, 67, 148, 237, 238, 240,
     246, 247, 248, 250, 251, 252, 253, 254, 255,
     330, 332, 344, 345
vanden Heuvel, H., 154
Vanrie, J., 100
Vanzetto, K., 297
Vasquez, K., 124
Vaughn, L. S., 90
Verette, J., 248
Verfaillie, K., 100
Vershure, B., 2

Vetter, T., 92
Vevea, J., 70
Vinokur, A. D., 229
Vohs, K. D., 68, 247, 263, 353
Voils, C. I., 178
Voinescu, L., 168
Vollrath, D. A., 323
Von Hippel, W., 5
Vygotsky, L. S., 354

Wachtmeister, C. A., 87
Wagner, G. P., 100
Wagner, W., 100
Wakefield, J. C., 4, 85
Walker, H. A., 320, 322, 327
Wall, S., 217
Wallbott, H. G., 86, 130
Waller, A. L., 269
Walster, E., 87
Walton, G. E., 95
Warner, M. S., 44
Wason, P. C., 20
Waters, E., 217
Watson, D., 126
Watson, T. L., 92
Weber, J. G., 149
Weber, M., 121
Webster, M. A., 92
Weghorst, S. J., 267
Wegner, D. M., 153, 321, 323, 327
Weiner, B., 124
Weiner, D., 194
Weiner, S. G., 217
Weisfeld, G. E., 91
Weisz, J. R., 72
Welch, I., 325
Wells, P. S., 151
West, R., 326
Westen, D., 296
Westermarck, E. A., 91
Wetherell, M., 301
Wheeler, L., 93
Wheelwright, S., 29
Whisler, E. W., 322
White, G. M., 123
Whitten, A., 60, 63
Whooten, D. B., 300
Whorf, B. L., 132
Wieselquist, J., 246
Wiest, C., 170
Wiggins, J. S., 99
Wilbur, C. J., 172
Wildschut, T., 248
Wilkinson, G. S., 244
Williams, G. C., 144, 145, 157

Williams, K. D., 16, 319, 329, 330, 333, 334
Wills, T. A., 211
Wilson, D. S., 118, 237, 245, 248, 250, 253, 256, 318, 335
Wilson, E. O., 143, 147, 237, 299, 360
Wilson, M., 2, 5, 264, 267, 269, 270, 271, 273, 274, 275, 304, 354, 359
Windschitl, P. D., 17
Winter, L., 28
Witte, E. H., 329
Wittenbaum, G. M., 324, 327
Woike, B. A., 86
Wolf, A. P., 91
Wolf, M., 227
Wolf, S., 325
Wood, C., 90
Wood, W., 200, 301, 311, 323, 357
Woodworth, G., 218
Worthington, E. L., Jr., 248
Wrangham, R. W., 226, 263
Wright, L., 117
Wu, S., 119
Wurf, E., 39
Wyland, C. L., 64
Wynne-Edwards, V. C., 144

Xu, J., 173

Yamagishi, T., 27, 168, 246, 253
Yates, W. R., 218
Yik, M. S. M., 359
Yoshikawa, S., 87
Young, A. W., 95
Young, A., 94
Young, R. C., 124
Yovetich, N. A., 248
Yuill, N., 29
Yuwiler, A., 225

Zaccaro, S. J., 68
Zahavi, Am., 299
Zahavi, Av., 299
Zahn-Waxler, C., 123
Zajonc, R. B., 6
Zanna, M. P., 173
Zarate, M. A., 166
Zebrowitz, L. A., 3, 6, 7, 85, 86, 87, 88, 90, 91, 95, 96, 97, 98, 100, 102, 168, 170, 175, 201
Zebrowitz-McArthur, L., 86, 88
Zeller, A., 64
Zilles, K., 128
Zimbardo, P. G., 263
Zimmerman, M. G., 325
Zuckerman, C., 327
Zuckerman, M., 87

Subject Index

Accuracy in social judgment, 15–32, 46, 49, 85–86, 89, 91, 95, 97, 98, 166–167, 189–206
  Accuracy model of romantic relationships, 191–192, 195
  Accuracy-satisfaction link, 194
  Empathic accuracy, 195
  see also Person perception; Personality judgment; Stereotypes
Aché society, 264, 267, 293, 299, 300
Adaptations,
  By-products and, 85
  Perceptual, 91, 92
  Social, 15–16
Adrenocorticotropic hormone (ACTH), 213
Affordances *see* Social affordances
Afrocentric facial features, 97
Aggregation Economies, 335
Aggression, 223–225, 263–283
  Among women, 272
  Costs and benefits of, 269
  Dominance and, 223–225
  Instinct theory of, 264
  In intimate relationships, 267–269
  Sex differences in, 270
  Verbal, 267, 272
  Victims of, 266, 270–272
Altruism, 237–256
Ambivalent sociality, 147–148, 156
Ambulance homicide theory, 273
American Sign Language, 94
Amygdala, 213
Anger, 121, 169–171, 175, 180
Anomalous face overgeneralization hypothesis, 98
Anosognosia, 44
Anterior cingulate cortex, 213
Anti-social behavior, 127
Art, 65, 346
Asperger's syndrome, 29
Assortative mating, 201
Attachment, 216, 219–223
  Adult, 219–223
  Styles, 216, 220–221
Attention,
  Education of, 91
Attentional weighting, 91, 92
Attraction, interpersonal, 9

Attractiveness *see* Physical attractiveness
Attunements, 82, 84–85, 88, 90–98, 100, 101
  Innate, 90–91
  Overgeneralization of, 95–98
  Varying with behavioral activities, 94–95
  Varying with experience, 91–93
  Varying with social goals, 93–94
Auditory looming, 23
Australopithecines, 58
Authority,
  Authority heuristic, 288, 293, 303–305, 309
  Authority ranking, 132
  Authority structures, 168
  see also Obedience to authority
Awe, 121

Baby faces, 87–88, 90, 93, 95–96, 100
  Babyface overgeneralization hypothesis, 95–96
Bayesian inference, 44–45, 193
Behavioral ecology, 10, 41
Behaviorism, 1
Belief in a dangerous world, 164, 169, 174
Berekhat Ram figurine, 65
Bias blind spot, 17
Biases and errors, 16–25, 42–47, 85
  Artifacts, 18–20
  Error management, 22–25
  Heuristics 20–22
  Sources of, 18–25
  see also Person perception; Personality judgment; Prejudice
Bioarchaeological record, 57–66, 264
Bipedalism, 123
Blindsight, 44
Brain size, 62–64
Brinksmanship, 275
Broca's area, 60, 64, 65
Bowerbirds, 299
Bullies, 266, 269
Burial practices, 65–66
By-products, 85

Causal attribution, 356
Chance, misconceptions of, 21
Cheater detection, 20, 29, 31, 40, 63, 241, 242, 246, 310

Cheater punishment, 250, 251
Cheating and social influence, 307–311
Chicken Little, 42
Chimpanzees, 164, 224, 263
Choking, risk of, 64
Climatic instability, 58
Club fights, 267
Coalition formation goal, 291, 292, 300, 307
Coalitional psychology, 164–166, 168–171,
    175–176
Coevolution,
    Gene culture, 354, 359–360
Cognition, 39–43, 48–49; see also Social
    cognition
Cognitive dissonance, 42, 47–48, 305–306
Cognitive neuroscience, 10, 11
Cognitive revolution 1–2, 6, 8–9, 10
    Behaviorist critiques of, 1–2, 3
Collective goal-directed behavior, 123
Collective self, 149, 152
Combinatorial explosion, 281
Commitment, 115, 119, 247, 248, 288, 293,
    305–307
    Commitment and consistency heuristic, 288,
        293, 305–307, 309
    Commitment model of emotions, 115, 119
Communal relationships see Relationships
Communication,
    Influence on culture, 348–350
Compassion, 120
Conditional strategies, 198–201
Confirmation bias, 17, 189
Conformity, 300–303, 325–326, 328
    Sex differences in, 301, 302
Conjunction fallacy, 19, 21
Contact hypothesis, 178
Contempt, 121
Conversational norms, 19; see also
    Communication
Cooperation, 237–256
Coordination problems, 319–329
Core configuration model, 150–154
Corpus collosum, 43
Corticotropin-releasing hormone (CRH), 213
Cost-benefit model, 331
Costly signalling theory, 244
Counterfactual thinking, 43
Cross-situational variability, 7–8
Cultural psychology, 11; see also Culture
Culture,
    Communication and, 348–350
    Constraints on, 345–350
    Cross-cultural differences, 47, 84, 93, 344,
        345, 351, 352–353, 356–360
    Cross-cultural similarities, 30–31, 345

Cultural "big bang," 65–66
Cultural learning, 333
Cultural transmission, 347–350
    Egalitarian, 133
    Evolution and, 30–31, 170, 177, 179,
        343–360
    Evolutionary foundations of, 255, 344–350
    Hierarchical organization, 132
    Social construction of, 348–350
    see also Universals and universality
Culture of honor, 269

Darkness, 24, 169, 173–174, 176
Defectors, 246, 252, 253
Defensive biases, 24
Deliberative mind set, 196
Deme, 150–151, 153
Depersonalized relationships, 152
Depression, 71; see also Emotions
Developmental biology, 10, 11
Differential parental investment, 4–5, 9, 190,
    197–199, 201, 270, 272, 295, 296, 301,
    304
Disease, 24, 163–164, 168–170, 172, 175–177,
    360
    Personal vulnerability to, 175–176
Discriminate sociality, 165
Disgust, moral, 163, 170–171, 178
Disgust, physical, 163, 169–172, 175–176,
    178–179
Disneyland, 42–43
Dissociative identity disorder, 44
Dissonance see Cognitive dissonance
Domain-general principles, 288
Domain-specific mechanisms, 287–292; see
    also Functional specificity
Dominance, 87–88, 93–94, 128–129, 223–225,
    304
    Competitions, 304
    Hierarchies, 128–129, 224, 267
Downward causation, 146, 149
Dryads, 1
Dud-alternative effect, 17
Dyadic selves, 153
Dynamic social impact theory, 348

Ecological theory, 81–102
    Basic tenets of, 82–85
Embarrassment, 121
Emotions, 68, 69, 86–87, 90, 96, 100, 115–134,
    163, 167, 170–175, 178, 250
    Altruism and, 123
    Appeasement and, 126
    Communication and, 125
    Coordinated interaction and, 125–126

Deficits in expression of, 126
Deficits in perception of, 126
Emotion cues, 86–87
Emotion overgeneralization hypothesis, 96
Facial expressions of, 90, 100, 130–131
Flexible extensivity, 129
Forgiveness and, 126
Frontal activation asymmetry, 122
Functions of, 117–118, 126–127
Levels of analysis and, 121–124
Moral intuition and, 124–125
Positive affect, 127
Potential vs. practice of experience, 131–132
Prejudice and, 163, 167, 170–175, 178
Problems of cooperation and, 120–121
Problems of reproduction and, 119
Relations with fitness, 68, 118–119
Self-conscious emotions, 126
Sexual desire and, 119
Social commitments and, 119–121
Social emotions, 117, 249, 250
Social functionalist framework of, 115–118,
    121, 126, 130
Status and, 124
see also entries for specific emotions
Empathic accuracy, 195
Empathy, 249
Encapsulation, 40–45, 48
Entitativity, 151
Environment of evolutionary adaptiveness
    (EEA), 318, 326
Envy, 121
Equality matching, 132
Equilibrium, 330–333
    Evolutionarily Stable, 331
    Mixed, 331–333
Error management theory, 22–25, 166, 298;
    see also Signal detection theory
Error paradigm, 20
Eureka task, 319
Evolutionary arms race, 31
Evolutionary cost-benefit analysis, 5–6, 8, 21,
    22, 23, 41, 64, 71, 199, 269–270; *see also*
    Error management theory
Evolutionary game theory, 6, 330–331, 336; *see
    also* Game theory
Evolutionary psychology, 1–11, 56, 74, 265, 270
    Critiques of, 3, 270
    Logic of, 2, 4–8, 265, 270
    Tools for theory-building, 4–6, 56, 74
Exaptation, 124
Exchange relationships *see* Relationships
Expectancy-value theory, 330
Expertise cues, 322
External agency illusion, 17

Facial action program, 131
Facial dominance, 87–88; *see also* Dominance
Fairness, 250
False consensus bias, 17, 189
Falsification, 3
Fantasized future environment, 279
Fantasized future killer, 279
Fear, 163, 167, 169–174, 178–179
Female social networks, 226
Fight-or-flight response, 218–219, 230
Fitness,
    Fitness overgeneralization hypothesis, 97–98
    Inclusive fitness, 5, 7, 274, 294, 295, 297
    Problems bearing on, 8, 15–16, 19, 116–119,
        167–170, 265–268, 289–290, 291
    Reproductive fitness, 7, 8, 68, 69
Folktales, 347–348
Food preferences, 84
    Cultural variation in, 84
Foot-in-the-door influence tactic, 305
Forgiveness, 248
Free-riding, 330–331, 333
Frequency dependent selection, 254
Freud, Sigmund, 10, 39, 48, 264
Functional flexibility, 8, 173–176, 269–270, 288
Functional specificity, 39, 40, 43, 45–46, 48,
    198–202; *see also* Domain-specific
    mechanisms
Functional magnetic resonance imaging
    (fMRI), 3, 29
Fundamental attribution error, 16–17, 22, 25,
    189

Gait, 88
Galvanic skin response, 45
Game theory, 6, 238–240, 330–333
Gebusi, 264
Gender differences *see* Sex differences
Gene's eye view, 143–144, 154, 156
Generalized exchange, 244, 250
Genetic relatedness *see* Kin and kinship
Genomics, 11
Gibsonian models of perception, 81–85
Glucocorticoids, 213–214
Goals, 16, 39, 42, 46–49, 66–73, 84, 88, 90,
    93–94, 101, 150, 289–291, 292, 295, 296,
    300–301, 304–305, 307, 349
Gossip, 322–323
Gratitude, 120
Grimm Brothers, 348
Group decision making, 323, 326–328
Group identification, 251, 255; *see also* Social
    identity
Group living, 62, 63, 143, 145, 155, 164, 168–170
    Survival problems of, 62–63, 164, 168–169

Group performance, 318–319, 334–335
Group selection, 143–146, 244, 245, 250, 335
Groups, 123, 143–157, 317–336
    Boundaries of, 154–156
    Core configurations of, 150–154
    Group roles and status, 123
    Identification with, 149, 152–155, 251, 255
    Size of, 251, 252, 255
    Stability of, 252, 253, 254
Guilt, 121, 249

Haystack model, 144
Hazard detection, 20
Health,
    Mental health, 222
    Physical health, 213–214, 217–218, 228
    see also Fitness
Height, 303
Helping behavior *see* Altruism
Heuristics, 20–22, 288, 289–307, 308, 321
    Authority, 288, 293, 303–305, 309
    Commitment and consistency, 288, 293,
        305–307, 309
    Fast and frugal, 22, 321, 325–328
    Liking heuristic, 288, 293, 296–298, 308
    Reciprocity, 288, 290, 292–296, 308
    Recognition, 22
    Representativeness, 21
    Scarcity, 288, 293, 298–300
    Social proof, 288, 293, 300–303, 308–309
Hidden profile, 324, 327–328
Hierarchical models, 145–147
Hindsight bias, 17
Homeostatic motives, 57, 67, 69, 70, 73
    Relation with reproductive fitness, 69
Homicide, 272–281
    Adaptations for, 272–281
    Byproduct hypothesis, 274, 281
    Fantasies about, 273–275, 278
    Rates of, 273
Homicide adaptation theory, 275–281
Homo erectus, 59, 60, 61, 62, 63, 64, 66, 67,
    73
Homo ergaster, 59, 60, 61, 62, 63, 64, 66, 67,
    73
Homo habilis, 59, 62, 64
Homo heidelbergensis, 60
Hunting and gathering, 61
Hypercognition and hypocognition, 129
Hypothalamic pituitary adrenal axis (HPA),
    213–216, 222–223, 230
Hypothalamus, 213

Ideal standards model, 200–202
Identity overgeneralization hypothesis, 96–97

Illusions,
    External agency illusion, 17
    Müller-Lyer illusion, 22, 45, 49
    Ponzo illusion, 22
    Positive illusions, 24, 49
    Transparency illusion, 17
Implemental mind set, 196
Implicit personality theories, 88
Incest, 91, 345
    Taboo against, 345
Inclusive fitness *see* Fitness
Infanticide, 278
Infidelity, 267, 269
Informational constraints, 22
In-group/out-group distinction, 149, 154–156,
    307–309
Innateness, 84, 85, 89, 90–91, 95, 357–359
Instrumentality, 330, 332–333
Inter-group bias, 244, 249, 251; *see also* Inter-
    group conflict; Prejudice
Inter-group conflict, 155, 263, 273
Inter-group differentiation, 155
Inter-group threats, 63
Intra-group cooperation, 63, 154–156
Intra-group processes, 317–336
Intrasexual competition, 266, 267, 270

Jealousy, 120, 267
Juvenile dependency, 15

Kin and kinship, 5, 294–295
    Cues indicating, 243–244, 251
Kin selection theory, 5, 243, 244, 249
Köhler Effect, 329
!Kung San, 264

Language, 27, 60, 64–65, 66, 128–129, 255
    Benefits of, 64
    Instinct, 27
    Origins of, 60
    Production of, 64–65
Larynx, 64–65
Leadership, 303–304, 320
    Height and, 303
    Sex differences in, 303–304
Learning processes, 57, 67, 68–69, 70, 73, 94,
    169, 177, 264, 265, 270, 310, 333, 344,
    354
    Learning motives, 57, 67, 68, 70, 73
    Observational learning, 94, 310, 264, 265
    Relation with reproductive fitness, 69
    Social learning, 265, 270, 344
Less-is-more effect, 22
Levels of organization, 146
Lewis and Clark Expedition, 317–318

Liking heuristic, 288, 293, 296–298, 308
Linda problem, 19, 21
Lorenz, Konrad, 264
Loss aversion, 299
Love, 119, 190–191, 197, 198
    Love-is-blind vs. love-is-wise paradox, 206
Low-ball influence tactic, 309
Loyalty, 247, 248, 252
Lucy (Australopithecus afarensis), 58

Macrodemes, 150–154
Majoritian group decision-making, 325–328
Male-male bonds, 225
Marriage, 352
Mass media, 264
Mate value, 268
Mating, 189–206, 289–291, 295, 296, 300–301,
    352, 350, 356–357
    Mate retention goal, 291, 296, 300–301
    Mate selection goal, 289–291, 295,
        300–301
    Mating trade-offs, 199
    see also Relationships
Mental health, 222
Meta knowledge, 321–323, 325
Meta-representations, 42
Mimesis, 60
Mimicry, 94, 310
Mind reading, 194–195
Minimal group studies, 155, 166
Modern living, 264
Modules and modularity, 27, 39–49, 100,
    167–168, 288
    Encapsulation as defining property, 40
    Enzymatic computation model, 40–41
    Massive modularity hypothesis, 40
Momentary affect, 124
Moral reasoning, 47–48
Morality, 47–48, 250, 345–346
Mother–child bond, 215, 217
Motivation,
    Gains, 329–330
    Losses, 329–330
    Problems, 319–320, 329–334
    see also Emotions; Goals
Müller-Lyer illusion, 22, 45, 49
Multilevel selection, 6, 154, 244, 245
Multiple selves, 48–49

Need for positivity, 190, 195–196, 202–205
Negative reinforcement, 268
Negativity bias, 246, 247
Neocortex, 62, 63, 64
Net-benefit criterion, 326, 334
Neuro-cultural theory, 131

Norms, 250, 251, 255, 256, 273, 345–346
    Gender norms, 273
    Moral norms, 345–346
    Sexual norms, 345, 350
    Stereotypes as, 349
Numerical thinking, 356

Obedience to authority, 304
Obligatory interdependence, 143, 147
Observational learning, 264, 265
Olfactory cues,
    Of fertility, 90
    Of symmetry, 91
Ontogeny, 190
Optimal distinctiveness theory, 148–150
Other mind problem, 122
Out-groups, 154–156
Overconfidence bias, 17
Overgeneralization hypothesis, 85, 95–98
    Babyface overgeneralization, 95–96
    Emotion overgeneralization, 96
    Fitness overgeneralization, 97–98
    Identity overgeneralization, 96–97
Oxytocin, 197–198

Pair-bonding, 219–223; *see also* Mating
Paranoid optimist, 24
Parasites and parasitism, 8, 310–311
Parasympathetic nervous system (PNS), 214
Para-ventricular nuclei (PVN), 213
Parent–child bond, 214–219
Parental care goal, 291
Parental investment *see* Differential parental
    investment
Perceptual experience, 91–93
Person–environment fit, 68, 71
Person perception, 81–102; *see also* Social
    cognition; Personality judgment
Personality disorders, 26, 44
Personality judgment,
    Accuracy of, 15–32
    Automaticity of, 28
    Biases in, 15–32
    Development of, 29
    Implicit personality theories, 88
    Influence of physical attractiveness, 87
    Personality judgment instinct, 15, 27–31
    Realistic accuracy model of, 26
    Universality of, 29–31
Personality traits,
    Big five, 30
    see also Personality judgment
Pessimistic bias, 17
Phantom limbs, 43
Phylogeny, 190

Physical attractiveness, 8, 87, 88, 90, 96, 96, 98, 360
    Impact on personality judgments, 87, 93
    Impact on social influence, 297
Physical health, 213–214, 217–218, 228
Planning fallacy, 17
Polygyny, 271
Ponzo illusion, 22
Positive illusions, 24, 49
Positivity,
    Need for, 190, 195–196, 202–205
    Seeking, 196, 202
Prefrontal cortex, 128
Prejudice, 155, 163–181, 244, 249, 251, 353–354
    Against African Americans, 163, 171, 174–175, 178–179
    Against feminist activists, 171–172
    Against foreigners, 175–177, 179
    Against fundamentalist Christians, 171–172
    Against gay men, 163, 172, 178
    Against immigrants, 172, 176–177, 179–180
    Against obese people, 24, 170, 175, 177
    Racial, 169–171, 174–175, 178–179
    Reducing, 172, 176–179
    Syndromes, 167, 169, 170–176
    Traditional view of, 173
Pride, 121
Prisoner's dilemma game, 238–239; see also Game theory
Process losses, 319–320
Producer–scrounger game, 331–334
Prosocial behaviour, 237–256
Prototype extraction, 91–92
Proximate causation, 190

Rape, 268
Realistic accuracy model, 26
Reciprocity, 115, 164, 166, 168–169, 288, 290, 292–296, 308, 309–310
    Reciprocal altruism, 115, 242, 244, 247
    Reciprocity heuristic, 288, 290, 292–296, 308
    Strong reciprocity principle, 309–310
Regulation, 212
Rejection see Social exclusion
Relational self, 152
Relational status 125
Relationships, 9, 152, 189–206, 211–232, 267–269, 294–295
    Aggression within, 267–269
    Communal, 294, 295
    Exchange, 294
    Parent-child, 214–219
    Personalized, 152
    Romantic, 9, 189–206

Same-sex, 223–228
    Short-term vs. long-term, 194, 199, 202, 203–204, 205
Religion, 346–348
Representativeness heuristic, 21
Reproductive exchange, 295–296
Reproductive fitness see Fitness
Reputation, 244, 250, 254, 266, 267, 269
Risky families, 217–219
RNA expression, 215

Same-sex ties, 223–228
Sapir–Whorf hypothesis, 132
Satisficing, 20–21
Scarcity heuristic, 288, 293, 298–300
Scenario building, 278–281
    Power of, 280–281
Scent see Olfactory cues
Scientific progress, 3
Self, the, 39–49, 55–74, 149, 152–154
    Brain size and, 62–64
    Collective self, 149, 152–154
    Definition of, 56–57
    Executive capacity of, 57
    Functions of, 66–73
    Modular approach to, 39, 46–49
    Private self, 63
    Projection of, 67
    Public self, 63
    Reflexive capacity of, 57
    Relational self, 152
    Representational capacity of, 56
    see also Symbolic self
Self-assessment, 69
Self-consistency, 47–48
Self-consistency theory, 48
Self-deception, 45, 48–49, 71
Self-defense, 266
Self-enhancement, 46–48, 70, 352–353
Self-esteem, 66–73, 268, 352–353
    And reproductive success, 68, 71
    Striving for, 71
Self-evaluation, 66–73
Self-improvement, 69
Self-interest, 148, 238
Self-protection, 24, 72, 74, 164, 166–176, 178–179, 291, 304
Self-referential biases, 189
Self-serving biases, 189; see also Self-enhancement
Selfish gene, 241, 242
Sex differences, 4–5, 199, 200, 202–204, 270–272, 301, 302
    In aggression, 270–272

In conformity, 301, 302
In leadership, 303–304
In romantic relationships, 199, 200,
    202–204
Sexual aggression, 268
Sexual dimorphism, 271
Sexual overperception bias, 23
Sexual selection, 4, 270, 272, 299–301, 304
Shaken baby syndrome, 278
Shame, 121
Signal detection theory, 41; *see also* Error
    management
Similarity,
    As kinship cue, 243–244, 251
    Impact on perception, 81
    Impact on social influence, 296, 297, 301
Sinister attribution error, 17
Social affordances, 83–84, 88–89, 99, 125
Social brain hypothesis, 70
Social categorization, 165–167
Social cognition, 15–32, 39–49, 81–102,
    165–167
    Contents of, 6–7, 39, 95–98, 163, 165–166
    Structure of, 39
    see also Person perception; Personality
        judgment; Prejudice; Self
Social compensation effect, 329
Social complexity, 63–64
    Relation with neocortex volume, 63–64
Social constructivists, 118
Social contracts, 40, 69
Social dilemmas, 154–156, 238–256, 330
Social exchange theory, 40, 238, 244–250, 345
Social exclusion, 16, 71
    Relation to physical pain, 16
Social functionalist framework, 115–118, 121,
    126, 130
Social goals *see* Goals
Social identity, 152–155
Social inclusion,
    Need for, 16, 349
Social influence, 287–312
    Attractiveness and, 297
    Authority and, 288, 293, 303–305, 309
    Cheating and, 307–311
    Commitment and, 288, 293, 305–307, 309
    Foot-in-the-door tactic, 305
    Impact of goal states, 289–291, 292, 295,
        296, 300–301, 304–305, 307
    Impact of heuristics, 288, 289–307, 308
    Liking and, 288, 293, 296–298, 308
    Low-ball tactic, 309
    Reciprocity and, 288, 290, 292–296, 308
    Scarcity and, 288, 293, 298–300

Similarity and, 296, 297, 301
    Social proof and, 288, 293, 300–303,
        308–309
Social intentions, 125
Social judgment, 15–32; *see also* Personality
    judgment
Social learning theory, 265, 270
Social loafing, 319–320, 329–330
Social networks, 61
Social norms *see* Norms
Social proof heuristic, 288, 293, 300–303,
    308–309
Social sanctions, 255, 256
Social shaping hypothesis, 212–213
Social-shardness biases, 323–328
Social status, 267, 269, 291, 300, 304–305
Social support, 222, 227–229
Social value orientation, 253
Socialization processes, 168, 179; *see also*
    Culture
Solitary confinement, 16
Spousal battery, 268, 269
Stalking, 268
Status *see* Social status
Status goal, 291, 300, 304–305
Stereotypes, 24, 165–167, 170–176, 177,
    179–180, 349
    Accuracy of, 166–167
    Kernel of truth in, 177
Stereotyping processes, 165–167; *see also*
    Prejudice
Stimulus imprinting, 91
Stone tools, 59, 60
Strange situation, 217
Strategic pluralism model, 198–202
Stress, 213–214, 216, 220–223
Supernatural beliefs *see* Religion
Symbolic self, 56–57, 61, 66–70, 73
    Capacities of, 56–57, 66–70
    Evolutionary origins of, 61–66, 73
    see also Self
Sympathetic nervous system (SNS), 213–214

Task groups, 151
Tattoos, 84
Tend-and-befriend, 226
Theory development, 2, 4–6, 356–357
Theory of mind, 63, 128
    Computational, 40
    Emotions and, 128
Thin slices of behavior, 28, 86
Threats, 164, 166–172, 179–180, 266–267
    Cues implying, 168–170
    To health, 168–172, 175–179

To personal freedoms, 171
To physical safety, 164, 166–176, 178–179
To reciprocity, 164, 166, 168–169
To values, 168, 171–172
Timeline of human evolution, 55–61, 73
Tiwi, 264
Trade-offs, 21, 22, 23, 71, 199, 269–270
Tragedy of the commons, 239, 240
Trait inferences, automaticity of, 28; *see also*
    Fundamental attribution error;
    Personality judgment
Transactive memory, 153, 321–322
Transparency illusion, 17
Trust and trustworthiness, 165–169, 174, 246, 252
Truth, quest for, 190, 195–196, 202–205

Ultimate causation, 190
Ultrasociality 115–116, 118, 164, 166, 171

Uncertainty, 279, 328, 336
Unitization, 91–92
Universals and universality, 29–31, 350–357
    Levels of, 355–356
Urban legends, 349

Valuation motives, 57, 67, 68, 70, 73, 74
Values, 168
Vasopressin, 197
Vigilance, 331, 333
Virtual environments, 100
Visual illusions *see* Illusions
Vocal cues, 88

Warfare *see* Inter-group conflict
Wason selection task, 20

Xenophobia, 251; *see also* Prejudice

Yanomamö, 264, 266, 267